Alexander Campbell
and Joseph Smith

PRAISE FOR

Alexander Campbell and Joseph Smith:
Nineteenth-Century Restorationists

"In this groundbreaking analysis of the life and thought of Alexander Campbell and Joseph Smith, RoseAnn Benson has produced the most extensively researched and deft treatment of these quintessentially American religious leaders to date. Benson's insider LDS insights, complemented by her careful examination of Campbell materials and consultation with Campbell scholars, make this an important addition to American religious studies."

—Douglas A. Foster, professor of church history in the
Graduate School of Religion and director of the Center for
Restoration Studies, Abilene Christian University

"Oftentimes, one's own cherished beliefs and religious interpretations are best studied in the context of other faiths and traditions. . . . Dr. Benson has written a balanced and compelling comparison between what she calls the 'revelatory restorationism' of Joseph Smith and the 'reasoned restorationism' of Alexander Campbell. Considering the fact that both religious movements began in America and that one of Mormonism's best known early leaders— Sidney Rigdon—came out of the Campbellite movement, this book is timely and most informative. Readers from both the Latter-day Saint and the various Disciples of Christ movements will find much to commend in this competent, highly readable study."

—Richard E. Bennett, professor of church history
and doctrine, Brigham Young University

Alexander Campbell
and Joseph Smith

NINETEENTH-CENTURY RESTORATIONISTS

ROSEANN BENSON

———

Forewords by
THOMAS H. OLBRICHT & ROBERT L. MILLET

On the cover: The Mantua Center Christian Church is the oldest Disciples of Christ (or Campbellite tradition) house of worship in Ohio. Photograph by Marianne Burton Millar. Cover and interior design by Carmen Durland Cole.

Published by Brigham Young University Press, Provo, Utah, in cooperation with Abilene Christian University.

Printed in the United States of America by Sheridan Books, Inc.

ISBN: 978-1-9443-9428-8
Retail: US $24.99

Library of Congress Control Number: 2017952626

Rose Isabelle Schlosser Benson (1923–2000)

and

Walter Latham Benson (1918–97)

A restoration of the ancient order of things is all that is necessary to the happiness and usefulness of christians. No attempt "to reform the doctrine, discipline and government of the church," (a phrase too long in use) can promise a better result than those which have been attempted and languished to death. . . . The thing proposed, is to bring the christianity and the church of the present day up to the standard of the New Testament.

—ALEXANDER CAMPBELL, 1825

Yea, the word of the Lord concerning his church, established in the last days for the restoration of his people, as he has spoken by the mouth of his prophets, and for the gathering of his saints to stand upon Mount Zion, which shall be the city of New Jerusalem.

—JOSEPH SMITH, 1832

Contents

ILLUSTRATIONS..ix

FOREWORDS

Thomas H. Olbricht..xi
Robert L. Millet...xiv

ACKNOWLEDGMENTS xix

INTRODUCTORY CHAPTERS

Chapter 1: Early American Christianity and the
           Beginnings of Two Restoration Movements..........................1
Chapter 2: Early Life of and Religious Influences
           on Alexander Campbell 9
Chapter 3: Early Life of and Religious Influences
           on Joseph Smith..29

SECTION I: RESTORATIONISM, PRIMITIVISM,
AND MILLENNIALISM 39

Chapter 4: Enlightenment versus Enthusiasm..57
Chapter 5: Alexander Campbell's Reasoned Restoration.....................69
Chapter 6: Joseph Smith's Revelatory Restoration 105

SECTION 2: SYSTEMS OF BELIEF.. 139

Chapter 7: Alexander Campbell's Foundational Beliefs...................... 143
Chapter 8: Joseph Smith's Articles of Faith 165
Chapter 9: Scriptural Commentaries and Emendations 201

SECTION 3: Conflict 215

Chapter 10: Conversions and Defections.................................. 221
Chapter 11: Alexander Campbell's "Delusions" and
      the Mormon Response... 251
Chapter 12: Waves of Crisis.. 273

SECTION 4: UNIQUE CONTRIBUTIONS OF
RESTORATIONISM 293

Chapter 13: Alexander Campbell's Unity and
      Millennialism... 295
Chapter 14: Joseph Smith's Expansive Eternalism 321
Epilogue: Final Thoughts on Two Restorationists.................... 339

APPENDICES

A. Delusions.. 361
B. The Constitution of the Mahoning Baptist
      Association... 381

ABOUT THE AUTHOR 385

INDEX.. 387

Illustrations

Map of United Kingdom, by Edward Dean Neuenswander 17

Alexander Campbell's 1809 Journal. Courtesy of Disciples
of Christ Historical Society, Nashville, Tennessee 18

Alexander Campbell's Mansion Home and
Study, by Edward Dean Neuenswander.. 70

Title page of the first edition of the Book of Mormon, 1830.
Courtesy of Kent P. Jackson 127

Thomas Campbell, c. 1834, by Edward Dean Neuenswander................. 145

Masthead of *Millennial Harbinger* 1, no. 1 (4 January 1830).
Courtesy of L. Tom Perry Special Collections, Harold B. Lee
Library, Brigham Young University 151

Alexander Campbell, c. 1815, by Edward Dean Neuenswander............. 153

Title page of Alexander Campbell, ed., *The Sacred Writings
of the Apostles and Evangelists of Jesus Christ*. Buffaloe, VA,
1826. Courtesy of Kent P. Jackson 204

Title page of Joseph Smith, *Holy Scriptures: Inspired Version*
(Herald Press, 1876). Courtesy of L. Tom Perry Special
Collections, Harold B. Lee Library, Brigham Young University 208

Map of Eastern United States, by Edward Dean Neuenswander 223

The Mantua Center, Ohio. Courtesy of Steve Hurd............................. 225

Map of Missouri and Illinois, by Edward Dean Neuenswander 280

Alexander Campbell, ca. 1860, by Edward Dean Neuenswander 342

Joseph Smith, ca. 1840, by Edward Dean Neuenswander 351

Foreword

THOMAS H. OLBRICHT

DISTINGUISHED PROFESSOR EMERITUS OF
RELIGION, PEPPERDINE UNIVERSITY

In this book, RoseAnn Benson has competently concluded a study never before attempted. She has set out to compare and contrast divergent visions of restorationism held by Alexander Campbell (1788–1866) and Joseph Smith (1805–44). Campbell was the key leader in the movement for which he preferred the designation Disciples of Christ. Smith was the founder of The Church of Jesus Christ of Latter-day Saints.

What is the importance of this study? One might argue that the comparison is warranted for the same reason that one climbs the proverbial mountain—because it is there! But a more pressing incentive is that these constituencies comprise the two largest indigenous religious bodies founded in America in the nineteenth century. These religious traditions reflect perhaps more than any other confessional groups the spiritual life and thought generated by the nineteenth-century American experience. Though the visions of these two men are profoundly divergent in specific ways, they nevertheless incorporate certain major motifs in American religious life of the time: primitivism, restorationism, evangelism, and denominationalism.

Smith and Campbell fathered religious bodies that at the beginning of the twenty-first century number into the millions and are found throughout the world. The largest constituency resulting from the work of Smith is The Church of Jesus Christ of Latter-day Saints, now headquartered in Salt Lake City, Utah, with now almost 6,000,000 members in the United States and approximately 9,000,000 elsewhere in the world. A second, smaller group is the Reorganized Church of Jesus Christ of Latter Day Saints, recently reconstituted as the Community of Christ, headquartered in Independence, Missouri, with about 250,000 members throughout the world. The total therefore comes to above 15,000,000.

The three largest religious groups that result from Alexander Campbell's efforts are the Christian Church (Disciples of Christ), with about 800,000 members in the world; the Churches of Christ, with about 3,000,000 members in the world, and 1,300,000 of these in the United States; and the Christian Churches/Churches of Christ, with about 1,200,000 members in the world. The total number therefore exceeds more than 5,000,000 persons. The heirs of Joseph Smith and Alexander Campbell have made a significant impact on religion not only in America but also across the globe.

These two religious bodies emerged at about the same time in the northeastern United States, and some of the early leaders of the Latter-day Saints came from the followers of Alexander Campbell, all of whom at that time were Baptists. Both of these groups proceeded from the assumption that original Christianity had departed from its moorings. Both Campbell and Smith were convinced that the biblical faith needed to be restored. Furthermore, they were convinced that creeds contributed to apostasy. What therefore was required was a return to the primitive faith as set forth in the ancient scriptures. A new start was imperative. It was only in this manner that Christians could be unified in the modern era. Despite these common aspirations, however, the visions of Smith and Campbell for the restored church diverged widely. Dr. Benson is largely occupied with the manner in which Smith and Campbell differed.

Benson first approached me about assessing her work several years ago. She thanked me for my suggestions and said I would receive additional essays from her again after she had read the changes proposed. When she wrote about six months later, she included another section of the book. I was impressed with how seriously she had taken my suggestions and at the more nuanced insights that resulted in what she had written. Benson then proposed that I continue to react to various versions of her manuscript, and that I have proceeded to do. It has taken some time for us to work through the major interpretations, since scholars, of course, differ. We have tried to achieve what best represents a consensus perspective among the major interpreters of Smith and Campbell.

I therefore have come to have great respect for this monograph, since Dr. Benson has put into it much effort and thought. I think it is a competent investigation of the outlooks of these two important American religious leaders. She has worked firsthand in their publications and appropriately reflected their visions. Competent scholars have critiqued her conclusions, so that even when she comments on the American backgrounds in their theological settings and the two movements over their longer history, her remarks are insightful.

Finally, the descendants of Alexander Campbell have felt free to critique his visions and understandings from the outset. Interpretative scholars from within the movement who have written on Campbell have therefore not shunned criticism of both Campbell and his heritage. It is the comments of these scholars upon whom Dr. Benson has depended in order to assess the views of Campbell. Insofar as she may have failed to properly evaluate Campbell, she by no means intentionally set out to distort his work. She has, I think, given her best effort to be fair to Campbell, even though she clearly rejects many of his perspectives.

Benson openly supports the vision and program of Joseph Smith. That she does so is understandable and lends authenticity to her observations upon the Latter-day Saints. In contrast with the Disciples, the scholars within The Church of Jesus Christ of the Latter-day Saints have not felt free to critique the visions of Joseph Smith. Among other reasons is that Joseph Smith claimed to have received his insights through direct revelation from God. As a result, the work before us, even though accurate in its depiction of Smith's perspectives, is not critical of his perspectives. Regardless, Benson's work will be a prolegomenon to any future study on the subject at hand.

Foreword

ROBERT L. MILLET

PROFESSOR EMERITUS OF ANCIENT SCRIPTURE
AND COORDINATOR OF RELIGIOUS OUTREACH,
BRIGHAM YOUNG UNIVERSITY

The population of the United States doubled in the first quarter of the nineteenth century. It was a time of revolution that some historians have called the "Second American Revolution," a time of upheaval and movement—social, political, economic, and religious. There was a movement in values and ideology as well as geography. Regarding the latter, Alexis de Tocqueville characterized the era as follows: "In the United States a man builds a house in which to spend his old age, and he sells it before the roof is on; he plants a garden, and leaves it just as the trees are coming into bearing."[1] Orestes Brownson, a prominent thinker of the time, explained: "No tolerable observer of the signs of the time can have failed to perceive that we are, in this vicinity at least, in the midst of a very important revolution; a revolution which extends to every department of thought, and threatens to change ultimately the whole moral aspect of society. Everything is loosened from its old fastenings, and is floating no one can tell whither."[2]

This was the age of restorationism, an era in America's history when men and women read the Bible, believed its story and message, and sought for a return to "the ancient order of things."[3] Many longed for the reestablishment of primitive Christianity; others desired once more to enjoy the spiritual gifts and outpourings that had once graced the ancients. A man named Robert Mason "believed that it was necessary to have prophets, apostles, dreams, visions and revelations in the church of Christ, the same as they had who lived in ancient days; and he believed the Lord would raise up a people and a church, in the last days, with prophets, apostles and all the gifts, powers, and blessings, which it ever contained in any age of the world." In speaking to one who would later become a leader among the Latter-day Saints, Mason declared:

> I was laboring in my field at mid-day when I was enwrapped in a vision.
> I was placed in the midst of a vast forest of fruit trees. I was very hungry,

and walked a long way through the orchard, searching for fruit to eat; but I could not find any in the whole orchard, and I wept because I could not find any fruit. While I stood gazing at the orchard, and wondering why there was no fruit, the trees began to fall to the ground upon every side of me, until there was not one tree standing in the whole orchard; and while I was marveling at the scene, I saw young sprouts start up from the roots of the trees which had fallen, and they opened into young thrifty trees before my eyes. They budded, blossomed, and bare fruit until the trees were loaded with the finest fruit I ever beheld. . . . As I was about to taste of it the vision closed. . . .

I then knelt upon the ground, and prayed unto the Lord, and asked him, in the name of Jesus Christ, to show me the meaning of the vision. The Lord said unto me: "This is the interpretation of the vision; the great trees of the forest represent the generation of men in which you live. There is no church of Christ, or kingdom of God upon the earth in your generation. There is no fruit of the church of Christ upon the earth. There is no man ordained of God to administer in any of the ordinances of the gospel of salvation upon the earth in this day and generation. But, in the next generation, I the Lord will set up my kingdom and my Church upon the earth. . . . You will live to see the day, and handle the fruit; but will never partake of it in the flesh."

When [he] had finished relating the vision and interpretation, he said to me, . . . "I shall never partake of this fruit in the flesh; but you will, and you will become a conspicuous actor in that kingdom." . . . He had this vision about the year 1800, and he related it to me in 1830.[4]

As late as 1838, Ralph Waldo Emerson stated in his famous "Divinity School Address" at Harvard that "the need was never greater of new revelation than now." He continued, "The Church seems to totter to its fall, almost all life extinct." Further, he said, "I look forward for the hour when the supreme Beauty, which ravished the souls of those Eastern men, and chiefly of those Hebrews, and through their lips spoke oracles to all time, shall speak in the west also."[5]

A century earlier, Roger Williams professed that the apostasy had so corrupted all Christian churches "that there can be no recovery out of that apostasy until Christ shall send forth new apostles to plant churches anew."[6] Williams united with the Baptists for a short time but then turned seeker—to wait for new apostles to restore Christianity. He felt that he had been misled and had also misled his followers. He became convinced there was no one who had been administered baptism "for the want of called administration."[7] In short, Williams held that there was "no regularly constituted church of Christ, on earth, nor any person authorized to administer any church ordinance, nor can there be until new apostles are sent by the great head of the Church, for whose coming I am seeking."[8]

John Wesley had also been a marvelous preacher and religious leader in the eighteenth century and became the father of Methodism. His brother Charles is responsible for many of the magnificent hymns sung in Christianity today. Though they were very close as brothers, Charles criticized John on one occasion when the latter ordained a man to an office without authority to do so. Charles wrote:

> How easily are bishops made
> By man or woman's whim?
> W[esley] his hands on C[oke] hath laid,
> But who laid hands on him?

> Hands on himself he laid, and took
> An Apostoic Chair:
> And then ordain'd his Creature C[oke]
> His Heir and Successor.

> Episcopalians, now no more
> With Presbyterians fight
> But give your needless Contest o're
> 'Whose Ordination's right?'

> It matters not, if Both are One,
> Or different in degree,
> For lo! Ye see in Prelate John contain'd in
> The whole Presbytery![9]

Such expressions of loss and the need for greater light and truth are echoed later by the two major nineteenth-century restorationists discussed in this book—Alexander Campbell and Joseph Smith. Both sought for "the ancient order of things" and for the return of the Christian gospel and church described in the New Testament. Both felt that the religions of their day were woefully deficient and in some cases extensively perverse. Both searched for the old-time religion in which Jesus and the apostles had ministered eighteen centuries earlier. While it may be convenient for some to lump the Mormon prophet with the head of the Disciples of Christ because of their similar identification of the problem, Dr. RoseAnn Benson has wisely and appropriately taken the time to tease out the doctrinal and practical differences between the teachings of the two leaders in order to provide a more accurate picture of their varied solutions to that problem. For far too long, Joseph Smith and Alexander Campbell have been studied separately, and in the process, nonspecialists have come away from a surface encounter with a list of superficial similarities or differences.

As one who has focused professionally more on theology than history, I find Dr. Benson's treatment to be just right—not so much historical detail that we drown in the past, but enough to provide a context for the doctrinal teachings. And while there are times when some readers may find themselves almost treading water in the pool of theological pronouncements, I find, once again, the mix to be right—one that enables studied theologians to wend their way through such topics as the Creation, the Fall, the Atonement, repentance, forgiveness, the church, the sacraments (ordinances), and the Second Coming without tedium. Dr. Benson has done her homework, has pored over thousands of pages of documents, and has produced a volume that is a worthy contribution to the field of religious and historical scholarship. She has laid a fine foundation for subsequent research in this field.

Much of my time for the last twenty years has been spent in outreach and interfaith relations, particularly between Latter-day Saints and evangelicals. It has proven to be a fruitful and productive time in my life—a refreshing and expanding decade in which much understanding has been gained while a great deal of misunderstanding has been corrected. After reading this manuscript through its several stages, I have been motivated by the thought that Latter-day Saints would be well-advised to begin a similar dialogue with their cousins of the age of restoration—with Disciples of Christ, the Church of Christ, and the Christian Church. With essentially the same historical roots (their early members having come principally from Protestant churches) and agreeing for the most part on the fact that an apostasy or falling away of the primitive Christian church had taken place, there would appear to be much room for conversation, especially about the origins and influences of present similarities and differences, as well as the future directions of the respective movements.

In the spirit of seeking for what once was, Thomas Jefferson, identified by most as a Deist, declared, "I adhere to the principles of the first age; and consider all subsequent innovations as corruptions of His religion, having no foundation in what came from Him."[10] To Timothy Pickering he wrote: "The religion builders have so distorted and deformed the doctrines of Jesus, so muffled them in mysticisms, fancies, and falsehoods, have caricatured them into forms so inconceivable, as to shock reasonable thinkers."[11] To Benjamin Waterhouse he lamented that although "happy in the prospect of a restoration of primitive Christianity, I must leave to younger athletes to encounter and lop off the false branches which have been engrafted into it by the mythologists of the middle and modern ages."[12]

The beloved Harry Emerson Fosdick commented boldly upon twentieth-century religion. "A religious reformation is afoot," he noted, "and at heart it is the endeavor to recover for our modern life the religion of Jesus as against the vast, intricate, largely inadequate and often positively false religion about Jesus. Christianity today has largely left the religion which he preached, taught and lived, and has substituted another kind of religion altogether. If Jesus should come back to earth now, hear the mythologies built up around him, see the creedalism, the denominationalism, sacramentalism, carried on in his name, he would certainly say, 'If this is Christianity, I am not a Christian.'"[13] I suppose to some extent both the followers of Alexander Campbell and Joseph Smith would identify with the sentiments of Reverend Fosdick. They agreed for the most part on the diagnosis and the malady; the medicine they prescribed has been noticeably different. For me, this book has helped to lay out the issues, the controversies, the points of conflict, and the areas of agreement between two indigenous American faiths involved in the religion-making enterprise. This study provides a story within the story. It is a story as old as the earth but as current as today's news: it is the story of humanity's quest for truth and understanding. This book certainly contributes to that noble quest.

NOTES

1. *Democracy in America*, 2 vols. (New York: Alfred A. Knopf, 1945), 2:164.
2. *Boston Quarterly Review*, 3 vols. (Boston: Cambridge Press, 1840), 3:265.
3. Alexander Campbell launched the series "A Restoration of the Ancient Order of Things" in the 1825 *Christian Baptist*.
4. Wilford Woodruff, "Leaves from My Journal," *Millennial Star*, 23 May 1881, 334–35.
5. Delivered before the senior class at the Harvard Divinity School, Cambridge, Massachusetts, 15 July 1838; in Sydney E. Ahlstrom, ed., *Theology in America* (Indianapolis: Bobbs-Merrill, 1967), 306, 315–16.
6. *Christenings Make Not Christians*, vol. 7 of *The Complete Writings of Roger Williams*, 31–41.
7. Cotton Mather, *Magnalia Christi Americana* (Hartford: Silas Andrus & Son, 1853), 2:498.
8. William Cullen Bryant, ed., *Picturesque America, or the Land We Live In* (New York: D. Appleton, 1872–74), 1:502.
9. John R. Tyson, *Assist Me to Proclaim: The Life and Hymns of Charles Wesley* (Grand Rapids, MI: Eerdmans, 2007), 311.
10. Albert E. Bergh, ed., "To the Reverend Jared Sparks," in *The Writings of Thomas Jefferson*, Monticello Edition (Washington, DC: Thomas Jefferson Memorial Association, 1904), 15:288.
11. "To Timothy Pickering," *The Writings of Thomas Jefferson*, 15:323.
12. "To Doctor Benjamin Waterhouse," *The Writings of Thomas Jefferson*, 15:391.
13. Cited in LeGrand Richards, *A Marvelous Work and a Wonder* (Salt Lake City: Deseret Book, 2014), 29.

Acknowledgments

*B*ooks are never written without considerable input from others—and especially first books. I express gratitude to Richard E. Bennett and Robert L. Millet for pushing me to write this book, reading and rereading my work; to Thomas Olbricht, who agreed to advise me so that my portrayal of Alexander Campbell was accurate; and to Elise Babbel Hahl, Gordon S. Benson, and Heather Hardy for making suggestions to my initial efforts in writing this book. Richard Bennett arranged for me to participate in a panel on restorationism, which helped launch this effort. Colleagues provided needed criticism and encouragement: Milton V. Backman, Davis Bitton, Richard D. Draper, Alonzo Gaskill, Daniel K Judd, Jonathan C. Liddell, Reid L. Neilson, David L. Paulsen, Keith W. Perkins, Noel Reynolds, Michael Rhodes, and Ron Walker. Other colleagues have loaned books or pointed me to resources: Alexander L. Baugh, J. Spencer Fluhman, Steven C. Harper, J. B. Haws, Andrew H. Hedges, Joseph Fielding McConkie, Craig J. Ostler, and Alan K. Parrish. Gifts of books from Noel Reynolds, Donald Q. Cannon, Robert J. Matthews, and Religious Education associate dean Richard D. Draper were invaluable aids. Ashley Caresse Logan helped replace citations to the *History of the Church* with citations to the new *Joseph Smith Papers*. George Miller, Felicity Ruggiero, and Roger Burns-Watson at the Alexander Campbell home in Bethany, West Virginia, were wonderful assistants in finding elusive quotations or resolving other questions. Carisse Berryhill, archivist at Abilene Christian University, shared her very helpful notations on Campbell's journals. Sara Harwell and Elaine Philpott, archivists at the Disciples of Christ Historical Society in Nashville, Tennessee, made all the Alexander Campbell journals in their care readily available for my examination. Doug Foster, director of Restoration Studies at Abilene Christian University, was a wonderful mentor and aided me in correcting certain points. The BYU Religious Studies Center team of Thomas A. Wayment, R. Devan Jensen, Brent R. Nordgren, Joany O. Pinegar, Carmen Durland Cole, Leah Welker, Kimball Gardner, Tyler Balli, Allyson Jones, and Leah Emal have been invaluable in aiding the completion of the book. Religious Education at Brigham Young University has funded trips to John Whitmer Society meetings and to Nashville, Tennessee, for research at the Disciples of Christ Historical Society. In the final analysis, however, it is my work, and it represents the writings and teachings of Joseph Smith and Alexander Campbell to the best of my research and understanding.

My parents, Rose Isabelle Schlosser and Walter Latham Benson, to whom this book is dedicated, are my family's transitional point between Alexander Campbell's Disciples and Joseph Smith's Mormons. I did not know of my Disciples heritage when I first began doing research on restorationism and Alexander Campbell. I had never connected the First Christian Church of my preschool childhood with the Disciples of Christ, and thus with Campbell. This book includes both sides of my family's restoration tradition and has become a quest for understanding my forebears and appreciating them as seekers. It has been an exceptional journey exploring Alexander Campbell's background, reading many of his publications, visiting his homestead in Bethany, West Virginia, and deciphering some of his journals housed in the Disciples of Christ Historical Society in Nashville, as well as learning more about Joseph Smith through his history, journal, and scriptural accounts, visiting his birthplace in Sharon, Vermont, and the home in upstate New York in which he grew to manhood. I am amazed and appreciative of the legacy of restorationist Christianity that flows from both sides of my family.

There is no such thing as true objectivity, but I have attempted to be open, balanced, and fair in my assessment of what each man attempted to accomplish. This book will not analyze Joseph Smith's claims to a prophetic calling or critique his announcements of visions and revelations. If Alexander Campbell had claimed to receive angelic ministrations, I would not critique his claims either but would adopt his perspective at face value. This is a book about the content of their teachings, not the veracity of their claims. Although these two men have diverging ideas on the meaning of restoration, each has made important contributions that made a significant impact on twenty-first-century Christianity and large groups of believers.

Early American Christianity and the Beginnings of Two Restoration Movements

*There is a Time of purity and Primitive Sincereity, there is a time
of Transgression and Apostacy, there is a time of the coming out
of the Babilonian Apostasy and Wilderness.*

—ROGER WILLIAMS, LETTER TO GEORGE FOX

*R*eformation and restoration have been pervasive and powerful themes throughout Christian history—perhaps the driving force underlying Protestantism and all efforts to purify Christianity—that continue even today in America as compelling ideas.[1] In American religious history, the urge for a return to an ancient and primitive standard began with the Puritans in the seventeenth century.[2] For example, Roger Williams was a seventeenth-century separatist minister who rejected the Church of England, which he considered an irredeemably corrupt institution, and became a Puritan for a time. He was a *seeker* who was looking for gospel purity—a restoration such as Alexander Campbell and Joseph Smith proposed two centuries later.[3] Williams set forth his own ideas of restoration. He was a strong proponent of religious toleration and the separation of church and state. In his letters, he wrote about a "time of transgression & apostasy" that would give way to the "time of the coming out of the Apostasy & Wilderness," which would lead to a time when a "restauration of the first pattern" would take place.[4] He had an unquenchable restorationist impulse that dominated his quest for God's pure church. Each section of this book begins with a quotation from Williams, taken from letters he wrote in the seventeenth century to George Fox, John Winthrop, and the English Parliament.

Seventeenth-century Puritans presaged the mid-eighteenth-century religious revival called the Great Awakening that influenced the northeastern seaboard's more educated and wealthy with the desire for more political and religious freedom. Revivals were the great engine that stoked Protestant growth in the new republic.[5] They were, however, controversial, both challenging and reinforcing traditional Protestant religions. The enthusiastic and emotional outpourings of the "born again" were thought to be crude and anti-intellectual by some.[6] The venerable Jonathan Edwards, however, defended revivalism in his 1746 *Treatise on Religious Affections*. For him, the passions, "affections," or "sense of the heart," were not in competition with human reason and will because all were grounded in the Great Being. Theology was the highest expression of rationality but also a window into the limits of reason.[7]

Half a century later, British loyalist Peter Oliver claimed that religious dissent led to a "Torrent of Enthusiasms" in which individuals claimed direct communication with the divine.[8] Harvard scholar David Holland points out, "The enthusiastic movements were considered dangerous primarily as the advocates of innovation."[9] These revivals had their greatest impact on the Protestant churches of New England with their undercutting of traditional and trained ministers and emphasis on personal salvation, introspection, and transformation as opposed to ritual and ceremony.[10] The weakening of authority held by "spiritual lords" and anticlerical sentiments accompanied the colonists' ideas of freedom from England. The revivals fed freedom of religion along with ideas of inalienable rights bestowed by God. The joining of religious and civic leaders for freedom against a state which would suppress these rights and liberties was a powerful alliance. Eighteenth-century Americans understood their fight for independence as against both civil and religious tyranny.[11]

In postrevolutionary America, a new Christian revival began called the Second Great Awakening. This movement at the end of the eighteenth century reached its peak during the 1830s and 1840s.[12] The "Great Reformation of the Nineteenth Century" was a battleground of theological ideas, appealing especially to the common folk—the less educated, less wealthy, and unchurched with a populist flavor and informal religious practices. It was an era characterized by spiritual regeneration, itinerant lay preachers, revivals and camp meetings, and restorationist ideals.[13] One scholar called the Second Great Awakening "the most influential revival of Christianity in the history of the United States."[14]

This movement began as the alliance between state and church began to unravel with the passage of the First Amendment, which according to Thomas Jefferson was intended to create a "wall of separation between church and state," allowing for religious liberty, diversity, and tolerance.[15] The removal of federal government jurisdiction over and financial support of religion led the individual states to adopt similar measures leading to free-market religions based in egalitarian, republican, and democratic ideology. The unprecedented religious freedom and Christian revivalism gave birth to restorationism, a primitive gospel movement to recover the primordial Christian doctrines and organization.[16] Although exhilarated by the prospects of the coming millennial era, many Americans by the 1820s sought progress not by looking forward to the end of history but by looking backward to its beginning in primitive Christianity.[17]

Alexander Campbell and Joseph Smith Jr. became prominent leaders in two very different restorationist movements.[18] They were contemporaries acutely aware and highly critical of each other. They jealously guarded their own flocks, were envious of the other's converts, and condemned those who left their flock. Campbell's restoration was a reasoned focus on New Testament essentials that he believed would bring unity in preparation for the Millennium—a rational approach reflecting the influence of the Enlightenment era. Smith's restoration, in contrast, was revelatory—an eclectic gathering from the Old and New Testaments, new sacred books, and even more. Abilene Christian University historian Douglas Foster points out that Campbell was restoring *to the church* ordinances and practices of the apostolic church that had been neglected, whereas Smith was restoring doctrines, practices, ordinances, and covenants *to a church that had ceased to exist* shortly after the time of the Apostles.[19]

HISTORY OF COMPARISONS

Comparisons between these two restoration traditions have a lengthy history. Richard Bushman suggests that in 1830, the Mormons bore a stronger resemblance to Campbell's restoration than to other Christian churches.[20] By the end of that year, each restoration tradition was well aware of the other, competing for converts—especially among seekers. Significant references to the other, as noted in this volume, are found in Campbell's *Millennial Harbinger* and Latter-day Saint publications *Messenger and Advocate*, *Times and Seasons*, and the *Evening and*

Morning Star—none complimentary of the other. In fact, Alexander Campbell was the very first to review and critique the Book of Mormon, Smith's signature revelatory output. His title reveals his point of view: "Delusions."[21] In 1842, John D. Lee and Alfonso Young, representing the restoration of Smith, and Abraham Sallee and Samuel Dewhitt who represented the Stone-Campbell restoration, spiritedly debated two propositions: (1) The Book of Mormon is man's work; and (2) Are the gifts and offices of the ancient Apostolic Church of Christ necessary in this age to constitute a perfect church or body?[22]

More recently, Churches of Christ scholar Richard T. Hughes presented an article titled "Two Restoration Traditions: Mormons and Churches of Christ in the Nineteenth Century"[23] to an interfaith dialogue conference in Washington, DC. Both restoration traditions were essentially ignored by Roger Finke and Rodney Stark in *The Churching of America, 1776–1990*,[24] implying that their impact on mainstream Christian churches was minimal. Some leading historians recognize only the movement of Thomas and Alexander Campbell as the major restoration church in their portrayal of American religious history.[25] In the index, Thomas and Alexander Campbell, the Disciples of Christ, Churches of Christ, and Christian Churches (or some part thereof) are listed under *restorationism*. Although they include Joseph Smith in their review, they ignore his claim of restoration—perhaps because the doctrines found in the Book of Mormon were not emphasized initially, falsely appearing not to have added enough novelty to the Christian tradition to make Mormonism more than a new Protestant sect. In a 2013 presentation by Churches of Christ scholar Douglas Foster to the John Whitmer Historical Society on the theme of restoration, Foster stated he believes that restoration is implied in Mormon scriptures; however, he was unable to find use of that term by reading and perusing indexes and argues that the designation of Smith's church as a "restoration movement" is a later development. A computer search of LDS scriptures, however, will demonstrate numerous examples of the use of restoration.[26]

BOOK ORGANIZATION

This book is a comparison of these two nineteenth-century men and the restoration movements they created with an in-depth examination of what restoration meant to both groups, as well as their beliefs, their interactions with each other, their similarities, their differences, and their unique contributions to Christianity. The introductory chapters give context in American history for restorationism and reveal the early life and influences on Alexander Campbell and Joseph Smith.

Section 1, "Restorationism, Primitivism, and Millennialism," explores the meanings of Christian restoration, primitivism, and millennialism and how Campbell and Smith's movements fit or did not fit into these categories. Chapter 4 introduces their divergent origins: Campbell from reason and his Enlightenment education, and Smith from enthusiasm and his acceptance of visions, visitations, and other extraordinary manifestations of spiritual gifts. Chapter 5 focuses on Campbell's reasoned and logical approach to the restoration of the church to its original New Testament form. Campbell's restoration was an orderly and rational reading of the scriptures in multiple languages attempting to ascertain their true meaning in the original Greek. Beginning in 1825, he published a thirty-two-part series, "A Restoration of the Ancient Order of Things," which identified some of his thoughts on restoration. Chapter 6 discusses Smith's visionary and revelatory approach to a restoration of God's "everlasting covenant." His reopening of prophetic dialogue between heaven and earth included a belief in past, present, and future revelation and the addition of new scripture. Key signature historical events are identified, including his First Vision, the coming forth of the Book of Mormon, and the establishment of a church that help organize and define Smith's restoration.

Section 2, "Systems of Belief," contextualizes nineteenth-century American religious life with its differing creeds and the splintering of Christianity into a host of new movements fostered by freedom, skepticism, and doctrinal debate. Chapter 7 examines three documents forming Campbell's theological foundation preceding the establishment of his own church: Thomas Campbell's 1809 *Declaration and Address;* Alexander's 1816 "Sermon on the Law"; and "A Statement of Belief," written in 1824 on behalf of his Wellsburg Baptist congregation as application for membership in a more liberal Baptist association. Joseph Smith's foundational beliefs came from his translation of the Book of Mormon and continuing revelation. Chapter 8 begins by discussing Doctrine and Covenants section 20, the first attempt to organize beliefs found in the Book of Mormon. Smith's 1842 "Articles of Faith" provides a succinct list to discuss the major parts of his theology. Chapter 9 discusses the biblical emendations of each man. Campbell published a New Testament with his insights on words from the Greek and scriptural notations. Smith produced a new translation of the Bible, with the addition of new verses and whole chapters he claimed to receive via inspiration and revelation.

The early nineteenth century brought about the perfect confluence of circumstances for restoration of the gospel: a revolutionary new country with religious freedom and a reawakening of religious fervor. Conflict between the two groups is discussed in chapter 10 with the introduction of Sidney Rigdon, a Reforming Baptist minister and one of the most prominent defectors from Campbell's movement. His conversion caused many of his congregants to consider the Mormon message more closely and was a factor in devastating the disciples' membership in several of the small towns in northeastern Ohio. Conversions and defections provided an acrimonious climate in which Campbell and others attacked Smith, accusing him of conspiring with Rigdon, to which Smith or his acolytes responded. The animosity climaxed in the tarring and feathering of Smith and Rigdon. Chapter 11 briefly relates the historical narrative of the Book of Mormon and is followed by Campbell's analysis of Smith and the Book of Mormon, titled "Delusions." Chapter 12 identifies several waves of contention and defection as Mormons struggled with understanding prophethood and weathered an extermination order from the Missouri governor.

Section 4, "Unique Contributions to Restorationism," discusses distinctive contributions to restorationism by Campbell and Smith. Chapter 13 focuses on Campbell's Millennialist thrust, his defense of restored Christianity through three signature debates, and his emphasis on the importance of Christian unity in ushering in the Millennium. It includes his "Prefatory Remarks," an 1850 retrospective look at some of the most important things he believed his restoration accomplished. Chapter 14 highlights Smith's unprecedented and expansive views of the eternal nature of God, man, and their relationship.

The epilogue contains a significant number of quotations and comments from peers and scholars in an attempt to assess the impact these two restorationists had on their followers, on outsiders, and on Christianity.

Notes

1. David Edwin Harrell Jr., epilogue to *The American Quest for the Primitive Church*, ed. Richard T. Hughes (Urbana: University of Illinois, 1988), 240.
2. Theodore Dwight Bozeman, "Biblical Primitivism: An Approach to New England Puritanism," in *The American Quest for the Primitive Church*, 20–21. Roger Williams was strongly opposed to the Puritan method of restoring the ancient order because they attempted to do it through secular means via government. C. Leonard Allen, "Roger Williams and 'the Restauration of Zion,'" in *The American Quest for the Primitive Church*, 43.

3. E. Brooks Holifield, *Theology in America: Christian Thought from the Age of the Puritans to the Civil War* (New Haven, CT: Yale University, 2003), 51. Roger Williams was a controversial figure because of his ideas on freedom of worship and clashes with the Puritans. In fact, Cotton Mather recorded that Williams refused to recognize any of the churches of Salem "as . . . *churches* of our Lord Jesus Christ." Williams was brought to trial, and upon sentencing, he and his followers left for southern New England and settled the city they called Providence. "There they proceeded not only unto the *gathering* of a thing like a church, but unto the *renouncing* of their *infant baptism*. . . . Mr. Williams . . . told them [his followers] 'that being himself misled, he had led them likewise out of the way;'" and "he was now satisfied that there was none upon earth that could administer baptism . . . [so] he advised them therefore to forego all . . . and wait for the coming of *new* apostles: whereupon they dissolved themselves, and became that sort of sect which we term *Seekers.*" Cotton Mather, *Magnalia Christi Americana* (Hartford: Silas Andrus & Son, 1853), 2:498. See also Narragansett Club, *Publications of the Narragansett Club* (Providence: Providence Press, 1866–74), 1:35–36.
4. C. Leonard Allen, "Roger Williams and 'the Restauration of Zion,'" *The American Quest for the Primitive Church*, 40–42. *Queries of Highest Consideration* was a tract written to counteract the recommendations of the Westminster Assembly and to persuade Parliament to embrace religious liberty rather than the officially established Church of England or the model of Scottish Presbyterianism. Edwin S. Gaustad, *Roger Williams* (New York: Oxford University Press, 2005), 75.
5. Edwin S. Gaustad and Leigh E. Schmidt, *The Religious History of America*, rev. ed. (San Francisco: HarperCollins, 2002), 147.
6. The dismissal by some people of spiritual experiences began early in American religious history. At Anne Hutchinson's 1637 trial, Governor John Winthrop labeled her immediate revelations "a delusion." Michael P. Winship, *The Times & Trials of Anne Hutchinson: Puritans Divided* (Lawrence: University Press of Kansas, 2005), 113. "Immediate" meant direct and without the medium of the scriptures.
7. Holifield, *Theology in America*, 103–4.
8. Douglass Adair and John Schutz, eds., *Peter Oliver's Origin and Progress of the American Rebellion: A Tory View* (Palo Alto, CA: Stanford University, 1961), 15–20.
9. David F. Holland, *Sacred Borders: Continuing Revelation and Canonical Restraint in Early America* (Oxford Scholarship Online, May 2001), 4.
10. Jon Butler, Grant Wacker, and Randall Balmer, *Religion in American Life: A Short History* (New York: Oxford University Press, 2003), 127–28.
11. Gaustad and Schmidt, *Religious History of America*, 121.
12. While the Second Great Awakening took place on American soil, its roots were in the Anglican reform ideas of John Wesley. Peter W. Williams, *America's Religions: From their Origins to the Twenty-first Century* (Urbana: University of Illinois, 1990–2002), 106.
13. Williams, *America's Religions*, 190–91; see also James D. Bratt, ed., *Antirevivalism in Antebellum America: A Collection of Religious Voices* (New Brunswick, NJ: Rutgers University Press, 2006), xvi.
14. Mark A. Noll, *A History of Christianity in the United States and Canada* (Grand Rapids, MI: William B. Eerdmans, 1992), 166. See also Harrell, epilogue to *The American Quest for the Primitive Church*, 240. Mark L. Staker, *Hearken, O Ye People: The Historical Setting for Joseph Smith's Ohio Revelations* (Draper, UT: Greg Kofford Books, 2009), 12–13.
15. Thomas Jefferson, "Letter to the Danbury Baptist Association, January 1, 1802," in Daniel L. Dreisbach and John D. Whaley, "What the Wall Separates: A Debate on Thomas Jefferson's 'Wall of Separation' Metaphor," *Constitutional Commentary* 16, no. 3 (Winter 1999): 18. Religious liberty, diversity, toleration, and plurality of

sects primarily occurred among Protestantism. The further a religion strayed from Trinitarian Protestantism, the further it moved down the scale of what was considered acceptable Christianity. Theoretically, religious freedom in America was unprecedented, especially in comparison to what there had been in the history of Europe; however, in some states, the dominant traditional churches continued to receive financial backing until the 1830s. Spencer Fluhman, *"A Peculiar People": Anti-Mormonism and the Making of Religion in Nineteenth-Century America* (Chapel Hill: University of North Carolina Press, 2013), 16, 24; Winfred Ernest Garrison and Alfred T. DeGroot, *The Disciples of Christ: A History* (St. Louis: Bethany Press, 1948), 258–59.

16. Robert West identified the postrevolutionary religious awakening differently. He divided the era into four distinctive movements: (1) the Second Great Awakening in the Eastern States; (2) the Great Revival on the Western frontier; (3) the Methodist movement; and (4) the primitive gospel movement. Robert Frederick West, *Alexander Campbell and Natural Religion* (New Haven, CT: Yale University, 1948), vi.

17. Butler et al., *Religion in American Life: A Short History* (New York: Oxford University, 2003), 213.

18. Earlier prominent restorationists of this era were New Englanders Abner Jones and Elias Smith, as well as others who joined together to form the Christian Connexion, James O'Kelly in Virginia and Barton Stone in Kentucky. Nathan O. Hatch, "The Christian Movement and the Demand for a Theology of the People," *The Journal of American History* 67, no. 3 (December 1980): 547. Barton Stone eventually united his followers with Alexander Campbell's followers to form one church in late 1831. The union is now referred to as the Stone-Campbell movement.

19. Douglas A. Foster, "Community of Christ and Churches of Christ: Extraordinary Distinctions, Extraordinary Parallels," *Restoration Studies* 14 (2013): 3.

20. Richard L. Bushman, *Joseph Smith and the Beginnings of Mormonism* (Urbana: University of Illinois Press, 1984), 180.

21. Alexander Campbell, "Delusions" *Millennial Harbinger* 2, no. 2 (February 1831): 85–96. When reprinted as a pamphlet, *An Analysis of the Book of Mormon; with an Examination of Its Internal and External Evidences, and a Refutation of Its Pretences to Divine Authority* was added to the title.

22. *Crihfield's Christian Family Library and Journal of Biblical Science*, July 1842. Craig Churchill of Abilene Christian University graciously sent me a copy of the debate which I had been unable to locate, cited in Richard T. Hughes, "Two Restoration Traditions: Mormons and Churches of Christ in the Nineteenth Century," *Journal of Mormon History* 19, no. 1 (Spring 1993): 34.

23. Hughes, "Two Restoration Traditions: Mormons and Churches of Christ in the Nineteenth Century," 34–51.

24. See Roger Finke and Rodney Stark, *The Churching of America, 1776–1990* (New Brunswick, NJ: Rutgers University Press, 1992).

25. See, for example, Noll, in *A History of Christianity in the United States and Canada* and *America's God* (New York: Oxford University, 2002); Jon Butler et al., *Religion in American Life*, and Peter Williams in *America's Religions*.

26. Foster, "Community of Christ and Churches of Christ: Extraordinary Distinctions, Extraordinary Parallels," 4–5. A computer search on lds.org resulted in numerous scriptures using the terms "restore," "restored," "restoring," and "restoration" in the context of restoring priesthood powers, restoring Zion, restoring knowledge of true principles and doctrines especially regarding Christ, and restoring the House of Israel. In addition to the examples given above, see also Doctrine and Covenants 27:6; 45:17; 84:2; 86:10; 103:13, 29; 124:28; 127:8; 128:17; and 132:40, 45; Book of Mormon: 2 Nephi 3:24; 30:8; Alma 37:19; Helaman 15:11; 3 Nephi 29:1; Joseph Smith Translation (JST), Matthew 17:10, 14; JST, John 1:22; and Articles of Faith 1:10.

2

Early Life of
and Religious Influences
on Alexander Campbell

*A*lexander Campbell was born near Ballymena in County Antrim, Ireland, in 1788 to Thomas Campbell and Jane Corneigle Campbell, both of whom held strong moral and religious convictions. Thomas grew up in a strict Anglican (Church of Ireland) home in County Down in northeastern Ireland.[1] In his early youth, Thomas's inherent love of the scriptures led him to associate with the Covenanters and the Seceders, movements within the Scottish Presbyterian Church he found more devotional than the ritualism of the Anglican Church.[2] The Anglicans were a formal religious tradition that retained much of the vestments, ceremony, liturgy, and architecture of the Catholic Church. Apparently, Thomas felt as others did, that the Anglican Church had become a mere shell of religious worship devolving into a cold, lifeless form of empty rituals.

Concerned for his own salvation, Thomas's distress became almost more than he could bear. While walking alone in the fields, he received the divine answer for which he had been seeking and felt the love and approval of God as never before. From this moment onward he considered himself consecrated to the service of God and specially "called," because he regarded "the feelings and sudden change of heart he experienced as proceeding from a direct divine influence."[3]

Thomas was sent to a nearby military regimental school for his education. His father was opposed to his change in religion but eventually relented, and Thomas entered the University of Glasgow to study divinity for three years. At the university, Thomas was thoroughly immersed in the antitraditional principles of the Scottish Enlightenment and natural theology.[4] The eighteenth-century Scottish philosophical theories were collectively known as Scottish Common Sense Realism. Francis Hutcheson and Thomas Reid were two of the major philosophers who dominated this movement at the university during the eighteenth century. These two Scottish thinkers promoted a reasoned approach to ethics based on universal human instincts.[5] Their system was made popular through a reading curriculum called Scotland's "theistic mental science," whose principles undermined long-accepted cultural, social, political, and religious foundations. The repudiation of tradition and history along with the authority of religious denominations, social hierarchy, and inherited government led eventually to the understanding that there were "self-evident truths" upon which society and individuals could be governed.[6] Scottish Common Sense philosophy, as it came to be known, was a defense of rational theology against skepticism, yet it guarded against excessive rationalism by emphasizing the limits of reason.[7] The philosophers were deeply concerned with moral action and how knowing could be channeled into proper ways of acting.[8] Some scholars have commented on the ubiquity of this philosophy and how it became "the official academic belief of the period," affecting not only secular but also religious thinking.[9]

In the seventeenth century, Francis Bacon developed an evidentiary style of thinking. It highlighted the glory of God's handiwork, which he believed would bring an understanding of all the hidden secrets of the universe. Applied to the physical sciences, this method involved organized observation by collecting data, conducting experiments, and carefully interpreting the results, thus learning the secrets of nature and ultimately how God worked. Combining Scottish rational thinking and Bacon's approach to the natural world, Hutcheson believed that by attending systematically to what moral sense communicated, one could develop an ethical construct that found beauty in virtuous actions. The main focus of Hutcheson's ethical philosophy was defined by the Baconian method: evidentiary data collection from which conclusions could be drawn. As applied to ethics, self-conscious examination became the evidence from which one drew broader conclusions about the nature of human existence.[10]

Once Thomas completed his literary coursework, he entered the Secession Presbyterian theological school of the Anti-Burghers. The Secession movement (Seceders) opposed patronage which allowed wealthy landowners to appoint pastors instead of the representative presbytery government, and the Anti-Burgher movement was opposed to public officials being required to swear an oath of allegiance to the Presbyterian Church of Scotland.[11] Seceders believed these requirements were political in nature, encroaching on religious freedom. Although freedom of political allegiance and local control became issues in the Campbell family, Thomas was more liberal and tolerant in his views and refused to become involved in the political and religious contention that pitted Catholics against Protestants and Irish against British.[12]

In time, Thomas became a probationary Anti-Burgher Seceder Presbyterian minister sent to a congregation that lacked a fixed ministry. Likely prior to this time, as he traveled back and forth between the University of Glasgow and his parents' home in the northern part of Ireland, he became acquainted with and married Jane Corneigle, a descendant of French Huguenots.[13] This faction of the Protestant Reformation became known as the Reformed Church in France, whose beliefs were greatly influenced by John Calvin.[14] They were highly critical of the doctrine and rituals of worship in the Catholic Church, believing instead that salvation came through simple faith in God and obedience to the teachings of the Bible. Persecution caused the Huguenots to flee from France for various other countries in 1681. Jane's ancestors had settled in County Antrim, in the northern part of Ireland. Her parents were strict Calvinistic Presbyterians, and she was raised memorizing and reciting scriptures. Both as a youth and as an older woman, her capacity for scripture memorization was legendary. Alexander had great praise for her, both as his mother and as his father's helpmeet in the Christian ministry.[15]

ALEXANDER CAMPBELL'S FORMATIVE YEARS

Alexander was born in 1788, the oldest of seven living children. During his formative years, Alexander's main interests were outdoor activities and sports, not study. He spent several years in boarding schools away from home, living with family members and others. Upon his return home at about the age of nine, his father desired to supervise his education; however, he found an uninterested son who was averse to the confinement required of serious study. Thomas determined to subdue Alexander's desire for sport and "to break him in to his books" by putting him to work as a farm laborer.[16] After working hard for several years, his intellectual nature began to assert itself. He had matured not only physically but also intellectually, gaining a love of reading and a desire to become "one of the best scholars in the kingdom."[17] Because Thomas Campbell was college educated and supplemented his preaching by teaching students, he was highly qualified to guide the education of young Alexander.[18] Consequently, Alexander became well educated in Greek; Latin; French; the Enlightenment philosophy of John Locke; the empirical, inductive, and nonspeculative style of Francis Bacon; and their mutual application to "common sense moral reasoning." He had a deep appreciation for Locke's Christian philosophy and reverence for the Bible. In particular, Alexander admired Locke's arguments in "Letters on Toleration," with its ideas on religious and civil liberty, along with his "Essay on the Human Understanding," with its notion that human knowledge and understanding began at birth and moved forward.[19] Locke's philosophy influenced Campbell's "view of the nature of man, the manner in which human knowledge originates, and the channels through which any communication from God must be made to man."[20] Campbell likely also appreciated Locke's words in *On the Reasonableness of Christianity as Delivered in the Scriptures*, a confirmation of evidence-based reasoning, a defense of faith against skepticism, and a rejection of the creeds of mainstream religions—all views he would adopt.[21] Alexander's reading interests illustrate that he enjoyed thinking deeply about the acquisition of knowledge found in Lockean epistemology. He also enjoyed applying Bacon's evidence-based style of reasoning to his study of the scriptures and would later use it in his defense of Christianity.

His religious training was as vigorous as his literary education. Every day, both morning and evening, the family worshipped by singing hymns, reading scriptures, memorizing Bible passages, and calling upon God in prayer.[22] These activities, along with the strong example of his father who believed in the "supreme superiority" of the Bible "above all human composition"—molded Alexander's character into the intellectual, well-spoken, and well-reasoned preacher that he would become.[23] In a memoir about his father, Alexander shared a rhetorical question his father had posited: "Are we living for time, or are we living for eternity?" Such were the discussions he remembers his father leading at family devotionals. His respect and admiration for his father's influence on his own life led him to confess that "whatever good, little or much, I may have achieved under God, I owe it all . . . to his paternal care and instruction, and especially to his example."[24]

In 1798, Thomas accepted a call as minister to a newly established Seceder church in Ahorey in northern Ireland. Sometimes on Sunday evenings, Thomas and Alexander would quietly visit a congregation of Independents in the nearby town of Richhill.[25] At these meetings, regionally well-known speakers such as Rowland Hill, James Alexander Haldane, and John Walker advocated a far more liberal point of view than the Seceder Presbyterians did. All of these men were highly educated, but each eschewed formal religion for independence and advocated itinerant preaching and nondenominational churches. Hill was denied ordination into the Catholic-influenced Church of England six times—likely because he taught a mix of Calvinist and Arminian ideas.[26] He preached without ordination in the open air, drawing opposition from both authorities and mobs. Haldane, initially part of the Church of Scotland (Presbyterian), left the church and, with his followers, organized "Churches of Christ" throughout Scotland and Ireland. Walker, a minister at Trinity College in Dublin for the Anglican Church of Ireland, resigned his position because his religious views had changed. His followers called themselves "The Church of God."

The fundamental principles of these Independent preachers apparently struck a resonant chord with Alexander. In the Anglican and Presbyterian Churches, people were encouraged to read—but not interpret—scripture, because interpretation was an exclusive part of the minister's calling. Within the Independent Church, however, the right to individually judge the meaning of scripture was a distinguishing characteristic and points to the influence of the Scottish Enlightenment. Their ideas exuded confidence in the ability of ordinary people to rationally and with common sense read the scriptures for themselves without the tainted erudition of the clerical elite.[27] Additionally, the Independents rejected the authority of the presbyteries, synods, assemblies, and conventions.

The ideas of independence likely percolated in young Alexander's mind as he contemplated his father's failed attempts to bring reform to their own congregation. Thomas had advocated for more frequent celebration of the Lord's Supper than the standard of twice a year and lamented that his recommendations were treated with indifference by the presbytery and synod. Further, Alexander could not help but observe the freedom of opinion and church governance the Independents enjoyed. The Scottish Independents in the Campbells' neighborhood were Haldanean adherents that partook weekly of the Lord's Supper and gave contributions for the poor; however, they opposed the New Testament practices of communal living and the washing of feet, and they believed that the miraculous gifts of the Spirit had ceased.[28] It appears that, initially, one effect the conflicting doctrines and practices had on Alexander "was to increase his reverence for the Scriptures as the only infallible guide in religion."[29]

In his late teens, Alexander began to pursue his own education and study with great passion, staying up late at night and rising early in the morning. Due to the size of his family, with six living siblings, it appeared that the opportunity to attend the university would not be possible.[30] In addition to his studies, he was an assistant at his father's school and a private tutor to local children whose parents could afford it. His father, excessively busy with all his teaching and congregational responsibilities, was discouraged by political and religious unrest, and this, coupled with the failure of his efforts to bring reform and greater unity among the churches of Ireland, caused him to grow increasingly ill over a period of years.[31] In June 1800, Thomas recorded in his journal that he felt "dull and heavy, weak and sickly, both in body and in mind."[32] Finally, his physician warned him he would die if he didn't give up his rigorous activities and recommended a long sea voyage as essential to his recovery. At the strong encouragement of his physician, family, and friends, Thomas Campbell determined to attempt a voyage to the New World.

Alexander made his father's departure possible by volunteering to fulfill his father's commitments at the school. At almost twenty, Alexander was described as "tall, athletic, and well-proportioned" and was quite capable of taking care of the family.[33] Additionally, he announced his own plan to immigrate to America when he came of age. Convinced on all accounts that he should go and make preparations for his family to follow, Thomas sailed in April 1807 from Londonderry, Ireland, on the ship *Brutus*. Upon landing in Philadelphia, he learned that the united Burgher and Anti-Burgher Presbyterians of the Associate Synod of North America were meeting in the city. He presented his papers and was assigned to the Chartiers Presbytery in southwestern Pennsylvania, with his base in the town of Washington.[34]

Almost a year and a half after Thomas's departure, delayed by a bout with smallpox, the Campbell family, consisting of seven children and mother, Jane, prepared to sail to America.[35] On 28 September 1808, as they boarded the *Hibernia* in Londonderry, Ireland, to sail for Philadelphia, Alexander noted, "The sailors were almost all young and inexperienced."[36] He had a strong premonition in a dream that the ship they were on was in grave danger.[37] In his reminiscences he described in horrifying detail what actually happened:

> On Monday 3 October at 3 o'clock we weighed anchor for as we thought the last time till we behold the [——] haven. The wind which was just now fair enough and a good sea blowing gale turned rather against us and soon we found we were unable to compete with it. We ran before it the whole night. [The] next morning we found ourselves on the coasts of Scotland and run into one of the western isles into a rocky shore and a very crooked cay. . . . We were told that Locham Daal [Loch Indaal] Cay was very dangerous, that many ships were wrecked there. On the night of 7th of October about 10 o'clock the wind rose so high that we were blown ashore and dash[ed] upon the rocks. In the midst of all this I got upon [the] deck the [main crew?] almost on her one side. For a little me thought that devouring flood must be the inevitable fate of every soul on board in about ½ an hour when the masts and rigging were all cut off. I began to weep a little but the long night [brought?] us down into despair.[38]

Alexander's description of the tempest and the threat of drowning was not an exaggeration. That night, another ship and a large sloop also wrecked on the rocks nearby, with no survivors.[39] During this harrowing experience, Alexander contemplated death and reexamined his priorities: "Kingdoms and scepters offered would not excite one wish. Their value here was like bubbles on a stream, not to be hunted after not to be desired . . . [and were] vain."[40] It appears he could clearly see the selfish and insignificant nature of most human ambitions as well as his own fragile mortal state. He recalled his father's life and devotion to God, and according to his biographer, "resolved that if saved from the present peril, he would certainly spend his entire life in the ministry of the gospel."[41] His family survived the shipwreck but was forced to delay its journey to America. The delay became providential for Alexander's further intellectual and spiritual development. The family determined to remain in Scotland for the winter, relocating to Glasgow while they awaited the next sailing season. Fortunately, Alexander was able to obtain several introductory letters for Greville Ewing, a noted Independent minister and reformer at the University of Glasgow. He secured passage from Bowmore to Glasgow for his family and went ahead to find lodgings.[42]

As the family recovered from its frightening ordeal, Alexander studied for a year under Professor Ewing as well as Professor George Jardine, who taught Scottish common sense reasoning and had been a student of philosopher Thomas Reid. During that year, Alexander began to record his personal thoughts and spiritual growth in a diary, in both shorthand and Latin. There he confessed "the usual deficiencies in spiritual-mindedness, self-consecration and attention to duty, and the usual longings after a higher spiritual life." In time, his reflections "gave place to broader and more elevated views, and to appropriate meditations upon certain portions of Scripture."[43]

As it had been during Thomas's time there, the University of Glasgow continued to generate Scottish Enlightenment ideas, similarly influencing Alexander's thinking. His father had provided an introduction to these ideas and now the university broadened and deepened his understanding, making him a capable and articulate spokesman for the application of common-sense moral reasoning to the scriptures.

In his school journal, titled "Juvenile Essays On Various Subjects by Alex Campbell in the University of Glasgow, 1808," he wrote essays and orations about the following topics, which give insight into some of his studies on Enlightenment thinking: "Defining Genius, its culture, the faculties it more completely defines, etc."; "Logic as the art of directing the powers of knowledge in the search of truth and communication"; "Socratic Dialogue"; "The Difference between a Judgment and a Proposition"; "On the Syllogisms"; and "On the Aristotilian [sic] Method of Dispute."[44]

Professor Ewing, Alexander's mentor at the University of Glasgow Seminary, was an advocate of the religious ideas of eighteenth-century reformers John Glas, Robert Sandeman, and Robert and James Haldane.[45] Glas advocated a reinstatement of the primitive order of the church. Some of Sandeman's main ideas included separation of church and state with local autonomy, weekly worship with the Lord's Supper and scriptural reading, and no creeds, very similar to the ideas of the Haldanes. Alexander was already familiar with James and Robert Haldane from occasional attendance at the meetings of the

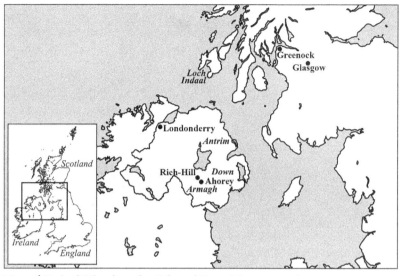

Map of United Kingdom, by Edward Dean Neuenswander.

Independents in Richhill with his father. Both of the Campbells were influenced by James Haldane's writings, or at least came to many of the same conclusions. Haldane's intent was to encourage scripture study, a point with which the Campbells strongly agreed; Thomas included it in his *Declaration and Address*, a prospectus for uniting Christians. The Campbells also believed that the New Testament contained all that was necessary for the Christian faith, but that "communalism" and the washing of feet were not essential practices. The Campbells believed in unity but forbore dictating a mode of baptism until studying it further. Haldane advocated that where possible, the laying on of hands should accompany the ordination to a particular office or work and the healing of the sick. Alexander subscribed to the laying on of hands for ordination but not for the healing of the sick, which he considered unique to the apostolic era. Haldane restricted laying on of hands for conveying the Holy Ghost to the Apostles. Neither he nor Campbell connected this ordinance with baptism.

Haldane listed other practices and ordinances observed by the apostolic church, including studying and proclaiming the gospel facts and truths, fasting, making contributions to care for the poor, partaking of the Lord's Supper, praying to and praising God, sanctifying the first day of the week, and participating in baptism. Alexander agreed with these practices and added confession and intercession to the list.[46]

Alexander Campbell's 1809 Journal. Courtesy of Disciples of Christ Historical Society, Nashville, Tennessee.

Haldane and the Campbells agreed on the extraordinary offices in the church of apostles, prophets, and evangelists who were chosen by the Lord himself. Haldane warned against conflating them with the stated offices of elders, bishops, preachers, ruling elders, widows, deacons (who could be both men and women), and pastors—all with a diversity of gifts among them to be used for the edification of the church; however, congregations should be independent. The Campbells embraced this view of church polity and agreed that the miraculous gifts of the Holy Spirit had ceased because those blessings were confined to the first ages before Christianity was established.[47]

The Haldane brothers and the Campbells shared a deep devotion to the words in the Bible and held out for the independence of spirit found in lay and itinerant preaching. The Haldanes focused on preaching the facts of the scriptures in Scottish Enlightenment fashion, appealing to the rational thinking and common sense of all Christians. Their knowledge of and focus on the scriptures made them highly successful—even among those whose views did not completely coincide with their own. They did not urge the addition of new gospel tenets but looked back to a revival of the Protestant Reformation begun by Luther and Calvin. The preaching of Christ crucified was the central tenet of their teaching—all differences regarding ordinances and church organization should be matters of "forbearance." They taught that it was the scriptural duty of every Christian, not just of ordained ministers, to warn sinners of God's wrath and to point to Jesus as the way, truth, and life.[48] Like the Haldanes, Alexander Campbell "resolved that he would preach the gospel without fee or reward."[49]

Campbell's scriptural journal of 1809 reflected his commitment to preparing to preach the gospel. His writings were filled with topics such as "The Heart Is Deceitful," "On the Being of God and on the Truth of Divine Revelation," "On God and Revelation," "Ministerial Character," "For Professions on Confessions of Faith from the Scriptures," "Proofs for the Sonship of Jesus, Christ Being Eternal," "Miracles," "Life of Paul: Remarks on the Life and Conversion of Paul," "Occupations of the Disciples," "Prophecies about Jesus: Quotations of Evangelists from the Prophets" [of the Old Testament], and "Parables and Similes of Jesus Christ." Perhaps the most interesting conclusion that he drew from reflecting on the parable of the talents was a link to democracy, leading him to claim that democracy was vindicated by religion.[50]

Additionally, he pondered deeply on faith, selecting Matthew 21:21–22 as his scriptural foundation regarding the withering of the fig tree and the promise of power to move mountains if one asks in faith. He noted that faith in these passages is opposed to doubt. "Belief then is to assent of the understanding to the truth of some proposition . . . one kind of evidence—ergo faith is the assent of the mind to the truths of the gospel."[51] This statement on faith embraced the Enlightenment philosophy in the collection of facts that appeal to the mind and was based on the Baconian evidentiary method. Leroy Garrett, Churches of Christ historian, asserts that this "scientific" approach to biblical interpretation was unique and strange to religious leaders in Campbell's day.[52]

Campbell accepted the Scottish Enlightenment philosophy as demonstrated by the Haldanes: faith in Jesus Christ rests upon the evidence furnished by the Holy Spirit in the scriptures that appealed to both the understanding and the heart. His understanding of faith embraced the Enlightenment practices that included rational thinking and Baconian reasoning, but with a distinctly spiritual aspect of the Holy Spirit aiding the heart in receiving the meaning of scripture. Faith created a testimony of Jesus Christ which was the foundation of personal trust in the Savior. Later, Alexander would argue "that where there was no evidence there could be no faith" and, therefore, no testimony of or trust in the Savior.[53]

Just as he had done with his father in Ireland, Alexander often took the opportunity to listen to preachers of different denominations and observe their strengths and weaknesses. He also was aware of the opposition of the clergy in the various churches to every attempt at reformation. Ewing continued to greatly influence Alexander's thinking regarding the principles of congregationalism and locally and independently run churches emancipated from the control synods and general assemblies; he also underscored the beliefs of the Haldane brothers.[54]

The influence of eminent men active in the Scottish Reformation and Enlightenment movements guided Alexander's thinking on existing denominations and in particular on his family's association with Presbyterianism. Following the end of the school year, the semi-annual communion time of the Seceder Presbyterians approached, and Alexander questioned whether he should participate. He underwent the required interview for someone who did not have papers from his former synod and was given the appropriate token to receive communion.[55] However, he still felt uncertain if he could conscientiously "recognize the Seceder Church as the Church of Christ." As the tokens were collected, he threw his on the plate but did not partake of the sacramental emblems. Thus, the token became the beginning of his separation from the Seceder Presbyterians.[56]

Several months later, passage became available for him and the rest of the family to sail for America. Finally, in August 1809, over two years after Thomas had left, the family resumed their journey, this time leaving from Greenock, Scotland, on the *Latonia*.[57] This trip was also full of danger and great distress, as Alexander recorded:

> Monday morning [the 7th] about 10 o'clock I was disagreeably surprised with the intelligence that the ship had sprung a leak. . . . [The] wind blew a very heavy gale so that the sea ran very high and we were [cold?] greatly tossed indeed[—]very apprehensive of danger from the heavings of this gale insomuch that we forgot the danger of the leak. This evening I went to see in the midst of many doubts and fears not knowing what might be my fate before I should see the sun of tomorrow. About midnight the wind fell and the danger of the gale was apparently gone. Next day I set to along with other passengers to pump in turn, to assist the sailors, and to know the extent of the leak.[58]

The trip was beset by gales and squalls, with brief respites of calm days. Between storms and seasickness, Alexander and other men assisted the sailors in pumping water to keep the ship afloat. Campbell recorded that many on board were certain that death was imminent. He turned to God with these personal thoughts: "Such was that dreadful squall and such its effects (on the ship), but thanks be to the God who raises the winds and quells the tumult of the Seas, that it did not prove fatal to us all, and may his great mercy bless us as a fatherly reproof to us all and instruct us by it to look in on habitual preparation for death when he calls for us."[59]

Arriving safely in New York on 29 September after the grueling fifty-four-day journey, Alexander began immediately to write a sermon based on John 5:39, "Search the scriptures; for in them ye think ye have eternal life: and they are they which testify of me," prefaced with these personal thoughts: "I have heard a voice from heaven from the judge of heaven and earth addressed to me, to you and all people."[60] He then laid forth his arguments regarding the duty to study the scriptures. It seems that this preface and the sermon that followed were the renewal of his vow of loyalty and service to God.[61]

Beginning on 5 October 1809, the family traveled the almost one hundred miles from New York to Philadelphia, and then westward another three-hundred-plus miles to Washington, Pennsylvania, where Thomas was living. En route, Alexander discovered that the hotel where they were lodging had neither locks nor bolts. He confessed that he felt like he had discovered a "golden age" where robbery and injustice were unknown and where Providence had created free institutions, equal rights, educational advantages, and moral and religious obligations among a purely Protestant community.[62] This exuberance about America may have been the foundation for his postmillennialist beliefs—great confidence that the millennial age could be created in the wonderful circumstances found in America and that this would bring forth the Second Coming of Christ.[63]

When Alexander and Thomas were reunited almost two weeks later, Alexander learned that his father had also experienced life-changing events. Similar to what had occurred in Ireland, neither the presbytery nor the synod was interested in his liberal ideas, and jealousy, animosity, envy, slander, and injustice characterized their treatment of Thomas to the point that he was convinced his life was in danger. He testified to his family that "nothing but the law of the land had kept his head upon his shoulders."[64] Thomas was censured and removed from his ministerial duties. Although indignant at the treatment of his father, Alexander rejoiced that he and his father, albeit in very different ways, had arrived at the same place in their religious sentiments.

At the time his family arrived in America in late September 1809, Thomas had just received the proofs for the *Declaration and Address*, his signature ideas on reform and restoration which would create Christian unity, a foundation on which the Millennial era could be built. This was the formal commencement of their reformation and restoration efforts.[65] Alexander read his father's words with great interest and approval.[66] Father and son were no longer associated with the Seceder Presbyterians, and Alexander soon joined his father in the non-denominational Christian Association of Washington, a diverse group of influential persons and families who were connected to various religious communities in the region, perhaps mainly Presbyterians, who adopted Thomas's sentiments in *Declaration and Address* as worthy of consideration by all Christians.

Although no longer attending school, Alexander continued to set high theological goals for himself with very specific means of accomplishing them. One of his resolutions for 1810 was to be "first in Theological Studies." He determined to accomplish this by daily effort: reading for a half hour from the scriptures in the original references; reading a chapter each in the Old and New Testaments (with Scott's notes), noting practical observations; and memorizing a verse, verses, or chains of verses to be repeated as a whole each Sabbath.[67] On Saturday evenings, he would reflect on his work and note in his journal whether it was fulfilled or not. He concluded his list of goals by asking for God's grace to attend him in his efforts. Just as he had desired when he was younger to become "one of the best scholars in the kingdom," now he wanted to be "first in Theological Studies."[68] He was competing against no one but his inner drive to know more than anyone else regarding the scriptures. Alexander Campbell's initial impulse was a "current reformation" within Christianity—specifically the Baptists. Later, he and his followers would refer to themselves as a "restoration movement," seeking to restore New Testament Christianity.

NOTES

1.   Thomas's father, the Scotch-Irish Archibald Campbell, converted from Catholicism to Anglicanism. Although the majority religion in Ireland was Catholicism and most of the Scottish immigrants were Presbyterians, Anglicanism was considered "the ascendency" religion and constituted the ruling class of Ireland. Membership would have given him privileges unavailable to Catholics or Presbyterians. The other two religious groups were considered dissenters. D. Newell Williams, Douglas A. Foster, Paul M. Blowers, eds., *Stone-Campbell Movement: A Global History* (St. Louis: Chalice Press; Nashville: Disciples of Christ Historical Society, 2013), 16–17.

2.   The Covenanters derived their name from the desire to mimic the Old Testament custom of covenants sworn by ancient Israelites. They bound themselves together in a National Covenant to maintain Presbyterian doctrines and policies as the sole form of religion in Scotland and protested against the king's efforts to change modes of worship. The Seceders protested from the official Presbyterian Church of Scotland because they claimed it did not recognize Christ as the supreme king, nor was it part of a covenant community.

     The Scottish General Assembly abolished patronage in 1690, when William and Mary reestablished Presbyterianism in the Church of Scotland; however, in 1712 the British Parliament reintroduced patronage into the Presbyterian Church of Scotland as an incentive for the Scottish landowners, as hereditary owners of the property on which the local church was built, to name a minister that supported Queen Anne rather than the Catholic Stuarts. When the Presbyterian Church of Scotland reluctantly allowed patronage to be reinstated, a group "seceded" from it. The Seceders refused to allow patronage at all and withdrew from the General Synod of the Church of Scotland in 1733, and formed their own Associate Synod. Williams et al., eds., *Stone-Campbell Movement*, 17.

3.   Robert Richardson, *Memoirs of Alexander Campbell*, 2 vols. (Germantown, TN: Religious Book Service, 1897), 1:23–24. Alexander Campbell designated Dr. Robert Richardson—longtime friend, family physician, and coeditor of and contributor to the *Millennial Harbinger*—as his official autobiographer. Richardson was tutored as a youth by Thomas Campbell, Alexander's father, and Walter Scott, who was appointed the chief missionary for Campbell's reformation in 1827. Richardson officially joined Campbell's restoration in 1829 and had access to papers and personal reminiscences of Campbell that other biographers did not. His *Memoirs* are considered an insider's perspective of Campbell and his restoration, and the first complete

and, to date, the most extensive account of his life. Douglas A. Foster, Director of the Center for Restoration Studies at Abilene Christian University, is currently at work on a critical biography. Other biographies are dismissed by researchers of restorationism as hagiographies and do not have the comprehensive view of Richardson and later scholars.

4.   Scottish Common Sense Realism "offered a defense of rational theology against the skepticism of eighteenth-century Scottish philosopher David Hume and yet provided a safeguard against rationalism by emphasizing also the limits of reason." Natural theology is a mode of Christian thinking that assumed unprecedented importance during the eighteenth century as it was contrasted with natural religion, the philosophy of the deists. Natural theologians claimed that "reason, reflecting on either the visible world or the workings of the human mind, could produce evidence for the existence of a transcendent God apart from the revelation in scripture or the tradition of the church. Natural theology pointed toward and confirmed truths above the capacity of reason to discover—truths accessible only through special revelation." Holifield, *Theology in America*, 5–7.

5.   Jonathan Edwards believed these moralists had accurately described moral sense but failed to realize that it could never attain the level of true virtue. The natural conscience could recognize secondary beauty found in order, symmetry, and proportion of natural objects and social relations but not discern the love and excellency of being in general. In other words, ethics belonged to divinity, because "moral philosophy was misleading without theology." Holifield, *Theology in America*, 120.

6.   David N. Livingstone, D. G. Hart, and Mark A. Noll, eds., *Evangelicals and Science in Historical Perspective* (New York: Oxford University Press, 1999), 104–5. The results of this movement were that the only two reliable sources for truth became the Bible and science.

7.   Holifield, *Theology in America*, 7.

8.   Paul C. Gutjahr, *An American Bible: A History of the Good Book in the United States, 1777–1880* (Stanford: Stanford University Press, 1999), 44.

9.   Quoted in Richard T. Hughes and C. Leonard Allen, *Illusions of Innocence: Protestant Primitivism in America, 1630 to 1875* (Chicago: University of Chicago Press, 1988), 154.

10. Mark A. Noll, *America's God: From Jonathan Edwards to Abraham Lincoln* (New York: Oxford University Press, 2002), 94.

11. The Seceder Presbyterians further divided between Burgher and Anti-Burgher over the "Burgess oath" that was required of city officials in Glasgow, Edinburgh, and Perth to keep Catholics out of public office after the 1745 Jacobite rebellion. City officials were required to swear support to the "true religion professed in this realm" and renounce Roman papistry. The Burgher Seceders believed this "true religion" could be interpreted as referring to the Seceder Presbyterian Church, whereas the Anti-Burgher Seceders did not, believing it to be interpreted as the Presbyterian Church from which they had seceded. Williams et al., eds., *Stone-Campbell Movement*, 17.

12. Williams et al., eds., *Stone-Campbell Movement*, 18. In Scotland, the official state religion was Presbyterian, whereas in Ireland it was the Anglican Church. Presbyterians believed Anglicans to be dissenters, and their political loyalty under question.

13. Richardson, *Memoirs of Alexander Campbell*, 1:22–27.

14. The five points of Calvinism are often expressed with the acronym TULIP: total depravity (meaning total inability and original sin), unconditional election, limited Atonement, irresistible grace, and perseverance of the saints (once saved always saved). However, this summary does not fully represent his views. It was developed for the 1618 Synod of Dordrecht (Council of Dort), which was held to settle the

controversy regarding ideas advocated by Jacob Arminius. See chapter 5 for a brief explanation of Calvinism, Arminianism, and the various aspects of TULIP.

15. Alexander Campbell, *Memoirs of Elder Thomas Campbell, Together with a Brief Memoir of Mrs. Jane Campbell* (Cincinnati: H. S. Bosworth, 1861), 309–11.

16. Richardson, *Memoirs of Alexander Campbell*, 1:32.

17. Richardson, *Memoirs of Alexander Campbell*, 1:32.

18. Richardson, *Memoirs of Alexander Campbell*, 1:1–2, 28–37.

19. Winfred Ernest Garrison, *The Sources of Alexander Campbell's Theology, Its Sources and Historical Setting* (St. Louis: Christian Publishing, 1900), 111–12; Richardson, *Memoirs of Alexander Campbell*, 1:33–34. See also Noll, *America's God*, 108.

20. Garrison, *The Sources of Alexander Campbell's Theology*, 92–94, 107–9, 156–57. See also Samuel Morris Eames, *The Philosophy of Alexander Campbell* (Bethany, WV: Bethany College, 1966), 19–26.

21. Interestingly, this 1695 publication had the effect of promoting the cause of deism for others. Although Locke had written that some of the truths of revelation might be above reason, although not contrary to it, John Toland, a proclaimed disciple of Locke, wrote that although he believed in biblical revelation, nothing in the gospel was contrary to reason, nor could truth be higher than reason. The Enlightenment and Locke's promotion of reason had become, for Toland, the highest order of revelation. Holifield, *Theology in America*, 160.

22. Richardson, *Memoirs of Alexander Campbell*, 1:35.

23. Richardson, *Memoirs of Alexander Campbell*, 1:39–40.

24. Campbell, *Memoirs of Elder Thomas Campbell*, iv.

25. When there were no Seeder meetings, "occasional hearings" to other churches were permitted but not encouraged. Richardson, *Memoirs of Alexander Campbell*, 1:60.

26. Calvinist and Arminian doctrines are considered the division in Protestant thought regarding soteriology (salvation). Presbyterians and Baptists (generally) were Calvinist, and the Methodists were Arminian. See chapter 5 for a discussion of both Calvinism and Arminianism. The 1618 international Synod of Dordrecht, held by Reformed Christians who followed Calvinistic ideas, condemned Arminianism.

27. Holifield, *Theology in America*, 291.

28. Richardson, *Memoirs of Alexander Campbell*, 1:60–73.

29. Richardson, *Memoirs of Alexander Campbell*, 1:75.

30. In addition to Alexander, who was the oldest child, Thomas and Jane had six more children: Dorothea, Nancy, Jane, Thomas, Archibald, and Alicia. Three other children died in infancy. Richardson, *Memoirs of Alexander Campbell*, 1:29, 77.

31. Between 1804 and 1806, Thomas had proposed to the synod the reuniting of the Burgher and Anti-Burgher factions of the Seeder Presbyterian Church in Ireland— after all, these factions were only a reality in Scotland! The Glasgow Synod quashed his proposal to permit the Irish churches to make their own decision, not even allowing a vote. Williams et al., *Stone-Campbell Movement*, 18.

32. Campbell, *Memoirs of Elder Thomas Campbell*, 200.

33. Richardson, *Memoirs of Alexander Campbell*, 1:96.

34. Williams et al., *Stone-Campbell Movement*, 19; Richardson, *Memoirs of Alexander Campbell*, 1:76–81.

35. Jane, the fourth of the living siblings, had contracted smallpox, which required confinement for several months; thus, rather than sailing in the spring of that year, they had to wait until the fall. Richardson, *Memoirs of Alexander Campbell*, 1:97.

36. Alexander Campbell, "Journal of a Voyage from Ireland towards America 1808," manuscript D, 12L, Disciples of Christ Historical Society, Nashville, Tennessee.

Manuscript D is the designation for the entire journal, 12 denotes the page (not numbered in the journal), and the letter *L* designates "left page" while *R* designates "right page." To date, this journal has not been transcribed.

37. Richardson, *Memoirs of Alexander Campbell*, 1:99–100. This dream was not recorded in Campbell's "Journal of a Voyage from Ireland towards America 1808." However, he may have considered it a sacred personal experience that he only shared with family and very close friends, such as his authorized biographer, Robert Richardson.

38. Campbell, "Journal of a Voyage from Ireland towards America 1808," 11R, 12L–R.

39. Eva Jean Wrather, *Alexander Campbell, Adventurer in Freedom: A Literary Biography* (Fort Worth: Texas Christian University, 2005), 62.

40. Campbell, "Journal of a Voyage from Ireland towards America 1808," 12L.

41. Richardson, *Memoirs of Alexander Campbell*, 1:102. Campbell did not record this commitment in his personal journal of the voyage.

42. Richardson, *Memoirs of Alexander Campbell*, 1:114–15.

43. Richardson, *Memoirs of Alexander Campbell*, 1:141–42. Campbell did not record this sentiment in his journal; however, his journal entries include notable academic and spiritual acumen.

44. Alexander Campbell, "Juvenile Essays on Various Subjects by Alex Campbell in the University of Glasgow, 1808," Manuscript B, Disciples of Christ Historical Society.

45. Richardson, *Memoirs of Alexander Campbell*, 1:177–79. John Glas and Robert Sandeman were eighteenth-century Scottish reformers who were connected by Sandeman's marriage to Glas's daughter as well as by some elements of their religious philosophy. Their followers were called respectively "Glasites" and "Church of Christ." *Encyclopedia of the Stone-Campbell Movement*, 335–56; Holifield, *Theology in America*, 294. According to "Sandeman, Robert," in *Encyclopedia of the Stone-Campbell Movement*, 669, "The role of faith in salvation, plurality of elders, and weekly communion are the clearest examples of a doctrinal relationship between Campbell and Sandeman." Campbell, however, vehemently denied any influence from Sandeman, professing to be an independent thinker. Some scholars argue that Campbell's idea of faith arising through the proclamation of the facts comes from Robert Sandeman and that his Christological ideas came from the Haldanes. Sandeman "proposed that neither good works nor a persuasion of being forgiven gave evidence of saving faith. . . . Faith meant intellectual assent to Christian teaching about redemption through Christ, and everyone who assented could be assured of salvation." Holifield, *Theology in America*, 139.

46. Alexander Campbell, *Christian System: The Christian System, in Reference to the Union of Christians, and a Restoration of Primitive Christianity, as Plead in the Current Restoration* (Cincinnati: Bosworth, Chase & Hall, 1871), 63.

47. James Alexander Haldane, *A View of the Social Worship and Ordinances Observed by the First Christians, Drawn from the Sacred Scriptures Alone: Being an Attempt to Enforce Their Divine Obligation; and to Represent the Guilt and Evil Consequences of Neglecting Them* (Edinburgh, Scotland: J. Ritchie, 1805). Haldane did not intend his book to set a standard for church order; however, many of his ideas resonated with Thomas and Alexander and became tenets of their restoration. Initially, Haldane advocated infant baptism, equating it with circumcision, but in 1808 embraced believers' baptism by immersion. In 1812, Alexander, through his own study, would also embrace believers' baptism by immersion.

48. Richardson, *Memoirs of Alexander Campbell*, 1:149, 160, 172, 178, 182.

49. Richardson, *Memoirs of Alexander Campbell*, 1:177.

50. Alexander Campbell, "A Diary Jany 1st 1809," Manuscript E, Disciples of Christ Historical Society, Nashville.

51. Campbell, "A Diary Jany 1st 1809," 76L.
52. Leroy Garrett, *The Stone-Campbell Movement* (Joplin, MO: College Press, 1983), 26.
53. Richardson, *Memoirs of Alexander Campbell*, 1:177–78;
54. Richardson, *Memoirs of Alexander Campbell*, 1:187–89.
55. Communion tokens were small square, circular, oval, or rectangular pieces of lead that were stamped with the minister's initials, the congregation, the date, or some other identifying mark. They were part of the Presbyterian ritual called "fencing the tables," meant to include or exclude communicants and maintain the boundaries between members and nonmembers, and those saved and unsaved. Leigh Eric Schmidt, *Holy Fairs: Scottish Communions and American Revivals in the Early Modern Period* (Princeton, NJ: Princeton University, 1989), 108.
56. Campbell's biographer called his reluctance an expression "not of communion, but of separation." Richardson, *Memoirs of Alexander Campbell*, 1:190. Other Churches of Christ scholars note that not partaking of the emblems may occur for a variety of reasons, such as concern for eating and drinking unworthily, as Paul warned in 1 Corinthians 11:27.
57. Campbell, "Journal of a Voyage from Ireland towards America, 1808," 12L. He titled this time period: "Second Part of my Journal from Scotland toward America, 1st August 1809."
58. Campbell, "Journal of a Voyage from Ireland towards America, 1808," 24R.
59. Campbell, "Journal of a Voyage from Ireland towards America, 1808," 27L.
60. Campbell, "Journal of a Voyage from Ireland towards America, 1808," 33L.
61. After Campbell's deliverance again from life-threatening storms, Richardson reported that Campbell renewed his vow of loyalty to God and promise of service in ministering the gospel. This sermon may be this recommitment. Richardson, *Memoirs of Alexander Campbell*, 1:198.
62. Richardson, *Memoirs of Alexander Campbell*, 1:210.
63. For further discussion on Millennialism, see chapters 8 and 13.
64. Richardson, *Memoirs of Alexander Campbell*, 1:220.
65. Richardson, *Memoirs of Alexander Campbell*, 1:237.
66. Campbell, *Memoirs of Elder Thomas Campbell*, 23.
67. "Scott's notes" refer to a five-volume Bible annotated by Calvinist Anglican Thomas Scott. It was first published in the United States between 1804 and 1809. Noll, *America's God*, 372.
68. Campbell, manuscript E29L; Richardson, *Memoirs of Alexander Campbell*, 1:32.

3

Early Life of
and Religious Influences
on Joseph Smith

*J*oseph Smith Jr. was born on 23 December 1805 in Sharon, Vermont, to Lucy Mack and Joseph Smith Sr.; the child was named after his father and was the third son of their nine children. Both families had roots in rural New England. Lucy was born in Gilsum, in the north-central part of New Hampshire, and Joseph was born in Topsfield, on the northeastern border of Massachusetts. Lucy and Joseph were deeply religious, but in different ways, and they could best be described as seekers rather than as affiliated with a particular denomination.

In about 1802, Lucy, as a young wife and mother of two children, recorded being visited by a Methodist exhorter when she was very ill with consumption that threatened to be fatal.[1] She did not want to converse with him because she was afraid "he will ask me if I am prepared to die"—thinking in her mind, "I do not know the ways of Christ."[2] That night she pleaded in private prayer for her life. She begged the Lord "that he would spare my life that I might bring up my children and comfort the heart of my husband, . . . and [I] covenanted with God if he would let me live I would endeavor to get that religion that would enable me to serve him right whether it was in the Bible or wherever it might be found even if it was to be obtained from heaven by prayer and Faith."[3]

Shortly after her miraculous recovery, Lucy began searching for a religion that would honor her covenant with God. She visited a minister whom she considered exceedingly devout, and who knew of her illness and marvelous rescue by God from death. During their conversation, however, his words regarding her illness and miraculous recovery lacked the testimony of Christ she expected, and she went away disappointed. She then heard about a pious minister who would be preaching at the Presbyterian church, so she went, hoping to hear the "bread of eternal life." Again she was disappointed, with what she described as "emptiness vanity vexation of spirit; . . . it did not fill the aching void nor satisfy the craving hunger of the soul."[4]

At this point, Lucy determined that she would continue to seek religious understanding on her own by listening and reading, but that God, rather than a minister, would be her spiritual guide. After pursuing this course for approximately eighteen years until her oldest son, Alvin, was twenty-two, she decided, "My mind would be easier if I were baptized and I found a minister who was willing to baptize me and leave me free from membership in any church."[5] Recognizing that baptism was an important commandment, Lucy obeyed; however, at this point in her life she remained nondenominational and was always hopeful of finding a minister or church that could satisfy her spiritual yearnings.

When the family moved to Tunbridge, Vermont, around 1807, Lucy began attending Methodist meetings, and Joseph Sr. acceded to her wishes and accompanied her, much to the chagrin of his father, Asael, and older brother, Jesse. At the turn of the nineteenth century, Methodism in America was a fast-growing religious movement noted for its enthusiasm and for being a more interactive faith than traditional churches. Joseph Smith Sr.'s family was well acquainted with the Bible; in fact, Asael was described as "a man of extraordinary retentive memory and possessed a great knowledge of the Bible, so much so that he could read it as well without the book as with it."[6] Asael belonged to a Universalist society that advocated salvation for all. He was also captivated by Enlightenment reasoning such as found in Thomas Paine's *Age of Reason*, urging his son Joseph to consider it. Jesse was Calvinist in his beliefs; both had opinions very different from enthusiastic and experiential Methodism. Although there were Calvinist and Arminian Methodist churches, Lucy and Joseph Smith Sr. were likely attending an Arminian Methodist church with enthusiastic impulses, which is what upset Asael and Jesse. The family was religiously minded and devoted to the scriptures but generally were seekers after a more satisfying religious faith than that provided in the creeds.[7] Stung by family criticism, Joseph Sr. stopped attending church with Lucy and requested she also stop going because it caused great division among their family and friends. Hurt and discouraged, Lucy walked to a nearby grove of wild cherry trees and prayed for the Lord to influence her husband "to receive the gospel whenever it was preached."[8] At that moment, she was exceedingly depressed about her family's religious standing, but that night she had her own very vivid dream of a beautiful meadow near her home with two majestic trees. During her dream, she contemplated the meaning and realized that the two trees represented her husband and his oldest brother Jesse; the former was "more pliable and flexible," while the latter was "stubborn and unyielding." She felt she was given to understand that "the breath of heaven which passed over them, was the pure and undefiled gospel of the son of God" and that her husband, Joseph, at a later time "would hear and receive [it] with his whole heart."[9]

In 1811, Joseph Sr. became more interested in religion. Lucy described it thus: "About this time my husband's mind became much excited upon the subject of religion; yet he would not subscribe to any particular system of faith, but he contended for the ancient order, as established by our Lord and Savior Jesus Christ and His Apostles."[10] Religious excitement was a term that could be interchanged with enthusiasm, and it included experiences such as dreams and visions, as opposed to the Enlightenment-directed rational and reasoned natural order of the universe. It is apparent that Joseph Sr. was a seeker after a church that mirrored the primitive Christian church of the New Testament and was open to personal spiritual experiences.

Shortly thereafter, beginning in April 1811 and over the next few years, at least until 1819, Joseph Sr. began having dreams in regard to his own and his family's salvation.[11] Lucy recorded seven of these dreams in her family memoir. His dreams exhibited "a desire for belief, healing, and direction."[12] However, they caused him to be "more confirmed than ever in the opinion that there was no order or class of religionists that knew any more concerning the Kingdom of God, than those of the world." Thus, he remained skeptical of all organized religions.[13] Joseph Sr. was careful with his religious sentiments. He accepted his dreams as heaven-sent, but this made him more aware of the disparity between what he felt in his heart and understood in his mind and what he knew of the religious denominations in his area.

At the outset of his married life, Joseph Sr. owned a farm and established a mercantile business and a ginseng exportation business;

however, the unethical dealings of a business partner, unfortunate business decisions of his own, and several seasons of poor crops left the family impoverished.[14] During this period, the family moved frequently, living in Tunbridge, Randolph, Sharon, Royalton, and Norwich, Vermont, then Lebanon, New Hampshire, and finally settling in Palmyra, New York, now completely indigent. He and his sons worked during the spring and summer clearing land, plowing, planting, harvesting, and doing odd jobs for hire. During the winter months, Joseph Sr. taught school. Lucy contributed her part to the family income by painting oil cloth coverings for table stands. The family experienced a short bout of prosperity in Palmyra, but generally it was difficult for Joseph Sr. to stay ahead of his bills and provide for his family.

High rates of child mortality and ill-informed medical care were common in early nineteenth-century America, and the Smith family became closely acquainted with death and debilitating disease. About 1797, the first child of Lucy and Joseph Sr. died at birth. In 1802, Lucy, after the births of Alvin and Hyrum, was considered so gravely ill from tuberculosis that she was expected to die. In late 1812 and early 1813, typhus fever caused Sophronia, the oldest daughter, to be so ill that the physicians ceased attending to her after three months because they believed her unable to recover and that death was imminent. Joseph Jr. had his own bout of typhus fever and experienced a new and innovative surgery for a serious bone infection during this same time. In 1823, their oldest son, Alvin, became ill with what Lucy called bilious colic, a blockage of the gallbladder. He was administered a large dose of calomel—a compound of mercury and chlorine—which in small doses has laxative and antiseptic properties. Within days, however, he died from the lethal overdose which remained lodged in the upper bowel, causing gangrene.[15]

All of these experiences tempered the lives of Lucy and Joseph Sr. Lucy openly turned to God to heal herself and her family both physically and spiritually. After the family bout with typhus fever and Joseph's bone infection, she testified, "We realized the blessing for I believe [we] felt more to acknowledge the hand of God in preserving our lives through such a desperate siege of disease pain and trouble than if we had enjoyed health and prosperity during the interim."[16] Lucy's expression of gratitude is likely speaking for the entire family, including Joseph Sr.; nevertheless, he remained aloof from many of the religious revivals surrounding Palmyra which became common in the early 1820s and refused to attend with Lucy and other family members.[17]

Joseph Smith Jr.'s Formative Years

The story previously mentioned about Joseph's bone infection began when, at about age seven, Joseph Jr. contracted a bacterial infection of typhus fever, which was followed a few weeks later by severe shoulder pain that caused him to scream aloud.[18] After weeks of suffering what the initial doctor diagnosed as a sprain, a closer examination revealed a large fever sore between the breast and shoulder area, likely the axillary lymph nodes, filled with pus. After the swelling in the shoulder area was lanced, pain concentrated in the marrow of his leg. For several more weeks there was no relief from the swelling and extreme leg pain. A surgeon made an eight-inch-long incision along the anterior tibialis muscle, relieving the pain for a short time, but as the incision healed, the pain was as excruciating as before. A second, deeper incision was made, revealing the bone, but as it began to heal, swelling caused the same unbearable pain. A council of seven surgeons found the infection in the bone so substantial that they considered it incurable and recommended amputation of the leg. Lucy appealed to the surgeons for one more attempt to save the leg by cutting out only the affected part of bone—apparently this was a new surgery that she had heard about. The surgeons acceded to her request. Joseph Jr. refused the cords to bind him to the bed and the brandy that was recommended for pain. His father held him as he screamed in pain while the surgeons removed part of his lower leg bone by boring into it from two angles and breaking off the infected area with forceps. Following surgery, Joseph Jr. recovered in Salem, Massachusetts, near the sea breezes, while living in the home of his uncle, Jesse Smith.[19] His ordeal caused him to walk with the aid of crutches for about four years and to slightly limp for the remainder of his life.[20]

As a result of his family's poverty, Joseph Jr. had little opportunity for formal education. In fact, he stated, "Being in indigent circumstances were obliged to labour hard for the support of a large Family having nine chilldren and as it required their exertions of all that were able to render any assistance for the support of the Family therefore we were deprived of the bennifit of an education suffice it to say I was mearly instructtid in reading and writing and the ground <rules> of Arithmatic which const[it]uted my whole literary acquirements."[21] Since his father taught school during winters to help meet the family's financial obligations, it is likely he taught Joseph Jr. in the basics of reading, writing, and arithmetic.[22] Due to his limited education, Joseph Jr.'s handwriting was always poor and his spelling and punctuation are perhaps best described as unique—and at least part of the reason he later almost always dictated to scribes.

Religious revivals were an intrinsic part of the Second Great Awakening. The early Methodist movement, known for its enthusiasm-driven beliefs in the supernatural, such as prophetic dreams, visions, and emotion-soaked revivals, acquired respect among some of the common folk. Camp meetings were led by highly charismatic lay preachers in multiday events filled with singing, shouting, falling down, and fervent preaching and praying. Some attempted to manipulate "excitements" to facilitate the decision to obey God's commandments, and some placed a bench called an "anxious seat" for those troubled by their conscience and in need of spiritual redemption. The New England region where Joseph lived was often a focal point for religious camp meetings. In fact, this area of upstate New York was later called the "burned over district" by Charles Finney because of all the religious revivals. One historian called revivals "calendrical festivals," special events for harvesting souls, and the high days of the year.[23] As part of their attempt to make money, the Smith family sold food to camp meeting attendees.

Sometime between the ages of twelve and fifteen, Joseph Jr. began his search for saving truth.[24] In recounting his early religious memories, it is apparent that Joseph had spent considerable time contemplating the religious enthusiasm he encountered in the region. His concern for the welfare of his "immortal soul" caused him to search the scriptures, having been "taught that they contained the word of God." Smith's apprehension was consonant with the impassioned preaching of the era that was calculated to arouse fear in the hearts of many concerning salvation and that increased the solemnity of all religious gatherings.[25] He became intimately acquainted with the beliefs of different denominations; however, he said that he "remained aloof from all these parties," although he "attended their meetings as often as occasion would permit."[26] Comparing their beliefs with what he found in the scriptures, he pondered the dissonance, contentions, and divisions among them, and became distressed at his own sins as well as at the apostasy of the denominations because he could find none "built upon the gospel of

Jesus Christ as recorded in the new testament."[27] As a young adolescent, he remembered vividly the "war of words and tumult of opinions" held by the convert-seeking Presbyterians, Baptists, and Methodists.[28] The consensus was that all were sinners, and he could not hope for salvation by his own efforts; the "Blood of the Lamb" alone could save him. The Calvinistic doctrines of predestination and regeneration clashed with the Armininian doctrine of salvation for all.[29] Smith revealed in detail his troubled feelings about the crucial questions of salvation in five first-hand accounts and five secondhand accounts given at different times over a period of twelve years to various individuals.[30] The following is a harmonization of these accounts with the official account written by Smith in 1838, noted as Joseph Smith—History (JS—H), as the foundation. The year and author of the different accounts is in parentheses.

JS—H 8: During this time of great excitement my mind was called up to serious reflection and great uneasiness [;] I became seriously impressed with regard to the all-important concerns for the welfare of my immortal soul (1832, JS). I began to reflect upon the importance of being prepared for a future state (1842/1843, JS) of existence: but how, or in what way, to prepare [my]self, was a question, as yet, undetermined in [my] own mind. [I] perceived that it was a question of infinite importance, and that the salvation of [my] soul depended upon a correct understanding of the same; [I] saw, that if [I] understood not the way, it would be impossible to walk in it, except by chance; and the thought of resting [my] hopes of eternal life upon chance, or uncertainties, was more than [I] could endure. . . . It also occurred to [my] mind that God was the author of but one doctrine, and therefore could not acknowledge but one denomination as his church; and that such denomination must be a people, who believe, and teach, that one doctrine (whatever it may be) and build upon the same. [I] then reflected upon the immense number of doctrines, now, in the world, which had given rise to many hundreds of different denominations (1840, Orson Pratt).

JS—H 9: My mind at times was greatly excited, the cry and tumult were so great and incessant (1838, JS). [I] wanted to get religion too [; I] wanted to feel and shout like the rest but could feel nothing (1844, Alexander Neibahr). The Presbyterians were most decided against the Baptists and Methodists, and used all the powers of both reason and sophistry to prove their errors, or, at least, to make the people think they were in error. On the other hand, the Baptists and Methodists in their turn were equally zealous in endeavoring to establish their own tenets and disprove all others (1838, JS).

JS—H 10: In the midst of this war of words and tumult of opinions, I often said to myself: What is to be done? Who of all these parties [,] whose feelings toward each other all too often were poisoned by hate, contention, resentment and anger [,] (1842, Orson Hyde) are right; or, are they all wrong together? If any one of them be right, which is it, and how shall I know it? (1838, JS). . . . The great question to be decided in [my] mind, was—if any one of these denominations be the Church of Christ, which one is it? Until [I] could become satisfied, in relation to this question, [I] could not rest contented (1840, Orson Pratt). I pondered many things in my heart concerning the situation of the world of mankind: the contentions and divisions, the wickedness and abominations, and the darkness which pervaded the minds of mankind. My mind became exceedingly distressed[,] for I [had] become convicted of my sins (1832, JS). The only alternative, that seemed to be left, was to read the scriptures, and endeavor to follow their directions (1840 Orson Pratt). . . . By searching the scriptures I found that mankind did not come unto the Lord but that they had apostatized from the true and living faith and [that] there was no society or denomination that built upon the Gospel of Jesus Christ as recorded in the New Testament (1832, JS).

JS—H 11: While I was laboring (1838, JS) in this state of perplexity (1841, JS) under the extreme difficulties caused by the contests of these parties of religionists, I was one day reading the Epistle of James, first chapter and fifth verse, which reads: *If any of you lack wisdom, let him ask of God, that giveth to all men liberally, and upbraideth not; and it shall be given him* (1840, Orson Pratt).

JS—H 12: This was cheering information to [me]: tidings that gave [me] great joy to guide [me] to the path in which [I] should walk It was like a light shining forth in a dark place (1840, Orson Pratt).

Smith pondered the idea that God would give wisdom to those that ask—even a fourteen-year-old youth.[31] Seeing this scripture as a way out of his "darkness and confusion," he determined to ask the Lord in prayer early in the spring of 1820. His initial question for God was, "Which of the sects is right (for at this time it had never entered into my heart that all were wrong)—and which I should join."[32] This was Joseph's first foray into personal vocal prayer; perhaps modeled after the practice of his mother Lucy who frequently walked into the woods to pray privately.[33]

His concerns included doctrinal disparities among the competing Protestant churches and dismay at some of the unchristian conduct of the ministers, but his most deeply held anxiety was for his eternal welfare. He had no thoughts but to find which currently existing church pleased God. As mentioned previously, he came from a visionary family.[34] Over the next ten years, Smith also claimed to receive many subsequent visions and visitations, formally organizing the Church of Christ on 6 April 1830 in Fayette, New York.[35]

NOTES

1. *Consumption* is an archaic and common term for the wasting of the body from a disease known today as pulmonary tuberculosis. The old term refers to an individual being consumed by the disease.

2. Lucy Mack Smith, *Lucy's Book: A Critical Edition of Lucy Mack Smith's Family Memoir*, ed. Lavina Fielding Anderson (Salt Lake City: Signature Books, 2001), 277. Lucy Mack Smith, History, 1844–1845, CHL [p. 3, bk. 1], http://joseph smithpapers.org.

3. Smith, *Lucy's Book*, 277–78; Smith, History, 1844–1845, CHL [p. 3–4, bk. 1], http://josephsmithpapers.org.
4. Smith, *Lucy's Book*, 280; Smith, History, 1844–1845, CHL [p. 4–5, bk. 1], http://josephsmithpapers.org.
5. Smith, *Lucy's Book*, 280–81; Smith, History, 1844–1845, CHL [p. 5–6, bk. 1], http://josephsmithpapers.org. Joseph, however, recorded in his official history that she and several of his siblings affiliated with the Presbyterian Church. Perhaps this occurred at a later date. Joseph Smith History 1:7 (Pearl of Great Price).
6. Richard Lloyd Anderson, *Joseph Smith's New England Heritage* (Salt Lake City: Deseret Book, 1971), 111.
7. Although associated with the Congregational Church and owning a pew in the local church, Asael also accepted Universalist teachings on salvation. Anderson, *Joseph Smith's New England Heritage*, 105–6, 191n129.
8. Smith, *Lucy's Book*, 292–93; Smith, History, 1844–1845, CHL [p. 10, miscellany], http://josephsmithpapers.org.
9. Smith, History, 1845, CHL [p. 50–51], http://www.josephsmith.papers.org.
10. Smith, History, 1845, CHL [p. 52], http://www.josephsmithpapers.org.
11. Smith, *Lucy's Book*, 294–98, 319–20, 324–25, 330; See also pages 169–70, which give an approximate chronology of dreams one, two, six, and seven.
12. Bushman, *Joseph Smith and the Beginnings of Mormonism*, 5.
13. Smith, *Lucy's Book*, 296; Smith, History, 1845, CHL [p. 53], http://www.josephsmithpapers.org.
14. Smith, *Lucy's Book*, 275, 281–86, 294, 298–99, 310–18. For greater detail on the Smiths' financial misfortunes, see Richard Lyman Bushman, *Joseph Smith: Rough Stone Rolling* (New York: Knopf, 2005), 18–19.
15. Smith, *Lucy's Book*, 168, 276–77, 300–310, 350–55.
16. Smith, *Lucy's Book*, 310; Smith, History, 1844–1845, CHL [p. 3, bk. 3], http://josephsmithpapers.org.
17. Smith, *Lucy's Book*, 357–58.
18. Typhus is what Lucy calls the fever that affected the family; however, typhoid fever is listed in the Critical Edition chronology. They are different bacteria and different diseases. See Smith, *Lucy's Book*, 169 and 300.
19. Smith, *Lucy's Book*, 303–10; Smith, History, 1844–1845, CHL [p. 2, bk. 3], http://josephsmithpapers.org.
20. Smith, *Lucy's Book*, 169.
21. Karen Lynn Davidson et al., eds., *Histories, Volume 1: Joseph Smith Histories, 1832–1844*, vol. 1 of the Histories series of *The Joseph Smith Papers*, edited by Dean C. Jessee, Ronald K. Esplin, and Richard Lyman Bushman (Salt Lake City: Church Historian's Press, 2012), 11.
22. Bushman, *Joseph Smith and the Beginnings of Mormonism*, 31. Others have speculated that Hyrum Smith, while caring for his brother after the leg operation, may have also aided in Joseph's education. This might have occurred after Joseph returned from his Salem, Massachusetts, recovery period.
23. Schmidt, *Holy Fairs: Scottish Communions and American Revivals in the Early Modern Period*, 215.
24. "Letter Book A," JS Letterbook 1 [ca. 27 Nov. 1832–ca. 4 Aug. 1835], JS Collection, CHL 1–2, http://josephsmithpapers.org.
25. Catharine C. Cleveland, *The Great Revival in the West, 1797–1805* (Gloucester, MA: Peter Smith, 1959), 36.
26. "History of Joseph Smith," *Times and Seasons*, 15 March 1842, 727, http://www.josephsmithpapers.org.

27. "Letter Book A," JS Letterbook 1 [ca. 27 Nov. 1832–ca. 4 Aug. 1835], JS Collection, CHL, 2, http://josephsmithpapers.org.
28. Joseph Smith—History 1:10.
29. Cleveland, *The Great Revival in the West*, 47.
30. The first vision account quoted was created by Matthew B. Christensen, *The First Vision: A Harmonization of 10 Accounts from the Sacred Grove* (Springville, UT: Cedar Fort, 2014), utilizing all the known recorded accounts of Joseph Smith's first theophany. Although the 1838 recital was an official account dictated by Joseph Smith and canonized as part of Joseph Smith—History in the Pearl of Great Price, the combination of all the other known accounts adds a much fuller description of the event and Joseph's feelings. Words and punctuation in brackets were added by Christensen to make grammatically complete phrases. For a full account of the now-known total ten accounts (in thirteen documents) of the primary historical sources of Joseph Smith's First Vision, see Dean C. Jessee, "The Earliest Documented Accounts of Joseph Smith's First Vision," in *Opening the Heavens: Accounts of Divine Manifestations, 1820–1844*, ed. John W. Welch with Erick B. Carlson (Provo, UT: Brigham Young University Press; Salt Lake City: Deseret Book, 2005), 1–36.
31. James 1:5. According to one account by Oliver Cowdery, Reverend George Lane, a Methodist minister, spoke in Palmyra during an 1820 revival—and it was through his preaching that Joseph Smith's mind became awakened. Cowdery, however, later changed the date to 1823. Oliver Cowdery, "Early Scenes and Incidents in the Church," *Latter Day Saints' Messenger and Advocate* 1, no. 3 (December 1834): 42, and 1, no. 5 (February 1835): 78. William Smith, Joseph's younger brother, gave credit to Reverend Lane for his brother's desire to approach God. According to William's recollections, however, Reverend Lane gave a talk entitled "What church shall I join," based on James 1:5, in 1822 or 1823, several years after Joseph dated his first vision. William Smith, *William Smith on Mormonism* (Lamoni, IA: Herald House Steam Book and Job Office, 1883), 6; *Deseret Evening News*, January 20, 1894, 11, cited in Larry Porter, "Reverend George Lane—Good 'Gifts,' Much 'Grace,' and Marked 'Usefulness,'" *BYU Studies* (Spring 1969): 336–38. See also Staker, *Hearken, O Ye People*, 131–33.
32. Joseph Smith—History 1:18.
33. Smith, *Lucy's Book*, 291–92, 455–56. A friend described Joseph Smith as "of lowly birth, a farm boy of common class, poor, illiterate and without distinction other than being religiously inclined; he attended revivals, was in these anxious circles honestly seeking religion and to learn which was the right church; and calling upon the Lord in simple faith that he might know." "Benjamin F. Johnson to George S. Gibbs, April–Oct. 1903," in E. Dale LeBaron, *Benjamin F. Johnson, Friend to the Prophets* (Provo, UT: Benjamin F. Johnson Family Organization, 1997), 229.
34. As previously noted, his mother Lucy recorded some of her own visions and those of her husband Joseph Smith Sr. in her family history. See Smith, *Lucy's Book*, 292–96, 318–20, 324–25, 329–30.
35. Joseph Smith's church organization went through several name changes. Initially, however, it was called the Church of Christ.

Restorationism, Primitivism, and Millennialism

After all my search, and examinations, and considerations,
I said, I do profess to believe that some come nearer to the first
primitive churches, and the institutions and appointments
of Christ Jesus than others. . . . I professed that if my soul
could find rest in joining unto any of the churches professing
Christ Jesus now extant, I would readily and gladly do it,
yea unto themselves whom I now opposed.

—ROGER WILLIAMS, LETTER TO GEORGE FOX, 1676

Restoration has a variety of definitions, all relative to the user. Hence, Alexander Campbell and Joseph Smith both called their religious work restoration, but how very different their methods were![1] Richard T. Hughes has given this broad and inclusive definition: "Restoration involves the attempt to recover some important belief or practice from the time of pure beginnings that believers are convinced has been lost, defiled, or corrupted. . . . [Therefore] restorationism assumes that at some point in Christian history a fall or apostasy occurred."[2] Restoration presupposes an earlier golden age and then a drift or falling away. A recovery of original truths, or "primal norms," has always been a foundational aspect of American thought.[3]

Apostasy

Belief in an apostasy in the early church was characteristic of Campbell and Smith, as well as many of their contemporaries.[4] Engaged in their restoration movements, both understood apostasy in relation to the confusion and strife they saw in Christianity as Protestantism continued to splinter into a multitude of sects. Campbell and Smith could agree that there had been ungodly additions to the Bible, most prominently the creeds. Campbell also believed there had been neglect of key aspects of the apostolic church which he intended to restore to the church. Smith announced that there had also been losses and over time began to focus on the loss of knowledge and doctrines.

Campbell's belief in apostasy sprang in part from the lack of an authentic and faithful history of Christianity; he lamented there was not a record of Christianity that was separate from the history of the Roman Catholic Empire. Campbell noted the collaboration between church and state until he believed they had become indistinguishable and their histories one. Although small groups began to separate early on from the Catholic Church in an effort to bring Christianity back to its primitive simplicity, their efforts were largely crushed. Nevertheless, even without a satisfactory history, Campbell identified the accommodation of doctrine to the prejudices of the Jews, Gentiles, and pagans as one of the most significant causes of Christianity's corruption,[5] and he bemoaned the fact that "most of the popular schemes, and dogmas, and institutes are Egyptian, Babylonish, or Roman."[6]

Campbell noted that in an effort to stem apostasy, there had been many famous reformations; however, they had been reformations of creeds and clergy rather than of religion itself. He proudly declared that Christianity could not be reformed because its author is infallible. Thus, "we have had reformations enough. . . . A restoration of the ancient order of things is all that is necessary."[7] He believed that the canonization of the New Testament marked the conclusion of Christianity's "pure beginning": "We [ought to] understand, believe and practise the doctrine of Christ delivered to us by his apostles."[8] He was convinced, that as important as the era of the Reformation was, the era of Restoration would far transcend it.[9]

As a fourteen-year-old boy, Smith was not thinking about the Reformation or creeds; his concern was finding truth and personal salvation. Pondering his quandary led Smith to search the scriptures. The great questions concerning his personal salvation tormented his thinking because he had "become convicted of [his] sins,"[10] and he "considered it of the first importance that [he] should be right, in matters that involve eternal consequences."[11] A desire for personal salvation led him into a grove of trees to "cry unto the Lord for mercy"[12] and to "ask of God . . . which of all the sects was right . . . and which I should join."[13] What Smith "sought first was to know was which church to join in order to submit himself to grace. The one issue could not be settled in his mind without addressing the other."[14]

Through his first visionary experience in 1820, he learned that humankind had apostatized from true faith in God and that none of the existing sects or denominations he knew about were founded upon the New Testament gospel of Jesus Christ. They were wrong because of their creeds, mistaken doctrines, and denial of the power of God.[15] There had been a serious departure from the New Testament pattern, and without saving truths, salvation would be in jeopardy. His "sense of an apostasy from the true Christian faith was ratified" in this theophany that included a monumental revelation that Christ's church in its pristine form did not currently exist on the earth.[16]

Smith's understanding of apostasy matured over the next thirteen years. He claimed to learn from visits of an angelic messenger, Moroni, the last prophet of the Book of Mormon, "that the apostasy encompassed more than the loss of a true Christian faith in the old world; it also included the dwindling of ancient covenant peoples, specifically the scattering of [the house of] Israel."[17] Further, the Book of Mormon puts forth the breadth and depth of the Apostasy[18] explaining that many "plain and most precious parts" of the gospel of Jesus Christ were taken away, especially many covenants of the Lord.[19]

By 1833, Smith noted signs that should follow believers in Christ—power to cast out devils, speak in tongues, heal the sick, and so on—and that they were lacking in the current Christian sects and denominations. He contended that from "the foregoing testamonies we may look at the Christian world and see the apostacy there has been from the Apostolic platform."[20] He then quoted Isaiah's lament that humankind had "transgressed the laws, changed the ordinances, and broken the everlasting covenant."[21] This perspective added to his understanding of the Apostasy: the corruption of the early church went further than human-created creeds and mistaken doctrines. It also included the loss of divine authority—the foundation of prophets and apostles—and therefore the loss of revelation and gifts of the Spirit.[22]

Both men recognized Christianity's apostasy from its pure beginnings and felt driven to return to the unadulterated gospel of ancient times. Campbell believed that the Great Apostasy had introduced extrabiblical creeds, innovations, and errors; Smith believed that and more. Like Campbell, Smith held to the ideal of uniting Christianity into one church, but in his view a fully restored church must be built upon a latter-day foundation of priesthood authority through apostles and prophets, revelation, gifts of the Spirit, and the promises of the Abrahamic covenant. Campbell, on the other hand, based his restoration on the teachings of the New Testament, with the early Christian church described in the Acts of the Apostles and especially the Epistles as the foundation. He believed that apostles, prophets, gifts of the Spirit, and revelation were no longer needed after the "pure beginning" had been established.

But they understood pure beginnings differently. Campbell believed the pure beginnings were with the early apostolic church as recorded in the Acts of the Apostles and the New Testament Epistles. Smith, in contrast, understood the pure beginnings to have been initiated with Adam and Eve in the Garden of Eden as recorded in Genesis—and a fuller restoration with Christ, as he organized his church. Both men believed that overwhelming reasons for a restoration were evident. Campbell believed that the incomplete Reformation meant that key ordinances and practices must be restored *to* the church. Smith believed, however, that the apostasy was so comprehensive that it required a redispensing of heavenly knowledge and authority—a reopening of the heavens and dialogue between God and humankind and a restoration *of* the church that had ceased to exist shortly after the time of the Apostles.

RESTORATIONISM AND PRIMITIVISM

As related to a historical movement, *restorationism* is often used interchangeably with *primitivism*, which in religious conversation refers to an effort to recover the Christian primordial doctrines and organization found in the New Testament. The Puritans brought to America a primitivist attitude which made them eager to discard "human inventions"—those vestments and ceremonies which had no biblical precedent.[23] Primitivists attempted to cast off nearly two thousand years of Christian theology as "spiritual barnacles" that had accumulated over time.[24] Restorationists continued that tradition. Although there were several restorationist movements in the nineteenth century, Disciples scholar Robert Frederick West attributed to Campbell the leadership of the nineteenth-century primitive gospel movement.[25] Most importantly, Campbell would argue that religious accretions after the writings of the Apostles were anathema to Christianity and caused some in the nineteenth century to turn away from God and others to believe in a disinterested God who watched humans from a distance.

George Marsden defines primitivism as "a type of Biblicism that appeals to the authority of Scriptures and therefore disparages the authority of traditions and tends toward historylessness."[26] This definition of primitivism accentuates the authority of the Bible and the original faith and practices of the early Christian church, and disparages the intervening centuries of historical traditions that attempted to interpret God's truths. Further, it is a type of biblicism that appeals to the authority of *sola scriptura*—the Protestant rallying cry of scripture alone. Marsden identifies Campbell's movement as the most overt of this type of biblicism. Gospel liberty and pure doctrine meant clearing away the accretions by well-meaning Christian Fathers of the previous centuries.[27] In his 1809 *Declaration and Address* (considered at length in chapter 7), Thomas Campbell advocated "returning to and holding fast by the original standard; taking the Divine word alone for our rule." Campbell's statement was later summarized with this pithy slogan: "Where the Scriptures speak, we speak; where the Scriptures are silent, we are silent."[28]

Joseph Smith also believed in the importance of the Bible, but he believed in the possibility of new revelation and in the precedence of lineal priesthood authority, both of which were significantly at odds with Protestant reliance for authority on the scriptures alone. Historian Spencer Fluhman notes that although Mormons consider their beliefs and practices as timeless, many of their roots are found in Judaism as well as Protestantism. Early Mormon converts were seekers with Protestant backgrounds—but the gulf between some of their previous beliefs and Smith's teachings seemed to widen as Smith received more revelations. Part of the difficulty for Mormons in historicizing their faith and disavowing connections to the early Christian Fathers and the Reformation springs from the ways Mormons "both drew on and repudiated their Protestant heritage."[29] Hughes describes this leapfrogging over the eighteen centuries of Christian history that precede the Mormon restoration as an aberration of the primordial norm and a completely ahistorical approach.[30]

Winton Solberg suggests that religious restorationism is a manifestation of chronological primitivism, the assumption being that the best time was in the beginning; the subsequent course of history has been downward.[31] Martin Marty maintains that the primitivist movements of both Campbell and Smith were not so much "escaping to the pristine past [as] trying to replicate it in the present."[32] They were unique primitivists: Campbell could be called a chronological primitivist looking back to the apostolic era; Smith could best be described as an anachronistic primitivist looking back to Old Testament and New Testament eras and revealing ancient doctrines and practices that seemed out of place in the nineteenth century.

Richard Hughes applies three descriptive labels to primitivism—*ecclesiastical, experiential,* and *ethical*—to describe the primary characteristics of any given restorationist movement. Using these categories, Hughes classifies the "American-born Churches of Christ [largely Campbell's] as ecclesiastical primitivists, chiefly concerned with reproducing the forms and structures they think characterized the most ancient churches." He describes Smith's "Mormons" as primarily experiential primitivists, "chiefly concerned with replicating a presumed spiritual dimension of the first age."[33]

In nineteenth-century America, a variety of religious groups exhibited a primitivist impulse, including the Shakers, Baptists, Disciples of Christ, Christians, and Mormons.[34] Franklin Littell divides restoration-minded groups into moderate reformers, or those seeking to make corrections within the current structure, and radical restitutionists, or those desiring to begin anew.[35] As should be apparent by now, Campbell belonged to the former classification and Smith to the latter.

Primitivists sought for timeless truths, absent human bias, and western cultural conditioning; however, primitivism ultimately produced a plethora of competing new Christian churches.[36] The proliferation of Protestant groups driven by the impetus for restoration, whether moderate or radical, produced "bitter jarrings and janglings of a party spirit" in the words of Thomas Campbell, as well as reinforcing the notion that Christianity had strayed from the Bible.[37] The primitive gospel movement was in part a reaction to sectarian conflict among mainstream Protestant churches but also the instigator of new sectarian divisions. Historian Marvin Hill lists several general characteristics of the primitivist movement: led by laymen with limited ministerial training who were critical of trained, professional clergymen; millennialist; opposed to Calvin's predestination ideas; and a belief that the Bible was the basis for Christian unity.[38] According to Hill, this last characteristic presented an unsolvable conundrum. Because churches were "free from European churchly traditions, each was inclined to disagree radically on matters of doctrine and church polity." In fact, each had different interpretations of the Bible; hence, the sectarian infighting would continue.

MILLENNIALISM AND PRIMITIVISM

In the unique restorationist view, millennialism and primitivism are linked in their idea that a resolution of the errant ways of the world would be brought about only by a restoration of the pristine purity of the ancient order.[39] Millennialism is the pinnacle of restorationist hope; it is the final triumphant re-creation of primordial purity.[40] Although not all Americans believed in Christian primitivism, many identified with millennialism.[41] In simple but imprecise terms, there are two ways to classify Millennialists, pre- and post-, depending on whether one believes that Christ will return prior to the one thousand years of peace and unity (premillennialist) or subsequently at the end of that time (postmillennialist). In addition to how and by whom the Millennium would come to fruition, essential differences in belief included literalist interpretations of biblical promises or allegorists who generally gave those promises a spiritualized or metaphorical interpretation.[42]

Both Campbell and Smith viewed their restorations as prologue to the Millennium, Campbell publishing the *Millennial Harbinger* beginning in January 1830 and Smith's followers in Missouri publishing the *Evening and Morning Star* beginning in February 1832. Campbell wanted to produce a journal that was a positive reflection of the need for religious reform and preparation for the Second Coming of Christ; hence the title was a herald of the coming millennial day. W. W. Phelps, Smith's printer, chose the name for their initial publication, symbolizing Mormon millennial expectations. The prospectus of the newspaper stated, "As the forerunner of the night of the end, and the messenger of the day of redemption, the Star will borrow its light from sacred sources and be devoted to the revelations of God . . . especially in these last days."[43] Both were influenced by the vision of the Apostle John in Revelation 14:6-7:

> And I saw another angel fly in the midst of heaven, having the everlasting gospel to preach unto them that dwell on the earth, and to every nation, and kindred, and tongue, and people,

Saying with a loud voice, Fear God, and give glory to him; for the hour of his judgment is come: and worship him that made heaven, and earth, and the sea, and the fountains of waters.

From his own experiences, Smith interpreted the angel from the biblical passage to be Moroni (the last Book of Mormon prophet, who had guardianship of that record), who "proclaimed himself to be an angel of God, sent to bring the joyful tidings that the covenant which God made with ancient Israel was at hand to be fulfilled, that the preparatory work for the second coming of the Messiah was speedily to commence; that the time was at hand for the Gospel in all its fullness to be preached in power, unto all nations that a people might be prepared for the Millennial reign."[44]

They both believed they were a part of the beginning of the millennial era by helping to establish God's kingdom in America in a more complete form than in any previous time of church history, a responsibility which they each equated with the building of Zion. They, along with many of their contemporaries, believed that the United States had a special destiny. "Conferences, sermons, books, plans and reforms of every sort addressed prophetic themes" in the late 1820s and early 1830s indicated a high interest in the Millennium. Millennial hymns were sung with fervor. Campbell's *Millennial Harbinger* printed this scripture on the masthead each month. Old Testament prophecies of Daniel, Zechariah, Jeremiah, and Ezekiel, as well as John's Revelation in the New Testament, were standard fare in sermons and in essays reprinted in the *Millennial Harbinger*.[45] Millennialist fever anticipated preparing for the imminent return of Christ. Many, including both Mormons and Campbell's followers, thought the emergence of the Millennium was imminent.[46]

Joseph Smith sought also to restore primitive Christianity through a restoration of all things. In the words of John Fullmer, an early Mormon convert, this included "embracing all the offices, powers and gifts, instituted by our Lord, and conferred upon his disciples before and after his ascension, and which distinguished the church of Christ during the apostolic age."[47] Smith was additionally challenging creedal Christianity by calling for the restoration of the purity of the gospel as given first to Adam and other Old Testament Patriarchs and then to the Apostles by Christ: "according to Mormon theology, God alone could 'restore' or reestablish that true faith."[48] Smith's restoration was not a reformation of Protestantism, but a restoration of the Abrahamic covenant, including all the promises of God to his children since the premortal council in heaven that were revealed in mortality to prophets as written in the Old and New Testaments, and revealed anew. This did, in time, lead to a church organization that was completely separate from and not part of Protestantism.

Grant Wacker calls both the Disciples of Christ and Latter-day Saints "restorers of ancient ways." He considers Smith more far-reaching than Campbell inasmuch as his restoration included not only the New Testament but the Old Testament as well.[49] In referring to Smith's innovative views, historian Jan Shipps identifies Latter-day Saints as reappropriators of the Judeo-Christian past.[50] This statement may be misleading—Smith was not restoring Old Testament forms such as the practices of the law of Moses. In restoring some features of Old Testament Israel, such as ancient covenants and priesthood keys, doctrines, and rituals given to Old Testament patriarchs, Smith also restored authority patterns that had previously guided the house of Israel—namely, prophets and an open canon.[51] Mark Noll acknowledges Campbell as "the upstart Restorationist"[52] but classifies the Latter-day Saints under Joseph Smith as nineteenth-century "outsiders,"[53] too far beyond Protestant Christianity to be recognized as occupying the same space as the "Millerites" or "Campbellites." Smith's restoration appears to some scholars to be "imaginative," "eclectic," "an amalgamation . . . that appears as sheer confusion," a "picking and choosing," and drawing on romanticism, apocalypticism, and the Enlightenment.[54] Historian E. Brooks Holifield argues that Smith's restoration leads to "realms of doctrine unimagined in traditional Christian theology."[55] It is apparent that a number of scholars, while more easily locating Campbell's main restoration focus under primitivism and Protestant reform, have greater difficulty in systematizing Smith's contributions other than labeling his restoration as radical.

Alexander Campbell's restoration movement fits more closely into the definitions of primitivism previously given. Campbell, although he considered himself a layman, was not poorly trained. He was well educated in languages (Greek, Latin, and French) and Enlightenment philosophy, and was familiar with European biblical commentaries. Richard Hughes, in fact, describes Campbell as "hardly a classical primitivist at all," characterizing his position instead as *rational progressive primitivism*."[56]

Although Joseph Smith's Latter-day Saints clearly had their own unique style of primitivism as well, Marvin Hill has pointed out that Mormon foundations were indeed grounded in the "primitive gospel."[57]

Campbell was seeking a recovery of the Christian primordial organiza-tion, behaviors, and doctrines based solely on the authority of the New Testament. Smith, in his sixth and seventh articles of faith, also declared a belief in the organization of the primitive church on a foundation of apostles and prophets, and all the gifts of the Spirit spoken of by the Apostle Paul.[58] His restoration was organizational, experiential, and eth-ical—it included both extraordinary biblical offices and extraordinary gifts of the Spirit, including direct communication with God, as well as a commitment to some of the ethical norms of Old and New Testament discipleship. But Smith claimed these offices, gifts, and moral imper-atives along with their accompanying doctrines, principles, and ordi-nances of the gospel had been redispensed several times throughout the millennia—for example, with Adam, Enoch, Noah, Melchizedek, Christ and his Apostles, and with the Nephites (Book of Mormon peoples) after Christ's visit to them. His restoration was inclusive of both the Old and New Testaments as well as additional scripture and revelation.

Mormons classify themselves as restorationist Christians and independent of Catholic, Orthodox, and Protestant traditions. They did not fit into Marsden's definition of primitivism that focuses on the Protestant notion of *sola scriptura*—a phrase that also implies without priesthood, tradition, or apostolic succession. Smith also placed great weight and authority on the Bible, believing it to be the word of God. Divine authority, however, could not be derived from interpretation of its pages. Additionally, since Latter-day Saints were not Catholic, Orthodox, or Protestant, both Christian tradition and history after the death of the Apostles had little influence on their doctrines. Accordingly, they fit Marsden's description of primitivism in the sense of being exces-sively free of tradition and history. With their unique position of not belonging to any existing Christian tradition—historical, creedal, or orthodox, but describing themselves as Bible-believing Christians of a different sort[59]—it is inherently more difficult to compare them with Campbell's Disciples, who, although not considered mainline, formal, or high church, are nevertheless still Protestant. It is extremely problematic to categorize Mormons using traditional Christianity as a model: they are not antiformal but have very ritualistic and symbolic ordinances, yet their Sunday services are free of high church ceremonies. They are not enthusiasm driven in the mode of charismatic worship; however, they believe in the continuing workings of all the gifts of the Spirit. They are not enlightenment rationalists, yet they believe that all truth comes from

God and should appeal to the heart and mind, whether found in the sciences or religion, and desire to embrace all that is true regardless of its source.[60] Historian James D. Bratt described Joseph Smith's church as an "extraordinary blend of the restorationist and futuristic."[61] His was a radical departure from every type of mainline Christianity. Mormonism is complex and fascinating, yet seemingly impossible to classify. Scholar A. Leland Jamison, with perhaps a bit of hyperbole, alleged, "The historical evolution of the Mormons furnishes the most thrilling chapter in the whole chronicle of American religion. By comparison, the adventures of the settlers in New England seem tame."[62]

Smith was a restorationist in terms of seeking to recover the primordial past, not based on the authority of scripture alone but on a foundation of covenants, priesthood authority with prophets, apostles, and, correspondingly, new revelation. Mormon scholar Terryl Givens asserts that "unlike the reformers who preceded him [or those who were contemporary with him], Joseph Smith insisted that his role was to usher in a new dispensation, a full restoration of Christianity in its pristine purity."[63] His was a restoration of *all* things, not just the *ancient order of* things from the New Testament Epistles.

Restoration as Part of the Second Great Awakening

Although both Alexander Campbell and Joseph Smith were nineteenth-century restorationists, they held very different ideas about how to accomplish a return to the primitive Christian church.[64] Constitutional disestablishment of state-sponsored religion created an era characterized by widespread interest in religious regeneration, revival, and restoration. Continuing disagreement about doctrine, practice, and church government by mainstream European Protestant churches such as the Anglican, Congregational, Presbyterian, and Lutheran churches caused further splintering of American Protestantism into a variety of new sects. The mix of so many religions, including traditional and upstart Protestant churches, was accompanied by the efforts of the Methodists and Baptists to evangelize the American populace, and the proliferation of non-Calvinist and innovative churches such as Free Will Baptists, Shakers, Millerites, and Unitarian/Universalists. Additionally, the dynamics of Enlightenment reason and unbridled charismatic emotionalism, more American than European, created great opposition and fueled the fires of debate and conflict over beliefs and practices.[65] The revivals of the era cultivated religious excitement that gave way to derogatory descriptors such as "enthusiasm," "fanaticism," and "extravagance," leading some to worry about a frenzied atmosphere leading to delusion.[66]

Alexander Campbell opposed the evangelical revivalism that took place in America because of its undisciplined religious emotionalism clearly at odds with his own rational, Enlightenment-inspired ideas. Joseph Smith found that the revivals in his area of western New York brought confusion. His deliverance from the "tumult of opinions" came through the professed authority of new revelations, visions, and angelic messengers.[67] From his study of the scriptures, Alexander Campbell deplored many of the theological and ideological "isms" popular in his day. Joseph Smith learned from his first theophany that human-created theologies were opposed to a true understanding of the power and authority of God as well as the nature of the Godhead.

Although a few Americans were "churched," belonging to one of several denominations that had migrated to the colonies, many others had not joined any congregation. According to Roger Finke and Rodney Stark, at the time of the [American] "Revolution only about 17 percent of Americans were churched."[68] Some of the unaffiliated were looking for the original gospel preached by Jesus. It was particularly among such "seekers" that restorationists such as Campbell and Smith found competition for converts.

Conclusion

Alexander Campbell and Joseph Smith are each unique primitivists and restorationists, holding contrasting and conflicting plans on how to restore the ancient order—Campbell by a careful reconstruction from a New Testament "blueprint" and Smith by revelation and the visitation of heavenly messengers. Further, although Campbell's ideas were considered radical by some mainstream religionists, he remained within the parameters generally accepted by Protestants. Smith's restoration incorporated multiple ancient and modern points of view—a complete break with traditional Christianity in all its forms.

Although Campbell and Smith both organized restoration churches within a year of each other, they were very different in important ways. Campbell was a gifted exegete reading the scriptures in multiple languages to lend unique insights and focused almost exclusively on New Testament Christianity for his key points of restoration. He was immersed in Enlightenment thought, meaning that he interpreted the scriptures using a rational and reasoned approach. From this method he formulated a picture of what he perceived needed to be pruned from the Protestant Reformation of Catholicism and the religions of his day—including his former Presbyterian Church and later regular Baptist Church—and from the New Testament Church what needed to be emphasized.

Joseph Smith, on the other hand, had not read or studied nearly as much as had Alexander, but at the age of fourteen he asked God for direction regarding his salvation. From the visions and angelic visitations that followed, he learned over time what he believed needed to be restored. As his faith matured, his focus was never in correcting the Protestant Reformation so much as in revolutionizing the whole of Christianity. "The *restoration* that Smith envisioned was more than the return of biblical principles, power, doctrine, ordinances, and authority. . . . It also meant rendering things not necessarily *as they once were*, but *as they should have been*."[69]

Both restorationists were returning to a "pure beginning," but they arrived at their conclusions by entirely different means—one by reason and the other by revelation—and therefore their directions and outcomes were very different. If restorationism is viewed as a continuum, Campbell and Smith are on opposite ends, one attempting to re-create through rational examination of the New Testament the ancient order of first-century Christianity, and the other revealing ancient covenants, doctrines, and rituals.

Campbell believed that the beginning was with Christ's Apostles, and Smith believed that Christianity began with Adam and Eve in the Garden and was redispensed at various other times, including during the mission of Christ and his Apostles. Early into his restoration proper, Smith pushed the "beginning" even further back. Ancient records that he translated by unique means described a council in heaven, a premortal group to which the plan of salvation was presented and ratified by all but a third part, and the premortal Christ accepted God's call to come to earth as Redeemer.

Campbell's restoration was a movement to restore the purity of primitive Christianity—the ancient order of things—primarily by discarding the divisive postapostolic creeds added over centuries of human interpretation and returning to the simple teachings of the New Testament.[70] He claimed he had "trimmed Christianity naked"; however, "our loss consists only of barren opinions, fruitless speculations, and useless traditions."[71] He eliminated nonscriptural beliefs and used inductive reasoning to reduce Christianity to what he deemed the core essential practices and principles that were presented in the New Testament. One of his primary assumptions was that the New Testament (particularly the Acts of the Apostles and the Epistles, especially the Epistle to the Hebrews) completely reflected the apostolic church with no need for further revelation.[72] From the Epistles, he could restore the correct forms, structures, and behaviors of the early church. His restoration was an attempt to complete the Christian Protestant reform that Luther had begun and not to begin a new sect or denomination.

In sharp contrast, Smith would not abide Campbell's rules of limiting himself to the New Testament. He was not just going back to primordial first-century Christianity; instead, he "saw himself as completing a work that had never been completely realized."[73] He ranged throughout the Old and New Testaments, even drawing upon prophets whose records were not in the Bible, and upon what he learned by revelation. Thus, he centered on restoring not only all the knowledge, covenants, and priesthood that have ever been taught by God; he expanded Christianity to encompass all truth given by God premortally and to humankind beginning with his words to Adam and Eve in the Garden of Eden, with the promise of even more revelation to come during the Millennium.

The scope of Smith's restoration is sweeping and, through Campbell's Enlightenment lens, beyond belief. In terms of restoration, one found sufficiency in the scriptures and the other found insufficiency; the one had a closed system approach and the other an open system. Key differences in these two restorationist approaches might be expressed as restoration by common sense reasoning with a reductionist approach to New Testament evidence and facts, juxtaposed against a restoration by revelation, personal visions, angelic visitations, and an almost incomprehensible expansion of the scriptural canon.

Smith and Campbell both drew on biblical promises to inform the foundations of their respective restorations. Campbell sometimes utilized the Old Testament to form the underpinnings upon which to base the New Testament teachings as he developed his views of restoration. He considered the Old Testament to be the Jewish portion of the Bible, however, and less instructive about Christianity than the New Testament. Smith's concentration, in contrast, included foundational doctrines in both the Old and the New Testaments, as well as in additional scriptures received through revelation. Each restorationist emphasized Christ, but from different perspectives: Campbell limited to the Bible, primarily the New Testament, and Smith unrestrained—including the Old Testament, New Testament, the Book of Mormon, as well as claims of extraordinary, unmediated interactions with otherworldly beings. Campbell was a man of the Book, and Smith was a man of the Books.[74]

Notes

1. Holifield and Mead, "Puritan and Enlightenment Primitivism: A Response," in *The American Quest for the Primitive Church*, 74.
2. Richard T. Hughes, "The Meaning of the Restoration Vision," in *The Primitive Church in the Modern World*, ed. Richard T. Hughes (Urbana: University of Illinois, 1995), x.
3. Hughes and Allen, *Illusions of Innocence*, 2.
4. See, for example, *Christian Disciple* 11 (September/October 1820): 346, 358, quoted in Richard E. Bennett and Amber J. Seidel, "Early Latter-day Saint Understanding of the Apostasy," in *Early Christians in Disarray*, ed. Noel B. Reynolds (Provo, UT: Brigham Young University Press, 2005), 74.
5. Campbell, "Notes of Apostacy, No. 1," *Millennial Harbinger* (New Series) 1, no. 1 (January 1837): 15–19.
6. Campbell, "Essays on Ecclesiastical Characters, Councils, Creeds, and Sects, No. 2," *Christian Baptist* 1, no. 9 (3 May 1824): 64.
7. Campbell, "A Restoration of the Ancient Order of Things, No. 1," *Christian Baptist* 2, no. 7 (7 February 1825): 126–28.
8. Campbell, "A Restoration of the Ancient Order of Things, No. 1," 128.
9. Campbell, "A Restoration of the Ancient Order of Things, No. 1," 128.
10. Dean C. Jessee, "Accounts of Joseph Smith's First Vision," *Opening the Heavens: Accounts of Divine Manifestations, 1820–1844* (Provo, UT: Brigham Young University Press, 2005), 5; Backman, "Joseph Smith's Recitals of the First Vision," 13; "Letter Book A," JS Letterbook 1 [ca. 27 November 1832–ca. 4 August 1835], JS Collection, CHL, 2, http://www.josephsmithpapers.org.
11. Jessee, "Accounts of Joseph Smith's First Vision," *Opening the Heavens*, 7; Backman, "Joseph Smith's Recitals of the First Vision," 13–14; JS, History [December 1834–May 1836?], verso of JS History, 1838–1856, vol. A-1, CHL, 120, www.josephsmithpapers.org.
12. Jessee, "Accounts of Joseph Smith's First Vision," *Opening the Heavens*, 15; "Letter Book A," JS Letterbook 1, 3, www.josephsmithpapers.org.
13. Jessee, "Accounts of Joseph Smith's First Vision," *Opening the Heavens*, 15; Backman, "Joseph Smith's Recitals of the First Vision," 14–16; Manuscript History of the Church, 1838–1856, volume A-1 [23 December 1805–30 August 1834], 3, www.josephsmithpapers.org.
14. Bennett and Seidel, "Early Latter-day Saint Understanding of the Apostasy," 72.
15. Jessee, "Accounts of Joseph Smith's First Vision," *Opening the Heavens*, 4–5, 23; Orson Hyde, *Ein Ruf aus der Wüste, eine Stimme aus dem Schoose der Erde: Kurzer Ueberlick des Ursprungs und der Lehre der Kirche "Jesus Christ of Latter Day Saints" in Amerika, gekannt von manchen unter der Benennung: "Die Mormonen"* (A Cry out of the Wilderness, A Voice from the Bowels of the Earth: A Short Summary of the Origin and Teaching of the Church [of] "Jesus Christ of Latter Day Saints" in America, Known by Many Under the Name "the Mormons") (Frankfurt: Im Selbstverlage des Verfassers, 1842), 13–30. The copy used herein is held at CHL.

English translation by Marvin H. Folsom, published in Dean C. Jessee, ed., *The Papers of Joseph Smith*, vol. 1, Autobiographical and Historical Writings (Salt Lake City: Deseret Book, 1989), 405–25. Milton V. Backman Jr., "Joseph Smith's Recitals of the First Vision," *Ensign*, January 1985, 11–13; Backman, "Confirming Witnesses of the First Vision," 35; Richard Lloyd Anderson, "Joseph Smith's Testimony of the First Vision," *Ensign*, April 1996, 10–21.

16. Bennett and Seidel, "Early Latter-day Saint Understanding of the Apostasy," 68, 73.
17. Bennett and Seidel, "Early Latter-day Saint Understanding of the Apostasy," 76.
18. Bennett and Seidel, "Early Latter-day Saint Understanding of the Apostasy," 77.
19. 1 Nephi 13:23–26 (Book of Mormon).
20. Manuscript History of the Church, 1838–1856, volume A-1 [23 December 1805–30 August 1834], 260, www.josephsmithpapers.org.
21. Isaiah 24:5.
22. In 1829, the Aaronic Priesthood was restored by John the Baptist, and the Melchizedek Priesthood was restored by Peter, James, and John. Joseph Smith and Oliver Cowdery were ordained Apostles. See Doctrine and Covenants 13; 27:7–8, 12; 21:1, 10.
23. Holifield, *Theology in America*, 29.
24. Grant Underwood, "Awash in a Sea of Faith," in *Lectures on Religion and the Founding of the American Republic*, ed. John W. Welch (Provo, UT: Brigham Young University Press, 2003), 98–99.
25. West, *Alexander Campbell and Natural Religion*, vii–viii. Earlier prominent Restorationists of this era were New Englanders Abner Jones, Elias Smith, and others who joined together to form the Christian Connexion, and Barton Stone, Richard McNemar, Robert Marshall, John Thompson, and John Dunlavy, who wanted to be called only Christians and whose influence extended throughout Ohio, Kentucky, and Tennessee.
26. George Marsden, "By Primitivism Possessed: How Useful is the Concept 'Primitivism' for Understanding American Fundamentalism?," in *The Primitive Church in the Modern World*, 34. Mark Noll noted, "When studying biblical primitivism, it does seem important to ask which part of the Bible functions as the standard, for it is rarely the entire text." Mark Noll, "Primitivism in Fundamentalism and American Biblical Scholarship: A Response," in *The American Quest for the Primitive Church*, 121.
27. Hughes and Allen, *Illusions of Innocence*, 157.
28. Thomas Campbell, *Declaration and Address*, Centennial Bureau, 1809. Although this quotation is not an original part of Thomas Campbell's *Declaration and Address*, Alexander Campbell added it later as a footnote. Garrison and DeGroot, *The Disciples of Christ: A History*, 159.
29. Fluhman, "*A Peculiar People*," 3.
30. Hughes and Allen, *Illusions of Innocence*, 6.
31. Winton U. Solberg, "Primitivism in the American Enlightenment," in *The American Quest for the Primitive Church*, 50.
32. Martin E. Marty, "Primitivism and Modernization: Assessing the Relationship," in *The Primitive Church in the Modern World*, 8.
33. Hughes, "The Meaning of the Restoration Vision," in *The Primitive Church in the Modern World*, xii.
34. Abner Jones and Elias Smith were early New Englanders who repudiated Calvinism and became part of the primitivist movement. James O'Kelly and Barton Stone also belonged to the primitivist movement. Whether initially Baptist, Methodist, or Presbyterian, they all rejected Calvinism. Marvin Hill, "The Role of Christian Primitivism in the Origin and Development of the Mormon Kingdom, 1830–1844"

(doctoral dissertation, University of Chicago, 1968), 19–30. See also Hughes and Allen, *Illusions of Innocence*, 12, 21.

35. Franklin Littell, *The Origins of Sectarian Protestantism* (New York: Macmillan, 1964), 79, quoted in John Howard Yoder, "Primitivism in the Radical Reformation: Strengths and Weaknesses," in *The Primitive Church in the Modern World*, 85.

36. Underwood, "Awash in a Sea of Faith," 99.

37. Thomas Campbell, *Declaration and Address*. See also, Nathan O. Hatch, *The Democratization of American Christianity* (New Haven: Yale University, 1989), 64–66.

38. Hill, "The Role of Christian Primitivism in the Origin and Development of the Mormon Kingdom, 1830–1844," 8–9.

39. Grant Underwood, "Millenarianism and Nineteenth-Century New Religions: The Mormon Example," in *Studies in Modern Religions, Religious Movements and the Bābī-Bahā'ī Faiths*, ed. Moshe Sharon (Boston: Brill, 2004), 123.

40. Theodore Dwight Bozeman, "Biblical Primitivism: An Approach to New England Puritanism," in *The American Quest for the Primitive Church*, 29.

41. Hatch, *The Democratization of American Christianity*, 184–85.

42. Grant Underwood, *The Millenarian World of Early Mormonism* (Urbana: University of Illinois Press, 1993), 4–5.

43. W. W. Phelps, "Prospectus for the Evening and Morning Star," 23 February 1832. A publication that began in 1840 was titled *The Latter-day Saints' Millennial Star*.

44. "Wentworth Letter."

45. Amos Hayden, *Early History of the Disciples in the Western Reserve, Ohio* (Cincinnati: Chase & Hall, 1875), 183–87.

46. Hatch, *The Democratization of American Christianity*, 184; Bushman, *Joseph Smith and the Beginnings of Mormonism*, 170. See also Pratt, *Autobiography of Parley P. Pratt*, 42, 121, 199.

47. John S. Fullmer, *Times and Seasons* 4, no. 2 (1 December 1842): 17.

48. Hill, "The Role of Christian Primitivism in the Origin and Development of the Mormon Kingdom, 1830–1844," 4n4.

49. Grant Wacker, *Religion in American History* (New York: Oxford University Press, 2003), 213–16.

50. Jan Shipps, *Mormonism: The Story of a New Religious Tradition* (Urbana: University of Illinois Press, 1987), 67–85.

51. See Richard J. Mouw, "What Does God Think about America?: Some Challenges for Mormons and Evangelicals," *BYU Studies* 43, no. 4 (2004): 11.

52. Mark A. Noll, *America's God: From Jonathan Edwards to Abraham Lincoln* (New York: Oxford University Press, 2002), 10.

53. Noll calls evangelical Protestants insiders and sectarian Protestants "outsiders," with Millerites on the border in between. Noll, *A History of Christianity in the United States and Canada*, 191–95.

54. Hughes, "Two Restoration Traditions," in *The Primitive Church in the Modern World*, 44–45; Hughes and Leonard, *Illusions of Innocence*, 145–46, 149; Marty, "Primitivism and Modernization: Assessing the Relationship," in *The Primitive Church in the Modern World*, 3.

55. Holifield, *Theology in America*, 335.

56. Richard T. Hughes, *Reviving the Ancient Faith* (Grand Rapids, MI: Eerdmans, 1996), 30.

57. Hill, "The Role of Christian Primitivism in the Origin and Development of the Mormon Kingdom, 1830–1844," 4.

58. See chapter 8 for an in-depth discussion of the articles of faith.

59. Phillip L. Barlow, *Mormons and the Bible: The Place of the Latter-day Saints in American Religion* (New York: Oxford University Press, 2013), xxiii. Jan Shipps

came to a similar conclusion in *Mormonism: The Story of a New Religious Tradition*, 69. Noll, *America's God*, 5, 76.

60. Manuscript History of the Church, 1838–1856, volume A-1 [23 December 1805–30 August 1834], http://josephsmithpapers.org. "Mormonism is truth."

61. James D. Bratt, ed., *Antirevivalism in Antebellum America: A Collection of Religious Voices* (New Brunswick, NJ: Rutgers University Press, 2006), xxvii.

62. As quoted in Barlow, *Mormons and the Bible*, viii.

63. Terryl Givens, *The Viper on the Hearth* (New York: Oxford University Press, 1997), 61.

64. Marvin Hill noted a characteristic of the nineteenth-century mind that ought to be recognized: "Joseph [Smith and also Alexander Campbell] thought that truth must be singular, not plural, and that the organization which represented God upon earth should likewise be singular. In taking this view, [they] in effect turned [their] back[s] upon the prevailing religious pluralism in the United States, rejecting it as the source of confusion and religious doubt." Hill, "The Role of Christian Primitivism in the Origin and Development of the Mormon Kingdom, 1830–1844," 55.

65. Williams, *America's Religions*, 147–48; Noll, *America's God*, 567; Staker, *Hearken, O Ye People*, 23.

66. Bratt, *Antirevivalism in Antebellum America*, xviii.

67. Joseph Smith—History 1:10 (Pearl of Great Price).

68. Finke and Stark, *The Churching of America, 1776–1990*, 15. See Williams, *America's Religions*, 190–91. Joseph Smith's mother, Lucy Mack Smith, called herself a "seeker." Lucy Mack Smith, *Lucy's Book: A Critical Edition of Lucy Mack Smith's Family Memoir*, 257–58, 278–80. See also Parley Parker Pratt, *The Autobiography of Parley P. Pratt*, ed. Scot Facer Proctor and Maurine Jensen Proctor, rev. ed. (Salt Lake City: Deseret Book, 2000), 13n9; Dan Vogel, *Religious Seekers and the Advent of Mormonism* (Salt Lake City: Signature, 1988).

69. Barlow, *Mormons and the Bible*, xxxvi; emphasis in original.

70. See Noll, *A History of Christianity in the United States and Canada*, 151.

71. Alexander Campbell, *Christianity Restored* (Bethany, VA: M'Vay and Ewing, 1835), 8–9; see also Hughes and Leonard, *Illusions of Innocence*, 107, 117. While Campbell believed that the inductive method helped join the primitive to the modern by opening up ancient truths, Hughes has written that Campbell's restorationism pointed backward in regression while his Millennialism pointed forward in progression, opposite directions which Hughes believed were incompatible. Hughes, *Reviving the Ancient Faith*, 29.

72. Thomas H. Olbricht, "Hermeneutics and the Declaration and Address," in *The Quest for Christian Unity, Peace, and Purity in Thomas Campbell's Declaration and Address*, ed. Thomas H. Olbricht and Hans Rollmann (Lanham, MD: Scarecrow Press, 2000), 254; Hayden, *Early History of the Disciples in the Western Reserve, Ohio*, 32.

73. Richard L. Bushman, *Mormonism: A Very Short Introduction* (New York: Oxford University Press, 2008), 5–6.

74. This expression comes from Richard Mouw in describing differences between what he termed classic Protestants in comparison to Mormons. Mouw, "What Does God Think about America?," 11.

4

Enlightenment versus Enthusiasm

Campbell and Smith viewed restoration from very different perspectives. Many of the nineteenth-century American religious-reformation congregants took two antithetical modes: enthusiasm driven or Enlightenment directed. Interestingly, "enthusiasm" initially meant "possessed by a god" or "god within," referring to the muses or gods of the Greeks and Romans. By the eighteenth and nineteenth centuries, it meant pretended inspiration, distinguished from true revelation.[1] In contrast, Enlightenment was defined as the "process of freeing human understanding from the accepted and customary beliefs sanctioned by traditional, esp. religious authority, chiefly by rational and scientific inquiry."[2] Enlightenment was the enemy of superstition and mysticism.

Both the Great Awakening and the Second Great Awakening were revivals that reenergized a seemingly complacent populace. The Great Awakening of the eighteenth century was focused on the New England elite, and some opposed the enthusiasm manifested. Well-known English revivalist George Whitefield came to America in the 1740s to generate religious excitement for Methodism. He traveled the length of the Eastern Seaboard twice, igniting the "Great Revival of Religion."[3] Charles Chauncy, pastor of the First Church in Boston, noted what he believed were errors in doctrine and accused revivalists of appealing to passion alone.

The Second Great Awakening spawned a new and dynamic religious fervor that was more popular, evangelical, ecstatic, personal, optimistic, and widespread. Visions, dreams, prophecies, and emotional spiritual outbursts became more acceptable to many.[4] But not all claims to religion were tolerable. Some religious leaders were concerned that "disestablishment had left too much room for religious expression" and that the anchor previously provided by formalist state-attached religions left Christianity dangerously unmoored.[5]

The Enlightenment skeptics in America took the form of Christian deists. These free-thinking rationalists believed that religious principles were part of the natural order and could be observed by anyone. Like Protestants, deists rejected inherited authority and had great confidence in the ability of humans and their future.[6] Reason and observation were sufficient evidence that a Creator existed according to this natural-religion philosophy, albeit a disengaged and noninterventionist God. Logic dictated that the universe was a self-sufficient machine that ran on its own.[7] From this viewpoint, the visions, visitations, revelations, and miraculous events were intrusions into the natural order and processes of the universe. Expressions of religious enthusiasm were considered eccentric, marginal, misguided, or even "fanatical" and "extravagant," which caused some religious leaders to worry about the creation of a frenzied atmosphere leading to disorder, manipulation, and delusion of a revival audience.[8]

With Campbell's restorationist views focused on a rational and reasoned interpretation of the scriptures, his reductionist approach to New Testament teachings, and his Enlightenment philosophy, it is not surprising that he viewed with alarm Smith's visions, revelations, additional scripture, and acceptance of some forms of religious enthusiasm. Campbell believed that all churches could come to agreement on the great doctrines and the positive ordinances and unite in one great Christian church if they would focus on the expressly stated teachings found in the New Testament. In Campbell's mind, Smith's expanding ideas from revelation and more scripture would prevent church unity, and therefore Smith's doctrines had to be condemned and disparaged. "From his platform of primitive Christianity, in fact, he [Campbell] launched a devastating attack on everything and everyone who did not agree with his vision of the ancient Christian faith."[9]

Campbell's Enlightenment-oriented academic and religious background and his opposition to modern-day extraordinary gifts of the

Spirit made him highly critical of the claims of prophets, the performance of miracles, and other signs of religious enthusiasm. As a defender of Christianity, he was highly sensitive to claims that did not fit within what he considered the proper order of rational religious practices. The claims of religious enthusiasm were threatening to the foundations of reasoned thinking upon which enlightened Christians based their beliefs. Campbell warned that "enthusiasm flourishes, [and] blooms under the popular systems." He exhorted his readers, "From all this scene of raging enthusiasm, be admonished, my friends, to open your Bibles and to hearken to the voice of God, which is the voice of reason. God now speaks to us only by his word. By his Son, in the New Testament, he has fully revealed himself and his will. This is the only revelation of his Spirit which we are to regard."[10] According to historian James Bratt, the term *enthusiasm* was an epithet that lumped together all forms of revival and was part of an antirevival movement.[11] Sober-minded rationalists such as Campbell worried that religious excitement—derogatorily referred to as "enthusiasm," "fanaticism," "extravagance"—and extreme emotionalism would manipulate truth and cause believers to be deluded into false forms of worship and, perhaps later, disbelief in "real" Christianity.[12]

From Campbell's perspective, each claimant to supernatural events had to be investigated and proved counterfeit to protect the integrity of the authentic prophets of the Bible. Because deists spoke with the authority of some of the great names of the European and American Enlightenment—Voltaire, Hume, Locke, Paine, and others—Alexander Campbell defended Christianity in Enlightenment terms that deists could accept as common sense and reasoned.[13] He wanted to keep the American deists within the bounds of Christ's gospel, unlike some of the deists in France and England who believed in God but rejected Christianity. Disciples of Christ scholar Robert F. West claimed that Campbell's rational defense of Christianity was crucial in rescuing America "from the threat of deism and unbelief."[14] One scholar, alluding to the revelation in Isaiah 40:3, called him "A Rational Voice Crying in an Emotional Wilderness."[15]

To denominate Campbell as strictly Enlightenment directed, however, does not give full credit to the nuances of his beliefs. He was not a traditional high church Christian; instead, he was an intelligent, well-read, reasoned thinker who initially sought Christian reform and then restoration. In his approach to reading the scriptures, he was neither skeptical nor speculative, but factual and faithful; he brought to his restoration both inductive and reductive approaches that were religious and not secular—reason in its proper perspective. For example, he maintained that "some philosophers have almost defied reason, and given to it a creative and originating power. They have so eulogized the light of reason and the light of nature, that one would imagine reason to be a sun, rather than an eye; a revelation, rather than the power of apprehending and enjoying it." Reason is only a "power bestowed on man. . . . It cannot make something out of nothing. . . . It is not light, but the power of perceiving and using it. And as the eye without light, so reason without tradition or revelation would be useless to man."[16] He believed in revelation—*past* revelation specifically—for the Bible was indeed the revealed word of God.

Smith was more enthusiasm driven, with his acceptance of visions, revelations, visitations, healings, and the extraordinary gifts of the Spirit; however, in describing his otherworldly experiences, he used phrases such as "our minds being now enlightened, we began to have the scriptures laid open to our understandings, and the true meaning and intention of their more mysterious passages revealed unto us in a manner which we never could attain to previously, nor ever before had thought of"[17] and "by the power of the Spirit our eyes were opened and our understandings were enlightened, so as to see and understand the things of God . . . from the beginning, *before the world was.*"[18] It was a very different type of enlightenment, and the emphasized phrase in the previous sentence was condemned specifically by Campbell as pursuing illicit knowledge or forbidden fruit. He mocked Smith and his former acolyte Rigdon as having "become wiser than any of the Prophets and Apostles of God."[19]

To characterize Smith exclusively as enthusiasm directed, however, is also too simplistic. He described revelation as appealing to both the mind and heart, thoughts and feelings, as mediated through the Holy Ghost and as "pure Intelligence" flowing into the mind and giving rise to strokes of ideas.[20] Mormon historian Davis Bitton noted that Smith's revelations had much in common with rationalistic Enlightenment: "Rejecting the traditional Christian creeds, Mormonism turned *away from* the mystery of the Trinity, the creation of the world *ex nihilo*, the depravity of fallen man, predestination, and a hell of eternal punishment *to* the Godhead as comprised of three individuals united in purpose, the creation of the world from previously existing matter, free will, the dignity and high destiny of man, and a graded salvation for all."[21]

RELIGIOUS RIVALS AND ENTHUSIASM

Campbell was decidedly anti-enthusiasm and particularly anti-emotionalism. He saw his approach to faith as rational and an alternative to the mindless piety of revivalism. He opposed the ideas of faith as a feeling and of conversion as an emotional experience brought upon by ministers who induced belief through fear or aroused emotions. He was adamantly opposed to the so-called miraculous presence of gifts of the Spirit in the modern day. He believed that gifts of the Spirit were essential but unique to the apostolic era but should not be expected until Christ returned. As a cessationist, he believed that the charismatic gifts of the Spirit accompanying the conversion of thousands were indispensable for the establishment of the New Testament church, but once it was formed in its pristine purity, the extraordinary gifts ended, and all who anticipated a restoration of spiritual gifts before the coming of Christ became "liable to all delusion."[22] He called the "Methodistic Enthusiasm" of his day "the shrieks and howling of the damned . . . thrown upon the canvass, with the wild and lurid coloring of a Rubens, and held up to the gaze of the weak and timid."[23]

Despite some overly emotional displays of enthusiasm in the nineteenth century, there also were many serious seekers after the pattern of the Christian Church, with its special offices and gifts of the spirit. For example, on a mission to Toronto, Canada, Mormon missionary Parley Pratt heard a prayer offered at the close of a nondenominational church meeting that echoed the lament of Roger Williams. "We have neither apostles, visions, angels, revelations, gifts, tongues, ordinances, nor a Christian ministry; we acknowledge that we are destitute of everything like the pattern of the true Church, as laid down in thy holy Word, and we pray thee to send whom thou wilt."[24] Thus, many seekers at that time were looking for the extraordinary offices and spiritual gifts manifested in the New Testament that would not be restored, Campbell asserted, until the end of the Millennium.

Interestingly, religious revivals in frontier America had their historical beginning in the sacramental season of post-Reformation Scottish Presbyterianism that migrated across the Atlantic in the early seventeenth century. Old World ways of organizing worship and devotion led to the reenactment of the sacramental festival in America from May to October each year, with attendance swelling between 1785 and 1815, reawakening large numbers of evangelical Presbyterians. The multiday meetings often began with basic Scottish forms: a Thursday fast, Friday sermon, Saturday meeting of preparation, lengthy Sabbath services with long tables for the administration of the Lord's Supper to those with proper tokens, and Monday thanksgiving service. Accompanying the daily communion meetings were "special outpourings of the spirit" that evidenced the power of God.[25]

By the early nineteenth century, such meetings also included Baptist and Methodist ministers, preaching, singing, praying, and ecstatic experiences alongside the traditional Scottish rituals. The center point of the meetings was the delivery of an action sermon followed by communion. The traditional Presbyterian gatherings for the sacrament had long been accompanied by religious ecstasy, and the influence of Methodists, Baptists, and Shakers markedly increased the range and prevalence of these behaviors. Although the "frontierization" of American Christianity had its own unique flavor, with camp revival meetings and a greater focus on conversionism rather than sacramentalism, according to historian Leigh Schmidt, it had its roots in Catholic Old World festivals.[26] From its beginning in Scotland, there were always detractors who believed the holy supper had become a "Theatrical Pomp," most notably critiqued in an eighteenth-century satirical poem by Robert Burns titled "The Holy Faire."[27] For Campbell, Enlightenment thinking replaced the evangelical rituals and ecstatic experiences of the past.

For those involved in leading revivals, it was not just a venue to convert the unchurched, it was also an event to reclaim backsliders and reheat the lukewarm.[28] The Methodists promoted a religion that was experienced and felt, and, therefore, emotional displays were an important part of worship.[29] By the early 1800s, the revivals attracted large numbers of families traveling from distances of thirty to even one hundred miles to attend the protracted meetings with numerous preachers speaking late into the night. The crowds of people exceeded the capacity of the inns and the homes of local Christians, which necessitated camping. Hence, the term "camp meeting" became synonymous with revival.

Profound feelings of the Spirit were felt by many seekers at these meetings; children, men, women, old and young, white and black were "struck down and exercised" by the Spirit in different ways.[30] Previous to this, many ministers had taught that the sinner's application to Christ for faith could take weeks or years. At an 1805 revival, however, Barton Stone (who later joined his restoration movement with Campbell's) observed that conversion could happen suddenly: "Many old and young, even little children, professed religion, and all declared the simple gospel of

Jesus Christ. I knew the voice and felt the power."[31] A neighbor reported that Emma Hale, future wife of Joseph Smith, "often got the power" when she was young, as did many in the area who had sincere religious feelings. "Getting the power was an important part of religious worship through[out] the Allegheny foothills where they lived."[32] Some of the camp participants manifested signs that were notable "for their intensity and variety and the astonishing ease and rapidity with which they were communicated (affecting at times an entire congregation)."[33] Some burst into prayer, exhortation, or tears of compassion. Some participants were terrorized by their experience and either tried to escape or called out to Jesus to have mercy on them as they fainted and swooned.[34] "Falling down became such a regular feature of the revival meetings, that it was customary to estimate the success of the meeting by the numbers who were affected in that manner."[35] Sometimes, those who were struck down awakened to deliver powerful sermons for an extraordinary "length of time, matter, and loudness of voice."[36] Others participated in what were termed "spiritual exercises" that included jerks, barking, dancing, visions, and happy, melodious singing that seemed to emanate from the breast.[37]

Smith reported that as a young boy, while attending a revival meeting with his mother and several of his siblings, "he wanted to get religion too, he wanted to feel and shout like the rest but could feel nothing."[38] Nevertheless, he incorporated some aspects of enthusiasm in his restoration. He embraced visions, revelations, and gifts of the Spirit as part of the restoration of the primitive church. Smith acknowledged the existence of conflicting opinions regarding the gifts of the Spirit:

> Some people have been in the habit of calling every supernatural manifestation, the effects of the spirit of God, whilst there are others that think there is no manifestation connected with it at all; and that it is nothing but a mere impulse of the mind, or an inward feeling, impression, or secret testimony, or evidence, which men possess, and that there is no such thing as an outward manifestation. It is not to be wondered at that men should be ignorant . . . of the nature, office, power, influence, gifts and blessings of the gift of the Holy Ghost[,] when we consider that the human family have been enveloped in gross darkness and ignorance for many centuries past without revelation, or any just criterion to arrive at a knowledge of the things of God, which can only be known by the spirit of God.[39]

REVELATIONS ON SPIRITUAL GIFTS

Arriving in Kirtland, Ohio, in late January 1831, nine months after organizing the Church of Christ, Smith found that ecstatic worship and religious enthusiasm had become a significant issue in the newly formed church. Lucy Mack Smith, his mother, recalled that Joseph found about one hundred members in the church: "They were fine brethren in general but that they had imbibed some very strange Ideas which it cost some pains to rid them of as the Devil had been deceiving them with a specious appearance of powe[r]." Joseph objected to the "strange contortions of the visage and unnatural Motions which they supposed as being occasioned by an operation of the power of God,"[40] declaring that "the Lord had sent him there, and he or the devil would have to leave. . . . After he arrived, the false spirits which had been operating through the members of the Church ceased for awhile."[41] Initially, there were no boundaries regarding extreme ecstatic experiences as part of missionary meetings or spiritual rebirth because God had not yet revealed any and Smith had not asked. In quick succession, between March and June 1831, Smith claimed three revelations that clarified what God found acceptable.

Returning to Kirtland in the spring of 1831, after a mission to Missouri, Parley Pratt was concerned with the manifestation of strange spiritual phenomena that were not edifying or in harmony with the doctrine and spirit of the gospel but that had crept into the newly organized church in his six-month absence. According to his report, between the period of time that the missionaries left and Joseph Smith arrived in late January, the fledgling church had become polluted by "a false and lying spirit."[42]

In March 1831, Smith received a revelation regarding the importance of directing all meetings by the Holy Ghost to prevent the problems they had been having with deception. In the revelation, every person was encouraged to earnestly seek after the best gifts by the power of the Spirit and receive them by that same power. Reviewing Paul's second epistle to the Corinthians and Moroni's last words in the Book of Mormon, the revelation sets forth a list of spiritual gifts, including a powerful testimony of the Savior, wisdom and knowledge, healing, the working of miracles, prophecy, speaking in tongues, interpretation of tongues, and so forth. The next part of the revelation governed the source of such manifestations and whether they were truly gifts from

God: "All these gifts come from God, for the benefit of the children of God. And unto the bishop of the church, and unto such as God shall appoint and ordain to watch over the church and to be elders unto the church, are to have it given unto them to discern all those gifts lest there shall be any among you professing and yet be not of God."[43] In Smith's restoration, the gifts of the Holy Ghost were rational, meaningful, purposeful, consistent with scripture, and contrary to the wild and foolish ideas of men or women.[44]

In May 1831, Smith received another revelation cautioning the church about "false spirits" and condemning some behaviors as "abominations." He warned "deceivers and hypocrites" in the church that they would be detected and "cut off."[45] Rather than a list of accepted or prohibited behaviors, the members were to judge by the Holy Ghost what was true or counterfeit. In the revelation, God revealed to Smith guidelines and principles: "Verily I say unto you, he that is ordained of me and sent forth to preach the word of truth by the Comforter, in the Spirit of truth, doth he preach it by the Spirit of truth or some other way? And if it be by some other way it is not of God. . . . He that receiveth the word of truth, doth he receive it by the Spirit of truth or some other way? If it be some other way it is not of God."[46]

In an additional revelation received in June 1831, a pattern was given for identifying those who were under the influence of God, because there were some who through "gross wickedness and hypocricy . . . who by a long face, and sanctimonious prayers, and very pious sermons had power to lead the minds'of the ignorant and unwary and thereby obtain such influence."[47] Talent in rhetoric or overwhelming emotion is not evidence of being under the influence of the Holy Ghost. Smith stated God's pattern to discern the spiritual character of individuals:

> Wherefore he that prayeth, whose spirit is contrite, the same is accepted of me if he obey mine ordinances. He that speaketh, whose spirit is contrite, whose language is meek and edifieth, the same is of God if he obey mine ordinances. And again, he that trembleth under my power shall be made strong, and shall bring forth fruits of praise and wisdom, according to the revelations and truths which I have given you. And again, he that is overcome and bringeth not forth fruits, even according to this pattern, is not of me. Wherefore, by this pattern ye shall know the spirits in all cases under the whole heavens.[48]

As a result of the growing crisis brought about by unrestricted enthusiasm and emotionalism, Smith, through revelation, "showed the brethren clearly the mistake under which they had been laboring"[49] and explained the discipline that he claimed God required. Thus, Smith recognized that not all enthusiastic expressions manifested in Kirtland were from God; however, guidelines were given so that the members were empowered to discern what was from God and what was not. Just as labeling Campbell as strictly Enlightenment directed is not accurate, neither is labeling Smith as strictly enthusiasm driven.

Charismatic expressions of faith were characteristic of the Second Great Awakening. Criticism of this type of religious experience was also common. Campbell completely rejected revivals and the extraordinary spiritual manifestations that accompanied them. As a youth, Smith was interested but unmoved by the revivals in his area and more circumspect in his remarks regarding charismatic gifts. He accepted the marvelous gifts of the Spirit taught by the Apostle Paul; however, he viewed some of the manifestations in the early Ohio period of the Church of Christ as coming from God and others as not.

NOTES

1. *Oxford English Dictionary*, s.v. "enthusiasm."
2. *Oxford English Dictionary*, s.v. "enlightenment."
3. Holifield, *Theology in America*, 93.
4. Staker, *Hearken, O Ye People*, 12–13.
5. Fluhman, "A Peculiar People," 9, 21.
6. Noll, *America's God*, 144.
7. Some seventeenth-century Enlightenment philosophers promoted deism as a comprehensive religion that would be an intellectual and social improvement on traditional Christianity. Ordinary human intelligence could understand God without the need for revelation, and this would "cleanse Christianity of its supernaturalist superstitions." Noll, *America's God*, 143–44.
8. Bratt, *Antirevivalism in Antebellum America*, xvii–xviii.
9. Hughes, *Reviving the Ancient Faith*, 22.
10. Campbell, "To the Readers of the Christian Baptist, Part IV," *Christian Baptist* 1, no. 8 (21 March 1824): 187–88,
11. Bratt, *Antirevivalism in Antebellum America*, xvii–xviii.
12. Bratt, *Antirevivalism in Antebellum America*, xviii.
13. West, *Alexander Campbell and Natural Religion*, vii; see also Richard Bushman, "Joseph Smith and Skepticism," in *Believing History: Latter-day Saint Essays*, ed. Reid L. Neilson and Jed Woodworth, (New York: Columbia University, 2004), 146–48.
14. West, *Alexander Campbell and Natural Religion*, viii.
15. John L. Morrison, "A Rational Voice Crying in an Emotional Wilderness," in *The Stone-Campbell Movement: An International Religious Movement*, ed. Michael W. Casey and Douglas A. Foster (Knoxville: University of Tennessee, 2002).
16. Campbell, "An Address," *Millennial Harbinger* 5, no. 8 (August 1841): 354.

17. Joseph Smith—History 1:74.
18. Doctrine and Covenants 76:12–13; emphasis in Campbell's commentary.
19. Campbell, "Mormonism," *Millennial Harbinger* 2, no. 7 (4 July 1831): 331.
20. History, 1838–1856, volume C-1 [2 November 1838–31 July 1842], 9 [addenda], http://josephsmithpapers.org; Doctrine and Covenants 8:2.
21. Davis Bitton, "Anti-Intellectualism in Mormon History," *Dialogue: A Journal of Mormon Thought* 1, no. 3 (1966); 114.
22. Alexander Campbell, "Queries," *Millennial Harbinger* 5, no. 3 (March 1834): 143.
23. Bratt, *Antirevivalism in Antebellum America*, 5.
24. Pratt, *Autobiography of Parley P. Pratt*, 179–80.
25. Leigh Eric Schmidt, *Holy Fairs: Scottish Communions and American Revivals in the Early Modern Period* (Princeton, NJ: Princeton University, 1989), 57.
26. Schmidt, *Holy Fairs*, 65. For example, the first two stanzas follow: "A robe of seeming truth and trust Hid crafty Observation; And secret hung, with poison'd crust, The dirk of Defamation: A mask that like the gorget show'd, Dye-varying on the pigeon; And for a mantle large and broad, He wrapt him in Religion. Hypocrisy A-La-Mode."
27. Schmidt, *Holy Fairs*, 170.
28. Underwood, "'Awash in a Sea of Faith,'" 100.
29. Catherine C. Cleveland, *The Great Revival in the West, 1797–1805* (Gloucester, MA: Peter Smith, 1959), 49.
30. Cleveland, *The Great Revival in the West*, 57–60. Cleveland quoted from several firsthand accounts. "McGready's Narrative of the Revival in Logan County," *New York Missionary Magazine* (1803), 192–94; *New York Missionary Magazine* (1802), 310–12.
31. Williams et al., *Stone-Campbell Movement: A Global History*, 12.
32. Staker, *Hearken, O Ye People*, 127.
33. Cleveland, *Great Revival in the West*, 87.
34. Richard McNemar, *The Kentucky Revival* (Cincinnati: 1808), 23, as cited in Cleveland, *The Great Revival in the West*, 60.
35. Cleveland, *Great Revival in the West*, 97–98.
36. Letter by Reverend Thomas Moore, Ten Mile, PA, 9 March 1803, printed in the *Massachusetts Missionary Magazine* 1 (1803): 198–99; as cited in Cleveland, *Great Revival in the West*, 95.
37. Cleveland, *The Great Revival in the West*, 98–103.
38. Dean C. Jessee, "The Earliest Documented Accounts of Joseph Smith's First Vision," 25.
39. History, 1838–1856, volume C-1 Addenda, 64, http://www.josephsmithpapers.org; Joseph Smith, "Gift of the Holy Ghost," *Times and Seasons*, 15 June 1842, 823.
40. Lucy Mack Smith, History, 1844–1845, 12, bk. 10, http://www.josephsmithpapers.org; Anderson, *Lucy's Book*, 506–7.
41. Philo Dibble, "Philo Dibble's Narrative," in *Early Scenes in Church History* (Salt Lake City: Juvenile Instructor, 1882), 78.
42. Pratt, *Autobiography of Parley P. Pratt*, 72.
43. Doctrine and Covenants 46:26–27.
44. "Baptism," *Times and Seasons* 3, no. 16 (15 June 1842): 823.
45. Doctrine and Covenants 50:4, 6, 8.
46. Doctrine and Covenants 50:17–20.
47. History, 1838–1856, volume C-1 [2 November 1838–31 July 1842], 872, http://www.josephsmithpapers.org.
48. Doctrine and Covenants 52:15–19.
49. Lucy Mack Smith, History, 1844–1845, p. 1, bk. 11, http://www.josephsmithpapers.org; Anderson, Lucy's Book, 507.

5

Alexander Campbell's Reasoned Restoration

Campbell sat in his hexagonal-brick study located near his two-story clapboard mansion home on 350 acres of farmland in the beautiful rolling hills of Bethany, Virginia (later West Virginia), reading, studying, and pondering the meaning of scriptures in multiple languages as he brought forth his restoration through reasoned thinking.[1] He proclaimed the Bible as his sole standard, contending that "the Holy Scriptures are all-sufficient, and alone sufficient."[2] This phrase was an echo of seventeenth-century Englishman William Chillingsworth, whose mantra was "The Bible, and the Bible only, is the Religion of Protestant."[3] As Campbell's father, Thomas, had recommended, he and his reformers developed the motto "Where the Scriptures speak, we speak; where the Scriptures are silent, we are silent."[4] His reasoning caused him to reject all accretions to the scriptures, aided his understanding of the correct mode of baptism, and assisted his thinking in writing over two dozen essays regarding some important elements of his restoration to the ancient order of the primitive church.

BAPTISM AND THE BAPTISTS

Early in Thomas and Alexander's ministry with the Christian Association of Washington, several members of the church claimed infant baptism was unscriptural. The Christian Association had

Alexander Campbell's Mansion Home and Study, by Edward Dean Neuenswander.

left the mode of baptism a matter of forbearance belonging to the chapter of nonessentials; therefore, Thomas and Alexander had not made it a term of communion.[5] Three years later, in the spring of 1812, the birth of Alexander and Margaret Campbell's first child occasioned his intensive scriptural study on the subject of baptism. His wife and her parents were Presbyterians who believed in pedobaptism. Alexander and his family also had all been baptized as infants. Up to this time, they had regarded the question of baptism as of relatively small importance in comparison with their much larger battles of overthrowing sectarianism and restoring the Bible to its primitive Christian focal point. As Alexander began his study, he became embarrassed that his previous position on baptism had been to "let it slip."[6] Christ had connected the ritual with salvation; therefore, it was important and could not be allowed "to slip." He now considered who should be baptized—infants or believers. In his research of the words in the original Greek, he learned the term *baptizo* was a transliteration rather than a translation and that the original Greek word meant "to dip" or "to immerse."[7] He quickly came to the realization that as Presbyterians, none in the family had been properly baptized. As a result, in June 1812, he and his wife, father, mother, and sister Dorothea were all immersed by a Baptist preacher, Matthias Luce (or Luse). Thereafter, Campbell preferred to substitute the word *immersion* when he wrote or spoke about *baptism*.

Their baptism was not according to Calvinistic Baptist practice, but "according to the pattern given in the New Testament," meaning that there was no need for each believer to recount a "religious experience" but simply confess that "Jesus is the Son of God."[8] Campbell noted that the controversy about how one was awakened unto Christ and the nature of their "experience" was not what the apostles had required, and neither should the Baptists.[9] "The Apostles did not command men to be baptized into their own experience, but into the faith then delivered to the saints."[10] The "reformers" became linked with the Baptists because they were the largest and most respected denomination that believed in the ordinance of baptism by what they now understood was the proper mode: immersion.[11] Campbell acknowledged, "I had no idea of uniting with the Baptists more than with the Moravians or the mere Independents. I had unfortunately formed a very unfavorable opinion of the Baptist preachers as then introduced to my acquaintance, as narrow, contracted, illiberal, and uneducated men. . . . I confess, however, that I was better pleased with the Baptist people than with any other community. They read the Bible, and seemed to care but little for anything else in religion than '*conversion*' and '*Bible doctrine*.'"[12]

"Isms," Creeds, and Confessions

Reflecting on his early religious training in the Scottish Seceder Presbyterian faith, Campbell lamented:

> [I was] compelled to memorize almost the whole New Testament and many passages in the Old. . . . The good effects of memorizing the New Testament were neutralized by the trash which the Westminster Divines had obliged me to interlard with it. This gave a coloring and a taste to all that I learned from the Scriptures. It was the same as if the Oracles of God had been translated into the Catechism—as if the spiritual meaning of the living word was decocted[13] into it. . . . I was alienated from the life of God by the very means which men had contrived to reconcile me to it.[14]

Campbell desired to correct the errors and innovations that had crept into Protestantism; he wanted to reform the church from within like his father had repeatedly attempted. He maintained that he had no system of his own to replace current systems, but that his only aim was to re-enthrone the New Testament and the ancient Apostles. He wanted to reunite Christianity based on Jesus's language in his intercessory prayer: a call for unity among the Apostles in Christ and among those who believed their words.[15] He determined that the way to accomplish this was to eliminate divisive, human-invented creeds and to distill the teachings and practices of the New Testament church to its essential core by using commonsense reasoning. Campbell based his ideas in the Enlightenment philosophy of John Locke and the evidentiary approach of Francis Bacon in his efforts to restore the ancient and pristine apostolic church.[16] From his perspective, the essence of the Christian church would be so obviously correct to all Christians that as soon as they were taught it, they would unite under one banner, creating the millennial church.[17]

Campbell complained that "if Christianity was persecuted by its enemies, it was corrupted by its friends."[18] He avowed, "We neither advocate Calvinism, Arminianism, Arianism, Socinianism, Trinitarianism, Unitarianism, Deism, or Sectarianism, but *New Testamentism*."[19] He claimed his restoration was more ancient than all of the previous "isms." His battle cry was "From all [these] isms may the Lord save us!"[20] He would contend for "Bibleism against all other *isms* both ancient and modern."[21] The implications of Campbell's criticism were that he did not believe in any of the current "reformed Protestant movements," nor did he believe in the Lutheran Church. He charged that Martin Luther had restored the Bible to its proper position of importance, but that after him, there was no Joshua to lead the people out of the wilderness and into the promised land. Luther's tenets became perverted into a new state religion and Protestants began to lust after the patronage and power of the Roman See, creating their own Protestant popes who assimilated the old church into the new and shackled the minds of people with creeds, manuals, synods, and councils, losing the spirit of the reformation and supplanting it with the spirit of the world.[22]

Interestingly, one of Campbell's main arguments was that since the Bible is from God, the principles therein must be accepted, not by reason, but simply because God revealed them. This is not the case with "isms," most of whose basic tenets Campbell rejected as follows.

Calvinism. The five points of Calvin-minded reformers were represented by the acronym TULIP.[23] The *total depravity of man* was a result of the Fall. Adam and Eve, representing all humankind, corrupted the souls of all their posterity through their sin, called by Augustine "original sin," rendering each unable "to turn to God, or to do anything truly good, and exposes it to his righteous displeasure, both in this world and that which is to come." *Unconditional election* referred to God's decision, made before the creation of the world, to choose certain members, a select number of elect individuals from

Adam's fallen posterity, for eternal glory according to his own purposes "without the least foresight of faith, good works, or any conditions performed by the creature," and that by his justice he could ignore the rest of humankind and consign them to dishonor and wrath for their sins. *Limited atonement* implies that Christ's Atonement is efficacious only for those whom God predestined or elected to be saved. Although Calvinists recognized that Christ's sacrifice was sufficient to atone for the sins of the whole world, they believed it was the will of God that his Atonement redeem only those who had been chosen. *Irresistible grace* refers to a person's inability to respond to the call to salvation excepting those individuals selected by Christ. In other words, Calvinists believed that all who have been elected will be sought out and found by God in his own time. Even if an individual comes to Christ and is converted, he cannot ascribe it to his own free will but to God, who is the only one capable of regeneration and salvation. *Perseverance of the Saints* means that once saved, an individual is guaranteed eternal life, and that those whom God elected to salvation can never completely fall from a state of grace. While one might fall partially, the mercy and faithfulness of God also gives the grace of perseverance.[24]

Campbell was an adamant opponent of Calvin's system of beliefs. In his view, this opinion of Christianity was pessimistic in its assessment that every aspect of human nature is lacking and corrupted, with the Savior choosing to limit whom he will save, and with predestination—that God has preselected certain individuals to salvation without the free-will efforts of individuals to choose salvation. Interestingly, the Presbyterian faith of Thomas and Jane Campbell was based in Calvinism, and Alexander did not want his restoration to take on an anti-Calvinist character. He declared his cause "no more anticalvinian than antiarminian."[25] His restoration was more ancient and venerable than the systems of either Calvin or Arminius, and theirs ought not be compared to his system that reached back to Christ and the Apostles.

The Calvinist term *irresistible grace* is not in the Christian scriptures, and on that basis Campbell called it speculative, declaring that "no mortal man was ever sanctified or saved by assenting to [it]; and I presume to say, never will be." He satirized two particulars of Calvinistic dogma: First, that "natural men are spiritually dead, and as unable to believe in the Messiah as they are to scale heaven by a rope of sand, or to create something out of nothing"; and second, that "God has foreordained a part of the world to everlasting life, and left the rest in their imbecile and bankrupt circumstances to sink down into everlasting death; that for these Christ died, and for a great portion of the human race no sacrifice was offered: no man can believe unless he to whom it is given."[26] In place of these ideas, Campbell taught what he considered to be the unvarnished truth regarding grace. He explained that grace, as described in the New Testament, "always signifies the favor of God towards sinners."[27]

Regarding God's plan of salvation, Campbell pointed out two extraordinary aspects: first, God, in his generosity, elected or called particular individuals—such as Abraham, Isaac, Jacob, Joseph, Moses, Aaron, Joshua, David, Paul, and others—to important positions to help others. Second, God gave humankind agency so that in regard to "spiritual and eternal blessings," each man or woman may choose "life and death, good and evil, happiness and misery," and each was commanded to make his or her own choice. Those who chose the good portion were then to "give all diligence to make [their] *calling* and *election* sure."[28]

Arminianism. This was a reform movement developed by Jacobus Arminius and his followers, called Remonstrants, in the early 1600s and associated in the eighteenth and nineteenth centuries with John Wesley and Methodism and certain groups of Baptists. The main differences between Calvinist and Arminian views are in regard to predestination and free will. Arminianism believes that the Fall of Adam and Eve affected humanity but did not predestinate humankind to depravity. God did, however, predestine some to salvation based on his foreknowledge of their faith or merits. So, unlike Calvinism, Arminianism acknowledges agency as a significant part of personal salvation. Free will in spiritual matters is aided by the prevenient grace (grace prior to full salvation) given by God so that original sin could be overcome, meaning that election is conditional based upon individual choice. In line with this idea is the notion that free will allows an individual to reject grace—no one is predestined to salvation. In contrast to Calvinism, Arminianism affirms that salvation requires the combined efforts of God, who calls, and humans, who must respond. Calvinism teaches limited salvation, whereas Arminianism teaches that all may be saved. The believers in Arminianism are mixed in their support of whether regeneration is absolute or whether those who at one time were saved can subsequently fall from grace.

Arianism. The Arian movement in many ways provoked the AD 325 Council of Nicaea and the development of a creed to define orthodox Christianity. Arianism posits that Jesus is subordinate to his Father because there was a time when he did not exist. In Arius's view, Jesus, the firstborn, was created, not begotten by the Father and therefore cannot be fully divine as the Father is. Jesus, according to Arius, can be of *like* but not the *same* substance or nature with the Father. Jesus was adopted by the Father as God's "Son" at the baptism of Christ—and in response to his faithfulness to the Father. These were non-Trinitarian beliefs that were rejected in the fourth-century councils as heretical.

Socinianism. This was also an anti-Trinitarian movement that developed in the sixteenth and seventeenth centuries. Their doctrines denied the preexistence of Jesus the Messiah, the Fall of Adam and Eve, God's omniscience, and other ideas central to traditional creedal Christianity. They believed that God was semiomniscient, in that he knows all things which will definitely happen, but he doesn't know things which might happen—things which we have a choice to do or not do, to change or not change. If he knew those things, in their view, humankind would be void of agency. Socinian thought circulated among the free thinkers such as Isaac Newton, Voltaire, and John Locke in the seventeenth and eighteenth centuries.

Trinitarianism. This is the traditional Christian belief in the full deity of Christ reaffirmed at the Council of Nicaea. God the Father, God the Son, and God the Holy Spirit are simultaneously united in their substance, but distinct and unique in their personhood. The precise nature of their oneness has been variously interpreted within Christian religions.

Unitarianism. Initially, this movement resisted becoming a separate denomination. They saw themselves as restoring the primitive Christianity of the New Testament churches, unmarred by the later corruptions of Augustine and Calvin, and in line with eighteenth century "catholick" (meaning universal) Congregationalists and Arminian liberals. Some early historians of Unitarianism believed theology was a minor interest and the preaching more practical and less doctrinal. Edward Hall, however, insisted that Unitarians affirmed "settled, clear . . . scriptural, rational" doctrines.[29] They were anti-Trinitarian, believing in one God. They sought an inclusive Christianity that circumscribed both believers in historic creeds and those who rejected them. They rejected the divine status of Jesus of Nazareth;

in some sense they believed that Jesus was the Son of God but that he was not the one God. Unitarianism also rejected original sin and predestination, having a more optimistic view of human nature.

Deism. This school of thought was called the religion of nature and was a type of rational theology that became very popular in the seventeenth and eighteenth centuries among freethinking intellectuals. Seventeenth-century Lord Edward Herbert of Cherbury considered deism the essential core religious belief of all humankind, including non-Christians such as Jews, Muslims, and pagans.[30] Deism emphasized logic and reason over divine revelation; it greatly influenced the American and French Revolutions and is considered to be the religious sentiment of some of the founding fathers. The creation was prime evidence that there was a Creator; however, a noninterventionist God let humans and events run their natural course. In addition to rejecting revelation, Deists also dismissed all the supernatural elements of Christianity, including miracles, prophecies, and the divinity and Resurrection of Christ. Doctrines such as original sin, the Genesis creation account, the inerrancy of scriptures, and as mentioned previously, the mystery of the Trinity, were dismissed as irrational beliefs unworthy of an enlightened age. God was a benevolent but distant creator who revealed himself through nature and human reason. Jesus was not divine, but he was admired as a wise and moral teacher. They observed the natural world with its order and precision, and found in it evidence for belief in God. Theirs was a minimalist view of religion that offered a rational and universal creed.

Sectarianism. This term refers to the setting up of boundaries in religious beliefs—particularly among Protestant churches that began in the fourteenth century during the time of John Wycliffe. Theological and political differences of opinion caused the proliferation of a multitude of Protestant sects in the Scottish Presbyterian Church in the nineteenth century and were evidence for Campbell of a pernicious practice. Often, part of sectarianism was the requirement of an individual to subscribe to a particular constitution of beliefs (or creed) and a confession of faith for fellowship. Campbell called Unitarian and Trinitarian beliefs "alike unphilosophic and unreasonable." He derided Calvin's hypothesis regarding the nature of the spirits of the Trinity as impossible to rationally oppose or defend on principles of reason. "Why then wage this warfare?"[31] Much of Campbell's disapproval was not with traditional Trinitarianism but the use of unscriptural terms to explain it, which made it speculative.[32] He also questioned how anyone called Christian could assent to Arian and Unitarian principles based on their explanations of the relationship between Father and Savior, which "confounds things human and divine." There are mortal names or titles that had their beginning in the Christian era at the time of Cesar Augustus that imply disparity; however, the eternal relationship is God, and the "word of God," which is perfectly equal.[33]

Each of the various schools of thought and theological differences mentioned by Alexander Campbell was antithetical in some way to his and his father's core beliefs and desire for unity as they studied the scriptures and applied logical thinking to their meaning and implications. Evidently, beginning in late 1809, at the reading of his father's *Declaration and Address*, Alexander became averse to the aforementioned doctrines, ideologies, and movements because they were the dividers of Christians; later, he vehemently opposed them because they were extrabiblical ideas and contrary to his understanding of the scriptures.

Creedalism. This term meant the doctrinal territory staked out by sectarians, the beliefs to which members must subscribe. Both Alexander and his father were put off by the splintering of Christianity and had no desire to start yet one more denomination, recognizing the need to return to the original standard of God, "free from all mixture of human opinions and inventions of men."[34] Alexander declared that his intent was to "build upon the Bible alone . . . to abandon the whole controversy about creeds and reformations, and to *restore* primitive Christianity, or to build alone on Apostles and Prophets, Jesus himself the chief cornerstone."[35] Of course, Campbell was primarily referring to his father and himself as leaders in this movement.

These observations led him to examine the platforms and constitutions of all the Protestant sects. He rejected outright the Augsburg, Westminster (the catechism of his former Presbyterian faith), and Philadelphia (promoted by the Baptists) Confessions, as well as the Wesleyan articles and creeds of faith, as possible foundations for restoring unity, peace, or success to the gospel of Christ.[36] In his criticism of them, he was not stating whether or not the list of beliefs was orthodox or heterodox, just that Christ and the Apostles had not composed them. His opposition was part of the credo "if the scriptures are silent, we are silent," and that Christian divisions over dogmas created by councils of men were hostile to God and the unity among men that Christ had prayed for. Campbell believed in a reasoned and logical methodology to understanding the scriptures; however, he was opposed to the "propositions, deduced by logical inferences, and couched in philosophical language" found in the creeds.

In the *Christian Baptist*, Alexander Campbell played devil's advocate to those arguing for the necessity of creeds or confessions. He suggested that if creeds or confessions were essential to unity, then the church could not be unified without them. Campbell argued that the apostolic church of the first century was unified without them. If creeds or confessions were necessary, then the New Testament was defective or insufficient. Campbell reasoned that if Christ, the author and founder of the Christian faith, had been defective in some manner, then humankind could seek to improve, reform, or adapt his religion. Since Christ foresaw and anticipated all the events of the world and arranged everything to man's benefit, his institution "can never be improved or reformed." While the religions of empires and countries or "the lives and conduct of disciples may be reformed," the religion of Christ could not be.[37] He believed the scriptures themselves were sufficient and that creedal language simply exacerbated misunderstandings and prevented Christians from achieving true unity. Campbell's premise, however, that the Christian churches were unified is not demonstrated in the New Testament Epistles. His willingness to submit, however, to Christ and the Apostles who had not seen fit to create creeds or confessions is a point well taken.

In his 1809 *Declaration and Address*, Thomas Campbell made the following clarification regarding his opposition to creeds and confessions:

> Although we may appear to our brethren to oppose them, yet this is to be understood only in so far as they oppose the unity of the Church, by containing sentiments not expressly revealed in the word of God; or, by the way of using them, become the instruments of a human or implicit faith, or oppress the weak of God's heritage. Where they are liable to none of those objections, we have nothing against them. It is the abuse and not the lawful use of such compilations that we oppose.[38]

Central to Alexander Campbell's teachings was disappointment with the Reformation because it continued the use of postbiblical creeds.[39] He implored, "Let the Bible be substituted for all human creeds."[40] In his mind, the salient question regarding creeds was "whether or not Christ shall be the author of the creed, and of the constitution and laws of his church? or shall a voluntary association of men . . . presume to exercise the power of changing, modifying, or improving it?"[41] Further, "to present . . . a sectarian creed composed, as they are all, of propositions, deduced by logical inferences, and couched in philosophical language, to all those who are fit subjects of salvation of Heaven . . . for their examination or adoption, shocks all common sense."[42] Campbell observed that "in the ancient order of things, there were no creeds or compilations of doctrine in abstract terms. . . . Therefore all such are to be discarded" because none "existed in the apostolic age," and further, "they are perfectly irrational, and consequently foolish and vain."[43]

As if that language was not strong enough, Campbell appealed to logic, reason, and the scriptures in several articles to show that creeds were simply absurd. (1) If one argues that confessions of faith or human creeds are plainer or easier to understand than the prophets of God, then "men are either wiser or more benevolent than God."[44] Instead, Campbell suggested that the "abstract and metaphysical dogmas of the best creeds now extant, are the most difficult of apprehension and comprehension."[45] (2) Creeds act as dividers rather than unifiers of the Christian church. If the apostolic church was united without creeds, they are not necessary or helpful to Christian unity. (3) Since creeds are composed of human speculation on the revelations of God, they necessarily include the imperfections and limitations of man's uninspired intellect and can never be placed on the same level as scripture. Thus, to suppose that unity and unanimity of agreement could occur under creeds "is in every way as irrational as to make a uniformity of features, of color, of height and weight, a bond of union."[46] (4) The number of items in the creeds—for example, the 33 chapters of the Presbyterian Confession with 171 dogmas—"is not amongst the least of their absurdities."[47] (5) In the business of our salvation we can depend only on pure truth. Thus, by depending on the scriptures rather than on creeds we protect ourselves from false ideas. If God's word is sufficient to save humankind, then creeds are not necessary. (6) We could better spend our time reading directly from the scriptures. Since creeds are uninspired human devices unauthorized by heaven, a more efficient use of time for those who wish to come to Christ would be to read directly from the prophets of God. Campbell contended that "the Bible is of itself as plain and intelligible as it can be made, and its pretended darkness a mere clerical fiction."[48] Further, he pointed out that creeds created by Synods must be fallible because their authors were fallible—and "it would be strange if man could explain the will of God more intelligently or benevolently than God himself had done it."[49] (7) Perhaps Campbell's most piercing argument was his citation of Jesus's intercessory prayer. He pointed out that the words of the Apostles regarding Christ are the basis of unity among the disciples of Christ. "The will of heaven . . . is that all who believe on the Messiah through the testimony of the apostles may be one; consequently, they do not will that those who believe on him through the Westminster divines shall be one." Thus, any attempt to unite Christians by creed is "an attempt to overrule the will of heaven."[50]

Campbell proclaimed the banner of "faith in Jesus as the true Messiah, and obedience to him as our Law giver and King, the only test of christian character, and the only bond of christian union, communion, and co-operation, irrespective of all creeds, opinions, commandments, and traditions of men."[51] He "imagined that once Christians abandoned their creeds and traditions and turned to the Bible and the Bible alone, the denominational structures would fall and all Christians would be united in the primitive Christian faith."[52] In other words, his creed was the Bible and the Bible only.

Although Campbell had strong beliefs on what constituted Christian doctrine, he did not develop a creed to which his followers were required to subscribe or recite weekly. He did, however, systematize his beliefs. For example, Campbell produced his 1835 book, *The Christian System, in reference to the Union of Christians, and a Restoration of Primitive Christianity, as plead in the current restoration.*

A Restoration of the Ancient Order of Things

Campbell's simple definition of restoration was "to bring Christianity and the church of the present day up to the standard of the New Testament."[53] He maintained that the "New Testament Scriptures are a perfect, complete and perspicuous rule of faith and practice, as far as respects Christianity."[54] In 1823, Campbell increased his audience and influence with the publication of a monthly periodical, the *Christian Baptist*, that gave his perspectives on the Christian faith with the message that "the restoration of primitive Christianity was the only means to the unity of all Christians, which, in turn, would usher in the millennial age."[55] Beginning in 1825, he wrote a thirty-two-part series entitled "A Restoration of the Ancient Order of Things," outlining what he believed were some of the essential tenets that belonged to a true restoration. The following paragraphs include some of his main points.

The Constitution of God. After his adamant rejection of creeds as previously discussed, the Constitution of God is a second major point from "Restoration of the Ancient Order of Things." Campbell's reasoned approach to reading the New Testament made it a kind of blueprint for restoring the ancient church.[56] According to Campbell, the only constitution of the kingdom of God was the New Testament, and this is what would unite the true disciples of Christ seeking salvation.

Crucial to Campbell's thinking and foundational to many of his arguments was a form of "covenant theology," referring to the dispensational relationship God had with humans. Central to Campbell's covenant theology was the belief that the plan of salvation developed in four successive stages or dispensations. (1) The first dispensation was "the primitive state of Edenic innocence" extending from the Creation to the Fall of Adam. In Eden, man was unmarred by sin and therefore needed no Savior. (2) The Patriarchal Age or dispensation extended from the time of Adam to Moses in which the family or tribe was the "highest social unit." This was a period of religious development in which previous revelations became codified. (3) The Mosaic or "Jewish dispensation, . . . the period of national religion," spanned Moses's day to Peter's sermon on the Day of Pentecost, in which God was king and "worship was symbolic, looking forward to the truths of the Christian dispensation," when the covenant was fixed and complete.[57] (4) The Christian dispensation continued from the day of Pentecost to the future Final Judgment and was "distinguished by the idea of the blotting out of sins, followed by the joy and peace of forgiveness."[58]

A favorite sermon of Campbell's illustrating covenant theology was based on Malachi 4:2 titled "The Sun of Righteousness," and it treated God's revelation as a progressive unveiling of light. The Patriarchal dispensation was the starlight age; the Mosaic dispensation was the moonlight age; John the Baptist was the twilight age; and the culminating dispensation was the sunlight age, or Christian era, that brought the Messiah, or the Sun of Righteousness.[59]

Covenant theology limited the importance of some parts of the Bible by placing the history of religious development on a vertical scale, the latest development being the highest and most important.[60] With this perspective, it appears that either God's plan evolved over time or humankind's ability to understand the plan progressed over time. In either case, this definition of dispensations is a progressive approach from simple to complex, and partial to complete. It also meant that doctrines and principles from the Old Testament were not transferable to the New Testament. For example, "Campbell had little use for Judaism, early Israel, or anything connected to pre-Christian priesthood" because it was from the Old Testament and a different dispensation.[61] Christian priesthood was a new creation that grew out of Christ's ministry, had no ties with prior dispensations, and had no need to pass authority from one dispensation to the next. Following the Protestant idea of a priesthood of all believers, Campbell believed no special commission was necessary to assume priesthood offices in church polity. Unlike Calvinists, who saw binding precedents in both the Old and New Testament, Campbell's replacement of the Mosaic dispensation with the Christian dispensation meant that the Calvinist system of preaching the law of Moses to prepare sinners for the gospel was unnecessary. The two great commandments to love God and neighbor superseded the Ten Commandments.[62] This subordination of Jewish law would lead the Baptists to charge that he was antinomian, meaning against the moral law.

Since Campbell recognized the church organization in the apostolic era, post-Resurrection and post-Ascension, only the Christian dispensation could provide the pattern for restoring the correct forms, structures, and behaviors of the primitive church. Thus, as Churches of Christ scholar Richard Hughes explained, in terms of the restoration of "the ancient order of things," the Old Testament and the four Gospels did not carry "normative weight for the church in his [Campbell's] day."[63] Although Campbell studied and illustrated some points of his sermons from the Old Testament, such as the aforementioned idea on the dawning of the Christian era from Malachi, it was not important in determining what was to be included in his restoration of doctrines, ordinances, or church offices.[64]

Pure Speech. Not only did Campbell argue against creeds and confessions of faith, but his "Restoration of the Ancient Order of Things" declared that "there must be an abandonment of the new and corrupt nomenclatures and a restoration of the inspired one," meaning that only scriptural terminology was acceptable.[65] Any departure from scriptural language was regarded as speculative. Campbell observed that the greatest contentions in Christianity were about what the Bible *did not* say rather than what is *does* say.[66] According to Campbell, God promised that "he would restore to the people 'a pure speech,'" and consequently, all must abolish what Campbell called "Babylonish," or corrupt phraseologies such as the following: "Trinity. . . . The Son is eternally begotten by the Father; the Holy Ghost eternally proceeding from the Father and the Son. . . . The common operations, and the special operations of the Spirit of God. Original sin, and original righteousness. . . . Free will. Free grace. Total depravity. Legal and evangelical repentance," and so forth.[67] Campbell declared that this "fixed style of expressing revealed truths to the exclusion of, or in preference to that fixed by the Spirit, and sometimes, too, at variance with it . . . is not the style of the oracles of God."[68]

In addition to the sophistry of nonbiblical language, he complained about context. Some people "select Bible terms and sentences and apply to them ideas totally different from those attached to them by the Holy Spirit." For example, Campbell considered the misused terms to include the following: "the natural man, spiritual man; in the flesh, in the spirit; regeneration, washing of regeneration; ministration of the Spirit, demonstration of the Spirit; power of God, faith of the operation of God, the grace of God; the letter, the spirit; the old and new covenant; word of God; the ministry of the word; truth of the gospel; mystery, election, charity, heretic, heresy, blasphemy, church communion, baptism, faith, etc."[69]

Campbell taught that not using biblical language "rejects the words of the Holy Spirit, and adopts others as more intelligible, less ambiguous, and better adapted to preserve a pure church." Misusing terminology "takes the terms and sentences of the Spirit, and makes them convey ideas diverse from those communicated by the Spirit."[70] His mandate was "we choose to speak of Bible things by Bible words, because we are always suspicious that if the word is not in the Bible, the idea that it represents is not there."[71] He maintained that confessions of faith, as well as additions to, subtractions from, transpositions of, and extractions from the Bible are hostile to the restoration of a pure speech.[72] Thus, Campbell held up the words of the Bible as the standard for pure speech, reiterating and underscoring his claim that "the Holy Scriptures are all-sufficient, and alone sufficient," and any other standard would prevent Christian unity.[73]

Christian Worship. In a fourth point from "Restoration of the Ancient Order of Things," Campbell asserted that there is a divinely instituted and uniform order to the true gospel that ought to be consistent in all Christian worship. Central to worship was the Lord's Supper. Although the Lord's Supper was formally initiated in the New Testament, with weekly celebration, a variety of practices emerged among Christian churches in the intervening centuries regarding the interpretation, procedure, and frequency of the ceremonial meal.

Campbell argued that the breaking of the bread was not only the steadfast practice of the ancient disciples but also an essential part of Christian worship by nature and design.[74] Like his father, he thought that partaking of communion twice a year as the Seceder Presbyterians practiced was not sufficient, but that the practice should be weekly. Campbell observed that the ancient disciples met on the first day of the week for this purpose, that the Apostle Paul set his churches in order declaring these same points, and that practices contrary to these have no "law, rule, reason, or authority" to contradict precedent and command.[75] Also included in the order that Campbell observed for worship were the following: scripture study, prayer, singing, fellowship, exhortation, and teaching.[76]

Campbell believed that "proper sanctification of the Lord's day" was worthy of the attention of all Christians and deplored that it was seldom taught.[77] He considered it the "pearl of days" and "just as preeminent amongst all the days of the week, as the Lord's Supper is among all the suppers of the week."[78] The idea of a sacred seventh day, in Campbell's estimation, appears to have been lost because it was not given as a commandment in the New Testament. Instead, he asserted that observance of the Sabbath began in the Jewish dispensation as part of the Decalogue and that therefore, the obligation to observe the seventh day ended at the conclusion of that dispensation. He believed that particular observances should be upheld but not by commandment, such as those mandated in the Ten Commandments and found in the previous dispensation. Campbell believed in worshipping on the Lord's

Day and in keeping a strict moral law, including abstinence from alcohol. However, he opposed a rigid law because the new covenant required worshipping God "in spirit and in truth."[79] It was the example of the Christian church in the New Testament that he followed, proclaiming the first day of the week as a celebration of Jesus's Resurrection.

Additionally, because the Christians in Jerusalem and those in the Apostle Paul's congregations made a weekly contribution for the poor, Campbell maintained that the giving of offerings was also a part of the religion of Jesus Christ. Campbell looked to the example of the Apostles as the basis for exhorting his followers to contribute to the needs of the poor. In fact, Campbell stated that the New Testament example, as rendered in 1 Corinthians 16:1, declared that the congregations on the first day of every week were to make a contribution for the poor saints. It was the responsibility of the Christian church to always care for the poor. Citing James 1:27, he declared that the sacrifice with which God is pleased is the relief of the orphans and widows of their afflictions.[80]

Psalms and Hymns. Another important part of Campbell's restoration of Christian worship was hymn singing, which in his opinion had "been corrupted by sectarianism." Sarcastically, he called them "our creed in metre," and as such they were indicators of "corrupt systems" and "a decisive characteristic of the grand apostasy."[81] He lamented that many believed they ought to sing "every notion, speculation, or opinion" and "every heretical or schismatical dogma."[82] Because the character and sentiments of many of the hymns that were in general use were not in accordance with the New Testament, he advocated using the scriptures as a standard by which one could judge what was appropriate.

In 1828, he first published his own collection of 125 selected hymns, entitled *Psalms, Hymns, and Spiritual Songs adapted to the Christian Religion.* These hymns were used in worship services and became popular reading for many of his followers.[83] Campbell's title of his hymnal mirrors Paul's sentiments in Ephesians 5:19, "Speaking to yourselves in psalms and hymns and spiritual songs, singing and making melody in your heart to the Lord." He considered that God consecrated and exalted humankind's singing and that hymns should "let not the little, low, selfish, schismatical, and sectarian topics find a place in this sublimest of all exercises known among men. Let not the rhapsodies of enthusiasm, nor the moonshine speculations of frigid abstraction, characterize what we, as Christians, call the praises of our God."[84] In his hymnal he excluded popular hymns deemed by him to include unscriptural sentiments. The preface of his book was a treatise on psalmody, clarifying differences between different ways of singing praise:

> Hymns directly address God in praise; psalms and spiritual songs indirectly praise him and are sometimes specially designed for the edification of man. . . . No exercise of social worship is more delightful, solemn, or sublime than singing the praises of the Lord. And when we address him in sacred song, care should be taken that the substance and form, or the matter and manner of our song, be such as will be acceptable to him.[85]

Campbell selected 125 texts for the first publication of a 3-by-5-inch hymnal. They were texts only, common in that day, but he also believed musical notes would be distracting to the importance of the words. He felt he could judge which of the popular Protestant hymns of his day followed the scriptures faithfully while carefully excluding Calvinist theology. Once again, he was consistent in advocating the verbalization of only what is in the scriptures. One scholar considered Campbell's hymnal as one of his "most important contributions to the Restoration Movement." Campbell believed strongly in the unity such a hymnal could create: "one people, one Bible and one hymn book." An essay on prayer concluded the hymnal. Initially, he did not write any hymns himself. However, in a later edition, he added five of his own texts. Although a "lover of good music," he admitted he was "born tuneless."[86]

Feasts of Charity. With some longing, Campbell's restoration noted the hope, joy, love, and confidence in God that animated the primitive Christians. A manifestation of this was the "feasts of charity" or "love feasts" mentioned in the New Testament.[87] He characterized this practice as a natural expression of the spirit of love which filled the early Christians. Campbell called any gathering of Christian family and friends for social eating and drinking a "love feast" and included praising God through hymn singing. His own personal table was often filled with guests for such events. He held that love feasts were part of the restoration of the ancient order found in the New Testament church; however, he never regarded them as a required part of Christian worship.[88]

Campbell was legendary among his friends and followers for the hospitality extended in his home. He loved to welcome visitors and place them at ease. He enjoyed sharing scriptural lessons or truths as conversation permitted. It was his way of sharing love for the gospel and the Savior with the many individuals who visited him.

Spirit of Christianity. Campbell declared that faith in Christ and obedience to him was the only true test of Christian character.[89] He believed that the spirit of the ancient Christians could be measured in their devotion and obedience to God, and the degree of their regeneration by the proportion of their likeness to God. For him, this spirit was an important component of his restoration.

Campbell illustrated his point with a well-crafted parable. A son was given responsibility for his father's vineyard, olive garden, and orchard while his father was gone. Because the son loved grapes more than any other fruit, he and the servants bestowed all their attention and effort on the vineyard and neglected the other two responsibilities. When the father returned and assessed his property, he requested an explanation as to why the olive garden and orchard had been neglected and destroyed whereas the vineyard had flourished. After the son explained that he had always considered the grape the most delicious, as it cheered the heart of both God and man, the father called his son unfaithful because he had served his own will instead of his father's.

In light of this parable, Campbell castigated those who observed only one aspect of the kingdom of God and ignored the others. Particularly, he noted that the Baptists, his own current faith tradition, were devoted to immersion, but when other aspects of the primitive church were brought up, they paid no attention.[90] He also compared his day to the ancient era, saying the latter "looked up to the throne of Jesus[,] . . . the praise of God[,] . . . [and] the apostles' doctrine was the food and support," whereas the former "[looked] around on the smiles of ecclesiastical rulers[,] . . . the praise of men[,] . . . while creeds and commentaries [were their] nourishment."[91] Indeed, he found the lack of true Christian spirit and character of his day extremely distressing.

Campbell's parable illustrates his celebrated reputation as a talented teacher and preacher of the gospel. The parable is similar to others in the New Testament, utilizing familiar symbols such as vineyards, orchards, olive gardens, and father and son; and the lesson that he drew from it is as pointedly sharp as some taught by the Savior.

Church Offices. Campbell organized his movement with many of the stated offices that he found taught in the New Testament epistles of Paul and Peter: priests, deacons, bishops, evangelists, preachers, and elders. He left out, however, the extraordinary offices of apostle and prophet that were also mentioned by Paul.[92] Campbell believed that "apostles, prophets, evangelists, pastors and teachers, were all supernatural characters, for a precise object, and for a limited time; that this object [had been] answered by their discourses and writings, and, that this limited time [had] expired."[93] Thus, he specifically "repudiated the claim of apostolic succession; of priestly supremacy, and the communication of any official grace by superiors to inferiors; or that the clergy had any inherent power in them as it respects ordination" found in the Roman Catholic Church.[94]

Deacons were servants to the entire congregation, and deaconesses were female public servants who officiated among the women only. The main responsibility of deacons was in the temporal affairs of the church, particularly the office of treasurer. They were to take care of contributions for the poor and handle their appropriate distribution as directed by the leadership. Under the stewardship of the deacons, funds were gathered each week for three contribution tables: (1) The Lord's table, (2) the bishop's table, and (3) the table for the poor. The church's treasury provided the bread and wine for the sacramental emblems, administered to the bishops according to their labors and their need, and cared for the poor, the widows, and the sick and afflicted.[95]

In Campbell's restoration, bishops, or overseers, presided and had oversight for only one congregation and were appointed after a congregation had come into existence. They were members of the congregation and appointed by the congregation because they held the qualifications set forth by the Apostles. Campbell differentiated the Christian bishop from the hireling by noting that the former claimed no inward call and did not set himself up to learn how to do the work, but was "chosen and ordained from his outward and visible qualifications," whereas the latter prepared himself by learning the "trade" of a preacher or minister, obtaining a license, and agreeing to preach for a particular amount of money.[96]

Campbell considered the designations of bishop and elder as terms sometimes used interchangeably: "The bishops of apostolic creation are sometimes called elders—because they were generally aged persons, and always amongst the oldest converts in the community in which they officiated."[97] He thought it incongruous that a young man between the ages of twenty and thirty could be called an elder; therefore, it was also unfitting for such an individual to hold the office of bishop.[98] In this instance, he must have questioned St. Paul's wisdom in appointing youthful Timothy to be bishop over the congregation in Ephesus.[99] The bishop was to be called and elected by "the voice of stretched out hand of the members entitled to choose."[100] In other words, the members of the congregation had the right to call, appoint, and ordain any person they chose without the assistance of any outside deacon, bishop, or other officer.[101] Ordination, Campbell stated, "if there ever was such an act peculiarly so called, consisted in the imposition of the hands of the senior members or elders of the congregation."[102] He declared that the office of evangelist, or proclaimer of the ancient gospel, was contingent upon need and was not a permanent office in the primitive church. Finally, Campbell attested that the one individual most worthy of the title preacher was the mother who taught her children about the Savior.[103]

Later, Campbell consolidated his thoughts by identifying three church offices that are necessary to maintain the perpetuity of the church: (1) bishops, whose office is to preside, to instruct, and to edify the church; (2) deacons, who sometimes acted as treasurers, almoners, stewards, doorkeepers, or messengers in caring for the temporal or spiritual needs of the church; and (3) evangelists, who do not serve the church directly but are sent out into the world to preach the gospel.[104]

Campbell parted ways with the Seceder Presbyterian practices at least partially because he was unwilling to relinquish any authority to a presbytery or synod. He advocated local control selected democratically and likely grew more adamant about this point after the way his father was treated, first in Ireland and then in Pennsylvania.[105] The congregation was the governing authority in religious matters. From Campbell's point of view, the selection of the man who should have the title as preacher was voted on by the particular congregation over whom he would preside and serve. With his approach to selecting church leadership, Campbell was on target with the postrevolutionary application of American democracy. The democratization of American Christianity embraced a "priesthood of all believers—religion of, by, and for the people."[106] Authority lay with the Bible. To express his point of view, Campbell quoted John Milton, explaining, "All Christians are a royal priesthood: therefore, any believer is competent to act as an ordinary minister according as convenience may require; provided only he be endowed with the necessary gifts, these gifts constituting his commission."[107] In Campbell's view of church government, each church was independent and had the exclusive authority to select its own preachers, who, after approval, were set apart by a formal ordination. Campbell did not regard this ceremony as conferring authority but as a public testimony that the person ordained possessed the necessary authority and was now committed to God to properly discharge those duties.[108]

Church Government. Campbell declared that once church leaders were selected by the membership, church government was an absolute monarchy and that "there is no democracy nor aristocracy in the governmental arrangements of the church of Jesus Christ."[109] Additionally, he promised that "if disciples meet not 'for doing business,' but for edification, prayer and praise, or discipline, they will never need any other platform or rules of decorum, than the writings of Paul, Peter, James, and John."[110]

From Campbell's view, centralized authority over true disciples of Christ was unneeded. If the leaders of the congregation noted the examples given in the scriptures, they would know how to run their meetings, and there was no need for a synod or presbytery to oversee or to exercise control over them. Fitting in with the democratic politics of the American Revolution, he was in favor of "congregation rights."

Church Discipline. Campbell devoted seven of his thirty-two restoration essays to church discipline. His thoughts on church discipline are perhaps best summarized in three ways. First, merciful: "Every part of the proceedings in reference to an offending brother must be distinguished by every possible demonstration of sympathy and concern for his good standing and character in the sight of God and man: and that final seclusion from the congregation must not be attempted until admonition, reproof, and persuasion, have failed to effect a real change in his views and behavior."[111]

Second, truthful: "While we show all tenderness for their persons . . . we are not to show the least partiality for their faults, or a disposition to diminish aught from the malignity of their trespasses. We ought to lay their sins before them in all their true colors, without extenuation or apology. . . . There is often too much care taken to diminish from, and make excuses for an immoral or unchristian act."[112]

And third, inclusive: "So long as a man evidently desires to please Christ, whatever we may think of his opinions, we are to love him as a brother."[113]

Excusing one's sins by attributing them to inconvenience or the hardness of the times was intolerable to Campbell. He called the breaking of promises, covenants, and obligations which were sacred oaths, a "great libel on Christianity."[114] Specifically, he cited financial speculation and incurring unreasonable debts as being in the spirit of "theft, lying, and slander," and contrary to Christianity.[115]

Campbell's views were compassionate but decisive on the importance of first calling to repentance those whose practices were contrary to Christian behavior, but he was also willing to apply the law of justice to cut offenders off if they persisted. His broad view illustrated that he understood well the lessons on apostasy that New Testament writers, notably Paul, warned about and the later nonscriptural practices that drove Martin Luther to protest against the Catholic Church.

In addition to the thirty-two essays, Campbell made other definitive and important statements of belief.

Godhead. Campbell explained that before the creation of the universe, the Godhead was called "God, the Word of God, and the Spirit of God"; after the development of the Christian system they were called "the Father, the Son, and the Holy Spirit."[116] Campbell was vehemently opposed to the use of the word *Trinity*. He found it irrational and unscriptural to reason that there were "three Divine persons in one Divine nature," or that they shared "one thought, purpose, will, and operation, and so [were] one God . . . because of the metaphysical technicalities, the unintelligible jargon, the unmeaning language of the orthodox creeds on this subject, and the interminable war of words without ideas to which the word *Trinity* has given birth."[117] He also declared that reason and revelation never confirmed that three distinct persons could exist in one God, nor that one God could be three in the same sense.[118] He complained that some "conceived of God as a mathematical unit; and as a thing cannot be both mathematically singular and plural—one and three, at the same time and in the same sense, they deny the true and proper divinity of the Son of God and of the Spirit of God."[119]

Although Campbell decried the word *Trinity* and found the explanation of it in the creeds to be obscure, nonscriptural, and unintelligible, he nonetheless believed Trinitarianism to be more plausible than Unitarian beliefs, which confined the "glory and attributes of divinity to the Father, and not allowing it to the Son or Holy Spirit."[120] He explained, "We do not perceive God by one of our senses; for if we could do this, it would be a proof that God is a material being," and "God has no materiality about him. Nor does the identity of the divine likeness belong to the personal portion—the corporeity of man."[121] In essence, then, Campbell believed God to be a spirit, invisible, "infinite, immutable, and eternal" full of "goodness . . . the necessary and essential idea or attribute of God." Although Campbell's views on God were similar to that of many of his contemporaries, he believed his explanations were clearer.[122] In his understanding of the Trinity, he emphasized the "economic" rather than the "immanent" Trinity, their relationship to humanity rather than their mysterious relationship to each other.[123]

Regarding Christ, Campbell affirmed that "before the Christian system, before the relation of Father, Son, and Holy Spirit began to be, his rank in the divine nature was that of the Word of God."[124] He differentiated between the terms "Son of God," which denotes a temporal relationship and the "Word of God," which implies an "un-originated" relationship. The "Word of God" is eternal; however, the "Son of God" began his life in the days of Augustus Caesar. Campbell quoted from Acts 13:33, "Thou art my Son, this day have I begotten thee," and deduced from this scripture that Jesus Christ became the Son of God on the day he was raised from the dead. Campbell explained the relationship between the Father and Son by stating, "While in the system of grace the Father is the one God, in all the supremacy of his glory, Jesus is the one Lord in all the divine fulness of sovereign, supreme, and universal authority."[125]

Campbell found the relationship between the Father and the Savior impossible to describe because "no relation amongst human beings can perfectly exhibit the relation which the Saviour held to the God and Father of All anterior to his birth. The reason is, that relation is not homogenial, or of the same kind with relations originating from creation. All relations we know any thing of are created, such as that of father and son." However, the relationship between God and the Savior "is an uncreated and unoriginated relation."[126]

The Spirit of God was the active operating agent in all of God's works, according to Campbell. It was the Spirit of God that made the body of Christ. Because of his role as the "immediate author and agent of the new creation, and of the holiness of Christians," he was also given the name "Holy Spirit."[127] Campbell most often referred to the Holy Ghost as the Holy Spirit or the Spirit of God, focusing on his function as a "positive divine spiritual influence upon the understanding and affections."[128] Campbell bore witness that humankind is indebted to the Spirit of God "for all that is known, or knowable of God, of the invisible world, and of the ultimate destinies of man." It is the "Spirit of God, who alone reveals to men the secrets of God. . . . A mighty agent in some work connected with the redemption of man."[129] In a nine-part series on the "Work of the Holy Spirit in the Salvation of Men," Campbell taught that the Holy Spirit is the "Spirit of Wisdom and the Spirit of Power" by which "it was the author of all the miracles, spiritual gifts, and prophecy."[130]

Campbell explained that divinity or godhead are terms which cannot be rationally apprehended. Campbell was not anti-Trinitarian as much as he was opposed to unscriptural terms and explanations. Reason, he maintained, could not explain the Trinitarian position. He was clear, however, on the Word of God, the Son of God, and the Holy Spirit.

Fall. He believed that the first law, meaning the prohibition of eating from the tree of knowledge, was a perfect test of loyalty and subordination for Adam and Eve. He saw the prohibition as a "positive" commandment; that is, it spelled out precisely what was to be done or avoided and was neither good nor evil by itself.[131] "This arrangement reminded him [Adam] of his origin, or his dependence, and accountability."[132] Campbell explained that since "man is made to be led by faith," then "the trial, on which our first parents were put by the Creator, was—whether they would be led by faith in God, or by their own views of expediency . . . whether they would reason out their own path, or be led by their creator. . . . The sophistry of the seducer consisted in making it appear better to disobey than to obey. . . . The sin of Eve began not in hearing but in listening."[133] In Campbell's mind, this transgression was "pure rebellion" and interpreted it as meaning "Thou shalt not reign over me."[134]

In speaking about the consequences of the Fall, Campbell began with Eve and her effect on Adam. The woman succumbed to the beauty of the fruit as well as to the allure of becoming wise.[135] As beautiful as Eve was at the time of her creation, Campbell taught that "the sting of sin transfused its poison through her whole personality—body, soul and spirit"—when she succumbed to the flattery of Satan. Adam, her admiring husband, oblivious to all but her charms and "overpowered by her former loveliness," took the fruit she handed him and ate it. At that moment his glory and dignity also vanished. Consequently, men were born as mere instinctive creatures beset with appetites and passions that make them easy prey for Satan.[136]

Campbell believed "all inherit a *fallen*, consequently a *sinful* nature, though all are not equally depraved"—thus no one is compelled to sin.[137] Campbell believed the original plan of God called for all his children to be born in the Garden; however, a remedial plan was in place long prior to the judgment of Adam, Eve, and the serpent.[138] According to Campbell, God's gospel plans, made prior to the foundation of the world, included plan A, that the Garden of Eden was the inheritance of Adam and Eve and to be the "cradle of the human race."[139] The estate was a grant—no work was required, just simple obedience. Plainly, he believed that the original plan of God called for Adam, Eve, and all their offspring to inherit Paradise eternally; however, God had a remedial plan in place that was adopted prior to their trial.[140] "One thing is evident, that none of our race were born in the garden of bliss, and that with the loss of Eden man lost his right and title to the earth and all that it contains."[141] As a consequence of transgression, paradise was forfeited—at least for a time.[142]

Faith and Works. Although Campbell clearly thought highly of the Protestant reformer Martin Luther, he noted that the excesses of the sixteenth century by the Catholic Church in penances, works of faith, and supererogation brought forth from Luther on the other side of the pendulum: *sole fide* or "faith alone."[143] Luther's emphasis on the Epistle to the Romans, with its accentuation of justification by faith, was Campbell's bone of contention with Luther.[144] Campbell had no such misgivings about the importance of faith and works, and commented on both the writings of Paul and James, quoting from James 1:25 and 2:21 on the importance of works.[145] In fact, he said, "There is such a close connection between faith, and works corresponding with it, that we can scarcely have any just conceptions of the one without the other."[146]

Campbell, although disappointed because of the Fall, declared that humans have reunited with Divinity through the Messiah, elevating man beyond his original glory in the Garden of Eden. Because of this redemption he professed, "God has gained more glory from creation, and also from man's apostasy, and the universe more bliss in the aggregate, than would have accrued to either Creator or creature, had sin never been conceived."[147] The Fall became a blessing to both God and humankind due to the intervention of the Savior. Although scriptures pronounce the creation of man and woman as good, and Campbell claimed that in their original state they were the epitome of human perfection, he also believed that the intercession of the Savior would make something even greater of them.

Faith and Conversion. Campbell opposed requiring a confession of an experience for membership or communion. He particularly "rejected the assumption that conversion depended on a mysterious change wrought by the Spirit."[148] Simple faith in credible evidence was sufficient. For example, he noted that the controversy about how one was awakened unto Christ and the nature of their "experience" was not what the Apostles had required.[149] "The apostles did not command men to be baptized into their own experience, but into the faith then delivered to the saints."[150]

It is important to note that Campbell's idea of faith emphasized reason.[151] Faith had to do with simple biblical facts and events attested to, not the feelings or experiences evoked by the Holy Spirit.[152] Faith, Campbell explained, was an "intelligent response of the mind to evidence rather than a Spirit-given emotional experience."[153] Faith in the facts was followed by testimony and belief, which were then confirmed by the doings of the Holy Spirit.[154] In 1811, Campbell wrote that "faith is an effect of almighty power and regenerating grace." A year later he clarified that "regeneration does not precede faith."[155] He emphasized a particular sequence regarding the development of faith: fact, followed by testimony and belief, which was then confirmed by the feelings of the Holy Spirit.[156] The Spirit worked in conjunction with the word of God in conversion.

One of the very important developments in Campbell's restoration was an 1827 contribution by Walter Scott,[157] considered a "clear-cut 'plan of salvation,'" the "order of the gospel," and which constituted the covenant phase of the "Plan of Salvation," meaning "the gospel restored." His plan of salvation was based on Peter's invitation in Acts 2:38 and simplified what the individual must do. The points were so elementary that he taught it to children with a "five-finger exercise," beginning with the thumb and touching each finger. Scott's five points were "faith to change the heart, repentance to change the life, baptism to change the state, remission of sins to cleanse the guilt, and the gift of the Holy Ghost to make one a participant in the Divine Nature." There were three things which an individual could do for the plan to have efficacy: "He must believe, upon the evidence, that Jesus is the Messiah, the Son of God; he must repent of his personal sins with godly sorrow and resolve to sin no more; and he must be baptized." Then there were three things that God promised to do: "deliver man from the guilt, power, and penalty of his repented sins; bestow the gift of the Holy Spirit; and grant eternal life."[158] While called the "five finger exercise," as can be seen, there were actually six steps in salvation—three for the individual and three for God. The effect on those who heard Scott and other reform-thinking Baptist preachers present this clear plan was immediate—hundreds sought baptism in Campbell's Reforming Baptist church.[159] For example, Parley P. Pratt recorded in his autobiography the anxiety he felt about his sins and the method by which they could be remitted. In his words, the local Regular Baptist minister required him to "experience a mysterious, indefinite and undefinable something called religion before we can repent and be baptized acceptably. But, if we inquire how, or by what means we are to come at this experience, he cannot tell us definitely" except that "it is the work of God in the soul; which he will accomplish in his own due time, for his own elect; and that we can do nothing acceptably til this is done."[160] When Pratt heard Rigdon preach Scott's simple steps to regeneration, he joined the Reforming Baptist church, believing that he had found the ancient gospel with principles he had discovered much earlier.[161]

CONCLUSION

Nineteenth-century Protestantism did not reflect Campbell's views of reformation and restoration. Speaking for himself and his father, he emphatically declared, "we are convinced, fully convinced, that the whole head is sick, and the whole heart faint of modern fashionable Christianity."[162] In fact, he felt that the Protestant Reformation had fallen into many of the same errors as the Roman Catholic Church. Although his writings praised the efforts of Martin Luther and all the Protestant Reformers to "dethrone the *Man of Sin*" spoken of by the Apostle Paul, Alexander Campbell maintained that the Reformation had become co-opted by those desiring power and authority.[163]

By the mid-1820s, Thomas and Alexander Campbell had a sizable following of believers who accepted their views on reform and restoration within the established Redstone and later Mahoning Baptist Associations of Pennsylvania and Ohio respectively. Finally, after many years of striving to stay within one of the dominant Protestant churches, Thomas and Alexander Campbell separated from the regular Baptists to continue the Protestant Reformation movement that they believed had been subverted by state and political interests.[164] The Campbells always recognized that a restoration of primitive Christianity would be a radical purging of the "gross and prevalent corruption" present in the professing church but believed they could unite all Christians under the "original simplicity, the primitive purity," and conservative position that "the Holy Scriptures are all-sufficient, and alone sufficient."[165] Their aims were more radical and sweeping than many realized—they were not satisfied with repairing defects in modern Christianity but in restoring all that they believed was original and pure "in letter, spirit, principle, and practice."[166]

Campbell's first goal was to unite Christianity by demonstrating from the scriptures the incorrect nature of the present Protestant churches with the accretion of non-biblical doctrines and practices and, with his prodigious talents in logic and reasoning, to convince others that the reformation begun by Luther was incomplete. The New Testament was normative for Campbell, and although his academic and religious knowledge was legendary, interpretation of the text invariably led to differences of opinion. As part of his efforts, he wrote dozens of essays focused on the restoration of the ancient order, primarily on the organization and officers of the church, the proper components of worship, and appropriate Christian comportment—or in other words, form, structure, and behavior. He was trying to reorder Christianity after what he read in the New Testament, but even some of the regular Baptists could not be convinced of his reformed agenda. The thirty-two-part series, "A Restoration of the Ancient Order of Things," is a convenient guide to many of Campbell's ideas. It is not, however, a complete enumeration of all his points on restoration. Chapter 7, "Alexander Campbell's Foundational Beliefs," will address some of his additional seminal ideas.

NOTES

1. Initially, Alexander and his wife lived with her parents on a large farm in Buffaloe, Virginia. In time, they were deeded the mansion house and farm. Richardson, *Memoirs of Alexander Campbell*, 1:459–60. Later, the town name was changed to Bethany.

2. Alexander Campbell, *Familiar Lectures on the Pentateuch* (St. Louis: Christian Publishing, 1867), 12.

3. Holland, *Sacred Borders*, 3.

4. Thomas Campbell's words in his 1809 *Declaration and Address* were "Where the Scriptures are silent . . . no human authority has power to interfere." The pithy phrase, "Where the Scriptures speak, we speak; where the Scriptures are silent, we are silent," was given at the close of Thomas Campbell's presentation to the Christian Association and adopted as a guide for the group's actions. This sentiment echoes that of Puritan Thomas Brooks (1608–80): "I dare not rise above what is written. Where the Scripture is silent, there I love to be silent and where the Scripture hath no tongue, there I desire no ears." Albert C. Outler, "'Biblical Primitivism' in Early American Methodism," in Hughes, *The American Quest for the Primitive Church*, 138.

5. Richardson, *Memoirs of Alexander Campbell*, 1:237–40.

6. Richardson, *Memoirs of Alexander Campbell*, 1:392–93.

7. A narrow definition of translating is the process of rendering the meaning of words from one language to another. Transliterating means replacing letters in one language to those of another, representing the same sounds. *Oxford English Dictionary*, s.v. "translating" and "transliterating."

8. Richardson, *Memoirs of Alexander Campbell*, 1:398.

9. Campbell, "A Restoration of the Ancient Order of Things, No. 3," *Christian Baptist* 2, no. 3 (4 April 1825): 140–41. Although Campbell was associated with the Baptists at this time, he considered himself a Reforming Baptist with a duty to help the Baptists see more clearly what the scriptures stated.

10. Campbell, "A Restoration of the Ancient Order of Things, No. 4," *Christian Baptist* 2, no. 11 (6 June 1825): 159.

11. Other groups practicing baptism by immersion came out of the Anabaptist (rebaptism of converts as adults) movement such as the Dunkers and Mennonites. The *Neue Taufer* (new Baptists) or "German Baptist Brethren" were commonly called "Dunkers" or "Tunkers." The Mennonite form of immersion was actually pouring. In contrast to the single complete immersion baptism of the Baptist Church, "Dunkers" observed trine forward immersion (or immersing three times face forward

from a kneeling position, once for each member of the triune). They also practiced laying on of hands to receive the Holy Spirit, feet washing, the holy kiss, and anointing with oil. Small numbers of Anabaptist groups were located in Pennsylvania and Ohio during the nineteenth century, remaining isolated by speaking "Pennsylvania Dutch" and observing other unique European ethnic practices.

12. Campbell, "Anecdotes, Incidents, Facts," *Millennial Harbinger* 5, no. 6 (June 1848): 345–46, emphasis in original.

13. An archaic expression meaning "to boil down or away," *Oxford English Dictionary*, s.v. "decoct."

14. Campbell, "Education—No. 2," *Millennial Harbinger* 1 (1 June 1830): 252–53.

15. See John 17. See also Campbell, "A Restoration of the Ancient Order of Things, No. 3," 139–42.

16. Campbell, "A Restoration of the Ancient Order of Things, No. 3," 140. Quoted in Hughes, *Illusions of Innocence*, 154–55. For more on Alexander Campbell's use of Lockean philosophy, Baconian inductive reasoning, and Scottish "consciousness" thinkers Reid and Stewart, see Morris Eames, *The Philosophy of Alexander Campbell* (Bethany, WV: Bethany College, 1966), 14, 19–27; see also Holifield, *Theology in America*, 298–99.

17. Hughes and Allen, *Illusions of Innocence*, 117; Alexander Campbell, "Millennium, No. 1," *Millennial Harbinger* 1, no. 2 (February 1830): 58.

18. Campbell, "Notes of Apostasy, No. 1," *Millennial Harbinger* (new series) 1, no. 1 (January 1837): 17. See also West, *Alexander Campbell and Natural Religion*, 2.

19. Campbell, "Address to readers of the Christian Baptist—No. 1," *Christian Baptist* 1, no. 5 (1 December 1823): 32; emphasis in original.

20. Campbell, "Trinity," *Christian Baptist* 4, no. 10 (May 1827): 338.

21. Campbell, "The Crisis," *Millennial Harbinger* 6, no. 12 (December 1835): 597–98.

22. Campbell, *Christian System*, 3.

23. The TULIP was based on Augustinian thought and the Council of Dort. For commentary on Calvin's Reformed Church, see the introduction. For a more extensive discussion of the various aspects of TULIP, see chapter 4.

24. Charles Buck, *A Theological Dictionary* (Philadelphia: J. J. Woodward, 1844), s.v. "Calvinism"; see also Holifield, *Theology in America*, 11.

25. Campbell, "The Crisis," *Millennial Harbinger* 6, no. 12 (December 1835): 597–98. In fact, Campbell suggested that the "chief difference between him [Calvin] and us, is, that we practise what we teach." Further, "we leave it to the good sense of the reader, whether John Calvin ought not to be called *a Campbellite*." Campbell, "Calvin on Baptism," *Millennial Harbinger* 4, no. 11 (November 1833): 546–47.

26. Campbell, "Essays on the Work of the Holy Spirit in the Salvation of Men, No. 8," *Christian Baptist* 2, no. 8 (7 March 1825): 131.

27. Campbell, "Essays on the Work of the Holy Spirit in the Salvation of Men, No. 9," *Christian Baptist* 2, no. 9 (4 April 1825): 137.

28. Campbell, *Christian System*, 33; emphasis in original.

29. Holifield, *Theology in America*, 197–98, 214.

30. Darren Staloff, "Deism and the Founding of the United States," in *Divining America: Religion in American History*, National Humanities Center.

31. Richardson, *Memoirs of Alexander Campbell*, 1:203.

32. See, for example, correspondence between Stone and Campbell in the 1827 *Christian Baptist* and 1840 *Millennial Harbinger*.

33. Campbell, "Trinity," *Christian Baptist* 4, no. 10 (May 1827), 330–31.

34. Thomas Campbell, *Declaration and Address of the Christian Association of Washington*, (Washington, PA: Brown & Sample, 1809), 73–74, in C. A. Young,

Historical Documents Advocating Christian Union (Joplin, MO: College Press Publishing, 1985), 71–209. See appendix A.

35. Campbell, *Christian System*, 5; emphasis in original; see also Ephesians 2:20.
36. Campbell, *Christian System*, 5.
37. Campbell, "A Restoration of the Ancient Order of Things, No. 2," 133.
38. T. Campbell, *Declaration and Address*, appendix A.
39. Campbell, "A Restoration of the Ancient Order of Things, No. 1," *Christian Baptist* 2, no. 7 (7 February 1825): 128.
40. Campbell, *Christian System*, 110.
41. Campbell, "The Creed Question," *Christian Baptist* 4, no. 9 (2 April 1827): 323–24.
42. Campbell, "The Foundation of Hope and Christian Union," *Christian Baptist* 1, no. 9 (5 April 1824): 60–61.
43. Campbell, "A Restoration of the Ancient Order of Things, No. 2," 133.
44. Campbell, "A Restoration of the Ancient Order of Things, No. 2," 133.
45. Campbell, "A Restoration of the Ancient Order of Things, No. 2," 133.
46. Campbell, "A Restoration of the Ancient Order of Things, No. 2," 134; see also "Philalethes on the Scriptures," *Millennial Harbinger* 1, no. 8 (August 1830): 337–40.
47. Campbell, "A Restoration of the Ancient Order of Things, No. 2," 134–35.
48. "Philalethes on the Scriptures," 337–40.
49. Campbell, *Memoirs of Elder Thomas Campbell*, 119.
50. Campbell, "A Restoration of the Ancient Order of Things, No. 8," 135.
51. Campbell, *Christianity Restored*, 9.
52. Hughes, *Reviving the Ancient Faith*, 27.
53. Campbell, "A Restoration of the Ancient Order of Things, No. 1," 128.
54. Campbell, "Walker Debate," in Richardson, *Memoirs of Alexander Campbell*, 2:28.
55. Hughes, *Reviving the Ancient Faith*, 22. Hughes also noted that Campbell's message in the Christian Baptist became ambiguous when he paired restoration with both unity and postmillennialism.
56. Hughes, *Reviving the Ancient Faith*, 12.
57. Garrison, *The Sources of Alexander Campbell's Theology*, 168–75.
58. According to Garrison, covenant theology was developed in the writings of Dutch theologians Cocceius and Witsius in the seventeenth century, accepted in Scotland in the eighteenth century, and partially adopted by the Seceder Presbyterian Church. Garrison, *Alexander Campbell's Theology*, 18, 156–58, 162–64, 168–74. According to Olbricht, the federal or covenantal theology was developed by Hugo Grotius and Johannes Cocceius. Thomas H. Olbricht, "Heumeneutic: *Christian System* and the Declaration and Address" in *The Quest for Christian Unity, Peace, and Purity in Thomas Campbell's Declaration and Address*, 252.
59. *Encyclopedia of the Stone Campbell Movement*, ed. Foster et al., 113.
60. Garrison, *Alexander Campbell's Theology*, 167–79; Eames, *The Philosophy of Alexander Campbell*, 25–26; Campbell, "Abrogation of the Sabbath," *Millennial Harbinger* 40, no. 3 (March 1869): 144; Richard T. Hughes, *Reviving the Ancient Faith* (Grand Rapids, MI: Eerdmans, 1996), 31. Campbell believed salvation was only through the blood of Christ; thus, those in previous dispensations were saved retroactively when Jesus atoned for their sins: "They were pardoned in anticipation of '*the redemption of the transgressions*' to be brought in under the new" Christian age. Campbell, "Atonement, No. 4," *Millennial Harbinger* [new series] 5, no. 1 (January 1841): 21. This view of the Bible was part of Campbell's arguments against infant baptism because the Presbyterians linked it to an Old Testament practice (circumcision) rather than New Testament baptism.
61. Staker, *Hearken, O Ye People*, 150.

62. Holifield, *Theology in America*, 295.
63. Hughes, *Reviving the Ancient Faith*, 31.
64. Campbell, "Journal of a Voyage from Ireland towards America 1808."
65. Campbell, "A Restoration of the Ancient Order of Things, No. 4," 159.
66. Campbell, *Christian System*, 126.
67. Campbell, "A Restoration of the Ancient Order of Things, No. 4," 159. For his thoughts regarding "purity of speech" on "the relation existing between Jesus Christ and his Father," see Campbell, "A Restoration of the Ancient Order of Things, No. 17," *Christian Baptist* 4, no. 8 (5 March 1827): 313.
68. Campbell, "A Restoration of the Ancient Order of Things, No. 4," 159.
69. Campbell, "A Restoration of the Ancient Order of Things, No. 4," 160.
70. Campbell, "A Restoration of the Ancient Order of Things, No. 4," 160.
71. Campbell, *Christian System*, 125.
72. Campbell, "Purity of Speech," *Christian Baptist* 4, no. 17 (5 March 1827): 314.
73. Campbell, *Lectures on the Pentateuch*, 12.
74. Campbell, *Christian System*, 311.
75. Campbell, "A Restoration of the Ancient Order of Things, No. 8," *Christian Baptist* 3, no. 3 (3 October 1825): 188–89; "A Restoration of the Ancient Order of Things, No. 5," *Christian Baptist* 2, no. 12 (4 July 1825): 165–66; "A Restoration of the Ancient Order of Things, No. 6," *Christian Baptist* 3, no. 1 (1 August 1825): 174–76; "A Restoration of the Ancient Order of Things, No. 7," *Christian Baptist* 3, no. 2 (5 September 1825): 181.
76. Campbell, "A Restoration of the Ancient Order of Things, No. 22," *Christian Baptist* 5, no. 6 (7 January 1828): 408.
77. Campbell, "The Sanctification of the Lord's Day," *Millennial Harbinger* (series 3) 7, no. 10 (October 1850): 541.
78. Campbell "The Sanctification of the Lord's Day," *Millennial Harbinger* (series 3) 7, no. 12 (December 1850): 661.
79. See John 4:23–24
80. Campbell, "A Restoration of the Ancient Order of Things, No. 10," *Christian Baptist* 3, no. 6 (2 January 1826): 210.
81. Campbell, "A Restoration of the Ancient Order of Things, No. 21," *Christian Baptist* 5, no. 5 (3 December 1827): 395–96.
82. Campbell, "A Restoration of the Ancient Order of Things, No. 22," *Christian Baptist* 5, no. 6 (7 January 1828): 406.
83. Isaac Watts produced a hymnal with the same title that was published the same year as Campbell's. Interestingly, Campbell included several of Isaac Watts's hymns in his own hymnal.
84. Alexander Campbell, *Psalms, Hymns, and Spiritual Songs, Original and Selected, Adapted to the Christian Religion* (Philadelphia: L. Johnson, 1828, 1843, 1856), 8.
85. Campbell, *Psalms, Hymns, and Spiritual Songs, Original and Selected, Adapted to the Christian Religion*, 5–6.
86. Jim Mankin, "Alexander Campbell's Contribution to Hymnody," *The Hymn, Discipliana and Restoration Quarterly* 49, no. 1 (January 1998): 11–12.
87. See Jude 1:12.
88. Campbell, "A Restoration of the Ancient Order of Things, No. 15," *Christian Baptist* 4, no. 4 (6 November 1826): 283–84; "A Restoration of the Ancient Order of Things, No. 22," *Christian Baptist* 5, no. 6 (7 January 1828): 408.
89. Campbell, *Christianity Restored*, 7.
90. Campbell, "A Restoration of the Ancient Order of Things, No. 20," *Christian Baptist* 5, no. 1 (6 August 1827): 362–63.

91. Campbell, "A Restoration of the Ancient Order of Things, No. 16," *Christian Baptist* 4, no. 5 (4 December 1826): 295.
92. He also did not list teacher or pastor but likely considered them as subsumed within the previously listed offices.
93. Campbell, "Essays on the Work of the Holy Spirit, in the Salvation of Men, No. 3, 'Spiritual Gifts,'" *Christian Baptist* 2, no. 3 (4 October 1824): 95–97.
94. Richardson, *Memoirs of Alexander Campbell*, 1:387.
95. Campbell, "A Restoration of the Ancient Order of Things, No. 19," *Christian Baptist* 4, no. 10 (7 May 1827): 335.
96. Campbell, "A Restoration of the Ancient Order of Things, No. 12," *Christian Baptist* 3, no. 9 (3 April 1826): 231–32.
97. Campbell, "A Restoration of the Ancient Order of Things, No. 13," *Christian Baptist* 3, no. 11 (5 June 1826): 243.
98. Campbell, "A Restoration of the Ancient Order of Things, No. 13," 243.
99. 1 Timothy 4: 12.
100. Campbell, "A Restoration of the Ancient Order of Things, No. 14," *Christian Baptist* 4, no. 1 (7 August 1826): 260.
101. Campbell, "A Restoration of the Ancient Order of Things, No. 14," 261.
102. Campbell, "A Restoration of the Ancient Order of Things, No. 14," 260; see also Campbell, *Christian System*, 83.
103. Campbell, "A Restoration of the Ancient Order of Things, No. 32," 585–86.
104. Campbell, *Christian System*, 79.
105. See chapter 7 for examples of how Thomas Campbell was poorly treated by the synod and presbytery in Ireland and America.
106. Hatch, *The Democratization of American Christianity*, 6, 12, 22–24, 34, 43, 69, 128.
107. John Milton, as quoted in Campbell, *Christian System*, 325.
108. Richardson, *Memoirs of Alexander Campbell*, 1:386–87.
109. Campbell, "A Restoration of the Ancient Order of Things, No. 23," *Christian Baptist* 5, no. 8 (3 March 1828): 428–29. Although this point of view may appear to be in opposition to his directions for selecting a bishop, I believe he is attempting to follow biblical precedent in his understanding of how a duly elected leader was to proceed.
110. Campbell, "A Restoration of the Ancient Order of Things, No. 24," *Christian Baptist* 5, no. 10 (5 May 1828): 441.
111. Campbell, "A Restoration of the Ancient Order of Things, No. 28," *Christian Baptist* 6, no. 5 (1 December 1828): 501.
112. Campbell, "A Restoration of the Ancient Order of Things, No. 29," *Christian Baptist* 6, no. 6 (5 January 1829): 509.
113. Campbell, "A Restoration of the Ancient Order of Things, No. 29," 510.
114. Campbell, "A Restoration of the Ancient Order of Things, No. 27," *Christian Baptist* 6, no. 3 (6 October 1828): 486.
115. Campbell, "A Restoration of the Ancient Order of Things, No. 27," 486.
116. Campbell, *Christian System*, 24.
117. Campbell, "To Brother Henry Grew," *Millennial Harbinger* 4, no. 4 (April 1833): 155.
118. Campbell, "To Brother Henry Grew," 155.
119. Campbell, *Christian System*, 20–21.
120. Buck, *A Theological Dictionary*, s.v. "Unitarians." Campbell used an analogy to explain Trinitarianism: it was like the "three personal relations" of human nature. Adam possessed all of human nature; Eve, coming out of him, possessed all his nature without subtracting anything from Adam; and a child coming from the two of them possessed all of their natures while remaining distinct from them. Campbell asserted, "Here, then, are three persons possessing one nature—three personal relations in one

common nature." Campbell, "Unitarianism as Connected with Christian Union, No. 3," *Millennial Harbinger* (series 3) 3, no. 8 (August 1846): 451.

121. Campbell, "Man in the Image of God," *Millennial Harbinger* (fifth series) 4, no. 2 (February 1861): 69; Campbell, *Familiar Lectures on the Pentateuch*, 87.

122. Campbell, *Christian System*, 20; Campbell, "Theology, Natural and Revealed," *Millennial Harbinger* (fourth series) 3, no. 5 (May 1853): 287–288; Milton V. Backman Jr., *American Religions and the Rise of Mormonism* (Salt Lake City: Deseret Book, 1970), 242.

123. *The Encyclopedia of the Stone-Campbell Movement*, ed. Foster et al., s.v. "God, Doctrine of," 357.

124. Campbell, *Christian System*, 22.

125. Campbell, *Christian System*, 23.

126. Campbell, "The Trinitarian System," *Christian Baptist* 4, no. 10 (7 May 1827): 333.

127. Campbell, *Christian System*, 24.

128. Campbell, "Christian Psalmody," *Millennial Harbinger* (third series) 1, no. 7 (July 1844): 292.

129. Campbell, "Essays on the Work of the Holy Spirit in the Salvation of Men, No. 1," *Christian Baptist* 2, no. 1 (2 August 1824): 81.

130. Campbell, "Essays on the Work of the Holy Spirit in the Salvation of Men, No. 1," 81.

131. Campbell, "History of Sin, Including the Outlines of Ancient History, No. 1," *Millennial Harbinger* 1, no. 3 (March 1830): 107.

132. Campbell, "Man in His Primitive State, and under the Patriarchal, Jewish and Christian Dispensations, No. 2," *Christian Baptist* 6, no. 2 (1 September 1828): 470.

133. Campbell, "Kingdom of Satan, No. 3," *Millennial Harbinger* (new series) 2, no. 3 (February 1838): 122–24.

134. Campbell, "History of Sin, Including the Outlines of Ancient History, No. 1," *Millennial Harbinger* 1, no. 3 (March 1830): 107.

135. Campbell, *Familiar lectures on the Pentateuch*, 80.

136. Alexander Campbell, *Popular Lectures and Addresses* (St. Louis: John Burns, 1861), 214.

137. Campbell, *Christian System*, 29; emphasis in original.

138. Campbell, *Christian System*, 30–31.

139. Campbell, "Address at Florence Academy," *Millennial Harbinger* (new series) 2, no. 12 (December 1838): 534.

140. Campbell, *Christian System*, 30–31.

141. Campbell, "Kingdom of Satan, No. 4," *Millennial Harbinger* (new series) 2, no. 4 (April 1838): 161.

142. Campbell, "Three Inheritances: Adam's Estate," *Millennial Harbinger* 3, no. 6 (June 1832): 251–52.

143. Campbell, *Christian System*, 4. "In the Roman Catholic Church: the performance of good works beyond what God commands or requires," *Oxford English Dictionary*, s.v. "supererogation." Luther called the Epistle of James an epistle of straw because he was unsure of its apostolic origin and could not reconcile Paul's emphasis on faith without the deeds or works of the law [of Moses] and James's emphasis on both faith and works.

144. Thomas Olbricht, "Alexander Campbell as a Theologian," Impact 21, no. 1 (1988), 22–37.

145. Campbell, *Christian System*, 174. In James 1:25, he replaced "works" with "ordinances" and identified "preaching the gospel . . . the reading and teaching of the Living Oracles—the Lord's day—the Lord's supper—fasting—prayer—confession of sin—and praise" as ordinances which contain the grace of God.

146. Campbell, "Faith and Works," *Millennial Harbinger* (October 1853): 446.
147. Campbell, "The Rank and Dignity of Man," *Millennial Harbinger* (new series) 2, no. 12 (December 1838): 540–41.
148. Holifield, *Theology in America*, 299–300.
149. Campbell, "A Restoration of the Ancient Order of Things, No. 3," *Christian Baptist* 3, no. 4 (4 April 1825): 140–41. Although Campbell was associated with the Baptists at this time, he considered himself a reformer with a duty to help the Baptists see more clearly what the scriptures stated.
150. Campbell, "A Restoration of the Ancient Order of Things, No. 4," *Christian Baptist* 3, no. 6 (6 June 1825): 159.
151. Garrison and DeGroot, *The Disciples of Christ*, 133, 162; Alexander Campbell, "The New Translation," *Christian Baptist* 4, no. 9 (2 April 1827): 326–27; Campbell, *Christian System*, 118–20.
152. Campbell, "The New Translation," 326–27.
153. Garrison and DeGroot, *The Disciples of Christ*, 133, 162.
154. Campbell, *Christian System*, 118–20.
155. Garrison and DeGroot, *The Disciples of Christ*, 133.
156. Campbell, *Christian System*, 118–20. See also *Encyclopedia of the Stone-Campbell Movement*, s.v. "faith," 328.
157. Hayden, *Early History of the Disciples*, 71, 81, 87; Garrett, *The Stone-Campbell Movement*, 218–19; Richardson, *Memoirs of Alexander Campbell*, 2:208. Garrison and DeGroot, *The Disciples of Christ*, 203
158. Garrison and DeGroot, *The Disciples of Christ*, 173, 187–88.
159. Hayden, *Early History of the Disciples*, 175.
160. Pratt, *Autobiography of Parley P. Pratt*, 10–11.
161. Pratt, *Autobiography of Parley P. Pratt*, 22.
162. Campbell, "Reply to Robert Cautious," *Christian Baptist* 1, no. 5 (1 December 1823): 33.
163. Campbell, *Christian System*, 3.
164. Campbell, *Christian System*, 5.
165. Richardson, *Memoirs of Alexander Campbell*, 1:267; Alexander Campbell, *Familiar Lectures on the Pentateuch* (St. Louis: Christian Publishing), 12.
166. Richardson, *Memoirs of Alexander Campbell*, 1:350.

6

Joseph Smith's Revelatory Restoration

*U*nlike Campbell, Smith had few moments of leisured literary reflection. He was never comfortably ensconced in his own home nor even his own private room until 1839, when he purchased a log house on the eastern bank of the Mississippi River in Nauvoo called the Homestead. His life was fraught with enduring persecution, living in the homes of others and relying upon the generosity of his followers; his life's work was bringing forth his restoration through revelation. Sometimes his revelations were the result of pondering scriptures, and sometimes they were the consequences of his questions on how to resolve difficult problems in the church. In addition to the Book of Mormon, Smith and later his scribes began recording his revelations in 1823. He selected for publication the most significant revelations received between 1823 and 1834, with the majority recorded between 1828 and 1832 and published in 1835.[1] Within a month after the organization of the Church of Christ in April 1830, Smith embarked on a reworking of the Bible, calling it an inspired translation. Although the majority of the work was completed by 1833, it was not published until 1867 by the Reorganized Church of Jesus Christ of Latter Day Saints. More about Smith's Bible translation is found in chapter 9.

On several points of Campbell's restoration of the ancient order of things, (1) opposition to -isms and creeds; (2) the constitution of God; (3) Christian worship; (4) psalms and hymns;

(5) feasts of charity; (6) church discipline, Smith did make some significant comments.

-Isms and Creeds. Like Campbell, Smith uniformly rejected the five points of Calvinism. Regarding the doctrines of election and predestination, Smith insisted, "Unconditional election of individuals to eternal life was not taught by the Apostles." Nevertheless, Smith clarified that "God did elect or predestinate, that all those who would be saved, should be saved in Christ Jesus, and through obedience to the gospel; but he passes over no man's sins, but visits them with correction, and if his children will not repent of their sins He will discard them."[2]

Smith was a vehement opponent of creeds but for reasons different from Campbell's. In the 1838 official record of his 1820 First Vision, Smith declared that in response to his question "which of all the sects was right," he was told among other things that the creeds of Christendom "were an abomination in his sight."[3] In other words, truth had been replaced by the false reasoning and philosophies of the early Christian Fathers, regardless of how well-meaning their efforts were, with which God was greatly displeased. Smith considered his First Vision a completely authoritative source coming from God himself. Creeds set limits on God and his ability to reveal additional light and knowledge; in other words, Smith believed the scriptures were very important but not sufficient.

In a statement about the confessions of the different denominations, Smith explained his own resistance to them: "They all have some things in them I cannot subscribe to though all of them have some thruth but I want to come up into the presence of God & learn all things but the creeds set up stakes, & say, hitherto shalt thou come, & no further—which I cannot subscribe to."[4] Although as a young man he was partial to the Methodists, Smith later professed that they "have creeds which a man must believe or be kicked out of their church."[5] Further, he declared, "The most prominent point of difference in sentiment between the Latter Day Saints & sectarians was, that the latter were all circumscribed by some peculiar creed, which deprived its members the privilege of believing anything not contained therein; whereas the L.D. Saints [had] no creed, but [were] ready to believe all true principles that exist, as they are made manifest from time to time."[6] Smith left open the door to further communication from heaven and lamented, "It is very difficult for us to communicate to the churches all that God has revealed to us, in consequence of tradition," meaning the creeds prevented him from sharing God's revelations with other churches.[7]

In response to the frequently asked question "Wherein do you differ from other sects?" Smith responded once with this statement: "We believe the Bible, and all other sects profess to believe their interpretations of the Bible, and their creeds."[8] By 1839, Smith recognized what creeds had wrought through the crucible of persecution for himself and his followers as he sat imprisoned for months. From jail in Liberty, Missouri, he wrote that the "hand of murder, tyranny, and oppression" were "supported and urged on and upheld by the influence" of the "inherited lies" found in the "creeds of the fathers," which were like an "iron yoke" filling "the world with confusion," limiting truth and especially an understanding of God."[9]

Constitution of God. Smith had an expanded view of what was included in the constitution of God. Although Doctrine and Covenants sections 20–22 have been referred to as the "constitution" of the Mormon Church, the true constitution consisted of the entire body of scripture.[10] It was more than the New Testament; it also included the Old Testament, the Book of Mormon, the Doctrine and Covenants, and the Pearl of Great Price as well as revelations given through a living prophet. Smith found value in all of God's words to his prophets in every dispensation, each of whom had testified of Jesus Christ and his birth, death, and Resurrection, and these words were the foundation of his restoration.[11] Smith taught that the first Christian dispensation began with Adam and that knowledge was redispensed at various times to prophets of God such as Enoch, Noah, Abraham, Moses, and, at the time of Christ, to Peter. Smith claimed that he became head of the final dispensation—what he called "the dispensation of the fulness of times"[12]—through the ministering of Peter, James, and John.[13] The constitution of God, from Smith's perspective, was an expansive gathering of revelation over millennia—a melding of the dispensations.

Christian Worship. Smith's initial revelations on church organization, church government, and the Lord's Supper gave few details for procedures in administering the Lord's Supper,[14] and early on, persecution, influence of converts from other religious backgrounds, and lack of church meeting houses, among other difficulties, caused the sacrament to be irregularly and inconsistently administered.[15] Over time, Smith's definition of what should be included in Sunday worship and the weekly administration of sacrament ordinances was similar to some of Campbell's statements. Significantly different, however, was the view that keeping the Lord's day holy and partaking of the sacrament were still commandments. Explicit instructions on how the Nephite Christians conducted church worship, as directed by Jesus, were recorded by the prophet Moroni.[16] Passages found in the Book of Mormon and repeated in the Doctrine and Covenants gave set prayers for blessing the sacramental emblems.[17]

Weekly participation in the Lord's Supper was central to the purpose for coming together. Smith's restoration included both the Old Testament and the New Testament commandments to honor the Lord. Unique to his restoration was the formal, ritual nature of the Lord's Supper. Scripted prayers that were revealed to Smith in two of his prophetic texts were pronounced by priesthood holders over the bread and wine.

Psalms and Hymns. In July 1830, Joseph Smith dictated a revelation for his wife, Emma, shortly after her baptism.[18] Among other things, she was directed to make a selection of sacred hymns for use in the church. In June 1832, the church's newspaper, *The Evening and the Morning Star,* began publishing Protestant hymn texts with doctrinal revisions by W. W. Phelps, the paper's editor, and in 1833, he added original Latter-day Saint hymns. Publication of Emma's collection, revised and prepared for printing by Phelps, was temporarily delayed because in 1833, a mob destroyed the printing press in Missouri. Published in 1835 in Kirtland, Ohio, *A Collection of Sacred Hymns, for the Church of the Latter Day Saints* was a 3×4½-inch book. It began with this preface:

> In order to sing by the Spirit, and with the understanding, it is necessary that the Church of the Latter Day Saints should have a collection of "Sacred Hymns," adapted to their faith and belief in the gospel, and, as far as can be, holding forth the promises made to the fathers who died in the precious faith of a glorious resurrection, and a thousand years' reign on earth with the Son of Man in his glory. Notwithstanding, the church as it were, is still in its infancy, yet as the song of the righteous is a prayer unto God, it is sincerely hoped that the following collection, selected with an eye single to his glory, may answer every purpose til more are composed, or be blessed with a copious variety of the songs of Zion.

Emma's hymnal was shorter than Campbell's, with the text of ninety hymns divided into sections titled Sacred Hymns, Morning Hymns, Evening Hymns, Farewell Hymns, On Baptism, On Sacrament, On

Marriage, and Miscellaneous, and an index organized alphabetically by the first line. The texts emphasize restoration ideals and key tenets, such as building a literal Zion in Missouri and preparing for an imminent Second Coming by creating a sense of community.[19] Interestingly, the two hymnals have twenty hymns in common; the most popular of these among Mormons today are "Guide Us [Me], O Thou Great Jehovah [Messiah]," "I Know That My Redeemer Lives," "How Firm a Foundation, Ye Saints of the Lord," and "O God! Our Help in Ages Past."[20]

Feasts of Charity. Newel K. Whitney, as bishop for Smith's church organization in Ohio, received divine instruction that part of his responsibility was to "travel round about and among all the churches, searching after the poor; to administer to their wants by humbling the rich and the proud."[21] How he organized his travels is unknown. "Fast meetings" were held in which individuals abstained from eating and then brought bread, butter, and other foods which thereafter were taken to the bishop's storehouse to be distributed among the poor, or else presented in a dinner that was organized for them.[22] Ann Whitney recalled one such event: "We determined to make a Feast for the Poor, such as we knew could not return the same to us; the lame, the halt, the deaf, the blind, the aged and infirm. The feast lasted three days, during which time all in the vicinity of Kirtland who would come were invited, and entertained as courteously and generously as if they had been able to extend hospitality instead of receiving it. . . . To me it was a feast of fat things indeed; a season of rejoicing never to be forgotten."[23]

Church Discipline. Smith organized councils beginning in Kirtland, Ohio, in 1831. One of the specific purposes of the council was church discipline. Certain elders of the church were to "sit in judgment" of the transgressions of individuals "according to the laws [of the church], by assistance of his counselors."[24] Smith also recognized the need for order in the church; a fair and impartial hearing for serious sins required either repentance or excommunication.

FOUNDATIONAL EVENTS AND REVELATIONS

Joseph Smith's vision of restoration was a sweeping expansion of the meaning of the term that was both experiential and revelatory. His revelatory approach to restoration recovered "lost possibilities and forgotten relics of the past," such as covenants, doctrines, rituals, and practices that interrupted the flow of traditional Christianity.[25] Persons, events, and places had historical and doctrinal implications. Recorded historical events had literal and doctrinal importance that drove Smith's questions, the asking of which also brought about historical events such as revelations and visions in peculiar and significant places for himself and sometimes others. Thus, as will be seen, trying to separate history from doctrine and vice versa is not completely possible in Smith's understanding of restoration.[26] Mormonism, then, is best described as a succession of historical events and not as a philosophy or series of arguments to be debated.

Smith's restoration began with claims of the reestablishment of immediate dialogue[27] between heaven and earth, through which the knowledge and understanding of doctrines, covenants, and priesthood keys[28] that were given to Adam and the ancient patriarchs were restored.[29] This means that communication between God and humans led to a redispensing of ancient gospel covenants and the restoring of both priesthood and "plain and precious" truths he believed had been lost from the biblical record.[30] Further, Smith proclaimed belief in past, present, and future revelation—to outsiders, an almost unfathomable enlargement in the meaning of the word *restoration*.[31] He probably spoke and dictated more about the past than he did about the future. Smith professed that his visions and revelations were "like an overflowing surge . . . before my mind."[32] It was his claim of revelation that allowed Smith to look both to the past and the future and to link them in a fashion that permitted growth and progress within the parameters of eternal doctrines and principles. A common way of thinking about Smith's prophetic career is as linearly advancing through ever-increasing stages of doctrinal development, complexity, and boldness in a systematic way; however, "the seeds of almost all his furthest-reaching innovations are present as early as 1830."[33] His restoration is actually more characterized by revelatory fits and starts, innovations and observations, and gatherings from disparate sources and "aha moments" when connections were made and many things came together in new ways. What follows is a simple way of chronologically systematizing five singular historical and foundational events describing the means by which the salvation taught in Smith's restoration had the power and authority to administer saving ordinances.

Smith's simple doctrinal summation ties the following events together: Christ was central to his restoration and everything else was secondary. Smith declared, "The fundamental principles of our religion are the testimony of the apostles and prophets concerning Jesus Christ, 'that He died, was buried, and rose again the third day, and ascended into heaven'; and all other things, are only appendages to [it], which pertain to our religion."[34] This summary is very similar to Campbell's statement in his 1824 Wellsburg church's application to join the Mahoning Baptist Association.

As noted in the introduction to this section, systematizing Mormon beliefs has eluded many scholars who have studied Joseph Smith and his restoration. The importance of the five historical events can only be understood in the context of the central nature of Christ to revelation and priesthood authority.

1. *The First Vision.* In the spring of 1820, during his fifteenth year, Joseph learned many things in his first encounter with Deity, commonly referred to as the First Vision and considered the initiating event of a new dispensation. The context of the vision—his personal thoughts, questions, and first attempt at a vocal prayer—was given in chapter 3, the "Early Life of and Religious Influences on Joseph Smith"; this is the substance of his experience. The following rendition of his theophany is a harmonization of five firsthand accounts and five secondhand accounts given at various times between 1832 and 1844 to different individuals, with the official account written by Smith in 1838, noted as Joseph Smith—History (JS—H), as the foundation. Much has been made by some that there are differences in the accounts. Audience, reexperiencing the event while retelling it, and spiritual maturity and understanding were likely important circumstances as he interpreted a singular and remarkable event over an eighteen-year period.[35] The main body of the experience can be divided into four parts: (1) opposition, (2) visitation, (3) question, and (4) answer.[36]

OPPOSITION

> JS—H 1:15: I immediately went out into the woods where my father had a clearing, and went to the stump where I had stuck my axe when I had quit work (1843, James White). After I had retired to the place where I had previously designed to go, having looked around me, and finding myself alone (1838, JS), in the place above stated or, in other words I made a fruitless attempt to pray (1835, JS). I knelt down and began to offer up the desires of my heart to God. I had scarcely done so, when immediately I was seized upon by some power which entirely

overcame me, and had such an astonishing influence over me as to bind my tongue so that I could not speak (1838, JS). My tongue seemed to be swollen in my mouth, so that I could not utter. I heard a noise behind me like some one walking towards me (1835, JS). Thick darkness gathered around me, and it seemed to me for a time as if I were doomed to sudden destruction (1838, JS). The adversary made several strenuous attempts to cool the passion of [my] soul. He clouded [my] mind with doubts, and brought to [my] mind all sorts of improper images to prevent [me] from attaining the object of [my] endeavors (1842, Orson Hyde); I strove again to pray, but could not; the noise of walking seemed to draw nearer, [and] I sprang upon my feet and looked round, but saw no person or thing that was calculated to produce the noise of walking (1835, JS).

JS—H 1:16: But, exerting all my powers to call upon God (1838, JS) [and] every energy (1842/1843, JS) to deliver me out of the power of this enemy which had seized upon me, and at the very moment when I was ready to sink into despair and abandon myself to destruction—not to an imaginary ruin, but to the power [and] influence (1842/1843, JS) of some actual being from the unseen world, who had such marvelous power as I had never before felt in any being—just at this moment of great alarm, I kneeled again, my mouth was opened and my tongue loosed [and as] I called on the Lord in mighty prayer (1835, JS), the dark cloud soon parted and light and peace filled [my] frightened heart [or in other words,] the overflowing mercy of our God came to uplift [me] and impart new impetus to [my failing strength] (1838, JS).

Visitation

JS—H 1:16: I saw a pillar of light (1838 recital) [or] fire (1835 recital) exactly over my head, which exceeded (1841, JS) the brightness of the (1838, JS) dazzling (1841) sun (1838 recital) in his meridian splendor (1841, JS), [and it] came down from above (1832 recital), which at first seemed to be at a considerable distance. As it drew nearer, it increased in brightness, and magnitude, so that by the time that it reached the tops of the trees, the whole wilderness, for some distance around, was illuminated in a most glorious and brilliant manner. [I] expected to have seen the leaves and boughs of the trees consumed, as soon as the light came in contact with them; but, perceiving that it did not produce that effect; [I] was encouraged with the hopes of being able to endure its presence (1840, Orson Pratt), which descended gradually until it fell upon me (1838, JS). It presently rested down upon me and filled me with unspeakable joy (1835, JS). [Indeed] it continued descending, slowly, until it rested upon the earth, and [I] was enveloped in the midst of it (1840, Orson Pratt).

JS—H 1:17: It no sooner appeared than I found myself delivered from the enemy which held me bound. When the light rested upon me (1838, JS) it produced a peculiar sensation throughout [my] whole system; and, immediately [my] mind was caught away, from the natural objects with which [I] was surrounded; and [I] was enwrapped in a heavenly vision (1840, Orson Pratt). [Furthermore,] I was filled with the Spirit of God, [and the] Lord opened the heavens upon me (1832, JS). A personage appeared in the midst of this pillar of flame, which was spread all around and yet nothing consumed (1835, JS), [having a] light complexion, blue eyes, a piece of white cloth drawn over his shoulders, his right arm b[are]. After a while (1844, Alexander Neibaur) another personage soon appeared (1835, JS) to the side of the first (1844, Alexander Neibaur) [who was] like unto the first (1835, JS). I saw two (1838, JS) heavenly (1842, Orson Hyde) [and] angelic (1830, Orson Pratt) Personages (1838, JS) who exactly resembled each other in features, and likeness (1842/1843, JS), [and] whose brightness and glory defy all description, standing above me in the air. One of them spake unto me, calling me by name and said, pointing to the other—*This is My Beloved Son. Hear Him!* (1838, JS).

QUESTION

JS—H 1:18: My object in going to inquire of the Lord was to (1838, JS) ascertain (1841, JS) which of all the sects was right, that I might know which to join (1838, JS). Consequently[,] as soon as possible (1841, JS) [and] no sooner, therefore, did I get possession of myself, so as to be able to speak, than I addressed this second person (1842/1843, JS) who stood above me in the light, saying ["]O Lord, what Church shall I join (1842/1843, JS) [?" And asking] which of all the sects was right (for at this time it had never entered into my heart that all were wrong (1838, JS) [because] I supposed that one of them (1841, JS) [was right].

ANSWER

JS—H 1:19: I was answered that I must join none of them, for they were all wrong; and the Personage who addressed me said that all their creeds were an abomination in his sight; that those professors were all corrupt

(1838, JS) because all of them were mistaken in their doctrine and not recognized by God as his church and kingdom (1842, Orson Hyde) [because] the Everlasting Covenant was broken (1843, Levi Richards); that: "behold the world lieth in sin at this time and none doeth good, no not one. They have turned aside from the Gospel and keep not my commandments (1842, Orson Hyde). They draw near to me with their lips, but their hearts are far from me, they teach for doctrines the commandments of men, having a form of godliness, but they deny the power thereof (1838, JS)[,] and mine anger is kindling against the inhabitants of the earth to visit them according to this ungodliness and to bring to pass that which hath been spoken by the mouth of the prophets and Apostles. Behold and lo, I come quickly[,] as it [is] written of me, in the cloud clothed in the glory of my Father["] (1842, Orson Hyde).

JS—H 19: He again forbade me to join with any of them (1838 JS). [I] was further commanded to wait patiently until a future time (1842, Orson Hyde), receiving a promise that (1842/1843) the true doctrine of Christ and the fullness of the gospel should be revealed to [me] (1842, Orson Hyde).

This was a stunning response to a simple prayer—opposition from a satanic force, an opening of the heavens amidst bright light that could be best described as resembling the fire of the sun, and a glorious personal visitation by heavenly beings who knew his name. Smith was introduced by God the Father to his beloved Son and was commanded to both see and hear him. He was able to clearly discern by the separate arrivals and communication with him that the Father and Son were separate beings of great glory, although he did not emphasize that point initially. "He was not prepared for the sweeping revelation that none of them [the sects] was the true church of Christ" because the human-created creeds had caused the corruption of true doctrine, particularly in regard to the power and authority of God.[37] Smith was to await further instruction from God, with the implications that future visions awaited him, that Christ was coming again soon, and that he would be taught more than he ever had imagined.[38]

Similar to other worshippers who gathered at revivals, Smith described his tongue being bound. His response, however, was significantly different. He did not interpret this experience as heavenly but described it as being from "the enemy" and sought God's help in overcoming it. It was after he was delivered from the enemy that he received the transcendent manifestation. His rejection of tongue binding as part of religious experience separated him from some of the enthusiasm-driven religionists of his day. Having a vision also separated him from the Enlightenment-directed, rational religionists.[39] His vision was personal, and he did not fully share it immediately with his family. His recounting of it in 1820 to a local Methodist clergyman was met with contempt, mocking, and reviling, encouraging him to keep his experience to himself.[40] Skepticism and persecution, however, did not cause him to retract his words, but it was not until twelve years later that he first recorded an account. Although initially not fully comprehending all that he received, he bore unashamed testimony of it. In a brief summary, a scribe recorded the following thoughts, feelings, and experiences:

> When he was a youth he began to think about these things but could not find out which of all the sects were right—"he went into the grove & enquired of the Lord . . . . — received for answer that none of them were right, that they were all wrong, & that the Everlasting covena[n]t was broken= he said he understood the fulness of the Gospel from beginning to end— & could Teach it & also the order of the priesthood in all its ramifications.[41]

Some significant points in this later reminiscence had to do with the "everlasting covenant" that was broken and the "order of the priesthood." At first, Smith did not fully understand the significance of these points. Over time, as he received additional revelations and messengers, he fleshed out more fully the account of his heavenly vision and the significance of the Abrahamic covenant and priesthood authority and power as they were restored through him to the church.

2. *Priesthood Ordination.* Smith recorded that in May 1829—prior to the organization of the church and while translating the Book of Mormon—he and Oliver Cowdery, his scribe, went into the woods to ask God regarding "baptism for the remission of sins."[42]

> JS—H 1:68: We on a certain day went into the woods to pray and inquire of the Lord. . . . While we were thus employed, praying and calling upon the Lord, a messenger from heaven descended in a cloud of light, and having laid his hands upon us, he ordained us, saying:
>
> JS—H 1:69: *Upon you my fellow servants, in the name of Messiah, I confer the Priesthood of Aaron, which holds the keys of the ministering of angels, and of the gospel of repentance, and of baptism by immersion for the remission of sins; and this shall never be taken again from the earth until the sons of Levi do offer again an offering unto the Lord in righteousness.*

JS—H 1:70: He said this Aaronic Priesthood had not the power of laying on hands for the gift of the Holy Ghost, but that this should be conferred on us hereafter; and he commanded us to go and be baptized, and gave us directions that I should baptize Oliver Cowdery, and that afterwards he should baptize me.

JS—H 1:71: Accordingly we went and were baptized. I baptized him first, and afterwards he baptized me—after which I laid my hands upon his head and ordained him to the Aaronic Priesthood, and afterwards he laid his hands on me and ordained me to the same Priesthood—for so we were commanded.

JS—H 1:72: The messenger who visited us on this occasion and conferred this Priesthood upon us, said that his name was John, the same that is called John the Baptist in the New Testament, and that he acted under the direction of Peter, James and John, who held the keys of the Priesthood of Melchizedek, which Priesthood, he said, would in due time be conferred on us, and that I should be called the first Elder of the Church, and he (Oliver Cowdery) the second. It was on the fifteenth day of May, 1829, that we were ordained under the hand of this messenger, and baptized.

Smith was not just observing the rite of baptism but claimed to be reinstituting the significance that it had anciently by restoring the power used by John the Baptist when he baptized Jesus and others.[43] Within a short time, Smith and Cowdery announced that the Apostles Peter, James, and John had also conferred upon them the keys of the Melchizedek Priesthood, emphasizing that priesthood was conferred by the laying on of hands by those who held it anciently.[44] Unfortunately, there is no record of the exact date; however, Mormon history scholar Larry Porter narrowed the time to between the middle and end of May 1829, within days or at most weeks of the visitation by John the Baptist. Porter further clarified: "Both scripture and history attest that the restoration of the keys and powers of the Melchizedek Priesthood took place as a necessary prerequisite to the reestablishment of Christ's church on the earth" because they "embraced all of the offices of the priesthood, including the keys of apostleship, the highest authority conferred upon men in the flesh."[45] The ancient apostolic order of the priesthood and accompanying gifts of the Spirit were an integral part of Smith's restoration because he claimed priesthood keys are the means by which all things are restored to their proper order. In an 1833 letter, he explained,

"The fundamental principles, government, and doctrine of the church are vested in the [priesthood] keys of the kingdom."[46]

3. *Coming forth of the Book of Mormon.* Smith claimed that in his first encounter with Deity, he was told not to join any church but that he was to wait patiently until the true doctrine of Christ and the fullness of the gospel would be revealed to him. In the fall of 1823, Smith, concerned again for his spiritual welfare, prayed to know his standing before God.[47]

Holding to the things he had learned from God in his First Vision, he passed through the next several years as boys his age commonly did, with work and lighthearted play.[48] As he matured, he recognized that perhaps his tendency toward levity and lack of focus on spiritual things was "not consistent with that character which ought to be maintained by one who was called of God as [he] had been."[49] His spiritual sensitivity caused him to ponder and worry about his weaknesses and imperfections.

Consequently, on 21 September 1823, before he went to bed, seventeen-year-old Smith recounted, "I betook myself to prayer and supplication to Almighty God for forgiveness of all my sins and follies, and also for a manifestation to me, that I might know of my state and standing before him; for I had full confidence in obtaining a divine manifestation."[50] He reported that while he was praying, his room began to grow light until it became "lighter than at noonday."[51] He described it as a pure and glorious brightness that "burst into the room . . . as though the house was filled with consuming fire."[52] Within the light was a personage, whose countenance he described "as lightning," wearing garments that were "pure and white above all whiteness." The "holy angel"[53] called Smith by name and announced that "he was a messenger sent from the presence of God . . . and that his name was Moroni."[54] The messenger proclaimed that he had been "sent to bring the joyful tidings that the covenant which God made with ancient Israel was at hand to be fulfilled, that the preparatory work for the second coming of the Messiah was speedily to commence; that the time was at hand for the Gospel in all its fullness to be preached in power, unto all nations that a people might be prepared for the millennial reign."[55] Warning Smith that his "name should be had for good and evil among all nations, kindreds, and tongues," Moroni also revealed that "there was a book deposited, written upon gold plates, giving an account of the former inhabitants of this continent, and the source from whence they sprang."[56]

Moroni quoted prophesies from the Bible, including parts of Malachi 3 and 4, with some variation from the way it reads in our Bibles. Moroni similarly quoted from Isaiah 11, Acts 3:22–23, Joel 2:28–32, declaring that many of these promises were soon to be fulfilled.[57] Oliver Cowdery later wrote that Moroni additionally quoted verses from Isaiah, Psalms, Jeremiah, and Deuteronomy.[58] From this list of scriptures comes the following passage: "I will reveal unto you the Priesthood, by the hand of Elijah the prophet, before the great and dreadful day of the Lord."[59] Priesthood was not a commission Smith could take upon himself. It would have to be revealed to him.

Regarding the book, the messenger gave Smith a brief sketch of the ancient civilization, including its laws and government as well as the people's relationship with God.[60] More importantly, Moroni testified that the plates contained the "fullness of the everlasting Gospel"—the gospel the Savior had delivered personally to those ancient people.[61] Smith was shown in vision that the plates were located in a hill he recognized as not far from his home.

As the vision concluded, the light gathered around the messenger until the room was dark again. This same vision was repeated two more times that night and then again the next morning. The repetition indelibly reinforced the message and the location of the plates in Smith's mind. When he went to the hill, he was easily able to locate the buried stone box in which the ancient golden plates were hidden.[62] Smith was not yet permitted to take the plates; Moroni told him to return to the hill each year on the anniversary date, 22 September, for further preparation. In a process that required meeting with the angel over a period of four years, Smith came and "received instruction and intelligence from Moroni . . . respecting what the Lord was going to do, and how and in what manner his kingdom was to be conducted in the last days."[63] As recorded in his 1832 history, on 22 September 1827, Smith was allowed to take the set of gold plates written in an ancient language after he had received visitations and tutoring from "many angels of God unfolding the majesty and glory of the events that should transpire in the last days."[64]

Smith described the records as thin 6x8-inch plates having the appearance of gold and bound together like a book with three rings holding the leaves together and covered with what he characterized as small, beautiful engravings similar to Egyptian characters. Smith also described a "curious instrument" that accompanied the plates. He explained that the instrument "consisted of two transparent stones set in the rims of a bow fastened to a breast plate."[65] Smith affirmed that this instrument was the medium through which he was enabled, by the gift and power of God, to translate the record. The common meaning of translation is to render from one language to another in a scholarly manner. Smith, however, considered the ability he had to translate as a gift of the Spirit, like the gift of speaking or interpreting tongues. Initially, he referred to the instrument as "interpreters"; however, by the fall of 1829, he called them "spectacles" and then began to use the Old Testament term "Teraphim," or "Urim and Thummim." Apparently, he and others later referred to all stones used for translation purposes by their ancient term, Urim and Thummim.[66] He never fully explained the translation process, saying, "It was not intended to tell the world all the particulars of the coming forth of the book of Mormon, & also said that it was not expedient for him to relate these things &c."[67] In addition to the interpreters found with the plates, Joseph Smith also translated using a personal seer stone he had found as a young man in New York, and which he had used previously to find hidden treasure or lost objects.[68]

During the fall and early winter of 1827 and 1828, individuals were trying to steal the plates, causing Joseph and Emma to move from his parents' home in Palmyra, New York, to Harmony, Pennsylvania, where Emma's parents lived. Smith began the translation in earnest in the spring and early summer of 1828, with Martin Harris as his primary scribe; however, 116 pages of manuscript were stolen when Harris borrowed them to show a few select family members. As a result of Smith's and Harris's carelessness, Moroni took back the plates and interpreters for several months.[69] After months of pleading for God's grace, Smith received the plates from Moroni on 22 September 1828. Emma may have acted as scribe for a short time, but the translation work was sporadic, and it appears little was accomplished.[70] In answer to a question about the veracity of Smith's claims regarding the translation process, Emma confessed, "Joseph Smith could neither write nor dictate a coherent and well-worded letter, let alone dictate a book like the Book of Mormon. And, though I was an active participant in the scenes that transpired, and was present during the translation of the plates, and had cognizance of things as they transpired, it is marvelous to me, 'a marvel and a wonder,' as much so as to anyone else."[71]

In the spring of 1829, Oliver Cowdery became acquainted with the Joseph Smith Sr. family. Cowdery was a schoolteacher who was boarding with the Smiths in their home in Palmyra, New York. He asked the Smiths about their son Joseph and about the rumors regarding the plates. After spending the day in study, Cowdery declared that "it had been put into his heart that he would have the privilege of writing for Joseph" after the school term was over.[72] On 5 April, Cowdery arrived in Harmony, Pennsylvania, and became Joseph's scribe on 7 April. Smith and Cowdery worked well together; however, they described a "spirit of persecution" and the threat of mobbing by the minister and members of the local Methodist Church, which made their translation efforts difficult.[73] At Smith's request, Cowdery wrote to ask his friend David Whitmer in Seneca County, New York, that they be allowed to come to the Whitmer farm in Fayette Township, where they could renew their translation in safety.[74] Cowdery continued to act as the principal scribe with others also assisting: David, John, and Christian Whitmer and Emma Smith.[75] Their translation efforts were made more laborious by the hot and humid summer days in which Smith and Cowdery worked long hours from morning till night. David Whitmer stated that they translated at his father's farm from 1 June to 1 July. Combined with the work they had accomplished in Harmony, Pennsylvania, in April and May, they spent about two-and-one-half months completing the translation of the plates, or approximately sixty-five to seventy-five working days.[76] According to Lucy Mack Smith, the completion of the translation brought forth the realization to Joseph that a dispensation of the gospel had been entrusted to him—and that it was just beginning.[77]

In addition to Smith, three other men—Oliver Cowdery, David Whitmer, and Martin Harris—beheld the records at the hands of an angel, saw the engravings, and bore testimony that God's voice told them the translation came by the power of God; therefore, they "knew of a surety that the work was true."[78] After returning to his parents' home in Palmyra with Cowdery and the Whitmer family, Joseph Smith took the males in the company—his father Joseph Smith Sr.; his two brothers Hyrum and Samuel; Christian, Jacob, Peter Jr., and John Whitmer; and their brother-in-law Hiram Page—to a nearby spot where Smith family members went to pray privately. Joseph showed the plates to these eight men, who were also allowed to hold them and examine the leaves closely. They bore testimony of this event and described the plates as having the appearance of gold and the inscriptions on the leaves as having the appearance of ancient and curious workmanship. The two very different descriptions by the three and eight witnesses balance the spiritual and material worlds.[79]

Work on the publication of the book began immediately. E. B. Grandin in Palmyra was contracted to print it. Cowdery was to copy the manuscript to take to the printer in the company of Hyrum Smith or Peter Whitmer Jr. The original manuscript remained in the home and was guarded by Peter Whitmer Jr. except when it was necessary for him to accompany Cowdery. Everyone in the vicinity seemed to know that Grandin was printing the Book of Mormon. At the print shop, a group of men who were angry about the forthcoming work were overheard to say: "This golden bible the smith's have got is destined to break down everything before it if there is not a stop put to it or an end made of it. For this very thing is going to be serious injury to all religious denominations and in a little while many of our excellent minister good men who have no means of obtaining a respectable livelihood except by their ministerial labor will be deprived of their sallaries which is their living. Shall we endure this gentlemen?" Plans were put into place to steal the manuscript during the day when only women were at home and to then throw it into the fire. Three men came to the Smith home and asked to see the gold bible, to which Lucy Mack Smith responded that they had no golden bible, but they had a translation from the plates. She gladly related the substance of the book, especially attempting to demonstrate the similarity of the principles to the gospel of Jesus Christ in the New Testament. Uninterested in her recitation, they attempted to coerce Lucy into showing them the manuscript, but they were unsuccessful. She had hidden it in a large chest that just fit under her bed, and she had no intention of retrieving it.[80]

Now concerned with the security of the manuscript left at the printing office, Hyrum Smith and Oliver Cowdery went one Sunday to make sure everything was safe. They found Abner Cole at work printing his own newspaper, *Dogberry Paper on Winter Hill*. Cole claimed he could not have the press during the day, so he was working on Sundays and evenings. Examining the prospectus of the newspaper, Hyrum and Oliver discovered that Cole promised his subscribers he would print a portion of "Joe Smith's Gold Bible" each week. In addition to plagiarizing manuscript pages, Cole had juxtaposed it in the paper with his own vulgar commentary. Ignoring copyright laws, Cole belligerently refused to stop printing it until Joseph came and threatened him with the law.

Finally, after submitting to arbitration, he stopped his printing of the Book of Mormon pages he had confiscated.[81]

Those living in the surrounding area, learning that the printing continued, met together and agreed that none of them would purchase the book. Concerned by the prospect of no sales and the Smith family's desperate financial circumstances, E. B. Grandin stopped printing. Smith, however, came with Martin Harris, who put up his farm as collateral in order that the printing continue. Three thousand copies of the Book of Mormon were published in late March 1830.[82]

This was Smith's first tangible contribution to his restoration and testament to his primary spiritual gift, the gift of translation, as "one who would bring forth records."[83] The book purports to be a second witness of Jesus Christ's premortal, mortal, and postmortal missions, covers a period of just over a millennium between approximately 600 BC and AD 450, and gives additional insights into the Old and New Testaments. Initially, the focus of Smith and the Mormon missionaries, however, was on the Book of Mormon's divine origin as primary evidence for Smith's claims and not on the text itself. The book was a "herald of something far greater than itself: a new church, a new dispensation, and a new American prophet." It was concrete evidence of a present God who took continuing interest in his children.[84]

4. *Organization of the Church*. By the spring of 1830, Joseph claimed to have received years of mentoring by angelic messengers. At some point—after being taught by the angel Moroni, translating the Book of Mormon, and receiving the Aaronic and Melchizedek Priesthoods—Smith learned that he was to restore the Church of Christ.

The official organization of the church on 6 April 1830, with six men and many others crowded into a small log home, was the culmination of a ten-year heavenly tutorial for Smith. However, the revelations and responsibilities had just begun. On the horizon were conferences; missionary work; further translation; gathering the members to Kirtland, Ohio, and Independence, Missouri; building temples; and calling the twelve apostles. Smith later reflected: "To find ourselves engaged in the very same order of things as observed by the holy Apostles of old, to realize the importance and solemnity of such proceedings; and to witness and feel with our natural senses, the like glorious manifestations of the powers of the Priesthood, the gifts and blessings of the Holy Ghost . . . combined to create within us sensations of rapturous gratitude."[85]

5. *Priesthood Keys.* On 3 April 1836, a week after the dedication of the temple in Kirtland, Ohio, Smith and Cowdery recorded that several prophets appeared to them in the temple, including Moses, Elias,[86] and Elijah.[87] Moses conferred the keys of the gathering of Israel, confirming the Savior's great commission to take the gospel to all nations, including the ten tribes, the living, and the dead;[88] Elias "committed the dispensation of the gospel of Abraham," meaning the Abrahamic covenant, with authority to extend eternally the blessings of family and posterity;[89] and Elijah stood before them, quoted the prophet Malachi, and announced the restoration of sealing powers, meaning the keys that could seal in heaven ordinances entered into on earth.[90] These three priesthood keys united the family of God in life on earth and for eternity.

From a Latter-day Saint point of view, God's pattern for the restoration of additional keys of priesthood authority is found in Matthew's account of the events on the Mount of Transfiguration. According to Smith, the Savior, with Moses and Elijah, gave additional priesthood keys to Peter, James, and John that were essential for the presidency of the New Testament church to have after the Savior's ascension into heaven.[91] Other than this brief recounting, neither the current Old Testament nor the New Testament seems to record clearly or completely a description of the keys and doctrines given first to Adam and restored anew in each of the succeeding dispensations.

Mormon scholar Robert Matthews asserted that the similarity of the events in the Kirtland Temple with those on the Mount of Transfiguration appears to certify that the main purpose of both visitations by holy beings was for the bestowal of additional priesthood keys in order to establish each dispensation, in the apostolic era and in the latter days, "on a solid and complete foundation, with power to preach the gospel, seal up the faithful to eternal life, and to communicate all of the gifts, powers, and graces of the gospel of Jesus Christ."[92] The establishment of the foundation of apostles and prophets through revelations from God and the ministrations of ancient prophets was the means by which Smith claimed to bring about a restoration of all things.

RESTITUTION OF ALL THINGS

Dispensations. Smith's vision of restoration was much broader than restoring the primitive church of the New Testament. It also included new revelation singular to the final dispensation, such as the millennial restoration of the ten tribes, the building of Zion, the return of earth to its Edenic state, and the eventual personal reign of Jesus Christ.[93] Jan Shipps, a non-Mormon and leading sociology scholar, has suggested that this new dispensation did not surpass previous dispensations—it fulfilled them.[94] Mormon scholars would not agree—the final dispensation both fulfilled and superseded all that had been previously revealed. Smith declared, "This dispensation comprehends all the great works of all former dispensations."[95] In other words, the final dispensation is like the ocean into which all rivers and streams flow.

Smith explained that the word *dispense* may refer either to a re-endowment of knowledge that was lost due to apostasy or to the transfer of priesthood keys and authority from one prophet to another. As Mormon philosopher Adam Miller expressed it, "A dispensation is an epoch forming retroactive configuration of history. . . . Only when the past is anachronistically and retroactively reconstituted can the lost and excluded elements of history be redeemed."[96] The final dispensation gathers together covenants, principles, doctrines, and ordinances that are ancient and seemingly out of proper sequence and time, because they are eternal. "Restoration, as Smith comes to understand the process, always builds upon the fragmentary remains of eternal truths, and thus diminishes the sense of historical and conceptual distances that separates one biblical dispensation from another."[97]

From his work translating the Bible and ancient Egyptian papyrus records, Smith restored and clarified knowledge of the dispensations of Adam, Enoch, Noah, Abraham, Moses, and Jesus Christ. With each new dispensation, God redispensed to particular prophets the glad tidings of saving truths and the keys of salvation, thus restoring doctrines and authority.[98] "The Keys have to be brought from Heaven whenever the Gospel is sent. When they are revealed from Heaven it is by Adam's Authority" because "the Keys were first given to him [Adam] and by him to others, [and] he will have to give an account of his stewardship and they to him." In other words, Adam "obtained the first Presidency and held the Keys of it from generation to generation."[99]

Smith taught that Adam knew the plan of salvation, was baptized, looked forward to the coming of Christ, and was the first link in a chain of authority and power that included the priesthood.[100] Adam and Eve were, therefore, the earth's first Christians, and all prophets after them, including Enoch, Noah, Melchizedek, Abraham, and Moses, also knew and taught of Christ.[101] The Book of Mormon illustrates a "centeredness on Christ, the Messiah, . . . one of the more remarkable—and daring—features of the Book of Mormon."[102] In a letter presumably dictated by Joseph Smith in Kirtland to his associates in Missouri, he wrote:

> For our own part, we cannot believe, that the ancients in all ages were so ignorant of the system of heaven as many suppose, since all that were ever saved, were saved through the power of this great plan of redemption, as much so before the coming of Christ as since; if not, God has had different plans in operation, (if we may so express it,) to bring men back to dwell with himself; and this we cannot believe, since there has been no change in the constitution of man since he fell; and the ordinance or institution of offering blood in sacrifice, was only designed to be performed till Christ was offered up and shed his blood, as said before, that man might look forward with faith to that time. It will be noticed that according to Paul, [see Galatians 3:8] the gospel was preached to Abraham. We would like to be informed in what name the gospel was then preached, whether it was in the name of Christ or some other name? If in any other name, was it the gospel?[103]

The central doctrine for all Christianity is Jesus Christ, and according to Joseph Smith, it has been that way since the days of Adam and Eve.

The new restoration was the last dispensing of truth before the Second Coming of Jesus Christ. This restoration was called the "dispensation of the fulness of times" by the Apostle Paul, signifying that everything pertaining to Christ, both in heaven and on earth, would be gathered together.[104] Smith brought the prophecy of Paul into a larger perspective by explaining that all ancient prophets, beginning with Adam, wanted to bring their people into the presence of God through the power of the priesthood: "There were Eliases raised up who tried to restore these glories, but did not obtain them; but they prophesied of a day when this glory would be revealed."[105] In this final dispensation, humankind would be successful in obtaining all the glory that God intended. In summary, Smith's thoughts on dispensations concluded with this thought: "Though there were different dispensations, yet all things which God communicated to His people were calculated to draw their minds to the great object, and to teach them to rely upon God alone as the author of their salvation, as contained in His law. From what we can draw from the Scripture relative to the teaching of heaven, we are induced to think that much instruction has been given to man since the beginning which we do not possess now."[106]

Smith described the restoration of the gospel of Jesus Christ as one of "vast magnitude and almost beyond the comprehension of mortals: its glories are past description and its grandeur unsurpassable. It is the theme which has animated the bosom of Prophets and righteous men from the creation of the world down through every succeeding generation to the present time, and it is truly the dispensation of the fulness of times, when all things which are in Christ Jesus, whether in heaven or on the earth shall be gathered in him and when all things shall be restored."[107] Smith claimed to preside over the final dispensing of gospel knowledge, and in an 1841 general conference of the church, he clarified that "the dispensation of the fulness of times will bring to light the things that have been revealed in all former dispensations, also other things that have not been before revealed."[108] Flowing into this new dispensation was all that had been revealed previously as well as new revelation for this unique, final period of time preparatory for the Second Coming of Christ and the Millennium.

In 1841, Smith believed that the time had finally arrived for the commencement of the "great and last dispensation to be ushered into the world." He declared, "The Lord uttered his voice from the heavens, an holy angel came forth and restored the priesthood and apostleship," and from this had "arisen the church of the saints."[109] Renewed to this generation were the restoration of the priesthood, keys, ordinances, spiritual gifts and blessings, and the promise of more.

Parley Pratt, a close contemporary of Smith, used New Testament metaphors in describing the restoration as a new tree with new fruit and wine requiring new bottles, new cloth, new garments, new leaven, and a new lump.[110] It was "a new covenant and spirit" that should "roll on till we have a new heaven and a new earth."[111] Thomas Parker, the author of arguably the first American biblical commentary, believed that Martin Luther's and John Wycliffe's efforts in the reformed church were the beginning of the Prophet Daniel's "stone cut out of the mountain without hands."[112] Joseph Smith believed he was to be one of the instruments in setting up the kingdom that would fill the whole earth and that was foretold by the Old Testament prophet.[113]

Restoration, Gathering, and Temples. The Book of Mormon uses the term *restoration* in the same way as the Bible does, particularly Isaiah, but in other ways as well. For example, in an ancient prophecy given by Joseph of Egypt and recorded in the Book of Mormon, Joseph Smith was promised that he would be made strong "in that day when my work shall

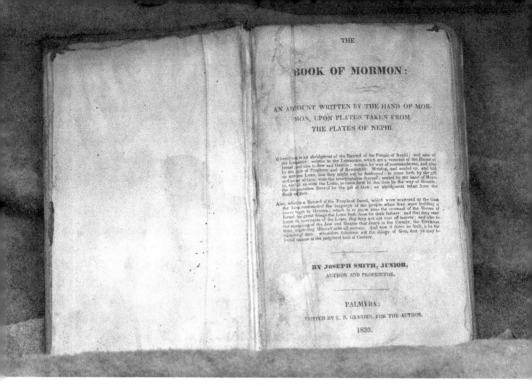

Title page of the first edition of the Book of Mormon, 1830. Courtesy of Kent P. Jackson.

commence among all my people, unto the restoring thee, O house of Israel."[114] Ancient American prophets recorded the promise of a restoration of the people of Israel to the "knowledge of Christ,"[115] to the "true church"[116] and the "true faith,"[117] and to the "knowledge of the covenant."[118] Speaking specifically about the latter-day remnant of Lehi's family (the central family at the beginning of the Book of Mormon narrative), God made this promise: "And the gospel of Jesus Christ shall be declared among them; wherefore, they shall be restored unto the knowledge of their fathers, and also to the knowledge of Jesus Christ, which was had among their fathers."[119] Ancient prophets called the Book of Mormon a significant part of the "marvelous work and a wonder," a sign that the promised latter-day restoration of the house of Israel had begun.[120] The Book of Mormon also repeated Isaiah's messianic promise regarding the gathering of the house of Israel: "When the day cometh that they shall believe in me, that I am Christ, then have I covenanted with their fathers that they shall be restored in the flesh, upon the earth, unto the lands of their inheritance. And it shall come to pass that they shall be gathered in from their long dispersion, from the isles of the sea, and from the four parts of the earth."[121]

Following the pattern of ancient prophets, Joseph Smith also spoke of the gathering of the house of Israel by quoting from the promises of Isaiah.[122] After the organization of the church in 1830, public meetings for preaching the gospel began, conferences were held, individuals were baptized, and the first missionaries were sent to the American Indians, who were designated in the Book of Mormon as members of the house of Israel through the lineage of Joseph of Egypt.[123] In late 1830 and early 1831, Smith claimed to receive two revelations commanding him and the New York members to gather to "the Ohio" to receive God's law and be "endowed with power from on high."[124] Later evidence of this zeal for gathering Israel to Zion was manifest when Smith sent members of the Quorum of the Twelve Apostles on missions to "preach the Gospel to the remnants of [the tribe of] Joseph" in the eastern United States, Canada, and British Isles and to dedicate the land of Palestine to receive the blessings promised to Abraham's posterity.[125]

Although he understood the reasons for such a gathering much earlier, Smith did not articulate them to the Saints until 1843. He explained that the "main object [of the gathering of Israel] was to build unto the Lord a house whereby He could reveal unto His people the ordinances of His house and the glories of His kingdom."[126] By 1843, the Kirtland Temple had been built, plans for the Nauvoo Temple were under way, and sites for other temples were selected in Independence, Far West, and Adam-ondi-Ahman, Missouri. Thus, like Isaiah and Nephi, Joseph Smith taught that once individuals are gathered to the gospel, they are then to build temples to receive further knowledge from God.[127] In Smith's restoration, the building of temples was an integral part of the gathering process.

Zion. The building up of Zion was always a primary objective for both Smith and Campbell.[128] Although the Mormon gathering began in Ohio only months after the church was organized and instructions for building a temple soon followed, Missouri was to be the true gathering place. It was called the land of promise, the setting for the city of Zion, and an everlasting inheritance. It was so designated because it was revealed to Smith to be the location of Adam-ondi-Ahman, the place where Adam gave his righteous posterity patriarchal blessings.[129] Initially, gathering was to a single city—the city of Independence was the central gathering site, and a temple lot was designated there.[130] Thus, in Smith's vision of the restoration, gathering was both historical and geographical—to the place of primordial beginnings. Later, due to persecution and an extermination order issued by the governor of Missouri, Smith announced a new place of gathering. Nauvoo, Illinois, became the hub, and the American continent, both North and South, was designated as the gathering place for Zion.[131]

CONCLUSION

From a Latter-day Saint perspective, the "restoration of all things," or initiating the "times of restitution of all things" in a "dispensation of the fulness of times," began in the woods near Smith's home when the heavens opened and God again spoke to man. In subsequent visitations, ancient prophets restored knowledge, power, and priesthood, authorizing Smith to establish a restoration of all things—the final dispensation in anticipation of the Second Coming of Jesus Christ.

Given that Joseph Smith's earthly ministry ended with his death on 27 June 1844, one might ask, "Is the restoration an accomplished fact?" The Latter-day Saint answer is both yes and no. Yes, the essential events have occurred: the reopening of dialogue between heaven and earth, the translation and publication of the Book of Mormon, the restoration of the Aaronic and Melchizedek Priesthoods, and the organization of the church with apostles, prophets, and priesthood keys. However, one of the purposes for which the restoration occurred—the final gathering of the house of Israel—is only in its beginning stages. Smith prophesied, however, concerning the future destiny of his restoration: "This church will fill North and South America—it will fill the world."[132] In an editorial in the Mormon journal *Times and Seasons*, presumably written or at least approved by Smith, the prophet acknowledged that it is only during the Millennium when the restoration will be accomplished: "In that day when the Lord shall come, he shall reveal all things—Things which have passed, and hidden things which no man knew, things of the earth, by which it was made, and the purpose and the end thereof—things most precious, things that are above, and things that are beneath, things that are in the earth, and upon the earth, and in heaven."[133] Then, at that day when all things are gathered together, the dispensation of the fullness of times will come to fruition.

Smith claimed he was an Elias—a preparer of the way for Christ.[134] In fact, in a contemporary of Smith, Lorenzo Snow, reported that Smith was once asked, "Who are you?" to which Smith smiled and responded, "Noah came before the flood. I have come before the fire."[135] In his inspired translation of Matthew 17, Smith gave additional insight to the answer given to Peter, James, and John after the Mount of Transfiguration experience: "And Jesus answered and said unto them, Elias truly shall first come, and restore all things, *as the prophets have written.* . . . The disciples understood that he spake unto them of John the Baptist, *and also of another who should come and restore all things, as it is written by the prophets.*"[136]

In a brief reiteration of visitations by ancient prophets, Smith claimed that from 1823 through 1842, he had visits from or communication with Michael the archangel (Adam), Gabriel (Noah), Raphael, John the Baptist, Peter, James, John, and other messengers "declaring their dispensation, their rights, their keys, their honors, their majesty and glory, and the power of their priesthood."[137] In 1833, Smith commented on the importance of making and keeping covenants.[138] Like Old and New Testament prophets, Joseph Smith claimed personal "dialogic revelations" from God of an ancient order.[139] Smith marveled at the experiences of his short, thirty-eight-year life. He exulted at the manifestations of Old and New Testament prophets and their priesthoods and the spiritual enlightenment given by the third member of the Godhead.

In summary, Smith's restoration of the ancient order included visions from on high, the ministering of angels, a new book of scripture, and the receipt of the priesthood and associated keys.[140] He claimed it was born out of a renewal of the revelatory relationship between God and his children. It was comprehensive in its nature: inclusive of the past and present and expansive of the future. Ancient prophets and biblical patterns were important in foreshadowing the future, but they were not all of the future. In preparation for Christ's return, the true principles, doctrines, and ordinances of the plan of salvation had to be revealed or redispensed in fulfillment of Peter's words regarding the "times of restitution of all things."[141] Smith's focus was first on the continuation of ancient covenants and second on priesthood keys—and a reopening of direct communication between heaven and earth was the means by which this occurred. Smith believed he had been "chosen to be an instrument in the hands of God to bring about some of His purposes": to restore the ancient order of God's kingdom and to oversee the restoration of the fullness of the gospel, the fullness of times, and the organization of God's church in anticipation of the Second Coming of Christ.[142] Shortly prior to his martyrdom, he boldly declared, "I intend to lay a foundation that will revolutionize the whole world."[143]

Why Joseph Smith? The question begs answering. He was young, uneducated, poor, and certainly one of the weakest of God's children in many ways. Why did he claim to have this unique experience and responsibility? Richard Brodhead, professor of English and American literature at Yale University, describes him as "apparently the lowest of the low."[144] As LDS scholar Terryl Givens claims, "God chose Joseph Smith not in spite of but because of his weakness."[145] According to Smith's own revelatory account, God designed that through someone weak in the eyes of the world he would reestablish his everlasting covenant,[146] and Smith appeared to be an enormously flawed human. In so many ways, he was an inconspicuous young man who made oversized claims.

Notes

1. Prior to this time, a collection of sixty-five revelations was published in 1833, titled the Book of Commandments. However, both the press and most of the uncut and unbound copies were destroyed.
2. Joseph Smith, History, 1838–1856, vol. C-1, created 24 February 1845–3 July 1845, CHL, http://www.josephsmithpapers.org.
3. Joseph Smith—History 1:19.
4. Joseph Smith, "Joseph Smith Diary," 15 October 1843, in *Words of Joseph Smith*, comp. and ed. Andrew F. Ehat and Lyndon Cook (Provo, UT: Religious Studies Center, 1980), 256.
5. Joseph Smith, "William Clayton Report," 8 April 1843, in *Words of Joseph Smith*, 184. See also Joseph Smith—History (Pearl of Great Price).
6. "History of Joseph Smith," *Latter-day Saints' Millennial Star* 20, no. 18 (1 May 1858): 277. Smith made these remarks on 1 January 1843 in response to questions by a group of political leaders, including Judge Stephen A. Douglas, soon to become a US representative from Illinois.
7. Minutes, Norton, OH, 21 April 1834, in Minute Book 1, 43–47, handwriting of Orson Hyde, CHL, 43, http://www.josephsmithpapers.org.
8. *Elders' Journal* 1, no. 3 (July 1838): 42, http://www.josephsmithpapers.org.
9. Doctrine and Covenants 123:7, 8, 12.
10. For additional details, see Robert J. Woodford, "The Articles and Covenants of the Church of Christ and the Book of Mormon," in *Sperry Symposium Classics: The Doctrine and Covenants*, ed. Craig K. Manscill (Salt Lake City: Deseret Book, 2004), 103–13; Richard Lloyd Anderson, "The Organization Revelations (D&C 20, 21, and 22)," in *Studies in Scripture*, ed. Robert L. Millet and Kent P. Jackson, vol. 1, *The Doctrine and Covenants* (Salt Lake City: Randall Book, 1985), 109.
11. *Elders' Journal* 1, no. 3, 41, http://www.josephsmithpapers.org.
12. Doctrine and Covenants 112:30; 128:18, 20.
13. Doctrine and Covenants 27:12–13.
14. Doctrine and Covenants 20:77, 79; 27:2–3.
15. Justin R. Bray, "The Lord's Supper in Early Mormonism," in *You Shall Have My Word: Exploring the Text of the Doctrine and Covenants*, ed. Scott C. Esplin, Richard O. Cowan, and Rachel Cope (Provo, UT: Religious Studies Center; Salt Lake City: Deseret Book, 2012), 64–65.
16. Moroni 6:5–9 (Book of Mormon).
17. Moroni 4–5 (Book of Mormon); Doctrine and Covenants 20:77, 79.
18. Doctrine and Covenants 25.
19. *A Collection of Sacred Hymns, for the Church of the Latter Day Saints* (Kirtland, OH: F. G. Williams & Co., 1835), http://www.josephsmithpapers.org.

20. Campbell, "Table of Contents," in *Psalms, Hymns, and Spiritual Songs, Original and Selected, Adapted to the Christian Religion*; Emma Smith, comp., "Index," in *A Collection of Sacred Hymns*, [i]–iv, 5–122, CHL, ii, iv, http://www.josephsmith papers.org.

21. Doctrine and Covenants, 1844 ed., 122. Robin Scott Jensen, Robert J. Woodford, and Steven C. Harper, eds., *Revelations and Translations, Volume 1: Manuscript Revelation Books*, vol. 1 of the Revelations and Translations series of *The Joseph Smith Papers*, ed. Dean C. Jessee, Ronald K. Esplin, and Richard Lyman Bushman (Salt Lake City: Church Historian's Press, 2011).

22. Staker, *Hearken, O Ye People*, 244.

23. Elizabeth Ann Whitney, "A Leaf from an Autobiography," *Woman's Exponent* 7, no. 9 (1 October 1878): 7; no. 11 (1 November 1878): 83; Isaiah 25:6.

24. Doctrine and Covenants 107:72, 78–81.

25. Adam Miller, *Rube Goldberg Machines: Essays in Mormon Theology* (Salt Lake City: Greg Kofford Books, 2012), 78.

26. Brigham Young also maintained that appreciating historical context was crucial to understanding the full import of Joseph Smith's revelations. Staker, *Hearken O Ye People*, xxxix. Louis Midgley described Mormonism as a "narrative theology." Martin Marty contrasts narrative theology with Protestant theologies that "combine the language of the Hebrew scriptures with mainly Greek philosophical concepts." Louis C. Midgley, "A Plea for Narrative Theology: Living in and by Stories," *Interpreter: A Journal of Mormon Scripture* 8 (2014): vii–xxi.

27. In the trial of Anne Hutchinson, part of her heresy was the claim to "immediate" revelation. This term means a revelation is received without the medium of the scriptures to bring forth the revelation. Smith's claims to revelation came about through meditation on scriptures and through questions and prayer. For Mormonism, this latter claim would mean the end of the Bible as the foundational source of religious truth. Winship, *The Times & Trials of Anne Hutchinson*, 112.

28. The term "priesthood keys" was a new concept not used among other Christian denominations. Smith used the term at least by 1832 to mean (1) authorizing priesthood power in specific offices and functions, such as the "key of the ministering of angels" in Doctrine and Covenants 84:26 and Joseph Smith—History 1:69; (2) unlocking information such as "keys of the mystery of those things which have been sealed" in Doctrine and Covenants 35:18 or "key of the mysteries of the kingdom" in Doctrine and Covenants 84:19; and (3) a sealing or binding power in Doctrine and Covenants 128:14.

29. Jan Shipps notes that at the organization of the Mormon Church, it was made clear that this was more than the primitive church. "The lack of a carefully drawn distinction between forms of authority drawn from the Old and New Testaments (and from the Book of Mormon) is an early signal that when the Mormon restoration was fully in place, it would be nothing less than the 'restoration of all things,'" Jan Shipps, *Sojourner in the Promised Land: Forty Years among the Mormons* (Urbana: University of Illinois, 2000), 236–37.

30. 1 Nephi 13:23–34 (Book of Mormon). Truth had been replaced by false ideas.

31. Articles of Faith 1:9 (Pearl of Great Price). Developments in church organization, procedure, and doctrine reflect "the principle of continuing revelation more than textual exegesis of either the Bible or the Book of Mormon." Terryl Givens, *By the Hand of Mormon* (Oxford: Oxford University Press, 2002), 198.

32. Andrew H. Hedges, Alex D. Smith, and Richard Lloyd Anderson, eds., *Journals, Volume 2: December 1841–April 1843*, vol. 2 of the Journals series of *The Joseph Smith Papers*, ed. Dean C. Jessee, Ronald K. Esplin, and Richard Lyman Bushman (Salt Lake City: Church Historian's Press, 2008), 360.

33. Terryl Givens, *Wrestling the Angel: The Foundations of Mormon Thought: Cosmos, God, Humanity* (New York: Oxford University Press, 2015), 4, 38.

34. History, 1838–1856, volume B-1 [1 September 1834–2 November 1838], 795–96, http://www.josephsmithpapers.org; Elders' Journal, Far West, Missouri, July 1838, vol. 1, no. 3, 44, http://josephsmithpapers.org.

35. Steven C. Harper, "Remembering the First Vision," in *A Reason for Faith: Navigating LDS Doctrine and Church History*, ed. Laura Harris Hales (Provo, UT: Religious Studies Center; Salt Lake City: Deseret Book, 2016), 7–19.

36. The following harmonized account was created by Christensen, *The First Vision: A Harmonization of 10 Accounts from the Sacred Grove*, utilizing the known recorded accounts of Joseph Smith's first theophany. Although an official account was dictated by Joseph Smith (the 1838 recital) and canonized as part of the Pearl of Great Price, adding the other accounts gives a much fuller description of the event and Smith's feelings. Words in brackets were added to make grammatically complete phrases.

37. Noel B. Reynolds, "What Went Wrong for the Early Christians?" in *Christians in Disarray*, 20.

38. For a separate collection of known recordings of the First Vision, see Jessee, "Accounts of Joseph Smith's First Vision," in *Opening the Heavens*, 1–33. It is important to note that at this time, Smith was not told to cease other "revelatory" activities that were part of accepted folk religious traditions. Hence, he was hired by Josiah Stowell (or Stoal), who had heard of his reputation for finding things that were "invisible to the natural eye," to help dig for Spanish silver that Stowell purportedly knew was near his property. Smith had discovered two stones, at least one of them by 1822. The history of the other stone is unknown. Smith, *Lucy's Book: A Critical Edition of Lucy Mack Smith's Family Memoir*, 360; Lucy Mack Smith, History, 1844–1845, bk. 3, 10–12, http://www.josephsmithpapers.org. Bushman, *Joseph Smith: Rough Stone Rolling*, 48–49.

39. Staker, *Hearken, O Ye People*, 136.

40. Joseph Smith—History 1:21; Michael Hubbard MacKay and Gerrit J. Dirkmaat, *From Darkness unto Light: Joseph Smith's Translation and Publication of the Book of Mormon* (Provo, UT: Religious Studies Center; Salt Lake City: Deseret Book, 2015), 2.

41. Levi Richards, Journal, 11 June 1843, extract, 16, http://www.josephsmithpapers .org. In an earlier account recorded by a scribe, Smith recalled, "I cried unto the Lord for mercy for there was none else to whom I could go and to obtain mercy and the Lord heard my cry in the wilderness and while in <the> attitude of calling upon the Lord <in the 16th year of my age> a piller of fire light above the brightness of the sun at noonday come down from above and rested upon me and I was filled with the spirit of god and the <Lord> opened the heavens upon me and I saw the Lord and he spake unto me saying Joseph <my son> thy sins are forgiven thee. go thy <way> walk in my statutes and keep my commandments. . . . My soul was filled with love and for many days I could rejoice with great Joy and the Lord was with me but could find none that would believe the hevnly vision nevertheless I pondered these things in my heart." "Letter Book A," JS Letterbook 1 [ca. 27 Nov. 1832–ca. 4 Aug. 1835], JS Collection, CHL, 3, http://www.josephsmithpapers.org.

42. Joseph Smith—History 1:68 (Pearl of Great Price); emphasis in original. Smith did not record this event until 1838.

43. Richard H. Brodhead, "Prophets in America, ca. 1830: Emerson, Nat Turner, Joseph Smith," *Journal of Mormon History* 29, no. 1 (Spring 2003): 64.

44. Joseph Smith—History 1:72. For a discussion of possible dates for the restoration of the Melchizedek priesthood, see Larry C. Porter, "The Restoration of the Aaronic and Melchizedek Priesthoods," *Ensign*, December 1996, 46; Anderson, "The Coming

of Ancient Apostles Before Church Organization: Accounts of Joseph Smith and Oliver Cowdery"; Bushman, *Joseph Smith and the Beginnings of Mormonism*, 107; for a different point of view on dating the restoration of the Melchizedek Priesthood, see Bushman, *Joseph Smith: Rough Stone Rolling*, 74–76, 118, 588n35.

45. Porter, "The Restoration of the Aaronic and Melchizedek Priesthoods," 46.
46. History, 1838–1856, volume A-1 [23 December 1805–30 August 1834], 285, http://www.josephsmithpapers.org.
47. Joseph Smith recorded both of the accounts given here: one account is from Joseph Smith's official history recorded in 1838 and is found in the Pearl of Great Price; the other account, "The Wentworth Letter," was written in March 1842 at the request of the editor of the *Chicago Democrat*.
48. Joseph Smith—History 1:21–27; Joseph Smith, Letter, Kirtland, OH, to Oliver Cowdery, Kirtland, OH, December 1834; *Latter Day Saints' Messenger and Advocate*, December 1834, 40; History, circa June 1839–circa 1841 [Draft 2], 5, http://www.josephsmithpapers.org.
49. Joseph Smith—History 1:28.
50. Joseph Smith—History 1:29.
51. Joseph Smith—History 1:30; History, 1838–1856, volume A-1 [23 December 1805–30 August 1834], 5, http://josephsmithpapers.org.
52. Joseph Smith, "Wentworth Letter"; History, 1838–1856, volume C-1 [2 November 1838–31 July 1842], 1281, http://josephsmithpapers.org.
53. History, 1838–1856, volume A-1 [23 December 1805–30 August 1834], 5, http://www.josephsmithpapers.org.
54. Joseph Smith—History 1:33. Moroni, the messenger or angel sent to Smith, was the last prophet in the Book of Mormon and the one who was given charge of hiding the plates. See Moroni 10:2 (Book of Mormon); see also the Book of Mormon title page.
55. Smith, "Wentworth Letter."
56. History, 1838–1856, volume A-1 [23 December 1805–30 August 1834], 5, http://josephsmithpapers.org.
57. Joseph Smith—History 1:36–41. See also Smith, "Wentworth Letter."
58. In 1835, Oliver Cowdery mentioned in two letters to the *Kirtland Messenger* additional passages of scripture quoted or paraphrased by Moroni that he remembered Smith telling him. Although Cowdery is a secondary source, Smith had likely rehearsed the event to him or in his presence many times. Kent P. Jackson, "The Appearance of Moroni to Joseph Smith," in *Studies in Scripture, Vol. 2: The Pearl of Great Price*, ed. Robert L. Millet and Kent P. Jackson (Salt Lake City: Randall Book, 1985), 360.
59. Malachi 4:5; JS—H 1:40.
60. Smith, "Wentworth Letter."
61. Joseph Smith—History 1:34.
62. Joseph Smith—History 1:42–51.
63. Joseph Smith—History 1:54.
64. Smith, "Wentworth Letter."
65. Smith, "Wentworth Letter."
66. Michael Hubbard MacKay, Gerrit J. Dirkmaat, Grant Underwood, Robert J. Woodford, and William G. Hartley, eds., *Vol. 1: July 1828–June 1831*, "Volume 1 Introduction," in *Documents*, vol. 1 of the Documents series of *The Joseph Smith Papers*, ed. Dean C. Jessee, Ronald K. Esplin, Richard Lyman Bushman, and Matthew J. Grow (Salt Lake City: Church Historian's Press, 2013), xxix–xxx.
67. Minute Book 2, 13, http://www.josephsmithpapers.org.
68. His personal seer stone was found in New York while he was digging either a well or for buried treasure with his neighbor, Willard Chase. In that era, "both treasure seeking and translating were likely perceived by Joseph's early converts as supernatural events. Early believers did not necessarily struggle with the fusion of Joseph the

treasure seeker and Joseph the translator." Michael Hubbard MacKay and Nicholas J. Frederick, *Joseph Smith's Seer Stones* (Provo, UT: Religious Studies Center; Salt Lake City: Deseret Book, 2016), 9, 37.

69. Martin Harris asked for permission to take the translated pages to let his wife read them "as he hoped that it might have a salutary effect upon his wife's feelings to read what was written." Joseph asked the Lord for permission and was told no. Martin begged again, and the Lord finally gave permission on the condition that Joseph would be responsible for the safety of the manuscript. Harris took a solemn oath that he would show it to only the five members of his immediate family. Unfortunately, he did not live up to this promise and showed the manuscript to everyone in the area who asked. The pages were initially locked in a box, but at some point they were stolen. Both Martin and Joseph were devastated. Joseph was perhaps even more distraught than Martin because he was afraid he had lost his call to be God's prophet and translate the record. After this, Martin was no longer permitted to act as scribe. Anderson, *Lucy's Book*, 411, 418–20; Lucy Mack Smith, History, 1844–1845, 5, bk. 7, http://josephsmithpapers.org.

70. Anderson, *Lucy's Book*, 429; Lucy Mack Smith, History, 1844–1845, 4, bk. 8, http://josephsmithpapers.org; Revelation, June 1829–E [D&C 17], 119, http://www.josephsmithpapers.org.

71. Joseph Smith III, "Last Testimony of Sister Emma," *Saints Herald* 26, no. 19 (October 1879): 290.

72. Anderson, *Lucy's Book*, 432; Lucy Mack Smith, History, 1844–1845, 1, bk. 8, http://www.josephsmithpapers.org.

73. "History of Joseph Smith," *Times and Seasons* 3, no. 19 (1 August 1842): 866; History, 1838–1856, volume A-1 [23 December 1805–30 August 1834], 18, http://www.josephsmithpapers.org.

74. Anderson, *Lucy's Book*, 446; Lucy Mack Smith, History, 1844–1845, 10, bk. 4, http://josephsmithpapers.org.

75. Emma Smith identified her brother, Reuben Hale, as a scribe, but this was likely in Harmony, Pennsylvania. Smith III, "Last Testimony of Sister Emma," 289. Joseph Smith also stated that both Emma and his brother Samuel had written a little in Harmony, Pennsylvania. Karen Lynn Davidson, David J. Whittaker, Richard L. Jensen, and Mark Ashurst-McGee, eds., *Histories, Volume 1: Joseph Smith Histories, 1832-1844*, vol. 1 of the Histories series of *The Joseph Smith Papers*, ed. Dean C. Jessee, Ronald K. Esplin, and Richard Lyman Bushman (Salt Lake City: Church Historian's Press, 2012), 16.

76. Except for the 116 stolen pages, the Book of Mormon was translated between 7 April, two days after Oliver Cowdery arrived, and 30 June 1829. For more on the translation time and speed, see John W. Welch and Tim Rathbone, "How Long Did It Take to Translate the Book of Mormon?," in *Reexploring the Book of Mormon*, ed. John W. Welch (Salt Lake City: Deseret Book; Provo, UT: FARMS, 1992), 3. For a critical analysis of two Book of Mormon manuscripts, see Royal Skousen, *The Original Manuscript of the Book of Mormon: Typographical Facsimiles of the Extant Text*, 2 vols. (Provo, UT: Neal A. Maxwell Institute, 2001).

77. Anderson, *Lucy's Book*, 452; Lucy Mack Smith, History, 1844–1845, 10, bk. 4, http://www.josephsmithpapers.org.

78. Anderson, *Lucy's Book*, 455; Lucy Mack Smith, History, 1844–1845, 12, bk. 8, http://josephsmithpapers.org; "Testimony of Three Witnesses," Book of Mormon.

79. Anderson, *Lucy's Book*, 455–57; Lucy Mack Smith, History, 1844–1845, 1–2, bk. 9, http://www.josephsmithpapers.org; "Testimony of Eight Witnesses," Book of Mormon. Martin Harris, in a newspaper interview, claimed that he had lifted the plates several times and estimated they weighed somewhere between forty and fifty pounds. Joel Tiffany, "Interview with Martin Harris," *Tiffany's Monthly*, May 1859,

163–70. Several of these eleven witnesses eventually left the church. However, none ever denied their testimony of these events or of the truthfulness of the Book of Mormon. For more information on these men, see Richard Lloyd Anderson, "Book of Mormon Witnesses," in *Encyclopedia of Mormonism*, ed. Daniel H. Ludlow (New York: Macmillan, 1992), 1:214–17.

80. Anderson, *Lucy's Book*, 460–62; Lucy Mack Smith, History, 1844–1845, 4, bk. 9, http://josephsmithpapers.org.

81. Anderson, *Lucy's Book*, 470–75; Lucy Mack Smith, History, 1844–1845, 9, bk. 9, http://josephsmithpapers.org.

82. Anderson, *Lucy's Book*, 475–76; Lucy Mack Smith, History, 1844–1845, 11–12, bk. 9, http://josephsmithpapers.org.

83. Richard L. Bushman, "The Book of Mormon in Early Mormon History," in *New Views of Mormon History: A Collection of Essays in Honor of Leonard J. Arrington*, ed. Davis Bitton and Maureen Ursenbach Beecher (Salt Lake City: University of Utah Press, 1987), 15.

84. Givens, *By the Hand of Mormon*, 61, 84–85. See also Noel Reynolds, "The Coming Forth of the Book of Mormon in the Twentieth Century," *BYU Studies* 38, no. 2 (1999): 8; Grant Underwood, "Book of Mormon Usage in Early LDS Theology," *Dialogue: A Journal of Mormon Thought* 17 (Fall 1984): 52, 53, 59.

85. History, 1838–1856, volume A-1 [23 December 1805–30 August 1834], 42, http://josephsmithpapers.org.

86. *Elias* is a Greek title which means "forerunner." For example, John the Baptist acted as an Elias for Jesus Christ, preparing the way for his first coming; Joseph Smith claimed to act as an Elias for Jesus Christ, preparing the way for his Second Coming. In this revelation, the particular messenger who restored the Abrahamic covenant was not given.

87. Doctrine and Covenants 110:11–16.

88. In 1830, Joseph began sending out missionaries to begin the gathering.

89. Genesis 12:1–3; 26:1–4, 24; 28:13–14; 35:9–13; 48:3–4.

90. Malachi 4:6; Doctrine and Covenants 49:11–14.

91. Matthew 17:1–3; Mark 9:2–9; History, 1838–1856, volume C-1 [2 November 1838–31 July 1842], 11 [addenda], http://www.josephsmithpapers.org; History, circa June 1839–circa 1841 [Draft 2], 52, http://www.josephsmithpapers.org. The Twelve Apostles had been ordained earlier to the priesthood by Jesus (see Matthew 10); however, Mormon scholars do not believe that all the keys for the fullness of blessings and the organization of the church had been given to them. Robert Matthews considers the giving of keys on the Mount of Transfiguration as the "single most important event in the ministry of the Savior between his baptism and the Garden of Gethsemane" in establishing God's kingdom on earth. Robert J. Matthews, "Tradition, Testimony, Transfiguration Keys," *Studies in Scripture, Vol. 5: The Gospels*, ed. Kent P. Jackson and Robert L. Millet (Salt Lake City: Deseret Book, 1986), 305–6.

92. Matthews, "Tradition, Testimony, Transfiguration Keys," 306.

93. Articles of Faith 9 and 10; *Bible Dictionary*, s.v. "Zion."

94. Shipps, *Mormonism: The Story of a New Religious Tradition*, 239.

95. History, 1838–1856, volume C-1 [2 November 1838–31 July 1842], 1238, www.josephsmithpapers.org.

96. Miller, *Rube Goldberg Machines*, 33.

97. Givens, *By the Hand of Mormon*, 24.

98. Alexander Campbell also spoke of dispensations, but, as explained in chapter 5, he did so with a different meaning. See Garrison, *Alexander Campbell's Theology*, 167–79; see also Eames, *The Philosophy of Alexander Campbell*, 25–26.

99. History, 1838–1856, volume C-1 [2 November 1838–31 July 1842], 11 [addenda], http://josephsmithpapers.org.

100. Moses 5:5–10; 6:64–67 (Pearl of Great Price). Quoting from the Apostle Paul, Smith taught, "Having made known unto us the mystery of his will, according to his good pleasure which he hath purposed in himself: That in the dispensation of the fulness of times he might gather together in one all things in Christ, both which are in heaven, and which are on earth; even in him." He then explained, "Now the purpose in himself in the winding up scene of the last dispensation is, that all things pertaining to that dispensation should be conducted precisely in accordance with the preceding dispensations. And again, God purposed in himself that there should not be an eternal fulness until every dispensation should be fulfilled and gathered together in one and that all things whatsoever that should be gathered together in one in those dispensations unto the same fulness and eternal glory should be in Christ Jesus; therefore he set the ordinances to be the same for ever and ever, and set Adam to watch over them, to reveal them from heaven to man or to send Angels to reveal them." History, 1838–1856, volume C-1 [2 November 1838–31 July 1842], 16 [addenda], http://josephsmithpapers.org.

101. Jacob 4:4–5; 7:11 (Book of Mormon). See also Galatians 3:6–29.

102. Givens, *By the Hand of Mormon*, 46. For example, "For we labor diligently to write, to persuade our children, and also our brethren, to believe in Christ, and to be reconciled to God; for we know that it is by grace that we are saved, after all we can do. And, notwithstanding we believe in Christ, we keep the law of Moses. . . . We talk of Christ, we rejoice in Christ, we preach of Christ, we prophesy of Christ, and we write according to our prophecies, that our children may know to what source they may look for a remission of their sins." 2 Nephi 25:23, 24, 26 (Book of Mormon).

103. "The Elders of The Church in Kirtland, to Their Brethren Abroad," *Evening and Morning Star* 2, no. 18 (March 1834): 287.

104. Ephesians 1:10.

105. History, 1838–1856, volume C-1 [2 November 1838–31 July 1842], 12 [addenda], http://www.josephsmithpapers.org.

106. "The Elders of the Church in Kirtland, to Their Brethren Abroad," *Evening and Morning Star* 2, no. 18 (March 1834): 287.

107. History, 1838–1856, volume C-1 [2 November 1838–31 July 1842], 1091, http://www.josephsmithpapers.org; First Presidency, Letter, Nauvoo, IL, to "The Saints Scattered Abroad," 15 September 1840, *Times and Seasons*, October 1840, 178, http://www.josephsmithpapers.org.

108. Joseph Smith, Discourse, Nauvoo, IL, 3 October 1841, in *Times and Seasons*, 15 October 1841, 2:578, http://josephsmithpapers.org. Minutes, Nauvoo, IL, 1–5 October 1841, in *Times and Seasons*, 15 October 1841, 2:578, http://joseph smithpapers.org.

109. Parley P. Pratt, "Grapes from Thorns and Figs from Thistles," *Millennial Star* 1 (1 January 1841): 237; see also *Times and Seasons* 3, no. 16 (15 June 1842): 816.

110. In the editorial there was an asterisk with this note: "New to this generation," which illustrates how Mormons viewed dispensations. Pratt, "Grapes from Thorns and Figs from Thistles," *Millennial Star* 1 (1 January 1841): 237; see also *Times and Seasons* 3, no. 16 (15 June 1842): 816.

111. Pratt, "Grapes from Thorns and Figs from Thistles," *Millennial Star* 1 (1 January 1841): 237; see also *Times and Seasons* 3, no. 16 (15 June 1842): 816.

112. Daniel 2:34–35, 45. Thomas H. Olbricht, "Biblical Primitivism in American Biblical Scholarship, 1630–1870," in Hughes, *The American Quest for the Primitive Church*, 86.

113. "Thomas Bullock Report," 12 May 1844, in *Words of Joseph Smith*, 367; emphasis added.

114. 2 Nephi 3:13 (Book of Mormon).
115. Mormon 9:36 (Book of Mormon).
116. 2 Nephi 9:2 (Book of Mormon).
117. Enos 1:14, 20 (Book of Mormon).
118. 3 Nephi 5:25 (Book of Mormon).
119. 2 Nephi 30:5 (Book of Mormon).
120. 2 Nephi 27:26 (Book of Mormon). See also 1 Nephi 13:34–42; 2 Nephi 27:6, 14, 26; 29:1–2; 3 Nephi 21; 29:1–4 (Book of Mormon).
121. 2 Nephi 10:7–8 (Book of Mormon); see also Isaiah 11:11–12.
122. "Millennium," *Times and Seasons* 3, no. 8 (15 February 1842): 687–702; History, 1838–1856, volume B-1 [1 September 1834–2 November 1838], 8 [addenda], http://www.josephsmithpapers.org.
123. John Whitmer, *From Historian to Dissident: The Book of John Whitmer*, ed. Bruce N. Westergren (Salt Lake City: Signature Books, 1995), 3; Doctrine and Covenants 28:8.
124. Doctrine and Covenants 38:32.
125. Whitmer, *The Book of John Whitmer*, 141.
126. Joseph Smith, "June 11, 1843," *Wilford Woodruff's Journal: January 1, 1841 to December 31, 1845*, ed. Scott G. Kenney (Midvale, UT: Signature Books, 1983), 2:240.
127. See for example Isaiah 11:12; 27:12; 40:11; 49:5, 18; 54:7; 56:8; 60:4; 66:18; 1 Nephi 10:14; 19:16; 21:5, 18; 22:12, 25; 2 Nephi 21:12; 29:14; 30:7 (Book of Mormon).
128. See chapter 13 for a few of Campbell's ideas on the topic of Zion in the context of millennialism.
129. "It was named Adam-ondi-Ahman; because . . . it is the place where Adam shall come to visit his people, or the ancient of days shall sit as spoken of by Daniel the Prophet." History, 1838–1856, volume B-1 [1 September 1834–2 November 1838], 798, http://josephsmithpapers.org; Discourse, between 26 June and 4 August 1839–A, as reported by Willard Richards, 63, http://www.josephsmithpapers.org.
130. Doctrine and Covenants 57:1–3.
131. Joseph Smith, "William Clayton Report," 8 April 1844, in *Words of Joseph Smith*, 362.
132. Joseph Smith, Reported by Wilford Woodruff in Conference Report, April 1898, 57.
133. Doctrine and Covenants 101:32–34.
134. Jackson, "The Appearance of Moroni to Joseph Smith," 240–43.
135. Lorenzo Snow, in Abraham H. Cannon diary, 1 January 1892, 16:30.
136. Joseph Smith Translation—Matthew 17:10–14 (in Matthew 17:11–13). Italics added indicate the portion that Smith added.
137. Doctrine and Covenants 128:20–21.
138. "Letter Book A," JS Letterbook 1 [ca. 27 November 1832—ca. 4 August 1835], http://www.josephsmithpapers.org.
139. Doctrine and Covenants 28:2. Terryl Givens defines dialogic revelation as a personal exchange with God in response to a question. Givens, *By the Hand of Mormon*, 48, 216.
140. History, circa Sumer 1832, 1, http://www.josephsmithpapers.org.
141. Acts 3:21.
142. Smith, "Wentworth Letter."
143. History, 1838–1856, volume F-1 [1 May 1844–8 August 1844], 18, http://www.josephsmithpapers.org.
144. Brodhead, "Prophets in America ca. 1830," 59.
145. Givens, *Wrestling the Angel*, 22.
146. Doctrine and Covenants 1:19–23.

Systems of Belief

First, what Precept or Pattern hath the Lord Jesus left you in his
last Will and Testament for your Synod or Assembly of Divines,
by vertue of which you may expect his presence and assistance.

—ROGER WILLIAMS, QUERY I,
IN *Queries of Highest Consideration*

$\mathcal{A}$ t the time of the American Revolution, only a small per-
centage—estimated at 17 percent of Americans—belonged
to one of several denominations that had migrated to the colonies.
Others were seekers that had not affiliated themselves with any
denomination, some of whom were looking for the original gospel
preached by Jesus.[1] The revolution and subsequent constitutional
disestablishment of the state-church relationship, with no state
monies sponsoring a particular religion, laid the groundwork for
religious pluralism that was relatively unknown elsewhere in the
world. Disestablishment of state patronage was gradual, but it was
complete by mid-1830.[2]

The era that followed was characterized by the advancement
of religious pluralism in the United States. With the Bible as the
sole religious standard and freedom from European rituals and
traditions socially and politically celebrated, disagreement on
any religious matter opened the door to more division. Sectarian
splintering occurred with disparity over any doctrine, practice, or

church polity, and it was followed by a confession of beliefs differentiating the new church from the old.

The early nineteenth century was a unique period in a new land, rich in free-thinking philosophy but also in God-fearing religionists and blessed with sufficient open territory that an individual was unrestrained as never before and might pursue personal and religious liberty as not previously conceived. Immigrants representing a great variety of social, political, and religious opinions differed often upon the essential as well as the trivial points of forming a new society. Heated controversies over points of religious doctrine engendered divisiveness and spiritual aggression that troubled the truly devout.[3] But the Bible was available for each individual to read; the Enlightenment and widely disseminated Scottish Common Sense philosophy encouraged individuals to apply rational thinking to the study of scripture; and unfettered religious freedom caused debate over doctrines, practices, and ideas that had been accepted or enforced for centuries.[4] Thus, Smith and Campbell were restorationists at the precise time when freedom, evidence-seeking skepticism, and doctrinal debate were part of the American religious landscape.

The cacophony of opposing opinions led to very unchristian-like contention among the various churches competing for new converts, a situation deplored by both Campbell and Smith.[5] Thomas Campbell, Alexander's father, abhorred sectarianism that brought forth contentious partisan feelings.[6] Smith, as a fourteen-year-old, observed that the contention between priests and converts was so intense "that all their good feelings one for another, if they ever had any, were entirely lost in a strife of words and a contest about opinions."[7]

Thomas and Alexander Campbell tried for years to fit in with contemporary Protestant churches, pushing their reform agenda from within organized Christian churches, in particular the Seceder Presbyterians—the main body of the Presbyterian Church in Ireland—and later the Baptists in America. Alexander Campbell and Joseph Smith were similarly motivated in their restorationist pursuits by a desire to transcend sectarian division in a manner both overwhelming and convincing: Campbell via reason and Smith via new revelation. Campbell and Smith saw at least part of their roles as removing boundaries within Christendom that had, through time, tradition, and official pronouncement become accepted as orthodox beliefs.

Chapter 7, which follows, is a representation of Alexander Campbell's core religious beliefs, examining (1) his father's 1809 *Declaration and Address*; (2) the unorthodox arguments he put forth in 1816 in the *Sermon on the Law*, comparing the law of Moses in the "Jewish" Old Testament to the covenant of Christ in the "Christian" New Testament; and (3) the 1824 Wellsburg application for membership in the Mahoning Baptist Association titled *A Belief of the Wellsburg Church*, which identified unalterable preconditions for affiliation. Campbell never made a succinct list of the articles of his faith; however, every effort has been made here to enumerate clearly those points he considered most important to his restoration, articulated over nearly five decades of writing.

Chapter 8 is based primarily on Joseph Smith's Articles of Faith, first published in 1842 in response to a query by John Wentworth, editor of the *Chicago Democrat*.[8] In the letter, Smith gave a brief overview of his own religious experiences, the contents of the Book of Mormon, and a general history of the Church to that point.[9] The conclusion consisted of thirteen succinct statements of belief. They reflect Smith's own thinking as well as the earlier writings of some of his close associates, Oliver Cowdery, Joseph Young, Parley P. Pratt, Orson Pratt, and Orson Hyde.[10] Although these articles of faith are not inclusive of all the principles and doctrines Smith taught, they do provide a systematic starting point for examining many foundational beliefs and for comparing them to Campbell's words on the same topics.

The letter to Wentworth had the perspective of twenty-two years since Joseph Smith's First Vision and twelve years since the official organization of the Church of Christ, during which time Smith claimed to have received scores of revelations that had been published in Latter-day Saint newspapers. The clear statements on beliefs, principles, ordinances, and doctrines reflect the unique Latter-day Saint position of being neither Catholic nor Protestant, but in their own words, "biblical Christians of a unique sort."[11]

Constitutions and confessions were the formula for most religious institutions—setting out boundaries of beliefs and membership. As discussed extensively in chapters 5 and 6, both Joseph Smith and Alexander Campbell vehemently opposed creeds and obligatory confessions of faith. Accordingly, the two following chapters are not commentary on creeds or catechisms in the traditional sense of the word, but instead, they are a more careful look at the respective beliefs Smith and Campbell embraced and formally expressed in their words and writings. Despite their noncreedal and nonconfessional nature, the various documents cited provide an organized format for discussing what these two men believed and taught.

NOTES

1. Finke and Stark, *The Churching of America, 1776–1990*, 15. See Peter W. Williams, *America's Religions* (Urbana: University of Illinois), 190–91. Joseph Smith's mother, Lucy Mack Smith, called herself a "seeker." Lucy Mack Smith, *Lucy's Book*, ed. Anderson, 257–58, 278–80; See also Pratt, *Autobiography of Parley P. Pratt*, 13n9; Dan Vogel, *Religious Seekers and the Advent of Mormonism* (Salt Lake City: Signature Books, 1988).

2. Fluhman, "A Peculiar People," 15, 24.

3. Cleveland, *The Great Revival in the West*, 35.

4. The American Bible Society, organized in May 1816, helped increase circulation of the scriptures with the stipulation that their Bibles would not contain notes of comments so that none would be offensive to any denomination.

5. Hatch, *The Democratization of American Christianity*, 21–22; Bushman, *Joseph Smith and the Beginnings of Mormonism*, 36, 39.

6. Campbell, "The Declaration."

7. Joseph Smith—History 1:6.

8. In response to Wentworth, Smith wrote an account of the Latter-day Saints up to that date and concluded with thirteen statements known as the Articles of Faith.

9. John Wentworth wrote a letter requesting that Joseph Smith write a document for Mr. George Bastow [Barstow], a friend of his, who was writing a history of New Hampshire. Although the book was published, Smith's manuscript was not in it. Barstow made 1819 the closing date of his study, and because the Mormons did not organize as a church until 1830, they were not included in his volume. Karen Lynn Davidson, David J. Whittaker, Richard L. Jensen, and Mark Ashurst-McGee, eds., *Histories, Volume 1: Joseph Smith Histories, 1832–1844*, vol. 1 of the Histories series of *The Joseph Smith Papers*, ed. by Dean C. Jessee, Ronald K. Esplin, and Richard Lyman Bushman (Salt Lake City: Church Historian's Press, 2012), 492. Smith's "chapter" was first published in the "Church History," *Times and Seasons* 3, no. 9 (1 March 1842): 3:706. David Whittaker has written a history of the publication of various editions of the Articles of Faith by both Latter-day Saint missionaries and outside sources. David J. Whittaker, "The 'Articles of Faith' in Early Mormon Literature and Thought," in Davis Bitton and Maureen Ursenbach Beecher, eds., *New Views of Mormon History: A Collection of Essays in Honor of Leonard Arrington* (Salt Lake City: University of Utah, 1987), 63–92. The complete text of the Wentworth Letter is in Appendix 12, "The Wentworth Letter," in Encyclopedia of Mormonism, ed. Daniel H. Ludlow (New York: Macmillan, 1992), 4:1750–55.

10. See, for example, Robert J. Woodford, *The Historical Development of the Doctrine and Covenants*, 3 vols. (PhD dissertation, BYU, 1974), 1:287–90; David J. Whittaker, "The 'Articles of Faith' in Early Mormon Literature and Thought," in Bitton and Beecher, *New Views of Mormon History*, 63–92; David J. Whittaker, *Encyclopedia of Mormonism*, s.v. "Articles of Faith." See also John W. Welch and David J. Whittaker, "'We Believe. . . .' Development of the Articles of Faith," *Ensign*, September 1979, 51–55.

11. Barlow, *Mormons and the Bible*, xxiii.

7

Alexander Campbell's
Foundational Beliefs

$\mathcal{A}$ ccording to historians of the Stone-Campbell movement, some of the most important documents explaining the beliefs of Alexander Campbell are the *Declaration and Address of the Christian Association of Washington* (1809), the "Sermon on the Law" (1816), and "A Belief of the Wellsburg Church" (1824).[1] Although Alexander Campbell was not the author of the *Declaration and Address*, it formed the foundation of his restoration. He was the author of the other two documents. The Sermon on the Law demonstrates his separation of the Old and New Testament covenants, clearly placing the importance of New Testament as central to his restoration. The brief declarations of the Wellsburg Church illustrate essential beliefs with which he would not compromise while remaining in the Baptist community. These three documents form the basis for examining Alexander Campbell's beliefs and teachings.

DECLARATION AND ADDRESS (1809)

Essential to Alexander Campbell's restoration was the *Declaration and Address of the Christian Association of Washington*, authored by his father. One cannot fully appreciate Thomas Campbell's singular contribution to the restoration movement without understanding the context of how it came about. Although Thomas Campbell was highly regarded by the small group of Seceder congregations as the most learned and talented preacher in southwestern Pennsylvania, the local Seceder clergy opposed his efforts to reform the church and promote Christian unity based on the Bible.[2] In 1808, the presbytery censured him for not adhering to the "Secession Testimony." Specifically, he had invited Presbyterians not of his Associate Synod to partake of the Lord's Supper, and he expressed in a sermon that there was no divine mandate for requiring a confession of faith, covenants, or fasting prior to administering the Lord's Supper.[3]

In a written protest to the synod, Thomas presented his case, which was referred to a committee. The committee upheld the censure, and Thomas was required to submit to their decision. Though convinced of the correctness of his teachings, he yielded to their reprimand in order to not give offense and in the naïve hope that he would be able to continue preaching with the Seceder Presbyterians. Continuing persecution from those in power finally caused Thomas to conclude, "I find myself in duty bound to refuse submission to their decision as unjust and partial; and also finally to decline their authority while they continue thus to overlook the grievous and flagrant mal-administration of the Presbytery of Chartiers. . . . The corruptions of that Presbytery now become also the corruptions of the whole Synod."[4] Unfortunately, the politics, sectarianism, and practices that caused divisions in Ireland had migrated with the leaders of the Presbytery of Chartiers and the Associate Synod of Philadelphia. He separated formally from all Christian communion and fellowship with the synod, and those who were unwilling to work together to heal religious dissensions and whose own points of testimony were more important to them, as he saw it, than the writings of the Bible.[5]

The censure, however, did not dissuade the large number of people who continued to be loyal attendees at Thomas Campbell's meetings each week. In time, he proposed that a special gathering should be held to formalize his ideas of Christian unity based upon the Bible alone. Many of those attending Thomas's meetings were still Presbyterians of some sort, and he did not propose separation from their churches. Their efforts were still vague sentiments of Christian union held together by the personal influence and integrity of Thomas Campbell. He and his followers opposed the intolerant and sectarian spirit which pervaded the existing religions. With the scriptures as their sole guide, none of these seekers would have to sacrifice truth, and all disagreements not definitively revealed in the Bible could be matters of opinion and forbearance.[6]

On 17 August 1809, his followers organized themselves into "The Christian Association of Washington," and Thomas began writing a mandate for unity and further reform within the Christian faith. By September of 1809, Thomas had completed his *Declaration and Address*, clarifying the objectives of the movement. It was not a document for separation, but an ecumenical call for Christians of all denominations using the original standard—the Bible and simple New Testament Christianity.[7] Although no longer affiliated with or under the jurisdiction of the Associate Synod of North America, Thomas did not believe that the "pious members" of that body were outside of Christ. The call to unity was a call to all those in that body and all others who strove to follow Christ to stop allowing the sectarian creeds and structures to keep them divided. The *Declaration and Address* was a call for Christians in every locality to come together to worship and work despite differences—modeled in the Christian Association.[8] It was Thomas's signature restoration contribution, consisting of a preamble of how the Christian Association came about, a "declaration" of nine points giving the purpose and plan of the society, and the "address," which was a more extended statement of the motives and intentions of the movement.[9]

Thomas Campbell, c. 1834, by Edward Dean Neuenswander.

Alexander noted in his father's memoirs that the "immediate cause" for the writing of the *Declaration and Address* was the violent censuring of Thomas by his erstwhile co-presbyters; and in the address portion, Thomas expressed his feelings that the judgment rendered against him was contrary to the law of Christ. In the document, Thomas was able to defend himself and make public his case for the Christian Association's position on unity and reform under the scriptures.[10]

At the time his family arrived in America in late September 1809, Thomas had just received the printer's proofs for the *Declaration and*

Address, which Alexander read with great interest and approval.[11] Thomas had put into writing some of the very ideas that Alexander had concluded from his study at the University of Glasgow. There, Alexander had already discontinued communion with the Seceder Presbyterian Church. It was with great rejoicing that Alexander discovered, during the first days of reunion with his father in America, that he, too, had left the Seceder Presbyterian Church and had put pen to paper in declaring religious reformation.[12]

The foundation for this reformation was self-reliance in reading the Bible. Thomas declared: "It is high time for us not only to think, but also to act, for ourselves; to see with our own eyes, and take all our measures directly and immediately from the Divine Standard."[13] Alexander had the conviction, energy, and intelligence to carry forward his father's mandate, testifying, "I have been so long disciplined in the school of free enquiry" that he could be influenced only by "the authority of evidence, reason, and truth."[14]

Initially, the Christian Association was not a church, but a singular group of like-minded Christians who desired reform. Both Thomas and Alexander believed that the word of God could be interpreted by the common sense manifested in all humans—a populist and anti-traditionalist point of view. Stripping away the accretions and dross of the past, including priestly interpretations, creeds, and confessions, would enable readers to grasp what the scripture clearly and literally intended.[15]

Some Churches of Christ scholars consider the *Declaration and Address* to be the greatest document that American Christianity has produced,[16] and one argued it was so fundamental to Campbell's restoration movement that it is doubtful Alexander ever added any new and important ideas or principles.[17] In 1861, having a long perspective on reformation and restoration, Alexander attested: "The *Declaration and Address* contains what may be called the embryo or the rudiments of a great and rapidly increasing community. It virtually contains the elements of a great movement of vital interest to every citizen of Christ's kingdom."[18] It was not the constitution of a specific church; instead, it was a bold statement on the beliefs of a society of Christians who advocated further reformation that had begun with Martin Luther and John Calvin. Thomas Campbell was primarily interested in restoring the beliefs and practices of the primitive Christian church that he believed would reduce the frictions among the various Christian denominations of his day.[19] Thomas advocated Christian unity by conforming to the model and practice of the primitive church that was expressly set forth in the New Testament. Thus, the reformation should match the original standard and form of Christianity found therein.

The "Divine Standard" was the Bible. It is "the word of God . . . contained in the Old and New Testaments and is the only rule to direct us how we may glorify and enjoy him."[20] The singular purpose of Campbell's society was to promote "simple evangelical Christianity, free from all mixture of human opinions and inventions of men."[21] The emphasis on *sola scriptura* is evident as the members of Campbell's association adopted the motto, "Where the Scriptures speak, we speak; where the Scriptures are silent, we are silent."[22] In other words, silence in the scriptures should limit rather than permit nonscriptural beliefs and practices common among churches. Thomas Campbell concluded that nothing ought to be included in faith, worship, or as a test of communion that is not of New Testament origin.[23] The uniqueness, then, of this document "lies in this vision that Christian unity could be achieved through a restoration of the primitive church."[24] The means of restoration was the primitive church of the New Testament and the logical end, the Campbells believed, would be unity among all Christians.

In the Address portion of his text, Thomas Campbell lamented the schisms, envying, strife, and confusion that were characteristic of religion in his day. Nevertheless, he saw great promise in the United States, "a country happily exempted from the baneful influence of a civil establishment of any peculiar form of Christianity."[25] His vision of a nation unfettered by religious restrictions fueled his enthusiasm for Christian unity in preparation for the creation of Zion. These statements were followed by a list of thirteen propositions that are briefly summarized here.[26]

Propositions one, two, ten, and eleven emphasized that the church of Christ should be a unified body with no schisms or uncharitable divisions because division among Christians is "antiscriptural . . . , antinatural," in violation of God's command, and "productive of confusion and of every evil work."[27] Introducing human opinions "into the constitution, faith, or worship of the Church" are the causes "of all the corruptions and divisions that ever have taken place in the Church of God."[28]

In a very mildly worded anticreedal statement, propositions three and five argued against requiring acceptance of articles of faith for communion except those which are expressly stated by Christ and his Apostles in the New Testament.

Propositions four, five, and six recognized that although the Old and New Testaments are inseparably connected, comprising the entire revelation of God, the New Testament is the perfect constitution for the worship, discipline, and government of the church. Because there is no human authority which can add to the commands and ordinances of Christ, "Nothing ought to be received into the faith or worship of the Church, or be made a term of communion among Christians, that is not as old as the New Testament."[29] Additionally, "inferences and deductions from Scripture premises . . . may be truly called the doctrine of God's holy word, yet they are not formally binding upon the consciences of Christians." Therefore, they cannot be made terms of communion and have no place in the church's confession.[30]

Propositions seven, eight, nine, and twelve called for simplicity in doctrinal information, profession of faith, and conduct conforming to that understanding and belief. The original church of Christ consisted of children as well as adults; therefore, a straightforward declaration of faith for admission into the church was sufficient, and a high degree of doctrinal information should not be the terms for communion. Individuals, however, must acknowledge humankind's "lost and perishing condition by nature and practice, and of the way of salvation through Jesus Christ."[31] Nevertheless, the church's "perfection and purity" can be achieved by receiving only those who "profess their faith in Christ and obedience to him . . . according to the Scriptures," retaining in communion only those whose temper and behavior manifest that profession, accepting ministers who are scripturally qualified and who teach only those articles of faith that are expressly revealed, and carefully observing "all Divine ordinances, after the example of the primitive Church, exhibited in the New Testament."[32]

Proposition thirteen directed that any other requirement for observance of ordinances that is not found in scripture "should be adopted under the title of human expedients, without any pretense to a more sacred origin, so that any subsequent alteration or difference in the observance of these things might produce no contention nor division in the Church."[33]

Unity through reformation and restoration was clearly the theme underlying Thomas Campbell's *Declaration and Address*. Each proposition was set forth to promote harmony and prevent division and discord among Christians. The *Declaration and Address* was printed and sent out for the consideration of those attending Thomas Campbell's meetings who were seekers yet in an "unsettled state as to a fixed Gospel ministry," as well as to ministers from a variety of churches.[34] Thomas Campbell sought to assure all other churches that the association had "no intention to interfere, either directly or indirectly with the peace and order of the settled Churches . . . to distract and divide congregations."[35]

Alexander Campbell's views on the need for the Christian Association can be found in this comment early in this commentary on the text of Isaiah 57:14: "The sects have all, in a good degree at least, held fast the substance, but none of them the form. . . . All the sects have been strenuously contending for their own confessions, but none of them for the faith once delivered to the saints in the form in which it was delivered."[36] He declared the Christian Association had attempted to (1) remove the stumbling block by eliminating private opinions as terms of communion; (2) gather out the stumbling stones of human invention; (3) point out the "old way," meaning from his point of view that the scriptures were perfect, infallible, and sufficient; and (4) lift up the standard of the New Testament as a perfect constitution for worship, discipline, government, and duties for the New Testament church.[37] It appears from Campbell's comments that among other errors, both he and his father considered the religious parties as "possessing the substance of Christianity but as having failed to preserve 'the form of sound words' in which it was originally presented."[38]

ALEXANDER'S FORAY INTO PREACHING

Soon after Alexander's arrival in America and his wholehearted approval of his father's *Declaration and Address*, his scriptural understanding and budding preaching ability surfaced. Encouraged by his father in 1810, Alexander, now twenty-two but not yet ordained, made his first attempt at public preaching to a small congregation in a private home.[39] In addition to the abundant respect that Thomas had garnered in the community, the great interest in the Christian Association and the rumors about the promising abilities of Alexander drew a much larger group for his first true sermon. As part of the Christian Association semiannual meeting on 1 November 1810, the *Reporter* announced that Alexander Campbell, VDS, would be delivering a discourse.[40] In his personal journal, he titled this section "Skeletons of Sermons." He began with "Sermon First, before the Christian Association in Washington, Nov. 1st 1810" and wrote a detailed sentence outline based on Isaiah

57:14 in connection with Isaiah 62:10, regarding the prophetic removal of the stumbling block, which resulted in a great revival of the Jews and the church by "fit persons raised up to maintain the Lord's cause—the cause of Zion."[41] Campbell declared that many had been engaged in the arduous work of writing and preaching to do their part in helping God make Zion, but their poor reception demonstrated the evils of division and evil causes of many of the parties. They refused "to be measured by the pure, original and catholic standard of the Holy Scriptures. They will only submit to be tried by their own standards, . . . their own opinions, as if the word had no certain, fixed or express meaning of its own, but just what they are pleased to give it."[42]

Although partial to the New Testament, and particularly the Epistles, Campbell employed Old Testament stories to make some of his points. For example, in order to illustrate the importance of covenants as taught in the book of Hebrews, he utilized the examples of Adam and Noah from the book of Genesis: "The sovereignty of God is imminently magnified in all his dealings with his peoples from the moment when Adam became conscious of existence until the present hour. God's dealings with his people have been in the [form?] of covenant. He made a covenant with Adam in the day when he was created. He declared a covenant to Adam after his fall." Campbell wrote "Sermon 2 on Noah's covenant." In this second sermon, he began by defining the term: "The original word translated covenant signifies a disposition, establishment, bargain or testimony . . . [and] denotes an establishment or constitution." He then returned to Hebrews 8:8–13 to outline his ideas on the "Covenant of Redemption," by which he means the new covenant.[43] In notes that have a date after 1811, he wrote about the "Work of Holy Ghost in Old Testament" and had a scriptural index of entries from Psalms to Amos, and Obadiah to Malachi.[44] Although there are a few sermons from the Old Testament—Genesis, Isaiah, Ecclesiastes, and Psalms— his primary focus was in the New Testament.

In his first year as a minister, Alexander became such a noted speaker that he preached 106 sermons.[45] He was described, "More imposing than handsome, he stood almost six feet tall and bore the mien of a cultured European. He was urbane, intellectual, and eloquent. . . . He was always informative, usually interesting, and occasionally scintillating."[46] His sermons were based strictly upon the rules of the Scotch Seceder clergy—that is, founded upon principles of logic and rhetoric. Thomas and Alexander customarily reviewed their discourses together,

THE MILLENNIAL HARBINGER.

No. 1. } BETHANY, VIRGINIA: } Vol. I.
MONDAY, JANUARY 4, 1830.

I saw another messenger flying through the midst of heaven, having everlasting good news to proclaim to the inhabitants of the earth, even to every nation and tribe, and tongue, and people—saying with a loud voice, Fear God and give glory to him, for the hour of his judgments is come: and worship him who made heaven, and earth, and sea, and the fountains of water.—JOHN.
Great is the truth and mighty above all things, and will prevail.

Masthead of *Millennial Harbinger* 1, no. 1 (4 January 1830). Courtesy of L. Tom Perry Special Collections, Harold B. Lee Library, Brigham Young University.

father teaching the son. "First, he ascertained whether or not the division of the subject had been such as to exhaust it; and secondly, whether or not the views or doctrines delivered were truly those of the text, taken in it proper connection with what preceded and what followed it."[47]

Early into his preaching career, Alexander and his father carried on an extensive correspondence on the principle of faith discussing such ideas as "faith of reliance," "faith of assurance," "historical faith, miraculous, temporary, and saving faith," "belief of truth," and faith "as an act or exercise of confidence in Christ."[48] Alexander's transcriptions of these letters gave his father the pseudonym *Philologus*, Greek for "lover of the word" and a Christian at Rome to whom the Apostle Paul sent his salutation in Romans 18:15. As for Alexander himself, he took the name *Philomathes*, Greek for "lover of learning." The letters demonstrate Alexander's extensive reading in the scriptures and the writings of eminent Christian thinkers which allowed him to develop his own ideas with the opportunity to see what his father thought of them. From his own efforts and correspondence with his father, he concluded that the primitive faith of the New Testament followers was a simple trust in Christ and that discipleship required only a simple confession of that fact.

In May 1811, the Christian Association built a modest house of worship near Buffalo Creek, Pennsylvania, in the Brush Run valley, calling it "The First Church of the Christian Association meeting at Crossroads and Brush Run." The church remained a nondenominational Christian movement until Thomas became convinced that due to continuing hostility, the "Christian Association should assume the character of an independent Church" in order to enjoy the privileges and performance of duties that belong to the church relationship.[49] Although Thomas had never wanted to start his own denomination, rejecting the sectarianism of his day and calling for unity, he finally yielded to the apparent requirements for his Christian movement to survive.

After learning in 1812 that the word *baptism* mean immersion, the Campbells and many of their associates in the Brush Run Church were immersed. Thereafter, the "reformers" became associated with the Regular Baptists because they were the only large denomination who shared what they now believed was the correct mode of baptism, as well as other essential beliefs. Campbell stated that the Baptists drew "nighest the old platform in the New Testatment, of any of the sects . . . [of] the Christian world. . . . In the general views of the kingdom of grace and of admission into it, in abhorrence of councils, synods, and authoritative tribunals, and in the necessity of faith, repentance, baptism, a new creature, and in many other items then sacred, but now sight of by many of that sect, we coridally united with them not for our benefit, but for theirs."[50]

Although initially reluctant to join, in the fall of 1813, the Brush Run congregation became part of the Redstone Baptist Association, theoretically an advisory council with no ecclesiastical, judicial, or executive powers, but only after Alexander obtained certain conditions: "We should be allowed to teach and preach whatever we learned from the Holy Scriptures, regardless of any creed or formula in Christendom."[51] The Redstone Association was an independent Baptist community that read from the scriptures, and some were very favorable to Alexander's style of preaching.[52] E. Brooks Holifield of the Candler School of Theology at Emory University claims that part of Campbell's popularity with some western frontier Baptists was because he linked his reform ideas with their populist inclinations of local control, biblicism, dislike of Calvinism, and suspicion of clerical elites. Thomas and Alexander hoped that all the individual congregations within their association would take up their points of view on reform. Alexander Campbell promoted a democratic spirit and an enlightened and rational theology with a reasonable and literal interpretation of the Bible, and many Baptists were persuaded.[53]

"Sermon on the Law" (1816)

Not all the members of the Redstone Baptist Association were in agreement about the inclusion of Campbell's Brush Run Church. Calvinist-leaning members considered the Campbells as religious innovators and charged them as inconsistent, dishonest, and Baptist in name only. There were substantial differences between regular Baptist beliefs and some of Alexander Campbell's ideas, such as the meaning and purpose of immersion and the importance of returning to the faith and practices found in the New Testament. Additionally, Campbell's rational manner of organized discourse in his sermons was quite different from the Baptist mode of preaching. It was generally more popular with the congregation but upsetting to preachers.[54] Campbell did not try to hide his principles and ideas, nor did he change his reasoned delivery style, hoping to convince the regular Baptists of his "higher ground."[55]

Alexander Campbell, c. 1815, by Edward Dean Neuenswander.

These differences became more apparent when Alexander was invited to speak at the Baptist church in Cross Creek, Ohio, as part of the Redstone Baptist Association meeting. On 30 August 1816, at the age of twenty-eight, Alexander Campbell preached his "Sermon on the Law."[56] Although some of the clergy in the association wanted Campbell to speak, others, aware of his liberal bent and heterodoxy, were vehemently opposed.[57]

In this mostly extemporaneous sermon, Campbell based his thoughts on Paul's writings in Romans 8:3: "For what the law could not do, in that it was weak through the flesh, God sending his own Son in the likeness of sinful flesh, and for sin, condemned sin in the flesh." First, Campbell defined "the law" in the Old Testament as meaning the law of Moses, and when that same term was used in the New Testament, it meant the whole legal or Mosaic dispensation unless it had some other distinguishing modifier.

Campbell began his sermon by pointing out that the Ten Commandments—commonly referred to as the moral law—are a law that regulates the conduct of individuals toward each other, and therefore cannot be called a moral law. He claimed that of the Ten Commandments, six of them are moral and define our relationship toward others but that the first four are respecting our duty to God. His second objection was that if the Ten Commandments are a moral law, then all morality should be contained in them, or that all immorality should be prohibited in them. He listed the immoralities of drunkenness, fornication, polygamy, retaliation, and so forth as not specifically mentioned. He charged that although many assume that these are comprehended in the commandments, the latitude of interpretation that some learned men had taken enlarged the Decalogue to absurd dimensions and defeated the division of the law of Moses. His third objection was based on the Apostle Paul denominating the ten precepts as the "ministration of condemnation and of death" that were to be done away with.[58] Nevertheless, Campbell embraced the two great Old Testament principles, "thou shalt love the Lord the God with all thy heart, soul, mind, and strength; and thy neighbor as thyself,"[59] because he believed they were foundational laws, meaning that they were of "universal and immutable obligation,"[60] but not part of the law of Moses. Campbell's reasoning appears curious since the New Testament claimed that "on these two commandments hang all the law and prophets";[61] thus, they were the basis of the law of Moses and the teachings of the prophets.

In the next section of the sermon, Campbell pointed out what the law could not accomplish: "In the first place, it could not give righteousness and life."[62] For example, Paul differentiated between his experiences as a Jew under the law of Moses and his experience as a Christian under the gospel, freed from the law. Campbell rewrote Paul's words in Romans 7:10 to explain them more clearly: "And the commandment (which I thought would give me) life, I found (to lead) to death." Therefore, "justification, righteousness, and eternal life, cannot by any means be obtained by the law."[63]

His second point was in regard to the demerit of sin in that the law did not define the degree of wickedness of particular sins, although it gave them descriptive names and showed that these actions were offensive to God, hurtful to the individual, and deserving of death. Campbell made the case that the life and sufferings of Christ were sufficient to make reconciliation for all the sins of his chosen race—or for all who in every age or nation believe in him.[64]

His third point was that the law was given to a particular group, the Jewish nation, and therefore designed for only a part of humankind; it was not a suitable rule of life for others. Although the law in and of itself was "holy, just and good," it "failed in that it was too high, sublime, and spiritual, to regulate so weak a mortal as fallen man."[65] It could not give righteousness and eternal life; however, the Eternal Father remedied this by sending his Only Begotten Son, who through his obedience and righteousness completed the reconciliation and redemption of sinners. All believers in Jesus Christ could "find righteousness and eternal life; not by legal works or observances, in whole or in part, but through the abundance of grace, and the gift of righteousness. . . . Hence it is that Christ is the end of the law for righteousness to every one that believeth."[66]

Campbell noted that Christ was above Moses and all the other prophets: he was the author and finisher, the Alpha and Omega—not the law itself. Then he arrived at his most important point: Christianity was based on a new covenant, which, although historically connected to the Old Testament and prophesied of in it, was, as two Disciples of Christ scholars put it, "radically different in principle and content."[67] Campbell separated Christianity from the Hebrew legal system, claiming that the coming of Christ rendered both the ceremonial and whole law of Moses obsolete. "Christians are not under the law in any sense," because "the law or ten commandments is not a rule of life to Christians any further than it is enjoined by Christ."[68]

Campbell concluded that all arguments and motives from the law or Old Testament that deduced baptism of infants, payment of tithes, observation of holy days and religious fasting preparatory to the Lord's Supper, sanctification of the seventh day, and establishment of national covenants or religion by civil law came from the Jewish laws and customs and "are inconclusive, repugnant to Christianity . . . , not being enjoined or countenanced by the authority of Jesus."[69] As part of his strict differentiation between Old and New Testaments, Campbell's congregation at the Brush Run Church refused to use the term "Sabbath" as the day of worship.[70] From Campbell's strong belief in developing dispensations, he argued that Old Testament law and practices were "irrelevant and immaterial" for the New Testament and therefore could not be used to validate Christian practices.[70] Accompanying that belief was his notion that "Christian ordinances were new ordinances having meanings that did not exist before Christ."[72]

In retrospect, Campbell credited this sermon as the true beginning of his restoration movement. His heretical statements on the law launched a "'seven years' war with some members" of the Calvinistic-oriented Redstone Baptist Association. In September 1823, his conflict with them reached a climax.[73] Campbell's teachings found in his "Sermon on the Law" and his application of them in debates defending baptism by immersion and defeating the baptism of infants by sprinkling caused the more conservative elements of the association to rise up in anger against his reforming ideas. Although Campbell was recognized as an outstanding orator, debater, and leader, the liberal bent in his teaching led the Redstone Baptist Association to secretly plan the exclusion of Campbell's Brush Run congregation from their association and to discredit Campbell. Having anticipated their charge of heresy, Campbell circumvented their attempt to excommunicate him from the association by organizing a new congregation at nearby Wellsburg, Virginia, to which he moved his membership prior to the annual Redstone Association meeting.[74]

Campbell's mode of thinking and teaching was distinct from the regular Baptist preachers. His reasoning on scripture and the rational organization of his presentation were compelling to many listeners and off-putting to his detractors. His use of New Testament scripture to teach the law and the gospel was considered a bold assault upon the theology and preaching methods of many of the Baptist preachers. The more orthodox Baptists of the Redstone Association were alarmed at what they considered Campbell's antinomianism because he referred only to the New Testament in defending the principles and ordinances of Christianity, completely ignored the Old Testament, and declared the law of Moses obsolete.[75] Of course, Campbell did not believe he was antinomian, because the New Testament comprised a law that superseded the Mosaic law of the Old Testament. Christians were saved under the law of Christ, not the law of Moses. Nevertheless, some in the Redstone Baptist Association criticized his sermon and made it the grounds for an impeachment trial for "damnable heresy" at their next annual meeting of the association. Later, Campbell would attribute his own efforts and the charitable views of several Mahoning Baptist Association members as saving him from public excommunication.[76]

"A BELIEF OF THE WELLSBURG CHURCH" (1824)

Alexander Campbell wrote "A Belief of the Wellsburg Church" as his new congregation's application for membership in the Mahoning Baptist Association, nearby, but separate and independent from the Redstone Baptist Association.[77] The Mahoning Association was formed in August 1820, taking its name from the Mahoning River near the border between Ohio and Pennsylvania. Although founded on the Philadelphia Confession of Faith, the Mahoning Baptist Association was more tolerant of doctrinal diversity. They knew of Campbell's reforming and restoring ideas and welcomed his congregation into their association.

Campbell's statements of belief made only a few key points:

1. "We have agreed to walk together in obedience to the authority and institution of our Lord and King . . . and recorded in the Holy Scriptures of the volume called the New Testament. Our views of this volume are briefly these:—We believe that the whole Christian religion is fully and explicitly developed in it, and that nothing is ever to be added thereto, either by any new revelations of the Spirit, or by any doctrines or commandments of men, but that it is, as presented to us, perfectly adapted to the all wise and holy ends of its all-wise and benevolent Author."

2. "From his volume, with the Old Testament Scripture, which we also receive as of divine inspiration and authority, we learn every thing necessary to be known of God, his works of creation, providence and redemption; and considering the Old Testament as containing the Jew's religion as fully as the New contains the Christian, we avial ourselves of both as containing every thing profitable for doctrine, for reproof, for correction and instruction in righteousness and to make the man of God perfect, thoroughly furnished unto every good work. But, we adhere to the New [Testament], as containing the whole Christian religion. The New teaches us and we solemnly declare our belief of it—that Jesus of Nazareth is the Son of God, the Savior, which was to come into the world; that died for our sins, was buried, and rose again the third day from the dead, and ascended to the right hand of the Majesty on high; that after his ascension he sent down the Holy Spirit to convince the world of sin, of righteousness, and of judgment, by giving testimony of the Savior, and by confirming the word of the apostles by signs, and miracles, and spiritual gifts; that every one that believeth by means of the demonstration of the Holy Spirit and the power of God, is born of

God, and overcometh the world, and hath eternal life abiding in him; that such persons; so born of the Spirit, are to receive the washing of water as well as the renewal of the Holy Spirit in order to [gain] admission into the Church of the living God." "And that such being the natural darkness and enmity of the children of men, and their hearts [are] so alienated from the life of God through the ignorance that is in them and by their wicked works, none can enter into this kingdom of heaven but in consequence of the regeneration or renewal of the Holy Spirit. For it is now, as it ever was, that only to as many as received Him, who are born not of blood, nor the will of the flesh, but of God, does He give power to become the sons of God, even to them that believe in His name. For we are born again not of corruptible seed, but by the incorruptible seed of the word of God, which abideth forever."

3. "Our views of the Church of God are also derived from the same source, and from it we are taught that it is a society of those who have believed the record that God gave of His Son: that this record is their bond of union; that after a public profession of this faith, and immersion into the name of the Father, Son, and Holy Spirit, they are to be received and acknowledged as brethren for whom Christ died. That such a society has a right to appoint its own bishops and deacons, and to do all and every thing belonging to a church of Christ, independent of any authority under heaven."[78]

Campbell maintained that Christianity was completely and plainly developed in the New Testament, and nothing needed to be added to it. Because he was a cessationist, not believing in the extraordinary gifts of the Spirit after the apostolic era, there could be no new revelations of the Spirit, and there should be no additional doctrines or commandments. An omniscient Father had given Christians the New Testament as a gift and blessing.

In his proposal for membership to the Mahoning Baptist Association, Campbell cast light upon some of the doctrines that had most disturbed the Redstone Baptist Association, that is, his emphasis on the singular authority of the New Testament and his unique views on dispensations. Although Campbell recognized the Old Testament as foundational scripture and was personally very familiar with it,[79] his main emphasis was the Christian dispensation contained in the New Testament. In perfect harmony with Baconian reasoning, he believed that the testimony of the eyewitnesses who had seen the miracles was the empirical evidence put forth in the Bible. True disciples would believe their words.

Some of the chief characteristics of this document include its independent spirit—Campbell was not begging for admission to the Mahoning Baptist Association; rather, he set forth the guidelines by which they would be willing to lend the Wellsburg Church's strength to the association. The application lacked anything resembling a creed. Instead, its emphasis was a complete reliance on and high regard for the Bible, the completeness of the New Testament for Christian practice and devotion, the central place of Christ, the importance of baptism by immersion, the place of the Holy Spirit in personal regeneration, and the requirement for local control over the church. Amos Hayden, an early Disciples of Christ historian, foresaw the seeds of Campbell's future religious reformation and restoration work in the words of this statement of belief which would be more fully fleshed out when he separated completely from the Baptists in 1830.[80]

SEPARATION FROM THE BAPTISTS

Eventually, despite their shared belief in baptism by immersion, the Regular Baptists and the Reforming Baptists separated. The three innovations and corruptions of all churches (including the Baptists) that Campbell criticized in the *Christian Baptist* were (1) the distinctions and pretensions of the clergy over the laity; (2) unauthorized organizations, societies, and "popular schemes" for doing the work of the church, including Bible and missionary societies and ecclesiastical structures such as synods, presbyteries, and conferences which claim control over local congregations; and (3) "the use of creeds as standards of orthodoxy or tests of fellowship."[81]

Although the Reforming Baptists considered themselves as belonging to the larger Baptist fellowship, the feelings were not mutual with some of the Regular Baptists. In 1824, the Redstone Association disfellowshipped Alexander Campbell's Brush Run Church.[82] By 1825, local separations from other Campbell churches took place continually and widely. Regular Baptist associations who held to the Philadelphia Confession began to separate themselves from the Reforming Baptists by withdrawing from them and starting new associations or excommunicating what they considered the unorthodox Campbell churches. Each faction lay claim to being the true Baptist Church and appointed representatives to the next meeting of the local association. The matter of who was the legitimate church was determined by the association, the majority of representatives siding with one side against the other. In most cases the aggressors in separation were the Regular Baptists. The Reforming Baptists were content to stay in associations with the Regular Baptists, provided they were given liberty in their testimony of what they regarded as errors in doctrine and practice. And, as a matter of principle, they did not desire to participate in division and sectarianism.[83] Individuals who were members of Regular Baptist Churches but espoused "Campbellite" sympathies were personally excommunicated. Nevertheless, Campbell and his followers continued to thrive. By 1827, followers of Alexander and Thomas Campbell's restoration movement began to call themselves "disciples." This was not so much the formation of a new organization, but the gradual separation of the various Reforming Baptists from their previous connections, allowing them to merge in a common cause.

Between 1827 and 1830, evangelistic efforts brought hundreds of converts to embrace the restoration of the ancient order. In addition, Campbell's reputation and prestige were enhanced in the early 1820s by winning debates against two Presbyterian ministers on the nature of baptism, the 1826 publication of his New Testament, the 1828 publication of his hymnal for singing and reading correct doctrine, the 1828 great debate with wealthy utopian socialist Robert Owen, and his 1829 participation as a delegate in the Virginia Constitutional Convention.[84]

By early 1830, the Mahoning Baptist Association chose to dissolve. They had radically altered from other Baptist associations, having accepted Campbell's reform and restoration ideas. The churches of the association had become Baptist in name only. They agreed that since there was no New Testament precedent for an association, the Mahoning Baptist Association ought to be dissolved. Campbell, however, opposed the dissolution of like-minded Christians and believed the congregations ought to continue working together.[85]

In mid-1830, Campbell ceased publishing the *Christian Baptist*, critical of Protestant and particularly Baptist failure to reform and restore true New Testament Christianity. In its place, he began to publish the *Millennial Harbinger*, also a monthly periodical but with a more positive focus in advocating Christian unity as preparation for the Millennium.

The most important event for the new disciples was their union with many of the western reformers led by Barton Stone.[86] These two independent groups were similar in objectives and familiar with each other's teachings since 1824, and in late December 1831 they chose to begin formally uniting with each other.[87] The two groups had much in common: both believed that the union of all Christians was a primary objective; for both, the only object of faith was Christ; both rejected creeds as tests of fellowship and encouraged liberty of opinion on all matters not clearly revealed; both rejected Calvin's "limited atonement"; both generally agreed on "the nature of faith and the ability of sinful men to believe the evidence about Christ as it was found in the scriptures"; both practiced believers' baptism by immersion for the remission of sins; and both chose scriptural names for the church, regarding other names as sectarian—although Campbell preferred the name Disciples, and Stone preferred Christians. The new churches expanded throughout the Midwest and were variously called Disciples of Christ, Disciples, Reformers, Churches of Christ, Christians, and Christian Churches.[88] While the church name and associations changed over the years, Campbell, his co-reformers, and his followers were always first and foremost restorationists, seeking to imitate the ancient apostolic order found in the New Testament.

Notes

1.   Hayden, *Early History of the Disciples in the Western Reserve*; Garrison and DeGroot, *The Disciples of Christ*; Richardson, *Memoirs of Alexander Campbell*; Thomas Olbricht, "Alexander Campbell as a Theologian," *Impact* 21, no. 2 (1988): 22–37.
2.   Richardson, *Memoirs of Alexander Campbell*, 1:223.
3.   Williams et al., eds., *Stone-Campbell Movement*, 19.
4.   Campbell, *Memoirs of Elder Thomas Campbell*, 18; see also Williams et al., eds., *Stone-Campbell Movement*, 20.
5   Campbell, *Memoirs of Elder Thomas Campbell*, 18. See also Richardson, *Memoirs of Alexander Campbell*, 1:225–30.
6.   Richardson, *Memoirs of Alexander Campbell*, 1:231–34.
7.   Williams et al., eds., *Stone-Campbell Movement*, 20.
8.   See "Unity, Christian," in Foster et al., *The Encyclopedia of the Stone-Campbell Movement*, 754.
9.   Thomas Campbell, *Declaration and Address*, in Charles Alexander Young, ed., *Historical Documents Advocating Christian Union* (Joplin, MO: College Press, 1985), 35. Many scholars have called the *Declaration and Address* the founding document for the followers of Thomas and Alexander Campbell. It is also the best document expressing the thoughts of the two major restoration groups that united: the Christians of Barton Stone and the Disciples of Christ of Alexander Campbell. Furthermore, it is one of the first documents expressing the importance of ecumenical thought in Christianity. Olbricht and Rollmann, eds., *The Quest for Christian Unity, Peace, and Purity in Thomas Campbell's Declaration and Address*.
10.   Campbell, *Memoirs of Elder Thomas Campbell*, 12

11. Campbell, *Memoirs of Elder Thomas Campbell*, 23.

12. Richardson, *Memoirs of Alexander Campbell*, 1:187–90, 219–21.

13. Campbell, *Declaration and Address*, 71.

14. Campbell, "Reply," *Christian Baptist* 3 (3 April 1826): 204.

15. Noll, *America's God*, 381.

16. William Warren Sweet, "Campbell's Position in Church History," *Christian Evangelist* 76, no. 36 (8 September 1938): 969. See also Bill J. Humble, "The Restoration Ideal in the Churches of Christ," in *The American Quest for the Primitive Church*, 220.

17. Charles Young, *Historical Documents Advocating Christian Union* (Joplin, MO: College Press, 1985), 34.

18. Campbell, *Memoirs of Elder Thomas Campbell*, 109.

19. Thomas H. Olbricht, "Hermeneutics and the Declaration and Address," 243.

20. Richardson, *Memoirs of Alexander Campbell*, 1:143.

21. Garrison and DeGroot, *The Disciples of Christ*, 147.

22. This quotation is found in a footnote as Thomas explained the circumstances of the coming forth of the *Declaration and Address* and not an original part of Thomas Campbell's important writing. The full quotation follows: "Having taken it for granted that the holy scriptures were all-sufficient, and alone sufficient, as the subject-matter for faith and rule of conduct; that as the Old Testament was all-sufficient for the Old Testament worshippers, so the New Testament Scriptures were all-sufficient for the New Testament worshippers; therefore, we conclude that where the scriptures speak, we speak; where they are silent, we are silent." Campbell, *Memoirs of Elder Thomas Campbell*, 19–20, from a letter written by James Foster Sr.

23. Olbricht, "Hermeneutics and the Declaration and Address," 248. The exact meaning of Campbell's statement is still under debate—some would advocate that the silence part meant that a belief or practice not mentioned in scripture should not be made a term of *fellowship*—that is, those interpretations or expedients that churches choose are acceptable but can never be required.

24. Humble, "The Restoration Ideal in the Churches of Christ," 221.

25. Campbell, *Declaration and Address*, 86.

26. Campbell, *Declaration and Address*, 107–14.

27. Campbell, *Declaration and Address*, 112–13.

28. Campbell, *Declaration and Address*, 113.

29. Campbell, *Declaration and Address*, 110.

30. Campbell, *Declaration and Address*, 110.

31. Campbell, *Declaration and Address*, 111–12.

32. Campbell, *Declaration and Address*, 114.

33. Campbell, *Declaration and Address*, 114.

34. Campbell, *Declaration and Address*, quoted from preface in Hiram J. Lester, ed., 175th Anniversary Abridged Edition.

35. Campbell, *Declaration and Address*, 128–29.

36. Richardson, *Memoirs of Alexander Campbell*, 1:340.

37. Richardson, *Memoirs of Alexander Campbell*, 1:341.

38. Richardson, *Memoirs of Alexander Campbell*, 1:348.

39. During this same period, Thomas naively applied for ministerial affiliation with the Presbyterian Synod of Pittsburg, part of the Presbyterian Church in the USA. His petition was rejected in October of 1810, probably in part because Alexander was preaching but not ordained, and likely because Thomas's previous reputation with the Associate Synod was known.

40. Campbell renounced the title of "Reverend" and chose instead *Verbi Divini Servus*, "Servant of the Word of God." Richardson, *Memoirs of Alexander Campbell*, 1:335n.

41. Campbell, "Skeletons of Sermons, Sermon First," manuscript D 34R.

42. Richardson, *Memoirs of Alexander Campbell*, 1:337–38.

43. "Manuscript D," 40R–43L

44. "Manuscript L, 1808–1812," Disciples of Christ History Society, Nashville, TN. I am indebted to Dr. Carisse M. Berryhill for a copy of her paper "A Descriptive Guide to Eight Early Alexander Campbell Manuscripts." These notes appear after a date of March 1811.

45. Richardson, *Memoirs of Alexander Campbell*, 1:312–17.

46. Foster et al., eds., *The Encyclopedia of the Stone-Campbell Movement*, s.v. "Alexander Campbell," 112.

47. Richardson, *Memoirs of Alexander Campbell*, 1:323–24. For an example of Thomas Campbell's "Method of Discoursing," see Campbell, *Memoirs of Elder Thomas Campbell*, 207–9.

48. Richardson, *Memoirs of Alexander Campbell*, 1:413–20.

49. Richardson, *Memoirs of Alexander Campbell*, 1:365–66.

50. "Introductory Remarks," *Millennial Harbinger* 1, no. 3 (2 January 1832): 4.

51. Richardson, *Memoirs of Alexander Campbell*, 1:441.

52. The purpose of a Baptist association was to give encouragement, counsel, and protection against heresy and imposters to the various churches in their geographical area.

53. Holifield, *Theology in America*, 290.

54. Richardson, *Memoirs of Alexander Campbell*, 1:437, 467.

55. Errett Gates, "The Early Relation and Separation of Baptists and Disciples" (PhD diss., University of Chicago, 1901), 124. See also Daryl Chase, "Sidney Rigdon— Early Mormon" (PhD diss., University of Chicago, 1931), 18–19.

56. Initially, Campbell printed a pamphlet of his discourse to counter misrepresentations of his views by the Baptists. Thirty years later, he reprinted it in the "Sermon on the Law," *Millennial Harbinger* (third series) 3, no. 9 (September 1846): 493–521. See also Richardson, *Memoirs of Alexander Campbell*, 1:469–80.

57. Richardson, *Memoirs of Alexander Campbell*, 1:469–71.

58. 2 Corinthians 3:7, 14.

59. Luke 10:27.

60. Campbell, "Sermon on the Law," 500.

61. Matthew 22:40.

62. Campbell, "Sermon on the Law," 501.

63. Campbell, "Sermon on the Law," 501–2.

64. Campbell, "Sermon on the Law," 504–5.

65. Campbell, "Sermon on the Law," 503.

66. Campbell, "Sermon on the Law," 504.

67. Garrison and DeGroot, *The Disciples of Christ: A History*, 165.

68. Campbell, "Sermon on the Law," 510.

69. Campbell, "Sermon on the Law," 519.

70. Richardson, *Memoirs of Alexander Campbell*, 1:432.

71. See chapter 5 for a discussion of Campbell's understanding of dispensations.

72. Garrison and DeGroot, *The Disciples of Christ*, 166–67.

73. Campbell, "Sermon on the Law," 493.

74. Campbell, "Anecdotes, Incidents, and Facts—#4," *Millennial Harbinger* (third series) 5, no. 10 (October 1848): 554–56. Richardson, *Memoirs of Alexander Campbell*, 2:68. Garrison and DeGroot, *The Disciples of Christ*, 171, 178.

75. Richardson, *Memoirs of Alexander Campbell*, 1:472. Antinomian literally means without law and is a pejorative term applied to extreme beliefs in justification by "grace alone." It is the theological opposite of "works righteousness." Antinomian belief declares that because Christians are saved by grace and not works or moral effort, saved man is free of all moral obligations or principles. Van Austin Harvey, *A Handbook of Theological Terms; Their Meaning and Background Exposed in Over 300 Articles* (London: Allen and Anwin, 1966), s.v. "antinomianism." The Redstone

Baptist Association accepted the Philadelphia Confession, described as Calvinistic in tone, as part of its standard of faith, which was decidedly not antinomian.

76. Campbell, "Sermon on the Law," 493; Richardson, *Memoirs of Alexander Campbell*, 1:479. See chapter 10 for more on the charitable individuals who saved him from excommunication.

77. Hayden, *Early History of the Disciples*, 26. Local control was the theoretical position of all the Baptist Associations.

78. Hayden, *Early History of the Disciples*, 31–33.

79. For example, under the title "Juvenile Essays on Various Subjects by Alexander Campbell in the University of Glasgow 1808," he recorded one of his topics as the "Classification/Division of the 18th Chapter of Proverbs." Manuscript B. In an 1809 journal, he wrote "Prophecies about Jesus: Quotations of Evangelists from the Prophets" and included prophecies from Isaiah, Micah, Hosea, Jeremiah, Judges, Psalms, Zechariah, and Malachi that are cited in the New Testament gospels of Matthew and Mark. Manuscript E, 76L.

80. Hayden, *Early History of the Disciples*, 33–34.

81. Garrison and DeGroot, *The Disciples of Christ*, 176.

82. Foster et al., eds., *The Encyclopedia of the Stone-Campbell Movement*, s.v. "Redstone Baptist Association," 629.

83. Gates, *The Early Relation and Separation of Baptists and Disciples*, 90–91.

84. See chapter 9 for a discussion of Campbell's New Testament translation, *The Living Oracles*. See chapter 5 for a discussion of Campbell's hymnal. See chapter 12 for a fuller discussion of Campbell's defense of Christianity through debate.

85. Hayden, *Early History of the Disciples*, 296. Richardson, *Memoirs of Alexander Campbell*, 2:328.

86. Richard Hughes compares these two leaders by saying that "if Alexander Campbell was essentially a rationalist, Stone was essentially a pietist." Hughes, *Reviving the Ancient Faith*, 11.

87. Garrison and DeGroot, *Disciples of Christ*, 208–12. There were a few differences: Barton Stone's Christians did not require immersion for membership but believed that baptism was a matter of opinion which required liberty; Stone's Christians appear to have distinguished between "elders" (ordained ministers) and "unordained preachers"; they had a "higher" understanding of the ministerial office and less fear of "clerical domination"; Stone's Christians were more in the mode of Methodist revivalist camp meetings to win converts, whereas Campbell's disciples were more evangelistic in a clear and rationalistic mode; disciples observed the sacrament of the Lord's Supper weekly; however, the Christians observed it less frequently. Stone rejected the orthodox doctrine of the Trinity and the idea of a substitutionary Atonement, while Campbell reflected more orthodox views of God and salvation. Although Barton Stone exercised great influence over later developments in the Disciples/Christian movement, it is not possible to examine them as part of this book.

88. Garrison and DeGroot, *Disciples of Christ*, 190–217. The three major groups today that result from the efforts of Alexander Campbell and Barton Stone are the Christian Church (Disciples of Christ), the Christian Churches/Churches of Christ, and the Churches of Christ. Foster et al., *Encyclopedia of the Stone-Campbell Movement*, xxi.

8

Joseph Smith's
Articles of Faith

Smith's experiences and beliefs were sufficiently different from the creeds and confessions of Protestantism that they immediately brought opposition. Beginning with the recounting of his First Vision in 1820 until his death in 1844, Smith's teachings rankled many. Smith did not begin with a system of beliefs, instead he began with a six-hundred-page revelation, the Book of Mormon.

A starting point for examining Smith's early restoration ideas can be found in Doctrine and Covenants 20, a revelation on church organization and government received at least partially by the summer of 1829 and recorded shortly after 6 April 1830, subsequent to the organization of the Church of Christ. In sixty-seven brief verses, doctrines of the Creation, the Fall, the Atonement, and baptism are affirmed; laws governing the principles of repentance, justification, and sanctification are set forth; and the responsibilities of priesthood holders and members are described, all drawing heavily on the Book of Mormon.

A second source of Smith's beliefs are listed in the March 1842 "Wentworth Letter," a very late and brief summary.[1] By this time the church was called the Church of Jesus Christ of Latter Day Saints (later hyphenated as Latter-day Saints). The document concluded with a list of unnumbered statements clarifying some beliefs of the "faith of the Latter-day Saints." These thirteen statements were later titled the Articles of Faith.

DEVELOPMENT OF THE ARTICLES OF FAITH

The Articles of Faith embody Smith's religious maturing of more than two decades of revelatory and experiential learning. They were not, however, a comprehensive summary of Smith's beliefs and teachings. For example, important doctrines such as the sacrament of the Lord's Supper, premortal life, resurrection, judgment, and kingdoms of glory were not included in these thirteen brief statements of belief. Instead, it appears that Smith was responding primarily to many of the conflicting creeds, confessions, and teachings of the proliferating sects and denominations in America's religious landscape while clearly setting forth central Latter-day Saint beliefs.[2]

Confessions of faith by other denominations also were declarative and affirmative statements of positions on such subjects as the Trinity, salvation in Christ, fallen humanity, baptism, a closed canon of scripture, and other important principles, ordinances, and doctrines. Smith's Articles of Faith reflect the doctrinal disagreements that existed among the splintering of denominations within nineteenth-century American Protestantism. The proliferation of new sects necessitated that each group delineate differences from others by statements of belief, some even requiring a profession of faith to their particular articles for membership and communion. Neither the term "articles of faith" nor personal or group statements of religious beliefs were new ideas.[3] In fact, the very creeds and confessions that Smith opposed also began each declaration of faith with the phrase "'we believe' or 'I believe.'"[4] Thus, the Articles of Faith fall into a genre of Christian confessions of faith that dates back even further than the Reformation, if the Apostles' Creed and the Nicene Creed are considered.

The Articles of Faith were not meant to be all-inclusive but to give a sense of Mormonism. Further, they were not meant to be recited weekly as part of a creedal ritual. Smith's sketch of Latter-day Saint beliefs was designed for individuals unfamiliar with the principles of the restoration that he taught.[5] Although Smith's Articles of Faith are neither a summary of beliefs nor a confessional requirement for membership and communion, they nevertheless do act as a declaration of many Latter-day Saint beliefs in the context of Protestant and Catholic confessions. Central doctrines, long debated in Christianity, are stated clearly and succinctly, and they provide a starting point for pronouncing Latter-day Saint doctrine in common with or different from other Christian faiths.

Reverend George Moore, a Unitarian minister in Nauvoo, Illinois, commented that "Smith makes it a point not to agree with anyone in regard to his religious opinions."[6] Moore's statement is an exaggeration;

however, in the first ten articles, Latter-day Saint doctrines do contrast sharply with commonly held Christian doctrines, such as belief in a God without body, parts, or passions; the nature of the Trinity; original sin; total depravity; limited atonement; predestination; infant baptism and baptism by sprinkling; priesthood of all believers; *sola scriptura*; *sola fide*; and postmillennialist expectations. The Articles of Faith also answer questions regarding free will, the balance between grace and works, church organization, priesthood authority, the continuation of spiritual gifts, prophecy, seership and revelation, and the literal nature of the Second Coming of Jesus Christ.

Mormon historian Richard Bushman rhetorically asks, "Did Joseph realize he was departing from Christian theology?" The answer is a qualified yes. Smith "was only vaguely aware of overthrowing entrenched theological traditions."[7] His revelations and sermons were never argumentative—they were merely the oracles he claimed had been revealed to him, many of which were contrary to current opinion or long-held Christian customs.

The thirteen statements are worded in a straightforward and nonargumentative manner; each stands on its own as an assertion of belief, and the first ten illuminate Latter-day Saints' unique place in Christendom.

ARTICLE 1: *We believe in God, the Eternal Father, and in His Son, Jesus Christ, and in the Holy Ghost.*[8]

The first article is a general statement on the Godhead, confirming Latter-day Saint fellowship with Christians through a profession of faith in Jesus Christ. Like many Christians, Latter-day Saints believe that the Godhead is made up of three beings. Although some might suppose this to be a typical Christian belief, post–Great Awakening Unitarians denied that the Godhead was a divine Trinity; the philosophical ramifications of Enlightenment thinking caused the rationalist and empiricist-driven deists to debate how one could know of God's existence, let alone his threefold nature.[9]

The definitive nature of Trinitarian doctrine set forth by ecumenical councils such as the Nicene Creed and other confessions during the fourth century was the result of two pressing demands: (1) to explain three divinities within strict monotheism and (2) to define God in a way that allowed for both his transcendence and humanness, his historical incarnation within time and his eternal existence outside of time.[10]

Despite not accepting the Trinity proclaimed by the creeds, Smith was quoted by New York journalist Matthew Davis as having said, "I believe, that there is a God, possessing all the attributes ascribed to him by all Christians of all denominations, that he reigns over all things in Heaven and on Earth; and that all are subject to his power. He then spoke, rationally, of the attributes of Divinity, such as foreknowledge, mercy, &c. &c."[11]

Latter-day Saints familiar with Joseph Smith's First Vision accounts and other revelations understand the first article of faith to define the Godhead as three separate beings; in its brief wording, however, Smith did not initially emphasize this separation.[12] Nevertheless, within the context of the Wentworth Letter, which includes an account of the First Vision, it is very clear that Smith rejected the traditional Catholic and Protestant doctrine of the Trinity expressed in the creeds and instead announced the unique Latter-day Saint belief in a Heavenly Father and his Son, Jesus Christ, as separate and distinct beings, and at the same time emphasized their oneness or unity in purpose.[13] In Smith's 1829 translation of the Book of Mormon, numerous passages declare that the Father, Son, and Holy Ghost are one God, focusing on their oneness in doctrine, divine nature, judgment, baptism, and redemption.[14] The Book of Mormon prophet Moroni emphasized the immutability of God, noting that "God is the same yesterday, today, and forever, and in him there is no variableness neither shadow of changing."[15] Moroni used this sentiment, also expressed by Paul, to illustrate that God performed miracles anciently and that his unchanging nature demonstrated he would continue to perform miracles. This concept reflects Smith's understanding of the nature of God.

Smith further clarified the nature of Father and Son as being divinely passible. Shortly after organizing the Church of Christ in April 1830, he began his work translating the Bible. He claimed that he received revelation enlarging upon the few words in Genesis 5:24 regarding Enoch, "and he was not; for God took him." Enoch and his city, called Zion, were blessed and taken to heaven. God showed Enoch those left on the earth, who, with the exception of Noah and his family, were under the power of Satan. Enoch witnessed God as he "looked upon the residue of the people, and he wept." Enoch asked the question all who believe in an impassible God would: "How is it that thou canst weep, seeing thou art holy, and from all eternity to all eternity?" God responded, "They are the workmanship of mine own hands, and I gave unto them their knowledge, in the day I created them; and in the Garden of Eden, gave I unto man his agency . . . and also given commandment, that they should love one another, and that they should choose me, their Father; but behold, they are without affection, and they hate their own blood."[16] God and all of heaven wept because Satan had become humankind's father and misery would be the natural consequence of this choice. A Book of Mormon prophet promised that Jesus "will take upon him death, that he may loose the bands of death which bind his people; and he will take upon him their infirmities, that his bowels may be filled with mercy, according to the flesh, that he may know according to the flesh how to succor his people according their infirmities."[17] Both of these restoration passages illustrate the compassion and passible nature of God. The Bible also speaks of God's great love that allows his Son to suffer for all his children and of the Son who willingly complies.

It appears that at least by August 1836 Smith's teachings concerning the material, anthropomorphic, and corporeal nature of God were known in Ohio. Truman Coe, a Protestant clergyman living in Ohio, published the following statement in the *Ohio Observer*: "They believe that the true God is a material being, composed of body and parts."[18] In 1841, Joseph Smith taught numerous times the corporeality of the Father and Son. Scribe William Clayton recorded that Smith revealed in a sermon "that which is without body or parts is nothing. There is no other God in heaven but that God who has flesh and bones."[19] A few weeks later, Smith remarked that "the Godhead . . . was not as many imagined—three heads and but one body . . . [but] the three were separate bodies."[20] Shortly thereafter, he declared that "the Son Had a Tabernicle & so had the father."[21] In 1843, he reiterated the nature of the Father's and Son's anthropomorphic corporality: "The Father has a body of flesh and bones as tangible as man's; the Son also."[22] Smith squared this statement with Paul's declaration that corruption (mortal flesh and blood) cannot inherit the kingdom of God by explaining that the Spirit of God flows in the veins of resurrected beings, not blood.[23]

Days before his martyrdom, Smith quoted from Revelation 3:6 that Christ "hath made us Kings and Priests unto God and his Father" and declared the translation of that verse correct. In response to the false accusations of apostates, he stated that for fifteen years he had taught a plurality of gods, declaring God to be a distinct personage, Jesus Christ to be a separate and distinct personage from God the Father, and the Holy Ghost to be a distinct personage or spirit. He maintained he had always taught that the Godhead consists of "3 distinct personages & 3 Gods."[24] Smith viewed the oneness of the Godhead as a "unity of heart, mind, purpose, and mutual indwellingness."[25]

Smith objected to those who believe "there is one God—the Far. Son & the H.G. are only 1 God—it is a strange God any how 3 in 1. & 1 in 3," Smith commented that "it is a curious thing anyhow. . . . [A]ll are to be crammed into 1 God"[26] (in sectarianism). In an earlier statement he noted that "Peter—[and] Stephen saw the Son of Man. Saw the son of man standing on the right hand of God.—3 personages—in heaven who hold the keys.—one to preside over all."[27] In Smith's mind, his initial vision agreed with the New Testament witnesses.

Whereas the Father and Son have bodies of flesh and bone, Smith explained that "the Holy Ghost . . . is a personage of Spirit" and is therefore able to dwell within us.[28] The role of Christ is that of mediator while the Holy Ghost is the witness or testator: "His Spirit will bear testimony to all who seek diligently after knowledge from him."[29] Additionally, Smith taught individuals to ask God to manifest the truth to them about his revelations, promising that an answer would come "by the power of His Holy Spirit," urging them not to "be dependent on man for the knowledge of God."[30]

In unambiguous terms, Smith set forth the nature of God the Father, God the Son, and God the Holy Ghost, along with their responsibilities, powers, and relationship to each other—and it was very different from traditional Christianity. The doctrine of the Godhead and the nature of its members, then, was not for Smith an incomprehensible mystery but a spiritual truth that was once lost but had been re-revealed by God to him in both vision and by revelation.[31] Smith taught that God is material, corporeal, and anthropomorphic. "God has a body of finite dimensions, occupies space, and rejoices and weeps" over his most important creation, humans.[32]

ARTICLE 2: *We believe that men will be punished for their own sins, and not for Adam's transgression.*

Smith taught that our first parents acted in harmony with God's divine plan because the Fall was foreordained.[33] In answering a question directed to him, Smith explained, "Adam Did Not Comit sin in [e]ating the fruit for God had Dec[r]eed that he should Eat & fall—But [also] in complyance with the Decree[,] he should Die."[34] The prohibition was a warning of the consequences that would follow. Further, Smith declared "that it [referring to Adam and Eve's transgression] is washed away by the blood of Christ, and that it no longer exists." Thus, with Adam's sin forgiven, there is nothing to be transmitted and "we are all born pure and undefiled."[35] Smith learned from his inspired translation of the Bible that Christ "atoned for original guilt"; therefore, children cannot be answerable for the sins of their parents because "they are whole from the foundation of the world."[36] Smith definitively separated himself from Calvin's teachings by preaching that there is no inherited sin or guilt, no total depravity of humankind.

In clarifying the divinely ordained role of Adam and Eve and discarding the doctrines of original sin and the depravity of humanity, Smith was nevertheless convinced of the fallen nature of humans and their need for redemption. He admitted, "I have learned in my travels that man is treacherous and selfish, but few excepted."[37] He went on to lament, "We are all subject to vanity while we travel through the crooked paths, and difficulties which surround us. Where is the man that is free from vanity? None ever were perfect but Jesus."[38] He also taught that natural inclinations rule man, for "in this world, mankind are naturly selfish, ambitious & striving to excell one above another."[39]

The stain of Adam's sin did not cause humankind to be born totally depraved; instead, Smith believed humans to be moral, responsible, and free agents. Journalist Mathew Davis, writing to his wife, reported that Joseph Smith taught the following: "Although it was fore-ordained he [mankind] should fall, and be redeemed, yet after the redemption it was not fore-ordained that he [mankind] should again sin. In the Bible a rule of conduct is laid down for him. . . . If he violates that law, he is to be punished for the deeds done in the body."[40] Smith placed the Latter-day Saints firmly in the Arminian doctrinal camp of believing in "free will," but he referred to it as "moral agency."[41]

Smith believed that God always intended for man to fall or become mortal since the growth necessary to become like God could not occur in the perfect environment of the garden, because it couldn't test humankind's faith. This idea emphasized the importance of mortality. The Book of Mormon makes this clear, stating, "If Adam had not transgressed he would not have fallen, but he would have remained in the garden of Eden. And all things which were created must have remained in the same state in which they were after they were created; and they must have remained forever, and had no end. And they would have had

no children; wherefore they would have remained in a state of innocence, having no joy, for they knew no misery; doing no good, for they
knew no sin."[42]

Thus, according to the Book of Mormon, learning to differentiate
between opposites, leaving Eden, and becoming mortal in order to have
children were all part of God's plan. Smith never clarified whether partaking of the fruit was symbolic or literal.

ARTICLE 3: *We believe that through the Atonement of Christ, all
mankind may be saved, by obedience to the laws and ordinances
of the Gospel.*

Article 3 points out the essential nature of the Atonement of Christ for
salvation.[43] Debated for centuries, the crucial issues regarding grace are
its relationship to free will and works and the severity of man's estrange-
ment from God.[44] Martin Luther, John Calvin, Jonathan Edwards, John
Wesley, Alexander Campbell, and other great theologians wrestled with
these questions as well as with the idea that certain individuals were
elected or predestined for salvation. Smith's statement in the third article of faith about "obedience to the laws and ordinances of the Gospel"
sounds like what might be called "works-righteousness"—anathema
for Luther and for Protestants in general.[45] The previous phrase in this
article, "through the Atonement of Christ, all mankind may be saved,"
links his doctrine clearly to the grace of Christ, the unmerited enabling
power available to all humans.

This article of faith emphasizes that "all mankind may be saved"—
a belief similar to that championed by Smith's Universalist-thinking[46]
grandfather, Asael Smith, and a rejection of Calvin's notions of the predestination of the elect and a limited atonement.[47] By uniting the two
phrases (1) "through the Atonement of Christ all mankind may be saved"
and (2) "by obedience to the laws and ordinances of the Gospel," Smith
asserted that the grace of Christ and his work of salvation are preeminent.
Humankind must, however, covenant with Christ through ordinances
to obey his law in order to be saved.[48] This is the meaning of the phrase
"work out your salvation with fear and trembling" that both Book of
Mormon prophet Alma and New Testament Apostle Paul used. In other
words, salvation requires the making and keeping of covenants through
ordinances.[49]

In the Book of Mormon, the prophet Nephi plainly declared
that Christ invites everyone to "come unto him and partake of his

goodness."[50] Salvation is free, and "all men are privileged the one like unto the other, and none are forbidden."[51] To make crystal clear that Christ will deny salvation to no one, Nephi identified the particular groups who are invited to come unto him: "black and white, bond and free, male and female; and he remembereth the heathen; and all are alike unto God, both Jew and Gentile."[52] The only caveat Nephi listed is that all must be persuaded to repent.[53] Nephi declared that "it is by grace that we are saved, after all we can do,"[54] meaning that notwithstanding or despite all we can do, our works are insufficient for salvation; but all who come unto Christ through repentance may be saved by his merits, mercy, and grace.[55] Thus, salvation is free and undeserved. It is neither a gift nor a reward; instead, it is a cooperative effort of humankind with God and available to all his children.

Book of Mormon prophet Lehi explained that the principle of agency is an invitation from God to all humans, who were created to act rather than be acted upon, thereby possessing the power to choose between "liberty and eternal life" or "captivity and death," the opposing forces of God and Satan.[56] Joseph Smith observed that "the devil cannot compel mankind to do evil. . . . Those who resist the Spirit of God, are liable to be led into temptation. . . . God would not exert any compulsory means, and the devil could not."[57] The power, then, to act or initiate change in fallen humanity is a gift of grace from God to all his children, which they may choose to accept or reject.

As mentioned earlier, according to Smith, God had only one plan, and it was in place before the earth was created, including the Savior and his redeeming sacrifice. Sending the Savior was not a recovery mission or recuperation from an unfortunate tragedy—the Fall—but it was part of the divine plan put forth initially. As God put forth his plan in premortality to all his spirit children, he queried, "Whom shall I send?" He was not asking a question as much as seeking confirmation from all the premortal spirits to affirm the chosen one, who answered: "Here am I, send me."[58] God the Father selected the Messiah, God the Son, who had planned with him to raise up repentant humankind, explaining, "And that which I have chosen hath pled before my face. Wherefore, he suffereth for their sins; inasmuch as they will repent in the day that my Chosen shall return unto me."[59] Faith in Jesus's redeeming grace and the works of covenant making and keeping were essential parts of God's salvation for each individual.[60]

ARTICLE 4: *We believe that the first principles and ordinances of the Gospel are: first, Faith in the Lord Jesus Christ; second, Repentance; third, Baptism by immersion for the remission of sins; fourth, Laying on of hands for the gift of the Holy Ghost.*

Smith connected the laws and ordinances necessary for salvation to the first principles and ordinances of the gospel. Faith in Christ, repentance, baptism by immersion, and the gift of the Holy Ghost are a reiteration of what Book of Mormon prophets called the "doctrine of Christ"—what Christ identified in the Book of Mormon as acceptance of "my doctrine" or "my gospel."[61] The preceding principles are found together at least three times and emphasize that these principles and ordinances are a beginning point after which one must endure to the end.

President Martin Van Buren in an 1842 interview inquired what made Smith's religion unique. Succinctly, Smith singled out baptism by immersion and the gift of the Holy Ghost by the laying on of hands as defining ordinances. He considered all other differences were contained within the gift of the Holy Ghost.[62]

Citing both the Holy Bible and the Book of Mormon, Smith wrote to a Rochester, New York, newspaper editor that God requires "all people, high and low, rich and poor, male and female, ministers and people, professors of religion and non-professors" to repent, be baptized for the remission of sins in the name of the members of the Godhead, and receive the Holy Spirit by the ordinance of the laying on of the hands by one who is ordained and sealed unto this power in order to fully enjoy the Holy Spirit of God and to escape the impending judgments of God.[63]

The steps for spiritual rebirth set forth in this article of faith were clearly defined and simple in comparison to most other churches and were also reserved for those old enough to be accountable for their sins. Smith's *ordo salutis*, the steps of salvation, used similar wording and were in the exact order that Campbell's associate Walter Scott taught, as discussed in chapter 5.

Faith. According to Smith's understanding, faith included an attitude of belief and a willingness to act on the belief, which is accounted for righteousness. Smith declared that "every word that proceedeth from the mouth of Jehovah has such an influence over the human mind—the logical mind—that it is convincing without other testimony."[64] "Faith [also] comes by hearing the word of God through the testimony of the servants of God," and it "is always attended by the Spirit of prophecy &

Revelation."[65] He elaborated by confirming that "miracles are the fruits of faith. . . . Where faith is, there will be some of the fruits; all gifts and power which were sent from Heaven were poured out on the heads of those who had faith."[66] Smith was more enthusiasm-driven than Campbell, but like Campbell, he did not require a confession of a faith experience for membership or communion, as did the Regular Baptists. Smith connected faith with reason and logic and also to gifts of the Holy Spirit, including miracles.

Repentance and Baptism. In translating the Book of Mormon, Smith learned that the practice of infant baptism was a "gross error" and "solemn mockery before God"[67] and stressed that repentance and baptism were for those who are accountable for their sins—revealed in the Doctrine and Covenants as age eight.[68] His own experience while translating the Book of Mormon, and discussed in chapter 6, was baptism by immersion under the hands of John the Baptist. Smith declared that "baptizing Children or sprinkling them or they must welter in Hell is a doctrin not true not supported in Holy writ & is not consistant with the Character of God."[69] Additionally, Smith learned from his translation work that "children are blessed; for behold, as in Adam, or by nature, they fall, even so the blood of Christ atoneth for their sins."[70]

Smith argued against a scriptural basis for pedobaptism. The Presbyterians claimed it was analogous to circumcision. Smith simply stated the ordinances were not the same: "Circumcision is not Baptism. Baptism is for the remission of sins. Children have no sins."[71] He explained that circumcision was the sign of the priesthood, which was given to Abraham.[72]

He also taught that the ordinance of baptism must be performed by those who have received priesthood authority. Significantly, those who had been baptized previously into other churches must be rebaptized, even if their baptism had been by immersion.[73] Accepting sectarian baptism was compared to "putting new wine into old bottles and putting old wine into new bottles."[74]

Smith taught that repentance and baptism were the entrance gate to further blessings, such as the gift of the Holy Ghost. Regeneration required both the baptism of water and the baptism of fire. The baptism of water was for the remission of sins, and the baptism of fire was the Gift of the Holy Ghost.[75] Smith explained the importance of baptism: "Baptism is a holy ordinance preparatory to the reception of the

Holy Ghost. It is the Channel and Key by which the Holy Ghost will be administered. The gift of the Holy Ghost by the laying on of hands cannot be received through the medium of any other principle, than the principle of Righteousness, for if the proposals are not complied with it is of no use but withdraws."[76] Smith declared that the gift of the Holy Ghost did not automatically follow baptism or prayer but was instead a separate priesthood ordinance conferred by the laying on of hands as it was in the New Testament.[77]

Gift of the Holy Ghost. Expounding on the declaration of the Apostle John from the texts of his English and German Bibles—"Except a man be born of water and of the Spirit, he cannot enter into the kingdom of God"[78]— Smith argued that you "might as well baptize a bag of sand as a man if not done in view of the getting of the Holy Ghost.—baptism by water is but ½ a baptism—& is good for nothing with[out] the other, —[that is, the baptism of] the Holy Ghost."[79] He followed this declaration with a rhetorical question, directing it by name to Alexander Campbell: "How are you going to save them with water alone? for John said his baptism was nothing without the baptism of Jesus Christ."[80] Had he responded directly to Smith, Campbell would have clarified that he believed a separate ordinance was unnecessary. He taught that the Holy Spirit, who dwelt in Jesus and who Jesus promised would dwell in his church, was received following a person's union with Christ, which occurred at immersion. Just as children at their birth inhale the spirit (air) of this world, so also do the regenerated who are born of the water receive the Spirit of the new kingdom into which they are reborn.[81] In his mind, the new covenant was a new institution adapted to a higher spiritual condition in which positive authority was unnecessary.[82]

These simple steps to salvation, taught by both Campbell and Smith, were in marked contrast to Calvinistic notions of many "stages of regeneration" and to the idea that an individual must be regenerated (elected or predestined) by God before he or she could have faith in Jesus Christ.[83] The two restorationists believed in the same principles and ordinances of the gospel and in the same order; however, their origin was different—Campbell's biblical and Smith's Book of Mormon—as were some of the meanings of the principles.

ARTICLE 5: *We believe that a man must be called of God, by prophecy, and by the laying on of hands by those who are in authority, to preach the Gospel and administer in the ordinances thereof.*

This article declares that the three antecedents necessary to authorize preaching the gospel and performing ordinances are (1) an individual must be called by inspiration of the Holy Spirit; (2) this calling must be certified by a particular priesthood ordinance—the laying on of hands; and (3) the individual announcing the calling to the one being called must have authority from God. The purpose of the priesthood is to administer saving ordinances, such as baptism.

When Reforming Baptist Parley Pratt first considered the steps for salvation, he was initially excited but then lamented, "He could find no one to minister in [them]. . . . One great link was wanting to complete the chain of the ancient order of things; and that was, the authority to minister in holy things—the apostleship, the power which should accompany the form. . . . Peter proclaimed this gospel, and baptized for remission of sins, and promised the Gift of the Holy Ghost, because he was commissioned so to do by a crucified and risen Savior. But who is Mr. Rigdon? Who is Mr. Campbell?"[84] Rigdon and Campbell had been baptized by the Regular Baptists, but who had ordained them? The Baptists could not claim apostolic office by succession as did the Catholics. Further, Rigdon and Campbell eventually left the Regular Baptists because in their opinion they did not teach the true gospel. When Rigdon was visited by Mormon missionaries in the fall of 1830, Pratt recorded, "At length Mr. Rigdon and many others became convinced that they had no authority to minister in the ordinances of God; and that they had not been legally baptized and ordained."[85]

The requirement of priesthood authority separated Latter-day Saints from all Protestant churches, whose rebellion against the power of the Catholic Church had eroded their respect for its authority. Smith set up a new hierarchy, but without inherited positions and requiring congregational sustaining.

Significantly, Smith implied in this article that he had received authority to administer in the ordinances of the gospel by the "laying on of hands." In fact, he recorded the 1829 visitations, first of John the Baptist to restore the Aaronic Priesthood and later of Peter, James, and John to restore the Melchizedek Priesthood to himself and Oliver Cowdery.[86] These claims regarding the priesthood held by ancient prophets bolstered Smith's argument that his church was indeed Christ's restored church.

ARTICLE 6: *We believe in the same organization that existed in the Primitive Church, namely, apostles, prophets, pastors, teachers, evangelists, and so forth.*

Article 6 is an open-ended statement about the organization that links the Church of Jesus Christ to the former-day Saints—those who lived during the first-century organization of Christ's church. Primitivist sentiment was common during Smith's era, and the connection between Smith's organization and that of the Apostle Paul's New Testament characterization of Christ's church in Ephesians 4:11 would have been clear to those who read this article of faith.

In the Wentworth Letter, Smith gave a brief overview of the Book of Mormon, in which he linked the church of the "western continent" to that of the "eastern continent." He stated that the Savior "planted the Gospel here in all its fulness, and richness, and power, and blessing; that [the ancient American church] had Apostles, Prophets, Pastors, Teachers, and Evangelists; the same order, the same priesthood, the same ordinances, gifts, powers, and blessings."[87]

By listing in this article of faith the same offices in the primitive church and referring in the Wentworth Letter to the Book of Mormon church organization, Smith tied the latter-day restoration to the ancient foundation of apostles and prophets, with Christ at the head in both Palestine and in the Americas.[88] Smith identified the same church offices as Campbell did, except for "deaconess." Additionally, he also included the offices of apostle and prophet—considered the "extraordinary" offices by James Haldane and Campbell.[89] Smith, through revelation, announced that an evangelist was a patriarch like Jacob (Israel), who pronounced a blessing on each of his twelve sons.[90] Joseph Smith Sr. became the first "evangelist," or patriarch, of the restoration. As Mormon historian Grant Underwood clarified, the connection between Latter-day and primitive church offices is in the nature of its organization (function) rather than its nomenclature (title).[91]

With Christ as the ultimate leader of the church, Smith organized a centralized church government that was to be administered by the senior Melchizedek Priesthood holder as leader of the Lord's church on earth. This man was sustained by all the membership (male and female) as an Apostle, with the mantle of prophet, seer, revelator, and president of the church. With his approach in selecting church leadership, Smith advocated an Old Testament patriarchal, hierarchical, and marginally democratic system.

Implied in the restoration of the same church organization as the primitive church is its purpose as the custodian of priesthood authority to perform essential saving ordinances. In this article of faith, Smith identified specific titles in the apostolic church rather than the responsibilities themselves—which linked his church to scripture and proper authority, adding "and so forth," to indicate that other titles might be used to carry out the responsibilities of the church.

ARTICLE 7: *We believe in the gift of tongues, prophecy, revelation, visions, healing, interpretation of tongues, and so forth.*

In article 7, another open-ended article, Smith listed several gifts of the Spirit that were part of the apostolic church: tongues, prophecy, revelation, visions, healing, and interpretation of tongues. The phrase "and so forth" at the end of the article indicates that the multitude of spiritual gifts discussed by Paul in 1 Corinthians 12–14 relating to the primitive church were also an integral part of the latter-day church. This article affirms the Savior's teaching that true believers would enjoy the "signs" of the true church—the gifts of the Spirit.[92]

Confusion about gifts of the Spirit caused young Parley P. Pratt to ask his Regular Baptist preacher "what Jesus meant when he said, 'these signs shall follow them that believe.' He replied, that it meant these signs should follow the Apostles only."[93]

In sharp contrast to both those who believed in the nonbiblical signs manifest in camp meetings and those who believed that signs had ceased, Smith noted that there were a variety of conflicting opinions regarding the gift of the Holy Ghost: "We believe in the gift of the Holy Ghost being enjoyed now, as much as it was in the apostles' days. . . . We also believe in prophecy, in tongues, in visions, and in revelations, in gifts, and in healings. . . . We believe in it [the gift of the Holy Ghost] in all its fullness, and power, and greatness, and glory . . . rationally, consistently, and scripturally, and not according to the wild vagaries, foolish notions and traditions of men."[94] In particular, Smith "gave an explanation of the gift of tongues: that it was particularly instituted for the preaching of the gospel to other nations and languages, but it was not given for the government of the church."[95]

In Doctrine and Covenants 46, Smith restated the Apostle Paul's point in 1 Corinthians that gifts of the Spirit were given to bless the church.[96] Smith went even further, declaring that the Spirit of God gives gifts to every individual, and the Lord gives unto the leader of the Church of Christ *all* the gifts to bless and benefit the whole church.[97] This leader in the Latter-day Saint Church is the senior high priest in the Melchizedek Priesthood and the president of the church. His responsibility is to be like Moses: "a seer, a revelator, a translator, and a prophet having all the gifts of God which he bestows upon the head of the church."[98] From this point of view, the same principles, ordinances, organization, priesthood offices, knowledge, and gifts of the Spirit as found in the ancient church were integral parts of Smith's restoration.

ARTICLE 8: *We believe the Bible to be the word of God as far as it is translated correctly; we also believe the Book of Mormon to be the word of God.*

Article 8 establishes the importance of scripture. In this article, Smith first stated a belief in the Bible and then placed the Book of Mormon next to it, calling each the "word of God." In the Wentworth Letter he explained that the Book of Mormon was to "be united with the Bible for the accomplishment of the purposes of God in the last days."[99] For Latter-day Saints, each book presupposes a belief in the other; unfortunately, many underestimate the importance of the Bible to Mormons.[100] For example, the Bible informs Mormonism's origins and character, thus making it a far more expansive and complex part of the religion than some realize. As Mormon scholar Philip Barlow explains, the Bible underlies Smith's "extravagant doctrines, policies, priesthoods, keys, revelation, ordinances and actions." He was "restoring proper relations and order in time and eternity."[101] Acceptance of the Bible and the Book of Mormon into the Latter-day Saint canon indicated that the ancient prophetic office, with the gifts of seership and revelation, was functioning and that the canon of scripture was open—the Book of Mormon acted as a second witness of the Bible and Jesus Christ.[102]

Sola scriptura, the doctrine of relying on "the scripture alone" as the anchor of religious authority, and "biblical inerrancy," the conviction that the original manuscripts of the Bible were "without error or mistake," were strongly held beliefs of Protestants, including Campbell, in the early American republic.[103] The balance, however, between biblical and traditional authority in the form of creeds was subject to debate.[104] Smith, having essentially completed his inspired translation of the Old and New Testaments by the time he wrote the Articles of Faith, added an interesting caveat to the Mormon belief in the Bible in contrast to the ideas of *sola scriptura* and biblical inerrancy: "as far as it is translated correctly." This statement probably referred more to transmission, such as copying, adding to, taking from, and interpreting, than to translation of language.[105] In 1832, referring to revelations he had thus far received, Smith commented, "It was apparent that many important points, touching the salvation of man, had been taken from the Bible, or lost before it was compiled."[106] In 1830, shortly after the publication of the Book of Mormon and organization of the Church of Christ, Smith claimed he was commanded by God to begin work on revising the Bible. He introduced a significant number of additions, clarifications, and revisions.[107] Notwithstanding errors and deletions, his high regard for the Bible and obedience to the laws of God was evident, as shown in this remark recorded by New York journalist Matthew Davis at a Washington, DC, lecture in 1840. Holding up the Bible, Smith made a remarkable statement to his audience: "I believe in this sacred volume. In it the Mormon faith is to be found. We teach nothing, but what the Bible teaches. We believe nothing but what is to be found in this Book."[108]

Early Latter-day Saint writers and missionaries almost always cited biblical rather than Book of Mormon passages in preaching the gospel.[109] After reading the Book of Mormon, early members in general did not pursue serious and persistent study of the text; what mattered most at that time was that such a book existed—a material witness that Smith's transcendent experiences actually occurred.[110]

The eighth article of faith encapsulates Smith's claim that the canon is not closed and that the prophetic office with the gifts of seership and revelation is functioning. It also affirms that the Bible *and* the Book of Mormon are "the word of God."

ARTICLE 9: *We believe all that God has revealed, all that He does now reveal, and we believe that He will yet reveal many great and important things pertaining to the Kingdom of God.*

The progressive nature of the Articles of Faith is particularly evident in article 9, which builds on previous statements regarding the Godhead, priesthood authority, prophetic and apostolic offices, the gift of prophecy, and an open canon. Despite the fact that most of the preachers of his day rejected his first vision, one Methodist preacher alleging that "it was all of the devil, that there were no such things as visions or revelations in these days; that all such things had ceased with the apostles,"[111] Smith announced that the heavens were again open because the kingdom of God was being established on the earth. The idea of direct, unmediated revelation from heavenly beings, although preposterous and offensive to many of his era, pervaded all that Joseph Smith did, beginning with the first vision and the many revelations he received until his untimely death.[112] This view of revelation was at the forefront of the conflict in Missouri. In "The Manifesto of the Mob," citizens of Jackson county considered the "pretended religious sect . . . styling themselves 'Mormons'" an important crisis to be dealt with peaceably or even forcibly. They deplored the Mormons' pretensions "to hold personal communication and converse face to face with the Most High God; to receive communications and revelations direct from heaven."[113] Smith's claims took aim at Christianity, asking a pointed question: "Did Christians truly believe in revelation? If believers in the Bible dismissed revelation in the present, could they defend revelation in the past?"[114]

Smith was once asked, "Is there anything in the Bible which licenses you to believe in revelation now a days?" He responded, "Is there anything that does not authorize us to believe so[?]; if there is, we have, as yet, not been able to find it." He then argued that if the canon of scriptures is full and therefore closed to more revelation, "there is a great defect in the book, or else it would have said so."[115] Belief in continuing written revelation presupposes that the canon cannot be closed and that more truth was revealed in the past and continues to the present day. The following quotation gives an idea of just how expansive Smith's views on revelation and open canon were:

> From what we can draw from the scriptures relative to the teaching of heaven, we are induced to think that much instruction has been given to man since the beginning which we do not possess now. This may not agree with the opinions of some of our friends who are bold to say that we have everything written in the Bible which God ever spoke to man since the world began, and that if He had ever said anything more we should certainly receive it. But we ask, does it remain for a people who never had faith enough to call down one scrap of revelation from heaven, and for all they have now are indebted to the faith of another

people who lived hundreds and thousands of years before them, does it remain for them to say how much God has spoken . . . [or] not spoken. . . . To say that God never said anything more to man than is there recorded, would be saying at once that we have at last received a revelation . . . for if any man has found out . . . that the Bible contains all that God ever revealed to man he ascertained it by an immediate revelation.[116]

In the Wentworth Letter, Smith included two specific heavenly experiences and a description of the Book of Mormon plates and the seer stones—which were "the medium" by which he "translated the record by the gift and power of God."[117] Thus, he made concrete claims both to new revelations and revelatory instruments. Taken alone, this article of faith intimates that only the canon of scripture is open— with *scripture* being defined as a revelation from God worthy of being recorded. The context of the Wentworth Letter, however, through specific references to heavenly visitations and an instrument—anciently called the "Urim and Thummim," which was used by Old Testament seers—provides clear evidence of his claims to prophecy, seership, and revelation through other means. Thus, "The Church of Jesus Christ of Latter-day Saints was not a static reproduction of the primitive Church, but was a growing, progressing church."[118] Article 9 is open-ended and expanding because of what it promises—continuing revelation to and for the church, which would be unveiled by great exertion. Through this principle, Smith declared that additional light and knowledge continues to be revealed to prophets, seers, and revelators today.

The words of Peter in the New Testament indicate that prior to the Second Coming of Jesus Christ, there would be a "restitution of all things, which God hath spoken by the mouth of all his holy prophets since the world began," and Smith believed he was to be the fulfiller of that promise.[119] Although many unique beliefs and practices of the Latter-day Saints are not mentioned explicitly in the Articles of Faith, this article makes clear the belief that restoration of truth is open ended, that additional truths are expected to be revealed, and that continuing revelation and open canon are linked.

ARTICLE 10: *We believe in the literal gathering of Israel and in the restoration of the Ten Tribes; that Zion (the New Jerusalem)*[120] *will be built upon the American continent; that Christ will reign*

personally upon the earth; and, that the earth will be renewed
and receive its paradisiacal glory.

Early American theologians wrote about the Millennium, looking forward to that era, however, with mixed views on how it would ultimately come to pass. For example, Puritan clergyman and seventeenth-century colonist John Cotton (1585–1652), preeminent minister of the Massachusetts Bay Colony, believed that the world stood on the verge of a millennial age. However, it would be a spiritual coming of Christ, not his final return, and he would use magistrates and ministers to build the earthly New Jerusalem.[121] Puritan minister Cotton Mather (1663–1728), in the early eighteenth century, wrote that an earthly Millennium inaugurated by Christ would bring about the resurrection of the saints destined to rule with him and the destruction of the earth by fire before transforming it. Then the New Jerusalem would descend as a material but ethereal city, hovering in the air above the restored earthly Jerusalem. The end of the Millennium would be climaxed by Armageddon and the Second Resurrection, which would include the righteous and the unrighteous.[122] Jonathan Edwards (1703–1758), Congregationalist preacher and theologian in the mid-eighteenth century, believed that the revivals he was leading and experiencing in New England as part of the Great Awakening reflected God operating in human history and prefaced the Second Coming of Christ.[123] He described the millennial era in terms of excellence, proportion, and beauty. It would be a period characterized by an orderly society, one church, and agreement on important doctrines—all of which would precede the return of Christ.[124] He claimed "there was a growing conviction among Americans that it was their own country that was especially chosen by God for great things."[125] His was a postmillennialist view of history, meaning that a thousand years of peace and prosperity would unfold gradually, culminating with the Second Coming of Christ.

The Church of Jesus Christ of Latter-day Saints, by its name—*Latter-day Saints*—links itself to the apostolic-era Saints as well as to the last days, or the culminating dispensation of time prior to the Millennium. The beliefs expressed in article 10 are not unique to Smith and his followers; they address the religious and secular ideas of many nineteenth-century Americans regarding the end of time and the divine role of America. Millennialism—in its various types—is a worldview, or a comprehensive way of explaining human history and ultimate salvation.[126]

American religious historian Nathan Hatch proposes that the first generation of Americans after the Revolutionary War may have anticipated the Second Coming of Christ more intensely than any generation since.[127] The struggle for liberty and the rights of mankind in the American Revolution was religiously significant in that it "prepared the way" for the Second Coming of Jesus Christ—the past was prologue to a glorious future. Many Americans in the nineteenth century felt that the United States was God's own country, a "redeemer nation," and perhaps even the stage for the Second Coming and the site of the New Jerusalem, generally understood figuratively to be a collection of Christians.[128]

Smith was a premillennialist, a minority position among traditional religionists of his day, believing that Christ would literally return to the earth to usher in peace and reign for one thousand years on the earth at the beginning of the Millennium. Part of premillennialist belief included "two comings, two physical resurrections, and two judgments."[129] The faithful dead would be resurrected at the premillennial coming of Christ. The rest of humanity would be part of a second resurrection at the conclusion of the thousand years.

In 1835, Charles Finney announced that "the millennium may come in this country in three years."[130] William Miller, also a contemporary of Campbell and Smith, forerunner to the Seventh-day Adventist movement and leader of thousands, famously calculated that the Second Coming would take place between 21 March 1843 and 21 March 1844.[131] Seven or eight young men came to visit Joseph Smith in February 1843 to inquire about Miller's prediction. Smith pointed out fallacies in Miller's "data" (possibly *date*) concerning the Millennium and preached "quite a sermon," explaining errors in the Bible translation Miller had used and indicating "many more things [were to take place] before Christ [would] come."[132]

Regarding the events of the last dispensation and those leading up to the Millennium, Smith prophesied that there would be a literal gathering of Israel, the literal restoration of the "lost" Ten Tribes of Israel, and the literal building of Zion (New Jerusalem) in America. These proclamations of the *literal* nature of ancient prophecies were new ideas for most Christians. Zion was a commonly held but vague ideal among American Protestants; however, the idea of a specific place, a city development plan, and the building of a temple was unique to Smith. Concerning the gathering of the house of Israel, Smith observed, "[It] is an item which I esteem to be of the greatest importance to those who are looking for salvation in this generation. . . . All the prophets that have written . . . in speaking of the salvation of Israel in the last days, goes directly to show, that it consists in the work of gathering."[133] For Smith, the building of Zion included both a spiritual and temporal gathering—a uniting of heaven and earth to bring about God's purposes. An editorial for the *Times and Seasons* made the following observations about the creation of Zion:

> The building up of Zion is a cause that has interested the people of God in every age; it is a theme upon which prophets, priests, and kings have dwelt with peculiar delight; they have looked forward with joyful anticipation to the day in which we lived; and fired with heavenly and joyful anticipations they have sung, and wrote, and prophesied of this our day. . . . We are the favored people that God has made choice of to bring about the Latter Day glory; it is left for us to see, participate in, and help to roll forward the Latter Day glory; "the dispensation of the fulness of times, when God will gather together all things that are in heaven, and all things that are upon the earth, even in one."[134]

In time, the "lost tribes of Israel" would also be gathered to their homelands.[135] One of the purposes for the gathering was to find protection from the apocalypse that would occur prior to Christ's literal one-thousand-year reign on the earth.[136]

Smith also taught that earth would be transfigured into a paradise, similar to the Edenic state lost at the Fall of Adam and Eve. He promised that "the earth shall yield its increase, resume its paradisean glory, and become as the garden of the Lord."[137] Perhaps most unique to Smith was that he saw all of these events as actual rather than merely symbolic or figurative promises. This article of faith includes the powerful fulfillment of God's covenants in very literal ways: the gathering, the city of Zion, the millennial reign of Christ, and a renewal of the earth to the beauty of Eden.

Smith's premillennialism included a belief that the Millennium would take place on the earth among a collective group of faithful Christians, would cause a complete transformation of life on earth, and would showcase a miraculous coming of Christ that was imminent and swift.[138] He also believed that humanity had important work to accomplish before the Second Coming; nevertheless, the Millennium would not be a product of man's accomplishment—it would be brought about by power and divine intervention.

The next three articles of faith are not unique to Joseph Smith's restoration; instead, they affirm their agreement with the basic tenets of the Constitution of the United States of America and Christian virtues.

ARTICLE 11: *We claim the privilege of worshiping Almighty God according to the dictates of our own conscience, and allow all men the same privilege, let them worship how, where, or what they may.*

This is the only article of faith that begins with "we claim" rather than "we believe," which gives it a stronger tone. During the colonial era, the families who separated themselves from the Church of England and escaped to practice religious freedom in the New World often felt justified in refusing that freedom to other religionists once they were entrenched in an area. With the United States Constitution announcing toleration for religious pluralism, however, most of the thirteen states followed suit and began to disestablish religious preferences and financial backing, some states taking longer than others, and some religions still experienced persecution throughout the nineteenth century.[139]

Smith claimed, "I am the greatest advocate of the C. [Constitution] of [the] U.S. . . . The only fault I can find with it is it is not broad enough to cover the whole ground."[140] Despite Smith's views of the Constitution's limitations, he announced in a revelation recorded in December 1833 that God had "raised up" wise men for the purpose of establishing the Constitution and the laws governing the United States in order to protect the rights of individuals to choose him.[141]

Basic to Smith's early training by his father was a belief in liberty of conscience regarding religious beliefs. In 1843, he declared:

> If it has been demonstrated that I have been willing to die for a Mormon, I am bold to declare before heaven that I am just as ready to die in defending the rights of a Presbyterian, a Baptist or a good man of any other denomination; for the same principle which would trample upon the rights of the Latter day Saints would trample upon the rights of the other denomination <Roman Catholics> or of any other denomination who may be unpopular and too weak to defend themselves. It is a love of liberty which inspires my Soul, civil and religious liberty to the whole of the human race.[142]

Latter-day Saints were victims of persecution motivated in great part by religious intolerance in New York, Missouri, Ohio, and Illinois.

In the Wentworth Letter, Smith gave a brief history of Latter-day Saint persecution and ridicule, beginning with the coming forth of the Book of Mormon and particularly delineating the inhumane treatment they received in four counties in Missouri. These experiences led Smith to declare in this Article of Faith the wisdom of the principle that government and public officials should maintain respectful neutrality in matters of worship.

Stronger statements on the institution of religion are found in the Doctrine and Covenants. Originally, section 134 of the Doctrine and Covenants included a preamble clarifying its purpose: "That our belief with regard to earthly governments and laws in general may not be misinterpreted nor misunderstood." This declaration, titled "Of Governments and Laws in General," was written by Oliver Cowdery, Smith's primary translation scribe, and it expressed God's sovereignty over humans and declared that they had no right to contravene the religious liberty of others in any way except when it infringes on the rights of others or is contrary to the laws of the land. Further, the declaration stated that civil government should confine itself to laws of protection against crime but never limit free exercise of religious belief, control conscience, or suppress the freedom of the soul.[143] The Latter-day Saints had been accused by their enemies of being opposed to law and order, and the statements in section 134 were a rebuttal to those false allegations.

That Smith accepted Cowdery's declaration as containing true principles is evident in this article of faith. In essence, Smith encouraged that he and his followers assert their God-given privilege to worship God in their own manner and allow all others the same right. From a religious point of view, Smith saw that religious freedom meant that the government recognized and protected an inalienable right from God to exercise religious beliefs and practices.

ARTICLE 12: *We believe in being subject to kings, presidents, rulers, and magistrates, in obeying, honoring, and sustaining the law.*

The early Latter-day Saints probably appeared to be insular, separatist, or at least clannish, because faithful members would gather to specific areas to build up Zion, to live the law of consecration, and to escape the impending destruction associated with the Second Coming of Christ.[144] Latter-day Saints were law-abiding citizens; however, their thoughts initially were more on building Zion than on the nature of government.[145]

In 1839, Smith declared that "the Constitution of the United States is a glorious standard[;] it is founded in the Wisdom of God. [It] is a heavenly banner."[146] In fact, Smith called the Constitution "true" in the same breath that he called God, the Bible, the Book of Mormon, the Book of Covenants, Christ, and ministering angels true. Nevertheless, he was sensitive to its failure to protect the religious rights of the Mormons. The government—regional, state, and national—failed to preserve his people's freedom of religion and made no provision for the punishment of government officials who refused to protect them against mobs or others who interfered with these rights.

As expressed in the 1842 Wentworth Letter, church members had been harshly, unfairly, and illegally treated, particularly by Governor Boggs of Missouri. The fact that Smith sought redress of the church's claims in the courts of Missouri and with United States president Martin Van Buren demonstrated that the Latter-day Saints recognized the importance of leaders and laws that could protect them.

While Smith declared in this article that men are subject to a variety of governments, he was also aware that the government of God is very different. It always promotes "peace, unity, harmony, strength and happiness; while that of man has been productive of confusion, disorder, weakness and misery."[147] Not defining a particular type of government, Smith affirmed that God loves order and good government and declared, "We believe that governments were instituted of God for the benefit of man; and that he holds men accountable for their acts in relation to them, both in making laws and administering them, for the good and safety of society."[148]

ARTICLE 13: *We believe in being honest, true, chaste, benevolent, virtuous, and in doing good to all men; indeed, we may say that we follow the admonition of Paul—We believe all things, we hope all things, we have endured many things, and hope to be able to endure all things. If there is anything virtuous, lovely, or of good report or praiseworthy, we seek after these things.*

This article does not declare belief in a particular doctrine; instead, it includes the "admonitions" of Paul to the Philippians and sentiments of Peter in his two epistles.[149] Like most restorationists, Smith felt a close affinity with the Apostle Paul. He quoted Paul, commented often on his teachings, and likened his own feelings when retelling his first vision to Paul's defense of his vision of Jesus Christ before King Agrippa.

Placing this as the culminating statement in a set of beliefs, Smith used this article to identify the relationship between all the previously stated doctrines and everyday ethical beliefs and actions. This ultimate statement taught that personal conduct must be consistent with professed beliefs and that honesty and all other virtues grow out of a belief in the gospel of Jesus Christ. Similarly, Jonathan Edwards's writings about "Holy Affections" or virtues explained that "strong inclinations of the soul that are manifested in thinking, feeling and acting" are essential to true spirituality because they lie at the heart of an individual. Nevertheless, "holy affections are not heat without light."[150] To Edwards, the practice of true religion and a holy Christian life were based in both beliefs *and* feelings, insisting that keeping the commandments and doing good works were "the chief of all the signs" regarding grace.[151] From this point of view, the holy virtues, devoid of the foundation of the doctrines of Christ, were a system of ethics lacking a firm foundation.

In the thirteenth article, Smith recognized that the revealed religion God restored through him had no saving power unless it was active in the lives of those who professed belief. While languishing with six others in jail in Liberty, Missouri, Smith penned a letter to the Saints who were being driven out of Missouri under an order of extermination in the winter of 1838–39. "How much more dignified and noble are the thoughts of God," he wrote, lamenting how low, mean, vulgar, and condescending had been their public as well as private interactions. He also exhorted the church members "to a reformation. . . . Let honesty, and sobriety, and candor, and solemnity, and virtue, and pureness, and meekness, and simplicity crown our heads in every place."[152] Religion is much more than mere mental assent to doctrines; living and seeking after the highest moral and ethical standards must become a natural part of an individual's life.[153] Regardless of government action or inaction, the Saints were to be good neighbors and good people, even among those who might feel threatened by them.

Just as the fruits of the Spirit accompany the gift of the Holy Ghost, so do morality, chastity, virtue, benevolence, and all other praiseworthy values follow as fruits of living gospel principles.[154] Smith stated, "We believe all things, we hope all things, we have endured many things, and hope to be able to endure all things." The New Testament Apostle Paul and the Book of Mormon prophet Moroni both identified essential gospel virtues as faith, hope, and charity—virtues that have the promise of helping an individual endure all the trials of mortality. Without them, an individual would not become like Christ, which is the essential quest of mortality.[155]

The final sentence in this article implores Latter-day Saints to seek good wherever and with whomever it may be found. These are worthy sentiments, but difficult in practice. Alexander Campbell probably would have liked this article of faith. He loved the epistles of Paul and Peter and believed that true Christianity is not merely the "acknowledgment of [it as] a good rule, but the walking by it that secures the happiness of society."[156]

CONCLUSION

Smith addressed many of the fundamental questions of Christianity—ideas that had divided Catholics and, later, Protestants since the "falling away" and the death of the original Apostles.[157] These divisions had continued to Campbell's and Smith's day. The multiplication of sects in America was based on differences of opinion and the freedom both to disagree and to start new churches.

Writing in the genre of Protestant confessions, Smith followed the established system in responding to a request for an explanation of the Latter-day Saint faith by writing the Articles of Faith. They begin with the Godhead as the overarching doctrine under which all other beliefs are subsumed, and are followed by the essential truths regarding the nature of man and the Atonement of Christ. Subsequent to these doctrines is the method through which salvation can be accessed individually. Next is the absolute necessity of having authority from God in order to perform the ordinances pertaining to salvation. After establishing the need for priesthood authority comes an explanation of the organization of the church in which that authority resides: first, the foundation of apostles and prophets through whom this authority is directed, and second, the gifts of the Spirit that follow acceptance of saving ordinances and are also signs of apostolic authority and the true church.

Furthermore, Smith's statements on scripture, both ancient and modern, illustrate its importance in helping believers learn the word of God, thus confirming the existence of both the primitive and latter-day prophetic office and gift of revelation. By restoring the ancient offices, Smith expressed indirectly that the priesthood keys for gathering Israel and reestablishing Zion were again on the earth. In order for these tasks to be accomplished, freedom to exercise moral agency must be unfettered, and governments must allow individuals to worship freely. Nevertheless, God requires order and obedience to civil authority, indicating that in his own time, freedom to act on choices must and will be available to all the earth's inhabitants. Finally, as a consequence of understanding and obeying the foregoing doctrines and principles of the gospel, honesty, loyalty, chastity, benevolence, and all the other Christ-like virtues will naturally grace and characterize the nature of such individuals.

Statements of belief were the norm for the religious faiths of Smith's day. Although Smith may have used similar terminology and format, many of his explanations were significantly different from the beliefs of other Christian groups, including Campbell's. In the new era of religious liberty, which spawned innumerable new denominations, Smith not only responded succinctly to the great theological questions but also put in place many of the foundational doctrines as part of the "restoration of all things" to which Mormonism is anchored.

NOTES

1. See Appendix 12, "The Wentworth Letter," in *Encyclopedia of Mormonism*, ed. Daniel H. Ludlow (New York: Macmillan, 1992), 4: 1750–55.

2. Not all Latter-day Saint scholars agree with this chapter's assessment that the Articles of Faith were written as a response to the religious controversies of Joseph Smith's time, but T. Edgar Lyon and Edward J. Brandt do. T. Edgar Lyon, "Origin and Purpose of the Articles of Faith," *Instructor* 87 (August–October 1952): 230–31, 264–65, 275, 298–99, 319; T. Edgar Lyon, "Doctrinal Development of the Church During the Nauvoo Sojourn, 1839–1846," *BYU Studies* 15, no. 4 (Summer 1975): 446; Edward J. Brandt, "The Origin and Importance of the Articles of Faith," in *Studies in Scripture*, vol. 2, *The Pearl of Great Price*, ed. Robert L. Millet and Kent P. Jackson (Salt Lake City: Randall Book, 1985), 18. David Whittaker states that T. Edgar Lyon was the first Latter-day Saint historian to suggest that the Articles of Faith were a response to the major religious questions of Joseph Smith's day. David Whittaker, "The 'Articles of Faith' in Early Mormon Literature and Thought," in *New Views of Mormon History: A Collection of Essays in Honor of Leonard J. Arrington*, ed. Davis Bitton and Maureen Ursenbach Beecher (Salt Lake City: University of Utah, 1987), 75. See also Stephen P. Sondrup, "On Confessing Belief: Thoughts on the Language of the Articles of Faith," in *Literature of Belief*, ed. Neal E. Lambert (Provo, UT: Religious Studies Center, 1981), 201–2. Welch and Whittaker, for example, posit that the lack of "argumentative language" makes this point of view unlikely. They emphasize Joseph Smith's declarative and affirmative approach to a broad scope of gospel principles. Welch and Whittaker, "We Believe . . . Development of the Articles of Faith," *Ensign*, September 1979, 54.

3.	Earlier statements of Mormon beliefs also are found in the writings of Oliver Cowdery, Joseph Young, Parley P. Pratt, Orson Pratt, and Orson Hyde. For a brief summary of these authors and their writings, see Whittaker, "The 'Articles of Faith' in Early Mormon Literature and Thought," 64, 67–73. See also, Woodford, "The Articles and Covenants of the Church of Christ and the Book of Mormon," 103–13; David Whittaker, "Articles of Faith," in *Encyclopedia of Mormonism*, 1:68–69; Pratt, *Autobiography of Parley P. Pratt*, 181–82.

4.	For example, see the New Hampshire Baptist Confession (1833), Philadelphia Articles of Faith (1790), and Winchester Profession (1803). Philip Schaff, *The Creeds of Christendom* (Grand Rapids, MI: Baker Books, 1931), 3:738–56; John H. Leith, ed., *Creeds of the Churches* (Chicago: Aldine Publishing, 1963), 354–60.

5.	In 1851, Elder Franklin D. Richards, a member of the Quorum of the Twelve Apostles and mission president in England, compiled previously published church literature for the British Latter-day Saints that included the Articles of Faith and titled the compilation the Pearl of Great Price, bringing them into Latter-day Saint usage and eventually into their scriptural canon. John A. Widtsoe, *The Articles of Faith in Everyday Life* (Salt Lake City: Presiding Bishopric of The Church of Jesus Christ of Latter-day Saints, 1951), 15; Brandt, "The Origin and Importance of the Articles of Faith," 18. The Pearl of Great Price was presented before the church in 1880 for approval under the direction of President John Taylor. Due to some confusion on the scriptural status of the Articles of Faith, they were presented again in 1890. H. Donl Peterson, "The Birth and Development of the Pearl of Great Price," in *Studies in Scripture*, vol. 2, *The Pearl of Great Price*, 12, 19–20.

6.	Donald Q. Cannon, "Reverend George Moore Comments on Nauvoo, the Mormons, and Joseph Smith," *Western Illinois Regional Studies* 5 (Spring 1982): 8, 10–11.

7.	Bushman, *Joseph Smith: Rough Stone Rolling*, 458.

8.	Smith used both "Holy Ghost" and "Holy Spirit" interchangeably but generally appeared to prefer "Holy Ghost." Campbell, on the other hand, exclusively used the term "Holy Spirit."

9.	Unitarians confined the "glory and attributes of divinity to the Father, and not allowing it to the Son or Holy Spirit." Buck, *A Theological Dictionary*, s.v. "Unitarians." Early on, Joseph Smith's father, Joseph Smith Sr., and grandfather Asael both flirted with Universalism, the "country cousin" of Unitarianism. Joseph Smith Jr., on the other hand, attended a debate club which, according to Bushman, "very likely . . . raised the question of how to know of God's existence." Bushman, *Joseph Smith and the Beginnings of Mormonism*, 28, 36, 55; Williams, *America's Religions: From Their Origins to the Twenty-First Century*, 220–22. See also Lyon, "Origin and Purpose of the Articles of Faith," 231.

10.	Givens, *Wrestling the Angel*, 70.

11.	Matthew Davis, in a letter to his wife, Mary Davis, 6 February 1840, History, 1838–1856, volume C-1 [2 November 1838–31 July 1842], 1014, http://www.joseph smithpapers.org.

12.	Doctrine and Covenants 20:17–29; 130:22. For a listing of First Vision accounts, see Jessee, "The Earliest Documented Accounts of Joseph Smith's First Vision," 1–33. In Smith's first and briefest recounting of this vision, written in 1832 by his own hand, he mentions only his conversation with Jesus. Later, he retells many more details of this vision, including the fact that God appeared first and introduced his Son, who then speaks to him. Karen Lynn Davidson, David J. Whittaker, Richard L. Jensen, and Mark Ashurst-McGee, eds. *Histories, Volume 1: Joseph Smith Histories, 1832–1844*, vol. 1 of the Histories series of *The Joseph Smith Papers*, edited by Dean C. Jessee, Ronald K. Esplin, and Richard Lyman Bushman (Salt Lake City: Church Historian's Press, 2012).

13. The Nicene Creed was formulated in the fourth century in response to theological disputes over the nature of Christ and the Godhead. It affirms the idea that the divinity of Christ is of the same substance as the divinity of God, thus guarding the unity of the Trinity. This creed is accepted by Roman Catholics and most Protestants. It also begins with the phrase "we or I believe." This doctrine, primarily the work of Augustine, was declared in response to the radical views of Marcion and Arius regarding Christ. "It is important to note that no important Christian theologian has argued that there are three self-conscious beings in the godhead. On the contrary, Augustine's favorite analogy for the triune god was one self-conscious-ness with its three distinctions of intellect, will, and the bond between them." Harvey, *A Handbook of Theological Terms*, s.v. "trinity." David Paulsen, a Latter-day Saint scholar, has described this Latter-day Saint view of the Godhead as a variation on "social trinitarianism." Paulsen, "Are Mormons Trinitarians?" *Modern Reformation* 12, no. 6 (November/December 2003): 40. Sterling McMurrin, using earlier phil-osophical terminology, wrote about the "tritheistic conception of the Godhead, where the Father, Son, and Holy Ghost are described as three ontologically separate beings." It appears that the former term refers to the united relationship among the members of the Godhead—how they are one—while the latter focuses on their indi-viduality—how they are separate. Both are accurate conceptions of Joseph Smith's teachings. For a more complete explication of the social model of the Godhead, including Smith's views compared with those of other Christians, see David Paulsen, "Are Christians Mormon? Reassessing Joseph Smith's Theology in His Bicentennial," *BYU Studies* 45, no. 1 (2006): 28–38.
14. See, for example, 2 Nephi 31:21; Alma 11:44; 3 Nephi 11:27, 36; Mormon 7:7 (Book of Mormon).
15. Mormon 9:9 (Book of Mormon); see also Hebrews 13:8.
16. Moses 7:28–29, 32–33 (Pearl of Great Price).
17. Alma 7:12 (Book of Mormon).
18. Truman Coe, "Mormonism," *The Ohio Observer* (Hudson), 11 August 1836, 1–2.
19. Joseph Smith, Discourse, Nauvoo, IL, 5 January 1841, in L. John Nuttall, journal, L. John Nuttall Papers, BYU, 7, http://www.josephsmithpapers.org.
20. Account of Meeting, [16 February 1841], as Reported by William P. McIntire, 11–12, http://www.josephsmithpapers.org.
21. Account of Meeting, [9 March 1841], as Reported by William P. McIntire, 14, http://www.josephsmithpapers.org.
22. Doctrine and Covenants 130:22. To examine the history of the Mormon understand-ing of the nature of God in the 1830s, see David Paulsen, "The Doctrine of Divine Embodiment: Restoration, Judeo-Christian, and Philosophical Perspectives," *BYU Studies* 35, no. 4 (1995): 4.
23. 1 Corinthians 15:50; Joseph Smith, 20 March 1842, in *Wilford Woodruff's Journal*, ed. Scott G. Kenney (Midvale, UT: Signature Books, 1983), 2:163.
24. Smith, 16 June 1844, "Thomas Bullock Report," in *Words of Joseph Smith*, 378.
25. Paulsen, "Are Christians Mormon?," 28. Ontological and metaphysical are phil-osophical abstractions regarding the existence of God. This view is sometimes referred to as Social Trinitarianism.
26. Smith, 16 June 1844, "Thomas Bullock Report," in *Words of Joseph Smith*, 380.
27. Smith, 11 June 1843, "Joseph Smith Diary," by Willard Richards, in *Words of Joseph Smith*, 212.
28. Doctrine and Covenants 130:22.
29. Letter to Moses Nickerson, 19 November 1833, 64–65, http://www.josephsmith papers.org.

30. Manuscript History of the Church, 1838–1856, volume A-1 [23 December 1805–30 August 1834], 227, http://www.josephsmithpapers.org.

31. See Paulsen, "Are Christians Mormon?," 30.

32. Givens, *Wrestling the Angel*, 101.

33. History, 1838–1856, volume C-1 [2 November 1838–31 July 1842], 1014, http://www.josephsmithpapers.org.

34. Account of Meeting, [9 February 1841], as Reported by William P. McIntire, 11, http://www.josephsmithpapers.org. Prior to eating from the tree of knowledge, Adam and Eve were called "innocent" and incapable of rebellion, see 2 Nephi 2:23 (Book of Mormon). In Latter-day Saint vocabulary, their disobedience is referred to as a *transgression* rather than a *sin*. See also Moses 3:17 (Pearl of Great Price).

35. History, 1838–1856, volume C-1 [2 November 1838–31 July 1842], 1014, http://www.josephsmithpapers.org. For two different views on the nature of humankind, see George T. Boyd, "A Mormon Concept of Man," and Rodney Turner, "The Moral Dimensions of Man: A Scriptural View," *Dialogue* 3, no. 1 (Spring 1968): 57–82.

36. Moses 6:54 (Pearl of Great Price). The "Joseph Smith Translation of the Bible" was begun in June 1830, with numerous individuals acting as scribes. Corrections were made to both the Old and New Testaments. The largest addition has come to be known as the "Book of Moses," which adds whole chapters to the Genesis account and is found in the Pearl of Great Price.

37. Manuscript History of the Church, 1838–1856, volume A-1 [23 December 1805–30 August 1834], 380–381, http://www.josephsmithpapers.org.

38. Manuscript History of the Church, 1838–1856, volume C-1 [2 November 1838–31 July 1842], 1202, http://www.josephsmithpapers.org.

39. Joseph Smith, 14 May 1843, in *Wilford Woodruff's Journal*, 2:230. See also Doctrine and Covenants 121:35–39.

40. Manuscript History of the Church, 1838–1856, volume C-1 [2 November 1838–31 July 1842], 1014, http://www.josephsmithpapers.org.

41. Doctrine and Covenants 101:78. Lyon, "Origin and Purpose of the Articles of Faith," 264. The term "moral agency" indicates that choice is a God-given blessing and means that all are accountable for their own sins at judgment, as recorded in Doctrine and Covenants 101:78. Charles Buck, an advocate of "free agency" as opposed to "free will," defined the latter term as an Arminian notion that "claims a part, yea the very turning point of salvation. . . . We need only certain helps or assistances, granted to men in common, to enable us to choose the path of life." On the other hand, "free agency" requires "an almighty and invincible Power to renew them" because "our hearts [are] by nature wholly depraved." Buck, *Theological Dictionary*, s.v. "free agency." Louis Midgely, writing on Calvin's idea of "free will," declares that it means "the human will is free to do as one desires" and at the same time insists that "all desires are strictly given to human beings and hence are firmly determined by God. So from this perspective, one is merely free to do what one was predestined to desire." Louis Midgely, "Confronting Five Point Calvinism," *Interpreter: A Journal of Mormon Scripture* 4 (2013): 85–92. Historian Mark Noll listed six beliefs regarding the nature of humans that refuted original sin and championed choice: "1) Humans did not *have* a sinful nature inherited from Adam but were influenced by the overwhelmingly comprehensive influence of the fall of humanity to *become* sinners; 2) Humans were by nature free, which meant an ability to choose with liberty against powerful motives or personal character as it had developed; 3) Thus, the great problem for humanity was that people chose to sin and, thus, because of those choices, were constituted sinful; 4) God was in no sense responsible for sin, either Adam's or anyone else's, and so he was completely free to condemn sinners and their sin because he had absolutely nothing to do with how

it came about; 5) God redeemed those individuals who, under the prompting of the Holy Spirit yet of their own free will, chose to turn to him in repentance and faith; 6) Finally, since redemption was God's loving response accomplished through the Holy Spirit prompting the sinner's choice, redeemed sinners could and should go on to seek the Christian perfection that God in Scripture promised to believers who sought him with their whole heart." Noll declared, "No major theologian affirmed all these countertraditional positions completely, or without explanation, but Unitarians, Finneyite revivalists, and sometimes New Haven theologians came close." Noll, *America's God*, 266–67. Joseph Smith would have agreed with all of the "countertraditional" positions that Noll listed.

42. 2 Nephi 2:22–23 (Book of Mormon).

43. Smith took issue with Luther and many Protestants in explaining salvation by grace. See 2 Nephi 25:23 (Book of Mormon); Mosiah 3:17 (Book of Mormon); Acts 4:7–12.

44. Bruce L. Shelley, *Church History in Plain Language*, 2nd ed. (Nashville: Thomas Nelson, 1995), 129. Pelagianism is identified as an early Christian heresy that denies the need for grace in salvation.

45. The origin of these issues stems from the Augustinian-Pelagian debates of the fourth and fifth centuries, which centered on original sin, humankind's depravity, and thus humankind's ability to exercise free will. Luther set forth *sola fide*, or salvation by faith alone. This was rejected by the Catholic Council of Trent in the sixteenth century, which said that salvation is by faith and works—sacraments and lives of moral rectitude. Catholic sacraments—baptism, Eucharist, reconciliation, confirmation, marriage, holy orders, and anointing of the sick—are similar to some Mormon ordinances. Today, some consider Latter-day Saints as non-Christians due to the false view that their beliefs are Pelagian—meaning saved by their righteous works.

46. Universalism or universal redemption is suggested in the Greek word *apocatasis* [apokatastasis], found in Acts 3:21, expanding the meaning of the "restitution of all things" to mean that all will be saved. Harvey, *A Handbook of Theological Terms*, s.v. "*apocatasis*."

47. Bushman, *Joseph Smith and the Beginnings of Mormonism*, 27, 36.

48. To appreciate the radical nature of this pronouncement, one must realize that from a Calvinist point of view, "only fringe theologians held that humans assisted in their own salvation." Noll, *America's God*, 28.

49. Alma 34:37 (Book of Mormon); Philippians 2:12.

50. 2 Nephi 26:33 (Book of Mormon).

51. 2 Nephi 26:28 (Book of Mormon).

52. 2 Nephi 26:33 (Book of Mormon).

53. 2 Nephi 26:27 (Book of Mormon).

54. 2 Nephi 25:23 (Book of Mormon). See also 2 Nephi 2:8 and Mosiah 4:19–20 (Book of Mormon).

55. 2 Nephi 2:8 (Book of Mormon).

56. 2 Nephi 2:14, 16, 27 (Book of Mormon).

57. History, 1838–1856, volume C-1 [2 November 1838–31 July 1842], 1202, http://www.josephsmithpapers.org.

58. Abraham 3:27 (Pearl of Great Price).

59. Moses 7:39 (Pearl of Great Price).

60. One of Campbell's first outlines from "Skeletons of Sermons" addressed God's relationship with humans as covenantal from the book of Hebrews, with Adam and Noah as examples. Alexander Campbell, "Journal of a voyage from Ireland towards America 1808," Manuscript D 40R to 43L.

61. 2 Nephi 31:2; 3 Nephi 11:31–40; 3 Nephi 27:13 (Book of Mormon).

62. *History of the Church*, 4:42.

63. Moroni 8:25–26. Smith simply declared, "A man may be saved, after the judgment, in the terrestrial kingdom, or in the telestial kingdom, but he can never see the celestial kingdom of God, without being born of water and the Spirit." "To the Honorable Men of the World," *Evening and Morning Star* 1, no. 3 (August 1832): 39. W. W. Phelps was the editor of the newspaper; however, this was an unsigned editorial, and Joseph Smith's input into it is unknown.

64. History, 1838–1856, volume E-1 [1 July 1843–30 April 1844], 1687, http://www.josephsmithpapers.org.

65. Report of Instructions, between 26 June and 2 July 1839, as Reported by Willard Richards, 15, http://www.josephsmithpapers.org.

66. History, 1838–1856, volume D-1 [1 August 1842–1 July 1843], 1530, http://www.josephsmithpapers.org.

67. See Moroni 8:5–15 (Book of Mormon).

68. See Doctrine and Covenants 68:25, 27.

69. Joseph Smith, 20 March 1842, in *Wilford Woodruff's Journal*, 2:160. See also Manuscript History of the Church, 1838–1856, volume C-1 [2 November 1838–31 July 1842], 1296, www.josephsmithpapers.org.

70. Mosiah 3:16 (Book of Mormon).

71. Smith, "Joseph Smith Diary," 9 July 1843, by Willard Richards in *Words of Joseph Smith*, 229–30.

72. "Baptism," *Times and Seasons* 3, no. 21 (1 September 1842): 904.

73. See Doctrine and Covenants 22:1–4.

74. Manuscript History of the Church, 1838–1856, volume C-1 [2 November 1838–31 July 1842], 1229, http://www.josephsmithpapers.org.

75. 2 Nephi 31:13, 14, 21 (Book of Mormon).

76. History, 1838–1856, volume C-1 [2 November 1838–31 July 1842], 8 [addenda], http://www.josephsmithpapers.org.

77. See Acts 8:16–18.

78. John 3:5.

79. Joseph Smith, "Joseph Smith Diary, July 9, 1843," by Willard Richards, in *Words of Joseph Smith*, 230.

80. Discourse, 7 April 1844, as Reported by *Times and Seasons*, 617, http://www.josephsmithpapers.org.

81. Campbell, "Brother Semple, Query 5," *Millennial Harbinger* 1, no. 8 (August 1830): 357–58.

82. Campbell, "Abrogation of the Sabbath," *Millennial Harbinger* 40, no. 3 (March 1869): 144.

83. One of the crusades by Methodists, Baptists, Christians, Universalists, and Disciples was against the Calvinist orthodoxy and its "ordered and predictable form of religious experience." Hatch, *The Democratization of American Christianity*, 170. See also Holifield, *Theology in America*, 42.

84. Pratt, *The Autobiography of Parley P. Pratt*, 22–23. Mr. Rigdon was Pratt's immediate Reforming Baptist minister, who followed Mr. Campbell's restoration teachings.

85. Pratt, *The Autobiography of Parley P. Pratt*, 52.

86. Joseph Smith—History 1:68–72; Doctrine and Covenants 13. Smith recorded that in May 1829—prior to the organization of the church, while translating the Book of Mormon—he and Oliver Cowdery went into the woods to ask God regarding "baptism for the remission of sins." In response to their prayer, John the Baptist appeared and conferred upon them the keys of the Aaronic Priesthood. Within a short time, Smith and Cowdery announced that Peter, James, and John had also conferred upon them the keys of the Melchizedek Priesthood. Doctrine and Covenants 27:12–13; 128:20.

87. Smith, "Wentworth Letter."
88. See Ephesians 2:20. None of the Protestant sects of the nineteenth century claimed the restoration of the priesthood, although a few individuals claimed to be prophets. Richard H. Brodhead, "Prophets in America ca. 1830: Emerson, Nat Turner, Joseph Smith," *Journal of Mormon History* 29, no. 1 (Spring 2003): 42–65.
89. These two callings were part of what James Haldane called "extraordinary," whereas the other offices he called "stated." Haldane, *A View of the Social Worship and Ordinances Observed by the First Christians*, 215.
90. History, 1838–1856, volume C-1 [2 November 1838–31 July 1842], 9 [addenda], http://www.josephsmithpapers.org; Genesis 49.
91. Grant Underwood, "The 'Same' Organization That Existed in the Primitive Church," in *Go Ye Into All the World: Messages of the New Testament Apostles*, 31st Annual Sidney B. Sperry Symposium, ed. Ray L. Huntington, Patty Smith, Thomas A. Wayment, and Jerome M. Perkins (Salt Lake City: Deseret Book, 2002), 168–69. Underwood discusses the meanings of the Greek words in Ephesians 4:11 that have been translated as apostles, prophets, pastors, teachers, and evangelists.
92. Mark 16:15–18.
93. Pratt, *Autobiography of Parley P. Pratt*, 12.
94. "Gift of the Holy Ghost," *Times and Seasons* 3, no. 16 (15 June 1842): 823; History, 1838–1856, volume C-1 Addenda, 64, http://www.josephsmithpapers.org.
95. History, 1838–1856, volume B-1 [1 September 1834–2 November 1838], 554, http://www.josephsmithpapers.org.
96. Doctrine and Covenants 46:10; 1 Corinthians 14:33.
97. Doctrine and Covenants 46:29; emphasis added.
98. Doctrine and Covenants 107:91–92.
99. Smith, "Wentworth Letter."
100. See 2 Nephi 3:12; 33:10; Mormon 7:8–9 (Book of Mormon).
101. Barlow, *Mormons and the Bible*, 29.
102. In 1982, a subtitle to the Book of Mormon, "Another Testament of Jesus Christ," was added.
103. Noll, *America's God*, 373.
104. Holifield, *Theology in America*, 29, 275, 344–45, 379.
105. In the seventeenth century, William Penn argued even "the utmost Dilligence" could offer no guarantee against "Translation, Transcription and Printing . . . Mistakes." Holland, *Sacred Borders*, 48.
106. "History of Joseph Smith, (cont.)," *Times and Seasons* 5, no. 14 (1 August 1844): 592; History, 1838–1856, volume A-1 [23 December 1805–30 August 1834], 183, http://www.josephsmithpapers.org.
107. Short additions, revisions, and clarifications can be found in the footnotes of the Latter-day Saint edition of the King James Bible. Larger additions are footnoted and can be found in an appendix at the end of the Latter-day Saint edition of the King James Bible. The greatest numbers of changes to the Bible are found in the Book of Moses (Genesis) and Matthew 24, found in the Pearl of Great Price.
108. Matthew Davis, in a letter to Mary Davis, History, 1838–1856, volume C-1 [2 November 1838–31 July 1842], 1014, http://www.josephsmithpapers.org.
109. Grant Underwood, "Book of Mormon Usage in Early LDS Theology," *Dialogue: A Journal of Mormon Thought* 17 (Fall 1984): 53.
110. Miller, *Rube Goldberg Machines*, 32.
111. Joseph Smith—History 1:21.
112. Givens, *By the Hand of Mormon*, 217.

113. "To His Excellency, Daniel Dunklin, Governor of the State of Missouri," *Evening and Morning Star* 2, no. 15 (December 1833): 114.
114. Richard L. Bushman, "A Joseph Smith for the Twenty-First Century," in *Believing History: Latter-day Saints*, ed. Reid L. Neilson and Jed Woodworth (New York: Columbia University, 2004), 273.
115. The questions posed were first recorded in *The Elder's Journal* 1, no. 2 (1837): 28–29 and answered in *The Elder's Journal* 1, no. 3 (1838): 43–44, http://www .josephsmithpapers.org. See also "History of Joseph Smith," *The Latter-day Saints' Millennial Star* 10, no. 16 (11 March 1854): 151. Some individuals have quoted Revelation 22:18 as confirmation that no more revelation should be added to the Bible; however, there is overwhelming consensus today among virtually all biblical scholars that this verse applies only to the book of Revelation, *not* the whole Bible. Nevertheless, it is not fair to critique Campbell or others of his era regarding what is accepted today.
116. "The Elders of the Church in Kirtland, to their Brethren Abroad," *Evening and Morning Star* 2, no. 18 (March 1834): 143.
117. Smith, "Wentworth Letter."
118. Lyon, "The Origin and Purpose of the Articles of Faith," 319.
119. Acts 3:20–21.
120. The parenthetical words are a clarification from the 1981 edition.
121. Holifield, *Theology in America*, 49.
122. Holifield, *Theology in America*, 77–78.
123. Butler et al., *Religion in American Life*, 130.
124. Holifield, *Theology in America*, 123–24.
125. Williams, *America's Religions*, 206. See also Hatch, *The Democratization of American Christianity*, 184; Winton U. Solberg, "Primitivism in the American Enlightenment," 65.
126. Underwood, "Millenarianism and Nineteenth-Century New Religions: The Mormon Example," 117.
127. Hatch, *The Democratization of American Christianity*, 184.
128. Williams, *America's Religions*, 206, 226. Holifield, *Theology in America*, 77.
129. Underwood, *Millenarian World of Early Mormonism*, 4.
130. Gaustad and Schmidt, *The Religious History of America*, 152.
131. Williams, *America's Religions*, 229–30.
132. Andrew H. Hedges, Alex D. Smith, and Richard Lloyd Anderson, eds., *Journals, Volume 2: December 1841–April 1843*, vol. 2 of the Journals series of *The Joseph Smith Papers*, edited by Dean C. Jessee, Ronald K. Esplin, and Richard Lyman Bushman (Salt Lake City: Church Historian's Press, 2008), 262–63.
133. Letter to the Elders of the Church, 16 November 1835, *Latter Day Saints' Messenger and Advocate*, 209, http://www.josephsmithpapers.org.
134. Editor, "The Temple," *Times and Seasons* 3, no. 13 (2 May 1842): 776. Joseph Smith was the general editor of the *Times and Seasons* in May 1842 and may have been the author of this editorial.
135. The "lost tribes of Israel" are the ten tribes belonging to the Northern Kingdom of Israel, who were taken captive by the Assyrians about 721 BC. Assyria transported part of the population to the north countries. Since that time, they have been referred to as the "lost ten tribes." Numerous Old Testament prophets promised their return, such as Isaiah 11:10–16; Jeremiah 3:18; 16:14–21; Book of Mormon prophecies, such as 1 Nephi 22:4–12; 2 Nephi 10:21–22; 3 Nephi 15:13–15; 16:1–5; and Doctrine and Covenants 133:26–35. LDS Bible Dictionary, s.v. "Israel, Kingdom of."

136. Doctrine and Covenants 115:6.
137. "The Government of God," *Times and Seasons* 3, no. 18 (15 July 1842): 855; History, 1838–1856, volume C-1 Addenda, 32, http://www.josephsmithpapers.org.
138. Underwood, *Millenarian World of Early Mormonism*, 5.
139. Williams, *America's Religions*, 181–82. Nevertheless, the state of Massachusetts held out until 1818. Anti-Catholicism was strong, and persecution of Mormons demonstrate that religious diversity did not allow much toleration. Even Campbell was vilified sometimes in the press. Fluhman, *"A Peculiar People,"* 16, 24; Garrison and DeGroot, *The Disciples of Christ*, 258–59.
140. Joseph Smith, "Joseph Smith Diary," 15 October 1843, by Willard Richards, in *Words of Joseph Smith*, 256.
141. Doctrine and Covenants 101:80.
142. History, 1838–1856, volume E-1 [1 July 1843–30 April 1844], 1666, http://www.josephsmithpapers.org.
143. Doctrine and Covenants 134.
144. The law of consecration requires those who enter into the covenant to be willing to sacrifice time, talents, and property for the building of the kingdom of God.
145. This is particularly evident later, when the Saints began practicing plural marriage, which they believed to be a mandate from God. This practice accelerated tensions between the Saints and federal legislation that made it illegal.
146. History, 1838–1856, volume C-1 [2 November 1838–31 July 1842], 912, http://www.josephsmithpapers.org.
147. "The Government of God," *Times and Seasons* 3, no. 18 (1842): 855; History, 1838–1856, volume C-1 Addenda, 32, http://www.josephsmithpapers.org.
148. Doctrine and Covenants 134:1.
149. See Philippians 4:8; 1 Peter 2:1, 17; 2 Peter 1:5–7.
150. Gerald R. McDermott, *Seeing God: Jonathan Edwards and Spiritual Discernment* (Vancouver: Regent College Publishing, 1995), 31, 34.
151. Holifield, *Theology in America*, 118.
152. History, 1838–1856, volume C-1 [2 November 1838–31 July 1842], 904[b], http://www.josephsmithpapers.org.
153. Lyon, "Origin and Purpose of the Articles of Faith," 299, 319.
154. Galatians 5:22–25.
155. See 1 Corinthians 13:4–7; Moroni 7:39–47 (Book of Mormon).
156. Campbell, *Christian System*, 4.
157. See 2 Thessalonians 2:3.

9

Scriptural Commentaries and Emendations

Since the time of the Puritans and through the nineteenth century, Americans have been called "people of the book," referring to the centrality of the Bible as the most printed, most distributed, and most read text in the nation.[1] Notably, both Campbell and Smith produced their own newly revised portions of the Bible. Campbell believed that "each religious party had sought to secure the Bible within its own sectarian cell," translating the Bible so that it comported with particular creeds, confessions, and practices founded on human innovations to particular theological tenets. His belief in the supremacy of the Bible and particularly in the importance of the New Testament for restoring the primitive church motivated his attempt to give his followers a purer version of the text as he understood it.

BIBLICAL CHANGES

The first English Bible printed in the United States was issued during the American Revolution. A new translation of the Bible in the nineteenth century was not an unusual event—in fact, the scriptures underwent numerous revisions, translations, and other modifications to meet a wide variety of changing ideological demands.[2] Between 1777 and 1833, more than eight hundred separate editions of the Bible (or parts thereof) were published in America.[3] Between 1808 and 1850, there were three new translations of the English Bible and ten new translations of the New Testament or the Gospels in the United States.[4] Campbell's new translation was included in this count; Smith's was not because it was unpublished until 1867. Many of these new Bibles were based on the Greek translation by Johann Jakob Griesbach, or were revisions replacing obsolete words and constructions.[5] Undoubtedly, Sidney Rigdon, Parley P. Pratt, and others made Smith aware of Campbell's translation that was first published in 1826.[6]

CAMPBELL'S NEW TESTAMENT EDITION

Alexander Campbell held to the notion of *sola scriptura* but believed that a better translation of the New Testament could be produced. In fact, he began thinking about this as a freshman at the University of Glasgow in 1810. He wrote in his personal notes, "Passages in the New Testament not right translated and therefore some of them are misunderstood," arguing his points on the basis of the Greek New Testament. For example, he commented and retranslated the following passages:

- Philippians 2:6: "Ought to be translated thus: 'who subsisting in Divine form did not reckon this ('which follows') robery [sic] that he should have things adequate to Godhead.'"
- John 1:18: "'None' not only no man but no existent being 'hath seen deity that is Godhead, being further and further in the bosom of the father,' that is knowing the secret of the father, 'hath revealed it' that is manifested the Godhead to man."
- Hebrews 1:8: "This verse is remarkably ill translated and should read 'But with relation to the son, (he says) thou (2) and God (1) (almighty), thy throne is forever and ever, the scepter of thy kingdom is a scepter of righteousness.'"
- Hebrews 4:3: "Ought to be thus translated: 'for we who believe enter into his rest, as he said, as I swore in my wrath, if thou shall enter into my rest, (I shall be forsworn) and besides when their works are finished as the foundation of the world God rested.'"[7]

These four passages stood out to him early in his study and may have been catalysts for his own translation of the New Testament completed sixteen years later. His two major criticisms of the commonly used King James Version were linguistic and theological.[8] In the preface to his 1826 edition of the New Testament, titled *The Sacred Writings of the Apostles and Evangelists of Jesus Christ, Commonly Styled the New Testament*, he wrote, "A living language is continually changing. . . . This constant mutation in a living language will probably render new translations, or corrections of old translations, necessary every two or three hundred years. For although the English tongue may have changed less during the last two hundred years . . . yet [because of] the changes which have taken place since the reign of James I do now render a new translation necessary."[9]

One of the main objectives of Campbell's translation, then, was simply to render the New Testament in the language of the nineteenth century. He noted that shortly after the completion of the Jewish and Christian writings, biblical Hebrew and Greek ceased to be spoken. The Bible thus preserved the meaning of the words in a way not possible otherwise. From Campbell's point of view, "we have, in writing, all the Hebrew and Greek that is necessary to perpetuate to the end of time, all the ideas which the Spirit of God had communicated to the world" in the words of unchangeable languages. Nevertheless, "the present version [King James] was made at a time when religious controversy was at its zenith; and . . . the tenets of the translators, whether designedly or undesignedly, did, on many occasions, give a wrong turn to words and sentences bearing upon their favorite dogmas."[10]

Specifically, Campbell believed that sixteenth-century Geneva translator Theodore Beza did "willfully and knowingly interpolate the scriptures, and torture many passages to favor their [Calvinist] system."[11] The reliance of the King James translators on this scholar introduced sectarianism and inaccuracies, and the translators who worked as a committee also allowed interpretive compromises. Further, Campbell believed that the capacity for making a more exact translation existed because of certain providential circumstances of his day: older and more reliable manuscripts were available, the original Greek was better understood, and scholarly debates in the eighteenth century had produced more critical knowledge of language. Better acquaintance with the idiomatic style of the apostolic writers would also prevent many of the errors of the King James translators, whose literal translations were correct but did not render a clear meaning.[12] A more reason-filled translation seemed a perfect way to offer biblical empirical evidence to resolve any misunderstandings in Christianity.[13]

In 1818, a New Testament was published in England from previously published work by three doctors. The Gospels were translated from Greek manuscripts by George Campbell (1778), the Epistles by James Macknight (1795), and the Acts and Revelation by Phillip Doddridge (1765). With these translations fully incorporated into his New Testament, Alexander Campbell set out to develop an American

Presented to James Asa. Runyon as a New Year's gift January 1842 by his affectionate Father Asa R. Runyon

THE

SACRED WRITINGS

OF THE

APOSTLES AND EVANGELISTS

OF

JESUS CHRIST,

COMMONLY STYLED THE

NEW TESTAMENT.

TRANSLATED FROM THE

ORIGINAL GREEK,

BY DOCTORS GEORGE CAMPBELL, JAMES MACKNIGHT. AND
PHILIP DODDRIDGE.

WITH PREFACES, VARIOUS EMENDATIONS, AND

AN APPENDIX,

Containing various translations of difficult passages—some Critical Notes
on the Language, Geography, Chronology, and History of the
New Testament—and Miscellaneous Tables designed to
aid every candid reader of the volume in acquiring
a satisfactory knowledge of its contents.

BY A. CAMPBELL.

THIRD EDITION:—REVISED AND ENLARGED.

PRINTED AND PUBLISHED BY ALEXANDER CAMPBELL.

BETHANY, BROOKE CO. VA.

1832.

Title page of Alexander Campbell, ed., *The Sacred Writings of the Apostles and Evangelists of Jesus Christ*. Buffaloe, VA, 1826. Courtesy of Kent P. Jackson.

publication with prefaces and critical notes to aid the reader, emendations from other translations of the Greek text, clarification of obscure passages and modernization of archaic readings, a new format designed for popular reading, and the daring "inclusion of the results of critical New Testament study."[14]

Perhaps most controversial to his new version was his change of the ambiguous word *baptism* to the definitive term *immersion* in almost every instance, including changing *John the Baptist* to *John the Immerser*. In 1812, during his studying of the New Testament, Campbell discovered *baptism* was a transliteration from the Greek rather than a translation. The transliterated word *baptizo* left open to opinion how the ritual should be administered. Believers in pedobaptism cited lexicons that defined the term as "to wash." Campbell argued from his lexicons that the word meant "to dip" or "immerse." Upon further study and examination of Latin, English, German, and French versions of the New Testament, as well as of Griesbach's Greek translation, Campbell found these versions often used words equivalent to immersion and never to sprinkling or pouring.[15] Campbell was convinced that the preservation of the Greek transliteration *baptizo* by King James and his translators was a "fraud to justify their kind of baptism, or at least to conceal that their practice was unscriptural."[16] If βάπτισμα had meant "immersion" in the first century, it should mean "immersion" in the nineteenth century. His was the first American New Testament translation to clarify the term and the "first shot in what would become the largest bible translation battle in early nineteenth-century America."[17]

Other important literary changes Campbell made included *angel* to *messenger, repent* to *reform, Christ* to *Messiah, hell* to *hades, grace* to *favor, conversation* to *behavior, testament* and *covenant* to *institution, church* to *congregation, Holy Ghost* to *Holy Spirit, preach* to *proclaim,* and *prevent* to *anticipate.* Some of the changes were due to previous meanings that had changed or to the theological baggage that had been attached to certain words. He also dropped the archaic *eth* from verb forms such as *do* and *keep*.[18] His was much more than just an *immersion* Bible; instead, it was a modernizing of the text by replacing archaic words with contemporary nineteenth-century English in an effort to avoid misunderstanding. Although convinced he had produced a superior Bible, he tried to avoid discord and recommended his Bible not as a substitute for the King James Version but to be used alongside it.[19]

Criticism of Campbell's New Testament version was fierce. He was accused of hubris, doctrinal error, and divisiveness. One Presbyterian critic opined that "all the alterations contended for, do not affect, either pro or con, one solitary article of the Christian system."[20] Obviously, he had not noted Campbell's clarification of baptism by immersion—a contradiction of the mode of Presbyterian baptism. A Tennessee Baptist questioned Campbell's motives: "The ambition of your life has been to become an acknowledged Reformer—a second Luther—to be the acknowledged head and leader of the whole Christian world and to receive the fragrant incense of its homage."[21] Regardless, prior to the 1881 Revised Version, Campbell's New Testament was arguably the best-selling Bible translation in America, partly due to his widespread movement and popular monthly newsletter. Unlike other American translations of the early nineteenth century, Campbell's Bible sold tens of thousands of copies and underwent sixteen editions, with additional revisions and numerous printings.[22]

Campbell's belief in the absolute primacy of the New Testament's portrayal of primitive Christianity over all creeds, traditions, and previous reformations prompted his aim to produce a literally accurate New Testament rendered in the living language.[23] He anticipated by decades many changes made in the modern-language translations of the twentieth century, including some of the most striking features of the Revised Standard Version, published in 1954.[24] Unabashedly, Campbell believed he had produced the most beautiful and correct printing of the New Testament published in America.[25]

SMITH'S INSPIRED BIBLE

In the spring of 1829, during the translation of the Book of Mormon, Smith dictated a revelation stating that there were additional "records which contain much of my gospel, which have been kept back because of the wickedness of the people" and that his scribe Oliver Cowdery was to assist him "in bringing to light" such scripture.[26] Book of Mormon passages also spoke of "plain and precious things" missing from the Bible and promised that these "plain and most precious parts of the Gospel of the Lamb" would be restored.[27] As Smith dictated these words, he may have understood them as a call to reexamine passages of the Bible rather than another extensive translation effort. After the publication of the Book of Mormon in the spring of 1830, Smith likely thought his scriptural translation efforts were complete. Instead, he was directed early that summer to begin what he would call an inspired version of the Bible.

Smith manifested a great love for the Bible, although his revelations indicate a loss of trust in the Christian clergy and their interpretation of it. Mormon historian Richard Bushman pointed out where the discrepancy lay: "They [Christian clergy] did not understand what the book meant. It was a record of revelations, and the ministry had turned it into a handbook. The Bible had become a text to be interpreted rather than an experience to be lived. In the process, the power of the book was lost. . . . It was the power . . . that Joseph . . . sought to recover."[28] An important part of Joseph Smith's significance is that he stood on the contested ground where Enlightenment, Pentecostal enthusiasm, and formal Christianity confronted one another, and his life posed the question "Do you believe God speaks?" At a time when the origins of Christianity were under assault by the forces of deist Enlightenment rationality, Smith attempted to return modern Christianity to its primitive origins through revelation.[29]

Smith's awareness of the lack of biblical clarity began as a teenager when he observed that "the teachers of religion of the different sects understood the same passages of scripture so differently as to destroy all confidence in settling the question by an appeal to the Bible."[30] When the angel Moroni visited him, he quoted from Malachi 4:5–6 "with a little variation from the way it reads in our Bibles."[31] Smith later would remark regarding the existing translations of the Bible, "I believe the Bible as it ought to be, as it came from the pen of the original writers."[32] From the revelations he had received, he knew that "many important points, touching the Salvation of men" had been removed or lost.[33] The Book of Mormon promised "other books, which [would] come forth by the power of the Lamb."[34] Smith would have interpreted those "other books" as including his translations and revelations found in the Book of Mormon, the Doctrine and Covenants, the Pearl of Great Price, and the new version of the Bible.

In June 1830, Smith dictated a conversation and vision that took the form of a revelation from God to Moses depicting the creation of the world, a prefatory background to the first chapter of Genesis, and thereafter following closely the first six chapters of Genesis.[35] After this revelation, Smith began a multiyear involvement with "translating" the Bible. Smith and Cowdery likely viewed the initial revelation, later titled "Visions of Moses," as providing insight into an important biblical figure and early events in his life. Subsequent revelations expanded not only the life of Moses but also narratives merely hinted

THE

HOLY SCRIPTURES,

TRANSLATED AND CORRECTED

BY THE

SPIRIT OF REVELATION,

BY

JOSEPH SMITH, Jr.,

THE SEER.

PUBLISHED BY THE

CHURCH OF JESUS CHRIST OF LATTER-DAY SAINTS.

PLANO, ILL.:

JOSEPH SMITH, I. L. ROGERS, E. ROBINSON,

PUBLISHING COMMITTEE.

1867.

Title page of Joseph Smith, *Holy Scriptures: Inspired Version* (Herald Press, 1876). Courtesy of L. Tom Perry Special Collections, Harold B. Lee Library, Brigham Young University.

at in biblical texts. As Smith's work on the Bible unfolded over the next several months, it became a revision and often an expansion of the King James Version of Genesis. Sidney Rigdon became Smith's new scribe as he continued working in Genesis, receiving additional information on Enoch in December 1830. Translation work was halted for the next few months as Smith and his followers moved from New York to Ohio. In March 1831, he was told to begin work in the New Testament.[36]

This was not a translation in the usual scholarly sense. Smith, unlearned in biblical languages, did not render Hebrew or Greek texts into English. Instead, he produced an inspired revision, "a translation of ideas rather than language,"[37] in which he endeavored to resolve inconsistencies, clarify and elaborate doctrine, and otherwise restore missing texts by revelation, with the lengthiest additions in Genesis. He also modified grammar or amplified the language of the King James Version. Smith's Bible has been variously called the "New Translation," "Inspired Translation," "Inspired Version," "Inspired Revision," and the "Joseph Smith Translation" (JST), which is the term used today.[38]

Oliver Cowdery, John Whitmer, Sidney Rigdon, Emma Smith, and Fredrick G. Williams all acted as scribes at different times; however, Sidney Rigdon served as the principal scribe.[39] Neither Smith nor his scribes left a record of how the work was accomplished. It appears that during much of the process, Smith read aloud directly from the Bible, a large 1828 Phinney King James Bible, and dictated his revision as he went.[40] The bulk of the additions and revisions were made by July 1833, when by working from Genesis through Revelation he had revised and added phrases, verses, and occasionally even whole chapters to the Bible. However, his sermons from 1833 to 1844 continued to clarify and correct passages not reflected in his earlier translation. It appears that because some of his translation process involved revelation, it was ongoing.[41] Doubtless he would have continued to make further changes had his life not been cut short at the age of thirty-eight.

According to Churches of Christ scholar Thomas Olbricht, legitimate pastoral ministry in nineteenth-century American Protestantism required knowledge of biblical Greek and Hebrew and familiarity with biblical commentaries in order to "ascertain the true meaning of the biblical text" and "to establish their case upon impeccable 'scientific' grounds."[42] Clearly, the Joseph Smith Translation did not follow the scholarly ecclesial standards of his day. Smith had no training in ancient languages at that time and thus did not work with Latin, Hebrew, or

Greek texts of the Bible.[43] Although some might try to represent his work as a rewording, paraphrasing, or commentary, Smith always referred to it as *inspired*. According to Mormon scholar Robert Millet, "In one sense, Joseph Smith was 'translating' the Bible in attempting to interpret it by revelation, to explain it by the use of clearer terms or a different style of language. In another sense, Smith was 'translating' the Bible, inasmuch as he was restoring in the English language ideas, events, and sayings that he claimed were originally recorded in Hebrew or Greek."[44] A reading of the Joseph Smith Translation provides insights into Smith's understanding of existing scriptures as well as new ideas about the gospel not found elsewhere.[45] Further, out of this biblical translation project came many important revelations which were later included in the Doctrine and Covenants. Thus, this translation work was a springboard for additional revelation.

Some have wondered if Smith was essentially "Mormonizing" the Bible—harmonizing it to fit his own doctrine. In June 1830, when the biblical translation began, there was little "Mormonism with which to Mormonize the Bible."[46] Smith had just completed his translation of the Book of Mormon and understood a few things differently, but his education was ongoing. Mormon scholar Robert J. Matthews called the Bible translation process "a type of spiritual education for the prophet himself."[47] Over a three-year period, Smith dictated changes to more than 3,400 verses from the King James translation of the Bible, including adding numerous verses regarding ancient patriarchs such as Adam, Enoch, Melchizedek, Abraham, Joseph of Egypt, and Moses.[48] From his work with the Bible came many seminal Mormon doctrines—premortal existence and details concerning the Creation, the Fall, and the Atonement—during the first few months of translation work on the book of Genesis, as well as unique revelations recorded in the Doctrine and Covenants such as three kingdoms of glory,[49] the olive leaf,[50] the status of the Apocrypha,[51] and a new and everlasting covenant, eternal marriage.[52]

Both Campbell and Smith brought forth new versions of the Bible. Restoration meant a revision of canonical scripture to meet the demands of ideology or God's command. Neither was audacious enough to call his efforts a replacement of the King James Version, the biblical standard of the day. Campbell's work was solely with the New Testament where he wrote scholarly commentary on the translations of three eminent British scholars. With his Greek background he could authoritatively translate particular passages, clarify the ordinance of baptism, and add insightful notes. Smith's work with the Old and New Testaments did not focus on these types of changes. Instead, what Smith brought forth was central to his restoration. If his work was to be part of the "restitution of all things," namely, those parts of the Bible which to his understanding had not survived the transmission of the text to the present day, then the text must, of necessity, be restored by revelation. Through his inspired translation of the Bible, Smith claimed to be a restorer of scripture that had previously existed. Both he and Campbell attempted to restore the original meaning of the biblical writers—one through scholarly methods and the other through inspiration and revelation.

Notes

1. Paul C. Gutjahr, *An American Bible: A History of the Good Book in the United States, 1777–1880* (Stanford: Standford University Press, 1999), 1.
2. Gutjahr, *An American Bible*, 3.
3. Margaret T. Hills, *The English Bible in America* (New York: The American Bible Society, 1961), 128.
4. Gutjahr, *An American Bible*, appendix 5, table 4.
5. Griesbach was an eighteenth-century German biblical textual critic, especially noted for his New Testament criticism. In his translation work, he sought to acquire a thorough understanding of a passage's setting and context in an effort to reproduce the author's original meaning, much more than grammar and philology. Gutjahr, *An American Bible*, 100. Abner Kneeland, John Gorman Palfrey, Samuel Sharpe, and others based their New Testament on the translation by Griesbach. Noah Webster attempted to render the King James Version more useful by removing obscure and questionable words and phrases.
6. Robert J. Matthews, *"A Plainer Translation": Joseph Smith's Translation of the Bible* (Provo, UT: Brigham Young University, 1975), 10.
7. "Extracts and Original Essays by Alexander Campbell, Glasgow 1809," Manuscript I, 89L–91L.
8. Cecil K. Thomas, *Alexander Campbell and His New Version* (St. Louis: Bethany Press, 1958), 172.
9. Alexander Campbell, *The Sacred Writings of the Apostles and Evangelists of Jesus Christ, Commonly Styled The New Testament* (Buffaloe, VA: Alexander Campbell, 1826).
10. Campbell, *The Sacred Writings of the Apostles and Evangelists of Jesus Christ*, v.
11. Campbell, *The Sacred Writings of the Apostles and Evangelists of Jesus Christ*, vi.
12. Campbell, *The Sacred Writings of the Apostles and Evangelists of Jesus Christ*, vii; Gutjahr, *An American Bible*, 102.
13. Lynn Savage Hilton Wilson, "Joseph Smith's Doctrine of the Holy Spirit Contrasted with Cartwright, Campbell, Hodge, and Finney" (PhD diss., Marquette University, 2010), 86.
14. Thomas, *Alexander Campbell and His New Version*, 40. The daring inclusion would likely refer to Griesbach's work.
15. Campbell, "Baptism," in *Christian System*, 56.

16. Campbell, "King James' Instructions to the Translators of the Bible—with Extracts and Remarks," *Christian Baptist* 2, no. 4 (1 November 1824): 106.
17. Gutjahr, *An American Bible*, 103.
18. For example, Campbell chose the broad word *institution* to replace *testament*, which was often attached to a *will* and also *covenant* because it connotes a *relationship between equals*, incorrect in defining the relationship between man and God; "the English word 'ghost' had come to signify a disembodied spirit of a dead person, and, consequently, ought never to be used to apply to the Spirit of God." Thomas, *Alexander Campbell and His New Version*, 28–36.
19. Gutjahr, *An American Bible*, 105.
20. "Biblical Repository," Second Series 1, 1839, 326, in Thomas, *Alexander Campbell and His New Version*, 73.
21. "Tennessee Baptist," Saturday, 10 June 1854 in Thomas, *Alexander Campbell and His New Version*, 73.
22. Gutjahr, *An American Bible*, 105. See also Kent P. Jackson, "The King James Bible in the Days of Joseph Smith," in *The King James Bible and the Restoration*, ed. Kent P. Jackson (Provo, UT: Religious Studies Center, 2011), 138–61.
23. Thomas, *Alexander Campbell and His New Version*, 26–43, 103–4, 184–87.
24. Thomas, *Alexander Campbell and His New Version*, 9–10, 18, 201–5.
25. Thomas, *Alexander Campbell and His New Version*, 19.
26. Doctrine and Covenants 6:26–27; Doctrine and Covenants 8:1, 11.
27. 1 Nephi 13:26–28, 32 (Book of Mormon).
28. Bushman, "A Joseph Smith for the Twenty-first Century," 274.
29. Bushman, "A Joseph Smith for the Twenty-first Century," 274.
30. Joseph Smith—History 1:12 (Pearl of Great Price).
31. Joseph Smith—History 1:36 (Pearl of Great Price).
32. Joseph Smith, 15 October 1843, "Joseph Smith Diary," by Willard Richards, in Ehat and Cook, *Words of Joseph Smith*, 256.
33. History, 1838–1856, volume A-1 [23 December 1805–30 August 1834], 183, http://www.josephsmithpapers.org.
34. 1 Nephi 13:39 (Book of Mormon).
35. "Selections from the Book of Moses," chapter 1, Pearl of Great Price.
36. Doctrine and Covenants 45:60; see also Doctrine and Covenants 76:15.
37. Staker, *Hearken, O Ye People*, 313.
38. The original manuscript and copyright are held by the Community of Christ, originally called the Reorganized Church of Jesus Christ of Latter Day Saints. Matthews, "A Plainer Translation," 12. For a typographic transcription of the original manuscripts, see *Joseph Smith's Translation of the Bible—Original Manuscripts*, ed. Scott H. Faulring, Kent P. Jackson, and Robert J. Matthews (Provo, UT: Religious Studies Center, 2004). For a history of the manuscript copies, scribes, and transcription, see Kent P. Jackson, *The Book of Moses and the Joseph Smith Translation Manuscripts* (Provo, UT: Religious Studies Center, 2005).
39. In a revelation given in response to Rigdon's recent conversion and trip to New York to meet the prophet, part of Rigdon's future responsibilities in relation to helping Smith were given: "And I have sent forth the fulness of my gospel by the hand of my servant Joseph; and in weakness have I blessed him; And I have given unto him the keys of the mystery of those things which have been sealed, even things which were from the foundation of the world. . . . And a commandment I give unto thee— that thou shalt write for him." Doctrine and Covenants 35:17–18, 20.
40. Matthews, "A Plainer Translation," 39.
41. Robert Millet, "Joseph Smith's Translation of the Bible: A Historical Overview," in *The Joseph Smith Translation: The Restoration of Plain and Precious Truths*, ed.

Monte S. Nyman and Robert L. Millet (Provo, UT: Religious Studies Center, Brigham Young University, 1985), 29–31, 33.

42. Thomas H. Olbricht, "Biblical Primitivism in American Biblical Scholarship, 1630–1870," Hughes, ed., *The American Quest for the Primitive Church*, 81, 94.

43. In 1830, when Smith began his translation of the Bible, he had no knowledge of any foreign languages. Beginning in the mid-1830s, he implored God to "give me learning even language: and end[ow] me with qualifications to magnify his name while I live." History, 1838–1856, volume B-1 [1 September 1834–2 November 1838], 672, http://www.josephsmithpapers .org. He studied the rudiments of biblical languages Hebrew and Greek. Later, he studied German with Alexander Neibaur. By 1844, he claimed in one of his sermons, "I have now preached a little Latin, a little Hebrew, Greek and German." Discourse, 7 April 1844, as reported by *Times and Seasons*, 617, http://www.josephsmithpapers.org.

44. Millet, "A Historical Overview," 26.

45. Robert J. Matthews, "Major Doctrinal Contributions of the JST," in *The Joseph Smith Translation*, 272.

46. Matthews, "The JST: Retrospect and Prospect—A Panel," in *The Joseph Smith Translation*, 292.

47. Matthews, "The JST: Retrospect and Prospect—A Panel," 292.

48. Matthews, "*A Plainer Translation*," 424–25.

49. Doctrine and Covenants 76.

50. Doctrine and Covenants 88.

51. Doctrine and Covenants 91.

52. Doctrine and Covenants 132.

Conflict

Since you both professe to want more Light, and that a greater
Light is yet to be expected; yea, that the Church of Scotland
may yet have need of a greater Reformation &c., we Querie,
how you can professe and Sweare to Persecute all others as
Schismatiques, Hereticks, &c., that beleeve they see a further
Light and dare not joyn with either of your Churches?

—ROGER WILLIAMS, QUERY 12,
Queries of Highest Consideration

Conflict between Campbell and Smith had its origins in 1830 in northeastern Ohio. Within a year of the Mormons moving to Ohio, opposition mounted in the Kirtland area against Smith for community disruption with his new revelations, and deep-seated anger rose at Rigdon's conversion and close association with Smith. Many of the revelations Smith received between late 1830 and early 1832 were outside accepted norms of Christianity and clearly separated Mormons from the beliefs of all other Christian denominations.[1] These new revelations were demanding and far-reaching, considered too much by some followers of Joseph Smith and those professing different religious beliefs.

Specifically, there were several major events and doctrinal ideas that exacerbated the strife and rivalry between the two men and their restorationist movements. In general, the events listed are chronological, but some occurred simultaneously and others lasted for several years.

1. In late October 1830, four Mormon missionaries stopped to preach in Kirtland, Ohio, a regional stronghold of Reforming Baptist ministers and disciples who followed Alexander Campbell. The missionaries were met with exceptional success by way of over one hundred baptisms in a few weeks—many of the new converts previously belonging to Reforming Baptist congregations.

2. The missionaries introduced into the religious landscape the belief in the extraordinary offices and spiritual gifts of the New Testament—including prophet, seer, revelator, visions, direct communication with God, the importance of priesthood authority, and a new book of scripture.

3. In early November 1830, Sidney Rigdon, an itinerant preacher to numerous Reforming Baptist congregations and a previously close ministerial confidant of Alexander Campbell, was baptized into Joseph Smith's Church of Christ, bringing with him many of his congregants.

4. In early December 1830, Rigdon traveled to New York to meet Joseph Smith and became his new scribe and close associate as Smith continued his work on what he called an inspired translation of the Bible.

5. In late January 1831, Joseph Smith moved his small New York and Pennsylvania congregations to the Kirtland, Ohio, area to join with the new converts.

6. In early February 1831, Campbell published his critique of the Book of Mormon in his monthly circular, the *Millennial Harbinger*, beginning a war of words between Campbell's *Millennial Harbinger* and the Latter-day Saints' *Messenger and Advocate* and *The Evening and the Morning Star*.

7. June 1831 began a series of new revelations to Joseph Smith regarding Zion as more than an idea, but as a particular place with individuals and families called out of small northeastern Ohio villages to move to Independence, Missouri, in order to begin a communal type of society requiring consecration of material goods in preparation for the Millennium.

8. February 1832 marked the receipt of a new revelation teaching an afterlife of "three degrees of glory" in contrast to heaven or hell.

9. While in New York and New Hampshire in 1836, Joseph Smith Sr. and John Smith (Joseph Smith's father and uncle) visited Alexander Campbell. John Smith recorded in his diary, "We told him to repent and washed our feet against him."[2] That same year, Rigdon also publicly

criticized his former mentors and friends. In a letter to Oliver Cowdery, Sidney Ridgon, editor of the *Messenger and Advocate*, wrote:

> We feel . . . at liberty to say, that we have all the evidence necessary to satisfy our mind, that Messrs. Campbell, and Scott, the leaders of that brotherhood, are not honest in their religion: they are men who think and act for themselves, independently, and they do know, that the same Jesus who said to his disciples "Go ye into all the world, and preach the gospel to every creature: he that believeth and is baptized shall be saved, and he that believeth not shall be damned." Also [Jesus] said "That signs shall follow them that believe &c.[3]

Campbell's personality did not allow him to be a passive recipient to the intrusion of Smith or others critical of his restoration. Churches of Christ scholar Caleb Clanton claimed that Campbell played the role of self-appointed religious flyswatter—especially in his early years—and brought upon himself accusations of heresy among other less enviable names.[4] At this time, Campbell's followers were nicknamed "Campbellites," and Smith's followers were called "Mormonites." The terms *Mormon, Mormonism,* and *Mormonites* were pejorative labels given by opponents of Smith and his church.[5] Similarly, *Campbellite* was used to distinguish Campbell's restorationist reformers from the more orthodox Regular Baptists; the term was also used at times as a derogatory epithet toward Campbell's followers.[6] When asked about the term Campbell responded, "It is a nickname of reproach invented and adopted by those whose views, feelings and desires are all sectarian—who cannot conceive of Christianity in any other light than an ISM."[7]

Both Campbellism and Mormonism were considered by many to be heretical movements and separate from the traditional Christianity of their day. "Evangelical Protestants in the Ohio Valley saw Campbell as something less than a true Christian: in their eyes he was the father of a heretical cult that despised the historic creeds, required immersion in water for regeneration, and stole sheep from their pastures by the thousands."[8] Some attacks on "Campbellites" included "Mormonites" in the same breath: The favored epithet for the Reforming Baptists was "Campbellite," and a common attack on the disciples was to lump the newcomers with odd and already ill-regarded sects. Thus, a missionary of the American Home Missionary Society (Presbyterian and Congregational) could denounce "the deluded Mormon and Campbellite" in Illinois. "The Friends to Humanity Association (Baptist) in Illinois, in its 1831 circular letter, complained that 'infidelity has assumed a thousand forms such as deism, atheism, Campbellism, Mormonism, Parkerism, and drunkenness.'" In another report from Illinois, "Scattered thro' this country we find Campbellism—Millerism—Mormonism—Antinomianism under different names and nearly all kinds & varieties of Error."[9]

Campbell preferred the scriptural name *Disciples of Christ* for his movement.[10] At its formal organization on 6 April 1830, Smith's group took the name *Church of Christ* and then in the mid-1830s used several different names: *Church of the Latter Day Saints*, *Church of Jesus Christ*, *Church of God*, and *Church of Christ of Latter Day Saints*. In 1838, the official name became *The Church of Jesus Christ of Latter Day Saints*.[11]

Inasmuch as Mormonism and Campbellism grew up in the same Second Great Awakening environment, the existence of common ground between them is understandable because both belonged to the larger nineteenth-century historical movement restorationism.[12] Even common folk recognized that, although not the same, the two groups were similar, as noted in this letter:

> A fresh cargo of Mormonites arrived in our neighborhood yesterday, between seventy and 100. I think they will take possession of this country for a while. they are crowding in as near the state line as they can get. they say that [they] can work miracles. . . . I do think they ought to be punished and I also think—(as Mr. Lykins says) that Alex. Campbell ought to claim them as his grand children for they preach very much like him. they are starving here at present. I know of a widow with eight children who it is said threw three thousand into the common stock and who is now living on boiled wheat.[13]

Historian and Latter-day Saint scholar Richard Lyman Bushman suggests that in 1830 the Mormons bore a stronger resemblance to "Campbellites" than to other Christian churches as suggested in the formula of faith, repentance, baptism by immersion for the remission of sins, and the Holy Ghost. That resemblance, along with a claim to priesthood authority, may account for the rapid conversion of so many of Campbell's followers to the Mormons in the fall of 1830.[14] Within a short time, however, the Church of Christ began to diverge significantly from Campbell's Disciples of Christ.

The chapters in this section discuss points of conflict between Campbell and Smith, between Smith and some of his followers, and between the Missourians and the Mormons. There were significant conversions, defections, and accusations between Campbell, Smith, and their adherents. Campbell was the first to read and critique Smith's major revelatory output, the Book of Mormon, and he deemed it a delusion. Smith was not only attacked from the outside by Campbell and others but also by some of his closest associates who challenged his prophetic style of leadership. The Missouri War challenged the rights guaranteed to Americans by the Constitution, and it demonstrated basic instincts of both human depravity and human kindness.

Notes

1. Staker, *Hearken, O Ye People*, 325–28. The vision is recorded in Doctrine and Covenants 76 and came about as Smith and Rigdon were pondering scriptures in the Gospel of John. From the revelations he had previously received, it seemed apparent to him that "many important points touching the salvation of man had been taken from the Bible, or lost before it was compiled. It appeared self-evident from what truths were left, that if God rewarded every one according to the deeds done in the body the term 'Heaven,' as intended for the Saints' eternal home, must include more kingdoms than one" (heading to Doctrine and Covenants 76). The vision that was shown to Smith and Rigdon included telestial, terrestrial, and celestial degrees of glory.

2. Davis Bitton, *Guide to Mormon Diaries and Autobiographies* (Provo, UT: BYU Press, 1977), 322. The symbolic "dusting of the feet" was not an action promoted by Joseph Smith Jr. In fact, in a letter published in 1832, he wrote the following: "Brethren, . . . you are to enlighten the world; you are to prepare the way for the people to come up to Zion; you are to instruct men how to receive the fulness of the gospel, and the everlasting covenants, even them that were from the beginning; . . . you are to set an example of meekness and humility before saints and sinners, as did the Savior; and when reviled you are not to revile again; you are to reason with men as in days of old, to bear patiently and answer as the spirit of truth shall direct, allowing all credit for every item of good. You are to walk in the valley of humility and pray for the salvation of all; yes, you are to pray for your enemies; and warn in compassion. . . . You are to preach the gospel, which is the power of God unto salvation, even glad tidings of great joy unto all people. Again, you are not to take the blessings of an individual, or of a church." History, 1838–1856, volume A-1 [23 December 1805–30 August 1834], 224, http://josephsmithpapers.org.

3. Sidney Rigdon, "For the Messenger and Advocate," *Messenger and Advocate* 2, no. 7 (June 1836): 297.

4. J. Caleb Clanton, *The Philosophy of Religion of Alexander Campbell* (Knoxville: University of Tennessee, 2013), 4–5.

5. Joseph Smith to Isaac Galland, 22 March 1839, Liberty, MO, *Times and Seasons*, February 1840, 51–56; Letter to Isaac Galland, 22 March 1839, http://josephsmith-papers.org.

6. Garrison and DeGroot, *The Disciples of Christ*, 193, 258.

7. Campbell, "Campbellism," *Christian Baptist* 5, no. 1 (6 August 1827): 97.

8. Haymes, quoted in Hughes, *Reviving the Ancient Faith*, 35–36.

9. Garrison and DeGroot, *The Disciples of Christ*, 258–59.

10. Garrison and DeGroot, *The Disciples of Christ*, 209. After Campbell joined forces with Barton Stone's *Christians*, some also took on that name.

11. Doctrine and Covenants 115:3–4. Dean C. Jessee, Mark Ashurst-McGee, and Richard L. Jensen, eds., *Journals, Volume 1: 1832–1839*, vol. 1 of the Journals series of *The Joseph Smith Papers*, ed. Dean C. Jessee, Ronald K. Esplin, and Richard Lyman Bushman (Salt Lake City: Church Historian's Press, 2008), Historical Introduction, 230.

12. Earlier prominent restorationists of this era were New Englanders Abner Jones, Elias Smith, and others who joined together to form the Christian Connexion. Holifield, *Theology in America*, 291. Also there were Barton Stone, Richard McNemar, Robert Marshall, John Thompson, and John Dunlavy, whose influence extended throughout Ohio, Kentucky, and Tennessee. Stone, *History of the Christian Church in the West, Part 2* (Lexington: College of the Bible, 1956).

13. Delilah McCoy Lykins to Isaac McCoy, 6 September 1831, "Isaac McCoy Papers," Manuscript Division, Kansas State Historical Society, Topeka.

14. Bushman, *Joseph Smith and the Beginnings of Mormonism*, 180.

10

Conversions
and Defections

The conflict between Campbell and Smith began with the conversion of Sidney Rigdon. He went from being one of Campbell's main ministers and evangelists to a scribe for Joseph Smith. Rigdon was considered persona non grata not only to Thomas and Alexander Campbell but also to many who lived in the Kirtland, Ohio, area and remained faithful acolytes to Campbell's restoration movement. Rigdon's immediate close association with Smith after his conversion led to accusations that he and Smith conspired to write the Book of Mormon based on an unpublished historical romance and that Smith stole doctrine from Campbell via Rigdon.

Rigdon, a Reforming Baptist minister who had been in Campbell's camp for nine years, joined with the Mormons in the fall of 1830. In an effort to set the record straight and to refute false accusations against Rigdon, the following was recorded in the Manuscript History of the Church: "As there has been a great rumor and many false statements have been given to the world respecting Elder Rigdons' connexion with the church of Jesus Christ, it [is] necessary that <a> correct account of the same be given so, that the public mind may be disabused on the subject."[1]

SIDNEY RIGDON: FROM RESTORATION PREACHER
TO APOSTATE AND MORMON CONVERT

About 1817, in his twenty-fourth year, Rigdon "professed religion" and joined the Regular Baptists in Pennsylvania. According to his son Wickliffe, Rigdon became a fine historian, Bible scholar, and orator—primarily through his own efforts. Although he wanted to attend school, he was forced to work on the family farm. He spent his evenings and spare time reading and educating himself in history, the Bible, and English grammar. Later, he was able to study theology with a Baptist minister and hone his talents as a preacher.[2]

During the winter months of 1818 and 1819, he resided with Reverend Andrew Clark in North Sewickley, Beaver County, in southwestern Pennsylvania, fulfilling the requirements to receive a license to preach and practice his skills as a Regular Baptist preacher. In May 1819, he moved to Warren, Ohio, and began to live with Adamson Bentley, also a Regular Baptist preacher, who became his new mentor. Within a year, Rigdon became an ordained preacher, met Phebe Brooks, sister-in-law to Bentley, and married her.[3]

Bentley and Rigdon read a transcript of Alexander Campbell's 1820 debate in southeastern Ohio with Seceder Presbyterian Reverend John Walker regarding the proper age and mode of baptism, and they wanted to learn more about Campbell's views. In their opinion, Campbell argued impressively against infant baptism, baptism by sprinkling, and using the Jewish Old Testament to defend ordinances or covenants in the Christian New Testament church. Rigdon found Campbell's arguments thoughtful and compelling. In the spring or summer of 1821, during a lengthy preaching circuit, the two men stopped at Alexander Campbell's home in Bethany, Virginia. According to a much later recollection by Campbell, the men sat up most of the night discussing everything from Adam to the Final Judgment, the various dispensations, and other topics of reformation and restoration. It was at this point that Rigdon became convinced that he had much to learn from Campbell's understanding of the scriptures, especially the ancient order of things in the modern day.[4] Bentley and Rigdon became converted to Campbell's reading of the scriptures and ideas on reformation and restoration. In fact, according to Campbell, Rigdon would declare as they departed that "if he had, within the last year, taught and promulgated from the pulpit one error, he had a thousand."[5] The two men returned to Warren, determined to preach the "ancient order of things" in the Regular Baptist churches

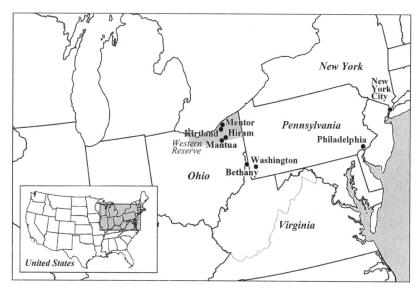

Map of Eastern United States, by Edward Dean Neuenswander.

in their area. Although still considered Regular Baptists, Rigdon and Bentley were now in Campbell's reformation camp. The two men were among the initial members of the Mahoning Baptist Association, and it was to this Baptist association that Campbell's new Wellsburg congregation would apply in 1823, sidestepping the excommunication effort by the Redstone Baptist Association mentioned in chapter 7.

In 1822, likely with Campbell's help, Rigdon received a position with the First Baptist Church of Pittsburg, a much larger town and congregation than Warren, Ohio, and a step upward in ministerial circles. Rigdon worked diligently, and "his peculiar style of preaching" brought in many new members; it soon became one of the most respectable churches in the city.[6] At that time, Rigdon was described as a "brilliant and eloquent young Baptist minister" with "more than ordinary ability as a speaker, possessing great fluency and a lively fancy which gave him great popularity as an orator," and one who espoused many of Campbell's reform ideas in his own congregation.[7] Rigdon's preaching of Campbell's reform ideas and refusal to teach the Philadelphia Confession of faith caused problems among the more orthodox Baptists of his church. A small faction of the First Baptist Church of Pittsburg opposed his reform ideas. The two groups separated, declaring "non-fellowship" and expelling each other from the Baptist Church. In September 1824, at the annual association meeting in Pittsburgh, the two groups appeared and argued as to which one should be accepted as the official Baptist church in Pittsburgh. A commission was organized to investigate charges of heresy brought against Rigdon "for not being sound in the faith."[8]

According to Reverend Williams, minister of the First Pittsburg Baptist Church beginning in 1827, Rigdon erred in teaching that (1) Christians are not under obligation to keep the moral law (the Ten Commandments), it having been abolished by the Savior; (2) the Jewish dispensation was not the best that God might have given to that nation, for it had made them threefold more the children of hell than they were before; (3) a change of heart consists merely in a change of views and baptism; (4) there is no such thing as religious experience; (5) saving faith is a mere crediting of the testimony given by the evangelists such as all persons have in the truth of any other history; and (6) it is wrong to use the Lord's Prayer, inasmuch as the reign of Christ has now commenced. Williams also testified that Rigdon spoke publicly about restoring the ancient order of things and advocated a "common stock system."[9] Campbell's ideas on separation of Old and New Testament teachings, simple faith in the facts of the gospel, and rejection of religious experience as a prerequisite for baptism were evident in these accusations. The investigation resulted in Rigdon's excommunication from the association; however, a majority of his congregation went with him.

Also in Pittsburg at that same time was Walter Scott, a preacher at a Scottish Haldanean/Sandemanian reform church, who became Rigdon's good friend in discussing the gospel. In 1824, the two men decided to unite their respective congregations, becoming the third church committed to Thomas and Alexander Campbell's reform movement.[10] With the loss of his position in the First Pittsburg Baptist Church, Rigdon began learning the tanning trade from his brother-in-law to support his wife and three children.

In 1826, Rigdon moved to Bainbridge, Ohio. In June, he was invited to preach a eulogy for the previous minister, Warner Goodall of Mentor, Ohio, and he delivered an impressive sermon. In 1827, the congregation in Mentor requested Rigdon to become its pastor. By this time, Scott had also moved to Ohio. Between 1827 and 1830, the evangelistic efforts by Walter Scott, Sidney Rigdon, Adamson Bentley, and "Raccoon" John Smith, all early 1820 devotees of Campbell, united to preach the ancient gospel as taught in the New Testament and brought hundreds of converts to embrace the restoration of the ancient order.[11]

The Mantua Center, Ohio. The church building was constructed in 1840. It is the oldest house of worship of the Disciples of Christ in Ohio. The historic church is still used for worship, and visitors are welcome to tour the inside. Sidney Rigdon came from the Disciples of Christ when he joined the Latter-day Saints. Photo courtesy of Steve Hurd.

As Rigdon traveled throughout northeastern Ohio, he was involved in preaching Campbell's reform and restoration ideas that he believed more closely approached the original Christian doctrines. He was an important influence in Portage County, especially in the village of Mantua, where he was elected bishop, as well as the towns of Hiram and Nelson.[12] He was described as a "great Campbellite preacher" and "an orator of no inconsiderable abilities . . . his language copious, fluent in utterance, with articulation clear and musical. Yet he was an enthusiast and unstable. His personal influence with an audience was very great . . . and just the man for an awakening. He was an early reader of Campbell's Christian Baptist . . . and brought out its views in his sermons," in which he was both sincere and candid.[13] Rigdon organized nine Reforming Baptist congregations and was a circuit preacher for seventeen congregations—including Mantua Center, Perry, Euclid, Birmingham, Waite, Hill, Elyria, and Hamden.[14] According to one account, Rigdon was second only to Walter Scott in his evangelizing efforts in the Western Reserve, holding numerous meetings and having a large following.[15]

In early 1830, Sidney Rigdon was approached by his congregation in Mentor, Ohio, regarding establishing a set reimbursement for his services. Although Rigdon now had a family of six children and lived in a small, unfinished frame home, he recorded that he was content with "having food and raiment." He told the leaders of the congregation that he could not sell his preaching abilities but would receive what they would willingly give. A committee purchased a farm and began erecting a home that would be suitable for his family and his numerous visitors.[16]

The Isaac Morley family, part of Sidney Rigdon's Reforming Baptist congregation in Kirtland, Ohio, owned an eighty-acre farm. In February 1830, he and several other families, including Titus Billings and Lyman Wight, joined to form a communal society based on Acts 2:44–45 and 4:32: "And all that believed were together, and had all things common; And sold their possessions and goods, and parted them to all men, as every man had need. . . . And the multitude of them that believed were of one heart and of one soul: neither said any of them that ought of the things which he possessed was his own; but they had all things common."[17] Eventually, the group numbered more than one hundred members. The Morley group's efforts were founded in an attempt to further restore a New Testament practice, and Rigdon, as a believer in the restoration of the ancient order of things, spoke often about this system and advocated its reestablishment. Although he was their spiritual leader and a proponent of communalism, for unknown reasons Rigdon never joined the "family," as they were called.

Rigdon's approval of common stock became one of several points of theological disagreement between Rigdon and Campbell. The tipping point in their friendship came when Rigdon had the audacity to publicly call out Campbell's restoration on the New Testament practice of common stock. In an August 1830 meeting of the Mahoning Baptist Association, Rigdon addressed the membership and argued that "to show our pretensions to follow the apostles in all their New Testament teachings, required a community of goods; that as they established their order in the model church at Jerusalem, we were bound to imitate their example." Campbell responded that such a practice was impractical and declared that New Testament communitarianism was a "special circumstance" that ended with Ananias and Sapphira and, further, that it was a voluntary practice not prevalent in the apostolic era. Purportedly, Rigdon was crushed by Campbell's thirty-minute rejoinder—although he should not have been surprised, because Campbell's views on communal societies were well known. In 1828, Campbell had debated Robert Owen, a wealthy English philanthropist and founder of several utopian societies, regarding his "A New Moral Order," a godless utopian communal society.[18] Further, Campbell was not about to allow Rigdon to dictate what should be part of his restoration movement.[19]

Parley P. Pratt was baptized into Joseph Smith's Church of Christ about 1 September 1830 and became a missionary for his new church a month later. Traveling west from New York with three other men, Pratt convinced his companions to stop in Mentor, Ohio, to see Rigdon, his "former friend and instructor in the Reformed Baptist Society." The men presented him with a Book of Mormon, testifying that it was a revelation from God. This was Rigdon's first acquaintance with the book. Despite doubts regarding the book's authenticity, Rigdon promised the missionaries, "I will read your book, and see what claim it has upon my faith, and will endeavor to ascertain whether it be a revelation from God or not."[20] Matthew Clapp, a member of Rigdon's congregation, stated that initially Rigdon "partly condemned it."[21] After listening to the missionaries preach to his Mentor congregation, Rigdon stood and declared to his followers that the information they had received "was of an extraordinary character, and certainly demanded their most severe consideration." Rigdon wrote in his own account that he became fully convinced of the truth of the work by a personal revelation.[22]

Whatever one might say about Rigdon—and he has his critics among the Regular Baptists, Reforming Baptists, and Mormons—it is apparent that Rigdon was willing to accept what he believed was truth, wherever he found it, and embraced it regardless of the cost. And cost it did. Rigdon was a popular and well-respected preacher. His congregation was building him a home, and his prospects were for continued esteem and abundance. The Church of Christ was generally unpopular, and Rigdon's character and reputation suffered at the hands of Campbell and his followers. When Rigdon informed Phebe of the consequences if they obeyed the gospel as taught by Joseph Smith, she declared, "I have weighed the matter, I have contemplated the circumstances. . . . I have counted the cost. . . . It is my desire to do the will of God."[23] They were baptized into Smith's Church of Christ about 8 November 1830.[24]

In a few short weeks, approximately 127 individuals joined Smith's restoration movement, many of whom had previously been followers of Campbell's restoration movement.[25] According to local Hiram, Ohio, Christian Church history, "Numbers who had accepted the position of the early Disciples were seduced to the new faith."[26] When prominent Disciples of Christ member Oliver Snow converted in Mantua and Simonds Ryder in Hiram, it was referred to "as a shock like an earthquake."[27] Many in Kirtland and Hiram of Campbell's restoration movement also joined with Smith's restoration movement.[28] Amos Hayden, an early Disciples of Christ historian, wrote, "Perhaps in no place except Kirtland, did the doctrines gain a more permanent footing than in Hiram. It entrenched itself there so strongly that its leaders felt assured of the capture of the town. Rigdon's former popularity in that region gave wings to their appeal."[29] Kirtland "was shaken as by a tempest under the outbreak of Mormonism."[30]

The Mantua Center Christian Church history marks 1830 as the "Mormon Episode"—the point when a number of members of Campbell's movement in northeastern Ohio were "lost" to Mormonism. Particularly the conversion of respected local citizens such as Sidney Rigdon, Oliver Snow, and Symonds Ryder was "a significant blow to the newly formed church at Mantua Center." Among Campbell's followers, there was a sense of alarm at the loss of so many leading individuals and families, calling it "the great Mormon defection [that] came upon us." The "outbreak of Mormonism" caused one prominent Disciple, Darwin Atwater, to lament that the church was "left small and inexperienced . . . and in a weak state, [and] in the midst of so much opposition, we were poorly prepared to take care of the church."[31] Methodists, Regular Baptists, and other unaffiliated seekers joined with the Mormons, but the vast majority of new converts were formerly followers of Campbell's movement.[32]

In a late 1868 reminiscence of the conversion of Campbell's followers to Smith, Simonds Ryder wrote, "To give particulars of the Mormon excitement of 1831 would require a volume."[33] The so-called Mormon defection in Mantua, Hiram, Mentor, and Kirtland likely offended many of the Disciples of Christ on several counts. First was Sidney Rigdon's defection to the perceived enemy and second was the loss of many members.

In May 1831, a northern Ohio newspaper reported, "Strange as it may appear, it is an unquestionable fact, that this singular sect have, within three or four weeks, made many proselytes in this county. The number of believers in the faith, in three or four of the northern townships, is said to exceed one hundred—among whom are many intelligent and respectable individuals."[34] With the influx of Mormons coming from New York and additional converts, some have estimated the number to be a thousand members at this time.[35]

A review of some of those who left Reforming Baptist beliefs and over time became prominent Mormon leaders reveals the impact their departure must have had on many of Campbell's restoration-movement congregations. Sidney Rigdon and Frederick G. Williams became Smith's counselors in the First Presidency; Orson and Parley Pratt, Orson Hyde, and Lyman Wight were ordained Apostles and members of the Quorum of Twelve; Levi Hancock became a member of the Quorum of Seventy; Edward Partridge and Newel K. Whitney became bishops, the former presiding over all the congregations in Missouri and the latter presiding over all the congregations in Ohio; Isaac Morley and Titus Billings became counselors to these bishops; John Murdock, a prominent missionary, baptized many people shortly after his own baptism; Eliza R. Snow became the second president of the women's organization, the Relief Society, and her brother Lorenzo became the fifth president, prophet, seer, and revelator of the church.[36] The contributions of these individuals to the growth of Smith's restoration movement can hardly be overstated.[37]

Within weeks after Rigdon was baptized, he came to Fayette, New York, in early December 1830 to meet Smith and find out what the Lord expected of him. In the revelation given through Smith, Rigdon was told that he had been a preparer of the way in his work as a Reforming Baptist preacher, just as John the Baptist had prepared the way for Christ. Rigdon immediately had new responsibilities in the Church of Christ, beginning with acting as a scribe for Joseph Smith's translation of the Bible (discussed in chapter 9). This work brought forth hours of discussion between Smith and Rigdon on the meaning of passages in the scriptures and revelatory clarification.[38]

Locating the site for the city of Zion became a focus for Smith in September 1830. In June 1831, Smith, Rigdon, and several others left Kirtland, Ohio, for Missouri with the promise from God that if they were faithful, the place for Zion (the New Jerusalem) would be revealed to them.[39] On the way, Smith met Walter Scott, one of Campbell's chief evangelists, in Cincinnati, Ohio. Their interview was not cordial. Like Campbell, Scott disagreed with Smith on the extraordinary gifts of the Spirit. Recalling their exchange, Smith stated, "Before the close of our interview, he manifested one of the bitterest spirits against the doctrine of the New Testament, ('that these signs shall follow them that believe,' as recorded in the 16th chapter of the gospel according to St. Mark,) that I ever witnessed among men."[40] In July, Smith learned that Independence, Missouri, was the center place and the location of a future temple.[41] In August, Rigdon dedicated the land for the gathering of the Saints, and Smith dedicated the temple site.[42]

By 1833, Smith was aware of Rigdon's shortcomings. While noting that Rigdon was sometimes selfish and prideful and lacked pure and steadfast love, Smith also complimented him, saying, "He is a <very> great and good man, a man of great power of words. . . . He is a man whom God will up hold, if he will continue faithful to his calling."[43] In 1834, Rigdon became a counselor and spokesman for Smith as well.[44] David Whitmer, a witness of the Book of Mormon, wrote, "Rigdon was a thorough Bible scholar, a man of fine education, and a powerful orator. He soon worked himself deep into Brother Joseph's affections, and had more influence over him than any other man living."[45] Rigdon's educational attainment was greater than Smith's, and he was considered the better preacher, but it was Smith's revelations and not Rigdon's sermons that provided the foundation of the Church of Christ. Whitmer, however, believed that errors had been introduced into the church and that Rigdon was the source of them.

WAR OF WORDS AND VIOLENCE

Campbell was stung by Rigdon's defection, and he was concerned about its consequences. In his 7 February 1831 edition of the *Millennial Harbinger*, Campbell addressed an open letter to his followers, the Wellsburg saints and the faithful brethren in Kirtland, expressing his sympathy for the trials and afflictions they were suffering as a consequence of Rigdon's apostasy along with some in their congregations. To reassure those remaining faithful to his followers, he began as did the Apostle Paul in several of his epistles: "Dearly beloved . . . , no other foundation can any man lay than is already laid; and that if a man or an angel from heaven should preach any other gospel than that which we have already received . . . he will be accursed when the Lord comes."[46] The letter was preceded by Campbell's critique of the Book of Mormon in his article titled "Delusions" and was followed by a disparaging article on Sidney Rigdon.[47]

In the latter article, Campbell expressed his regret, surprise, and condemnation that Rigdon had renounced the ancient gospel. By doing so, Campbell declared that Rigdon had been insincere in his profession of it—in other words, Rigdon was a hypocrite. Campbell believed Rigdon had "fallen into the snare of the Devil in joining the Mormonites." Campbell vigorously attacked Rigdon by ascribing to him instability with a "peculiar mental and corporeal malady. . . [with] fits of melancholy succeeded by fits of enthusiasm accompanied by some kind of nervous spasms and swoonings which he has, since his defection, interpreted into the agency of the Holy Ghost." Campbell concluded his vituperative tirade by declaring that "every person who receives the book of Mormon is an apostate from all that he ever professed, if, indeed, he ever professed to receive or value any thing we have ever spoken or written on the subject of christianity."[48] Thus began a steady twelve-year back-and-forth war of words between Campbell and Smith, converts and defectors.

In February 1831, Smith began teaching principles he claimed were revealed to him pertaining to the law of consecration. The consecration of personal property for the care of the poor became formalized through the bishop of the church and his counselors with an unbreakable deed.[49] Consecration was also part of the law for the creation of Zion and the building of temples.[50] In an 1868 reminiscence, Symonds Ryder, a brief convert from the Disciples of Christ, claimed he learned about consecration when Smith, Rigdon, Pratt, and others went to Missouri to lay the foundations for the city of Zion and a temple in Independence; "they left their papers behind," allowing him "an opportunity to become acquainted with the internal arrangement of their church." From the papers he concluded that "a plot was laid to take their property from them and place it under the control of Joseph Smith" to form a communal society, and that "this common fund would allow certain persons to live without work."[51] Ryder, baptized into the Church of Christ about June 1831, returned in September 1831 to his former Disciples community in Hiram and was described thereafter as a faithful elder, defender, teacher, and preacher to the congregants in northeastern Ohio.[52]

During this time, Ezra Booth, a former Methodist clergyman, joined with the Church of Christ in February 1831. His conversion was a short-lived five months. In the fall of that year, he published nine letters in the *Ohio Star*, giving his reasons for renouncing Smith and Mormonism, stirring up even more animosity against Smith and his followers.

The spring of 1832 brought the religious conflict to a climax in the form of mob violence toward Smith and Rigdon, who were at this time living at or near the Johnson Farm in Hiram, Ohio. On 25 March 1832, disguised with blackened faces, a mob of approximately twenty-five to thirty people from Shalersville, Hiram, Garrettsville, Nelson, Mantua, and possibly Freedom "gathered to seek revenge for what they perceived as the deception of the Mormon leaders."[53] According to a late reminiscence of Symonds Ryder, some "who had been the dupes of this deception determined not to let" Smith's so-called plot to defraud them "pass with impunity, and a company was formed of citizens . . . [who] proceded to headquarters in the darkness of night, and took Smith and Rigdon from their beds, and tarred and feathered them both, and let them go."[54] The mob was made up of those who felt they had fallen victim to a scheme, meaning some were apostate Mormons, and others who had family members who had joined with the Mormons, and still others who saw an opportunity to rid the community of two problem makers.

Smith dictated his version of what happened. Sidney Rigdon was dragged out of his house by the feet until his head was bloody and he became unconscious. Smith, when he saw him, supposed him dead and began to plead with the mob:

> You will have mercy and spare my life, I hope:— To which they replied, "God dam ye: call on yer God for help, we'll show ye no mercy;— and the people began to shew themselves in every direction: one coming from the orchard had a plank, and I expected they would kill me, and carry me off on the plank. . . .The mob . . . held a council, and as I could occasionally over-hear a word, I suppose it was to know whether it was best to kill me. They returned after a while when I learned that they had concluded not to kill me, but pound and scratch me well, tear of[f] my shirt and drawers and leave me naked. . . . They ran back and fetched the bucket of tar, when one exclaimed, "God dam it,—Let us tar up his mouth;" and they tried to force the tar paddle into my mouth. . . . They then tried to force a phial into my mouth, and broke it in my teeth.[55] All my

clothes were torn off me . . . and one man fell on me and scratched my body with his nails like a mad cat, and then muttered out, "God dam ye, that's the way the Holy Ghost falls on folks."[56]

In a later reminiscence of the event, Rigdon declared:

A mob of 20 or 30 ruffians came damming & roaring against us—our houses were surrounded. . . . At last there got some hundreds of them. . . . They broke into my house I was dragged out of my bed, was put on a large wood pile—some were putting it on me. My head went thump thump upon the hard frozen ground—they then threw a quantity of pitch on me . . . [and also attempted to throw] a something else on me I feel and the next morning when I went to the same place I found it was a quantity of aqua fortis [nitric acid] that they were going to throw on me.[57]

Smith described Rigdon's condition as "crazy" and delirious for days after his ordeal. "His head [was] highly inflamed, for they had dragged him by his heels, and those, too, so high from the earth he could not raise his head from the rough frozen surface, which lacerated it exceedingly."[58]

Initially, at least some participants believed they had done a service to the community and "ended the Mormon absurdity in Hiram."[59] The bitingly satirical headline in the *Hudson Ohio Observer and Telegraph* read, "Triumphs of the Mormon Faith." In an unsigned letter to the editor, the author wrote regarding the tarring and feathering of Smith and Rigdon. His sarcastic barb stated, "I call this a base transaction, an unlawful act, a work of darkness, a diabolical trick. But bad as it is, it proves one important truth which every wise man indeed knew before, that is, that Satan has more power than the pretended prophets of Mormon."[60]

One of the side effects of this incident was surely unintended. John Murdock's wife, Julia Clapp Murdock, had died giving birth to twins, Julia and Joseph. Unable to care for the infants, John gave them to Emma and Joseph Smith, who had lost premature twins born the very same day. Already sick, baby Joseph was sleeping separately from Julia to prevent spreading his illness. Joseph was taking care of the little boy when the mob came and dragged him out, leaving the door open. After that extended exposure to the cold winter air, baby Joseph died a few days later. The family of Judge Orris Clapp was highly regarded as members of the Disciples, and his son Matthew Clapp married Alexander

Campbell's sister, Alicia Campbell. Julia Clapp, sister to Matthew, married John Murdock, and both joined with the Mormons; hence, little Joseph was Alexander's nephew by marriage, and the grandson of a prominent Disciples family.[61]

In 1833, Doctor Philastus Hurlbut, a former Methodist preacher and short-lived convert to Mormonism, made public accusations about Smith and the Church of Christ. That year, Joseph Smith wrote to William Phelps and others that "we are suffering great persecution on account of one man by the name of Docter Hurlburt who has been expeled from the chirch for lude and adulterous conduct and to spite us he is lieing in a wonderful manner and the peapl[people] are running after him and giveing him mony to b[r]ake down mormanism which much endangers <our lives> at preasnt[present]."[62]

Perhaps smarting from Rigdon's perceived treachery, several followers of Campbell's reform movement advanced money to Hurlbut to discredit Smith. "Hurlbut was hired by a local committee in Ohio 'to obtain affidavits showing the bad character of the Mormon Smith family' and to 'completely divest Joseph Smith of all claims to the character of an honest man, and place him at an immeasurable distance from the high station he pretends to occupy.'" In 1833, Hurlbut traveled to Ohio, New York, and Pennsylvania, collecting statements about the Smith family. Hurlbut's efforts to uncover embarrassing information from Smith's neighbors in New York was easy. They recollected the family's low character, purporting that they were unwilling to work for a living; instead, they were involved in money digging. It is true that in 1826, after being hired by Josiah Stowell to find buried silver, Joseph was accused of being a disorderly person and brought to trial on the charge of "glass looking" with a peep stone to find lost objects and buried treasure. Magic and the miracles of Christianity were intermingled until well into the nineteenth century to find lost objects, Native American artifacts, or Spanish bullion. Not only were the Smiths looking for treasure in the Palmyra area in the 1820s but so were many of their neighbors.[63] The combination of folk tradition and religion was a common part of the culture among virtually all Yankees of that generation—strange by today's standards, but a harmless and accepted activity then.[64]

Hurlbut purchased a copy of Solomon Spaulding's 1812 historical romance, *Lost Manuscript Found*, and collected affidavits from his friends and family who alleged there were similarities between

Spaulding's manuscript and the Book of Mormon. Hurlbut claimed that before Rigdon publicly embraced Mormonism, he and Smith had conspired to alter Spaulding's novel that linked the American Indians and the Jews to produce the Book of Mormon.[65] Although the affidavits claimed that the two books shared names and similar plotlines, the manuscript of the novel itself demonstrated both of these claims to be unfounded. Rigdon vehemently denied accusations of conspiracy. In 1833 or 1834, speaking before a large congregation among whom were some who believed Hurlbut and Howe's accusations of collusion with Smith, Rigdon declared, "I testify in the presence of this congregation, and before God and all the Holy Angels up yonder, (pointing towards heaven), before whom I expect to give account at the judgment day, that I never saw a sentence of the Book of Mormon, I never penned a sentence of the Book of Mormon, I never knew that there was such a book in existence as the Book of Mormon, until it was presented to me by Parley P. Pratt, in the form that it now is." But the rumor was started and has continued in some form into the twenty-first century.[66]

Hurlbut sold his research to Eber D. Howe, who published it (but not Spaulding's novel), along with Booth's accusatory letters to the *Ohio Star*, quotations from Campbell's "Delusions," and a collection of other anti-Mormon sentiments in his 1834 book titled *Mormonism Unvailed* [*sic*].[67] Howe furthered Hurlbut's claims by adding dates to the purported Rigdon-Spaulding theory of the origin of the Book of Mormon. He argued that after Rigdon discovered the unpublished novel sometime between 1823 and 1824 while in Pittsburgh, he conspired with Smith and reworked it to create the Book of Mormon. Howe's collection of accusations are at least part of the source for the claim that Mormonism sprang from a Reforming Baptist preacher and follower of Alexander Campbell's movement, Sidney Rigdon, and, therefore, that Mormonism is a breakoff of Campbellism.[68]

In his new position with the Church of Christ, Rigdon fired off his own barbs against Campbell's restoration. In a seven-part series published in *The Evening and the Morning Star*, printed in Kirtland, Ohio, beginning in early 1834, Rigdon compared the restorations of the day with thinly veiled references to Walter Scott and Alexander Campbell. It appears that Rigdon took the opportunity to defend himself and vent his anger on his former colleagues for their public accusations and condemnation of him. Since they had refused to restore all of the New

Testament practices, he felt justified about those things they had ignored. In his first article he wrote the following regarding communalism:

> All the religious societies in our country, (or nearly all,) will direct us to the Acts of the Apostles, and to the notable day of pentecost for the time that the gospel was first proclaimed; and to Jerusalem for the first gospel church that was organized. They will show us what was required of men in order that they might become christians: That they must repent and be baptized for the remission of sins, and then receive the gift of the Holy Spirit. But here that matter ends, even with those who are the most tenacious for the scriptures, and for the order of the new testament, they will follow this church no farther. Instead of following them to a full display of their faith in the equal distribution of their goods, they will fly off in a tangent, and endeavor to prove that this was all the church that so disposed of their property. They are very cautious in the mean time, never to notice what Paul said to Titus: "For this cause left I thee in Crete, that thou shouldst set in order the things that are wanting, and ordain elders in every city as I had appointed thee."[69]

In his final article in the series, Rigdon wrote on another point of contention between himself and Campbell: manifestations of the Holy Spirit in the modern day. Campbell was a cessationist, and Rigdon firmly believed everything from the apostolic area, including extraordinary gifts of the Spirit as manifest on the day of Pentecost—an integral part of the restoration of the ancient order of things. Without the gifts of the Spirit, such as faith in mighty miracles, Rigdon believed a restoration could only be considered imaginary—a deft jab at Campbell. On the subject, Rigdon wrote the following:

> But notwithstanding all these pretended reformations, there are none of them who ever pretend to restore to the world that which it has lost, namely, the religion of heaven: they all with one consent, admit that that has disappeared. . . . I say their religion, because, take away their faith by which they wrought their mighty works, and what is left? nothing but a form, an empty sound, mere idle pretentions, without virtue or efficacy. . . . But what renders this peculiarly strange is, that the sects, though they confess that the religion of the ancients has ceased, and that the gift of the Holy Spirit is no more, yet, they claim to themselves the promises made to the people who enjoyed the gifts of the Holy Spirit, and who had power sufficient with God to obtain all gifts, and revelations sufficient for both this world, and that which is to come; but by

what authority they claim them, we have yet to learn. . . . The promises of God were never public plunder, to be applied according to the whims or caprices of men, nor according to the prejudices, nor prepossessions of any age; but were founded upon definite and fixed principles, suited precisely to the people to whom they were given, and rarely applicable to any other people, but those to whom they were immediately given. . . . And it was because of their peculiar circumstances that they obtained all promises they did obtain.[70]

Decrying the opposition to Joseph Smith and his restoration, Oliver Cowdery, as editor of *The Evening and the Morning Star*, made reference to the writings of Campbell, Hurlbut, and Howe in the fall of 1834: "One man has cried 'delusion,' another 'false prophets,' a third has reported a long catalogue of falsehoods of his own making, to blast the characters of men whom he never saw nor had a spark of evidence against." He also declared that there would be a fourth man who would see through these untrue claims and embrace the gospel.[71]

In 1835, Campbell printed a brief blurb from Howe's book *Mormonism Unvailed*, pronouncing it an "honest" representation of the facts.[72] Howe was the source of Campbell's accusations that Smith was a "money-digger, juggler, and diviner of stolen goods."[73]

Joseph Smith finally responded to Howe, Campbell, Hurlbut, and others in a "letter to the Elders of the Church of the Latter Days" in December 1835. Pertaining to Eber Howe, Smith asked, "Is not this the kingdom of heaven that is raising its head in the last days . . . even the church of the Latter day saints,—like an impenetrable, immovable rock in the midst of the mighty deep, exposed to storms and tempests of satan, but has, thus far, remained steadfast and is still braving the mountain waves of opposition, . . . urged onward with redoubled fury by the enemy of righteousness, with his pitchfork of lies, as you will see fairly represented in a cut, [of] 'Mormonism Unveiled'?" Smith's comments directed to Alexander Campbell were even harsher, with a reference to what Campbell had called him in his February 1831 critique of the Book of Mormon, "Delusions": Elymus [Elymas], sorcerer and an atheist.

And we hope that this adversary of truth will continue to stir up the sink of iniquity, that people may the more readily discern between the righteous and wicked. We also would notice one of the modern sons of Sceva, who would fain have made people believe that he could cast out devils, by a certain pamphlet (viz. the "Millenial Harbinger,") that went the rounds through our country, who felt so fully authorized to brand Jo Smith, with the appellation of Elymus the sorcerer, and to say with Paul, O full of all subtilty and all mischief, thou child of the devil, thou enemy of all righteousness, wilt thou not cease to pervert the right ways of the Lord! We would reply to this gentleman—Paul we know, and Christ we know, but who are ye? And with the best of feelings, we would say to him, in the language of Paul to those who said they were John's disciples, but had not so much as heard there was a Holy Ghost, to repent and be baptised for the remission of sins by those who have legal authority, and under their hands you shall receive the Holy Ghost, according to the scriptures.[74]

In a sort of postscript to Campbell, Smith declared Hurlbut and Howe disreputable men. He said, "The right honorable Doctor Philatus Hurlbut who is the legitimate author of 'Mormonism Unveiled,' is not so much a doctor of physic, as of falsehood, whereas reverend Eber Howe is the illegitimate author of 'Mormonism Unveiled.' In order to give currency to the Millennial Harbinger, Campbell ought to point out to his readers that that Mr. Hurlburt, was bound over to court, for threatening to take my life."[75]

Rigdon continued his own verbal dispute with Campbell regarding gifts of the Spirit. In an 1836 letter to Oliver Cowdery, Rigdon wrote:

We feel in the mean time at liberty to say, that we have all the evidence necessary to satisfy our mind, that Messrs. Campbell, and Scott, the leaders of that brotherhood, are not honest in their religion: they are men who think and act for themselves, independently, and they do know, that the same Jesus who said to his disciples "Go ye into all the world, and preach the gospel to every creature: he that believeth and is baptized shall be saved, and he that believeth not shall be damned." Also [Jesus] said "That signs shall follow them that believe &c."[76]

Walter Scott, former preaching and evangelizing friend from his days in Pittsburg, took sharp aim in his monthly publication the *Evangelist*, and Rigdon responded. He rebuked Scott, his brother-in-law Adamson Bentley, and Alexander Campbell in an 1836 letter to the editor of the *Latter Day Saints' Messenger and Advocate* on the topic of the right to claim the gift of the Holy Ghost following baptism for the remission of sins. Rigdon called them "destitute of candor" in their failure to investigate this aspect of the New Testament, "proving that after all his pretentions, he is an unbeliever in the ancient gospel." He accused Scott in particular of taking the "liberty of leaving out what he pleases and explaining the rest to suit himself." For example, he teaches baptism for the remission of sins, but modifies the Apostle Peter's Day of Pentecost promise of the gift of the Holy Ghost, which includes "prophesying, seeing visions, dreaming dreams."[77]

Rigdon also blasted Symonds Ryder in a published letter for making "without cause or provocation" what Rigdon deemed an unmanly and unrighteous attack of slander and abuse on himself and other members of the church of the Latter Day Saints. He accused Ryder and other followers of Walter Scott and Alexander Campbell as not at liberty to think for themselves. Rigdon maintained that the Bible was not their primary source, but the writings of the *Evangelist* and the *Millennial Harbinger* and called this a barefaced and impudent scheme imposed by Scott and Campbell.[78] Ryder, however, was a short-lived convert to Mormonism who quickly returned to Campbell's fold.

In 1839, Campbell republished a critique from the *Boston Daily Advertiser* about the "Mormon Bible." The article included statements from Matilda Davison, widow of Solomon Spaulding, concerning the "origin of the 'Book of Mormon,' or 'Golden Bible,'" along with Campbell's own editorial, which reiterated some of the main points he had made in his original 1831 critique.[79] In 1842 and 1843, Campbell serially reprinted in his *Millennial Harbinger* extracts from the pamphlet *Mormonism Exposed*, by LaRoy Sunderlund, and a diatribe titled *Mormonism in Agony.*[80] In conclusion to his series on Mormonism Exposed, Campbell wrote:

> I have now paid my share of attention to the meanest, vilest, and most infamous humbug ever promulgated in any age, language, or country under these broad and high heavens. It is a sacramental seal of the Devilism of the nineteenth century—an impersonation of Bible ignorance, infidel impudence, and heaven-defying impiety. I have printed in sequence the whole expose of its revealed abominations. I have been asked to do this by my brethren in Great Britain as well as by those in America, and I have done it faithfully for the common benefit of the whole community.
>
> I am acquainted with the early history of Mormonism perhaps as fully as any one of its historians. I have marked its progress, and I opine, upon all its premises, that it would be more difficult to exaggerate its enormous wickedness than any other species of delusion, fraud, or fiction ever palmed upon the world. It is much more execrable than the

Koran, though because of the light of the age it has not room to plant itself in the earth; and yet it is such an indication of the ignorance and gullability of all masses of religionists, that it is humiliating and mortifying in the superlative degree, to notice its headway in this country and in other places, though its votaries are scarcely more than a tithe of what its lying oracles would have the community to believe. Meanwhile we must refer all future inquiries to the documents already spread upon our pages, from which, if they cannot learn its monstrous impiety, they could not be taught by any human tongue.[81]

Campbell's twelve-year history with Smith and his restoration gave him a perspective on the Mormons that perhaps no one else had. He was convinced that Smith had deluded his gullible followers with a more abominable hoax than the Qur'an and was exaggerating his success by reporting ten times the number of actual converts.

Clearly the war of words by both sides was to attack and defend, prevent defections, and keep converts. Parley Pratt began the Mormon invasion of Reforming Baptist territory in northeastern Ohio by visiting his former preacher and friend Sidney Rigdon. Campbell immediately responded to the challenge by publishing his judgment on Smith and the Book of Mormon. Neither side held back, especially Pratt and Rigdon in attacking Campbell and his points of view, and neither did Campbell, Booth, Hurlbut, Howe, Bentley, or Scott in attacking Smith.

Stolen Doctrine

Sidney Rigdon, Parley Pratt, Orson Hyde, John Murdock, Isaac Morley, and Lyman Wight were preachers or influential men in Campbell's restoration and brought some of his beliefs with them. There can be no question that Smith exchanged ideas with former followers of Campbell's restoration movement. Integrating converts from a variety of religious traditions meant that initially, aspects of their previous religion were sometimes incorporated into local churches until Joseph told them to do otherwise. They would have assumed that what they had learned or been teaching was correct until revelation dictated it false. Rigdon, as a constant companion and scribe to Smith, would have brought many of his previous teachings to the forefront in their study of the Bible which would have helped focus the questions that came to their minds as they worked on Smith's inspired version of the Bible.[82] In October 1833, Rigdon was given additional responsibilities in his work with Smith.

The two men were to work together closely, Smith revealing truth and Rigdon testifying of it with great power.[83] Smith's conversations with his contemporaries certainly influenced his reading and studying and led him to ponder many ideas. What is unique is that his questions drove him to ask God, which resulted in revelation. It was not his native intellect or the ideas he heard from others to which he gave credit to his restoration, but to God. Whatever gospel truths that Thomas and Alexander Campbell, Walter Scott, and Adamson Bentley had taught and discovered in their study of the scriptures could also be accepted by Mormons. Joseph Smith declared that receiving truth is a fundamental principle of Mormonism—that is, "We believe that we have a right to embrace all, and every item of truth, without limitation," regardless of its source.[84] In other words, he believed that if an idea is true, it belongs in Mormonism.

Scott, a major preacher and missionary for Campbell's reform movement, published his own monthly paper, the *Evangelist*. In an 1843 edition, he titled a paragraph "Mormonism—The Means by which it stole the True Gospel." He declared, "It is well known that the Mormons preach the true gospel and plead for immediate obedience to it on the part of the hearers, as the advocates of original Christianity do. This was not an original measure of Mormonism; for, indeed, baptism for the remission of sins is a phrase not found in their book. A few of their leaders took it from Rigdon."[85] Scott was certain that Rigdon learned about baptism for the remission of sins during the 1823 McCalla versus Campbell debate on infant baptism by sprinkling as opposed to baptism by immersion for believers. Campbell reprinted Scott's paragraph and corrected the false claims in the *Evangelist* by stating, "Baptism for remission is, however, taught in the Book of Mormon. . . . It is found variously and frequently stated in the Book of Mormon."[86]

In 1841, Adamson Bentley, Rigdon's brother-in-law and Reforming Baptist preacher who remained in Campbell's movement, recalled that in 1827 Rigdon had stated that "in the plates dug up in New York there was an account not only of the Aborigines of this country but also it was stated that the Christian religion had been preached in this country during the first century just as we were preaching it on the Western Reserve."[87] Contrary to his 1831 assertion in "Delusions" that Smith was the author of the Book of Mormon, Campbell became convinced the year Bentley was talking about was actually 1826, that "Sidney Rigdon had a hand in the manufacture of the religious part of the Book of

Mormon," and that he had "stolen" doctrine regarding baptism from his former associates in the Reforming Baptist movement. Walter Scott, Adamson Bentley, and Alexander Campbell's comments regarding Rigdon and his association with Joseph Smith and the Book of Mormon were late reminiscences—at least fifteen years after Rigdon purportedly helped write the Book of Mormon. Tensions between Rigdon and his family and former colleagues were high.

Nevertheless, the similarity between the two restoration movements in naming the same basic principles and ordinances of the gospel led Mormon historian T. Edgar Lyon to comment, "Casual observers assumed that The Church of Jesus Christ of Latter-day Saints was but one phase of the 'Campbellite agitation.'"[88] Campbell and Smith had some things in common; however, emphasizing their commonalities at the expense of their great differences—or to place Rigdon as the source for Campbell's or Smith's restoration—gives an inaccurate picture of both restoration movements.

There is no evidence that Rigdon ever claimed, even after he left the Mormons, to have had doctrine revealed to him separately from Smith, although he was a recipient of several powerful manifestations from God. He did claim, however, to have contributed significantly through his service to both the "Campbellites" and the "Mormonites."[89] Campbell's foundational documents demonstrate that he was his own man, however much Rigdon added as a preacher and evangelist. On the whole, Smith claimed that what he received regarding doctrine, polity, and practice came by revelation from God, and Rigdon never objected to Smith's claim.

Campbell's attempt to reform the Baptists with a restoration to the ancient order of things convinced many individuals of the flaws and shortcomings of the Protestant Reformation, turning them into independent seekers. Smith's restoration, a much more expansive attempt to return to ancient covenants as well as to embrace newly revealed teachings, appealed to some of those same independent seekers. Rivalry, strife, and conflict over territory, converts, and doctrine were inevitable.

Recently, Craig Blomberg of Denver Seminary listed a number of Latter-day Saint doctrines and practices that were both Christian and parallel to Campbell's restoration movement and argues that their desires for restoration and other similarities between the two religions imply that Smith borrowed from Campbell or that Mormonism grew out of Campbellism.[90] For example, after noting that Sidney Rigdon, a close associate of Campbell later became Smith's "right hand man," he quoted George Arbaugh, a twentieth-century Lutheran minister and professor who claimed that "Mormonism was transformed by revelation from a Campbellite sect to a unique religion."[91] Arbaugh's main thesis on Mormonism was based on the convergence of three factors, all of which related to Sidney Rigdon: founding the "Mormon" church, acquiring the Book of Mormon (Spaulding manuscript), and appointing Joseph Smith as prophet.[92] Significantly, both Abner Cole (pen name Obadiah Dogberry) and Alexander Campbell, who wrote their versions of the origin of the Book of Mormon in 1829 and in early 1831, declared Smith as the sole author. Emma Smith also stated that Sidney and Joseph did not meet until after the Book of Mormon was translated and published.[93] Arbaugh contended, however, that "Mormons borrowed outright, so that Mormonism is in a sense a split-off from the Campbellite Church."[94] Historian Marvin Hill maintains that Christian primitivism "was too diffused among the early Mormons for it to have been purloined from the Campbellites. . . . The primitive gospel beliefs of the Mormons were essential to the movement and did not need to be surreptitiously taken from the Disciples."[95] Churches of Christ historian Richard Hughes also refutes the assertion that early Mormons had "filched from us" key doctrines of baptism and forgiveness of sins as an explanation for early Mormon successes among Campbell's followers.[96]

Unfortunately, Blomberg agrees with Arbaugh's assessment that Smith gathered much of his doctrine from Campbell via Rigdon, and if this hypothesis were correct, Mormonism could be considered Christian since the Disciples of Christ are accepted members of the Christian community.[97] It is difficult to imagine who would be more offended by Blomberg's claim that the only way Mormonism could be considered Christian would be if Mormonism is a Campbellite sect—Joseph Smith or Alexander Campbell.

The 1830 missionary efforts in northeastern Ohio by former Reforming Baptist Parley Pratt and his companions culled a number of new members from the local congregations of Campbell's disciples, bringing them into Smith's Church of Christ. Sidney Rigdon was a highly regarded preacher to a number of Reforming Baptist churches in Ohio and a successful evangelizer of many to Campbell's restoration of the ancient order. As such, he was a key convert for the Mormons and a devastating blow to Campbell's followers. Many from his various congregations followed his lead into the Mormon Church. Although numbers of converts to Mormonism are estimated in late 1830 as over one hundred, their previous affiliation was not recorded. Numbers in each of the individual Disciples congregations were small, but the impact of even a few families leaving could be overwhelming. Rigdon and Campbell had already begun to separate on communalism and gifts of the Spirit that Rigdon thought should be part of a true restoration of the ancient Christian church. His baptism into a different restoration tradition was the clean break that was already in process. Rigdon's talents in preaching the gospel and knowledge of the Bible were immediately put to use by Smith. One Churches of Christ historian questioned whether Rigdon was a Benedict Arnold.[98] The desertion of one so highly regarded and important in that area of Ohio deeply rankled Thomas and Alexander Campbell, former ministerial and missionary companions Adamson Bentley and Walter Scott, and those from Rigdon's congratations who did not join him in converting. Tarring and feathering as well as accusations of conspiring with Smith and stealing Campbell's doctrine were manifestations of how deeply felt Rigdon's defection was.

NOTES

1. History, 1838–1856, volume A-1 [23 December 1805–30 August 1834], 61, http://www.josephsmithpapers.org.
2. John Wickliffe Rigdon, "I Never Knew a Time When I Did Not Know Joseph Smith," ed. Karl Keller, *Dialogue: A Journal of Mormon Thought* 1, no. 4 (Winter 1966): 19–20.
3. Daryl Chase, "Sidney Rigdon—Early Mormon" (PhD diss., University of Chicago, 1931), 9–10, 12.
4. Richardson, *Memoirs of Alexander Campbell*, 2:44–45.
5. Campbell, "Anecdotes, Incidents, and Facts," *Millennial Harbinger* 5, no. 6 (June 1848): 523.
6. History, 1838–1856, volume A-1 [23 December 1805–30 August 1834], 63, http://josephsmithpapers.org.
7. J. J. Haley, *Debates That Made History: The Story of Alexander Campbell's Debates with Rev. John Walker, Rev. W. L. McCalla, Mr. Robert Owen, Bishop Purcell, and Rev. Nathan L. Rice* (St. Louis: Christian Board of Publication, 1840), 40; Richardson, *Memoirs of Alexander Campbell*, 2:47.
8. Chase, "Sidney Rigdon," 14.
9. Richard S. Van Wagoner, *Sidney Rigdon: A Portrait of Religious Excess* (Salt Lake City: Signature, 1994), 31.
10. Hayden, *Early History of the Disciples*, 64; Richardson, *Memoirs of Alexander Campbell*, 2:99. As noted in the introduction, Alexander Campbell's religious mentor at Glasgow had been an advocate for the reform ideas of Robert Sandeman and John Glas. Their reform was referred to as Sandemanian. According to Rigdon's recollections, Walter Scott was a member of the Sandemanian Church in Pittsburg. History, 1838–1856, volume A-1 [23 December 1805–30 August 1834], 64, http://josephsmithpapers.org.

11. Walter Scott is given primary credit for the large number of conversions. "Walter Scott," *Encyclopedia of the Stone-Campbell Movement,* 675. See also Chase, "Sidney Rigdon," 24.
12. Staker, *Hearken, O Ye People,* 279.
13. Whitney, "A Leaf from an Autobiography," 51; Hayden, *Early History of the Disciples,* 191–92.
14. Richard McClellan, "Sidney Rigdon's 1820 Ministry: Preparing the Way for Mormonism in Ohio," *Dialogue: A Journal of Mormon Thought* 36, no. 4 (Spring 2003): 156–57. *Mentor Christian Church Scrapbook* (Mentor, OH: Mentor Christian Church, 1978), 5.
15. Joseph R. Jeter, "Some We Lost: A Study of Disaffections from the Disciples of Christ," *Discipliana* 61, no. 1 (Spring 2001): 7.
16. Rigdon, "I Never Knew a Time When I Did Not Know Joseph Smith," 21.
17. Van Wagoner, *Sidney Rigdon,* 31. Some have postulated that the Isaac Morley communal society was influenced by the teachings of Samuel Underhill, a member and promoter of Robert Owen's beliefs on communalism in Kendal, Ohio, close to Kirtland.
18. More on this debate is found in chapter 13.
19. Hayden, *Early History of the Disciples,* 298–99; Garrison and DeGroot, *The Disciples of Christ,* 197; Van Wagoner, *Sidney Rigdon,* 54.
20. "History of Joseph Smith," *Times and Seasons* 4, no. 19 (15 August 1843): 289.
21. M. S. C. (Matthew Clapp), "Mormonism," *Evangelical Inquirer* 1, no. 10 (7 March 1831): 221.
22. "History of Joseph Smith," *Times and Seasons* 4, no. 19 (15 August 1843): 290, http://www.josephsmithpapers.org.
23. "History of Joseph Smith," *Times and Seasons* 4, no. 20 (1 September 1843): 304. History, 1838–1856, volume A-1 [23 December 1805–30 August 1834], 75, http://josephsmithpapers.org.
24. History, 1838–1856, volume A-1 [23 December 1805–30 August 1834], 74–75, http://josephsmithpapers.org.
25. According to Steven Hurd, some accounts record that as many as five hundred people in the Western Reserve joined the Mormons between 1830 and 1831. Steven M. Hurd, comp., *On the Principle of Faith: The Story of Mantua Center Christian Church 1827-2002* (self-published), 37. Mark Staker gives a record of the approximate number of baptisms between 3 November 1830 and 12 November 1830 as fifty-eight, however their previous affiliation is not noted. See Staker, *Hearken, O Ye People,* xix–xx, 285. Parley P. Pratt recorded that within two to three weeks of their arrival, they "baptized one hundred and twenty-seven souls, and this number soon increased to one thousand." Pratt, *Autobiography of Parley P. Pratt,* 52.
26. Eliot Irving Osgood, *Centennial History of the Hiram Church, 1835-1935* (Hiram, OH: Hiram Christian Church and the Hiram Historical Society, 1935), 5.
27. Hayden, *Early History of the Disciples,* 239–40.
28. Hayden, *Early History of the Disciples,* 252; see also Hurd, comp., *On the Principle of Faith,* 37–38.
29. Hayden, *Early History of the Disciples,* 220.
30. Hayden, *Early History of the Disciples,* 195.
31. Darwin Atwater, "Letter to Amos S. Hayden," in Hayden, *Early History of the Disciples,* 239; see also Hurd, comp., *On the Principle of Faith,* 37–38.
32. Staker, *Hearken, O Ye People,* 325.
33. Hayden, *Early History of the Disciples,* 220.

34. *Western Courier*, Ravenna, Ohio, 26 May 1831. Levi Jackman Autobiography, L. Tom Perry Special Collections, Harold B. Lee Library, Brigham Young University, Provo, UT.

35. Thomas M. Spencer, "Introduction," in *The Missouri Mormon Experience*, ed. Thomas M. Spencer (Columbia: University of Missouri Press, 2010), 2.

36. Although Eliza R. Snow's father, mother, and sister joined Smith's group in 1831, she remained part of the Disciples until 1835. She had been associated with Campbell's restoration movement through Sidney Rigdon and was attracted to his rational teachings. She had "hoped his new light led to a fullness—was baptized, and soon learned that, as well they might, he and his followers disclaimed all authority, and my baptism was of no consequence." Jill Mulvay Derr and Karen Lynn Davidson, "A Wary Heart Becomes 'Fixed Unalterably': Eliza R. Snow's Conversion to Mormonism," *Journal of Mormon History* 30, no. 2 (Fall 2004): 98. Her brother Lorenzo converted to the Mormons in 1836 at the age of twenty-two.

37. Milton V. Backman Jr., "The Quest for a Restoration: The Birth of Mormonism in Ohio," *BYU Studies* 12, no. 4 (Summer 1972): 364. See also Max H. Parkin, "Kirtland: A Stronghold for the Kingdom," *The Restoration Movement: Essays in Mormon History*, ed. F. Mark McKiernan, Alma R. Blair, Paul M. Edwards (Independence, MO: Herald House, 1979), 63–65.

38. Doctrine and Covenants 35:3–6, 20. For example, in 1832, as the two were contemplating John 5:29 regarding resurrection, they received a revelation referred to as "the Vision," which consisted of 119 verses describing three degrees of glory for resurrected beings.

39. Doctrine and Covenants 52:2–5. One entered into the new covenant through what Smith called the first principles and ordinances of the gospel—faith, repentance, baptism, and the gift of the Holy Ghost.

40. History, 1838–1856, volume A-1 [23 December 1805–30 August 1834], 126, http://www.josephsmithpapers.org.

41. Doctrine and Covenants 57:1–3.

42. Matthew C. Godfrey, Mark Ashurst-McGee, Grant Underwood, Robert J. Woodford, and William G. Hartley, eds., *Documents, Volume 2: July 1831–January 1833*, vol. 2 of the Documents series of *The Joseph Smith Papers*, ed. Dean C. Jessee, Ronald K. Esplin, Richard Lyman Bushman, and Matthew J. Grow (Salt Lake City: Church Historian's Press, 2013), 12–14. To the Latter-day Saints at that time, "to bring forth Zion" meant building a city for the gathering of the Saints as a refuge against tribulations and calamities. Bushman, *Joseph Smith: Rough Stone Rolling*, 168.

43. History, 1838–1856, volume A-1 [23 December 1805–30 August 1834], 380, http://www.josephsmithpapers.org.

44. Doctrine and Covenants 90:6; 100:9.

45. David Whitmer, *An Address to All Believers in Christ* (Richmond, MO: David Whitmer, 1887), 35.

46. Campbell, "Letter," *Millennial Harbinger* 2, no. 2 (7 February 1831): 98.

47. "Delusions" is discussed in greater detail in chapter 11.

48. Campbell, "Sidney Rigdon," *Millennial Harbinger* 2, no. 2 (7 February 1831): 100–101.

49. Doctrine and Covenants 42:30–35.

50. The law of consecration is that of sacrifice—freely made—of time, talents, and property for the building of the kingdom of God. "In order to erect the Temple of the Lord, great exertions will be required on the part of the Saints, so that they may build a house which shall be accepted of by the Almighty, and in which his power and glory shall be manifested. Therefore let those who can, freely make a

sacrifice of their time, their talents, and their property, for the prosperity of the kingdom, and for the love they have to the cause of truth." History, 1838–1856, volume C-1 [2 November 1838–31 July 1842], 1148, http://josephsmithpapers.org; "A Proclamation, To The Saints Scattered Abroad; Greeting," *Times and Seasons* 2, no. 6 (15 January 1841): 277.

51. Symonds Ryder, "Letter to Amos Hayden," in Hayden, *Early History of the Disciples*, 221; Symonds Ryder in Hurd, comp., *On the Principle of Faith*, 38; Allanson Wilcox, in Hurd, comp., *On the Principle of Faith*, 38–39.

52. Hayden, *Early History of the Disciples*, 253.

53. Hurd, comp., *On the Principle of Faith*, 39; Staker, *Hearken, O Ye People*, 348.

54. Ryder, "Letter to Amos Hayden," in Hayden, *Early History of the Disciples*, 221.

55. Dr. Richard Dennison had brought at least three vials of nitric acid. One group argued for tarring and feathering, another for murder, and a third for castrating Smith. Staker, *Hearken, O Ye People*, 351–52.

56. Joseph Smith, History, 1838–1856, vol. A-1, created 11 June 1839–24 August 1843, CHL, http://josephsmithpapers.org; emphasis in the original.

57. Sidney Rigdon, April 1844 Conference, Nauvoo, IL., in Staker, *Hearken, O Ye People*, 349. Thomas Bullock recorded Rigdon's words in shorthand. This is Staker's reconstruction of Bullock's notes.

58. Joseph Smith, History, 1838–1856, vol. A-1, created 11 June 1839–24 August 1843, CHL, http://josephsmithpapers.org.

59. Local folklore maintains that Perlea Moore, a Campbell follower, provided the feathers. Hurd, comp., *On the Principle of Faith*, 39. See also "History of Joseph Smith," *Times and Seasons* 5, no. 15 (15 August 1844): 611–12; Anderson, ed., *Lucy's Book*, 558–59; Rigdon, "I Never Knew a Time When I Did Not Know Joseph Smith," 25–26. See also Symonds Ryder, a letter written to "Bro. Hayden," in Hayden, *Early History of the Disciples*, 221; Garrison and DeGroot, *The Disciples of Christ*, 300–301; Susan Easton Black, "Joseph's Experience in Hiram, Ohio: A Time of Contrasts," in *Regional Studies in Latter-day Saint Church History, Ohio*, ed. Milton V. Backman Jr. (Provo, UT: Brigham Young University, 1990), 36–39; Bushman, *Joseph Smith: Rough Stone Rolling*, 178–80.

60. "Triumphs of the Mormon Faith," *Hudson Ohio Observer and Telegraph* 3, no. 6 (5 April 1832).

61. Staker, *Hearken, O Ye People*, 45, 61; Hayden, *Early History of the Disciples*, 193–94.

62. Hurlbut sought to discredit the Smith family by gathering affidavits from people who claimed to have known the Smiths in New York and Pennsylvania. The affidavits were strangely repetitive in phraseology and generalities and portrayed the Smiths as indolent deceivers, "entirely destitute of moral character and addicted to vicious habits." Richard Lloyd Anderson, "Joseph Smith's New York Reputation Reappraised," *BYU Studies* 10, no. 3 (Spring 1970): 280–90.

63. According to current research, between 1820 and 1827 ten local Palmyra/ Manchester residents were known to have possessed personal seer stones. MacKay and Frederick, *Joseph Smith's Seer Stones*, 8–9.

64. Richard L. Bushman, "Joseph Smith and Money Digging," in *A Reason for Faith: Navigating LDS Doctrine & Church History*, ed. Laura H. Hales (Provo, UT: Religious Studies Center; Salt Lake City: Deseret Book, 2016), 2–4; MacKay and Frederick, *Joseph Smith's Seer Stones*, 16–17.

65. Spaulding's novel cast the first settlers of America as descendants of the lost tribes of Israel who were discovered by a Roman ship blown off course. Spaulding died in 1816, and his manuscript was left with a printer who never published it. Campbell, "The Mormon Bible," *Millennial Harbinger* (new series) 3, no. 4 (June 1839): 267. Richardson, *Memoirs of Alexander Campbell*, 2:344–46. Solomon Spaulding lived

from 1761 to 1816. A facsimile copy titled *Lost Manuscript Found* was published in 1886 in Salt Lake City by Deseret News Company.

66. Statement by Phineas Bronson, Hiel Bronson, and Mary D. Bronson, quoted in Rudolph Etzenhouser, *From Palmyra, New York, 1830, to Independence, Missouri, 1894* (Independence, MO: Ensign Publishing House, 1894), 388. In an 1884 interview with Nancy Rigdon Ellis, Rigdon's daughter, she recalled when her father first saw the Book of Mormon. Although only eight at the time, she remembered it clearly "because of the contest which soon arose between her father and Pratt and Cowdery, over the Book of Mormon." She stated, "I saw them hand him the book, and I am as positive as can be that he never saw it before. He read it and examined it for about an hour and then threw it down, and said he did not believe a word in it." Nancy Rigdon Ellis, interview with E. L. Kelley and W. H. Kelley, 14 May 1884, in *The History of the Reorganized Church of Jesus Christ of Latter Day Saints*, 8 vols., ed. Joseph Smith III and Heman C. Smith (Independence, MO: Herald House, 1967), 4:451–52. See also Rigdon, "I Never Knew a Time When I Did Not Know Joseph Smith," 15–42; Matthew Roper and Paul J. Fields, "The Historical Case against Sidney Rigdon's Authorship of the Book of Mormon," *Mormon Studies Review* 23, no. 1 (2011): 113–25.

67. Benjamin Winchester, *Plain Facts, Shewing the Origin of the Spaulding Story, Concerning the Manuscript Found, and Its Being Transformed into the Book of Mormon: With a Short History of Dr. P. Hulbert* (Bedford, England: G. J. Adams, 1841); originally published in 1840 in Philadelphia as *The Origin of the Spaulding Story, Concerning the Manuscript Found*. See also *Personal Writings of Joseph Smith*, rev. ed., comp. and ed. Dean C. Jessee (Salt Lake City: Deseret Book; Provo, UT: Brigham Young University, 2002), 301, 354; Rigdon, "I Never Knew a Time When I Did Not Know Joseph Smith," 41–42. See also Givens, *By the Hand of Mormon*, 160. The full title of the book is *Mormonism Unvailed* [sic] *or a Faithful Account of that Singular Imposition and Delusion from Its Rise to the Present Time with Sketches of the Propagators and a Full Detail of the Manner in which the Famous Golden Bible was Brought before the World, to which Are Added Inquiries into the Probability That the Historical Part of the Said Bible Was Written by One Solomon Spaulding, More than Twenty Years Ago, and by Him Intended to Have Been Published as a Romance* (Painesville, OH: self-printed and published), 1834.

68. Winchester, *Plain Facts*. In the intervening century, the Spaulding manuscript theory has been shown to be false, along with the accusation that Rigdon had prior knowledge of Joseph Smith and the Book of Mormon, or that he helped write it. See Roper and Fields, "The Historical Case against Sidney Rigdon's Authorship of the Book of Mormon," 113–25; Givens, *By the Hand of Mormon*, 160–61.

69. See Titus 1:5. Sidney Rigdon, "Faith of the Church in these Last Days," *The Evening and Morning Star* 2, no. 17 (February 1834): 130. See also an editorial, "The Ancient Order of Things," *Messenger and Advocate* (September 1835): 183–84, likely written by Rigdon, advocating the complete restoration of the ancient things, and not a part of it only, including the offices of the New Testament and the extraordinary gifts of the Spirit.

70. Rigdon, "Faith of the Church of the Christ in these Last Days," *The Evening and the Morning Star* 2, no. 24 (September 1834): 186.

71. Oliver Cowdery, "Address to the Patrons of the Evening and the Morning Star," *The Evening and the Morning Star* 2, no. 24 (September 1834): 185.

72. Eber D. Howe, "Mormonism Unveiled," reprinted in *Millennial Harbinger* 1, no. 6 (January 1835): 44–45.

73. Campbell, "Mormonism," *Millennial Harbinger* 2, no. 7 (4 July 1831): 332.

74. Joseph Smith, Letter, Kirtland, OH, to the elders of the church, December 1835, *Latter Day Saints' Messenger and Advocate*, December 1835, 225–30, Letter to the Elders of the Church, 30 November–1 December 1835, 227, http://www.josephsmithpapers.org.

75. In 1836, Hurlbut threatened Smith's life, resulting in a $200 fine and restraining order. Dean C. Jessee, Mark Ashurst-McGee, and Richard L. Jensen, eds., *Journals, Volume 1: 1832–1839*, vol. 1 of the Journals series of *The Joseph Smith Papers*, ed. Dean C. Jessee, Ronald K. Esplin, and Richard Lyman Bushman (Salt Lake City: Church Historian's Press, 2008), 216.

76. Sidney Rigdon, "For the Messenger and Advocate," *Messenger and Advocate* 2, no. 7 (June 1836): 297.

77. Rigdon, "For the Messenger and Advocate," *Messenger and Advocate* 2, no. 4 (June 1836): 243–44.

78. Rigdon, "For the Messenger and Advocate," *Messenger and Advocate* 2, no. 7 (June 1836): 297–98.

79. Campbell, "Mormon Bible," *Millennial Harbinger* (new series) 3, no. 7 (June 1839): 265.

80. "A Serial Reprinting of La Roy Sunderland's *Mormonism Exposed*," *Millennial Harbinger* (new series) 6, no. 9, through (new series) 7, no. 8 (September 1842–August 1843); Sunderland's book was published in 1842 by New York Watchman in New York City. Campbell, "Mormonism in an Agony," *Millennial Harbinger* (new series) 6, no. 8 (August 1842): 358–62.

81. Campbell, "Remarks on the Mormon Expose," *Millennial Harbinger* (new series) 7, no. 8 (August 1843): 351.

82. Staker, *Hearken, O Ye People*, 320–24.

83. Doctrine and Covenants 100:9–11.

84. Letter to Isaac Galland, 22 March 1839, 54, http://josephsmithpapers.org; Willard Richards, "Joseph Smith Diary," Sunday, 9 July 1843, in *Words of Joseph Smith*, 229. In the spring of 1833, Smith received this passage: "Truth is knowledge of things as they are, and as they were, and as they are to come" (Doctrine and Covenants 93:24).

85. The date of this publication is not certain but believed to be September 1843. See "Uncle Dale's Readings in Early Mormon History (Newspapers of Ohio)," http://www.sidneyrigdon.com/dbroadhu/oh/evan1832.htm#000043.

86. Walter Scott, "Mormonism—The Means by which it stole the True Gospel," reprinted from the *Evangelist*, in *Millennial Harbinger* (third series) 1, no. 1 (January 1844): 39.

87. Adamson Bentley, "Solon," reprinted from the *Evangelist*, in *Millennial Harbinger* (third series) 1, no. 1 (January 1844): 39. A similar late account regarding mounds, antiquities, and Aborigines was recorded in a letter from Darwin Atwater to Amos Hayden in 1873. Hayden, *Early History of the Disciples*, 239–40.

88. Lyon, "Origin and Purpose of the Articles of Faith," 265.

89. Rigdon complained, "The reason why they were called Campbellites, was, in consequence of Mr. Campbell's publishing the [*Christian Baptist*], and it being the means through which they communicated their sentiments to the world; other than this, Mr. Campbell was no more the originator of that sect than Elder Rigdon." Rigdon, *Times and Seasons* 4, no. 13 (15 May 1843): 193; Rigdon, "I Never Knew a Time When I Did Not Know Joseph Smith," 39.

90. Craig Blomberg, "Is Mormonism Christian?," in *The New Mormon Challenge*, ed. Francis J. Beckwith, Carl Mosser, Paul Owen (Grand Rapids, MI: Zondervan, 2002), 322–23. For example, Blomberg highlights the similarity of their views on

anticreedalism, care of the poor and communion as part of worship, Sabbath keep-ing, dispensationalism, steps in salvation, necessity of faith and works, apostasy, reformation and restoration, anti-Calvinism, church name and organization, cleri-cal titles and paid clergy, tithes and offerings, new translation of the scriptures, mis-sionary zeal, Millennialism and establishing Zion, and Smith and Campbell as char-ismatic and iconoclastic founders of new movements. Unfortunately, Blomberg overemphasizes their similarities and omits their foundational differences on many of these points.

91. Blomberg, "Is Mormonism Christian?," 315–23. See George Bartholomew Arbaugh, *Revelation in Mormonism: Its Character and Changing Forms* (Chicago: University of Chicago, 1932), 217.

92. Arbaugh, *Revelation in Mormonism,* 9. Rigdon was a scribe, counselor, and spokes-man, but not a prophet. A Rigdon biographer, Richard Van Wagoner, misquoted Robert J. Matthews by writing, "The material of the early manuscripts (Joseph Smith Translation), which extended at least through the first seven chapters of Genesis in the handwriting of Oliver Cowdery and John Whitmer, was further revised and rewritten by Rigdon." Instead, Matthews states that "[the first seven chapters of Genesis] were further revised by the prophet and rewritten in the handwriting of Sidney Rigdon." Van Wagoner, *Sidney Rigdon,* 73; Robert J. Matthews, "The 'New Translation' of the Bible, 1830–33: Doctrinal Development During the Kirtland Era," *BYU Studies* 11, no. 4 (Summer 1971): 406.

93. Joseph Smith III, "Last Testimony of Sister Emma," *Saints' Herald* 26, no. 19 (October 1879): 289.

94. George Bartholomew Arbaugh, *Gods, Sex, and Saints: The Mormon Story* (Rock Island, IL: Augustana Press, 1957), 10.

95. Hill, "The Role of Christian Primitivism," 60.

96. Hughes, "Two Restoration Traditions," 40–41.

97. Blomberg, "Is Mormonism Christian?," 322–23.

98. Lloyd Knowles, "Sidney Rigdon, the Benedict Arnold of the Restoration Move-ment?," *Stone-Campbell Journal* 6, no. 1 (2003): 3–25.

11

Alexander Campbell's "Delusions" and the Mormon Response

The Book of Mormon purports to unfold the history of ancient America, from its first settlement by a colony that came from the time of the tower, when the languages were confounded, about the beginning of the fifth century of the Christian era. Smith wrote:

> We are informed by these records that America in ancient times has been inhabited by two distinct races of people. The first were called Jaredites, and came from the tower. The second group came directly from the city of Jerusalem, about six hundred years before Christ. They were principally from the house of Israel, of the descendants of Joseph[, who was sold into Egypt, and called Nephites and Lamanites]. The Jaredites were destroyed about the time that the Israelites came from Jerusalem, who succeeded them in the inheritance of the sacred land. The principal nation of the second group [Nephites] fell in battle at the close of the fourth century. The remnant are the Indians [Native Americans] that now inhabit this country.

The book also records the appearance of Jesus Christ to this continent after his resurrection;

> that he planted the gospel here in all its fulness, and richness, and power, and blessing; that they had apostles, prophets, pastors, teachers and evangelists; the same order, the same priesthood,

the same ordinances, gifts, powers, and blessings, as were enjoyed on the eastern continent, that the people were cut off in consequence of their transgressions, that the last of their prophets who existed among them was commanded to write an abridgment of their prophecies, history, &c., and to hide it up in the earth, and that it should come forth and be united with the Bible for the accomplishment of the purposes of God in the last days.[1]

As seen in this summary, the Book of Mormon has a biblical ring to its message, bringing together elements from the Old and New Testaments. For example, it refers to a people who were at the tower which Smith identified as the Tower of Babel when the languages were confounded,[2] and it mentions the tribes of Israel, naming specifically the tribe of Joseph and his son Manasseh. The book references Zedekiah, the last king of the Southern Kingdom of Judah, as well as the prophet Jeremiah. In addition, the book quotes extensively from the writings of Isaiah. The Book of Mormon also concentrates on elements from the New Testament, such as the birth of Jesus Christ to the virgin Mary, his baptism at the hands of John, and his atoning sacrifice. Uniquely, the record describes the resurrected Christ's visit to the descendants of the house of Israel in America where he personally showed them the marks of his crucifixion, performed miracles, taught the Sermon on the Mount, instituted the sacrament of the Lord's Supper, and organized his church among them.[3] In the words of Paul Gutjahr, American studies and English scholar, the Book of Mormon "was perhaps the most audacious rendering of Christ's life to appear in the nineteenth century."[4] Historian Gordon Wood's evaluation of the Book of Mormon noted that in a time of intense conflict over biblical interpretation, Smith's contribution "cut through these controversies and brought the Bible up-to-date. It was written in plain biblical style for plain people. It answered perplexing questions of theology, clarified obscure passages of the Bible, and carried its story into the New World. And it did all this with the assurance of divine authority."[5]

The Book of Mormon's main story is a microcosm of the history of the house of Israel in a thousand-year span: a family's divinely guided journey from the old promised land to a new promised land, their fracture into opposing parties vying for power, their eventual wholesale rejection of the Messiah, and the genocidal civil war that resulted. The Book of Mormon is a "voice from the dust"—records hidden in the ground of a people long dead.[6] It is about the loss of possibilities—a reminder of what might have been. As Mormon scholar Hugh Nibley expressed it, the tragedy of the Book of Mormon is not what became of the Nephites, but what the Nephites became.[7] Despite the historical narrative, the Book of Mormon "is meant to be revelatory in a universal way, revealing the world from beginning to end, and revealing it in such a way as to usher in the coming of the Messiah."[8]

In the first week of his arrival in Kirtland, Ohio, in February 1831, Smith was greeted by the publication of Campbell's critical review of the Book of Mormon. Campbell was the first to actually examine and present a detailed critique of the Book of Mormon. He viewed it through the lens of his Enlightenment learning, superior academic education, and perhaps also the stinging loss of some of his converts, and he was convinced that both Joseph Smith and his "golden bible" were delusions.

"Delusions: An Analysis of the Book of Mormon"

In the fall of 1830, Walter Scott visited the Isaac Morley farm in Kirtland, Ohio. This was the location of a Reforming Baptist group practicing communal living—members of Sidney Rigdon's community. Scott acquired a copy of the Book of Mormon during this time, likely from his good friend Rigdon, and sent it to Alexander Campbell along with information on how it was purportedly translated.[9] In the 7 February 1831 *Millennial Harbinger,* less than a year after the printing of the Book of Mormon and organization of the Church of Christ, Alexander Campbell published what he considered a reasoned refutation of Smith and the Book of Mormon. The critique was titled "Delusions." In pamphlets published in 1832, however, an enlarged and more descriptive title became "Delusions. An Analysis of the Book of Mormon; with an Examination of Its Internal and External Evidences, and a Refutation of Its Pretences to Divine Authority."[10] It is notable that the term *delusion* was also used in the sixteenth century to describe Anne Hutchinson's revelations in her trial before Governor Winthrop and other men of the Massachusetts Bay Colony. She claimed to receive immediate revelation, meaning that it was received with or without the medium of the Bible. This reception of revelation without the Bible appeared to signal the "end of the Bible as the foundational source of religious truth" and, in the eyes of some, negated the need for ministerial authority to guide the people. This concern would have applied to Smith's Book of Mormon and the threat his restoration movement brought.[11]

A significant issue at the outset is the belief in a closed canon (the impossibility of additional scripture) and a rejection of immediate revelation—both of which are foundational premises that inform Campbell's thinking and commentary.

Campbell's critique is a mixture of reason, mockery, and exaggeration, both humorous and unamusing in a combination of rhetorical devices that gain and generally hold the attention of readers.[12] Only a few truly dedicated biblical scholars would have appreciated his strongly reasoned arguments; however, all could appreciate his humorous comparison of the Book of Mormon to a lowly cave-dwelling "bat" and the Bible to the soaring "American Eagle." By linking Book of Mormon peoples to Quakers, Episcopalians, Calvinists, Methodists, and Freemasons, he used terms familiar to all his readers.[13] His tone was skeptical and exaggerated to demonstrate how illiterate the author and his book were.

He began his comments with a disparaging personal assessment of Joseph Smith, comparing him to the long tradition of false prophets, such as Pharaoh's court impostors, Jannes and Jambres, who contended with Moses;[14] the false prophets of the Jewish era, including diviners, soothsayers, and magicians; and the many false messiahs since the crucifixion of Christ. Since the Great Apostasy began, and especially at the time of the Reformation, there have been, according to Campbell, countless radical Protestants such as Munzer, Stubner, and Stork;[15] and eighteenth-century reformer Ann Lee of the Shakers.[16] While not giving details on the "Barkers, Jumpers, and Mutterers of the present age," or a Miss Campbell "who . . . came back from the dead and had the gift of tongues,"[17] Campbell mentioned them as further evidence that "every age of the world has produced impostors and delusions" along with dupes who believe them. After the comparison of Smith to such known frauds and declaring that all who had joined his restoration had been deceived, Campbell began his examination of "the most recent and impudent delusion which has appeared in our time . . . THE MORMONITES . . . [and] their bible."[18] It appeared obvious to Campbell that Joseph Smith was merely one more in a long line of charlatans whose "purported miracles were no evidence for divine authority, unlike the miracles on which Christianity was based."[19]

Following this introduction, Campbell quoted from the title page of the Book of Mormon, detailed the structure of the book, and recited many of the storyline's main points—including the names of prophets and leaders. He called the book a romance, but then corrected himself because this term was too innocent for such a fraudulent production. Campbell noted the book began with a family who lived in Jerusalem at the time of King Zedekiah: Lehi, his wife, Sariah, and their four sons. He called Lehi "a greater prophet than any of the Jewish prophets, [who] uttered all the events of the christian era, and developed the records of Matthew, Luke, and John, six hundred years before John the Baptist was born." He remarked that the "Nephites [so-named after Lehi's fourth son], like their father, for many generations were good Christians, believers in the doctrines of the Calvinists and Methodists, and preaching baptism and other Christian usages hundreds of years before Jesus Christ was born!"[20] Before Nephi died, "he had preached to his people everything that is now being taught in the state of New York." He noted that Book of Mormon prophet Enos "was a contemporary with Old Testament Nehemiah, and may we not say how much wiser and more enlightened were the Nephites in America than the Jews at their return to Jerusalem!"[21] Referencing King Benjamin from the Book of Mormon, Campbell was perplexed by the combination of sacrifice under the law at a new temple and preaching regarding Christian institutions, found in what he called Benjamin's patriarchal valedictory address.[22]

In essence, Campbell wondered how the Nephites were writing about Christ in ways that the Jews did not know. Besides this, Campbell had several other questions about the Book of Mormon. How could Book of Mormon prophets know so many details about Christian doctrine before the New Testament era or before the Reformation? How could the Book of Mormon claim to be of ancient origin and yet mention details such as "the mother of Christ would be a virgin called Mary," except that Joseph Smith just wrote it in? How could the prophet Nephi claim his people believed in Christ, teaching, preaching, and prophesying about him hundreds of years before his birth? Why did the Jews of Jerusalem practice the rituals of the law of Moses while the Nephites not only practiced the rituals but also understood the symbolic meanings that pointed to Christ's future sacrifice? How could the Nephites know more than the Jews about Christ so many years out of proper time and order?

Campbell noted the strange, nonsequential character of prophecy in the Book of Mormon. Any historian would find it disconcerting to find Hebrew prophets predicting with precision the details of Jesus's parentage, ministry, and Atonement hundreds of years prior to his birth while purporting to be of ancient origin. The book is unapologetically both Christ centered and anachronistic—out of proper order and time—in ways that confused and irritated Campbell, a passionate Bible scholar.[23] The Book of Mormon did not conform to the separation of the Old and New Testaments as Campbell understood them.

Campbell further alleged that the Book of Mormon invented Freemasonry, a covenant between individuals to "aid one another in all things, good and evil."[24] The Book of Mormon does not mention Freemasonry nor this promise. Significantly, Campbell gave substantial detail regarding the visitation of Christ to the Nephites.

Throughout the rest of his rehearsal of the Book of Mormon story, Campbell periodically added commentary and exclamation marks to emphasize his incredulity at what he saw as absurd statements. He noted the civilization's concluding wars, commenting that "Mormon appears next in the drama, the recording angel of the whole matter, who, by the way, was a mighty general and great christian; he commanded in one engagement forty-two thousand men against the Lamanites!!! He was no Quaker!"[25] Campbell was likely emphasizing his pacifist beliefs in regard to Christians and warfare with these comments. Campbell made geographical assumptions, as had many of Smith's converts: "The Lamanites took South America for themselves, and gave North America to the Nephites."[26] Campbell also exclaimed, "Mormon was very orthodox, for he preached in these words, A. D. 362:—'That Jesus was the very Christ and the very God.' He must have heard of the Arian controversy by some angel!!"[27] Campbell's statement demonstrated his skepticism that Mormon, who is contemporaneous with this controversy but on a different continent, could possibly state so definitively that Christ is God.[28]

After Campbell had finished reciting many of the events in the Book of Mormon and mentioning the testimony of eleven witnesses, he begged forgiveness of his readers for bringing the "bible of the Mormonites" to their notice. He was examining it as a service to many investigators from a variety of denominations who believed "its pretensions to divine authority; for it purports to be a revelation from God."[29] This was Campbell's point in the title of his critique: the book is a delusion because it did not agree with his understanding of the Bible.

Campbell then examined internal evidences to further prove his conclusion that the Book of Mormon was a fantasy. He begins this section of his critique by stating: "It admits the Old and New Testaments to contain the revelations, institutions and commandments of God to Patriarchs, Jews, and Gentiles, down to the year 1830, and always, as such, speaks of them and quotes them. This admission blasts its pretensions to credulity. No one with his eyes open can admit both the Bible and the book of Mormon come from God. Since we know the Bible came from God then the book of Mormon did not."

Campbell began his doctrinal analysis of the Book of Mormon by making ten points that proved, in his view, that it could not have come from God and that Smith, "as ignorant and impudent a knave as ever wrote a book," must be its real author.[30] Discussion of each of the points of Campbell's criticism will be followed with explanatory commentary by Oliver Cowdery, who responded to Campbell's 1831 *Millennial Harbinger* "Delusions" four years later with his own 1835 *Messenger and Advocate* article titled "Delusion."[31] Joseph Smith's words or Latter-day Saint scriptures will provide the rest of the commentary. It should be noted that Campbell's point of reference is the Bible only, whereas both Cowdery and Smith cite the Bible, but also inform their response with latter-day revelation, such as that found in the Doctrine and Covenants.

1. Priesthood. Campbell saw Smith's approach to priesthood as a fatal flaw in the book. According to him, Smith had based "his whole book upon a false fact, or a pretended fact, which makes God a liar. Campbell cited several Old Testament passages regarding the priesthood that was given to the tribe of Levi and the high priest office that was given to Aaron and his sons, exclaiming that according to Paul, "Jesus himself was excluded from officiating as priest on earth according to the law. This Joseph Smith overlooked in his impious fraud."[32] Campbell concluded that because Lehi and his family descended from the tribe of Joseph, rather than the priestly tribe of Levi, and the Book of Mormon describes sacrifices and ordinations almost six hundred years prior to the coming of Christ; either "the God of Abraham or Joseph Smith must then be a liar!!"[33] Campbell rightly pointed out that Lehi's family are from the tribe of Joseph and that they administered the priestly rituals usually associated only with the tribe of Levi under the law of Moses. Campbell wondered how Smith could have made an error of such huge proportions.

Oliver Cowdery responded to the question of priesthood author-ity by asking his own: "How did it *happen* that Moses had authority to consecrate Aaron a priest? Where did he get his authority?" Cowdery explained that "Moses received the holy priesthood, after the order of Melchesedek, under the hand of Jethro, his father-in-law . . . [and] with this authority . . . and by commandment [Moses] ordained Aaron to a priesthood less than that [Aaronic], and that Lehi was a priest after this same order [that Moses had, meaning the Melchizedek Priesthood]."[34] In January 1841, Smith would elaborate on these statements: "All priest-hood is Melchizedek; but there are different portions or degrees of it. That portion which brought Moses to speak with God face to face [Melchizedek] was taken away; but that which brought the ministry of angels [Aaronic] remained. All the prophets had the Melchizedek Priesthood and [were] ordained by God himself."[35]

2. Promised Land. Campbell began his second point with "This ignorant and impudent liar . . . makes the God of Abraham, Isaac and Jacob, violate his covenants with Israel and Judah, concerning the land of Canaan, by promising a new land to the pious Jew." The story of a devout Jewish prophet (Lehi) leaving the temple and the land of Jerusalem, which land had been promised to his fathers, was to Campbell "so monstrous an error, that language fails to afford a name for it."[36] He accused Smith of making Lehi "more happy in forsaking the institutions of Moses, more intelligent in the wilderness, and more prosperous in adversity, than even the Jews in their best days, in the best of lands, and under the best of all governments!!!"[37] Because of this seeming mistake, Campbell branded Smith an "imposter" who was ignorant of the history of the Jews, the nature of covenants of promise, and the curses of the law.[38]

Campbell demonstrated in this criticism that he had read the sto-ryline of the first book in the Book of Mormon. Lehi was a devout Jewish prophet who left his homeland, the promised land of Moses and Joshua. The claim that Lehi was happier, more intelligent, and more prosperous is, however, more than the text indicates. The storyline found in the first forty-three pages of the Book of Mormon details great difficulties, including threats of death in Jerusalem, relocation from his home to caravanning in a wilderness, hatred between some of his sons, hunger, thirst, fatigue, birth of children, death, all while spending over eight years crossing the desert, then building and sailing a ship across the ocean and enduring a terrible storm before arriving in a new promised land.

Cowdery responded to Campbell's statements regarding Lehi's leaving the promised land by acknowledging that Canaan was promised to Abraham and his posterity but that God had never said he would not give them more. In fact, "Jacob declared that his blessings had prevailed above those of his progenitors unto the *utmost bound of the everlasting hills*, and that he confers them upon the head of his son Joseph, of whom Lehi was a descendant."[39] The prophet Moses also blessed Joseph's posterity with a land: "His glory is like the firstling of his bullock, and his horns are like the horns of unicorns: with them he shall push the people together to the ends of the earth: and they are the ten thousands of Ephraim, and they are the thousands of Manasseh."[40] Cowdery interpreted the two passages cited here to mean that the descendants of Joseph—his sons Ephraim and Manasseh and the Book of Mormon patriarch and prophet Lehi—were blessed with promised lands and a large posterity which, as Moses prophesied, would gather the house of Israel from the "ends of the earth" at a later time. From this point of view, Cowdery then rhetorically asked, "Why all this parade about the blessing of Joseph, if he were only to inherit an equal proportion of the land of Canaan?"[41]

The Book of Mormon recorded that lands of promise were given and maintained contingent upon obedience to God's laws.[42] The first few pages of the Book of Mormon indicate that the prophet Jeremiah was a contemporary of Lehi in Jerusalem.[43] The book of Jeremiah reveals passages that describe a society divided by allegiance to Egypt or Babylon; a complacent people because they lived in the temple city; and problems with changed ordinances, false prophets, and grossly wicked rulers.[44] Cowdery's argument rested upon the fact that the promises made to Abraham were in force only if the house of Israel remained faithful. Old Testament accounts of both the Northern Kingdom of Israel and the Southern Kingdom of Judah testify of wickedness in the house of Israel which ultimately caused them to be scattered by their enemies, Assyria and Babylon respectively. The tribes of Israel would remain "lost" until God redeemed them as part of the "restoration of all things," which Smith explained would be the literal gathering of Israel both spiritual (to Christ's everlasting gospel) and temporal (geographical).[45]

3. Kingship. Campbell questioned the large number of Jews in the New World and the new dynasty set up even before the birth of Christ. He pointed out that in the Book of Mormon "the scepter . . . has departed from Judah. . . . king Benjamin is a wiser and more renowned king than king Solomon."[46] Here again, Campbell's move beyond the text is an exaggeration. His main concern seems to be that Smith had removed kingship from its rightful heir, the tribe of Judah. Referring to the adage that "'the more marvellous, the more credible the tale,' and the less of fact, and the more of fiction, the more intelligible and reasonable the narrative," Campbell believed Smith had fooled many.[47]

Neither Cowdery nor Smith ever addressed the issue of kingship; however, the existence of kings and rulers in the Book of Mormon is in keeping with the civilization's Near Eastern heritage. That Christ was the rightful king over the house of Israel was never challenged by the Book of Mormon kings; they were simply governing a remnant of the house of Israel in another part of the world.

4. Temple Worship. Campbell was distraught that "[Smith] represents the temple worship as continued in his new land of promise contrary to every precept of the law."[48] In Campbell's mind, this was contrary to Jewish law because God's only house of prayer was in Jerusalem. The Nephites should have been like the Jews in the old world, turning their faces in the direction of Jerusalem and weeping for the temple that had been destroyed. He referred to the Nephite "wigwam temple," apparently not noting that Nephi described the temple he constructed as "after the manner of the temple of Solomon," with fine workmanship, though without all the precious things of Solomon's temple.[49]

Cowdery responded to Campbell's concern by quoting from the Old Testament: "But will God indeed dwell on the earth? behold, the heaven and heaven of heavens cannot contain thee; how much less this house that I have builded?"[50] Cowdery followed this quotation with two questions: "If God's presence and glory fill the heavens, is he not sufficient to fill more than one small house like that built at Jerusalem? and has not a man, endowed with the holy priesthood, after the order of Melchisedek, authority to build a house to the honor of his name, and especially, when the worship of that [temple] at Jerusalem was corrupted, or it thrown down?"[51]

In 1843, Smith explained his perspective on the purpose of temples, declaring that throughout all scripture and time, the house of Israel was to gather to build temples in order to receive ordinances and blessings that God had reserved for his children.[52] The underlying premise for Campbell's disagreement on this issue appears to be that he viewed the house of Israel and all its blessings as a fixed, one-time covenant, superseded in the New Testament by Christ, whereas Smith viewed it as more of an ongoing, ever-applicable covenant.

5. *Law of Moses.* Campbell claimed, "Nephi and Smith's prophets institute ordinances and observances for the Jews, subversive of Moses, 500 years before the Great Prophet came."[53] Campbell's specific concerns about the Nephites' observance of the law of Moses were not detailed. His problems likely resided in non-Levites officiating in law-of-Moses rituals and in his feeling that the Nephites preempted the fulfillment of the law of Moses by teaching Christian doctrines before the coming of Christ. The purpose of adherence to the law of Moses was made clear in the Book of Mormon: the Nephites understood that the law of Moses had been given to point them to Christ who would come to earth.[54] Additionally, they recognized the need to practice it, including temple rituals, until Christ fulfilled the law with his atoning sacrifice and visitation to them.[55]

6. *Secrets.* Campbell argued that Smith embarrassed himself with "his ignorance of the New Testament matters and things. The twelve Apostles of the Lamb, are said by Paul, to have developed certain secrets, which were hid for ages and generations, which Paul says were ordained before the world to their glory, that they should have the honor of announcing them.[56] But Smith makes his pious hero Nephi, 600 years before the Messiah began to preach, and disclose these secrets concerning the calling of the Gentiles, and the blessings flowing through the Messiah to Jews and Gentiles."[57] Accordingly, Smith has Nephi express every truth found in the writings of the Apostles concerning these secrets, even quoting from Romans 11. "Paul says these things were secrets and unknown until his time; but Smith makes Nephi say the same things 600 years before Paul was converted!"[58] In Romans 11:13–27, Paul taught his Gentile converts their place in the Lord's plan of salvation for the house of Israel that they might not "be ignorant of this mystery." Paul wrote that God chose or foreordained the house of Israel according to the election of grace, although some members would be broken off because of unbelief. Using symbols, he explained that the Gentiles were a "wild olive tree" grafted into the "good olive tree," the house of Israel, when they believed in Christ. This symbolism is significantly expanded in the Book of Mormon.[59] It seems that the main point

of Campbell's criticism is the time and space between the account of Paul, which he would consider original, and the account found in the Book of Mormon. Written by a prophet who preceded Lehi's family, a section of the Book of Mormon gives an extended version of Paul's brief statements about the destiny of the Jews and the adoption of the Gentiles and therefore also greatly precedes the Apostle Paul. From a Book of Mormon point of view, this lengthy allegory would have been well known since Old Testament times among the Jews. The prophet Jacob, living somewhere between the fifth and sixth centuries before the coming of Christ, quoted Zenos's allegory of the olive tree. Zenos was a prophet whose writings were recorded on the brass plates, which Lehi's family brought with them.[60] Campbell concluded his point by declaring that either Paul or Joseph Smith was a false prophet and challenged, "Mormonites, take your choice!"[61]

7. Prophecies. Campbell next made the point that truths, errors, and doctrinal controversies found in New York were also found in the Book of Mormon. His accusation is that this is further evidence that Joseph Smith is the author and that the Book of Mormon is the product of Smith's milieu.

> This prophet Smith, through his stone spectacles, wrote on the plates of Nephi, in his book of Mormon, every error and almost every truth discussed in N. York for the last ten years. He decides all the great controversies—infant baptism, ordination, the trinity, regeneration, repentance, justification, the fall of man, the atonement, transubstantiation, fasting, penance, church government, religious experience, the call to the ministry, the general resurrection, eternal punishment, who may baptize, and even the question of freemasonry, republican government, and the rights of man. . . . How much more benevolent and intelligent this American Apostle, than were the holy twelve, and Paul to assist them!!! He prophesied all these topics, and of the apostasy, and infallibly decided, by his authority, every question. How easy to prophecy of the past or of the present time!![62]

In mentioning Smith's "stone spectacles," the seer stones that Smith claimed to use in his translation, Campbell answered his own question of why the Book of Mormon seems so anachronistic. Smith asserted he was a seer; therefore, he saw the past, present, and future as the head of the dispensation of the fullness of times, charged with bringing all of God's words together. Smith claimed to restore ancient covenants, priesthood power and authority, temple worship, knowledge about the Godhead, and many other important doctrines, principles, ordinances, and rituals. Smith used theological vocabulary regarding Christ, common to the nineteenth century, and at the same time, he claimed the Book of Mormon to be an ancient record. Hence, it is difficult to determine to what historical period the book belongs—to nineteenth-century rural America or to fifth-century BC Hebrew refugees.[63] The book is anachronistic in ways that made Campbell certain it and its prophecies were false.

The Book of Mormon does respond to some of the Christian controversies Campbell mentioned and explained why these controversies existed: many "plain and precious" truths and covenants of the Lord were removed from the Bible after the death of the Apostles.[64] From Campbell's list, the Book of Mormon does resolve many Christian questions such as infant baptism,[65] ordination, call to the ministry, who may baptize,[66] regeneration and religious experience,[67] repentance,[68] justification,[69] the Fall of man,[70] the Atonement and Resurrection,[71] fasting,[72] church government,[73] and the rights of man.[74] The Book of Mormon, however, does not treat directly the nature of the Trinity (in comparison to Joseph Smith's first vision and revelations recorded in the Doctrine and Covenants), although it does refer to "one God." Further, it does not mention republican government, transubstantiation, penance, or freemasonry, items also on Campbell's list.[75]

8. Geography and History. Campbell claimed Smith was "better skilled in the controversies in New York than in the geography or history of Judea. He makes John baptise in the village of Bethabara and says Jesus was born in Jerusalem."[77] In the Book of Mormon, Nephi speaks of "a prophet who should come before the Messiah, to prepare the way of the Lord" and states, "And my father said he should baptize in Bethabara, beyond Jordan; and he also said he should baptize with water; even that he should baptize the Messiah with water."[77] This is similar to the King James Version of John's Gospel: "These things were done in Bethabara beyond Jordan, where John was baptizing."[78] The first point of Campbell's criticism is unclear.

The second criticism was pointed at the Book of Mormon verse that states, "He shall be born of Mary, *at Jerusalem* which is the land of our forefathers."[79] The common Book of Mormon phrase "land of Jerusalem" is repeated forty times and is a generic reference to the larger ancestral place "from whence we came." It is used broadly to refer to the Nephites' former and now irrecoverable homeland, their previous "land of inheritance" or "land of our forefathers." These two criticisms are concluded by Campbell with triple exclamatory marks: "Great must be the faith of the Mormonites in this new Bible!!!"[80]

Campbell chided Smith for referring to the relatively recent inventions of the mariner's compass and steamboat that "Nephi knew all about . . . 2400 years ago."[81] Smith called the compass Campbell was referring to as "the marveelus directors which was given to Lehi while in the wilderness."[82] The Book of Mormon calls it the "Liahona" and described it as a round, brass "ball of curious workmanship" that was a gift from God with the capability to direct them through the desert and across the sea.[83] According to the Nephites, the spindles did not work by principles of magnetism like a common compass, but instead "according to the faith and diligence and heed which we did give unto them."[84] As for the steamboats, Campbell did not indicate where he found them in the text—they are not mentioned in the Book of Mormon.[85]

9. Christian Institution. Campbell observed that Smith "represents the christian institution as practised among his Israelites before Jesus was born" and "his Jews are called christians while keeping the law of Moses."[86] The idea of Christians prior to the Christian dispensation would have been perplexing to Campbell—an anachronistic eccentricity in the Book of Mormon. In 1830, Smith likely could not have explained this doctrine and certainly not from the Book of Mormon. The term *dispensation* is not mentioned in it.[87]

10. Summary. Campbell's reading of the Book of Mormon caused him to exclaim that although "the book professes to be written at intervals and by different persons . . . for uniformity of style, there never was a book more evidently written by one set of fingers, nor more certainly conceived in one cranium . . . than this same book." Since "Joseph Smith is a very ignorant man and called the author on the title page, I cannot doubt for a single moment that he is the sole author and proprietor of it."[88] Additionally, the book is full of what Campbell called "Smithisms," or certain evidence that Joseph Smith was its author. "It is patched up and cemented with 'And it came to pass'—'I sayeth unto you'—'Ye saith unto him'—and all the King James' *haths, dids* and *doths*—in the lowest imitation of the common version; and is, without exaggeration, the meanest book in the English language." To compare the Book of Mormon to the Bible was, in Campbell's opinion, a complete misrepresentation of gargantuan proportions, similar to trying to "compare . . . a mouse to a mammoth."[89]

In the initial publications of the Book of Mormon, Smith listed himself as author and proprietor to satisfy New York state copyright laws; however, he always maintained that he was merely the translator of the Book of Mormon, never its author. In a letter to his wife, Matthew Livingston Davis, journalist and Washington correspondent for the *New York Enquirer*, wrote that when Smith spoke about the Book of Mormon he was careful to impress upon his audience that it "was communicated to him direct from Heaven. If there was such a thing on Earth, as the author of it, then he (Smith) was the author; but the idea that he wished to impress was, that he had penned it as dictated by God."[90]

Having completed his summary of internal evidences against Smith's claims, Campbell "entered into an imaginary dialogue"[91] regarding external evidence with Oliver Cowdery, David Whitmer, and Martin Harris, witnesses whose testimonies about the plates, God, and an angel are found in the preface to the Book of Mormon. "I would ask them how they knew that it was God's voice which they heard—but they would tell me to ask God in faith. *That is, I must believe it first, and then ask God if it be true!!*" Campbell believed that faith comes from evidence furnished by the Holy Spirit in the scriptures and the mind assenting to these facts. In light of this, he pointed out a peculiar Book of Mormon paradox. In the closing pages of the Book of Mormon, the reader is directed to ask God if the book is "not true."[92] By asking whether the book is not true, one must begin, as Campbell noted, by assuming that the book is true. This is what eighteenth-century writer Samuel Taylor Coleridge called "that willing suspension of disbelief for the moment, which constitutes poetic faith." Coleridge desired to direct his readers to the supernatural that familiarity and selfishness preclude by paraphrasing from Isaiah 6: "We have eyes, yet see not, ears that hear not, and hearts that neither feel nor understand."[93] The setting aside of skepticism places the onus of discovery upon the reader rather than the writer.

Noting that Mormons believe in spiritual gifts as a sign among true believers, Campbell asked, "Have they wrought any miracles?" In asking this question, Campbell uncovered a second paradox in the Book of Mormon: the idea that there is "no witness [miracle] until after the trial of [one's] faith."[94] From Campbell's reasoned point of view, *assuming* that something is true before *knowing* that it is—that one must have faith in order to receive a miracle—was backwards, irrational, and a circular process.

Campbell went on to reject the collective testimonies of the eight additional witnesses, disparaging their signed affidavits and certification as hollow proof. Their claim to have handled the plates caused him to facetiously assert, "So did I." Campbell thought Smith still had the plates and challenged:

> Let him show them. Their certificate proves nothing. . . . If this prophet and his three prophetic witnesses had aught of speciosity about them or their book, we would have examined it and exposed it in a different manner. I have never felt myself so fully authorized to address mortal man in the style in which Paul addressed Elymas the sorcerer as I feel towards this Atheist Smith. His three witnesses, I am credibly informed, on one of their horse-swapping and prophetic excursions in the Sandusky country [Ohio], having bartered horses *three* times for *once* preaching, represented Walter Scott and myself as employed in translating these plates, and as believers in the book of Mormon.[95]

The basis of his attack on the sworn word of eleven witnesses in addition to Smith's was that Smith ought to show the plates to him and other more credible individuals. Hence, from his point of view, he had proven his hypothesis: the Mormon Bible was a grand delusion.

Impressively, Campbell did read the Book of Mormon closely and was able to summarize much of the storyline that accompanied the doctrine, even as he dismissed it, noted grammatical errors, downplayed any similarity to the Bible, and decried Smith's ignorance of the basic facts about Jewish and Christian history. Nevertheless, as historian Richard Bushman noted, he "at least acknowledged the Book of Mormon's treatment of theological issues and gave it credit for attempting to decide 'all the great controversies'" of religion in recent New York history.[96]

Campbell's republication of his critique in pamphlet form the next year was even more widely circulated than the *Millennial Harbinger*.[97] Missionary Parley Pratt wrote of its use by a clergyman in Toronto, Canada, to disrupt their large meetings, which they estimated to be in the thousands, with quotations from "Delusions."[98]

Campbell's defense of the Bible and especially the New Testament in his publications and public debates would have made it impossible for him to consider the Book of Mormon as anything but a fraud. His concern for his followers abandoning his movement to join Smith's movement made his critique especially pointed. His extensive study of the Bible shaped his views and he found the Book of Mormon contrary to his conception of dispensations as progressive—instead principles and ordinances considered Christian were known and practiced six hundred years before the birth of Christ. The Book of Mormon claimed that ancient Israelites in America lived the law of Moses but taught Christian principles. These New Testament teachings and rituals were anachronistic and that fact could not be squared with Campbell's ideas about dispensations and separation of the Old Testament from having anything to do with the restoration of the New Testament Church. It should not be surprising that his "Delusions" was harsh.

On 24 September 1834, Smith finally responded to Campbell's critique in *The Evening and the Morning Star*. Writing to Oliver Cowdery, the editor, he countered Campbell's harsh comments about him with his own stinging criticism of Campbell:

> I never have rejoiced to see men of corrupt hearts step forward and assume the authority and pretend to teach the ways of God—this is, and always has been a matter of grief; therefore I cannot but be thankful, that I have been instrumental in the providence of our heavenly Father in drawing forth, before the eyes of the world, the *spirits* by which certain ones, who profess to be 'Reformers, and Restorers of ancient principles,' are actuated! . . . Mr. Campbell was very lavish of his expositions of the falsity and incorrectness of the book of Mormon . . . [in a] lengthy article, in which he undertook to prove that it was incorrect and contrary to the former revelations of the Lord. Perhaps, he is of the opinion that he so completely overthrew the foundation on which it was based. . . . I have never written Mr. Campbell, nor received a communication from him but a public notice in his paper. . . . I take this course to inform the gentleman, that while he is breathing out scurrility he is effectually showing the honest [reader], the motives and principles by which he is governed, and often causes men to investigate and embrace the book of Mormon, who might otherwise never have perused it. I am satisfied, therefore he should continue his scurrility; indeed, I am more than gratified, because his cry of *Joe* Smith! *Joe* Smith! *false* prophet! *false* prophet! must manifest to *all* men the spirit he is of, and serves to open the eyes of the people. . . . I am your brother in the testimony of the book of Mormon.[99]

Smith did not counter Campbell's specific criticisms of the Book of Mormon, but claimed he was "content to sit awhile longer in silence and see the great work of God roll on, amid the opposition of this word in the face of every scandal and falsehood which may be invented and put in circulation."[100] He believed that the work of men could be easily destroyed, but not so with pure religion. "There is a power attendant on truth that all the arts and designs of men cannot fathom. . . . The vain cry of 'delusion' from the giddy multitude," the sneers, the frowns, the raging of those in power cannot prevent the influence of the Book of Mormon.[101]

Campbell's "Delusions," Smith's rejoinder, and Cowdery's "Delusion" are striking illustrations of the intense verbal rivalry between members of the two restorationist movements. The passionate, candid voice of Alexander Campbell was true to the Enlightenment approach he cherished and his role as a defender of rational Christianity. He left no one wondering where he stood regarding Joseph Smith or the "golden bible" that he considered detrimental to the unity of Christ's church. Neither did Joseph Smith mince words about the importance of the Book of Mormon to his restoration. He asserted, "Take away the Book of Mormon, and the revelations, and where is our religion? We have none."[102]

NOTES

1. Smith, "Wentworth Letter."
2. See Genesis 6:1–9; Ether 1:5, 33 (Book of Mormon).
3. See also Bushman, *Joseph Smith: Rough Stone Rolling*, 84–88.
4. Gutjahr, *An American Bible*, 151.
5. Gordon S. Wood, "Evangelical America and Early Mormonism," *New York History* 61, no. 4 (October 1980): 358–86.
6. Miller, *Rube Goldberg Machines*, 29.
7. Hugh Nibley, *Since Cumorah* (Salt Lake City: Deseret Book, 1988), 388.
8. Miller, *Rube Goldberg Machines*, 29.
9. Staker, *Hearken, O Ye People*, 108.
10. Campbell, "Delusions: An Analysis of the Book of Mormon with an Examination of Its Internal and External Evidences, and a Refutation of Its Pretences to Divine Authority," *Millennial Harbinger* 2, no. 2 (7 February 1831): 85–96.
11. Winship, *The Times & Trials of Anne Hutchinson*, 112–13.
12. Rod A. Martin, *Psychology of Humor: An Integrative Approach* (Burlington, MA: Elsevier, 2008), 104–5.
13. Jared Michael Halvorsen, "'Extravagant Fictions': The Book of Mormon in the Antebellum Popular Imagination" (master's thesis, Vanderbilt, 2012), 67–70.
14. Jannes and Jambres were mentioned by Paul in 2 Timothy 3:8, and their exploits were referred to in Exodus 7:10–12.

15. Sixteenth-century reformers Thomas Munzer, Nicholas Storch, and Mark Stubner dubbed the "Zwickau prophets," were part of the "radical Reformation," sometimes called the "left wing Reformation." They are often associated with the Anabaptist movement. It is not clear if Campbell was critical of the radical reformation of the latter two groups or particular doctrines that they, at least in name, had in common with the "Mormonites." Campbell specifically mentioned Thomas Munzer's teaching that "all Christians should put their possession into one common stock, and live together in that state of equality . . . and that polygamy was not incompatible with either the Old or New Testament." Campbell, "Delusions," *Millennial Harbinger* 2, no. 2 (February 1831): 85–86.

16. Campbell wrote Anna Lesse but obviously meant Ann Lee. Campbell noted that the Shakers also advocated "common stock."

17. Campbell, "Delusions," 85.

18. Campbell, "Delusions," 85.

19. Richard L. Bushman, "Joseph Smith and Skepticism," in Neilson and Woodworth, eds., *Believing History*, 152.

20. Campbell did not specify which doctrines of the Calvinists and Methodists that he believed the Nephites were teaching.

21. Campbell, "Delusions," 87.

22. Mosiah 1–5 (Book of Mormon).

23. Miller, *Rube Goldberg Machines*, 33–34.

24. Campbell, "Delusions," 89.

25. Campbell, "Delusions," 89.

26. Campbell, "Delusions," 89–90.

27. Campbell, "Delusions," 90. The Arian controversy predates the Nicean Council of AD 325. It appears that Arius argued that Christ is both subordinate and inferior to God the Father because "there was a time when the Son was not." From Arius's point of view, this meant that Christ was finite, the Father's divinity was greater, and that they were neither coequal nor coeternal. The Nicene Creed attempted to stem the controversy by using the term homoousios, meaning "consubstantial" and of the same substance or essence, or separate persons but the same being to describe the metaphysical oneness of the Father and the Son.

28. Campbell was correct in stating that neither the prophet Mormon nor Joseph Smith taught Arianism. Jesus Christ is subordinate to his Father, but not because of the statements of the Nicene Creed. Smith taught that "christ came according to the words of John, & he was greater than John because he held the keys of the Melchesedic Priesthood & the kingdom of God & had before revealed the priesthood to Moses. Yet christ was baptized by John to fulfill all righteousness." Joseph Smith, 22 January 1843, in *Wilford Woodruff's Journal*, 2:216. In other words, the premortal Christ had priesthood authority and appeared to Moses and other Old Testament and Book of Mormon prophets for the purpose of dispensing that power. He is the Father of heaven and earth, and the Creator of all things from the beginning and is the God who condescended to come to earth to redeem his people. He has always been a member of the Godhead, but subordinate to his Father as his Son, to whom he obeyed, praised, and prayed.

29. Campbell, "Delusions," 91.

30. Campbell, "Delusions," 91.

31. A four-year gap between Campbell's critique and Cowdery's rebuttal can best be explained by the huge responsibilities that Cowdery shouldered in helping Smith organize Zion in Independence, Missouri, traveling as a missionary, and wading through persecution and difficulties in both Missouri and Ohio.

32. Campbell, "Delusions," 91.

33. Campbell, "Delusions," 92.
34. Cowdery, "Delusion," *Messenger and Advocate* 1, no. 6 (March 1835): 91; emphasis in original.
35. William Clayton, "Extracts from William Clayton's Private Book," 5 January 1841, *Words of Joseph Smith*, comp. and ed. Ehat and Cook, 59. Joseph Smith, Discourse, Nauvoo, IL, 5 January 1841, in L. John Nuttall, Journal, 4–8, L. John Nutall Papers, Vault MSS 790, L. Tom Perry Special Collections, Harold B. Lee Library, Brigham Young University, Provo, Utah.; Account of Meeting and Discourse, 5 January 1841, as Reported by William Clayton, 5, http://www.josephsmithpapers.org. See also Doctrine and Covenants 84:18–28; 107:18–20. With this ten-year learning perspective, Smith could have explained that Lehi, whose prophetic call is detailed on the first few pages of the Book of Mormon, held the Melchizedek Priesthood—and Lehi's family, although they were of the tribe of Joseph, could minister in sacrificial ordinances. Accordingly, Lehi could ordain his sons to that same priesthood, and they too could administer the sacrifices and ordinances of the law of Moses in their temple. However, in 1831, this greater understanding had not yet been received.
36. Campbell, "Delusions," 92.
37. Campbell, "Delusions," 92.
38. Campbell, "Delusions," 92.
39. Cowdery, "Delusion," 91; see Genesis 49:26; emphasis in original.
40. Deuteronomy 33:17.
41. Cowdery, "Delusion," 91–92.
42. 2 Nephi 1:3–11, 20 (Book of Mormon).
43. 1 Nephi 1:4; 5:13; 7:14 (Book of Mormon).
44. Jeremiah 2:13, 18; 7:1–15; 26:20–23; 28; 29.
45. Editor, "The Temple" *Times and Seasons* 3, no. 13 (2 May 1842): 776; Joseph Smith was general editor of the *Times and Seasons* in May 1842.
46. Campbell, "Delusions," 92.
47. Campbell, "Delusions," 92.
48. Campbell, "Delusions," 92.
49. 2 Nephi 5:16 (Book of Mormon).
50. 1 Kings 8:27.
51. Cowdery, "Delusion," 92.
52. Joseph Smith, "June 11, 1843," in *Wilford Woodruff's Journal*, 2:240.
53. Campbell, "Delusions," 93.
54. 2 Nephi 25:23–24 (Book of Mormon).
55. 3 Nephi 1:24–25 (Book of Mormon).
56. Campbell is likely referring to 1 Corinthians 2:7 and Romans 6:25–26.
57. Campbell, "Delusions," 93.
58. Campbell, "Delusions," 93.
59. 1 Nephi 10:14; 15:13–16; Jacob 5 (Book of Mormon).
60. See Jacob 5 (Book of Mormon).
61. Campbell, "Delusions," 93.
62. Campbell, "Delusions," 93.
63. Miller, *Rube Goldberg Machines*, 33–34.
64. 1 Nephi 13:26 (Book of Mormon).
65. See Mormon 8:5–15 (Book of Mormon).
66. See Mosiah 18:18; Mosiah 25:19; Alma 5:3; 13:8; Moroni 3:3–4 (Book of Mormon).

67. Phrases such as "mighty change of heart," "receiving his image in your counte-nance," and "spiritually born of God" are used to define "regeneration." Alma 5:13–14 (Book of Mormon).
68. See 3 Nephi 11:33–37; 2 Nephi 2:21; Moroni 7:34; Alma 34:15 (Book of Mormon).
69. See 1 Nephi 16:2; 2 Nephi 2:5 (Book of Mormon).
70. See 2 Nephi 2:15–25 (Book of Mormon).
71. See 2 Nephi 2:7–8; 2 Nephi 9:5–10; Alma 40 and 41 (Book of Mormon).
72. See Omni 1:26; Alma 6:6 (Book of Mormon).
73. See 2 Nephi 6:2; Mosiah 25:19–22; Moroni 2 and 3 (Book of Mormon).
74. See 2 Nephi 2:13–14, 16, 27 (Book of Mormon).
75. The types of government represented in the Book of Mormon are some combina-tion of patriarchs, kings, prophets, and judges. Transubstantiation and penance are Catholic, not Mormon, doctrines. The Gadianton robbers, bound together by secret oaths and combinations, were interpreted by some as related to the Masons and appeared to "Campbell like an anti-Masonic view of Masonry." Bushman, "The Book of Mormon and Its Critics," in *Believing History*, 118–19.
76. Campbell, "Delusions," 93.
77. 1 Nephi 10:7–9 (Book of Mormon).
78. John 1:28.
79. Alma 7:10, emphasis added. Additionally, the use of at and land indicate that the location in question was a greater area that included the small distinct town of Bethlehem located only a short distance away from Jerusalem. It is improbable that Smith would not have known that Jesus was born in Bethlehem. Daniel C. Peterson, Matthew Roper, and William J. Hamblin, "On Alma 7:10 and the Birthplace of Jesus Christ," *FARMS Preliminary Report*, Neal A. Maxwell Institute, BYU, 1995.
80. Campbell, "Delusions," 93.
81. Campbell, "Delusions," 93.
82. Revelation, June 1829–E [D&C 17], 119, http://www.josephsmithpapers.org.
83. 1 Nephi 16:10 (Book of Mormon). Webster's 1830 dictionary defines a compass as an instrument for directing the course at sea or in the desert. Loren Blake Spendlove, "Understanding Nephi with the Help of Noah Webster," *Interpreter: A Journal of Mormon Scripture* 11 (2014): 119.
84. 1 Nephi 16:28 (Book of Mormon).
85. Despite the fact that there were three different groups who came to the Americas over the course of the Book of Mormon record, details on their mode of travel are brief or lacking entirely. It is recorded that Nephi built a ship of "curious workmanship," as shown to him by God, with wind as the force driving his boat (1 Nephi 18:2, 9 Book of Mormon). The Jaredites were directed by God to build eight small, lightweight barges that were "tight like a dish," or waterproof. Campbell humorously called them "made like ducks . . . swimming and diving" their way to the promised land. Actually, their mode of travel, described in the Book of Mormon "as a whale in the midst of the sea," was perhaps by ocean cur-rent (Ether 2:16, 24 Book of Mormon). The means by which the third group, the descendants of King Zedekiah through his son Mulek, came to the Americas is not included in the record. Later in the record, a man named Hagoth built ships so that many could travel to the north lands, but this was also by sail (Alma 63:5 Book of Mormon).
86. Campbell, "Delusions," 93.
87. Between late 1831 and 1832, Smith might have been able to begin explaining his view of succeeding Christian dispensations, which was quite different from

Campbell, who saw them as incrementally building on the previous one and culminating in the Christian dispensation. As Smith worked on his inspired translation of the Bible, he received additional revelation about Adam. Adam was taught about Christ, the sacraments or ordinances, the plan of salvation, and priesthood long before the so-called "Christian era" (Moses 6 Pearl of Great Price). Smith believed there were few differences between earlier and later dispensations, as each dispensation had prophets; however, God has reserved additional light and knowledge for the final dispensation. His inspired translation of Genesis and Egyptian papyrus contain information regarding Adam, Enoch, Noah, Abraham, and Moses.

88. Campbell, "Delusions," 93.
89. Campbell, "Delusions," 95; emphasis in the original.
90. History, 1838–1856, volume C-1 [2 November 1838–31 July 1842], 1015, http://www.josephsmithpapers.org; emphasis in original.
91. Bushman, "Joseph Smith and Skepticism," in *Believing History*, 155.
92. Moroni 10:4 (Book of Mormon).
93. Samuel Taylor Coleridge, *Samuel Taylor Coleridge*, ed. H. J. Jackson (Oxford: Oxford University Press 1985), 314.
94. Ether 12:6b (Book of Mormon).
95. Campbell, "Delusions," 96; emphasis in original.
96. Bushman, "The Book of Mormon and Its Critics," 114–17.
97. Alexander Campbell, *Delusions: An Analysis of the Book of Mormon with an Examination of Its Internal and External Evidences, and a Refutation of Its Pretences to Divine Authority* (Boston: Benjamin H. Green, 1832).
98. Parley P. Pratt, "Dear Brother Cowdery," *Messenger and Advocate* 2, no. 8 (May 1836): 319.
99. Letter to Oliver Cowdery, 24 September 1834, 192, http://josephsmithpapers.org.
100. Letter to Oliver Cowdery, 24 September 1834, 192, http://josephsmithpapers.org.
101. History, 1834–1836, 52, http://www.josephsmithpapers.org.
102. Minutes and Discourse, 21 April 1834, 44, http://www.josephsmithpapers.org.

12

Waves of Crisis

*J*ust as Campbell was opposed by some of the staunch Regular Baptists from at least 1816 until he completely severed ties with them in 1830 and by the Mormons in 1830 and 1831, so too did Smith have difficulties. Smith's claims to prophethood were challenged from without as discussed in chapters 10 and 11 by Campbell, Scott, Bentley, and others, but also from within the membership of the church. Some early converts, such as Booth, Howe, Ryder, and Hurlbut, became members for a short time, left, then provided inside accounts of Smith's perceived weaknesses and follies. Although these individuals presented obstacles for Smith and his fledgling church, there were others whose dissension, opposition, and loss were much more keenly felt.

Smith's restoration was so unique in American religious history—a throwback to biblical precedents—that some were wont to negate it in the new era of American religious freedom. Smith and his followers grappled with questions regarding his role as prophet, seer, and revelator. Smith was already outside Protestant tradition, preaching from the Bible, Book of Mormon, and his revelations. Was he also to lead his community in other aspects of life? Was he to be like Enoch and Moses, who gathered their followers into a new way of organizing themselves, where the purpose of their efforts was to work together to build the kingdom of God on earth?[1]

In the newly formed republic, what were the rights of free men, and what were the responsibilities of Latter-day Saints? Could Smith cross traditional American boundaries—rights fought for in the Revolutionary War—and insert himself in the temporal affairs of his followers? Should religious values permeate all aspects of life? Where was the line between individualism and obedience to a self-proclaimed prophet? Questions regarding the role of prophetic leadership caused deep rifts among some church members.[2]

KIRTLAND, OHIO

In the late summer of 1836, following a season of great spiritual renewal culminating in the dedication of the Kirtland Temple and the visitation of angelic messengers, the tide turned quickly. The rapid influx of Saints gathering to Kirtland, now numbering about two thousand members among three thousand inhabitants, accelerated the demand for property, homes, and goods. Although some members began to prosper, the church itself was deep in debt from caring for the poor, purchasing property to settle newcomers—many of whom had sold their property elsewhere at a discount and arrived unable to purchase land at the going rate—publishing *A Book of Commandments for the Government of the Church of Christ* and a hymnal, helping send out missionaries, and especially building the temple. There was a steadily rising level of poverty among the membership in Kirtland. Church leaders, including Smith, had debts that were primarily in short-term notes, but their assets were in nonliquid land and buildings. Smith could not bear to demand hard cash from his impoverished followers, resulting in a cash-flow problem.[3] Helping the poor in Kirtland acquire property at a reasonable price would help both them and the church by producing additional income through land sales.

Warren Cowdery, editor of the church newspaper *Messenger and Advocate*, reminiscing on the post-Pentecostal season, wrote that some of the Saints were "guilty of wild speculation" and dreams of worldly wealth.[4] Enterprises of all types grew up along the canals and throughout the Western Reserve as part of a national trend. Speculation led to a great demand for money, leading to a lending boom. Everyone planned to get rich, and this same spirit "was taking deep root in the church."[5] The closest bank to Kirtland was the Geauga Bank in Paineville with a monopoly on all the lending activity in the area, influencing growth and investment. Returning home in the fall of 1836 after a summer of missionary efforts, Heber C. Kimball recorded his thoughts on the "spirit of speculation that was prevailing in the Church. Trade and traffic seemed to engross the time and attention of the Saints." Some individuals who previously "could hardly get food to eat . . . [were now] men of supposed great wealth; in fact, everything in the place seemed to be moving in great prosperity, and all seemed determined to become rich."[6] In November 1836, Smith and other church leaders chastised the Saints and warned them to repent or serious consequences awaited them.[7]

In early November 1836, to relieve church debt Smith and other leaders proposed incorporating a bank to be called the Kirtland Safety Society to increase the amount of money available. The bank was intended to help resolve temporal needs of the poor then gathering to Kirtland. The state legislature, many of whom were hard-money Democrats, was biased toward specie, or hard currency such as gold, silver, and copper, and turned down the request for a bank charter. The problem was that this meant the economy could only grow as fast as specie was mined and minted by the federal government. Bank notes or currency, on the other hand, with only a fractional reserve of specie were needed to increase the money supply for loans and thereby increase economic growth.[8] Whigs and soft-money Democrats encouraged commercial institutions to issue notes, considering the actions of the majority, hard-money Democrats, unlawful and unconstitutional.[9] To provide the currency needed for economic development, Smith, Rigdon, and Cowdery, with other church leaders and with the apparent aid of legal counsel, created a private joint-stock company called the Kirtland Safety Society Anti-Banking Company that was like other unchartered banks in Ohio. It was typical to operate a bank unchartered for a short period, thus providing a track record for the state legislature to appraise in deciding to issue a charter; however, a charter would continue to be sought to give greater confidence to the investors.[10] Rather than just the wealthy purchasing stock, those who invested in the Safety Society included "men, women, blacks, whites, Mormons, non-Mormons, merchants, farmers, old, young, wealthy, and poor."[11]

On 9 January 1837, the Safety Society opened its doors for business. Smith supported the institution and invited church members from abroad to purchase stock in the new enterprise.[12] Wilford Woodruff described in his journal his initial reaction to returning to Kirtland after two and one-half years away: there had been "wonderful progress."

Previously, many had been impoverished and his brothers in the church "poor, despised, & even looked down upon." Now, the community had been transformed. In their midst was a fine temple, a printing shop, and the Kirtland Safety Society, in addition to commercial, mercantile, and small manufacturing firms. The promise of prosperity brought cheerful countenances and industry in the form of new homes and markets.[13] Little did Woodruff know of the maelstrom swirling at the highest levels in the church or of the difficulties the financial institution was already beginning to experience.

At the same time the Safety Society was established, wild speculation was sweeping the country. The high demand for redemption of Kirtland Safety Society notes in the first weeks of operation caused it to suspend specie payments and replace the backing of the notes with land values that were deeply discounted.[14] Behind the scenes, Grandison Newell on the Geauga Bank board of directors opposed the Safety Society by traveling throughout the area buying all their notes possible and immediately redeeming them for specie.[15]

Speaking in a meeting at the temple, Brigham Young warned a quorum of priesthood holders not to murmur against Smith, likely referring to both financial and spiritual problems. If the Saints wanted a Moses figure to lead them and do what he had done, then Smith was that man. If they wanted, however, to demand their rights as Americans over their responsibilities to the church, then there was a dilemma.[16]

In February, Sidney Rigdon echoed a similar warning, exhorting the Church members "to union that they might be prepared to meet every trial & difficulty that awates them."[17] Nevertheless, an undercurrent of murmuring had already begun. On the last day of the month, Smith and Rigdon each spoke on the temporal affairs of the church, hopeful that the Kirtland Safety Society could bless their financial circumstances and encourage the Saints to be unified.[18] The national bank crisis, the Panic of 1837 began in the middle of the month in New York and was followed by a seven-year general economic depression.[19] In late February, Woodruff recorded that Smith rose up "in the power of God" to defend himself against the complainers. While he had been away on church business, a group of dissenters planned to depose him and place David Whitmer as head of the church.[20]

In March, as the Panic of 1837 spread westward, banks throughout the country began closing. By April, economic problems with the Safety Society were apparent to all. At one meeting Smith, proclaimed in the name of God that those who professed to be his friends but who turned traitors to oppose the bank currency had given power to the enemy and caused the poor to remain that way.[21] Further, Smith warned regarding speculation, for "the Safety Society could not survive its practice of lending money without sufficient resources."[22]

In May, the national "crisis of confidence" in the banks also included more of Mormon opinions regarding their prophet. Woodruff wrote that the "spirits of murmering, complaining, & of mutiny" had continued to the point "until many & some in high places had risen up against Joseph. . . . And they were striving to overthrow his influence & cast him down."[23] Some believed he was a "fallen prophet." Warren Parrish, former clerk and cashier in the Safety Society was accused of "peculation," meaning embezzlement in the sum of $25,000 from the bank.[24] Within weeks, Smith became deathly ill. The stress and contention had worn him down, and some were certain that he would not survive.[25]

In early June, disgruntled members of the Quorum of Twelve Apostles and other disaffected church leaders attempted to defend their quarrel against Smith. With Smith ill, Sidney Rigdon, counselor to Smith, was in charge of a meeting at the temple, and after a time chose to hear no more from dissenters and closed the meeting. Smith finally began to recover but was still too ill to attend meetings. At the end of the month, Parrish arrived at a meeting early and took the seat usually reserved for Smith, openly defying the prophet in his absence.[26] Mary Fielding compared this challenge of Smith to the rebellion of Korah against Moses and Aaron.[27] At this time, Heber C. Kimball claimed that not twenty men in Kirtland still believed Smith was a prophet.[28] Kimball's hyperbolic statement illustrates his own deep feelings on the apostasy of members of the Quorum of Twelve Apostles: Parley and Orson Pratt, David Patten, Frederick G. Williams, and Smith's Safety Society clerk, Warren Parish. Bushman maintains that "apostasy was rife, but many remained loyal followers, and the church was not near collapse."[29] The apostasy was among some of the leadership, not many of the rank-and-file membership.

Before 7 July, Smith officially resigned his position as treasurer of the Safety Society and disposed of his personal investments, convinced that "no institution of the kind . . . would be suffered to continue its operations in such an age of darkness, speculation, and wickedness."[30] It appears that with the change in leadership at the Safety Society that

Parrish recirculated banknotes, forged signatures, signed new notes, and made loans that would not fall due until September when it was apparent to many by then that the Safety Society would have shut their doors.[31]

Warren Cowdery suggested in the July issue of the *Messenger and Advocate* that Smith had crossed traditional American boundaries of liberty and caused his followers to surrender their rights and privileges as independent citizens. He accused Smith of setting himself up as infallible and using ecclesiastical tyranny akin to principles of popery.[32] In very Protestant America, to denounce Smith as acting like the pope with a system of priests ruling over the people—in other words, what was then called "priestcraft"—was the height of personal condemnation. Others disagreed with the defectors regarding Smith's vigorous leadership style and authority. Mary Fielding felt the crisis was brought about not because Smith or his counselors tried to exert too much influence, but because some leaders and members needed to be more submissive to his leadership.[33]

In August, Smith continued to warn the members and friends of the church "to beware of speculators, renegades, and gamblers, who are duping the unwary and unsuspecting by palming upon them those bills, which have no worth here. . . . I know [these practices] to be detrimental to the best interests of the society as well as to the principles of religion."[34]

With no state backing, other financial institutions decided not to accept the Kirtland Safety Society notes as legal tender, and the bank was forced to close its doors. The lack of a state banking charter was key to its early demise, creating financial handicaps, bad publicity, and great personal risks to the backers.[35] Those who did business with the bank expected to benefit from their transactions. Although Smith had provided his creditors with assets and was buying and selling land at market prices, the economic reversals in Kirtland and the country involved a change in economic conditions that even a reasonably prudent businessman probably would not have anticipated.[36] Creditors were angry, Smith was fined by the state, and many of the two hundred who invested in the bank blamed Smith for their losses. The investors who were church members "questioned his authority and ability to receive divine direction."[37]

Some of the dissenters developed a new plan to oppose Smith. The dissenters set up a new church organization with the intent to take control of Smith's church, force the First Presidency from office, and oust them from Kirtland. They were derisively referred to by those faithful to Smith as "black legs," a contemptuous metaphor perhaps referring to these individuals as disease-producing black canker (scurvy). In turn, the "black legs" ridiculed those who remained loyal to Smith by calling them "lick-skillets," an insulting and derisive nickname in a "culture of honor, since it implied servility and a humiliating lack of manhood."[38] Metaphorically, it described their unwavering obedience to do everything Smith asked as if "licking" the last morsel from the pan. George A. Smith later recalled that if "a man would stand up in the streets and say he was Joseph's friend, could not receive a greater compliment than to being called a lick-skillet" because at that time Smith had few friends.[39] Kirtland had devolved into two groups: those who rejected the First Presidency's leadership in economic affairs and viewed Smith as a fallen prophet even while accepting his earlier revelations and those who saw other causes for the failure of the bank and were willing to follow Smith's prophetic leadership.

At the 3 September 1837 conference, Kirtland church members put the Safety Society fiasco behind them, and the majority sustained the leadership. By this time, the Pratt brothers, Orson Hyde, and other members of the Quorum of Twelve Apostles had returned to Smith's side. The 1837 Kirtland crisis was an apostasy that cost close to a third of the top leadership in the church, but few of the regular members. Some of the elite, more well educated, and more prosperous, including Warren Parrish, Book of Mormon witnesses Martin Harris, Oliver Cowdery, and David Whitmer, and Apostles Lyman and Luke Johnson and John F. Boynton were among those who continued to dissent.[40] Surprisingly and paradoxically, the trials had the net effect of strengthening Smith and those who stayed with him.[41] During the Kirtland era, Smith had further set in place the organization of the church with Twelve Apostles and sent them on missions to Great Britain. He had essentially finished his work on the Bible and translated the Book of Abraham scrolls. Those who remained faithful were convinced of Smith's prophetic calling despite his personal failings and the continuing struggles of the church.

The dissenters and anti-Mormons not only openly opposed Smith and Rigdon but also pursued vexatious lawsuits and threatened their lives. Smith recorded, "The bitterness of the spirit of apostate mobocracy . . . continued to rage and grow hotter . . . until Elder Rigdon and

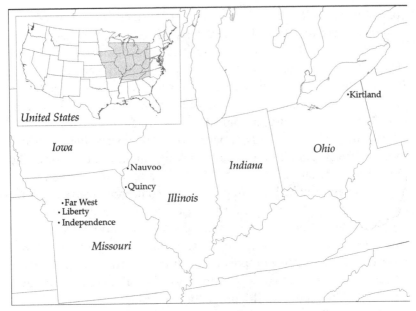

Map of Missouri and Illinois, by Edward Dean Neuenswander.

myself were obliged to flee from its deadly influence."[42] In January 1838, the two men with their families made a winter migration of almost 900 miles overland to Missouri under pursuit by men armed with pistols seeking their lives until they were out of the state of Ohio, arriving in Far West mid-March.[43]

FAR WEST, MISSOURI

Smith's problems, however, were not over. The church in Missouri was in the midst of its own crises. As noted in chapter 6, Smith had designated Missouri as the location of Zion in the summer of 1831. The area around Independence was referred to by some as the "New Jerusalem." Rather than set a time frame for the Second Coming, Smith had named a place of gathering.[44] Shortly after the revelation was received, families were asked to settle in Jackson County. Soon, an agent purchased large tracts of land, a press helped to standardize, publish, promote and publicize church doctrine and organization,[45] and Smith established a communitarian system where individuals willingly deeded their property to the bishop and in return received a stewardship in "Zion." The goal was for every family to have sufficient for their own needs and to help the poor. The call to settle in Missouri was about creating a community that was united religiously and communally.[46] That goal, however, was not likely to include many Missourians whom Smith observed in 1831 as having a "leanness of intellect, ferocity, and jealousy of a people that were nearly a century behind the times" and who "roamed about without the benefit of civilization, refinement and religion."[47]

By mid-1833, close to one-third of Jackson County consisted of Mormon settlers, numbering approximately 1,200.[48] Their millenarian perspective, the "great reversal" regarding the imminent return of Christ, accompanied by the disruption of the current social order, helped foster an "us versus them" mentality.[49] Additionally, high numbers of Mormons were New Englanders who were either ambivalent toward slavery or at least not proslavery and believed that God intended to give them this "sacred land." These ideas did not sit well with the frontier Missourians who had come a few years earlier, mostly from the Carolina piedmont region of the upper south—Virginia, North Carolina, Kentucky, and Tennessee.[50] Missouri proslavery inhabitants praised the 1820 Missouri Compromise that made them a slave state even though they were part of the Louisiana Purchase and north of 36.5 degrees north latitude. They were westward-looking entrepreneurs who valued the wealth embedded in western land and whose sense of manifest destiny justified exploitation. They believed the land belonged to them, which warranted the goal of removing the earlier inhabitants (American Indians) and not sharing that land with unwanted settlers.[51] The two groups—proslavery southerners and eastern Mormons— clashed culturally. They were described as "oil and water," a "noxious blend," and "a keg of gunpowder beside a campfire."[52]

Fear of Mormon political and economic control and the enthusiastic thrust of their religion led the 1833 non-Mormon citizens to resolve to "save" their county from Mormon domination by demanding that settlement by Mormons cease and that current Mormon settlers must leave. Their "worst fear envisioned Mormon abolitionists descending upon them in droves to proselytize Native Americans while dictated at every turn by the undemocratic authority of direct revelation."[53] Disgruntled individuals began nighttime predations: breaking windows, shooting at homes, and shouting abuses. David Pettigrew reported that while he was in his own field working his neighbor shouted, "We are determined to drive you away from this Country and we will Stop you from emigrating here." When Pettigrew replied that Mormons did not interfere with the rights of others and kept the laws of the land, his neighbor rejoined: "That is to no purpose . . . . The old laws and Constitution are all worn out, and we are about to frame a new One." A few days later at a religious meeting, representatives of the mob came to inform the Mormons of their intention:

> There is great difficulty between us, and we are sent by the Authority, and a large body of men <are> already Collected together at Independence, and all are under arms, and now the proposals are these, If you will forsake your Mormon prophet religion, and become of Our Religion, we will become your brothers, and will fight for you, and we will protect you in any difficulties or troubles you may have, we will Stand by you and never forsake you, but if you will not, why will fall you. Our men are now all under Arms, and it has been with great difficulty they have been Kept back, and now you have Some Knowledge of your Situations. We feel for, and beg of you to consider your Situation and Save yourselves, from the calamity which will Soon follow, Should you fail to comply with our request. Forsake your Prophet Religion, for we will not suffer Mormonism amongst us.[54]

An 1833 removal petition sent to the governor described the Mormons as "deluded fanatics." Had they been "respectable citizens in society" and thus merely religiously "deluded," they "would have been entitled to our pity rather than our contempt and hatred." They were described as the "very dregs" of society; "lazy, idle and vicious," in contrast to the other residents who were "fearless, honest, and independent citizens." This view made it "extremely natural" for the Missourians to "feel disposed to rid themselves of such a pest."[55] The resulting mob action of four to five hundred Missouri vigilantes destroyed the printing office, threw the press out the upper floor window, confiscated the contents of what was being printed, and tarred and feathered Bishop Edward Partridge and Charles Allen.[56] Partridge reported his response to the mobbers who stripped him of his hat, coat, and vest in preparation for tarring and feathering: "If I must suffer for my religion, it was no more than others had done before me. That I had lived in the county for two years and I was not conscious of having injured any one in the county, therefore I could not consent to leave it."[57] Removal petitions continued as more Mormons immigrated to the state and were moved from one county of Missouri to another.

By 1836, some of the complaints centered around the nationalities of the Mormons: they were from "different parts of the world," their alien status justifying a "war of extermination" or removal from the state.[58] As the Missourians perceived them, the Mormons were far too inclusive—allowing different nations, colors, and classes of people to join with them. Further, their own text promoted the ideal that God invites everyone to come to him: all are alike to him, including the black man, the slave, the heathen, and the Jew.[59] Mob violence and the lack of protection by local and state authorities caused the Mormons to move from Jackson County to Clay County, then Ray County from which Caldwell County was created in 1836 by the legislature as a safe haven for the Mormons. Others moved further north into Daviess County.

By 1838, significant problems existed from without and within the church. Two church leaders, W. W. Phelps and John Whitmer, were accused of misusing church funds and were excommunicated. Two other significant leaders and Book of Mormon witnesses, Oliver Cowdery, assistant president of the church, and David Whitmer, president of the church in Missouri, also were accused of serious infractions. In April 1838, Cowdery maintained he had a difference of opinion with Smith. He declared: "I will not be influenced, governed, or controlled, in my temporal interests by any ecclesiastical authority or pretended revelation whatever, contrary to my own judgment. . . . The three great principles of English liberty . . . are 'the right of personal security, the right of personal liberty, and the right of private property.'" He was unwilling to give up his American principles "for anything less liberal, less benevolent, or less free." He considered Smith as attempting "to set up a kind of petty government, controlled and dictated by ecclesiastical influence, in the midst of this National and State Government." Additionally, he complained that this effort "to controll me in my temporal interests, I conceive to be a disposition to take from me a portion of my Constitutional privileges and inherent rights. I only, respectfully, ask leave, therefore, to withdraw from a society assuming these they <have> such right."[60] David Whitmer also did not support Smith's use of political and economic influence to advance the church's aims, but preferred a separation of church and state affairs.[61] He wrote a letter to John Murdock stating that he, too, had decided to "withdraw from your fellowship and communion."[62] By this time, all three of the original witnesses to the Book of Mormon were excommunicated, and three of the group of eight witnesses were either excommunicated or alienated from the church.[63] One can only imagine Smith's somber feelings at the loss of such close friends and longtime associates, particularly Oliver Cowdery, Martin Harris, and John and David Whitmer—a dark and tragic time in church history. Fortunately, Oliver Cowdery, Martin Harris, W. W. Phelps, and some of the other leaders later returned to the church; however, the Whitmers did not.

A secret group of Mormons formed in this highly charged era, the "Danite Band"—organized most likely by Sampson Avard. The group went through several very different stages of development. Initially, they were established under the guise of ridding Caldwell county of Mormon apostates and dissenters and enforcing the law of consecration. After the dissenters were forced out, their new purpose was to defend and protect individuals and property and to influence state and county elections in favor of Mormons or at least those who would defend their rights. At some point, Avard repurposed the group and secretly taught his followers to rob their "enemies'" for the perverted purpose of consecrating the spoils for building up the kingdom of God.[64] Although there was a legitimate state militia composed of Mormons organized in Far West and Diahman called the "Armies of Israel," they were distinct groups with different purposes—the former having open membership to all able-bodied men for defense, and the latter a secretive and closed paramilitary group with signs, passwords, and blood oaths for pillaging and burning the property of non-Mormons. Some Danites were also part of the legitimate militia, confounding separation of the two groups' operations. Avard convinced his followers that he had the approval of church leaders, and because they were bound to secrecy they were forbidden to ask—his indoctrination was thorough, blurring the lines of his illegitimate activities by sacralizing his methods.[65]

Smith's initial statements indicate that he viewed the group as protective of individuals and property. In mid-December 1838, however, Smith asserted, "We have learned . . . that many false and pernicious things which were calculated to lead the Saints far astray and to do great injury have been taught by Dr. Avard as coming from the Presidency."[66] In March 1839, Smith again repudiated the Danite band, calling Avard wicked and clarifying that the only Mormon covenant was the everlasting covenant contained in the scriptures and the things God has revealed. "Pure friendship always becomes weakened the very moment you undertake to make it stronger by penal oaths and secrecy."[67]

While dealing with challenges from within the church, hostilities with the Missourians continued to increase. Mormons had always been considered outsiders. Their beliefs were foreign to accepted Christianity of that day. By 1830 there was "a well-established color line that segregated citizens and subjects, civilized and savage, free and slave," but where did the Mormons fit in?[68] Although by native birth and skin color they looked like Protestants, their conversion to Mormonism marginalized them as a socially inferior class of people; a separate race. "Race, then, was a socially invented category and not a biological reality. It was employed by the white Protestant majority to situate Mormons at various distances away from the top of a racial hierarchy and thereby justify discriminatory policies against them. . . . Outsiders were convinced that Mormonism represented a racial—not merely religious—departure from the mainstream."[69] They were not certain where to situate the Mormons in their self-composed hierarchy of races; "nonetheless, some were convinced that Mormons represented a backward racial descent."[70] Mormon and then Mormonite became pejorative labels to distinguish them from their neighbors. Over time, these labels allowed outsiders to conflate Smith's followers to a homogenous group with not only common religious beliefs but also physical degeneration, and intellectual inferiority, making them liable to superstition, delusion, and ultimately leading to racial decline. This shared identity was used to justify the removal of the Mormons from several counties in Missouri and eventually the state.[71] The label made them a distinct group and differentiated them from citizens who could claim basic rights to life, liberty, and property.

Animosity continued to accelerate the violence between Mormons, vigilantes, and the state militia, culminating with what has been called the "Missouri Mormon War," a three-month conflict from August to November 1838. Four key events highlighted the war: (1) the 6 August election-day brawl involving as many as sixty men that occurred in Gallatin when non-Mormons attempted to prevent Mormons from voting; (2) the 25 October Battle of Crooked River between the official Missouri militia and the Mormons; (3) the 27 October "Extermination Order" issued by Governor Lilburn Boggs that gave Mormons the choice of leaving the state voluntarily or being forced out by the militia; and (4) the 30 October surprise attack at Haun's Mill by a mob-militia that left seventeen Mormons dead and thirteen others wounded.

On 31 October, "under the presumption they had been invited to discuss ways of diffusing the volatile situation," five Mormon leaders under a flag of truce approached the camp near Far West under the command of Missouri militia leader General Lucas.[72] In accordance with Governor Boggs's executive order, Lucas immediately arrested the men, among them Smith, Rigdon, and Pratt. At a court-martial, the men were found guilty in absentia, and Lucas drafted an order of immediate execution. Fortunately, the men were under the custody of Brigadier General Alexander Doniphan, who vehemently opposed the decision, informing Lucas that he considered the order illegal, had no intention to obey it, and threatened legal action if it was carried out. The men, under heavy guard, were moved from Far West to Independence to Richmond for trial and then to Liberty for incarceration.

The men spent the winter, December 1838 until late April 1839, in Liberty Jail, a tiny 14-by-14½-foot unheated, underground dungeon with two small grated windows for ventilation, and accessed by a trap door. The inmates' comments paint a painful picture: "grates and screeking iron doors," "dirty straw couches," "the nauseous" smell, the "grimace of the guard night and day," "weary joints and bones," and "this hell surrounded with demons."[73] Neither pen, nor tongue, nor angels could fully portray the horrific experience. In March, after months in jail, Smith cried out to the Lord, "O God, where art thou? And where is the pavilion that covereth thy hiding place? How long shall thy hand be stayed, and thine eye, yea thy pure eye, behold from the eternal heavens the wrongs of thy people and of thy servants, and thine ear be penetrated with their cries?"[74] His desperate call was not just for himself and his inmates but also for the people who had put their trust in him as a prophet and were suffering because of that belief.

Mormon historian Mark Staker sums up "the attempt of Mormons to establish a religious community in western Missouri's rough frontier" with this description: "fraught with sharp religious competition, imprudence, bravado, and numerous complex issues of cultural difference by both believers and non-believers."[75] Missouri was an excruciatingly painful and difficult time in Mormon history: some of it due to the Missourians, but some of it brought upon the Mormons by their own actions. In a revelation to Smith, the Lord declared they had been afflicted because of their transgressions and that they needed to be chastened. There had been "jarrings, and contentions, and envyings, and strifes, and lustful and covetous desires among them; therefore by these things they polluted their inheritances." Additionally, since they had been slow in hearkening to God, God had been slow to answer their prayers of distress. He had not cast them off, despite their imperfections, calling them "his jewels," and promised he would yet be merciful, but they must be chastised.[76]

QUINCY, ILLINOIS

While the men were in jail, approximately ten thousand Mormons fled the state with very little—their weapons, homes, livestock, and belongings had been taken from them. Insufficient food, clothing, footwear, bedding, or means of travel, caused most to leave Missouri as quickly as possible. They had until late March to comply with the state mandate, but many began leaving in January amid threats from local vigilantes, running out of food and supplies and not being allowed to replenish them, and being warned that Smith would not be released from prison until they had left Missouri. They traveled through bitter cold, snow, hail, rain, and deep mud. When they reached the Mississippi, they sometimes had to camp for days along the bank until the river thawed and they could cross by boat.[77]

Quincy, Illinois, was the closest settlement to Far West that had ferryboats and scores of Mormons already living there who were willing to help. In late February, the *Quincy Whig* reported the Mormons were "coming in from all quarters, . . . bringing with them the wreck of what they could save from their ruthless oppressors. . . . They appear, so far as we have seen, to be a mild, inoffensive people, who could not have given cause for the persecution they have met with."[78] The Mormons were considered "objects of charity" who have been "thrown upon our shores destitute, through the oppressive people of Missouri, common humanity must oblige us to aid and relieve them all in our power."[79] City leaders and residents opened their farms, sheds, huts, and tents to the refugees. Despite having been robbed of their "corn, wheat, horses, cattle, cows, hogs, wearing apparel, houses and homes" and with widows entirely destitute, what the Mormons wanted was work.[80] The Quincy Democratic Association and citizens' committee passed a resolution stating that the "Strangers recently arrived here from the State of Missouri, known by the name of the 'Latter Day Saints,' are entitled to our sympathy and kindest regard, and that we recommend to the Citizens of Quincy to extend to them all the kindness in their power to bestow, as persons who are in affliction."[81] In contrast to how the Mormons were viewed in Missouri, Quincy's "good Samaritan" response was a most welcome respite. Quincy's compassion is credited by Mormon historian Richard E. Bennett with saving the Saints as a people and perhaps even saving the institutional church.[82] The Mormons remained in Quincy for only a few months before purchasing property and moving up river to Commerce, Illinois, and renaming it Nauvoo.

Aftermath

When Smith arrived in Quincy in April 1839, having earlier solicited the members to write petitions for redress and affidavits regarding property losses and their suffering in Missouri, he began collecting them. Of the 678 petitions which have survived, the losses totaled $2,275,789 in that day.[83] In late October, Smith, Rigdon, and several other men left for Washington, DC, to meet with the Illinois congressional delegation and President Martin Van Buren. A December newspaper reported on the Mormon delegation: "Several of the Mormon leaders are at present in the city. Their object is to obtain recompense for losses sustained by them in consequence of the outrages committed on them in Missouri . . . at which the heart sickens. . . . They appear to be peaceful and harmless, and if fanaticism has led them into error, reason, not violence, should be used to reclaim them."[84]

Congressman John Reynolds of Illinois introduced Smith to Van Buren. Just before entering the office of the president Reynolds reported, "the prophet asked me to introduce him as a 'Latter Day Saint.' It was so unexpected and so strange to me, . . . but he repeated the request, . . . [and] I introduced him as a 'Latter Day Saint,' which made the President smile."[85] Smith and members of his delegation met with the president at least once, and perhaps twice.[86] Later, at dinner with Judge Stephen A. Douglas, Smith recounted the Missouri persecution and reported his reception by Van Buren: "Gentlemen Your cause is just, but I can do nothing for you."[87] Other weighty matters of the country subordinated the problems of the Mormons.[88] In the national scheme of things, Missouri votes were more important than the Mormons in Van Buren's desire to be reelected.[89]

Smith endured years of lawsuits, persecutions, and disappointments. Some men would have been crushed; Smith instead continued to rise up. He recognized that God's timetable both for settling accounts with their persecutors and for establishing a New Jerusalem in Missouri were in the future. He had not given up on his fellow church leaders— even some whose defection was deeply personal, nor had he given up on the foundational principles of the Constitution. An editorial published 1 October 1843 in the Nauvoo *Times and Seasons* queried "Who Shall Be Our Next President?" It did not suggest any specific names but concluded that the candidate must be "the man who will be the most likely to render us assistance in obtaining redress for our grievances."[90] In early November, Smith wrote letters to the leading presidential candidates John C. Calhoun, Lewis Cass, Richard M. Johnson, Henry Clay, and Martin Van Buren describing the Missouri persecutions, asking, "'What will be your rule of action relative to us as a people', should fortune favor your ascension to the chief magistracy?"[91] Van Buren had already given his answer. Calhoun, Cass, and Clay responded expressing little sympathy for the cause of the Mormons. On 29 January 1844, at a meeting in the Nauvoo mayor's office, the Quorum of Twelve Apostles and citizens of Nauvoo unanimously nominated Smith to be a candidate for president of the United States.[92]

NOTES

1. For more on the Mormon view of Enoch, see Moses 7:18–19, 69 (Pearl of Great Price).
2. Ronald K. Esplin, "Joseph Smith and the Kirtland Crisis," in *Joseph Smith, the Prophet and Seer,* ed. Richard N. Holzapfel and Kent P. Jackson (Provo, UT: Religious Studies Center; Salt Lake City: Deseret Book, 2010), 263.
3. Marvin S. Hill, C. Keith Rooker, and Larry T. Wimmer, "The Kirtland Economy Revisited: A Market Critique of Sectarian Economics," *BYU Studies* 17 (Summer 1977): 420–23.
4. Warren A. Cowdery, *Messenger and Advocate* 3, no. 8 (May 1837): 509.
5. "History of the Church, *Millennial Star* 16, no. 1 (7 January, 1854): 11.
6. Orson F. Whitney, *Life of Heber C. Kimball* (Salt Lake City: Kimball Family, 1888), 111.
7. *Wilford Woodruff's Journal,* 1:111.
8. R. McKay White, "The Kirtland Safety Society: The Myths, the Facts, and the Prophet's Good Name," 2009, http://www.fairmormon.org/Misc/KSS.pdf.
9. The *Painesville Republican* of 19 January 1837, for example, declared the law an outrage upon equal rights insisting that no legislative body has the constitutional right to grant privileges to one set of men in regard to the use of money and prohibit the enjoyment of like privileges by others," in Hill, Rooker, and Wimmer, "The Kirtland Economy Revisited," 456–57; Special Report of the Auditor of State [of Ohio]: Railroad Companies, Pub. Doc. No. 44, 5 January 1843, 17–40, in Dale W. Adams, "Chartering the Kirtland Bank," *BYU Studies* 23, no. 4 (1983): 3–6.
10. Staker, *Hearken, O Ye People,* 448.
11. Staker, *Hearken, O Ye People,* 464.
12. "Notice," *Messenger and Advocate,* January 1837.
13. *Wilford Woodruff's Journal,* 1:108.

14. *Cleveland Daily Gazette*, 24 January 1837; *Painesville Telegraph*, 27 January 1837; *Cleveland Daily Herald and Gazette*, 1 May, 8 and 17 July 1837; in Hill, Rooker, and Wimmer, "The Kirtland Economy Revisited," 434.

15. James Thompson, "Statement," 3, in Staker, *Heaken, O Ye People*, 484. Although Newell boasted that "he had forced the Mormon's to leave Kirtland" is an overstatement, he may also have influenced the Bank of Geauga's refusal to accept Safety Society notes further exacerbating its difficulties.

16. *Wilford Woodruff's Journal*, 1:121.

17. *Wilford Woodruff's Journal*, 1:121.

18. *Wilford Woodruff's Journal*, 1:124.

19. Causes of the nationwide financial panic included speculative and inflationary selling of public lands and some of previous president Andrew Jackson's economic policies including his opposition to the renewal of the national bank charter.

20. *Wilford Woodruff's Journal*, 1:125.

21. *Wilford Woodruff's Journal*, 1:138.

22. Leland Homer Gentry and Todd M. Compton, *Fire and Sword: A History of the Latter-day Saints in Northern Missouri, 1836–39* (Salt Lake City: Greg Kofford Books, 2011), 75.

23. *Wilford Woodruff's Journal*, 1:147–48.

24. *Life of Heber C. Kimball*, 113. Roberts, *Comprehensive History*, 1:405; "Argument to argument where I find it; Ridicule to ridicule, and scorn to scorn," http://www.josephsmithpapers.org. Luke Johnson was the likely informant to Joseph Smith that Parrish robbed "the Kirtland Bank of twenty-five thousand dollars at one time, and large sums at others." Staker, *Hearken, O Ye People*, 535.

25. Mary Fielding to Mercy Fielding, 15 June 1837, Church History Library, The Church of Jesus Christ of Latter-day Saints, Salt Lake City; Hill, Rooker, and Wimmer, "The Kirtland Economy Revisited," 435.

26. Esplin, "Joseph Smith and the Kirtland Crisis," 279; Bushman, *Joseph Smith: Rough Stone Rolling*, 338.

27. See Numbers 16.

28. *Heber C. Kimball*, 5:63.

29. Bushman, *Joseph Smith: Rough Stone Rolling*, 332.

30. *Millennial Star* 16, no. 13, in *History of the Church*, 2:405; http://www.josephsmithpapers.org.

31. Staker, *Hearken, O Ye People*, 533–34.

32. Warren Cowdery, "Editorial," *Messenger and Advocate* 3, no. 10 (July 1837): 638.

33. Mary Fielding to Mercy Fielding, 15 June 1837.

34. "Caution," *Messenger and Advocate* 3, no. 11 (August 1837): 560.

35. Hill, Rooker, and Wimmer, "The Kirtland Economy Revisited," 435.

36. Hill, Rooker, and Wimmer, "The Kirtland Economy Revisited," 394.

37. Alexander Baugh, "Joseph Smith in Northern Missouri, 1838," in *Joseph Smith, the Prophet and Seer*, 292.

38. Staker, *Hearken, O Ye People*, 535.

39. George A. Smith, in *Journal of Discourses* (London: Latter-day Saints' Book Depot, 1881), 11:12.

40. Esplin, "Joseph Smith and the Kirtland Crisis," 26; Gentry and Compton, *Fire and Sword*, 77.

41. *Wilford Woodruff's Journal*, 1:134, 138.

42. History, 1838–1856, volume B-1 [1 September 1834–2 November 1838], 780, http://www.josephsmithpapers.org.

43. Smith and the other founders of the bank continued for several years to repay the bulk of their debts. Adams, "Chartering the Kirtland Bank," 11.

44. Thomas M. Spencer, "Persecution in the Most Odious Sense of the Word," in *The Missouri Mormon Experience*, ed. Thomas M. Spencer (Columbia: University of Missouri Press, 2010), 2.

45. Ronald E. Romig, *Eighth Witness: The Biography of John Whitmer* (Independence, MO: John Whitmer Books, 2014), 147.

46. Doctrine and Covenants 72:15–18, 24; 58:7.

47. http://www.josephsmithpapers.org.

48. Spencer, "Persecution in the Most Odious Sense of the Word," 4.

49. Grant Underwood, "Mormonism, Millenarianism, and Missouri," in *The Missouri Mormon Experience*, 51.

50. Spencer, "Persecution in the Most Odious Sense of the Word," 5–6; Richard E. Bennett, "The Nauvoo Legion and What Mormons Learned in Missouri," in *The Missouri Mormon Experience*, 140.

51. Steven C. Harper, "'Overwhelmingly Democratic': Cultural Identity in Jackson County, Missouri, 1827–1833," *Mormon Historical Studies* 9, no. 2 (Fall 2008): 3, 6.

52. Alexander L. Baugh, *A Call to Arms: The 1838 Mormon Defense of Northern Missouri* (Provo, UT: BYU Studies, 2000), 6–7; Spencer, "Persecution in the Most Odious Sense of the Word," 17.

53. Harper, "Overwhelmingly Democratic," 1; Staker, *Hearken, O Ye People*, 183.

54. David Pettigrew, "Autobiography and Diary," 1840–61, 17–18.

55. "Regulating the Mormonites," *Daily Missouri Republican*, 9 August 1833; "The Mormons," *Sangamo Journal* (Springfield, IL), 7 December 1833.

56. "Book of Commandments, 1833," *The Joseph Smith Papers*, http://www.josephsmithpapers.org.

57. Edward Partridge, *The Utah Historical and Genealogical Association* 7 (July 1916): 108. This sketch was attributed primarily to Orson F. Whitney, "The Aaronic Priesthood," *Contributor*, 1884.

58. "The Missouri Mormon War," in *Document containing the orders, correspondence, etc. in relation to the disturbances with the Mormons; and the evidence given before the Hon. Austin A. King, Judge of the fifth Judicial circuit of the State of Missouri, at the court house in Richmond, in a criminal court of inquiry, begun November 12, 1838, on the trial of Joseph Smith, Jr., and others, for high treason and other crimes against the State* (St. Louis Mercantile Library Association), https://www.sos.mo.gov/archives/resources/findingaids/miscMormonRecords/doc.

59. 2 Nephi 26:33 (Book of Mormon).

60. Oliver Cowdery to Edward Partridge, Far West, Missouri, 12 April 1838, http://www.josephsmithpapers.org.

61. Romig, *Eighth Witness*, 314.

62. David Whitmer to John Murdock, Far West, Missouri, 13 April 1838, http://www.josephsmithpapers.org.

63. Nevertheless, none of the Book of Mormon witnesses denied their experience with Smith and the gold plates. William McLellin thirty-seven years later about an event on July 22, 1833 with Oliver Cowdery and David Whitmer. Alone in the woods after having been chased by mobbers, he asked the two men "Is that book of Mormon true"? Cowdery responded with great solemnity, "Brother William, God sent his holy Angel to declare the truth of the translation of it to us, and therefore we *know*. And though the mob kill us, yet we must die declaring its truth." Whitmer, one of the missionaries who brought the message of the restoration to McLellin in 1831 reiterated his testimony that he gave then and reaffirmed Cowdery's statement: "Oliver has told you the solemn truth, for we could not be deceived." Hiram Page, also a witness was stripped and beaten mercilessly with a hickory switch sixty or seventy times on his back because "he was

a damned Mormon." He was given the opportunity to deny that "damned book" [Book of Mormon], but he refused asking the mob, "how can I deny what I know to be true?"

64. Gentry and Compton, *Fire and Sword*, 222–23; Baugh, *A Call to Arms*, 9. Mitchell K. Shaeffer, "The Testimony of Men," *BYU Studies* 50, no. 1 (2011): 100–102, 109.

65. Gentry and Compton, *Fire and Sword*, 221–54.

66. http://www.josephsmithpapers.org.

67. http://www.josephsmithpapers.org.

68. Harper, "Overwhelmingly Democratic," 13.

69. W. Paul Reeve, *Religion of a Different Color: Race and the Mormon Struggle for Whiteness* (New York: Oxford University Press, 2015), 4.

70. Reeve, *Religion of a Different Color*, 8.

71. Reeve, *Religion of a Different Color*, 20–21.

72. Dean C. Jessee, *"Walls, Grates and Screeking Iron Doors": The Prison Experience of Mormon Leaders in Missouri, 1838–1839,"* in *New Views of Mormon History*, 19.

73. Jessee, "Walls, Grates and Screeking Iron Doors," 25.

74. Doctrine and Covenants 121:1–2.

75. Staker, *Hearken, O Ye People*, 183.

76. Doctrine and Covenants 101:1–9.

77. William Hartley, "The Saints' Forced Exodus from Missouri," in *Joseph Smith, the Prophet and Seer*, 347–61.

78. *Quincy Whig*, 23 February 1839.

79. "The Mormons," *Quincy Whig*, 2 March 1839.

80. History, 1838–1856, volume C-1 [2 November 1838–31 July 1842], 890, http://www.josephsmithpapers.org.

81. History, 1838–1856, volume C-1 [2 November 1838–31 July 1842], 889, http://www.josephsmithpapers.org.

82. Richard E. Bennett, "'Quincy—the Home of Our Adoption': A Study of the Mormons in Quincy, Illinois, 1838–1840," *Mormon Historical Studies* 2, no. 1 (Spring 2001): 115.

83. Hartley, "The Saints' Forced Exodus from Missouri," 375.

84. *Adams Sentinel* (Gettysburg, PA), 30 December 1839.

85. John Reynolds, *My Own Times: Embracing Also the History of My Life* (Belleville, IL: B. H. Perryman and H. L. Davidson, 1855), 575.

86. Ronald O. Barney, "Joseph Smith Goes to Washington, 1839–40," in *Joseph Smith, the Prophet and Seer*, 407–8.

87. History, 1838–1856, volume D-1 [1 August 1842–1 July 1843], 1552, http://www.josephsmithpapers.org.

88. The historical context of Van Buren's comments includes lingering economic difficulties from Andrew Jackson's presidency, the beginning of the Underground Railroad secreting slaves to the North and liberating them, the election to Congress of the first abolitionist, the forced removal of a comparable number of Cherokee Indian by the federal government from Georgia to what is now Oklahoma, troubles with Great Britain, and Van Buren's belief in the protection of states' rights.

89. Barney, "Joseph Smith Goes to Washington, 1839–40," 393, 411–12.

90. *Times and Seasons*, 1 October 1843, 343–44.

91. Joseph Smith to John C. Calhoun, 4 November 1843, http://www.josephsmith papers.org; emphasis in original.

92. Richard Neitzel Holzapfel, "The Prophet's Final Charge to the Twelve, 1844," in *Joseph Smith, the Prophet and Seer*, 497–99. See also Arnold K. Garr, *Joseph Smith: Presidential Candidate* (Orem, UT: Millennial Press, 2007).

Unique Contributions of Restorationism

Although the fame and found is great of Reformation we Querie, Whether a dead soule is capable of any Reformation. . . . Allegations may be brought from the corruptions of the Church of the Jewes and the Churches of Christ: but We doe not use to define a Man by his Diseases, nor a Garden by Weeds, nor a Citie by a Tumult, or an Army by a Rout or disorder, especially when we treat upon an Institution or Restauration.

—ROGER WILLIAMS, QUERY 5,
Queries of Highest Consideration

*I*n retrospect, one of the most important questions for this volume is "What did Alexander Campbell and Joseph Smith leave as restoration legacies?" Both Mormons and Disciples of Christ are shaped by their interpretation of scripture—and their definition of what constitutes scripture. This section focuses on some of the important ideas that Alexander Campbell and Joseph Smith brought to the American religious scene. Both men made important scriptural contributions. An entire chapter in this section is devoted to their biblical emendations.

For Campbell, New Testament structures, forms, and behaviors were important, but nothing was as crucial as Christian unity, a concern not to be minimized. He intended to identify the key attributes of the New Testament church and thereon unify all Christians worldwide to bring forth the Millennium. Campbell, with his well-constructed monthly newsletters advocating restoration, which began in 1823 and continued throughout his life, made him regionally well known. He was the consummate scriptorian and this, coupled with his lively intellect, made him a formidable defender of apostolic Christianity to an even wider audience. He promoted intellectual independence and trust in the ability of common individuals to understand the Bible—the foundation for his ecclesiastical *novus ordo seclorum*, a new order of the ages, was a restoration of the New Testament church, particularly as depicted in the writings of Paul.[1]

Smith claimed to have received his vision of restoration by revelation. "Direct experience with truth" was clearly remarkable.[2] Premortal life, an expanding canon, and kingdoms of glory hereafter are just a sampling of his distinctive teachings on the eternal nature of God's plan for his children. Smith's vision of restoration was a dynamic process involving the intersection of "angels and men, resurrected beings and earthly prophets, crisscrossing time and dispensations" in something akin to reversing gospel entropy by bringing order to seemingly disparate groupings.[3] Smith's claims to revelation are not, however, without their detractors. W. D. Davies proposes this dilemma: "Progressive and continuous revelation is certainly an attractive notion, but equally certainly it is not without the grave danger of so altering and enlarging upon the original revelation as to distort, annul, and even falsify it. This is the fundamental question which all the more traditional Christian communions and—indeed, the NT itself—pose to Mormonism."[4] As Samuel S. Hill Jr. observes, Smith's restoration was not a "derivation or a deviation or a reactionary response. . . . It is a *sui generis*, a one of a kind religious tradition."[5]

NOTES

1. Noll, *America's God*, 231.
2. M. Catherine Thomas, *The God Seed: Probing the Mystery of Spiritual Development* (Salt Lake City: Digital Legend, 2014), 17.
3. Givens, *Wresting the Angel*, 33.
4. W. D. Davies, "Reflections on the Mormon 'Canon,'" in Givens, *By the Hand of Mormon*, 196.
5. Samuel S. Hill Jr., "Comparing Three Approaches to Restorationism: A Response," in *The American Quest for the Primitive Church*, 232.

13

Alexander Campbell's Unity and Millennialism

$\mathcal{A}$lexander Campbell's religious focus was preparing for the coming millennial age by unifying the Christian church through identifying, restoring, and defending "the ancient order of things"—the ordinances, practices, and faith of the early Christian church that had been neglected. Campbell rejoiced in the freedom of religion that he found as he landed on the shores of America in 1809. As he read his father's newly printed *Declaration and Address*, he embraced the restoration of the ancient gospel that he found in it. With the passage of time, Alexander had an even greater appreciation for what his father had composed. He asserted, "The Declaration and Address contains what may be called the embryo or the rudiments of a great and rapidly increasing community. It virtually contains the elements of a great movement of vital interest to every citizen of Christ's kingdom."[1] He believed its foundation in New Testament forms and structures could undo sectarian divisions to bring about the unity of all Christians and lead to the conversion of the world. This universal conversion would bring forth the millennial day of peace and be followed by the Second Coming of Christ.[2]

Campbell asserted that the foundation of Christian unity could not be found in the creeds, but instead in strict adherence to "gospel facts" found within the scriptures.[3] Campbell began by working within Christianity, most notably within the Baptist Church; nevertheless, there were doctrines and practices in the church with which he did not agree. Through his preaching, his debating, and his writing of pamphlets, books, and a monthly publication titled the *Christian Baptist* (later the *Millennial Harbinger*), Campbell sought to convince others to unite behind his reasoned understanding of the Bible and particularly the New Testament. He was convinced from his study of the New Testament that by discarding the various creeds and historical traditions, the essence of the Christian church would be so obvious to all Christians that as soon as they were taught it, they would unite under one banner and the Millennium would begin. Campbell was so convinced of the imminent uniting of Christians that he declared the "Ancient Gospel [was] long enough, broad enough, strong enough for the whole superstructure called the Millennial Church, . . . alone [to be] the instrument of converting the whole human race, and of uniting all Christians upon one and the same foundation."[4]

Of the present, however, he complained, "There is no platform in any of the great sects of christendom on which to rear this glorious superstructure. They are all *too narrow* and too weak." By narrow, he meant that all sects embraced "opinions, inferences, or deductions" from the scriptures. Basing a religion or a faith upon inferences from the scriptures made it an "intellectual operation," and the intellectualization of religion requires "men to be well trained by logic and philosophy" to understand and interpret the suppositions of a creed. He believed that Christianity must unite and sects be destroyed along with their creeds in order for the government of Christ and his religion to appear. Such sects are weak both individually and collectively because they do not provide the foundation of the Christian or "Millennial Church."[5]

He believed there was a core of basic beliefs and practices around which all reasonable Christians could unite. Unity was the means by which the greater end was achieved: the "grand design" of the Christian religion "to reconcile and unite men to God, and to each other, in truth and love, to the glory of God, and their own present and eternal good," as Christ had prayed for in his intercessory prayer.[6]

CHRISTIAN APOLOGIST

As Alexander's oratorical skills as a preacher became more well known, he was invited to defend the Baptist practice of immersion. Initially, both he and his father were opposed to public controversy regarding religious beliefs, particularly in the form of "disputes," as debates were called then. Thomas Campbell was especially opposed to the use of debates to contend for the faith, concerned that the goal would be victory rather than truth. Alexander was already very familiar with written and oral persuasion, having studied "Logic as the art of directing the powers of knowledge in the search of truth and communication," "Socratic Dialogue," "The Difference between a Judgment and a Proposition," "On the Syllogisms," "On the Aristotilian [sic] Method of Dispute," and Bacon's evidentiary strategy as a student at the University of Glasgow.[7] Eventually, Alexander convinced his father that openly defending revealed gospel truth was his public duty.[8] The presentation of opposing points of view for the audience to judge for themselves and accept or reject had a sort of egalitarian attractiveness. In the nineteenth century, debates were quite popular in the United States and drew large crowds, which appealed to Alexander in promoting his reformation and restoration ideas.[9]

Ten years after his introductory engagement into preaching, and against his initial inclinations and convictions, Alexander began successfully debating for his views on reformation Christianity. Many of these debates went on for days, some for weeks, with large audiences. Campbell loved to speak extemporaneously. His public defense of primitive Christianity made him arguably one of the most well-known Christian apologists of antebellum America. He published "transcripts" of his debates in the *Christian Baptist* from his own notes and those of his followers' records who were present. The wide distribution of his debates in his own press and by others made him a household name in America by the 1840s. Further, Campbell was an excellent debater for Christianity and his restoration ideas because he had read and studied the Bible better than any of his opponents. Just as he had desired when he was younger to become "one of the best scholars in the kingdom," and as a budding preacher to be "first in Theological Studies," now he had become just that.[10] He defended his use of debate based on the writings of early Christian apologists, believing that controversy was simply another name for "opposition to error," and thus important for improvement of the Christian faith. Without it, the Jewish and Christian religions would not have been established, nor the Protestant Reformation.[11] He modeled his approach on the inductive reasoning of Francis Bacon and quoted the great scientist and later Christian philosopher Isaac Newton: "Everything is to be submitted to the most minute observation. No conclusions are to be drawn from guesses or conjectures. We are to keep within the certain limits of experimental truth. We first ascertain the facts, then group them together, and after the classification and comparison of them, draw conclusions."[12] He wanted his arguments and those of his opponents to be "examined by the improved principles of the inductive philosophy, by those very principles which right reason and sound experimental philosophy have sanctioned as their appropriate tests."[13]

Some of those with whom he debated acknowledged his superior talents, and although some Regular Baptists were initially pleased at his defeat of Presbyterian ministers regarding the practice of pedobaptism and defense of immersion, they found his points of view on the scriptures too different from their beliefs. Although "disputing" was, at best, controversial, Campbell deemed it necessary propaganda because of the importance of his restoration efforts, and his role as the predominate leader.[14] If debate could teach truth, it could unify Christians in preparation for the Millennium, so debate he would.

Walker Debate. Campbell's speaking reputation could not be denied, and in June 1820 he was issued an invitation by a Baptist preacher, John Birch, to debate the Reverend John Walker, a Seceder Presbyterian minister at Mount Pleasant, Ohio, on the subjects and action of baptism.[15]

One scholar called this debate Campbell's "beginning of the war against sectarian creeds and divisions."[16] At that time, Mount Pleasant, Ohio, was primarily a Quaker farming community with the rest of the population Calvinistic, either Baptist or Seceder Presbyterian. The Seceder Presbyterians vehemently opposed Campbell because he had left their church, having failed to initiate any reforms, and had joined with the Baptists. Recent immersions of former Seceders into the Baptist Church and sermons by Reverend Walker defending infant baptism by sprinkling had brought the ordinance to the forefront. Reverend Walker challenged the Baptists to a debate and Alexander Campbell was chosen to represent their views. Although Campbell disagreed with the Baptists on many other points, he accepted the opportunity to represent the truth on this matter with the hope that it would lead to additional opportunities to teach essential restoration ideas.[17]

On 19 June 1820, Walker and Campbell met before a large assembly to commence the two-day debate. The opening remarks by Reverend Walker, a single paragraph of 124 words, illustrate how poorly prepared he was for the intellect of Alexander Campbell. Walker defended the baptism of infants by sprinkling using the Old Testament covenant of circumcision as the reasoning for infant baptism: as circumcision was the seal for the Jews, so is baptism the seal for Christians. Since the lawgiver and husband were the same, he considered the two rituals analogous. Campbell made short work of this argument: (1) the ritual of circumcision derived from the Old Testament, Jewish law, and literal descent from Abraham, not the New Testament and Christian Church established by Christ and his Apostles; and (2) baptism required more than a genealogical relationship; it required faith in Jesus Christ. Additionally, baptism differs greatly from circumcision in many respects, but perhaps foremost in that baptism is for the remission of sin and the gift of the Holy Spirit, neither of which are connected to circumcision.[18]

The second point of the debate was based on covenants. Walker stated the pedobaptist belief that the Jewish dispensation found in the Old Testament connected with the Christian dispensation found in the New Testament. Because the first covenant included infants, so should the second covenant. Campbell described the former covenant as carnal, temporal, and national in nature in comparison to the latter covenant, with its emphasis on the moral, spiritual, and personal covenant ratified in Christ through the Holy Spirit, and, therefore, not the same at all. Campbell cited Jeremiah to argue that the new covenant was in contrast to the old covenant and Hebrews 8:6 to argue that the new covenant was described as a "better covenant which was established upon better promises."[19]

The third point of the debate was on the antiquity of the practice of pedobaptism by sprinkling. Walker insisted that the "term *baptizo* signifies to wash, and that this washing must have been done by sprinkling, and not dipping."[20] He also argued that the scriptures teach: "Baptism has a respect to the blood of sprinkling that justifies us[21] . . . [therefore] it is very suitable to administer Baptism in such a way . . . that this reference may be seen," and "why, then should we act . . . in baptizing, so as to indicate that it was the quantity, not the quality, that relieved our souls, or affected our state?"[22]

Campbell conceded both ancient practice and tradition, but maintained that these points did not make the practice right. Through the quotation of an eminent Greek translator and critic, Presbyterian Dr. George Campbell, Alexander Campbell turned the tables on his Presbyterian opponent.[23] The Greek verb *baptizein*, as all Greek scholars and lexicons corroborated, "signifies to dip, to plunge, to immerse,"[24] and that strict obedience to this mode was required because "the only Baptism of divine authority is immersion."[25] In fact, he argued that corruptions had been introduced into the Church in the first two centuries and that the first mention of pedobaptism was by Tertullian late in the second century, almost 150 years after the apostolic era, and this early Christian Father disapproved of it. Campbell concluded his remarks by stating that faith in tradition and custom were not sufficient to warrant a practice that was not scriptural.

The main conclusions that could be drawn from Campbell's arguments were first, that circumcision and baptism are not related in purpose, so the subject was wrong; and second, that baptism meant immersion, not sprinkling, so the mode was also wrong.

Although the topic of the multiday debate was ostensibly regarding infant baptism by sprinkling, "the chief point debated, however, was the identity of the covenants on which the Jewish and Christian institutions rested, as asserted by Mr. Walker" and countered by Campbell quoting "Paul's account of the 'new covenant.'"[26] Walker fought for the oneness of the covenant, and Campbell utilized his ideas previously expounded in the "Sermon on the Law" to argue for the separation and distinction between the old and new covenants. Campbell's emphasis on the succession of dispensations, and thus on a succession of covenants, was meant to separate baptism from circumcision and free Christianity from Jewish precedents in the Old Testament. Campbell won the debate. Even the Presbyterians, believers in infant baptism by sprinkling, felt he had triumphed.[27] Some of the Baptists were ecstatic to have such a brilliant thinker who could defend and vindicate so ably their practice of immersion.[28]

Against such an ill-prepared opponent, Campbell utilized some of his debate time to emphasize keys points of his own reform, such as the supreme authority of the scriptures and the necessity for a definitive command from God for ritual practices such as baptism of infants. Initially reluctant to debate Mr. Walker but having seen the effect of the debate, Campbell began to hope that his reform and restoration principles might be extended on a larger scale to influence a wider audience.[29]

Although the moderator closed the debate, Campbell believed there was further need to discuss these points in greater depth and threw out an invitation to any pedobaptist in good standing within his religious community to debate him on the point that "infant sprinkling is a human tradition and injurious to the well being of society, religious and political."[30]

The debate with Walker was published and widely read by both Baptists and Presbyterians, but mostly in the region where Campbell lived. Likely the most gratifying result for Campbell was the admiration of many Baptists for his ability to defend their mode of baptism, making them a more fruitful audience for his additional reform ideas.

Maccalla Debate. Campbell's ideas on baptism sharpened, and he continued to voice different facets of his views on baptism through debate. In the Walker debate, Campbell declared baptism as symbolic of the salvation already received by those who have believed, a representation of the completed work by God, essentially the same understanding as Baptists.

In October 1823, Presbyterian Reverend William L. Maccalla (also spelled McCalla), a trained lawyer, took up the challenge to debate Campbell. One scholar called this debate by Campbell the "war against sectarianism and disunion."[31] Accompanying Campbell on the three-hundred-mile journey from Bethany, Virginia, to Washington, Kentucky, was Sidney Rigdon.[32] Unfortunately, there is no record of the discussion that took place as they traveled together; it likely was an energetic and fascinating conversation. Rigdon took notes during the week-long debate, and when the record of the debate was prepared, he gave Campbell a certificate affirming the correctness of the version which was published in May 1824.[33]

Again, at this debate, Campbell was the defender of the Baptist ordinance of baptism by immersion and Maccalla was the defender of Presbyterian belief in pedobaptism by sprinkling.[34] Maccalla gave two major points which he intended to prove: there is a divine command by God authorizing infant baptism (that is, the infants of believers), and there is both probable and positive evidence of the apostolic practice of infant baptism. Campbell began with two propositions stated in the Presbyterian Confession: "Those things which are necessary to be known, believed and observed for salvation, are so clearly propounded and opened in some place of Scripture or other, that not only the learned but the *unlearned* . . . may attain unto a sufficient understanding of them." The second part of the Confession that he quoted said, "Baptism is a sacrament of the New Testament, ordained by Jesus Christ."[35] Thus, Campbell used Maccalla's own denomination's beliefs to limit the scope of the debate to the scriptures and particularly the New Testament. While Campbell's previous debate topics had been concerned with the subjects of baptism, penitent believers, and the mode of baptism, in this debate he focused on the design and effect of baptism.

Maccalla began the debate by making the case that the Abrahamic covenant was a true and visible Church of God and that the Christian Church is a branch of it. Therefore, "Jewish circumcision before Christ and Christian baptism after Christ are the same seal, though in different forms."[36] In other words, Maccalla based his arguments on the very same points as Walker had, but with somewhat greater oratorical ability. When Maccalla claimed that he could produce scriptural proof of a divine command authorizing infant baptism, Campbell, having read and studied the scriptures thoroughly, knew Maccalla was wrong: there was no such command.

During the discussion on the mode of baptism, Campbell had the easy task of pointing to Greek lexicons that the word *baptism* meant to dip, to plunge, or to immerse. Maccalla argued that in exceptional cases, sprinkling was a viable substitute for those who were too ill to be plunged into cold water and for convenience of the administrator, who must perform it regularly. By this time in the debate, however, Maccalla's inability to respond to Campbell's arguments from the scriptures was apparent, but this particular point was ignored when the audience looked at the small and sickly Presbyterian debate moderator, who obviously would have had difficulty performing such an ordinance, compared with the tall and portly Baptist moderator.

Campbell argued that the purpose of baptism was the "washing of regeneration" of an individual's personal sins of which he had repented, not the removal of original sin, in which Campbell did not believe. In setting down his opposition to original sin, Campbell radically departed from a doctrine that was widely accepted in the Christian community by Catholics and the sixteenth-century Protestant reformers alike.[37] Since Peter promised on the day of Pentecost that remission of sins accompanied baptism,[38] and because an infant's capacity for virtue or sin was only latent, there was no purpose for infant baptism. Rather, "the benefit and design of baptism for penitent believers . . . [secured] for them the forgiveness of the sins of which they [had] repented." Nevertheless, Campbell did not preach "water salvation"; baptism was the formality of that which actually occurred through the blood of Christ.[39] Campbell continued to connect "real" forgiveness and salvation with faith in Christ, but began to draw a closer relationship between baptism and remission of sins. He considered baptism as the "formal" act that remits sins.[40] The purpose and mode of baptism was fully understood and publicly taught in this debate; however, it wasn't until 1827 that Walter Scott developed a clear and practical application of the ordinance as part of faith, repentance, and receiving the Holy Spirit.[41]

The debate on pedobaptism was over; Campbell had clarified that baptism was a sign of remission of sins for those who had faith in Jesus Christ and thus could not be for infants who had never sinned. Maccalla had annoyed the Baptists for some time by criticizing their distinctive beliefs, and his defeat raised Campbell's reputation in their estimation. Maccalla, however, did not go home accepting defeat but continued to argue his points to change public opinion and to prejudice the minds of others against Campbell and his reforming ideas.

Having secured the rapt attention of the Baptists, Campbell now took the opportunity to lead them into "a more rational mode of reading, interpreting and using the Bible . . . and to more extended and correct views of the nature and polity of the kingdom of Christ."[42] He presented to the audience copies of his publication, the *Christian Baptist*, dedicated to some of the points he had made during his debate and to additional points of restoration. Campbell was now convinced that public debate was a viable means of propagating truth and exposing error. As a result of the Maccalla debate, Campbell's reputation and influence were extended to a much larger geographical area than where he was previously known, the small area at the convergence of Ohio, Pennsylvania, and Virginia. His talents were now also recognized in the state of Kentucky.

Because of his oratorical and critical-thinking skills along with his encyclopedic knowledge of the scriptures, Campbell was hugely successful in arguing against the pedobaptist point of view. His reputation also drew a large crowd to view the debates and reached many more in his re-publication of the arguments. As a result, he concluded that days-long debates were worth hundreds of sermons in presenting truth and exposing error.[43]

Owen Debate. Of all of his debates, the one that brought Campbell international fame was his defense of Christianity against the Welsh-born skeptic and social reformer Robert Owen, which one scholar called the "conflict between Christianity and infidelity."[44]

As Campbell was honing his debate skills against pedobaptists, he was also unknowingly preparing for the biggest debate of his life. Beginning with the January 1827 *Christian Baptist*, he answered questions addressed to him from an anonymous deist, "Mr. D, a sceptic."[45] His first priority in debating had been reformation and restoration. His second priority now became answering the challenge of skeptics, deists, and atheists against the Bible and Christianity.[46]

Owen, a wealthy industrialist, social reformer, and philanthropist, had attempted to build utopian communities first in Orbiston and New Lanark, Scotland (near Glasgow), and then in New Harmony, Indiana, based on principles found in his book *A New View of Society: Or, Essays on the Formation of the Human Character*. Convinced by his success in New Lanark, Owen considered his system a practical experiment in human communalism. Owen advocated "a New Moral World" of happiness, enlightenment, and prosperity through education, science, technology, and communal living. He proposed the development of small communities of about 1,200 people settled on 1,000 to 1,500 acres and living together in one large building with a public kitchen and public dining. Each family was to have a private apartment with responsibility for children until age three, after which the community would be responsible for child care except at meals and other times deemed appropriate. The economic base of the community was agricultural, but a wide variety of employment was also available. The goal was for the township to be self-contained. He hoped that his township ideas would spread until communalism became the master plan for the entire world. Most Owenite communities focused on economic cooperation and "rejected religion as a corrupting influence used to take advantage of others."[47] Of his 4 July 1826 speech, the *Painesville Telegraph* in Ohio wrote that Owen proclaimed independence from a trinity of evils: private property, irrational systems of religion, and marriage based on individual property.[48] Initially, Campbell took a wait-and-see approach to Owen's ideas on economic reform; however, from the outset, he had concerns regarding his religious skepticism and ideas on marriage.[49]

Although Owen had previously invited other Christian ministers to debate him on his new ideas, none had accepted. Campbell could no longer wait for some other Christian apologist to take up the verbal challenge against a system that was being taught in his area of the country. In 1828, Campbell declined to debate the lesser-known Samuel Underhill, who advocated the principles of Owen's new system in Kendal,

Ohio, but offered to debate Owen on the merits of the old system versus the new system. Owen visited Campbell at his home in Bethany and agreed to an eight-day debate. As the two men were walking the farm, they passed by the family burial ground and Owen stated, "There is one advantage I have over the Christian—*I am not afraid to die.*" Campbell replied by asking, "Since you have no *fear* in death; have you any *hope* in death?" After Owen replied "No," Campbell, pointing to a nearby ox replied, "Then you are on a level with that brute. He has fed til he is satisfied, and stands in the shade whisking off the flies, and has *neither hope nor fear in death.*"[50] Clearly, Owen had met his match!

Campbell's assessment of skeptics was that they were "generally more witty than wise, more pert than prudent, more talkative than learned"—this likely was also his opinion of Owen.[51] Owen found Campbell to be an "acute, clever, and I believe, sincere man, who will make the most of his cause. I have no doubt that truth will ultimately prevail."[52]

Campbell delineated Owen's four main points in opposition to Christianity and found them untenable though worthy of debate: "1. That all the religions of the world were founded upon the ignorance of mankind. 2. That they have been and are the real sources of vice, disunion, and misery of every description. 3. That they are *now* the only real bar to the formation of a society of virtue, intelligence, sincerity, and benevolence. 4. That they can no longer be maintained except through the ignorance of the mass of the people, and the tyranny of the few over the mass."[53]

Campbell recognized that their debate considered some of the most foundational and far-reaching questions for Christians such as: "What is man?"; "Whence came he?"; "Is he mortal or immortal?"; and "Is there no object of future hope?"[54] From the perspective of almost a century, Disciples of Christ historian Jesse J. Haley considered the debate crucial to saving the Mississippi Valley from communalism. The goal of the utopian movement in the United States was to cure poverty, unhappiness, and unrest by abolishing all restraints. Some utopian communities advocated "individual sovereignty" in marriage. This meant it was left to couples to be married formally or not, live together or separately, have their relationship public or private, and dissolve the relationship at will with no restrictions. Rings for those who chose to wear them consisted of a red thread which was understood to mean "married."[55]

Campbell focused his criticism on what he identified as Owen's overarching premise, "Man is not a free agent." From this fundamental principle, Owen deduced, "No man forms his own character but that every man's character is formed for him," and "merit and demerit, praise and blame, reward and punishment belong not to man, nor in truth, to any being in the Universe." Campbell claimed that this is the "soul or life of the entire system."[56] Campbell called his defense of free will *reductio ad absurdum*, a philosophical method that attempts to prove the falseness of a premise by demonstrating that its logical consequence is contradictory. Campbell pointed out that under Owen's premise there is no moral difference between the actions of a machine or anyone of biblical or scientific note; man, fish, oyster, tree, or watch are equally free agents, and none are virtuous, praiseworthy, or good, and therefore none can be vicious, blameworthy, or evil. Further, the metaphysics of placing an idiot, madman, or philosopher on the same plane with each other and objects such as animals, vegetables, and ores is truly absurd.[57] Another major objection to Owen's social system was its foundation on atheism and infidelity. Campbell claimed that Owen's New Harmony was an effort to organize pagan philanthropy in the midst of a Christian nation.[58]

In debating Owen and his "infidel" ideas, Campbell believed he demonstrated that Christianity is an institution founded upon facts and documents, whereas infidelity is nothing—a mere negation that assails Christianity but offers no substitute. Illustrating his Enlightenment training, he contended, "I have never read, nor heard a philosophic, rational, logical argument against Christianity; nor have I ever seen or heard a rational, philosophic, or logical argument in favor of any form of skepticism or infidelity."[59] Campbell was persuaded that skepticism was a great threat to his ideals of Christian unity. The eight-day debate, attended by an average of 1,200 per day, catapulted Campbell into the spotlight. At the conclusion of the debate, he became a well-known and respected national figure.

Restoration, Unity, and the Millennium

To characterize Campbell's primary motives as restoration and Christian unity is to misinterpret him. In addition to defending Christianity, Campbell's main goal was bringing forth the Millennium. In his mind, the "restoration of primitive Christianity would bring

Christian unity, which, in turn, would bring the millennial dawn."[60] In other words, the purpose of his restoration was to unite Christians, and unity would bring the Millennium, the end objective.[61] Although these ideals were first expressed by Thomas Campbell, the task of applying them to the everyday questions of faith, ordinances, and worship became his son's lifework.[62] Churches of Christ scholar Richard Hughes wrote that "Campbell's ultimate concern was for the kingdom of God, the millennium on earth. . . . [His] millennial dream was one of the constant factors upon which his other, penultimate commitments [restoration and unity] shifted and changed."[63]

As a young man arriving on the shores of America in 1809, Campbell felt he had discovered the perfect convergence of opportunity and advantages among a largely Protestant population.[64] He saw the rise of America as preface to the creation of millennial Zion that preceded the Second Coming of Jesus Christ.

By 1825 he concluded, "In so far as the ancient order of things, or the religion of the New Testament, is restored, just so far has the Millennium commenced, and so far have its blessings been enjoyed."[65] In an 1830 speech, Campbell compared the celebration of 4 July 1776 to the Jewish Passover, calling them days to be remembered with great gratitude. The American Revolution was a foreshadowing of an even greater revolution, the emancipation of the mind from superstition and preparation for the millennial reign of heaven.[66]

Campbell's optimistic worldview "imagined that human progress would usher in the kingdom or rule of God (the Millennium) and that Jesus would return only at the conclusion of that golden age."[67] He had great faith in American democracy and in the power of its exceptionalism to create a millennial society and expected Christ's literal return after one thousand years of human-wrought peace.[68] Campbell's postmillennialist view agreed with many religious denominations in America in the eighteenth and nineteenth centuries. They recognized that "the kingdom of God was not simply going to arrive but needed hard human work for it to be ushered in."[69] In this respect, they believed that expanding American values such as liberty, equality, and good moral choices would cause the kingdom spoken of in the book of Revelation to gradually unfold, leading to a sort of "civil millennialism," climaxed after one thousand years by the Second Coming of Jesus.[70]

Early on, Campbell demonstrated his interest in Revelation 14:6–7. In 1809, while at the University of Glasgow, as part of his "Skeletons of Sermons," Campbell quoted, outlined, and explained this particular passage written by the Apostle John. He clarified that angels were messengers and sometimes called seraphim or "burners." Their zeal was emblematic of the "ministry of reform." Highlighted was "their zeal for piety; and reformation." That they "bring God's tidings is figured out under the term 'fly.' They can and do return as a flash of lightning." In his analytical method of rhetorical questions and discussion, he recorded: "What had the angel with him? The everlasting gospel. Did you ever hear this gospel: what is it?" He defined this phrase point by point. The gospel is everlasting on account of (1) authority, (2) duration of its plan, and (3) propitiation and mercy of salvation.[71] He further explained the passage by writing:

> The gospel was born by the angel but defection, apostasy and false religion had stained true religion. With a loud voice it was to cry—denotes connecting intensity of zeal and magnitude of concern. What does it declare? (1) From God, (2) Give glory to God, (3) For the hour of His judgment is coming. What is the cause of his judgment? (1) It is either a departure in principles or in practice from the records of his will. (2) He will be avenged on all them that do either unless they repent.[72]

Twenty-one years later, Campbell printed this passage from Revelation 14:6–7 with his own slightly different translation on the masthead of his monthly publication, the *Millennial Harbinger*, from 1830 to 1864, as a signal to his readers of a new emphasis in his writing.[73] In this new publication, Campbell exhibited a milder tone than he had in the *Christian Baptist* because he was exhilarated by the progress "of the reformatory principles, the union of so many of different parties in the primitive faith" and was convinced "that the millennial period anticipated by the Church was nigh at hand. He felt assured that a reformation such as he advocated . . . could leave no room for any other religious reformation, and must of necessity be the very last effort possible to prepare the world for the coming of Christ."[74] The *Millennial Harbinger* was key in disseminating the ideas that he believed would help bring about the coming of Christ.[75]

In the first edition, right under the masthead, he stated the prospectus for the publication: "This work shall be devoted to the destruction of Sectarianism, Infidelity, and Antichristian doctrine and practice. It shall have for its object the developement, and introduction of that political and religious order of society called The Millennium, which will be the consummation of that ultimate amelioration of society proposed in the Christian Scriptures."[76] The Millennium, a political and religious order, would be the consummation of humankind's efforts to eradicate earthly problems and to restore the primitive church.

"The premillennialism apocalyptic date-setting of William Miller . . . helped Campbell to develop and publicize his postmillennial alternative as the 'Protestant view' in the *Millennial Harbinger*."[77] Churches of Christ scholar Anthony Dunnavant clarified Campbell's Millennialism in five steps: (1) God prepared this nation with religious freedom in order to (2) restore the ancient gospel and order of things which would result in (3) the unity of all Christians which would (4) usher in the Millennium after which (5) Christ would return.[78] The Millennium was the "divinely ordained climax and stage of history in which sectarianism, 'popery,' the union of kingcraft and priestcraft, skepticism, and paganism would be overcome." In other words, "Christ was not to appear magically upon the physical clouds to accomplish it but he would ultimately reign in the hearts and lives of people."[79]Although the end time was not yet, Campbell initially predicted that given the signs of the times, it would soon commence.[80]

Restoration was the means by which a reunion to true Christianity, that which had existed in the Apostolic era, could be achieved. Roman Catholic historian Richard Tristano identified what he called the two motives of the Restoration Movement—a truth motive and a unity motive. According to Tristano, the truth motive, or the idea that Christian truth can be found in the teaching and practices of the New Testament alone, is a radical interpretation of *sola scriptura* because it eliminates the opinions contained in creeds, church councils, and theological disputes. The unity motive, an emphatic rejection of sectarianism, could be achieved if the clear and precise descriptions of the New Testament essentials of belief and practice were identified and adhered to. Campbell's efforts were in identifying and adhering to only these beliefs and practices that should eliminate disagreement among sects and lead to unity. The true church of Christ ought not be divided into a variety of diversely believing bodies.[81] The unity Tristano identifies in Thomas and Alexander's efforts was a restoration movement that went far beyond what is commonly called Protestant ecumenism—it is the more ancient concept of Catholic Christian unity—the universal church.[82]

To Campbell, the idea of clear and precise descriptions must have seemed achievable if one could deduce from Greek manuscripts and New Testament translations and commentaries what the original sense of each passage had been. The Reformation had upturned the previous "unity" of Catholicism, creating a proliferation of sects. Uniting the sectarian world via New Testament restorationism explained by Enlightenment and Baconian reasoning was a lofty, but impossible goal. Tristano's criticism of Campbell in ignoring historical creeds, church councils, and theological disputes and attempting to recreate a universal church was a very Roman Catholic point of view.

Historically, unity was important to the restoration movement as a clearly stated purpose in Thomas Campbell's 1809 document *Declaration and Address*.[83] He was exhausted from the sectarian contention and quarreling and instead advocated measures that would "restore unity, peace, and purity to the whole Church of God."[84] He believed that through their efforts—Thomas, Alexander, and their Christian Association of Washington [Pennsylvania]—they could return Christians to an apostolic purity, fostering unity that in turn would bring peace. In setting forth his call to unity and peace and purity, Thomas declared that it was the duty of all Christians to promote the interests of Zion, the millennial day. "The time to favor her [Zion] is come; even the set time."[85] Apparently, in Thomas Campbell's mind, Zion's hour had arrived in 1809, and the main consideration for Christians should be agreement. He exhorted his followers to seek for the "removal of contentions, for the healing of divisions, for the restoration of a Christian and brotherly intercourse one with another, and for the promotion of each other's spiritual good" that Zion may be brought forth in the midst of troublesome times.[86] Although Thomas Campbell was the author of the words, it is evident that his son, Alexander, agreed wholeheartedly.

In the preface to the *Christian System*, Alexander Campbell simply stated, "Our opposition to creeds arose from a conviction, that whether the opinions in them were true or false, they were hostile to the union, peace, harmony, purity, and joy of Christians; and adverse to the conversion of the world to Jesus Christ."[87] Therefore, they prevented the advent of the millennial day. Thomas Campbell wrote in the *Declaration*: "Rejecting human opinions and the inventions of men as of any authority, or as having any place in the Church of God, we might forever cease from further contentions about such things."[88] Creeds were extrabiblical, unauthorized, and uninspired. In Alexander's mind, they, along with paid clergymen, promoted the sectarianism he disdained.

Although the Campbells remained in the Protestant realm, they maintained their independence from the confessional requirements of even the Baptists with whom they were associated for many years. Instead, the Campbells advocated unity amid diversity, meaning unity on the essential elements of the New Testament, and allowing diversity of opinion on all other points.[89] From his study of the New Testament, Alexander Campbell held strong beliefs on what constituted Christian doctrine, and the creeds and confessions did not express it. Those doctrines not definitively spelled out in the scriptures should not be points of contention or division.

In the preface beginning the 1840 *Millennial Harbinger*, Campbell reflected on his part in the "great drama of human existence, . . . the progress of a great revolution—a reformation" with obligations and responsibilities to society: "The question is variously propounded; but the substance is, *Who shall rule in Zion?*—Jesus or the Pope?—Christ or Antichrist?—the twelve Apostles or twelve hundred Synods and Councils?—the New Testament or a human Creed?—the Word of the Lord or the Opinions of Men?—Union or Schism?—Catholicity or Sectarianism?—one Lord, one faith, one baptism, or three Lords, three faiths, and three baptisms?"[90]

Campbell painted the lack of Christian unity in black and white terms. His stark contrast dictated that he thought it must be one or the other. His part in the "great revolution" or "reformation" was to think clearly and logically and place before his readers and listeners the choices that the various religious movements gave them in contrast to his. "The issue is between—whether the church began in Jerusalem or in Rome—whether the acts of the Apostles, or the acts of four or seven general Councils, shall be first, last, or midst in deciding what the gospel is. . . . A hundred sects, or even two, cannot be right: all may, however, be wrong. All, indeed, are wrong that are built on anything but the one foundation of Apostles and Prophets, Jesus Christ himself the chief corner stone. There cannot be two houses built upon the same foundation."[91] In these two quotations, Campbell clearly summarized what he thought were opposing views between his restoration and all others. He laid the blame for disunity at the feet of Catholics, sectarian Protestants, and certainly Smith. Smith also claimed to build on the foundation of apostles and prophets with Christ as the chief cornerstone, but he believed in latter-day apostles and prophets yet again communing with Christ.

The *Declaration* spelled out the means by which unity could be achieved: "Returning to and holding fast by the original standard; taking the Divine word alone for our rule; the Holy Spirit for our teacher and guide . . . and Christ alone . . . for our salvation."[92] It was a call to return to the ancient order of things, the standard set up by the apostolic church. Alexander Campbell believed that by reading the scriptures, he could uncover the essential forms and structures of the first-century church as described in the New Testament, doctrines on which all Christians should be able to agree. In the *Declaration and Address*, Thomas Campbell assumed that scripture would convey the same ideas to everyone. He understood that differences of opinion existed; even so, he believed these differences were not intrinsic to the passage but in the inferences made from them.[93]

The only doctrines to be taught, Thomas Campbell explained, should be those "expressly revealed and enjoined in the word of God."[94] Since both Campbells distinguished clearly between the Old and New Testaments, the path to unity could lie only in the Christian dispensation.[95] The teachings of the Christian dispensation were what the Campbells considered the essentials that would establish unity and on which all could agree. This claim meant that all teachings that could not be specifically validated as a belief or practice among the ancient Christians must be discarded, and all that was sanctioned in the primitive church must be adopted.[96] The Campbells believed that if Christians would conform to the model and adopt the practices of the primitive church—as clearly exhibited in the New Testament with a "Thus saith the Lord," as directly stated or approved by precedent—the Campbells and their followers could restore the original unity, peace, and purity designed by Christ. The Campbells maintained that most of the differences among Christians were either matters of "private opinion, or inventions of men."[97]

The Campbells, although advocating a return to certain New Testament practices, chose not to follow the early Christian practice mentioned in Acts 2:44 of having "all things common," perhaps wisely recognizing that without the extraordinary offices of prophets and apostles they did not know how to organize and direct such a community. They believed the extraordinary spiritual gifts were needful for the apostolic age but not their own; perhaps a response to their Enlightenment training and also to the excesses of some enthusiasm practices. Christ did pray for unity, peace, and purity in his final teachings to Apostles, but it was never achieved by his followers, as noted in the Epistles, nor would the Campbells be able to create this ideal despite their great efforts.

In one of the first issues of the *Millennial Harbinger*, Alexander Campbell asked a series of rhetorical questions: "Will sects ever cease? Will a time ever come when all disciples will unite under one Lord, in one faith, in one immersion, in one hope, in one body, in one spirit, and in adoring one God and Father of all? Will divisions ever be healed? Will strife ever cease among the saints on Earth?" He answered his own questions with a "yes," but not by everyone joining a particular existing sect, inasmuch as all sects have some opinions or customs which must be eliminated. How, then, he asked, will it be done? He responded, "By abandoning opinions, and founding all associations upon the belief of gospel facts."[98] These gospel opinions would be what Campbell considered nonessentials, deductions or inferences on which agreement is not necessary.[99] During the years, points of contention arose, pitting opinions against principles. Since principles are more important than opinions, Alexander declared that even formerly deeply held opinions ought to be thrown overboard.[100] Recognizing that humans seldom are capable of giving up their opinions, Campbell then advocated, "We ask them only not to impose them upon others . . . as private property."[101]

The Campbells believed that although their Protestant neighbors had some parts of Christianity, they had failed to retain the pure scriptural admonitions by which they were originally taught.[102] A major objective in their restoration was to persuade each to abandon every human accretion or religious invention and to adopt "sound words"— meaning scriptural terminology—as the true basis of unity.

Both Thomas's *Declaration* and Alexander's thirty-two essays on "A Restoration of the Ancient Order" focused primarily on issues that created division or unity. To Christians who refused to unite, Alexander Campbell warned: "The sin of schism in the Christian Church of the present day is the capital sin of the age against the Lord's anointed; if not personally against himself, against his mission, his teachings, his gospel, his intercessory prayer."[103] If the great prayer of the Savior found in John 17 encouraged unity among all Christians, then those who refused to unify, according to Campbell, could not truly be considered Christians. In late 1831, largely at fellow restorationist Barton W.

Stone's instigation, many of the Campbell followers, the Disciples of Christ, united with Stone's Christians to form an alliance of Christian congregations.[104] Despite their differences, Christian unity was the all-important ideal in their understanding of restorationism as a movement that would bring forth the Millennium. Campbell demonstrated by this action that he was willing to set aside Stone's more revival and enthusiasm-driven background in order to highlight their important restoration beliefs and to dissolve one more denomination.

In short, Campbell's idea of unity was a reduction of Christianity to the explicit commandments found in the writings of the Apostles—a minimalist perspective.[105] In contrast, as will be elaborated in chapter 13, Joseph Smith's perspective was one of expansion—new revelations, scriptures, temples, and covenants. Campbell saw this approach as detrimental to Christian unity and purity of the first order. The "Mormonites" were therefore not true Christians in his view and ought to be roundly condemned.

Even though two of the main themes of Campbell's restoration were unity and purity of doctrine, the latter leading to the former, he met with limited success in uniting Christian denominations under his restoration movement. By the mid-1820s, Campbell conceded that a uniting of sects might not be desirable, perhaps because the various sects failed to heed the call in the *Declaration and Address* and his writings in the *Christian Baptist* to unite under the banner of the ancient apostolic order. Viewing such a unity as dangerous, he contended, "I have no idea of seeing, nor wish to see, the sects unite in one grand army." He suggested, rather, that *individuals* who loved the Lord—what Campbell called disciples—should unite. He believed that in time these disciples would bring about the downfall of hireling priesthoods and of all who opposed unity and purity.[106]

Speaking on an essential doctrine, Campbell wrote that baptism was a principle and ordinance on which disciples ought to unite. For him, baptism by immersion was an expected duty of all believers to open a way for union and cooperation among Christians. He reasoned that baptism by immersion gave the recipient "a constitutional right of citizenship in the universal kingdom of Jesus," whereas any other type of baptism gave "rights of citizenship only in some provinces of that kingdom."[107] By this he meant that all sects accepted the baptism of an individual who had been immersed as a confession of faith, whereas any other type of baptism such as sprinkling or pouring would only be acceptable by some sects. He believed that the ordinance of baptism by immersion could be a beginning point for Christian unity. He wrote, however, that anyone who did not desire to accept this baptism, or to know and do the will of God was separated from pure doctrine and therefore the unity he espoused. Campbell was unconcerned with the issue of authority to perform ordinances because he accepted the Reformation's rejection of the Catholic Church. Whether or not he would have accepted baptisms by immersion performed by Smith's followers would have been an interesting (although apparently unanswered) question.

Other essential points of Christian unity Campbell would have expected all true disciples of Christ to agree upon would include the major points of his thirty-two essays on "A Restoration of the Ancient Order," such as the New Testament as the foundational constitution of the church, the use of scriptural language in hymns, weekly worship and communion, caring for the poor, and the spirit of Christianity as discussed in chapter 5.

Conclusion

Campbell stated that if he were to classify what he called the important schools of thought in Christianity he would choose Christian *faith*, Christian *worship*, and Christian *morality*. Modern schools, much to his chagrin, added to these human *philosophy* and human *tradition*. It was the addition of these latter two schools that caused division and a deficiency in doctrinal purity, which prevented unity.[108]

The following is a representative summary of Campbell's foundation for Christian union: "*Let* The Bible *be substituted for all human creeds;* Facts, *for definitions;* Things, *for words;* Faith, *for speculation;* Unity of Faith, *for unity of opinion,* the Positive Commandments of God, *for human legislation and tradition;* Piety *for ceremony;* Morality *for partisan zeal;* The Practice of Religion, *for the mere profession of it: and the work is done.*"[109] For Campbell, unity was possible for the honest Christian who read and studied the Bible. Likeminded individuals would unite under the banner of faith in the facts presented in the scriptures. Communities of pious and moral individuals would actually practice true religion. Campbell saw his mission as presenting the facts of the Bible in his preaching, writing, and debating to unite the faithful in following the commandments of God found in the New Testament in order help usher in the Millennium.

In 1850, with the perspective of twenty-eight volumes of writing, Alexander looked back and reminisced on some of the crucial accomplishments of his restoration.[110] By this time, his followers were spread throughout the United States, Canada, England, Scotland, Ireland, New Zealand, and Australia with between 250,000 and 300,000 members. He identified signature accomplishments of his movement: (1) The role of the scriptures. In concert with all Protestants, the scriptures were the basis of his restoration. Within the Bible, however, the New Testament was particularly important in restoring principles, doctrines, practices, and polity to the Church. (2) The centrality of Jesus Christ. The church of Christ is built upon the testimony of the apostles and prophets of Jesus Christ as the chief cornerstone. He is the rock upon whom the Christian church is built and upon whom lies the only hope for sinners. Campbell declared this as the "grand central truth of Christianity" accompanied by "the truth that Jesus is the Christ, the Son of the Living God."[111] These testimonies ought to be a sufficient declaration for baptism—unlike the requirements of some churches for a special experience or parental vows as prerequisites. (3) Foundational principles for the New Testament church. Campbell's explication of the Christian church regarding practices and worship came from the New Testament, and within the New Testament, the foundation of apostles and prophets. From their writings, he spent much of his time clarifying baptism and its mode and meaning, the importance of weekly partaking of the Lord's Supper, the ministry of church leaders, and church polity or organization. (4) The canon within the canon. Although Campbell called the Acts of the Apostles "an authentic and invaluable history of primitive Christianity,"[112] his reductionist approach placed more importance on the epistles, especially the writings of Paul. Romans was central and was to be interpreted in light of Hebrews because it identified the structure, practices, and doctrines of the apostolic church.[113] The New Testament, rather than the Old, and nothing beyond determined the nature of Christianity. Just as in the Old Testament account of the Creation when God ceased speaking, the universe was perfect and complete, so when the Messiah and his Apostles ceased speaking, Christianity was perfect and complete. Campbell considered "every new institution, custom, law, or ceremony annexed thereunto, was only and wholly human, and unwarranted."[114]

Campbell's optimism that his work would aid the dawning of the golden millennial era was shattered in the last few years of his life by the

Civil War that erupted in 1861. His perception that America was the place for restoration of the teachings, practices, and unity of the New Testament church was certainly devastated by the hatred, divisiveness, and killing that took place between the North and South.[115]

NOTES

1. Campbell, *Memoirs of Elder Thomas Campbell*, 109
2. Campbell, *Christian System*, 113.
3. *Encyclopedia of the Stone-Campbell Movement*, ed. Foster et al., s.v. "Eschatology," 304.
4. Campbell, "Millennium, No. 1," *Millennial Harbinger* 1, no. 2 (1 February 1830): 58.
5. Campbell, "Millennium, No. 1," 54–56.
6. Thomas Campbell, *Declaration and Address*, 1809; see also John 17.
7. Campbell, "Juvenile Essays on Various Subjects by Alex Campbell in the University of Glasgow 1808."
8. Richardson, *Memoirs of Alexander Campbell*, 2:13–17.
9. Richard J. Cherok, *Debating for God: Alexander Campbell's Challenge to Skepticism in Antebellum America* (Abilene, TX: Abilene Christian University, 2008), 19.
10. Richardson, *Memoirs of Alexander Campbell*, 1:32; Campbell, manuscript E.
11. Campbell, "Religious Controversy," *Millennial Harbinger* 1, no. 1 (4 January 1830): 42.
12. Robert Owen and Alexander Campbell, *Debate on the Evidences of Christianity; Containing an Examination of the Social System, and all of the Systems of Scepticism of Ancient and Modern Times* (London: R. Groombridge, Panyer Alley, 1839), 253.
13. Owen and Campbell, *Debate on the Evidences of Christianity*, 253.
14. J. J. Haley, *Debates That Made History: The Story of Alexander Campbell's Debates with Rev. John Walker, Rev. W. L. McCalla, Mr. Robert Owen, Bishop Purcell, and Rev. Nathan L. Rice* (St. Louis: Christian Board of Publication, 1840), 15–16.
15. Alexander Campbell, *Debate on Christian Baptism, between Mr. John Walker, a Minister of the Secession, and Alexander Campbell*, 2nd ed. (Pittsburgh: Eichbaum and Johnston, 1822); Richardson, *Memoirs of Alexander Campbell*, 2:14–15.
16. Haley, *Debates That Made History*, 23.
17. Haley, *Debates That Made History*, 26–27.
18. Campbell, *Debate on Christian Baptism*, 12–13, 17.
19. The probable citation is Jeremiah 31:31–33. Other possibilities include Jeremiah 32:40; 50:5.
20. Campbell, *Debate on Christian Baptism*, 133.
21. Likely Walker was referring to Hebrews 12:24 or 1 Peter 1:2.
22. Campbell, *Debate on Christian Baptism*, 121–22.
23. Richardson, *Memoirs of Alexander Campbell*, 2:26.
24. Campbell, *Debate on Christian Baptism*, 125.
25. Campbell, *Debate on Christian Baptism*, 124.
26. Richardson, *Memoirs of Alexander Campbell*, 2:21.
27. Richardson, *Memoirs of Alexander Campbell*, 2:31.
28. Haley, *Debates That Made History*, 16.
29. Richardson, *Memoirs of Alexander Campbell*, 2:49.
30. Haley, *Debates That Made History*, 37.
31. Haley, *Debates That Made History*, 33.
32. By the time of this trip, Rigdon was in some trouble with the Regular Baptists of Pittsburg because of his reform teachings and conveniently left town to travel with Campbell. See chapter 10.

33. Campbell, *A Debate on Christian Baptism by Alexander Campbell* (Buffaloe, VA: Campbell & Sala, 1824), ix.

34. For a complete record of correspondence and the debate see Alexander Campbell, *A Public Debate on Christian Baptism, between The Rev. W. L. Maccalla, a Presbyterian Teacher, and Alexander Campbell* (London: Simpkin and Marshall, Stationers' Hall Court, 1842; Kansas City: Old Paths Book Club, 1948).

35. Richardson, *Memoirs of Alexander Campbell*, 2:75 (emphasis in original).

36. Richardson, *Memoirs of Alexander Campbell*, 2:79.

37. Irenaeus is credited with setting forth the idea that all humans are part of Adam and his sin but are still capable of righteous choices. Augustine developed the idea further by identifying sexual desire (concupiscence) as the mode by which Adam and Eve transmitted their fallen nature. In Augustine's view, all of humanity was present in Adam when he sinned, and therefore all have sinned and all inherit his guilt. As a result, infants need to be baptized for original sin or they would go to hell.

38. Acts 2:38.

39. Garrison and DeGroot, *The Disciples of Christ*, 172–73; Richardson, *Memoirs of Alexander Campbell*, 2:71–90.

40. *Encyclopedia of the Stone-Campbell Movement*, s.v. "baptism," 58.

41. Richardson, *Memoirs of Alexander Campbell*, 2:84.

42. Richardson, *Memoirs of Alexander Campbell*, 2:87.

43. Richardson, *Memoirs of Alexander Campbell*, 2:90.

44. Haley, *Debates That Made History*, 57.

45. Campbell, "To Mr. D—," *Christian Baptist* 4, no. 6 (1 January 1827): 121–25.

46. Cherok, *Debating for God*, 18.

47. Staker, *Hearken, O Ye People: The Historical Setting for Joseph Smith's Ohio Revelations* (Salt Lake City: Greg Kofford Books, 2009), 38.

48. "We Observe in the New Harmony Gazette," *Painesville Telegraph* 5, no. 7 (25 August 1826): 3.

49. Staker, *Hearken, O Ye People*, 40.

50. Richardson, *Memoirs of Alexander Campbell*, 2:242–43 (emphasis in original).

51. Owen and Campbell, *Debate on the Evidences of Christianity*, vi.

52. Robert Owen to James M. Dorsey, 14 July 1828, Indiana Historical Society, Indianapolis.

53. Campbell, "A Debate on the Evidences of Christianity," *Christian Baptist* 6 (4 August 1828): 23.

54. Haley, *Debates That Made History*, 59.

55. Haley, *Debates That Made History*, 8.

56. Campbell, "Mr. Robert Owen," *Christian Baptist* 7, no. 1 (3 August 1829): 19.

57. Campbell, "Mr. Robert Owen," 19.

58. Haley, *Debates That Made History*, 72.

59. Owen and Campbell, *Debate on the Evidences of Christianity*, iv.

60. Hughes, *Reviving the Ancient Faith*, 11.

61. Hughes, *Reviving the Ancient Faith*, 45.

62. Bill J. Humble, "The Restoration Ideal in the Churches of Christ," in *The American Quest for the Primitive Church*, 221, 223.

63. Hughes, *Reviving the Ancient Faith*, 45.

64. Richardson, *Memoirs of Alexander Campbell*, 1:210.

65. Campbell, "A Restoration of the Ancient Order of Things, No. 1," *Christian Baptist* 2, no. 7 (7 February 1825): 128.

66. Campbell, *Popular Lectures and Addresses*, 374–75.

67. Hughes, *Reviving the Ancient Faith*, 3.

68. *Encyclopedia of the Stone-Campbell Movement*, s.v. "Eschatology," 305. With this perspective, it is little wonder that the US Civil War was devastating to Campbell and "contrary to his perception of America as the place where the New Testament church would be restored in its teachings, practices, and unity." Foster, "Community of Christ and Churches of Christ," 10.

69. Williams, *America's Religions*, 181–82, 206.

70. Noll, *America's God*, 566; Williams, *America's Religions*, 206.

71. Campbell subdivided these three further into a list of six. The gospel is everlasting on account of its effects as (1) a bargain or covenant, (2) righteousness, (3) salvation, (4) consolation, (5) strength, and (6) everlasting glory. Alexander Campbell, "Journal of a Voyage from Ireland towards America 1808," manuscript D, 56, Disciples of Christ Historical Society, Nashville, Tennessee. Although part of the same manuscript, he titled this time period: "Second Part of My Journal from Scotland toward America, 1st August 1809."

72. Campbell, "Journal of a Voyage from Ireland towards America 1808," 56R.

73. Reflecting his own 1826 translation of the New Testament, Campbell's version is slightly different from the King James version quoted above: "I saw another *messenger* flying through the midst of heaven, having everlasting *good news* to *proclaim* to the inhabitants of the earth, to every nation, and tribe, and tongue, and people; saying with a loud voice, Fear God and give glory to him, for the hour of his *judgments* is come; and worship him who made heaven, and earth, and sea, and the fountains of water." Emphasis added indicates the primary differences from the KJV.

74. Richardson, *Memoirs of Alexander Campbell*, 302–3.

75. *Encyclopedia of the Stone-Campbell Movement*, s.v. "Millennial Harbinger," 517.

76. Campbell, "Prospectus," *Millennial Harbinger* 1, no. 1 (4 January 1830): 1.

77. *Encyclopedia of the Stone-Campbell Movement*, s.v. "Eschatology," 305.

78. Anthony L. Dunnavant, "Basic Themes of the Stone-Campbell Movement," *Discipliana* 46 (June 1986): 17.

79. West, *Alexander Campbell and Natural Religion*, 164.

80. By 1860, Campbell was more circumspect in his views on the timing, and at the commencement of the Civil War, absolutely devastated by the events that were totally contrary to his conception of America and its role as the location of the restoration of the New Testament church. Foster, "Community of Christ and Churches of Christ," 10. See also West, *Alexander Campbell and Natural Religion*, 165.

81. Richard M. Tristano, *The Origins of the Restoration Movement: An Intellectual History* (Atlanta: Glenmary Research Center, 1988), 3.

82. Tristano, *Origins of the Restoration Movement*, 3.

83. Thomas Campbell, *Declaration and Address*, in *Historical Documents Advocating Christian Union*, ed. Charles Alexander Young (Joplin, MO: College Press Publishing, 1985), 71–209. See appendix A.

84. Campbell, *Declaration and Address*, 73.

85. Campbell, *Declaration and Address*, 87.

86. Campbell, *Declaration and Address*," 87.

87. Campbell, *Christian System*, 9.

88. Campbell, *Declaration and Address*, 73.

89. Hughes and Allen, *Illusions of Innocence*, 172.

90. Campbell, "Preface," *Millennial Harbinger* (new series) 4, no. 1 (January 1840): 3.

91. Campbell, "Preface," 3.

92. Campbell, *Declaration and Address*, 73.

93. Campbell, *Declaration and Address*, Article 5, 75–76.

94. Campbell, *Declaration and Address*, Article 2, 74.

95. Alexander Campbell's beliefs on dispensations were discussed in great detail in chapter 5. The Christian dispensation extended from the day of Pentecost to the final judgment. Garrison, *Alexander Campbell's Theology*, 167–79; Eames, *The Philosophy of Alexander Campbell*, 25–26; Campbell, "Abrogation of the Sabbath," *Millennial Harbinger* 40, no. 3 (March 1869): 144; Hughes, *Reviving the Ancient Faith*, 31.

96. Tristano, *The Origins of the Restoration Movement*, 75, 94.

97. Campbell, *Declaration and Address*, Article 5, 75–76.

98. Campbell, "Millennium—No. 2," *Millennial Harbinger* 1, no. 4 (5 April 1830): 145.

99. Tristano, *The Origins of the Restoration Movement*, 75.

100. Campbell, *Christian System*, 9.

101. Campbell, "Millennium—No. 2," 145.

102. Campbell, "A Restoration of the Ancient Order of Things, No. 2," *Christian Baptist* 2, no. 8 (7 March 1825): 133–34; Richardson, *Memoirs of Alexander Campbell*, 1:348.

103. Campbell, "Grace, Faith, Repentance, Baptism, Regeneration," *Millennial Harbinger* (fifth series) 2, no. 3 (March 1859): 130.

104. Churches of Christ scholar Richard Hughes contends that originally there were two competing traditions in the Churches of Christ: apocalyptic revivalism led by Barton Stone, and Enlightenment progressivism led by Alexander Campbell. Their alliance gave a prolific writer such as Campbell a larger arena of influence. Though these two churches combined, this book will focus only on the writings and teachings of Alexander Campbell. Hughes, "Two Restoration Traditions: Mormons and Churches of Christ in the Nineteenth Century," in *The Primitive Church in the Modern World*, 42.

105. Tristano, *The Origins of the Restoration Movement*, 18.

106. Campbell, "A Restoration of the Ancient Order of Things, No. 3," *Christian Baptist* 2, no. 9 (4 April 1825): 140.

107. Campbell, "Christians Among the Sects," *Millennial Harbinger* (new series) 1, no. 7 (December 1837): 564.

108. Campbell, *Christian System*, 124; emphasis in the original.

109. Campbell, *Christian System*, 110; emphasis in the original.

110. Campbell, "Prefatory Remarks," *Millennial Harbinger* (series 3) 7, no. 1 (January 1850): 3–8. Olbricht, "Alexander Campbell as a Theologian," 24–25.

111. Campbell, "Prefatory Remarks," 3.

112. Campbell, "Notes of Apostacy, No. 1," *Millennial Harbinger* (new series) 1, no. 1 (January 1837): 17.

113. Thomas Olbricht, "Hermeneutics and the Declaration and Address," in *The Quest for Christian Unity, Peace, and Purity in Thomas Campbell's Declaration and Address*, 243, 254.

114. Campbell, "Prefatory Remarks," 3.

115. Foster, "Community of Christ and Churches of Christ," 10.

14

Joseph Smith's
Expansive Eternalism

" *I* can taste the principles of eternal life," Smith declared in his last conference address 7 April 1844. "So can you. They are given to me by the revelations of Jesus Christ and I know you believe it."[1] Eternity, as Smith understood it, was "without beginning of days or end of years."[2] If God sets his hand on creation, humans, or ordinances, they have the capability of becoming eternal.

In Doctrine and Covenants 19 (revealed to Smith in the summer of 1829), a unique idea is put forth regarding the terms *endless* and *eternal,* which are defined in the context of punishment and suffering. The revelation clarifies that "it is not written that there shall be no end to this torment." Instead, these terms are descriptors of God: "For, behold, I am endless, and the punishment which is given from my hand is endless punishment, for Endless is my name." Eternal punishment and endless punishment are God's punishment—not unceasing punishment.[3] From these passages, it appears that the terms *endless* and *eternal* sometimes describe a quality of life rather than a period of time.[4] Accordingly, endless and eternal life describe God's life—his existence, character, and nature—which he desires to share with his children.[5] Illustrating how differently Smith and Campbell saw the meanings of these words, prominent Baptist Robert Semple, a reader of the *Millennial Harbinger,* inquired about these very concepts: "What are your views of the future punishment of wicked men? Is it eternal and without end?" Campbell responded:

"Their destruction is an everlasting destruction, and their punishment an endless punishment. If men are not now saved by the gospel, it is impossible that they can escape the condemnation of hell: for after death no means more efficacious can be used to save them from sin than those employed here:—and if uncured by these, they are incurable for ever. *Sic stat sententia.* [meaning] Thus stands the decree."[6]

Smith explained, "God dwells in eternity, and he does not view things as we do."[7] Several unique doctrines that Smith taught fall under the heading of *eternalism*—or God's perspective of time and eternity—and are discussed in this chapter under the overarching umbrella of the plan of salvation, which embodies principles Smith claimed were revealed to him as part of his restoration, such as premortal existence as spirits, the creation of the earth, the priesthood, ordinances, and the Resurrection. These revelations are contained in the Book of Mormon; Doctrine and Covenants; the Book of Moses, which was part of his Bible translation; the Book of Abraham, which he translated from Egyptian papyri scrolls; and other sermons and teachings recorded by his scribes.[8]

Plan of Salvation

In the Book of Mormon, a summary of the plan of salvation includes three essential elements: the Creation, the Fall, and the Atonement (which includes the Resurrection).[9] Smith taught, "At the first organization in heaven we were all present and saw the Savior chosen and appointed, and the plan of salvation made and we sanctioned it."[10] The Book of Mormon calls the plan of salvation "the merciful plan of the great Creator" and "the great plan of redemption."[11] From Smith's perspective, it is the way God guides humankind through the processes of premortal existence, birth, salvation, and, ultimately, exaltation.[12]

Premortal Existence of the Spirit

Smith taught that the spirit of man was eternal and substantial.[13] Many sectarians of his day believed that the spirit continues on after death, however, it did not exist prior to birth. Smith, in contrast, believed that the spirit existed prior to mortal birth and would continue to exist after death because of its eternal nature.[14] He taught further that "the first step in the salvation of men is the laws of eternal and self-existent principles."[15] Smith explained that spirit material "existed from Eternity & will exist to Eternity. Any thing created cannot be Eternal."[16] Speaking on the immutability of the spirit of humankind, he argued, "If the soul of man had a beginning it will surely have an end," thereby exposing what he believed to be poor logic in saying that "the spirit of man had a beginning and yet [has] no end."[17]

According to Smith's revelations, there were two creations—one spiritual and one physical. God organized everything spiritually "before it was in the earth, and before it grew . . . before they were naturally upon the face of the earth. . . . And I, the Lord God, had created all the children of men.[18] All things were created spiritually, before they were naturally (physically) placed upon the face of the earth. Included in this order of creation was humankind, for God said to Adam, 'I made the world, and men, before they were in the flesh.'"[19] Smith received additional revelation indicating a premortal or spiritual existence: Moses's and Abraham's descriptions of Satan's premortal rebellion and expulsion from heaven, including details not in the accounts of Isaiah and John;[20] Enoch's vision of the "spirits that God had created";[21] and Smith's own revelation that declared humankind's creation was "before the world was made."[22]

Smith also explained the nature of spirit matter: "The Spirit by many is thought to be immaterial, without substance." He declared instead that "Spirit is a substance; that it is material, but that it is more pure, elastic, and refined matter than the body; —that it existed before the [physical] body, can exist in the body, and will exist separate from the body, when the body will be mouldering in the dust; and will in the resurrection be again united with it."[23]

Because the spirit material from which humans are made was not created, it is coeternal with God. It has substance but is purer and more refined than the body. From this perspective, although a member of the Godhead, Christ is everyone's elder brother because he was the firstborn of all God's spirit children, thereby receiving by birthright his royal station in the premortal realms.[24] Smith's revelations describe Christ as "from everlasting to everlasting"[25] and "from all eternity to all eternity."[26] The great advancement, obtained by keeping the first estate in premortality, was the uniting of the spirit with a body, which would be redeemed by the Savior. Mortality was the grand prize.[27] Smith declared, "We came to this earth that we might have a body and present it pure before God in the Celestial Kingdom. The great principle of happiness consists in having a body."[28]

Notwithstanding our ignorance of God's plans, Smith declared, "The great Jehovah contemplated the whole of the events connected with the earth, pertaining to the plan of salvation, before it rolled into existence." He knew of and comprehended the Fall of Adam and had planned humankind's redemption prior to the Creation. From this perspective, humankind was never intended to live in the Garden of Eden; Adam and Eve's Fall was part of God's eternal plan, and Christ had already been foreordained to perform his redeeming sacrifice.[29] The plan of salvation was in place to provide an atoning sacrifice through his Son—by whose merits, mercy, and grace alone humankind could find redemption.[30]

CREATION OF HEAVEN AND EARTH

Using reason and inspiration, Smith clarified what he believed Genesis 1:1 meant: "In the beginning God created the heaven and the earth." He analyzed each part of the first Hebrew word in the Bible: *Berosheit*: *baith* (*be*) means in, by, and through; *rosh* means head; and *sheit* is a grammatical ending. Smith declared that Moses, the inspired man who recorded this passage initially, did not write the prefix *baith*. A Jew without authority rewrote the word, changing the meaning of the original first phrase of the Old Testament. When it was first recorded, Smith declared it read, "'The head one of the Gods brought forth the Gods,' that is the true meaning of the words. . . . Thus the head God brought forth the Gods in the grand council. . . . The head God called together the Gods, and set in grand council. The grand counsellors sat in yonder heavens, and contemplated the creation of the worlds that were created at that time."[31]

The Genesis phrase "in the beginning" gave rise to the notion of *ex nihilo*—the idea that material elements did not exist before the Creation. Smith rebuked "the learned men who are preaching salvation [that] say, that God created the heavens and the earth out of nothing."[32] Smith called these men unlearned because they declared his teachings on the subject blasphemy and him a fool. He explained, "God had materials to organize the world out of chaos; chaotic matter, which is element, and in which dwells all the glory. Element had an existence from the time he had. The pure principles of element, are principles that can never be destroyed. They may be organized and re-organized; but not destroyed."[33] "Earth, water, &c all these had their existence in an elementary state from Eternity."[34] Smith claimed the second Hebrew word in Genesis 1:1, *baurau*, translated as *create*, means "to organize; the same as a man would organize a ship" and would be more accurately translated as *formed* or *organized*.[35] Additionally, Smith taught that the second phrase describing the earth and translated as "without form and void" in Genesis 1:2 should read "empty and desolate."[36] Putting this altogether, Smith could have said, "The head God gathered the Gods together in a grand council in order to form and organize the earth out of eternal and already existing elements producing what was then an empty and desolate planet."

Smith's pronouncements regarding the nature of elements appear to be in harmony with early Greek philosophy that "nothing comes from nothing," and with ideas on the conservation of mass and energy in closed systems as expressed by scientists in the eighteenth century.[37] Benjamin F. Johnson, a contemporary and friend of Smith, claimed that Smith was the first to describe "substantialism" as belief in the "eternity of matter." Smith further explained

> that no part or particle of the great universe could become annihilated or destroyed; that light and life and spirit were one; that all light and heat are the 'Glory of God' which is His power, that fills the immensity of space, and is the life of all things, and permeates with latent life, and heat, every particle of which all worlds are composed; that light or spirit, and matter, are the two first great primary principles of the universe, or of Being; that they are self-existent, co-existent, indestructible, and eternal, and from these two elements both our spirits and our bodies were formulated.[38]

Smith's ideas of *creatio ex materia* contradicted *creatio ex nihilo*, an idea accepted by Augustine, Luther, Calvin, Wesley, and Matthew Henry. From Smith's point of view, God's creative work is a magnificent process of organizing eternally existing materials by using eternally existing energy, in accordance with eternally existing laws. As Mormon historian Davis Bitton explained, Mormonism came close to Enlightenment rationalism in its attitude towards science. God had spatial qualities and called the material world into existence from preexisting materials. There was no dichotomy between spirit and matter, although they differed in density or quality. The laws of nature were inherent in the universe and not derived by God, who by using them brought to fruition his divine purposes.[39]

MELCHIZEDEK PRIESTHOOD: AN EVERLASTING POWER

Priesthood is one of humankind's most direct access to power and authority from God. Smith claimed revelation to explain the higher priesthood:

The Melchizedek Priesthood holds the right of presidency, and has power and authority over all the offices in the church in all ages of the world, to administer in spiritual things . . . [and] a right to officiate in all the offices in the church. . . . The power and authority of the higher, or Melchizedek Priesthood, is to hold the keys of all the spiritual blessings of the church—to have the privilege of receiving the mysteries of the kingdom of heaven, to have the heavens opened unto them.[40]

Regarding the Apostle Paul's words that speak of Christ, Melchizedek, and priesthood in Hebrews 5 and 12, Smith explained that Christ was a "priest forever, after the order of Melchisedec, and the anointed son of God, from before the foundation of the world."[41] Christ's priesthood, Smith explained, was an everlasting principle. Priesthood, meaning God's power, has always existed with God and will continue to exist "from Eternity . . . to Eternity, without beginning of days or end of years."[42] In fact, it existed before "the morning stars sang together, or the Sons of God, shouted for joy."[43]

Smith declared that the Melchizedek Priesthood holds the keys (power to direct and preside) of the kingdom of God on earth, which keys must be brought from heaven whenever the gospel is restored, and that the priesthood "is the Channel through which all knowledge, doctrine, the plan of Salvation and every important matter is revealed from Heaven."[44]

Smith believed that he had been ordained in heaven before the world was created to the office of prophet, designated to lay the foundation of God's work in the last or seventh dispensation in the Grand Council.[45] At that grand council all who were to be prophets, priests, or leaders were also ordained. The scriptural basis for these declarations regarding the Grand Council in Heaven came from Smith's translation of the Egyptian papyri containing the Book of Abraham. He learned that prior to the mortal creation of humankind, God gathered his "noble and great" spirit children together and foreordained them to be his rulers on the earth. Regarding Abraham, he declared, "Thou art one of them; thou wast chosen before thou wast born."[46]

With this understanding of receiving earthly responsibilities in premortality, Smith taught that Adam and Eve, as spirit children, prior to being placed in the Garden of Eden, were foreordained to their particular mission in life, which was to bring mortality to the spirit children of God. Adam was set apart by God to "introduce the principles of life among the people, of which the Gospel is the grand power and influence, and through which salvation can extend to all peoples, all nations, all kindreds, all tongues, and all worlds."[47] According to Smith's revelations, Adam—called the "Ancient of Days" in Daniel 7,[48] meaning first and oldest of all mortals—received the priesthood during the Creation and had dominion given to him over all other living creations. When the gospel is redispensed upon the earth, priesthood keys must be brought from heaven, and all this is done by the authority of Adam.[49]

Without attempting to explain everything he knew and understood regarding the "laws that govern the body and spirit of man [and] their relationship to each other," Smith simply stated it had been revealed to him that "the spirits of men are eternal, that they are governed by the same priesthood that Abraham, Melchisdedek [sic], and the Apostles were; that they are organized according to that priesthood which is everlasting[,] . . . that they all move in their respective spheres, and are governed by the law of God."[50]

RITUALS AND ETERNAL ORDINANCES

An integral part of Mormonism is formalized ritual in both language and performance that convey both the literal and symbolic nature of the words and the actions of ordinances. Campbell was formal in the mode of baptism and in the necessity of weekly distribution of the Lord's Supper; in general, however, he would have agreed with the anti-formalism of many of the nineteenth-century religious movements, especially in comparison with Anglican, Presbyterian, and Catholic liturgical worship services. Mormon worship services are also relatively informal in comparison with these denominations; however, there are some very formal rituals. Specific rituals that must be done with exactness include the words and mode of the baptismal ordinance, the sacrament prayers prior to the weekly distribution of the Lord's Supper, and the acknowledgment of Melchizedek Priesthood authority prior to giving blessings. Initially meetings held under a grove of trees were sufficient for Sabbath-day worship, partaking of the Lord's Supper, giving blessings, and the closest body of water for the ordinances of living baptism. In August 1840, Smith began to teach the ordinance of baptism for deceased ancestors. Addressing a widow who had lost a son that had not been baptized, he called the principle "glad tidings of great joy," in contrast to the prevailing Christian tradition of that day that all unbaptized are damned. Baptisms for the dead began to be performed immediately in the Mississippi River near Nauvoo. However, by January 1841, Smith declared additional revelation that the ordinance belonged to the temple the Saints were commanded to build. In 1842, Smith announced, "The church is not now organiz'd in its proper order, and cannot be until the Temple is completed."[51]

Smith's restoration vision would find its greatest fulfillment in the temple and its ordinances. Temples were built and set aside for special rituals that were too sacred for groves or meetinghouses. Smith spoke of temples as "an house whereby he [God] Could reveal unto his people the ordinances of his house and glories of his kingdom & teach the people the ways of salvation. For [there] are certain ordinances & principles that when they are taught and practiced, must be done in a place or house built for that purpose."[52] These ordinances have precise words and rituals to be performed by the participants that must take place at a holy place dedicated for that purpose.

Temples were so important to Smith that, despite the impoverished conditions of his people, he directed the building of a temple in Kirtland, Ohio, and later in Nauvoo, Illinois. Additionally, plans were made and cornerstones laid for several more temples in Missouri. In the fourteen years Smith led the church as prophet, seer, and revelator, he dedicated numerous locations for the construction of "houses of the Lord": Independence, Far West, and Adam-ondi-Ahman in Missouri; Kirtland; and Nauvoo. During his lifetime, one temple was built, Kirtland, and Nauvoo was under construction at his death.[53]

Smith taught that all things created here on earth have only a temporary existence unless God lays his hand upon them. For example, in 1843, Smith recorded a revelation stating that "all covenants, contracts, bonds, obligations, oaths, vows, performances, connections, associations, or expectations" end at death unless they are approved, ratified, and sealed for time and all eternity.[54] Smith explained that this list referred to ordinances such as baptism, conferring of the gift of the Holy Ghost, ordination to the priesthood, and temple covenants for both the living and the dead.[55]

In light of Smith's teaching, Mormons believe New Testament passages connecting them to the primitive church and Christ's pronouncement to Peter at Caesarea Philippi take on great significance: "I will give unto thee the keys of the kingdom of heaven: and whatsoever thou shalt bind (seal) on earth shall be bound in heaven: and whatsoever thou shalt loose on earth shall be loosed in heaven."[56] According to Smith, he was ordained to the Melchizedek Priesthood under the hands of Peter,

James, and John, who had received this authority from Christ.[57] In April 1836, Smith and his associate president, Oliver Cowdery, announced that Elijah the prophet had returned, as Malachi promised, and revealed to them the priesthood keys necessary "to turn the hearts of the fathers to the children, and the children to the fathers," meaning the sealing of families as eternal family units.[58] In a Sunday address early in 1844, Smith explained that the word *turn* [in this passage] should be translated *bind* or *seal*,[59] meaning the sealing of families as eternal family units.[60] For this purpose, Mormons build temples wherein they perform ordinances for themselves as well as by proxy for the dead. This, Smith maintained, "is the Chain that binds the hearts of the fathers to the Children & the Children to the Fathers which fulfills the mission of Elijah."[61]

Regarding the plan of salvation, and specifically performing vicarious baptisms for the dead, Joseph Smith captured the interdependence of Mormon salvation; "without us they could not be made perfect nor we without them. . . . This is the spirit of Elijah that we redeem our dead & connect ourselves [to those] which are in heaven."[62] Few saw the grand plan of God that Smith saw, and he may have seen it a bit differently than we understand it today:

> The great designs of God in relation to the salvation of the human family are very little understood by the professedly wise, and intelligent generation in which we live; various and conflicting are the opinions of men concerning the plan of salvation; the requisitions of the Almighty; the necessary preparations for heaven; the state and condition of departed spirits; and the happiness, or misery that is consequent upon the practice of righteousness and iniquity.[63]

Smith saw God's relationship with his children uniquely disparate from many of the seventeenth- and eighteenth-century theologians who used fear as a means of exacting obedience:

> While one portion of the human race are judging and condemning the other without mercy, the great parent of the universe looks upon the whole of the human family with a fatherly care, and paternal regard. . . . He will judge them 'not according to what they have not, but what they have;' those who have lived without the law, will be judged without law, and those who have a law, will be judged by that law.[64]

From this statement, Smith demonstrated his understanding of God's omniscience, omnipotence, and love. "He knows the situation of both the living and the dead, and has made ample provision for their redemption."[65]

In another example, marriage between a man and woman is pronounced efficacious "until death do you part" unless there is someone with power to bind the marriage on earth and also in heaven.[66] Smith's revelation claimed, "A man must enter into an everlasting covenant with his wife in this world or he will have no claim on her in the next."[67] The essential qualifier, according to Smith, is that one "who is anointed, both as well for time and for all eternity," having been "appointed on the earth to hold this power," must preside over the marriage ceremony.[68]

Smith is also known for entering into plural marriage. Included in the "restitution of all things" spoken of by Peter was the restoration of past principles.[69] Likely as part of his Old Testament study of Genesis in mid-1830 and early 1831, Smith had questions regarding how God justified the practice of plural marriage by some of the great patriarchs: Abraham, Isaac, Jacob, Moses, David, and Solomon.[70] The Book of Mormon definitively stated God's law of marriage, "For there shall not any man among you have save it be one wife; and concubines he shall have none," with one caveat: "For if I will, saith the Lord of Hosts, raise up seed unto me, I will command my people; otherwise they shall hearken unto these things." The answer to the Old Testament question was clear: God gave additional wives to Abraham, Isaac, Jacob, Moses, and initially David, to raise godly children. In David's case, however, his overreaching beyond what was given to him by the prophet Nathan brought forth this condemnation: "David and Solomon truly had many wives and concubines, which thing was abominable before me, saith the Lord."[71] The Book of Mormon forbade plural marriage unless the Lord specifically commanded otherwise; adultery was a forbidden practice and promised punishment.[72] From the twenty-first century, it is extremely difficult to understand this practice—it was even difficult for many at the time Smith instituted it.

Finally, although covenants are entered into for eternity, the individual must claim that blessing through faithfulness. Citing the Apostle Paul's explanation of the "Doctrine of Election," which exhorted "us to make our calling and election sure," Smith taught, "This is that sealing power spoken of by Paul in other places (Ephesians I. 13. 14. 'In whom ye also trusted, that after ye heard the word of truth; the gospel of your salvation, in whom also after that ye believed, ye were sealed with that Holy Spirit of promise, which is the earnest of our inheritance, until the redemption of the purchased possession unto the praise of his glory.') That we may be sealed up unto the day of redemption."[73] In other words, the Holy Ghost has the power to bind in heaven the covenants that were entered into on earth. Nevertheless, priesthood keys cannot countermand the moral agency of humans. Smith declared that "the anointing & sealing—[must be]—called, elected and made sure."[74] Therefore, the ordinances performed by the living for themselves or on behalf of the dead are valid upon acceptance of the ordinance and faithfulness to the gospel covenant, resulting in one's life being "sealed by the Holy Spirit of promise."[75]

Temples, the symbolic primordial connection between heaven and earth, were essential locations where Smith's vision of eternity could be taught and carried out. Marriages could be performed for eternity and family units sealed everlastingly. Further, ordinances could be performed vicariously in behalf of those who never had the opportunity in mortality to receive the full blessings of the gospel. Smith illustrated the importance of the principle of vicarious baptism with this hypothetical example: "The case of two men, brothers, equally intelligent, learned, virtuous and lovely, walking in uprightness, and in all good conscience. . . . One dies, and is buried, having never heard the gospel of reconciliation; to the other the message of salvation is sent, he hears and embraces it, and is made the heir of Eternal life. Shall the one become a partaker of glory, and the other be consigned to hopeless perdition? Is there no chance for escape? Sectarianism answers none!" Smith taught the doctrine of baptism for the dead, declaring the "wisdom and mercy of God, in preparing an ordinance for the salvation of the dead, being baptized by proxy, their names recorded in heaven, and they judged according to the deeds done in the body."[76] For Smith, the temple stood as a binding link between heaven and earth; time and eternity; past, present, and future; husbands and wives; parents and children; and individuals to Christ. Ordinances and rituals such as baptism, the Lord's Supper, priesthood blessings, and those performed in the temple had eternal ramifications requiring exactness in mode and word with a formality not often associated by some with Mormonism.

RESURRECTION INTO THE ETERNITIES

Earlier in this chapter, the human spirit was defined by Smith as having substance. To understand Smith's views on resurrection, it is essential to understand his definition of the soul. Regarding the soul, Smith identified it as consisting of the spirit and the body;[77] it is not the classical idea of an "invisible, immaterial, non-spatial, and indivisible substance."[78] The soul is a composite of two materials: one is more refined than the other, the other is corporeal, meaning fleshy, having both spatial characteristics and existing in temporality, meaning consisting of matter. This idea rejected the "radical divide between body and spirit, the earthly and the heavenly" proposed by most sectarians.[79] Thus, resurrection consists of the reuniting of the spirit, now blessed by the grace of Christ according to our deeds and desires during mortality, with a perfect body; there is physicality to the resurrected body.[80] A resurrected soul is the great gift, the inheritance of all God's children, redeeming them from the effects of a fallen body regardless of their deeds in mortality.[81] Smith declared that "spirit and element, inseparably connected, receive a fullness of joy."

Early in 1832, significantly prior to most of the preceding doctrine was revealed and developed, Smith and Rigdon were working together in their translation of the Gospel of John. "It appeared self-evident" to them "that if God rewarded everyone according to the deeds done in the body, the term 'Heaven,' as intended for the Saints' eternal home, must include more kingdoms than one." After translating John 5:29 concerning the "resurrection of life" and the "resurrection of damnation," Smith and Rigdon pondered the nature of these two resurrections. Then they received a grand vision of the "three degrees of glory" recorded in Doctrine and Covenants section 76. This was one of the most distinctive revelations that radically separated Mormon beliefs from Campbell's beliefs.

The first doctrine clarified in the vision was that "they who have done good" come forth "in the resurrection of the just; and they who have done evil, in the Resurrection of the unjust," phrases parallel to the terms "life" and "damnation" used by John.[82] Smith identified the individuals who would come forth in the Resurrection of the just as those who had "received the testimony of Jesus," had been "baptized after the manner of his burial," had "receive[d] the Holy Spirit," had overcome the world "by faith," and had been "sealed by the Holy Spirit of promise." He called these individuals "just men made perfect through Jesus . . . whose bodies are celestial, whose glory is that of the sun, even the glory of God."[83] The highest manifestation of future glory in the celestial kingdom is deification: "They have received of his fullness, and of his glory . . . they are gods, even the sons of God."

By emphasizing the likeness of man to God in substance, materiality, and a preexisting human identity gives rise to a unique Mormon belief in human theosis—or the idea that man may become like God.[84] Smith emphasized that God and humankind are alike in some ways; they are coeternal spirits, anthropomorphic, and corporeal. Additionally, God's purposes are aligned with their advancement, as Smith recorded in the Book of Moses, "this is my work and my glory to bring to pass the immortality and eternal life of man."[85] This intimate picture of God's desire expresses his love for humankind, and is articulated in the commandment for his children to love one another as God loves them.

A second group belonging to the Resurrection of the just are those who inherit the "terrestrial world"—a place that differs in glory from the celestial "even as that of the moon differs from the sun."[86] Smith identified this group of individuals as "honorable men of the earth, who were blinded by the craftiness of men." They are individuals "who are not valiant in their testimony of Jesus."[87]

A third group Smith and Rigdon saw in vision was "the telestial, which glory is that of the lesser, even as the glory of the stars differs from that of the glory of the moon."[88] This group is part of the Resurrection of the unjust because these individuals did not receive Christ or the tenets of his gospel—they are "liars and sorcerers, and adulterers, and whoremongers, and whosoever loves and makes a lie."[89] They must remain in hell in the postmortal spirit world until Christ finishes his millennial work before they are resurrected.[90] Nevertheless, once resurrected, they will find that "the glory of the telestial . . . surpasses all understanding."[91] Rewards of differing degrees of light described by Smith as celestial, terrestrial, and telestial are similar to Paul's comparison of resurrection as like the glory of the sun, moon, and stars.[92]

SUMMARY

Two months before his death, Smith delivered one of the final and most complete presentations on eternalism. In this address, he stated that he wished to start at the beginning, the Creation, in order for his audience to understand "the mind, purposes, decrees, &c. of the great Eloheim, that sits in yonder heavens."[93] Smith instructed those gathered that understanding God from the beginning was essential for understanding the character of God and their relationship to him, also essential for comprehending themselves. For example, he declared that "God was a self exhisting being. Man exhists upon the same principle."[94] Therefore, he could also point out that since neither God nor man had a beginning or end: "God never had power to create the spirit of man. God himself Could not create himself. Intelligence is eternal & it is self exhisting."[95] Thus, God, finding "himself in the midst of spirit and glory, because he was greater, and because he saw proper to institute laws, whereby the rest could have a privilege to advance like himself."[96] The ramifications of these pronouncements "made individual persons radically free."[97] Neither their nature nor their choices were predetermined. Each man and woman must choose whether or not he or she will ally with God. The freedom in this vision of eternity is dizzyingly expansive.

Smith came to his understanding of God, the cosmos, and eternity from his claim of personal, intimate revelation. Smith's assertion to be a prophet, seer, and revelator—one who could bring together the past, present, and future—made his pronouncements so broad and expansive that they were unlike any other restoration movement.[98] His explanation of eternity encompassed the whole gospel plan because "every principle proceeding from God is eternal, and any principle which is not eternal is of the Devil,"[99] meaning all that which is temporal will be destroyed at Christ's Second Coming. Accordingly, the Creation, Fall, Atonement, Judgment, and Resurrection were taught to the spirit children of God, and all but a "third part" accepted the plan of God for their redemption.[100] All mortals were also spirit children consisting of a refined substance prior to birth on the earth. Priesthood authority was the power by which preexisting elements were organized and took form. It is also the power by which ordinances are performed. God's eternal plan includes precise rituals and ordinances for his children, which, when performed by proper priesthood authority and based upon the faithfulness of the individual, allow them to be recognized and welcomed into exaltation—God's quality of life, meaning endless and eternal. Smith's restoration is a commitment to nontraditional and revolutionary beliefs about the Creation, the nature of God and humankind, and ordinances to eternally seal their relationship.

Notes

1. Joseph Smith, in *Wilford Woodruff's Journal*, 2:386, http://www.josephsmith papers.org.
2. Moses 6:67 (Pearl of Great Price).
3. Doctrine and Covenants 19:6, 10, 11–12.
4. The Hebrew (*olam*) and the Greek (*aeon*) translated as *eternal* appear to have originally had meanings such as "long duration," the period from antiquity to

futurity, indefinite futurity, continuous existence, an age, an epoch, relative time, or prolonged time. The earliest connotations of *olam* were "hidden or distant time belonging to the remote and inscrutable past or future from the standpoint of the present." Francis Brown, *The New Brown, Driver, and Briggs Hebrew and English Lexicon of the Old Testament*, based on the lexicon of William Gesenius, trans. Edward Robinson, ed. Francis Brown (Lafayette, IN: Associated Publishers and Authors, 1981), s.v. "olam"; *Theological Dictionary of the New Testament*, ed. Gerhard Kittel and Gerhard Friedrich, trans. Geoffrey W. Bromiley (Grand Rapids: W. B. Eerdmans, c. 1985), s.v. "aeon." Sterling McMurrin explains that the word *eternal* in this sense does not mean timeless but un-begun and endless time. Sterling McMurrin, *The Theological Foundations of the Mormon Religion and the Philosophical Foundations of Mormon Theology* (Salt Lake City: Signature Books, 2000), 13.

5. Givens, *Wrestling the Angel*, 266.

6. Campbell, "Brother Semple," Query 7, *Millennial Harbinger* 1, no. 8 (August 1830): 358.

7. Smith, in *Wilford Woodruff's Journal*, 2:386.

8. As part of a traveling display, an entrepreneur brought Egyptian papyri scrolls and mummies to Kirtland, Ohio, in 1835. Several Mormons purchased them and Smith began translation of the scrolls during the summer and fall of that year. The Book of Abraham was published in 1842. After Smith's death most of the artifacts were sold to the Chicago Museum and were burned in the Great Fire of 1871.

9. 2 Nephi 2:14–26; 9:6, 12; Alma 18:36, 39; 22:12–14 (Book of Mormon).

10. Account of Meeting and Discourse, 5 January 1841, as Reported by William Clayton, 7, http://www.josephsmithpapers.org.

11. 2 Nephi 9:6; Jacob 6:8 (Book of Mormon).

12. Givens, *Wrestling the Angel*, 300.

13. Doctrine and Covenants 93:29, 33.

14. Although the human body is finite, the spirit has within itself foundational existence, which Smith called "intelligence," Abraham 3:22 (Pearl of Great Price). See also McMurrin, *Theological Foundations*, 5.

15. Account of Meeting and Discourse, 5 January 1841, as Reported by William Clayton, 7, http://www.josephsmithpapers.org.

16. Report of Instructions, between 26 June and 4 August 1839–A, as Reported by Willard Richards, 64, http://www.josephsmithpapers.org; Doctrine and Covenants 93:29.

17. Account of Meeting and Discourse, 5 January 1841, as Reported by William Clayton, 6, http://www.josephsmithpapers.org; Smith, in *Wilford Woodruff's Journal*, 2:385.

18. Moses 3:5 (Pearl of Great Price); see Doctrine and Covenants 29:31–32. Doctrine and Covenants 131:7.

19. Moses 6:51 (Pearl of Great Price).

20. Moses 4:1–4 and Abraham 3:27–28 (Pearl of Great Price); compare to Isaiah 14:12–15; Revelation 12:4–9.

21. Moses 6:36 (Pearl of Great Price).

22. Doctrine and Covenants 49:17; 93:23.

23. History, 1838–1856, volume C-1 [2 November 1838–31 July 1842], 1307, http://www.josephsmithpapers.org. See also Doctrine and Covenants 131:7–8.

24. Robert Millet, *A Different Jesus? The Christ of the Latter-day Saints* (Grand Rapids, MI: Eerdsmans, 2005), 20. Doctrine and Covenants 93:21.

25. Doctrine and Covenants 61:1.

26. Doctrine and Covenants 39:1.

27. See Jude 1:6.

28. Account of Meeting and Discourse, 5 January 1841, as Reported by William Clayton, 7–8, http://www.josephsmithpapers.org. See also Jude 1:6.
29. 2 Nephi 2:22–25 (Book of Mormon).
30. 2 Nephi 2:6–8 (Book of Mormon).
31. Discourse, 7 April 1844, as Reported by *Times and Seasons*, 614, http://www.josephsmithpapers.org. He also used "the Father of the Gods" in the same discourse to describe the head God.
32. Discourse, 7 April 1844, as Reported by *Times and Seasons*, 615, http://www.josephsmithpapers.org.
33. Discourse, 7 April 1844, as Reported by *Times and Seasons*, 615, http://www.josephsmithpapers.org.
34. History, 1838–1856, volume C-1 [2 November 1838–31 July 1842], 11 [addenda], http://www.josephsmithpapers.org.
35. Discourse, 7 April 1844, as Reported by *Times and Seasons*, 615, http://www.josephsmithpapers.org; Account of Meeting and Discourse, 5 January 1841, as Reported by William Clayton, 6, http://www.josephsmithpapers.org.
36. Account of Meeting and Discourse, 5 January 1841, as Reported by William Clayton, 6, http://www.josephsmithpapers.org.
37. The law of conservation of mass states that mass cannot be created or destroyed, and the law of conservation of energy states that energy cannot be created or destroyed—but they can be changed. These were once thought to be separate and distinct laws, but Einstein in his theory of special relativity showed that mass and energy are equivalent as expressed in his well-known equation $E=mc^2$. Although mass can be converted into energy and energy into mass, the total quantity of mass-energy in the universe remains constant. Thus, we now have the law of conservation of mass-energy, or the first law of thermodynamics.
38. Benjamin F. Johnson to George S. Gibbs, 1903, in LeBaron, *Benjamin Franklin Johnson*, 223.
39. Bitton, "Anti-Intellectualism in Mormon History," 115.
40. Doctrine and Covenants 107:8–9, 18–19.
41. "Baptism," *Times and Seasons* 3, no. 21 (1 September 1842): 905.
42. Report of Instructions, between 26 June and 4 August 1839–A, as Reported by Willard Richards, 63, http://www.josephsmithpapers.org.
43. History, 1838–1856, volume C-1 [2 November 1838–31 July 1842], 16 [addenda], http://www.josephsmithpapers.org.
44. History, 1838–1856, volume C-1 [2 November 1838–31 July 1842], 16 [addenda], http://www.josephsmithpapers.org.
45. Joseph Smith, "Thomas Bullock Report," in *Words of Joseph Smith*, 367; Smith, "George Laub Journal," in *Words of Joseph Smith*, 370.
46. See Abraham 3:22–23 (Pearl of Great Price).
47. John Taylor, in *Journal of Discourses*, 21:94.
48. Daniel 7:9, 13, 22.
49. Report of Instructions, between 26 June and 4 August 1839–A, as Reported by Willard Richards, 63, http://www.josephsmithpapers.org.
50. History, 1838–1856, volume C-1 [2 November 1838–31 July 1842], 1307, http://www.josephsmithpapers.org. "Try the Spirits," *Times and Seasons* 3, no. 11 (1 April 1842): 745.
51. Nauvoo Relief Society Minute Book, 36, http://www.josephsmithpapers.org.
52. Smith, in *Wilford Woodruff's Journal*, 2:240.
53. The walls of the Nauvoo Temple were beginning to rise at the time of Smith's murder. Work on the temple continued steadily until most of the Latter-day Saints left Nauvoo under duress of mob violence early in the spring of 1846. Orson Hyde and

others stayed behind the main body of the Latter-day Saints who had crossed the Mississippi to Iowa and worked to finish the interior of the temple.

54. Doctrine and Covenants 132:7. Although recorded in 1843, historical evidence indicates that some of the principles involved in this revelation had been revealed as early as 1831.

55. Joseph Smith, quoted in *Wilford Woodruff's Journal*, 2:341–42. Temple covenants including sealing (marriage) of husband and wife.

56. Matthew 16:19.

57. Mark 3:14.

58. Malachi 4:5–6; Doctrine and Covenants 110:13–15.

59. Smith, in *Wilford Woodruff's Journal*, 2:341. In Doctrine and Covenants 128:18, Smith used the phrase "welding link of some kind or other between the fathers and the children."

60. See Doctrine and Covenants 110:13–15.

61. Smith, in *Wilford Woodruff's Journal*, 2:341.

62. Smith, in *Wilford Woodruff Journal*, 2:362.

63. History, 1838–1856, volume C-1 [2 November 1838–31 July 1842], 1321, http://www.josephsmithpapers.org. See also Smith, "Baptism for the Dead," *Times and Seasons*, 15 April 1842, 760.

64. History, 1838–1856, volume C-1 [2 November 1838–31 July 1842], 1321, http://www.josephsmithpapers.org.

65. History, 1838–1856, volume C-1 [2 November 1838–31 July 1842], 1322, http://www.josephsmithpapers.org.

66. Doctrine and Covenants 132:7.

67. "William Clayton Diary," in *Words of Joseph Smith*, 233; Doctrine and Covenants 132:15.

68. Doctrine and Covenants 132:7.

69. Acts 3:21.

70. Doctrine and Covenants 132:1, 34–38.

71. Jacob 2:24, 27, 28, 30 (Book of Mormon).

72. With these prohibitions as part of the revelation Joseph received, as well as his own reticence, he was torn by the command to take plural wives. Plural marriage, part of the larger revelation recorded in Doctrine and Covenants 132, was a difficult practice for Smith and others to accept who were called to take additional wives. Likely few welcomed the restoration of a biblical practice entirely foreign to their sensibilities. The Lord commanded the adoption—and later the cessation in 1896—of plural marriage, with few instructions. The challenge of introducing a principle as controversial as plural marriage is impossible to overstate. What possibly could have driven Smith to teach "a practice that put his life and his work in jeopardy, not to mention his relationship with Emma?" The history of Joseph Smith demonstrates that he acted on God's commands to him that in turn invited opposition, ostracism, persecution, beatings, mockery in the press, and imprisonment and ended in murder. It appears that plural marriage was one commandment Smith initially resisted. It was an Abrahamic test for both Joseph and Emma. According to a plural wife of Smith, Helen Mar Kimball, Joseph warned, "The practice of this principle would be the hardest trial the Saints would ever have to test their faith." Only a spiritual witness of its truthfulness allowed Smith and other Latter-day Saints to accept this principle—and even then, with great reluctance. Richard L. Bushman, *Joseph Smith: Rough Stone Rolling* (NY: Alfred Knopf, 2005), 441; Steven C. Harper, *Making Sense of the Doctrine & Covenants: A Guided Tour through Modern Revelations* (Salt Lake City: Deseret Book, 2008), 481; Helen Mar Whitney, *Woman's Exponent* 10 (1 November 1881): 83; https://www.lds.org/topics/plural-marriage-in-kirtland-and-nauvoo.

73. History, 1838–1856, volume C-1 [2 November 1838–31 July 1842], 8 [addenda], emphasis in original, http://www.josephsmithpapers.org.

74. "Joseph Smith Diary by Willard Richards," in *Words of Joseph Smith*, 244.

75. Doctrine and Covenants 132:12–18.

76. History, 1838–1856, volume C-1 [2 November 1838–31 July 1842], 1229–30, www.josephsmithpapers.org. See also *Times and Seasons* 2, no. 24 (15 October 1841): 577–78.

77. Doctrine and Covenants 88:15.

78. Miller, *Rube Goldberg Machines*, 39.

79. Givens, *Wrestling the Angel*, 57. Monism is the philosophical term applied to the theory or idea that things are of the same reality or substance.

80. Luke 24:39.

81. The Book of Mormon describes the reunion of the body after death as follows: "Now, there is a death which is called a temporal death; and the death of Christ shall loose the bands of this temporal death, that all shall be raised from this temporal death. The spirit and the body shall be reunited again in its perfect form; both limb and joint shall be restored to its proper frame, even as we now are at this time.... Now, this restoration shall come to all, both old and young, both bond and free, both male and female, both the wicked and the righteous; and even there shall not so much as a hair of their heads be lost; but every thing shall be restored to its perfect frame, as it is now, or in the body.... Now, behold, I have spoken unto you concerning the death of the mortal body, and also concerning the resurrection of the mortal body. I say unto you that this mortal body is raised to an immortal body, that is from death, even from the first death unto life, that they can die no more; their spirits uniting with their bodies, never to be divided; thus the whole becoming spiritual and immortal, that they can no more see corruption." Alma 11:42–45 (Book of Mormon). See also Doctrine and Covenants 88:16.

82. Doctrine and Covenants 76:17.

83. Doctrine and Covenants 76:50–70.

84. For a fuller discussion of theosis, see Givens, *Wrestling the Angel*, 256–315.

85. Moses 1:39.

86. Doctrine and Covenants 76:71.

87. Doctrine and Covenants 76:73, 79.

88. Doctrine and Covenants 76:81.

89. Doctrine and Covenants 76:82, 103.

90. Doctrine and Covenants 76:84–85.

91. Doctrine and Covenants 76:89.

92. Doctrine and Covenants 76:25–38; 1 Corinthians 15:40–42.

93. Discourse, 7 April 1844, as Reported by *Times and Seasons*, 613, http://www.josephsmithpapers.org.

94. Smith, in *Wilford Woodruff's Journal*, 2:385; Discourse, 7 April 1844, as Reported by Wilford Woodruff, 137, http://www.josephsmithpapers.org.

95. Smith, in *Wilford Woodruff's Journal*, 2:386; Discourse, 7 April 1844, as Reported by Wilford Woodruff, 137, http://www.josephsmithpapers.org.

96. Discourse, 7 April 1844, as Reported by *Times and Seasons*, 615, www.josephsmithpapers.org.

97. Bushman, *Joseph Smith: Rough Stone Rolling*, 535–36.

98. Miller, *Rube Goldberg Machines*, 25.

99. Account of Meeting and Discourse, 5 January 1841, as Reported by William Clayton, 6, http://www.josephsmithpapers.org.

100. See Abraham 3:22–28 (Pearl of Great Price); Doctrine and Covenants 93:31; Isaiah 14:12–14; Revelation 12:7–9.

Final Thoughts on Two Restorationists

Although you both professe your Holynesse, Diligence,
Zeale, Courage, Selfe-deny all, Patience, and the one of you the
incomparable spirit of your Fathers in the work of Reforma-
tion; yet we Querie, Whether there hath not been as Holy, Able
and Zealous men since the Aposacie . . . have there not been as
excellent and heavenly Reformers as your selves and Fathers,
whose professed Reformation you now dislike. Who shall out-
shine many of the Waldensian Reformers for Holynesse, Zeale,
patience? Where is, or hath that pretious man been found, who
hath (for personall excellencies) outshined Luther?

—ROGER WILLIAMS, QUERY 6,
Queries of Highest Consideration

Although a superficial examination of Alexander Campbell and Joseph Smith might conclude that the two men taught the same restoration doctrines, they are, in fact, as the last fourteen chapters have illustrated, quite different—on such matters as the nature of the Trinity, the meaning of faith, the gift of the Holy Ghost and manifestations of gifts of the Spirit, revelation, the organization of the church and church offices, priesthood authority, tithing, millennialism, and many other doctrines, principles, and practices. Most uniquely, Smith's views on eternity set him apart not just from Campbell but also from all others. One of the greatest differences between the two restorations is that although both looked to a primordial past and to the millennial future, only Smith claimed to do so through the medium of revelation. Smith was not like Martin Luther or even Alexander Campbell, who pored over the scriptures to revise interpretations of Christian doctrine, or King Josiah, who discovered scrolls that had been neglected when the Jerusalem temple closed. He aspired to be more like Moses, bringing down wholly "new tablets from the mount, to a people still possessed of shadowy recollections of a former, fuller knowledge of Jehovah."[1] Churches of Christ scholars Richard Hughes and Leonard Allen expressed the key differences between Campbell and Smith this way: "If Campbell's movement exalted rationality and shackled the Spirit to the 'facts' and propositions of scripture, Smith's movement exalted the Spirit and revolted against the stark, earth-bound premises of the Disciples."[2]

Much more could be written about both Campbell and Smith. In retrospect, however, one of the most important questions for this volume is "What did Alexander Campbell and Joseph Smith leave as restoration legacies?"

Both men were idealists. Theirs was the hope that in some way their restoration would help prepare for the Millennium. In many ways, the religious tension between them highlighted differences in American culture: enthusiasm versus Enlightenment, rural folk magic versus accepted practices, and sacred land versus manifest destiny. This volume placed them in a nineteenth-century restorationist context and focused on some of their central beliefs, noted their similarities and differences, and highlighted what I believe to be their distinctive contributions. Today, Campbell's unique view of dispensations and adamant denunciation of infant baptism and creeds would probably not give pause to many mainline Protestant groups. He was a restorationist, but he never claimed to be a prophet receiving revelation, as Smith did. For that reason, Smith's movement still causes questions about his supernatural claims and divinely ordained status.

ALEXANDER CAMPBELL'S LEGACY

Alexander Campbell was husband to Margaret Brown, and after her death he married Selina Bakewell. He was the father to fourteen children, ten of whom preceded him in death. His friends fondly called him the "sage of Bethany" and the "Bishop of Bethany." Although Protestant by background, he had separated himself from mainstream, formal

Protestantism and preferred to be referred to simply as a Christian and a disciple. His movement, in contrast to most Protestant denominations, taught four simple steps to salvation: faith, repentance, baptism, and the Holy Spirit—with no creeds or confessions. He was at the forefront of an ecumenical movement for the unity of all Christians amidst a diversity of opinions. He applied reason to his interpretation of scripture and made friends and enemies as he sought to reform and restore ancient Christianity.

Campbell had many proponents, some of whom were well known in American political circles. He was a proud delegate to the Virginia Constitutional Convention in 1829 and 1830, which placed him in the company of founding fathers and former presidents James Madison and James Monroe. Campbell juxtaposed the great political happiness of individuals under the political institutions developed in the United States to the even greater happiness found by those who followed the Christian system which was bestowed on them by a gracious God.[3] He gave credit to the Protestant reformers for America's national privileges and civil liberties and contrasted them with those in Spanish America, England, Spain, Portugal, and Italy. He made no secret of his animosity to what he perceived as the impious, haughty, and arrogant pretensions and the tyrannical rule of the Holy Roman See.[4]

He was acknowledged as "the greatest promoter of this reformation," meaning the "restoration of the ancient order of things" and a return to primitive Christianity. He was one of its chief founders and strongest publishers and its foremost debater, speaker, and leader. During his lifetime, he produced more than sixty volumes of his thinking.[5] He was probably as well known as any religious figure of the mid-frontier between 1830 and 1860.[6] Campbell was equally comfortable discussing mutual problems with his neighborhood farmers, enjoying the company of a British consul, or sitting as a dinner guest of President James Buchanan in the White House.[7] Some of the notable guests who sat around his dinner table included Jefferson Davis, future president of the Confederacy; James A. Garfield, trustee of Bethany College, president of Bethany's daughter institution, Hiram College, and future president of the United States; and Judge Jeremiah Black, US attorney general under President Buchanan. When Campbell traveled to Europe in 1847 on a speaking tour, he carried a letter of introduction from former secretary of state Henry Clay lauding Campbell as one of "the most eminent citizens of the United States, distinguished for his learning and ability, for his successful devotion to the education of youth, for his piety and as the head and founder of one of the most important and respectable religious communities in the United States."[8]

Although written in 1843, over twenty years before his death, the following quotation points to Campbell's own evaluation of his life's work:

> I thank God and take courage from every effort, however imperfect it may be, to open the eyes of the community to the impotency and wickedness of schism.... The reformation for which we plead grew out of a conviction of the enormous evils of schism and partyism.... The abjuration of human creeds ... as the permanent causes of all sectarianism, was set forth as a preliminary step to the purification of the church.... The restoration of a pure speech, or the giving of Bible names to Bible ideas, followed in its train, and ... we have been led, step by step, to our present position, each one of the prime movers adding to the common stock something of importance, until matters have issued in one of the most extensive moral and ecclesiastical movements and revolutions of the present age.[9]

Alexander Campbell, ca. 1860, by Edward Dean Neuenswander.

Campbell saw himself as carrying the banner for Christian unity by fighting against creeds and restoring the pure language of the scriptures. He saw his restoration movement as a crucial part in the revolution against sectarian Christianity.

Late in his life, Campbell undertook the responsibility to help place Bethany College, his own creation, on firm financial footing and to secure funds for replacing a building that had burned. Of these efforts he stated, "If I did not feel that it is the Lord's work, and that he will be my helper, I would shrink from the task. I sometimes feel like asking to be relieved from further service, but it seems I cannot hope to rest from my labors, till I am called also to rest with my fathers.... Therefore, all my days shall be given to the Lord."[10] Campbell wore out his life in dedication to the tasks he believed God had given him.

Walter Scott, credited as one of the major contributors to the Campbell restoration movement, wrote that three successive steps had been taken in returning the gospel to its original institution: "First the Bible was adopted as sole authority in our assemblies, to the exclusion of all other books. Next the Apostolic order was proposed. Finally the True Gospel was restored." Richard Hughes suggests that what Scott meant is that "Thomas Campbell had restored the Bible as authoritative, Alexander Campbell had restored the 'ancient order' (worship and organization of the church) through his articles in the *Christian Baptist*, and he himself [Scott] had restored the ancient gospel by means of the five-point plan of salvation."[11] Thus, contemporary and coreligionist Walter Scott recognized Alexander Campbell's crucial influence in restoring the primitive New Testament gospel. Toward the end of his life, when he was writing his autobiography, Barton Stone acknowledged Campbell as "the greatest promoter of this Reformation of any man living." In a kind and generous compliment, Stone observed, "I will not say there are no faults in brother Campbell; but that there are fewer, perhaps, in him, than any man I know on earth; and over these few my love would draw a veil, and hide them from view forever."[12]

One Presbyterian minister, on hearing Campbell preach on the exaltation of the risen Christ found in Psalm 24, proclaimed his discourse "the most impressive demonstration of divine eloquence he had ever heard."[13] Campbell captivated well-known Americans with his speaking ability. Former president James Madison, who served with Campbell on the Virginia Constitutional Convention of 1829, declared that while Campbell had acquitted himself well during the convention, "it is as a theologian that Mr. Campbell must be known. It was my pleasure to hear him very often as a preacher of the gospel, and I regard him as the ablest and most original expounder of the Scriptures I have ever heard."[14] General Robert E. Lee quoted words written about John Milton and redirected them as compliments about Campbell. Lee said Campbell was "a man who, if he had been delegated as a representative of his species to one of the many superior worlds, would have suggested a grand idea of the human race."[15]

Judge Jeremiah Sullivan Black, chief justice of Pennsylvania and later attorney general of the United States, also testified of Campbell's unusual speaking talent. He described Campbell's ability to hold his audience spellbound—not by eloquence or human wisdom but with logic, explanation, and clear argument. "But all this," Black declared, "does not account for the impressiveness of his speeches, and no analysis of them can give any idea of their power."[16]

Right Reverend John B. Purcell, bishop of Cincinnati and Campbell's debate opponent in 1837, had high words of praise: "Campbell was decidedly the fairest man in debate I ever saw, as fair as you can possibly conceive. He never fought for victory. . . . He seemed to always be fighting for the truth, or what he believed to be the truth. In this he differed from other men. He never misrepresented his case, nor that of his opponent."[17]

Robert Graham, president of the University of Kentucky, admired everything about Campbell. He found him an excellent lecturer and superior to all he knew at the pulpit, appealing to old, young, educated, and uneducated. In his opinion, "no one could listen to him and not confess him to be one of the greatest men of his age."[18] Similarly, Dr. Heman Humphrey, a Presbyterian doctor and former president of Amherst College, heard Campbell speak twice. He described him as "the most perfectly self-possessed, the most perfectly at ease in the pulpit, of any preacher I ever listened to. . . . In laying out his work his statements are simple, clear and concise, his topics are well and logically arranged, his manner is calm and deliberate, but full of assurance. . . . In listening to him you feel that you are in the presence of a great man."[19] In 1850 he wrote, "Mr. Campbell has for more than twenty years wielded a power over men's minds, on the subject of religion, which has no parallel in the Protestant history of this country, nor of the Romish either."[20]

George D. Prentice, the editor of the *Louisville Journal*, called Campbell "unquestionably one of the most extraordinary men of our time." Although not agreeing with Campbell's point of view, Prentice noted that "his achievements [give him] a place among the foremost spirits of our age . . . [belonging] only to the world's first leaders in thought and action." Prentice vouched for Campbell's character and declared his intellectual gifts "among the clearest, richest, [and] profoundest." Particularly he believed that Campbell's abstract thinking and pure thought processes had "few, if any, living rivals." Prentice pronounced him "a part of the common treasure of society . . . [belonging] to no sect or party, but to the world."[21]

Campbell, a few years prior to his death, published a volume of his *Popular Lectures and Addresses*. In the publisher's preface to the book, an unnamed editor wrote, "No man of the present age has been more frequently before the public, both in his addresses, debates, and writings than Alexander Campbell; and the impress of his mind he has left on the age, and will leave to future generations."[22]

At Campbell's death on 4 March 1866, William Kimbrough Pendleton, his son-in-law and a later coeditor of the *Millennial Harbinger*, eulogized Campbell's long career with the following words: "His great fame attracted to his public appointments vast concourses of hearers, and he was accustomed to address such almost daily, for several hours at a time—and not unfrequently two or three times a day. . . . Throngs would collect to hear him *talk* [and] . . . his tours would be almost an endless monologue. Nobody wished to talk in his presence."[23] Joseph King, a pastor in the Christian Church at Allegheny City, Pennsylvania, declared the following in a memorial sermon:

> Mr. Campbell was no ordinary man. He was a "great man" in every sense of the word. He was wonderfully gifted. He had the talents of an angel almost, and he consecrated them, without reserve, to the service of Christ. He wielded a power and exerted an influence which no other man in the nation exerted. And I think it no exaggeration to say that the greatest mind in the nation passed to the better land, when Alexander Campbell breathed his last. He was an independent thinker, a vigorous writer, a logical debater, a polished, classical speaker, and a most courteous Christian gentleman.[24]

Alexander's eloquence was noted it seemed by all who heard him—young and old. In a book published in 1867, just a year after Campbell's death, the editor to Campbell's *Familiar Lectures on the Pentateuch* wrote this dedication: "To the students of Bethany College who have listened to 'the old man eloquent,' and will readily recognize in these lectures much that is familiar, is this attempt to revive sweet memories."[25]

In 1875, at the unveiling and dedication of a marble bust of Alexander Campbell in Bethany, Virginia, Judge Jeremiah Black reminisced with the following accolades:

> As a great preacher, he will be remembered with unqualified admiration by all who had the good fortune to hear him in the prime of his life. The interest which he excited in a large congregation can hardly be explained. The first sentence of his discourse "drew audience still as death," and every word was heard with rapt attention to the close. It did not appear to be eloquence; it was not the enticing words of man's wisdom; the arts of the orator seemed to be inconsistent with the grand simplicity of his character. It was logic, explanation and argument so clear that everybody followed it without an effort, and all felt that it

was raising them to the level of a superior mind. Persuasion sat upon his lips. Prejudice melted away under the easy flow of his elocution. The clinching fact was always in its proper place, and the fine poetic illustration was ever at hand to shed its light over the theme.[26]

More recently, Pepperdine University Churches of Christ scholar Thomas Olbricht, examining Campbell's contemporary relevance, claimed that Campbell's heirs—the Christian Church (Disciples of Christ) and the Christian Churches/Churches of Christ—"owe much more to him than [they] acknowledge."[27] Robert Oldham Fife, a professor at Milligan College and Emmanuel Christian Seminary, echoing similar sentiments, declared, "On both sides of the Atlantic, Alexander Campbell was among the best known religious leaders of his generation." Fife queried, "What other American religious leader was invited to speak to the London Society of Skeptics?" Yet "he is less known, or grossly misunderstood, by many modern religious leaders, even less known to American historians and almost completely unknown to the American public." Fife further lamented, "Joseph Smith, the obscure charlatan, is far more well known in this country than Alexander Campbell."[28]

Other current scholarship cites Campbell's defense of Christianity against all comers as having "established him as the most significant apologist for the Christian religion in antebellum America."[29] Campbell challenged Enlightenment-inspired, philosophical skeptics and free-thought societies, corresponded with individuals answering questions regarding differences between Christianity and Judaism, condemned the Transcendentalist movement, and as noted earlier in this book responded to "the snare of the Devil"—Joseph Smith and the Book of Mormon—with his article "Delusions." Aptly, his grave monument reads, "Defender of the faith once delivered to the saints."

JOSEPH SMITH'S LEGACY

Smith's conception of revelation was unique among Christians of the nineteenth century. He taught that dialogue between heaven and earth was not limited to biblical times but also occurred in his day, what he called the latter days. At the dawn of his foray as a prophet of God and again at its sunset, Joseph Smith made clear that he felt compelled in his life's mission by God. As a fourteen-year-old he declared that despite the persecution he received, "I had seen a vision; I knew it, and I knew that

God knew it, and I could not deny it, neither dared I do it; at least I knew that by so doing I would offend God, and come under condemnation."[30] As a thirty-seven-year-old, he asserted, "If I had not actually got into this work, & been called of God, I would back out, . . . but I cannot back out. I have no doubt of the truth."[31] To those who could not accept his testimony he granted forbearance: "I don't blame any one for not believing my history; if I had not experienced what I have I could not have believed it myself."[32]

Persecuted and forced out of New York, Ohio, and Missouri by those who disagreed with his religious teachings, one city offered him and his followers refuge. When Smith arrived in Quincy, Illinois, in April 1839 after his incarceration in Missouri, a St. Louis reporter wrote, "We had supposed from the stories and statements we had read of 'Jo Smith' (as he is termed in the papers) to find him a very illiterate, uncouth sort of man; but from a long conversation, he appears intelligent and candid, and divested of all malicious thought and feeling toward his relentless persecutors."[33]

In late 1839 and early 1840, Smith spent the winter in Washington, DC, attempting to obtain redress from the federal government for the Missouri persecution. One newspaper reporter wrote the following of the situation:

> Joe Smith, the leader and prophet of the sect, who professes to have received the golden plates on which the Mormon creed was transcribed, and who has figured so conspicuously in fight, is a tall muscular man, with a countenance not absolutely unintellectual. On the contrary, [he] exhibits much shrewdness of character. . . . His general appearance is that of a plain yeoman, intended rather for the cultivation of the soil, than the expounding of prophecy. Without the advantage of education, he has applied himself, with much industry to the acquisition of knowledge; . . . he converses very fluently on the subject nearest to his heart, and whatever may be thought of the correctness of his opinions, no one who talks with him, can doubt that his convictions of their truth are sincere and settled. His eye betokens a resolute spirit, and he would doubtless go to the stake to attest his firmness and devotion.[34]

Matthew Davis, a New York journalist, also in Washington, and curious to understand Smith's teachings, listened to him give a lecture in 1840 and wrote to his wife the following:

He is not an educated Man: but he is a plain, sensible, strong minded man. Everything he says, is said in a manner to leave an impression that he is sincere, There is no levity, no fanaticism, no want of dignity in his deportment. He is apparently from 40 to 45 years of age, rather above the middle stature, and what you ladies would call a very good looking man. In his garb there are no peculiarities, his dress being that of a plain, unpretending Citizen. He is, by profession, a farmer; but is evidently well read.[35]

As the newspaper article and Matthew Davis had commented on Smith's lack of education, so did John Taylor, an educated follower who noted, "He was ignorant of letters as the world has it, but the most profoundly learned and intelligent man that I ever met in my life."[36]

James Arlington Bennet—an attorney, newspaper publisher, educator, and author—wrote to Smith in 1843 regarding his restoration movement, calling him a "philosophical divine." He complimented him on his bold "plans & measures, together with their unparalleled Success" which so far, according to Bennet, had thrown a charm over Smith and singled him out "as the most extraordinary man of the present Age."[37] Responding to Bennet's generous compliments six months prior to his death, Smith made his own assessment of his contributions to Christianity. First, Smith clarified the proper use of Bennet's phrase "boldness of the plans and measures" and declared that they "should be denominated the righteousness of the cause, the truth of the system and power of God." Smith recognized the hand of God in all his accomplishments, including "the boldness of the plan of preaching and <the boldness of the measures—> declaring repentance and baptism for the remission of sins; and a reception of the Holy Ghost, by laying on <of the> hands agreeably to the authority of the priesthood; and the still more bold measures of receiving direct revelation from God . . . [and] the gathering of the Saints." Smith considered himself extraordinary only insofar as "truth is mighty and will prevail; and that one man empowered from Jehovah, has more influence with the children of the kingdom than eight hundred million led by the precepts of men."[38]

In 1844, just weeks before Smith was killed, Josiah Quincy—a nineteenth-century writer, publicist, and future mayor of Boston—visited him in Nauvoo, Illinois. Although skeptical of what Smith told him, he wrote many years later, "At some future time, the question may be asked, 'What great American has done more to mold the minds and destiny of his countrymen than any other man upon this continent?'

Absurd as it may seem to some, it is not improbable that the answer to this question will be, Joseph Smith, the Mormon prophet."[39]

On 7 June 1844, the *Nauvoo Expositor* press, founded by apostate Mormons and others, printed its only issue, which was critical of Smith and some of his teachings. On 10 June, Mayor Smith and the Nauvoo City Council declared the press to be a nuisance and ordered the city marshal to destroy it. On 12 June, this action brought officers from Carthage, Illinois, to arrest Smith for destruction of the press and charge him with committing riot by declaring martial law. Smith sought help from the Nauvoo Municipal Court through a writ of habeas corpus "from being thrown into the power of the mobocrats" and was discharged. That same day, Thomas Sharp wrote an inflammatory editorial in his *Warsaw Signal*, a neighboring county newspaper. It stated, "War and extermination is inevitable! *Citizens* ARISE, ONE and ALL!!!—Can you *stand* by, and suffer such INFERNAL DEVILS! to ROB men of their property and RIGHTS, without avenging them. We have no time for comment, every man will make his own. LET IT BE MADE WITH POWDER AND BALL!!!"[40]

On 14 June, in defense of his actions, Smith wrote Illinois governor Thomas Ford regarding the actions he and the city council had taken: "The press was declared a nuisance under the authority of the charter as written in 7th section of Addenda, the same as in the Springfield charter."[41] Governor Ford promised Smith that no harm would come to him if he would allow himself to be taken to jail in Carthage to stand trial.[42] Others knew differently. Smith submitted to arrest but lamented, "I am going like a lamb to the slaughter, but I am calm as a summer's morning. I have a conscience void of offense toward God and toward all men. If they take my life I shall die an innocent man, . . . and it shall be said of me He was murdered in cold blood."[43] Frank Worrell, an officer of the guard of Carthage Jail, predicted on 27 June, "We have had too much trouble to bring Old Joe' here to let him ever escape alive. . . . You'll see that I can prophesy better than Old Joe,' that neither he nor his brother, nor anyone who will remain with them, will see the sun set today."[44] On that same day, Governor Ford left Carthage for Nauvoo in order to issue a warning to the Mormons: "A great crime has been done by destroying the *Expositor* press and placing the city under martial law, and a severe atonement must be made, so prepare your minds for the emergency."[45] Late that afternoon, a mob estimated to be between one hundred and two hundred armed men with blackened faces, many from the disbanded Warsaw militia, stormed the Carthage Jail. Smith was shot five times while trying to jump from a window—likely to save the lives of the other men who were with him in the jail cell. He died at the age of thirty-eight not only as a prophet-leader but also as the mayor of Nauvoo, Illinois, the lieutenant general of the Nauvoo Legion, and a candidate for president of the United States.

After Smith's martyrdom, Willard Richards, who was present in the jail with Smith on that fateful afternoon, wrote the following heroic summary of many of Smith's accomplishments in the eyes of his followers:[46]

> In the short space of twenty years, he has brought forth the Book of Mormon, . . . the revelations and commandments which compose this book of Doctrine and Covenants, and many other wise documents and instructions for the benefit of the children of men; gathered many thousands of Latter-day Saints, founded a great city, and left a fame and name that cannot be slain. He lived great, and he died great in the eyes of God and his people; and like most of the Lord's anointed in ancient times, has sealed his mission and his works with his own blood.[47]

Unfortunately, the false allegations of early anti-Mormon writers Philastus Hurlbut and Eber Howe, the mistaken accusations of Walter Scott and Adamson Bentley, and Campbell's own enmity against the radical Mormon leader had prejudiced him sufficiently that when news of Joseph and Hyrum Smith's murder reached him, Campbell wrote the following in the September 1844 issue of the *Millennial Harbinger*: "Joseph Smith and his brother have been providentially cut off in the midst of their diabolical career," calling Smith "the money-digger, the juggler, and the founder of the Golden Bible delusion."[48] Nevertheless, Campbell deplored the lawless behavior of those who murdered the brothers.

In an 1855 memoir, John Reynolds, governor of Illinois from 1830 to 1834 and US congressman from 1834 to 1839, wrote about meeting Smith in Washington, DC:

> I had received letters, as well as the other Democratic members of congress, that Smith was a very important character in Illinois. . . . He stood at the time fair and honorable, as far as we knew . . . , except his fanaticism on religion. The sympathies of the people were in his favor. . . . In all the great events and revolutions in the various nations of the earth nothing surpasses the extraordinary history of the Mormons. The facts in relation to this singular people are so strange,

so opposite to common-sense, and so great and important, that they would not obtain our belief if we did not see the events transpire before our eyes. No argument, or mode of reasoning, could induce any one to believe that in the nineteenth century, in the United States, and in the blaze of science, literature, and civilization, a sect of religionists could arise on delusion and imposition.... This sect, amid persecutions and perils of all sorts, has reached almost half a million souls, scattered over various countries within twenty-five or thirty years.[49]

Reynolds met with Smith over the winter of 1839 in regard to his petitions on behalf of the Mormons and became well acquainted with him. He described him as "a person rather larger than ordinary stature, well proportioned, and would weigh ... about one hundred and eighty pounds. . . . In his appearance amiable and benevolent. He did not appear to possess any harshness or barbarity in his composition, nor did he appear to possess that great talent and boundless mind that would enable him to accomplish the wonders he performed." Reynolds, unable to reconcile Smith's background and education with his accomplishments, made this prediction: "No one can fore tell the destiny of this sect, and it would be blasphemy, at this day, to

Joseph Smith, ca. 1840, by Edward Dean Neuenswander.

compare its founder to the Saviour, but, nevertheless it may become veritable history, in a thousand years, that the standing and character of Joseph Smith, as a prophet, may rank equal to any of the prophets who have preceded him."[50]

In 1855, Brigham Young, successor to Smith as president of the Mormon Church, exuberantly declared, "I feel like shouting Hallelujah, all the time, when I think that I ever knew Joseph Smith, the Prophet whom the Lord raised up and ordained, and to whom He gave keys and power to build up the kingdom of God on earth."[51] Another of Smith's close associates, Orson Pratt, called him "the great Seer of the last days, who, as an instrument in the hands of the Lord, laid the foundation of the Kingdom of God, preparatory to the second coming of the Messiah to reign with universal dominion over all the Earth."[52] Parley Pratt, a former adherent of Campbell's beliefs, testified as he lay dying in 1857, "I die a firm believer in the Gospel of Jesus Christ as revealed through the Prophet Joseph Smith. . . . I know that the Gospel is true and that Joseph Smith was a prophet of the living God."[53]

In 1992, Harold Bloom—a Jewish modern-American literary and religious critic, although skeptical of the possibility of Christian restorationism because he did not believe in the legitimacy of the primitive church—stated, "Whatever his lapses, Smith was an authentic religious genius, unique in our national history." In critiquing the Wentworth Letter, Bloom acknowledged its dignity, its simple eloquence, and the confidence "of a religious innovator who is so secure in the truth of his doctrine that he can state its pith with an almost miraculous economy." He praised the letter as a celebration of "the organization of a people on the basis of a spiritual idea." Even though he believed Smith's insights indicated genius in Bible reading, he also believed they were a creative misreading of early Jewish history. In particular, he commented that this reading of the Bible "found its way back to elements that Smith rightly intuited had been censored out of the stories of the archaic Jewish religion." It was "Smith's radical sense of theomorphic patriarchs and anthropomorphic gods" that Bloom called "an authentic return to J, or the Yahwist, the Bible's first author."[54] Bloom marveled at what he called Smith's "intuitive understanding of the permanent religious dilemmas of our country."[55] What impressed Bloom the most was "the sureness of his instincts, his uncanny *knowing* precisely what is needful for the inauguration of a new faith. . . . The Mormons, like the Jews before them, are a religion that became a people," thus assuring their survival.[56] In Bloom's mind, there was no doubt "that Joseph Smith was an authentic prophet." He queried, "Where in all of American history can we find his match?"[57] He declared, "There is no other figure remotely like him in our entire national history, and it is unlikely that anyone like him ever can come again." In his own prophetic hyperbole, Bloom continued, "We do not know Joseph Smith. . . . He requires strong poets, major novelists, accomplished dramatists to tell his history, and they have not yet come to him."[58]

Robert V. Remini, in a recent biography on Smith, drew the following conclusions about him and his restoration movement:

> To a large extent Smith and his Church were products of a uniquely American milieu. The Jacksonian age with its democratic thrust and reach for perfection provided the conditions and impetus for sudden

and massive changes throughout the country. . . . During the Second Great Awakening those forces brought about the violent death of a decent man who claimed to be a prophet of God. But they could not extinguish his message or the promise he made to his followers of their ultimate triumph. They could not prevent the Church of Jesus Christ of Latter-day Saints from achieving global recognition and acceptance.[59]

Terryl Givens, a Mormon literary scholar, identified what he called Smith's greatest accomplishment—the creation of a community. The quality of this community, not its rate of increase, is what Givens claims has made Smith's contributions lasting. In Givens's estimation, Smith's greatness lies in the fact that his movement transcended his historical era and invigorates people throughout the world today. Givens summarized Smith's restoration as bringing back "a correct understanding of the divine nature, of human nature, and of their relationships to each other."[60]

Richard Hughes declared that Smith "clearly draws on the biblical vision in ways that dwarf every other nineteenth-century American preacher or would-be prophet. For Joseph refused to confine himself to the New Testament or the Old Testament or to certain sections of the Bible that he found most useful. Instead, Joseph ranged throughout the Bible and drew from it all." He was "unwilling to confine [himself] to a single book or to a single sacred epoch as did traditional restorationists" and was "like [a] bee sucking nectar first from this flower and then from the next." He moved with ease "from the primitive church to Moses to the prophets of Abraham to Adam and finally to the coming millennium."[61]

Richard Bushman, Joseph Smith's most noted biographer, wrote:

Joseph Smith's experiences can be compared to reports from the visionaries of his time, just as he can be linked to other nineteenth-century cultures—universalism, rational skepticism, republicanism, progress, revivalism, magic, communitarianism, health reform, restorationism, Zionism, and a host of others. But no one of these cultures or even all of them added together encompasses the whole of his thought. Joseph went beyond them all and produced a culture and society that the visionaries around him could not imagine. Visions and revelations lay at the core of [his] restoration.[62]

Despite what these men said, Smith knew that his story strained credulity, declaring, "No man knows my history; I cannot tell it. I shall never undertake it; if I had not experienced what I have, I should not have known [believed] it myself."[63] While some see him primarily as a product of the nineteenth century, impacted by the currents of his day, he claimed his restoration came from without—from visions, angels, revelations from God, and direction of the Holy Spirit and not his own abilities. Nevertheless, his creativity and energy had to organize those transcendent events into a coherent human endeavor.[64]

Mormon philosopher David Paulsen reviewed a number of theories and theorists suggesting naturalistic origins to the doctrines taught by Joseph Smith and came to the following conclusion: "All explanations to date are, at best, partial, neither individually nor collectively even beginning to account for all Mormon doctrines considered severally let alone for their unique synthesis in the teachings of Joseph Smith. . . . There is no cultural antecedent."[65] Bushman discovered that while culture may have shaped Smith's questions, it was not the source of his answers. In fact, he "is best understood as a person who outgrew the culture."[66]

CONCLUSION

Common experiences for Alexander Campbell and Joseph Smith included religiously minded fathers whom they deeply admired. Thomas Campbell was "churched" but withdrew from his father's church. He sought answers about his own salvation and eventually felt called by the Spirit to become a minister. Joseph Smith Sr. grew up in a family of "seekers." As he studied the scriptures and listened to preachers, he was not content with any church; however, he had dreams that he would find salvation for himself and his family.[67] Both Campbell and Smith confessed that in their teen years they were boys with the usual distractions and follies of their age; however, as they matured, their reflections became more serious and appropriate for what they were to become.[68] Both discovered that Presbyterianism was not the right church for them.[69] They had unique spiritual experiences that brought them closer to God. Alexander feared for his life, with legitimate apprehensions. For example, both of the times he and his mother and siblings set sail for America, he feared that they could have drowned. These experiences caused him to reflect deeply on life's purposes and convinced him that he would preach the gospel all his days. Joseph's formative experiences included a typhus fever infection that lodged in his leg, causing the doctors to contemplate amputation, as well as the death of a beloved older brother. Both Campbell and Smith experienced sobering realities at young ages.

Their differences on reason-driven and revelation-directed Christianity caused the religious movements they initiated to be very different, even though they started out with several ideas in common: (1) each heeded the counsel of Jude, "earnestly contend[ing] for the faith which was once delivered unto the saints;"[70] (2) each searched for truth by carefully examining the scriptures; (3) each believed that faith should appeal to the head and the heart;[71] and (4) each emphasized the principles of faith and repentance, followed by the ordinance of baptism by immersion for the remission of sins, and receipt of the Holy Ghost. Additionally, (5) both taught of an apostasy in the early Christian church and determined that the Protestant Reformation was not sufficient to restore Christ's church; (6) both rejected the five central doctrinal statements connected with Calvinism, as well as the creeds and confessions of faith that were commonly recited and required for communion; (7) both characterized the Apostle John's revelation (Revelation 14:6–7) as defining their points in their respective restoration and millennial ideas; (8) both sought unity and the undoing of sectarianism by offering what each hoped would prove irresistible grounds for Christian union; and (9) each started a denomination with names that indicated absolute faith in the Son of God—the Disciples of Christ and the Church of Christ.[72]

Both of these restorers of the ancient order shared their understanding of the gospel of Jesus Christ in their sermons and writings. Campbell believed all people could understand the New Testament if they would each individually apply the tools of the Enlightenment—with reasoned logic and rational thinking, they too, by deduction, could come to the same conclusions he had. Thus, clergyman and layman stood as equals in interpreting the scriptures. According to Smith's followers, one of his greatest contributions was receiving revelation and sharing his visionary experiences with others. From the beginning, Smith invited his associates to share in his otherworldly experiences. "God hath not revealed any thing to Joseph, but what he will make known unto the Twelve & even the least Saint may know all things as fast as he is able to bear them."[73] His ability to connect his followers with heaven was an important key to his success.[74]

Alexander Campbell and Joseph Smith were seekers for the pristine church of Jesus Christ. They each felt an internal drive, a divine commission, a certitude in the direction they took in bringing forth their restorations. From their efforts came their respective restoration movements and churches. The well-educated Campbell utilized the tools of the Enlightenment to read the scriptures, pointing out where the Reformation had failed to reject extrabiblical forms and structures. Smith, with little formal education, testified he had been enlightened by God and added numerous visions and revelations to his newly expanded canon. Both men believed a restoration was essential—their prayerful reveries of how to accomplish that goal were divergent—one reducing and the other ever expanding. Campbell, living a long life to age seventy-seven, wore out his life in service to God in "restoring the ancient order of things"; Smith lived to a little more than thirty-eight years, dedicating most of his life to his prophetic responsibility to "restore the dispensation of the fullness of times" before dying a martyr's death.

Because there is no central organization and congregations are autonomous, the number of Campbell's followers is an estimate. Henry Webb estimates that during Campbell's lifetime, his Disciples of Christ followers numbered 350,000 by 1870 and 1,120,000 by the turn of the century.[75] The two major restoration movements that derive from Alexander Campbell and Barton Stone are the Christian Church (Disciples of Christ) and the Christian Churches/Churches of Christ. From Smith's movement, Nauvoo, the last city he and his people settled and developed, contained approximately 10,000 inhabitants; the religious affiliation of many but not all would have been Mormon. There were numerous breakoffs from Smith's movement after his death; however, the major group which went west to Utah with Brigham Young numbered about 16,000 by 1852, and 80,000 had made the trek by 1869. These approximations demonstrate that Campbell had a much larger number of adherents in the nineteenth century—as much as four times as many—than Smith by 1870.

What then is the *sine qua non*—the indispensable ingredient? For Campbell, although forms and structures were important, unity leading to the Millennium was the essential component. For Smith, on the organizational level it was apostles and prophets who have priesthood keys, and on an experiential level it is the revelation and the extraordinary gifts of the Spirit, including visions, visitations, revelations, and miracles of all sorts. As one examines Campbell's and Smith's claims, their basic premises are so very different: scholarship versus apostleship; reasoned, enlightened, biblical acumen versus priesthood authority from God received by the laying on of hands; subtraction of scriptures to core practices versus the addition of scripture and revelation. Their epistemologies are confounding: thoughtful analysis by the power of rational thinking versus asking in faith, nothing doubting; doctrine by reasoning through the scriptures versus doctrine through revelation from heaven. One was a brilliant theologian for God; the other claimed to be a prophet of God. One embraced Christian rationalism and the sufficiency of the scriptures; the other embraced spiritual gifts and revelatory new canon.

How can these two men be evaluated? One way might be to assess how closely they reached the goal of restoring the ancient order of things. By taking what Campbell advocated in his numerous writings and comparing them to the New Testament, one can appraise how closely he came to imitating apostolic Christianity. Similarly, one can note how closely Smith came to imitating any one of several dispensations, including the Adamic and apostolic eras. Their thinking and writing can be apprehended by intellectual means; however, one must turn also to the test of the Holy Spirit as reflected in the feelings and impressions of the heart. Campbell's restoration occurred primarily by reasoned thinking and should be comprehended the same way. Just as Smith's restoration occurred primarily through personal revelation, his restoration must be comprehended the same way.

Even though Campbell and Smith understood restoration differently, one's admiration for their idealism within a generally skeptical and cynical nineteenth-century society increases as they are studied more thoroughly. Gospel purity for Campbell came through the pronouncements of the apostolic New Testament church. Gospel purity for Smith came through collecting everything Jehovah had ever revealed, did then reveal, or would yet reveal. Whatever gospel purity means for the reader, the striving for purity in Christianity in order to restore the church of Christ appears as perhaps a naive effort. And yet the efforts of Alexander Campbell and Joseph Smith to reform and restore purity in Christ's message and church continue to impact spirituality in the United States and throughout the world.

Notes

1. Givens, *By the Hand of Mormon*, 48.
2. Hughes and Allen, *Illusions of Innocence*, 153.
3. Campbell, *Christian System*, 180.
4. Campbell, *Christian System*, 3.
5. Archibald McLean, *Alexander Campbell as a Preacher* (New York: Fleming H. Revell, 1908), 1.

6. Foster et al., *Encyclopedia of the Stone-Campbell Movement*, 113.
7. Richardson, *Memoirs of Alexander Campbell*, 2:499, 543; Foster et al., eds., *Encyclopedia of the Stone-Campbell Movement*, 115.
8. Richardson, *Memoirs of Alexander Campbell*, 2:548.
9. Campbell, "Christian Union, No. 10, Evangelical Alliance, No. 5," *Millennial Harbinger* 3, no. 4 (1847): 253–54; Richardson, *Memoirs of Alexander Campbell*, 1:541.
10. Campbell, "Our Projected Tour for Bethany College," *Millennial Harbinger* 5, no. 1 (January 1858): 47–48.
11. Hughes, *Reviving the Ancient Faith*, 53. See chapter 5 for a discussion of Scott's five points: faith, repentance, baptism, remission of sins, and gift of the Holy Spirit.
12. Richard Collins, *Collin's Historical Sketches of Kentucky* (Covington, KY: Collins, 1882), 426.
13. Foster et al., *Encyclopedia of the Stone-Campbell Movement*, 112–13.
14. Richardson, *Memoirs of Alexander Campbell*, 2:313.
15. Champ Clark, "Alexander Campbell, Barton W. Stone, and Walter Scott," in *Centennial Convention Report: One Hundredth Anniversary of the Disciples of Christ* (Cincinnati: Standard Publishing, 1909), 378.
16. McLean, *Alexander Campbell as a Preacher*, 10.
17. Haley, *Debates That Made History*, 14.
18. McLean, *Alexander Campbell as a Preacher*, 11.
19. Richardson, *Memoirs of Alexander Campbell*, 1:582.
20. Foster et al., *Encyclopedia of the Stone-Campbell Movement*, 113.
21. McLean, *Alexander Campbell as a Preacher*, 43–44.
22. Campbell, *Popular Lectures and Addresses*, v.
23. W. K. Pendleton, "Death of Alexander Campbell," *The Millennial Harbinger Abridged* 2, no. 15 (1902): 572.
24. Joseph King, "A Memorial Sermon on the Occasion of the Death of Alexander Campbell," *The Millennial Harbinger Abridged* 2, no. 15 (1902): 584.
25. Campbell, *Familiar Lectures on the Pentateuch*, iii.
26. Mary Black Clayton, *Reminiscences of Jeremiah Sullivan Black* (St. Louis: Christian Publishing, 1887), 76.
27. Thomas H. Olbricht, "The Relevance of Alexander Campbell for Today," *Restoration Quarterly* 30, nos. 1–2 (1988): 168.
28. Robert Oldham Fife, "Campbell's Future Influence on Disciples of Christ, Christian Churches, and Churches of Christ," *Impact* 21, no. 1 (1988): 9, 11.
29. Cherok, *Debating for God*, 159.
30. Joseph Smith—History 1:25.
31. Andrew H. Hedges, Alex D. Smith, and Richard Lloyd Anderson, eds., *Journals, Volume 2: December 1841–April 1843*, vol. 2 of the Journals series of *The Joseph Smith Papers*, ed. Dean C. Jessee, Ronald K. Esplin, and Richard Lyman Bushman (Salt Lake City: Church Historian's Press, 2008), 337.
32. History, 1838–1856, volume E-1 [1 July 1843–30 April 1844], 1979, www.josephsmithpapers.org.
33. *St. Louis Daily Missouri Republican* (St. Louis), 3 May 1839.
34. *Adams Sentinel* (Gettysburg, PA), 30 December 1839.
35. History, 1838–1856, volume C-1 [2 November 1838–31 July 1842], 1014, http://www.josephsmithpapers.org.
36. John Taylor, in *Journal of Discourses*, 21:63.
37. Letter from James Arlington Bennet, 24 October 1843, 1, http://www.josephsmithpapers.org.
38. Letter to James Arlington Bennet, 13 November 1843, 2, http://www.josephsmithpapers.org.

39. Josiah Quincy, *Figures of the Past* (Boston: Roberts Brothers, 1893), 376–77. Perhaps Quincy's prophecy has come to pass. In the spring 2015 *Smithsonian* magazine collection series, the "One-Hundred Most Significant Americans of All Time," Joseph Smith ranked first among "religious figures."

40. Thomas Sharp, *Warsaw Signal*, 12 June 1844, 2.

41. Joseph Smith to Thomas Ford, 22 June 1844, Joseph Smith Collection; "History, 1838–1856, volume F-1," 144; *History of the Church*, 6:539.

42. Letter from Governor Ford to Joseph Smith, 22 June 1844, *History of the Church*, 6:533–37; *Message of the Governor of the State of Illinois, in Relation to the Disturbances in Hancock County, December 21, 1844* (Springfield: Walters & Weber, Public Printers, 1844), http://www.idaillinois.org/cdm/ref/collection/isl/id/16828.

43. Doctrine and Covenants 135:4.

44. Willard Richards, Journal, 10:39, 27 June 1844, CHL, "History of Joseph Smith," *Millennial Star* 24, no. 28 (12 July 1862): 438–39.

45. *History of the Church of Jesus Christ of Latter-day Saints*, ed. B. H. Roberts, 2nd ed. rev. (Salt Lake City: Deseret Book, 1978), 6:623.

46. LaJean Purcell Carruth and Mark L. Staker, "John Taylor's June 27, 1854, Account of the Martyrdom," *BYU Studies* 50, no. 3 (2011): 25–62.

47. Doctrine and Covenants 135:3.

48. Campbell, "Death of J. Smith, The Mormon Impostor," *Millennial Harbinger* (third series) 1, no. 9 (September 1844): 410; Campbell, "Mormonism," *Millennial Harbinger* (new series) 6, no. 9 (September 1842): 418–20. The first notice of Smith's death in the *Millennial Harbinger* was an inaccurate account. J. Creath Jr., "Death of Joseph Smith," *Millennial Harbinger* (third series) 1, no. 8 (August 1844): 383. To Campbell's credit, a third story was printed in the *Millennial Harbinger* refuting the inaccuracies of Creath's account and decrying the "spirit of mobocracy" which had prevailed. J. W. Davidson, "The Murder of the Smiths," *Millennial Harbinger* (third series) 1, no. 11 (November 1844): 519–20.

49. Reynolds, *My Own Times: Embracing Also the History of My Life*, 575.

50. Reynolds, *My Own Times: Embracing Also the History of My Life*, 575, 564.

51. "Sermon by President Brigham Young," in *Journal of Discourses*, 3:51.

52. Orson Pratt, *The Seer* 1, no. 1 (January 1853): 1.

53. John A. Peel, as quoted in Steven Pratt, "Eleanor McLean and the Murder of Parley P. Pratt," *BYU Studies* 15 (Winter 1975): 248.

54. Harold Bloom, *The American Religion: The Emergence of the Post-Christian Nation* (New York: Simon & Schuster, 1992), 82–84, 127.

55. The documentary hypothesis attributes the Torah (five books of Moses) to at least four different authors: the Yahwist, the Elohist, the Deuteronomist, and the Priestly writer—each writing independent and parallel narratives.

56. Bloom, *The American Religion*, 40, 82–83.

57. Bloom, *The American Religion*, 95.

58. Bloom, *The American Religion*, 126–27.

59. Robert V. Remini, *Joseph Smith* (New York: Viking Penguin, 2002), 181–82.

60. Terryl L. Givens, "'Lightning Out of Heaven': Joseph Smith and the Forging of Community," *BYU Studies* 45, no. 1 (2006): 9.

61. Richard T. Hughes, "Joseph Smith as an American Restorationist," in *The Worlds of Joseph Smith: A Bicentennial Conference at the Library of Congress*, ed. John W. Welch (Provo, UT: Brigham Young University, 2006), 38.

62. Richard Bushman, "The Visionary World of Joseph Smith," in *Believing History*, 211.

63. Discourse, 7 April 1844, as reported by *Times and Seasons*, 617, http://www.josephsmithpapers.org; Discourse, 7 April 1844, as reported by Thomas Bullock, 22, http://www.josephsmithpapers.org.

64. Richard Bushman, "Joseph Smith as Translator," in *Believing History*, 244.
65. David Paulsen, "The Search for Cultural Origins of Mormon Doctrines," in *Excavating Mormon Pasts: The New Historiography of the Last Half Century*, ed. Newell G. Bringhurst and Lavina Fielding Anderson (Salt Lake City: Greg Kofford Books, 2004), 50.
66. Bushman, *Joseph Smith and the Beginnings of Mormonism*, 7. See also Richard L. Bushman, "The Secret History of Mormonism," review of *The Refiner's Fire: The Making of Mormon Cosmology, 1644–1844*, by John L. Brooke, *Sunstone* 19, no. 1 (March 1996): 67.
67. Anderson, *Lucy's Book*, 294–98, 319–20, 324–25, 330. See also pages 169–70, which give an approximate chronology of dreams one, two, six, and seven. Lucy Mack Smith, History, 1844–45.
68. Richardson, *Memoirs of Alexander Campbell*, 1:141; Joseph Smith—History 1:28.
69. Joseph Smith—History 1:20; Richardson, *Memoirs of Alexander Campbell*, 1:190.
70. Jude 1:3b.
71. Although Campbell appears to focus primarily on evidences or facts, he believed the Holy Spirit in the scriptures appealed to both the understanding of the mind and the heart. Richardson, *Memoirs of Alexander Campbell*, 1:177–78. Smith recorded in Doctrine and Covenants 8:2–3 that the Holy Spirit confirms truth through the mind and the heart.
72. The church organized by Joseph Smith in 1830 was originally called the Church of Christ. As noted earlier, the church went through several name changes until 1838.
73. Report of Instructions, between 26 June and 2 July 1839, as Reported by Willard Richards, 17–18, http://www.josephsmithpapers.org.
74. Bushman, *Joseph Smith: Rough Stone Rolling*, 560.
75. Henry Webb, *In Search of Christian Unity: A History of the Restoration Movement* (Abilene, TX: Abilene Christian University, 1990), 243.

Delusions

Alexander Campbell, *Millennial Harbinger* 2, no. 2
(7 February 1831): 85–96.

*E*very age of the world has produced imposters and delusions. Jannes and Jambres withstood Moses, and were followed by Pharaoh, his court, and clergy. They for some time supported their pretensions, much to the annoyance of the cause of the Israelites and their leader Moses.

To say nothing of the false prophets of the Jewish age, the diviners, soothsayers, magicians, and all the ministry of idols among the Gentiles, by which the nations were so often deceived, the imposters which have appeared since the Christian era would fill volumes of the most lamentable details ever read. The false Messiahs which have afflicted the Jews since the rejection of Jesus of Nazareth, have more than verified all the predictions of the Faithful and True Witness. No less than *twenty-four* distinguished false Messiahs have disturbed the Jews. Many were deceived, and myriads lost their lives through their impostures. Some peculiar epochs were distinguished for the number and impudence of these impostors. If the people had fixed upon any year as likely to terminate their dispersions, and as the period of their return, that year rarely failed to produce a Messiah. Hence, in the twelfth century no less than *ten* false Messiahs appeared.

The year 1666 was a year of great expectation, and gave birth to one of the most remarkable of the false Christs. "Great multitudes marched from unknown parts, to the remote deserts of Arabia, and they were supposed to be the ten tribes of Israel, who had been dispersed for many ages. It was said that a ship was arrived in the north part of Scotland, with sails and cordage of silk, that the mariners spoke nothing but Hebrew, and on the sails was this motto: 'The Twelve Tribes of Israel.' Then it was said that Sabatai Levi appeared at Smyrna and professed to be the Messiah." The Jews gave up their business and attended to him. He obtained one Nathan in Jerusalem to pass for his Elias, or forerunner. Nathan prophesied for him, and the Jews became very penitent, and reformed under the expectation that the Messiah would appear in two years. "Some fasted so long that they died—some endured melting wax to be dropped on their flesh—some rolled in snow—many whipped themselves. Superfluities in dress and household were dispensed with; property was sold to large amounts, and immense contributions were made to the poor. Though he met with much opposition, his followers increased, and began in large numbers to prophesy and fall into ecstacies. Four hundred men and women prophesied of his growing kingdom, and young infants who could hardly speak, would plainly pronounce, 'Sabatai, Messiah and Son of God.' The people were for a time possessed, and voices were heard from their bowels. Some fell into trances, foamed at the mouth, recounted their future prosperity, their visions of the Lion of Judah, the triumphs of Sabatai.

"When he was brought before the Magistrates, some affirmed they saw a pillar of fire between him and the Cadi or Magistrates, and others actually swore that they saw it. This the credulous Jews believed.—Those who would not believe in him were shunned as excommunicated persons, and all intercourse with them was prohibited.

"The Grand Seignor, determined to try his faith by stripping him naked and setting him a mark for his archers; but rather than subject himself to this test, he turned Mahomedan, to the great confusion of the Jews."

We have been thus particular in giving a view, of the incidents of the life of this impostor, as a specimen of the others; and because of some remarkable analogies between him and the present New York imposter.

Numerous have been the imposters among christians since the great apostacy began; especially since, and at the time of the Reformation. Munzer, Stubner and Stork, where conspicuous in the beginning of the 16th century. "These men taught that among christians, who had the precepts of the Gospel to guide them, and the Spirit of God to direct them, the office of magistracy was not only unnecessary, but an unlawful encroachment on their spiritual liberty; that [p. 86] the distinctions occasioned by birth, rank, or wealth, should be abolished; that all Christians should put their possessions into one common stock, and live together in that state of equality, which becomes members of the same family; and that polygamy was not incompatible with either the Old or New Testament. They related many visions and revelations which they had from above, but failing to propagate their views by these means, they attempted to propagate them by arms. Many Catholics joined them, and in the various insurrections which they effected, 100,000 souls are said to have been sacrificed."

Since the Millennium and the evils of sectarianism have been the subjects of much speaking and writing, impostures have been numerous. In the memory of the present generation, many delusions have been propagated and received. The Shakers, a sect instituted by Anna Lesse, in 1774, have not yet quite dwindled away. This Elect Lady, as they style her, was the head of this party, and gave them a new Bible. "They assert that she spoke seventy-two languages, and conversed with the dead. Through her all blessings flow to her followers—She appointed the sacred dance and the fantastic song, and consecrated shivering, swooning and falling down, acts of acceptable devotion. They are for a common stock, and rank marriage among the works of the flesh—they are plain in their apparel, and assume the aspect of the friars and nuns of Catholic superstition."

The Barkers, Jumpers, and Mutterers of the present age, need not be mentioned here. Nor need we detail the history of Miss Campbell, who in Good Old Scotland a year or two since, came back from the dead and had the gift of tongues; who was believed in by several ministers of the Scotch Church. But we shall proceed to notice the most recent and the most impudent delusion which has appeared in our time. The people that have received this imposture are called

THE MORMONITES.

I have just examined their bible, and will first notice its contents. It is called "The Book of Mormon, an account written by the hand of Mormon upon plates taken from the plains of Nephi, wherefore it is an abridgement of the Record of the people of Nephi, and also of the Lamanites, written to the Lamanites, which are a remnant of the House of Israel, and also to Jew and Gentile: written by way of Commandment, and also by the Spirit of Prophecy and of Revelation."—"By *Joseph Smith, Junior, Author and Proprieter.*"—From plates dug out of the earth, in the township of Manchester, Ontario county, New York—Palmyra, printed by E. B. Grandin, for the Author, 1830. It is a collection of Books said to have been written by different persons during the interval of 1020 years—The 1st and second Books of Nephi occupy 122 pages; the Book of Jacob the brother of Nephi occupies 21; that of Enos 3; that of Jarom 2; that of Omin 4; the Words of Mormon 3; the Book of Mosiah 68; that of Alma 186; that of Helaman 44; that of Nephi the son of Helaman 66; that of Mormon 20; that of Ether 35; and that of Moroni 14 pages; making in all 588 octavo pages.

This romance—but this is for it a name too innocent—begins with the religious adventures of one Lehi, whose wife was Sariah, and their four sons, Laman, Lemuel, Sam, and Nephi. Lehi lived in Jerusalem all his life, up till the 1st year of Zedekiah, King of Judah, and when the prophets appeared foretelling the utter destruction of Jerusalem, Lehi humbled himself, and after various visions and revelations, started with his sons into the wilderness. Lehi, before his departure, forgot to bring with him the records of his family, and that of the Jews; but Nephi, his younger son, with much pious courage returned and succeeded in getting upon plates of brass the Records of the Jews from the Creation down to the 1st year of Zedekiah, King of Judah—and also the prophets including many prophecies delivered by Jeremiah.

From the records it appeared that this Lehi was a son of Joseph. He prevailed on one Ishmael and his family to accompany him into the wilderness, whose daughters the sons of Lehi took for wives. [p. 87] Lehi was a greater prophet than any of the Jewish prophets, and uttered all the events of the christian era, and developed the records of Matthew, Luke, and John, 600 years before John the Baptist was born.—These pilgrims travelled several days journey in some wilderness, "a south, South-east direction, along the borders of the Red Sea." A ball with pointers on it, inscribed with various intelligence, legible at proper times, was the pillar and index in passing through the wilderness for many, very many days. By their bow and arrow they lived for eight years, travelling an easterly course from Jerusalem, until they came to a great sea. By divine revelation Nephi constructed a ship, and although opposed by his unbelieving brethren, being greatly assisted by the Holy Spirit, he succeeded in launching her safely, and got all his tribe, with all their stock of seeds, animals, and provisions, safely aboard. They had "a compass" which none but Nephi knew how to manage; but the Lord had promised them a fine land, and after many perils and trials, and a long passage, they safely arrived at the land of promise. Nephi made brazen plates soon after his arrival in America, for that was the land of promise to them, and on these plates be marked their peregrinations and adventures, and all the prophecies which God gave to him concerning the future destinies of his people, and the human race.

After his father's death, his brethren rebelled against him. They finally separated in the wilderness, and became the heads of different tribes, often in the lapse of generations making incurations upon each other. The Nephites, like their father, for many generations were good Christians, believers in the doctrines of the Calvinists and Methodists, and preaching baptism and other christian usages hundreds of years before Jesus Christ was born!

Before Nephi died, which was about 55 years from the flight of Lehi from Jerusalem, he had preached to his people every thing which is now preached in the state of New York, and anointed or ordained his brother Jacob priest over his people, called the Nephites. Jacob brought up his son Enos "in the nurture and admonition of the Lord," gave him the plates, and left him successor in office over the people of Nephi. Enos says "there came a voice to me, saying, Enos thy sins are forgiven thee, and thou shalt be blessed. And, I sayeth, Lord how it is done. And he sayeth unto me, Because of thy faith in Christ, whom thou hast not heard nor seen." page 143. Enos died 179 years from the hegira of Lehi; consequently, this happened 431 years before Jesus Christ was born. He was a contemporary with Nehemiah, and may we not say how much wiser and more enlightened were the Nephites in America than the Jews at their return to Jerusalem!!

Enos gave the plates to Jarom, his son. In his time "they kept the law of Moses and the Sabbath day holy to the Lord." During the priesthood and reign of Enos, there were many commotions and wars between his people and the Lamanites. Then the sharp pointed arrow, the quiver, and the dart were invented. Jarom delivered his plates to his son Omni, and gave up the ghost 238 years from the flight of Lehi. Omni died 276 years from the hegira, and gave the plates to his son Amaron, who in the year 320, gave them to his brother Chemish; he, to his son Abinadom; he to his son Amaleki; and he having no son, gave them to the just and pious King Benjamin.

King Benjamin had three sons, Mosiah, Helorum, and Helaman, whom he educated in all the learning of his fathers. To Mosiah he delivered up the plates of Nephi, the ball which guided them through the wilderness, and the sword of one Laban, of mighty renown. King

Benjamin addressed his people from the new temple which they had erected, for they had, even then, built a temple, synagogues, and a tower, in the New World.

King Benjamin assembled the people to sacrifice according to the law around the new temple; and he enjoined upon them, at the same time, the christian institutions, and gave them a patriarchal valedictory. After they had heard him speak, and had offered up their sacrifices, they fell down and prayed in the following words: "O have mercy, and apply the atoning blood [p. 88] of Christ, that we may receive forgiveness of our sins, and our hearts may be purified; for we believe in Jesus Christ the Son of God, who created Heaven and Earth and all things, who shall come down upon the children of men." "Then the Spirit of the Lord fell upon them and they were filled with joy, having received a remission of their sins." [Book of Mormon] p. 162.[1]

King Benjamin ordered his people to take upon them the name of Christ, and in these remarkable words,—"There is no other name given whereby salvation cometh; therefore I would that you should take upon you the name of Christ, all you that have entered into the covenant with God that ye should be obedient unto the end of your lives." [Book of Mormon] p. 166. They all took upon them the name of Christ; and he, having ordained them priests and teachers, and appointed his son, Mosiah, to reign in his stead, gave up the ghost 476 years after Lehi's escape from Jerusalem, and 124 before Christ was born. Mosiah gave up the plates of brass, and all "the things which we had kept" to Alma, the son of Alma, who was appointed "chief judge and high priest," the people willing to have no King, and Mosiah died 569 years from the time Lehi left Jerusalem.

In the 14th year of the judges, and 69 years before the birth of Jesus, they sent out missionary priests, who preached through all the tribes of the country against all vices, "holding forth the coming of the Son of God, his sufferings, death and resurrection—and that he should appear unto them after his resurrection: and this the people did hear with great joy and gladness."—[Book of Mormon] p. 269.

Alma's book reaches down to the end of the 39th year of the judges. These were wonderful years—many cities were founded, many battles were fought, fortifications reared, letters written, and even in one year a certain Hagoth built an exceeding large ship, and launched it forth into the West Sea. In this embarked many of the Nephites. This same ship builder the next year built other ships—one was lost with all its passengers and crew.—[Book of Mormon] p. 406.

Many prophecies were pronounced; one that in 400 years after the coming of Christ, the Nephites would lose their religion. During the time of the judges, many were called Christians by name, and "baptism unto repentance" was a common thing. "And it came to pass that they did appoint priests and teachers throughout all the land, and over all the churches." [Book of Mormon] p. 349. "And those who did belong to the church were faithful; yea all those who were true believers in Christ took upon them gladly the name of Christ, or christians, as they were called, because of their belief in Christ." [Book of Mormon] p. 301. "And it came to pass that there were many who died, firmly believing that their souls were redeemed by the Lord Jesus Christ: thus they went out of the world rejoicing." [Book of Mormon] p. 353. "The word was preached by Helaman, Shiblon, Corianton, Amnon, and his brethren, &c. yea, and all those who had been ordained by the holy order of God, being baptized unto repentance, and sent forth to preach unto the people." [Book of Mormon] p. 362. This happened in the 19th year of the judges, 72 years before the birth of Jesus. Before this time synagogues with pulpits were built, "for the Zoramites," a sort of Episcopalians, "gathered themselves together on one day of the week, which day they called the day of the Lord."— "And they had a place which was high and lifted up, which held but one man, who read prayers, the same prayers every week; and this high place was called Rameumptom, which being interpreted, is the *Holy Stand.*" [Book of Mormon] p. 311.

The book of Helaman reacheth down to the 90th year of the judges, and to the year preceding that in which the Messiah was born. During the period embraced in Helaman's narrative, many ten thousands were baptized. "And behold the Holy Spirit of God did come down from heaven, and did enter into their hearts, and they were filled as with fire, and they could speak forth marvellous words." [Book of Mormon] p. 421. Masonry was invented about this time; for men began to bind themselves in secret oaths to aid one another in all things, [p. 89] good or evil. [Book of Mormon] p. 424. Powers of loosing and binding in heaven were conferred upon Nephi, the son of Helaman, and all miraculous powers, such as the Apostles possessed. One Samuel, also foretold that "the Christ would be born in five years, and that the night before should be as light as day; and that the day of his death should be a day of darkness, like the night." [Book of Mormon] p. 445.

The book of this Nephi commences with the birth of the Messiah, 600 years from the departure of Lehi from Jerusalem. In the midst of the threats of the infidels to slaughter the faithful, the sun set; but lo! the night was clear as mid-day, and from that period they changed their era, and counted time as we do. A star also appeared, but it is not stated how it could be seen in a night as bright as day—but it was universally seen throughout all the land, to the salvation of the pious from the threats of their enemies.

The terrors of the day of his death are also stated, and in the 34th year from his nativity, after his resurrection, he descended from heaven and visited the people of Nephi. Jesus called upon them to examine his hands and his sides, as he did Thomas, though none of them had expressed a doubt. Two thousand five hundred men, women and children, one by one, examined him, and then worshipped him. He commanded Nephi to baptize, and gave him the words which he was to use, viz: "Having authority given me, of Jesus Christ, I baptize you in the name of the Father, and of the Son, and of the Holy Ghost. Amen." He commissioned eleven others, who with Nephi, were his twelve American Apostles, and promised himself to baptize their converts "with fire and with the Holy Spirit."

He delivers them the sermon upon the mount, and some other sayings recorded in Matthew, Mark, Luke, and John. He healed all their diseases, and prayed for their children; but the things spoken were so great and marvellous that they could not be spoken nor written.

He ordained one to administer the supper, who alone had authority to dispense it to the disciples baptized in his name. The only new commandments which were given to the American christians on his occasional visits which were repeated, were—"Pray in your families unto the Father, always in my name, that your wives and your children may be blessed." "Meet often, and forbid no man from coming unto you when you shall meet together." [Book of Mormon] p. 492.

Nephi was chief among the 12 Apostles: he baptized himself, and then baptized the eleven, whose names were Timothy, Jonas, Mathoni and Mathoninah, Kumen, Kumenonhi, Jeremiah, Shimnon, Jonas, Zedekiah, and Isaiah. "They were baptized in fire and the Holy Ghost." Not a new word, however, should be written in addition to those found in the New Testament; for although he spake for several days to these American disciples, none of the new and marvellous sayings could be uttered or written!! He inspected the plates of Nephi, and only found one omission, which was that he failed to mention the resurrection of many saints in America at the time of the tempest and earthquake. He commanded these Nephites to be called christians.

The book of Nephi the son of Nephi, gives, in 4 pages, the history of 320 years after Christ. In the 36th year, all the inhabitants of the land were converted. There was a perfect community, and no disputations in the land for 170 years. Three of the American Apostles were never to die, and were seen 400 years after Christ; but what has become of them no one can tell, except Cowdery, Whitmer and Harris, the three witnesses of the truth of the plates of Nephi, be these three immortal men. Towards the close of the history of Nephi or the record of Ammaron, sects and divisions and battles became frequent, and all goodness had almost left the continent in the year 320.

Mormon appears next in the drama, the recording angel of the whole matter, who, by the way, was a mighty general and great christian; he commanded in one engagement 42,000 men against the Lamanites!!! He was no Quaker! This dreadful battle was fought A.D. 330. The Lamanites took [p. 90] South America for themselves, and gave North America to the Nephites. Mormon was very orthodox, for he preached in these words, A. D. 362:— *"That Jesus was the very Christ and the very God."* He must have heard of the Arian controversy by some angel!!

Moroni finishes what Mormon, his father, left undone, and continues the history, till A.D. 400. He pleads that no one shall disbelieve his record because of its imperfections!! and declares that none who receive it will condemn it on account of its imperfections, and for not doing so, the same shall know greater things. [Book of Mormon] p. 532. *"He that condemneth it shall be in danger of hell fire."* He laments the prevalency of free masonry in the times when his Book should be dug up out of the earth, and proves that miracles will never cease; because God is the same yesterday, to-day, and forever—consequently must always create suns, moons, and stars, every day!! He exhorted to "take heed that none be baptized without telling their experience, nor partake of the Sacrament of Christ unworthily"!! [Book of Mormon] p. 537.

Moroni, in the conclusion of his Book of Mormon, says if his plates had been larger we would have written in Hebrew; but because of this difficulty he wrote in the "Reformed Egyptian," being handed down and altered unto us according to our manner of speech." [Book of Mormon] p. 538. "Condemn me not," says he, "because of mine imperfections; neither my father, because of his imperfections, neither them which have written before him; but rather give thanks unto God that he hath made manifest unto you our imperfections, that you may learn to be more wise than we have been." [Book of Mormon] p. 538. A very necessary advice, indeed!!

Moroni writes the book of Ether, containing an account of the people of Jared, who escaped from the building of the tower of Babel unconfounded in his language. These people of Jared, God marched before in a cloud, and directed them through the wilderness, and instructed them to build *barges* to cross seas; and finally they built eight barges, air tight, and were commanded to make a hole in the top to admit air, and one in the bottom to admit water, and in them were put 16 windows of *molten stone,* which when touched by the finger of Jesus, became as transparent as glass, and gave them light under "the mountain waves," and when above the water. He that touched these stones, appeared unto the brother of Jared, and said, "Behold I am Jesus Christ, *I am the Father and the Son.*" Two of these stones were sealed up with the plates, and became the spectacles of Joseph Smith, according to a prediction uttered before Abraham was born. It was also foretold in the Book of Ether, written by Moroni, that he that should find the plates should have the privilege of shewing the plates unto those who shall assist to bring forth this work, and unto *three* shall they be shown by the power of God: wherefore they shall of a surety known that these things are true." [Book of Mormon] p. 548.

And the eight barges, air-tight, made like ducks, after swimming and diving 344 days, arrived on the coasts of the land of promise. The Book of Ether relates the wars and carnage amongst these people. In the lapse of generations they counted two millions of mighty men, besides women and children, slain; and finally, they were all killed but one, and he fell to the earth as if he had no life. So ends the book of Ether. [Book of Mormon] p. 573.

The book of Moroni details the manner of ordaining priests and teachers, the manner of administering ordinances, and the epistles of Mormon to his son Moroni. Moroni seals up the record A.D. 423, and assures the world that spiritual gifts shall never cease, only through unbelief. And when the plates of Nephi should be dug up out of the earth, he declares that "men should ask God the Eternal Father, in the name of Christ, if these things were not true." "If with a sincere heart and real intent, having faith in Christ, such prayers are made, ye shall know the truth of all things." [Book of Mormon] p. 586.

The testimony of Oliver Cowdery, David Whitmer, and Martin Harris, asserting that they saw the plates, is appended. They also testify that they know [p. 91] that they have been translated by the gift and power of God, for his voice has declared it unto them.

Another testimony is appended signed by four Whitmers, one Hiram Page, and three Smiths, affirming that they saw the plates, handled them, and that Smith has got the plates in his possession.

Such is an analysis of the book of Mormon, the Bible of the Mormonites. For noticing of which I would have asked forgiveness from all my readers, had not several hundred persons of different denominations believed in it. On this account alone has it become necessary to notice it, and for the same reason we must examine its pretensions to divine authority; for it purports to be a revelation from God. And in the first place, we shall examine its internal evidences.

INTERNAL EVIDENCES.

It admits the Old and New Testaments to contain the revelations, institutions and commandments of God to Patriarchs, Jews, and Gentiles, down to the year 1830—and always, as such, speaks of them and quotes them. This admission at once blasts its pretensions to credibility. Admitting the Bible now received to have come from God, it is impossible that the book of Mormon came from the same Author. For the following reasons:—

I. Smith, its real author, as ignorant and impudent a knave as ever wrote a book, betrays the cloven foot in basing his whole book upon a false fact, or a pretended fact, which makes God a liar. It is this:—With the Jews, God made a covenant at Mount Sinai, and instituted a priesthood, and a high priesthood. The priesthood he gave to the tribe of Levi, and the high priesthood to Aaron and his sons for an everlasting priesthood. He separated Levi, and covenanted to give him this office irrevocably while ever the temple stood, or till the Messiah came. "Then, says God, Moses shall appoint Aaron and his sons, and they shall wait on their priest's office, and the stranger, (the person of another family,) who cometh nigh, shall be put to death." Numbers iii.10. "And the priests, the sons of Levi, shall come near; for them the Lord thy God hath chosen to minister unto him, and to bless in the name of the Lord, and by their word shall every controversy and every stroke be tried." Deut. xxi. 5. Korah, Dathan, and Abiram, with 250 men of renown, rebelled against a part of the institution of the priesthood, and the Lord destroyed them in the presence of the whole congregation. This was to be a memorial that no stranger invade any part of the office of the priesthood. Num. xvi. 40. "Fourteen thousand and seven hundred of the people" were destroyed by a plague for murmuring against this memorial.

In the 18th chapter of Numbers the Levites are again given to Aaron and his sons, and the priesthood confirmed to them with this threat—"The stranger that cometh nigh shall be put to death." "Even Jesus," says Paul, "were he on earth, could not be a priest, for he was of a tribe concerning which Moses spake nothing of priesthood." Heb. vii.13. So irrevocable was the grant of the priesthood to Levi, and of the high priesthood to Aaron, that no stranger dare approach the altar of God which Moses established. Hence, Jesus himself was excluded from officiating as priest on earth according to the law.

This Joseph Smith overlooked in his impious fraud, and makes his hero Lehi spring from Joseph. And just as soon as his sons return with the roll of his lineage, ascertaining that he was of the tribe of Joseph, he and his sons acceptably "offer sacrifices and burnt offerings to the Lord."—p. 15. Also it is repeated, p. 18—Nephi became chief artificer, ship-builder and mariner; was scribe, prophet, priest and king unto his own people, and "consecrated Jacob and Joseph, the sons of his father, priests to God and teachers—almost 600 years before the fulness of the times of the Jewish economy was completed." p. 72. Nephi represents himself withal as "under the law of Moses," [Book of Mormon] p. 105. They build a *temple* in the new world, and in 55 years after they leave Jerusalem, make a new priesthood which God approbates. A high [p. 92] priest is also consecrated, and yet they are all the while "teaching the law of Moses, and exhorting the people to keep it!!" p. 146, 209. Thus God is represented as instituting, approbating and blessing a new priesthood from the tribe of Joseph, concerning which Moses gave no commandment concerning priesthood. Although God had promised in the law of Moses, that if any man, not of the tribe and family of Levi and Aaron, should approach the office of priest, he would surely die; he is represented by Smith as blessing, approbating, and sustaining another family in this approbated office. The God of Abraham or Joseph Smith must then be a liar!! And who will hesitate to pronounce him an imposter? This lie runs through his records for the first 600 years of his story.

II. This ignorant and impudent liar, in the next place, makes the God of Abraham, Isaac and Jacob, violate his covenants with Israel and

Judah, concerning the land of Canaan, by promising a new land to the pious Jew. If a company of reprobate Jews had departed from Jerusalem and the temple, in the days of Zedekiah, and founded a new colony, it would not have been so incongruous. But to represent God as inspiring a devout Jew and a prophet, such as Lehi and Nephi are represented by Smith,—with a resolution to forsake Jerusalem and God's own house, and to depart from the land which God swore to their fathers so long as they were obedient; and to guide by a miracle and to bless by prodigies a good man in forsaking God's covenant and worship—is so monstrous an error, that language fails to afford a name for it. It is to make God violate his own covenants, and set at nought [sic] his own promises, and to convert his own curses into blessings. Excision from the commonwealth of Israel, and banishment from Jerusalem and the temple, were the greatest curses the law of Moses knew. But Smith makes a good and pious Jew the subject of this curse, and sends him off into the inhospitable wilderness, disinherits him in Canaan, and makes him more happy in forsaking the institutions of Moses, more intelligent in the wilderness, and more prosperous in adversity, than even the Jews in their best days, in the best of lands, and under the best of all governments!!! The imposter was too ignorant of the history of the Jews and the nature of the covenants of promise, to have even alluded to them in his book, if he had not supposed that he had the plates of Moses in his own keeping, as he had his "molten plates" of Nephi. To separate a family from the nation of Israel, was to accumulate all the curses of the law upon that family. Deut. xxix. 21.

III. He has more of the Jews, living in the new world, than could have been numbered any where else, even in the days of John the Baptist; and has placed them under a new dynasty. The sceptre, with him, has departed from Judah, and a lawgiver from among his descendants, hundreds of years before Shiloh came; and King Benjamin is a wiser and more renowned King than King Solomon. He seems to have gone upon an adage which saith:— "the more marvellous, the more credible the tale," and the less of fact, and the more of fiction, the more intelligible and reasonable the narrative.

IV. He represents the temple worship as continued in his new land of promise contrary to every precept of the Law, and so happy are the people of Nephi as never to shed a tear on account of the excision, nor turn an eye towards Jerusalem or God's temple. The pious Jews in their captivity turned their faces to Jerusalem and the holy place, and remembered God's promises concerning the place where he recorded his name. They hung their harps upon the willow trees, and could not sing the songs of Zion in a foreign land; but the Nephites have not a single wish for Jerusalem, for they can, in their wigwam temple, in the wilderness of America, enjoy more of God's presence than the most righteous Jew could enjoy in that house of which David had rather be a door-keeper, than to dwell in the tabernacles of men. And all this too, when God's only house of prayer, according to his covenant with Israel, stood in Jerusalem.

V. Malachi, the last of the Jewish prophets, commanded Israel to regard [p. 93] the law of Moses till the Messiah came. And Moses commanded them to regard him till the Great Prophet came. But Nephi and Smith's prophets institute ordinances and observances for the Jews, subversive of Moses, 500 years before the Great Prophet came.

VI. Passing over a hundred similar errors, we shall next notice his ignorance of the New Testament matters and things. The twelve Apostles of the Lamb, are said by Paul, to have developed certain secrets which were hid for ages and generations, which Paul says were ordained before the world to their glory—that they should have the honor of announcing them. But Smith makes his pious hero Nephi, 600 years before the Messiah began to preach, and disclose these secrets concerning the calling of the Gentiles, and the blessings flowing through the Messiah to Jews and Gentiles, which Paul says were hid for ages and generations, "which in these ages was not made known unto the sons of men, as it is now revealed unto us the holy Apostles and prophets, by the Spirit; that the Gentiles should be fellow heirs and of the same body and partakers of his promise in Christ by the gospel." Smith makes Nephi express every truth found in the writings of the Apostles concerning the calling and blessing of the Gentiles, and even quotes the 11th chapter of Romans, and many other passages before he had a son grown in the wilderness able to aim an arrow at a deer. Paul says these things were secrets and unknown until his time; but Smith makes Nephi say the same things 600 years before Paul was converted! One of the two is a false prophet. Mormonites, take your choice!

VII. This prophet Smith, through his stone spectacles, wrote on the plates of Nephi, in his book of Mormon, every error and almost every truth discussed in New York for the last ten years. He decides all the great controversies;—infant baptism, ordination, the trinity, regeneration, repentance, justification, the fall of man, the atonement, transubstantiation, fasting, penance, church government, religious experience, the call to the ministry, the general resurrection, eternal punishment, who may baptize, and even the question of free-masonry, republican government, and the rights of man. All these topics are repeatedly alluded to. How much more benevolent and intelligent this American apostle, than were the holy Twelve, and Paul to assist them!!! He prophesied of all these topics, and of the apostacy, and infallibly decided, by his authority, every question. How easy to prophecy of the past or of the present time!!

VIII. But he is better skilled in the controversies in New York than in the geography or history of Judea. He makes John baptise in the village of Bethabara, [Book of Mormon] (page 22) and says Jesus was born in Jerusalem, p. 240. Great must be the faith of the Mormonites in this new Bible!!! The mariners compass was only known in Europe about 300 years ago; but Nephi knew all about steam boats and the compass 2400 years ago.

IX. He represents the christian institution as practised among his Israelites before Jesus was born. And his Jews are called Christians while keeping the law of Moses, the holy Sabbath, and worshipping in their temple at their altars, and by their high priests.

X. But not to honor him by a too [two] minute examination and exposition, I will sum up the whole of the internal evidence which I deem worthy of remark, in the following details:—

The book professes to be written at intervals and by different persons during the long period of 1020 years. And yet for uniformity of style, there never was a book more evidently written by one set of fingers, nor more certainly conceived in one cranium since the first book appeared in human language, than this same book. If I could swear to any man's voice, face or person, assuming different names, I could swear that this book was written by one man. And as Joseph Smith is a very *ignorant* man and is called *the author* on the title page, I cannot doubt for a single moment that he is the sole author and proprietor of it. As a specimen of his style the reader will [p. 94] take the following samples—Page 4th. In his own preface:— "The plates of which hath been spoken." In the last page, "the plates of which hath been spoken." In the certificate signed by Cowdery and his two witnesses, he has the same idiom, "which came from the tower of which hath been spoken;" [Book of Mormon] page 16, "we are a descendant of Joseph." "The virgin which thou seest is the mother of God." "Behold the Lamb of God the Eternal Father," [Book of Mormon] p. 25; "Ye are like unto they," "and I saith unto them," [Book of Mormon] p. 44. "We did arrive to the promised land;" [Book of Mormon] p. 49, "made mention upon the first plate," [Book of Mormon] p. 50.

Nephi 2400 years ago hears the saying of a Pagan who lived 634 years after him—"The God of nature suffers." [Book of Mormon] p. 51. "The righteous need not fear, for it is they which shall not be confounded." [Book of Mormon] p. 58. Shakespeare was read by Nephi 2200 years before he was born—"The silent grave from whence no traveller returns," [Book of Mormon] 61. "Your own eternal welfare" was a phrase then common in America, [Book of Mormon] p. 62. "Salvation is free" was then announced. "That Jesus should rise from the dead" was repeatedly declared on this continent in the reign of Nebuchadnezzar. And at the same time it was said, "Messiah cometh in the fulness of time that he might redeem the children of men from the fall;" [Book of Mormon] p. 65. "The fall" was frequently spoken of at the Isthmus of Darien 2400 years ago.

I had no object, says Nephi, in the reign of Zedekiah, "but the everlasting salvation of your souls." [Book of Mormon] 66. "I had spake many things," "for a more history part are written upon mine other plates." [Book of Mormon] 69. "Do not anger again because of mine enemies," p. 70. "For it behoveth the Great Creator that he die for all men." "It must needs be an infinite atonement." "This flesh must go to its mother earth." "And this death must deliver up its dead," [Book of Mormon] p. 70, were common phrases 2300 years ago—"for the atonement satisfieth the demands of his justice upon all those who have not the law given them," [Book of Mormon] p. 81. The Calvinists were in America before Nephi. "The Lord remembereth all they," [Book of Mormon] 85. "The atonement is infinite for all mankind," [Book of Mormon] p. 104. The Americans knew this on the Columbo 2400 years ago. "His name shall be called Jesus Christ the Son of God." An angel told this to Nephi 545 years before it was told to Mary, [Book of Mormon] p. 105. "And they shall teach with their learning and deny the Holy Ghost which giveth them utterance;" this prophecy was at that time delivered against us, [Book of Mormon] p. 112. "My words shall hiss forth unto the ends of the earth," [Book of Mormon] p. 115. "Wherein did the Lamb of God fill all the righteousness in being baptised by water," [Book of Mormon] 118. This question was discussed 2300 years ago. "The baptism by fire and the Holy Ghost" was preached in the days of Cyrus, [Book of

Mormon] p. 119. "The only true doctrine of the Father and of the Son and of the Holy Ghost which is one God without end. Amen," [Book of Mormon] p. 120. This was decided in the time of Daniel the Prophet. "I glory in plainness," says Nephi. "Christ will show you that these are his words in the last day," [Book of Mormon] p. 122. Too late to prove your mission, Mr. Nephi!

"After that ye have obtained a hope in Christ, ye shall obtain riches if you seek them." So spoke Jacob in the days of Ezekiel the Prophet. "They believed in Christ and worshipped the Father in his name," [Book of Mormon] p. 129. This was said by Jacob in the time of Daniel. "Do as ye hath hitherto done," says Mosiah, [Book of Mormon] page 158. These Smithisms are in every page. "And his mother shall be called Mary." [Book of Mormon] p. 160. "The Son of God and Father of heaven and earth." [Book of Mormon] p. 161. "The infant perisheth not, that dieth in his infancy." "For the natural man is an enemy of God and was from the fall of Adam, and will be forever and ever," [Book of Mormon] p. 161. This was spoken by King Benjamin 124 years before Christ. He was a Yankee, too, for he spoke like Smith, saying, "I who ye call your king." "They saith unto the king," [Book of Mormon] p. 182. This was another Joseph Smith called Mosiah. "They were baptised in the waters of Mormon, and were called the church of Christ," p. 192. This happened 100 years before Christ was born. "Alma, why persecuteth thou the church of God," [Book of Mormon] p. 222. "Ye must be born again; yea, born of God—changed from their carnal and fallen state to a state of [p. 95] righteousness," [Book of Mormon] 214. This was preached also 100 years before Christ was born. "These things had not ought to be," [Book of Mormon] 220.

"I, Alma, being consecrated by my father Alma to be a high priest over the church of God, he having power and authority from God to do these things, [Book of Mormon] (p. 232) say unto you, except ye repent ye can in no wise enter into the Kingdom of Heaven." [Book of Mormon] 237. "He ordained priests and elders, by laying on his hands, to watch over the church"—"Not so much as a hair of the head shall be lost in the grave"—"The holy order of the high priesthood." [Book of Mormon] p. 250. The high priesthood of Alma was about 80 years before Christ. "The Lord poured out his spirit to prepare the minds of the people for the preaching of Alma, preaching repentance." [Book of Mormon] p. 268. Alma was a Yankee of Smith's school, for he saith: "The light of everlasting light was lit up in his soul." [Book of Mormon] p. 47.

During the pontificate of Alma men prayed thus: "If there is a God, and if thou art God wilt thou make thyself known unto me," [Book of Mormon] p. 286. Alma "clapped his hands upon all they which were with him." [Book of Mormon] p. 313. "Instruments in the hand of God" were the preachers of Alma, [Book of Mormon] p. 323. Modest and orthodox men, truly! "If ye deny the Holy Ghost when it once hath place in you, and ye know that ye deny, behold this is the unpardonable sin." [Book of Mormon] p. 332. So Alma preached. "And now my son, ye are called of God to preach the Gospel." [Book of Mormon] p. 340. "They were high priests over the church." [Book of Mormon] p. 350. "The twenty and second year of the judges this came to pass." [Book of Mormon] p. 364. "They were valiant for courage." [Book of Mormon] p. 376.

These are but as one drop out of a bucket compared with the amount of Smithisms in this book. It is patched up and cemented with "And it came to pass"—"I sayeth unto you"—"Ye saith unto him"—and all the King James' *haths, dids* and *doths;* in the lowest imitation of the common version; and is, without exaggeration, the meanest book in the English language; but it is a translation made through stone spectacles, in a dark room, and in the hat of the prophet Smith from the *reformed Egyptian!!!* It has not one good sentence in it, save the profanation of those sentences quoted from the Oracles of the living God. I would as soon compare a bat to the American eagle, a mouse to a mammoth, or the deformities of a spectre to the beauty of Him whom John saw in Patmos, as to contrast it with a single chapter in all the writings of the Jewish or Christian prophets. It is as certainly Smith's fabrication as Satan is the father of lies, or darkness the offspring of night. So much for the internal evidences of the Book of Mormon.

Its external evidences are, first, the testimony of the prophets Cowdery, Whitmer, and Harris; who saw the plates and heard the voice of God; who are disinterested retailers of the books. I would ask them how they knew that it was God's voice which they heard—but they would tell me to ask God in faith. *That is, I must believe it first, and then ask God if it be true!!* 'Tis better to take Nephi's proof which is promised to us in the day of final judgment! They say that spiritual gifts are continued to the end of time among the true believers. They are true believers—have they wrought any miracles? They have tried; but their faith failed. Can they shew any spiritual gift? Yes, they can mutter Indian and traffic in new Bibles.

"But Smith is the wonder of the world." So was the Apocalyptic beast! "an ignorant young man." That needs no proof. Gulliver's travels is a heroic poem in comparison of this book of Smith. "But he cannot write a page." Neither could Mahomet, who gave forth the Alcoran. "Smith is an honest looking fellow." So was Simon Magus, the sorcerer. "But he was inspired." So was Judas, by Satan.

Its external evidences are also the subscriptions of four Whitmers, three Smiths, and one Page, the relatives and connexions of Joseph Smith, junior. And these "men handled as many of the brazen or golden leaves as the said Smith translated." So did I. But Smith has got the plates of which hath been spoken. Let him shew them. Their certificate proves nothing, save [p. 96] That Smith wrote it, and they signed it. But Smith gives testimony himself. There is one who says: "If I bear testimony of myself, my testimony ought not to be regarded."

If this prophet and his three prophetic witnesses had aught of speciosity about them or their book, we would have examined it and exposed it in a different manner. I have never felt myself so fully authorized to address mortal man in the style in which Paul addressed Elymas the sorcerer as I feel towards this Atheist Smith. His three witnesses, I am credibly informed, on one of their horse-swapping and prophetic excursions in the Sandusky country, having bartered horses *three* times for *once* preaching, represented Walter Scott and myself as employed in translating these plates, and as believers in the book of Mormon. If there was any thing plausible about Smith, I would say to those who believe him to be a prophet, hear the question which Moses put into the mouth of the Jews, and his answer to it—"And if thou say in thy heart, *How shall we know the word which the Lord hath not spoken?*"—Does he answer, *"Ask the Lord and he will tell you"*?—Does he say "Wait till the day of judgment and you will know"? Nay, indeed; but—"When a prophet speaketh in the name of the Lord, if the thing follow not nor come to pass, that is the thing which the Lord hath not spoken; the prophet hath spoken it presumptuously: *thou shalt not be afraid of him.*" Deut.xviii. 8. Smith has failed in every instance to verify one of his own sayings. Again, I would say in the words of the Lord by Isaiah, "Bring forth your strong reasons, saith the King of Jacob: let them bring them forth and show us what shall happen: let them show the former things what they mean, that we may consider them, and know the latter end of them—show the things which are to come hereafter, that we may know that you are prophets: yea, do good or do evil, that we may be dismayed and behold it together. Behold you are nothing, and your work of naught: an abomination is every one that chooseth you." Is. 41: 21–23.

Let the children of Mormon ponder well, if yet reason remains with them, the following passage from Isaiah 44, and if they cannot see the analogy between themselves and the sons of ancient imposture, then reason is of as little use to them as it was to those of whom the prophet spake —

"The carpenters having chosen a piece of wood framed it by rule and glued the parts together, and made it in the form of a man, and with the comeliness of a man, to set it in a house. He cut wood from the forest which the Lord planted—a pine tree, which the rain had nourished, that it might be fuel for the use of man: and having taken some of it he warmed himself; and with other pieces they made a fire and baked cakes, and of the residue they made gods and worshipped them. Did he not burn half of it in the fire, and, with the coals of that half bake cakes: and having roasted meat with it did he not eat and was satisfied; and when warmed say, 'Aha! I am warmed, I have enjoyed the fire?' Yet of the residue he made a carved god, and worshipped it, and prayeth to it, saying, 'Deliver me, for thou art my God.'

"They had not sense to think; for they were so involved in darkness that they could not see with their eyes, nor understand with their hearts: nor did any reason in his mind, nor by his understanding recollect, that he had burned half of it in the fire, and on the coals thereof baked cakes, and had roasted flesh and eaten, and of the residue had made an abomination; so they bow themselves down to it. Know thou that their heart is ashes, and they are led astray and none can deliver his soul. Take a view of it, will you not say, 'There is indeed a lie in my right hand?'"

"Remember these things, O Jacob, even thou Israel, for thou art my servant. I have made thee my servant; therefore O Israel do not thou forget me. For, lo! I have made thy transgressions vanish like a cloud—and thy sins like the murky vapor. Return to me, and I will redeem thee."

A. CAMPBELL.

February 10, 1831.

Note

1. The Book of Mormon page numbers that Campbell cited are from an original 1830 edition, which were in paragraphs rather than verses, and differ from the page numbers in the 2013 edition.

The Constitution of the Mahoning Baptist Association

1826

*T*he Mahoning Association, a voluntary Baptist union, was formed in August 1820. The purpose of a Baptist association was to give encouragement, counsel, and protection against heresy and imposters.[1] Two of the association's early leaders were Adamson Bentley and Sidney Rigdon, who had met Campbell in 1821 and were enthralled with his restoration views.[2] In 1823, when Campbell's Wellsburg congregation was on the brink of being expelled from the Redstone Baptist Association, he was welcomed by his old friends into their Baptist association. Ecclesiastical authority was not vested in the association, allowing for complete local control which was just what Campbell wanted.[3]

The objectives and limitations of the association were followed by a list of thirteen brief statements of belief accompanied by a New Testament scriptural reference. Since Alexander Campbell wrote his church's application to join the Mahoning association, it is fair to assume he agreed in general with the constitution, especially since a New Testament citation was given for each article of belief.[4]

CONSTITUTION

It is our object to glorify God. This we would endeavor to do by urging the importance of the doctrine and precepts of the gospel in their moral and evangelical nature, commending ourselves to every man's conscience in the sight of God; not pretending to have authority over any man's (conscience,) nor over the churches, whose representatives form this association. But we act as an advisory coun-sel [sic] only, disclaiming all superiority, jurisdiction, coercive right and infallibility; and acknowledging the independence of every church; which has received authority from Christ all duties enjoined respecting the government of his church in this world.

Article 1: *Three persons in the Godhead—the Father, the Word, and the Holy Ghost; and these three are one. John v: 7.*

Article 2: *Eternal and personal election to holiness, and the adop-tion of children by Jesus Christ the Redeemer. Eph. i: 4, 5.*

Article 3: *The condemnation of all mankind in consequence of Adam's transgression. Rom. v: 16, 18.*

Article 4: *The depravity of all mankind, in all the faculties of the soul, the understanding, will, and affections. Col. 1:18; Acts xxvi:18; Eph. iv. 18, 23; John v: 40; Rom. viii. 7.*

Article 5: *Particular 5 redemption by the blood of Jesus Christ. Rom. v: 9; Isa. xxxv. 10; John vi: 37, 39.*

Article 6: *Pardon of all sin through the merits of Christ's blood to all true believers. 1 John i: 7; Col. i:14; Acts x: 43.*

Article 7: *Free justification by the righteousness of Christ imputed to all true believers. Jer. xxxiii: 6; 1 Cor. i: 30; Rom. ix: 5, 18, 19.*

Article 8: *The irresistible power of the Holy Ghost in regeneration. Eph. ii: 1; John i: 13.*

Article 9: *The perseverance of the saints in grace, by the power of God unto eternal life.*

John x: 27, 28, 29; Col. iii: 3, 9; John x: 29.

Article 10: *Water baptism, by immersion of the whole body of the party, so as to be buried with Christ by baptism; and not by sprinkling or pouring, as the manner of some is. Mark i: 9, 10; John iii: 23; Acts viii: 38, 39; Rom. vi: 4; Col. ii: 12; Heb. x: 22.*

Article 11: *The subjects of baptism: those who repent of their sins and believe in Christ, and openly confess faith in the Son of God. Matt. iii: 8; Acts viii: 37; x: 47.*

Article 12: *The everlasting punishment of the finally impenitent in as unlimited sense as the happiness of the righteous. Matt. xxv: 41–46; Mark iii: 29; Rev. xiv: 11.*

Article 13: *We believe that the first day of the week is the Lord's day, and that it ought to be held sacred to the memory of Christ's glorious resurrection, and devoted in a special manner to the duties of religion.*

Notes

1. Hayden, *Early History of the Disciples*, 25.
2. Hayden, *Early History of the Disciples*, 19.
3. Hayden, *Early History of the Disciples*, 26.
4. See chapter 3 for Campbell's letter of application to the Mahoning Baptist Association.
5. "Particular" redemption is a traditional view of the Atonement: Christ's death might have significance for all humanity in general, but according to scripture, the saving benefit applies only to those who were redeemed. Noll, *America's God*, 267.

About the Author

*R*oseAnn Benson is a former adjunct professor in community and public health at Utah Valley University and was previously an adjunct professor of ancient scripture and Church history and doctrine at Brigham Young University. She has published research on restoration movements in the peer-reviewed *Journal of Mormon History*, *Journal of Book of Mormon Studies*, *Religious Educator*, and academic books. She has presented at the BYU Church History Symposium, BYU Easter Conference, BYU Religious Education Student Symposium, Mormon History Association conference, John Whitmer Historical Association conference, and Sidney B. Sperry Symposium. She has a PhD from Southern Illinois in community and school health with an emphasis in nutrition. She has an MA from BYU in ancient Near Eastern studies with an emphasis in religious education and an MS in exercise science with a minor in health science. She has also been a head women's swimming and diving coach at several NCAA Division I universities.

Index

A

Aaronic Priesthood, 54n22, 115–16
Abrahamic covenant, 46–47, 123, 302
Adam. *See also* Fall; original sin
  in Campbell's sermons, 150
  dispensation of, 272n87
  foreordination of, 326–27
  and keys of salvation, 124
aeon, 334–35n4
agency, 74, 173, 195–96n41, 306, 331, 334
Allen, Charles, 282
American Bible Society, 142n4
American Revolution, 185, 307
Anabaptist groups, 98–99n11
angels, 308
Anglican Church, 9, 23n1
Anti-Burgher movement, 11, 24n11
antinomian belief, 82, 156, 163n75
apocatasis, 196n46
apostasy, 40–42, 277–80, 283–84
Arbaugh, George, 243
Arianism, 75, 269nn27–28
Arius, 269n27
Armies of Israel, 284
Arminianism, 74
Articles of Faith, 141, 191–92
  development of, 165–67
  first, 167–70
  second, 170–72
  third, 172–73
  fourth, 174–76
  fifth, 177–79
  sixth, 178–79
  seventh, 179–80
  eighth, 180–81
  ninth, 181–83

Articles of Faith (*continued*)
  tenth, 183–87
  eleventh, 187–88
  twelfth, 188–89
  thirteenth, 189–91
Associate Synod of Philadelphia, 144
Atonement, 73, 171–73
Augustine, 318n37
Avard, Sampson, 284

B

Babylonish, 83
Bacon, Francis, 10, 12
baith, 324
baptism
  authority for, 177
  in Brush Run Church, 152
  Campbell debates regarding, 298–303
  in Campbell's New Testament, 205
  Campbell on unity through, 314–15
  Campbell's views on, 69–71, 100n60, 156, 222, 296–97
  and conflict between Joseph Smith and Alexander Campbell, 241
  in fourth article of faith, 174–76
  groups practicing immersive, 98–99n11
  Haldane and Campbell's views on, 26n47
  of infants, 69–70, 100n60, 175, 222, 298–303, 318n37
  of Joseph Smith and Oliver Cowdery, 116
baptism for the dead, 327–28, 331

Baptists, 70–71, 153, 159–61
baptizein, 299–300
baptizo, 205
Barstow, George, 142n9
baurau, 324
"Belief of the Wellsburg Church, A"
  (Campbell), 143, 157–59
Benjamin, King, 255
Bennet, James Arlington, 348
Bentley, Adamson, 222–23, 241–42
Berosheit, 324
Bethany College, 342
Beza, Theodore, 203
Bible. *See also* New Testament; Old
  Testament
  American editions of, 201–2
  Campbell's New Testament edition
    of, 201, 202–6, 210–11
  comparison of Book of Mormon to,
    264–65
  in eighth article of faith, 180–81
  and immediate revelation, 253–54
  Joseph Smith Translation, 105,
    108, 168–69, 181, 195n36, 206–11,
    250n92
  language of, 83–84
biblicism, 43, 48, 54n26, 69, 98n4,
  144–47
bishops, 88–89
Black, Jeremiah Sullivan, 343, 345–46
"black legs," 279
Bloom, Harold, 352
body/bodies
  of God and Jesus Christ, 169, 170
  resurrection of, 331–33, 338n81
  in soul, 332
bone infection of Joseph Smith, 33
Book of Abraham, 335n8
Book of Mormon. *See also* "Delusions"
  (Campbell); gold plates
  authorship of, 264–65
  coming forth of, 117–22, 135n76
  and conflict between Joseph Smith
    and Alexander Campbell, 241–42
  content of, 251–53
  in eighth article of faith, 180–81
  explanation of apostasy in, 41
  Hurlbut's attack on, 234–35
  importance of, 268
  Jesus Christ as focus of, 137n102
  lost manuscript pages of, 119, 135n69
  modes of travel to Americas in,
    271n85
  receiving testimony of, 265–66

Book of Mormon (*continued*)
  restoration in, 126–27
  Sidney Rigdon on, 227, 248n66
  types of government in, 271n75
Book of Moses, 207–9
Booth, Ezra, 232, 273
Brush Run Church, 151–53, 156, 159
Buck, Charles, 195n41
Burgess oath, 24n11
Burghers, 11, 24n11

C

Calhoun, John C., 289
Calvinism, 24–25n14, 72–74, 99n25, 106
Campbell, Alexander. *See also* conflict,
  between Joseph Smith and Alexander
  Campbell; "Delusions" (Campbell);
  restoration legacy of Alexander
  Campbell
  authority of, 177
  on baptism, 69–71, 100n60, 156, 205,
    222, 296–97, 298–303, 314–15
  belief in apostasy, 40–42
  "A Belief of the Wellsburg Church,"
    143, 157–59
  break between Rigdon and, 226–27
  on Calvin, 99n25
  as Christian apologist, 296–306
  common experiences of Joseph
    Smith and, 354
  common ideas of Joseph Smith and,
    355–56
  and *Declaration and Address*, 145–46
  differences between Joseph Smith
    and, 339–40
  dream of, 26n37
  and enthusiasm, 58–60
  followers of, 356
  formative years of, 11–23
  on gift of Holy Ghost, 176
  history of comparisons with Joseph
    Smith, 3–4
  influence on Sidney Rigdon, 222–25
  legacy of, 340–46
  and Mahoning Baptist Association,
    381
  and millennialism, 45–48
  New Testament edition of, 201,
    202–6, 210–11
  on primitivism, 43
  public preaching of, 149–52
  on punishment of wicked, 321–22
  reacts to martyrdom of Joseph
    Smith, 350

Campbell, Alexander (*continued*)
  on reformation, 71–80
  rejects religious pluralism, 56n64
  republishes critique of Book of
    Mormon, 239
  restorationism of, 3, 50–53, 69,
    80–98, 356–57
  and revivalism, 49–50, 61
  Sandeman's influence on, 26n45
  on sectarianism, 140
  separates from Baptists, 159–61
  "Sermon on the Law," 143, 153–56
  on Trinitarianism, 102–3n120
  and Zwickau prophets, 269n15
Campbell, Archibald, 23n1
Campbell, George, 203
Campbell, Jane, 25n35
Campbell, Jane Corneigle, 9, 11
Campbell, Margaret, 70
Campbell, Thomas
  and Alexander Campbell's formative
    years, 11–13, 14
  applies to Presbyterian Synod of
    Pittsburg, 162n39
  changing beliefs of, 22
  and Christian Association of
    Washington, 152
  on creeds and confessions, 78
  Declaration and Address of
    the Christian Association of
    Washington, 22, 43, 78, 143–49,
    161n9, 162n22, 295, 310, 312
  Haldanes's influence on, 17–19
  opposes debates, 296–97
  promotes reunion of Burgher and
    Anti-Burgher factions, 25n31
  religious background of, 9–11, 354
  restorationism of, 97
  reviews sermons with Alexander,
    150–51
  on sectarianism, 140
  on unity, 310–11
Campbellites, 217, 249n89
camp meetings, 62–63
Carthage Jail, 349–50
Cass, Lewis, 289
Catholic Church, 40, 196n45
celestial kingdom, 332–33
charity, feasts of, 86–87, 109
Chauncy, Charles, 57
Cherbury, Lord Edward Herbert of, 76
Christian Association of Washington,
  22, 145–49, 151–52. See also
  Declaration and Address of the

Christian Association of Washington
  (T. Campbell)
Christian Baptist, 78, 81, 159–60,
  249n89. See also *Millennial Harbinger*
Christian deism, 58
Christianity
  as based on new covenant, 155–56
  and Campbell's critique of Book of
    Mormon, 263–64
  Campbell's defense of, 303–6
  spirit of, 87
Christian System (A. Campbell), 310
Christian worship, 84–85, 107–8
chronological primitivism, 44
church discipline, 90–91, 109
church government, 90
church offices, and Campbell's
  restorationism, 87–90
Church of Jesus Christ of Latter-day
  Saints, The
  attacks on, 230–40
  fundamental principles of, 110–11,
    174–76
  organization of, 122, 132n29, 178–79,
    218
  problems of, in Far West, 280–87
  problems of, in Kirtland, 274–78
  Sidney Rigdon joins, 227–30
church-state separation, 3, 49, 139
circumcision, 175, 299–300, 302
civil obedience, 188–89
Civil War, 316–17, 319n68, 319n80
Clark, Andrew, 222
Clay, Henry, 289, 341–42
Cole, Abner, 121–22, 243
Coleridge, Samuel Taylor, 265
Collection of Sacred Hymns, for the
  Church of Latter Day Saints, A, 108–9
common stock. *See* communalism
communalism, 226–27, 236, 245n17,
  280–81, 304. *See also* consecration
communion tokens, 27n55
compass, 264, 271n83
confessions, 77–78
confessions of faith, 166
conflict
  between Joseph Smith and
    Alexander Campbell, 215–19, 221
  doctrine as source of, 240–44
  Sidney Rigdon as source of, 221–30
  words and violence in, 230–40
congressional delegation, 288
consecration, 231, 246–47n50, 280–81
  See also communalism

conservation of mass and energy, laws of, 336n37
Constitution, 187, 189
Constitution of God, 81–82, 107
conversion
    Alexander Campbell on, 95–96
    and revivalism, 62–63
corporeality of God and Jesus Christ, 169, 170
Cotton, John, 184
Council of Trent, 196n45
Covenanters, 23n2
covenants, 172, 299–300
covenant theology, 81–82, 100n58
Cowdery, Oliver
    apostasy of, 283
    and coming forth of Book of Mormon, 119–21
    and conflict between Joseph Smith and Alexander Campbell, 237
    priesthood keys conferred upon, 123, 197n86
    priesthood ordination of, 115–17
    on religious freedom, 188
    responds to "Delusions," 258, 259, 260, 269n31
    and visitation of Moroni, 134n58
    as witness of gold plates, 291n63
Cowdery, Warren, 278
creatio ex materia, 324–25
creatio ex nihilo, 324–25
Creation, 323–25
creeds and creedalism, 77–80, 106–7, 310–11

D

Danite band, 284
David, 330
Davis, Matthew, 347–48
Davison, Matilda, 239
deacons and deaconesses, 88–89
death(s)
    Owen and Campbell on, 305
    in Smith family, 32
debate(s)
    with John Walker, 298–301
    popularity of, 296–97
    and restoration legacy of Alexander Campbell, 297–98
    with Robert Owen, 303–6
    with William L. Maccalla, 301–3
Declaration and Address of the Christian Association of Washington

(T. Campbell), 22, 43, 78, 143–49, 161n9, 162n22, 295, 310, 312
degrees of glory, 219n1, 332–33
deification, 332–33
deism, 58, 66n7, 76
"Delusion" (Cowdery), 257, 268
"Delusions" (Campbell)
    content of, 253–57, 361–80
    doctrinal analysis of, 257–67
    as first critique of Book of Mormon, 4
    Joseph Smith responds to, 237–38, 267–68
    publication of, 216, 253–57
Dennison, Richard, 247n55
depravity of man, 72, 171
discipline, church, 90–91, 109
disestablishment of state-church relationship, 3, 49, 139
dispensation of the fulness of times, 125–26, 129, 137n100
dispensations, 81–82, 107, 123–26, 271–72n87
Doctrine and Covenants 20, 165
doctrine of Christ, 174
Doddridge, Phillip, 203
Dogberry Paper on Winter Hill, 121–22
Doniphan, Alexander, 286
dream(s)
    of Alexander Campbell, 15, 26n37
    of Joseph Smith Sr., 31
    of Lucy Mack Smith, 31
Dunkers, 98–99n11
dusting of feet, 219n2

E

Edwards, Jonathan, 2, 24n5, 184, 190
Egyptian papyri and mummies, 335n8
elders, and Campbell's restorationism, 88–89
election, unconditional, 72–73, 106
Elias, 123, 130, 136n86
Elijah, 123, 329
endless, 321
energy, law of conservation of, 336n37
Enlightenment, 16, 19–20, 57–60, 140
Enoch, 168–69
Enos, 255
enthusiasm
    Campbell's views on, 58–60
    defined, 57
    Joseph Smith as driven by, 60
    and revelations on spiritual gifts, 64–66
    revivalism and, 61–63

eternal, 321, 334–35n4
eternalism of Joseph Smith, 321–22,
  333–34
  Creation, 324–25
  Melchizedek Priesthood, 325–27
  plan of salvation, 322
  premortal existence, 322–24
  resurrection, 331–33
  rituals and ordinances, 327–31
ethical primitivism, 44, 48
Evangelist, 241
evangelists, and Campbell's
  restorationism, 89
Evening and the Morning Star, The,
  45–46, 216, 235–37
Ewing, Greville, 16, 20
experiential primitivism, 44, 48

F

faith
  Alexander Campbell on, 19–20,
    94–96, 265–66
  confessions of, 166
  in fourth article of faith, 174–75
Fall
  in Arminianism, 74
  in Calvinism, 72
  and Campbell's restorationism,
    93–95
  in plan of salvation, 324
  in second article of faith, 170–72
false prophets, 254
families, sealing of, 329–30
Far West, Missouri, 280–87
fast meetings, 109
feasts of charity, 86–87, 109
feet, dusting of, 219n2
Fielding, Mary, 277–78
Fife, Robert Oldham, 346
final dispensation, 123–24, 126, 137n100
Finke, Roger, 4
Finney, Charles, 185
First Amendment, 3
First Baptist Church of Pittsburg,
  223–24
First Vision
  accounts of, 38n30, 133n36, 133n41,
    193n12
  and Joseph Smith's opposition to
    creeds, 106
  in Joseph Smith's restorationism,
    111–15, 346–47
Ford, Thomas, 349

foreordination, 326–27
Foster, Douglas, 4
free agency, 195n41. *See also* agency
Freemasonry, 256, 271n75
free will, 195n41. *See also* agency

G

Gadianton robbers, 271n75
Garrett, Leroy, 20
gathering of Israel, 126–28, 183–87,
  199n135, 259
Genesis 1:1, 324–25
Gentiles, 261–62
geography, and Campbell's critique of
  Book of Mormon, 263–64
German Baptist Brethren, 98–99n11
gifts of the Spirit. *See* spiritual gifts
Glas, John, 16, 26n45, 244n10
God. *See also* Godhead
  Alexander Campbell's conception
    of, 92
  Constitution of, 81–82, 107
  in first article of faith, 167–70
  government of, 189
  Joseph Smith's conception of, 329–
    30, 333–34
  in Socinianism, 75
Godhead
  and Campbell's restorationism,
    91–93
  in first article of faith, 167–70
  and Nicene Creed, 194n13
gold plates, 117–21, 135–36n79, 266,
  283–84, 291–92n63. *See also* Book of
  Mormon
gospel purity, 357
gospel virtues, 189–91
government
  in Book of Mormon, 271n75
  church, 90
grace
  irresistible, 73–74
  in third article of faith, 172–73
Graham, Robert, 344
Grandin, E. B., 121–22
Great Awakening, 2, 57
Griesbach, Johann Jakob, 202, 211n5

H

Hagoth, 271n85
Haldane, James Alexander, 13, 16–19,
  26n47
Haldane, Robert, 16–19

Hale, Reuben, 135n75
hands, laying on of, 17, 177–79
Harris, Martin, 119–20, 122, 135–36n79
Hayden, Amos, 159
Hebrews 1:8, 202
Hebrews 4:3, 202
Hibernia, 15
Hill, Rowland, 13
history, and Campbell's critique of Book
of Mormon, 263–64
Holy Ghost. *See also* Godhead; spiritual
gifts
Alexander Campbell's conception of,
93, 360n71
in Articles of Faith, 167–70, 179
gift of, 174–76
Joseph Smith's conception of, 360n71
Sidney Rigdon on, 236–37
hospitality, 86–87
Howe, Eber D., 235, 237–38, 273
Huguenots, 11
Humphrey, Heman, 344
Hurlbut, Philastus, 234–35, 238, 247n62,
273
Hutcheson, Francis, 10
Hutchinson, Anne, 7n6, 132n27, 253
hymns, 85–86, 108–9

I

illness, in Smith family, 32–33
immediate revelation, 253–54
Independence, Missouri, 216, 280–81
Independent Church, 13–14
infant baptism, 69–70, 100n60, 175, 222,
298–303, 318n37
Irenaeus, 318n37
irresistible grace, 73–74
-isms
Alexander Campbell on, 72–77
Joseph Smith on, 106–7
Israel, gathering of, 126–28, 183–87,
199n135, 259

J

Jackson County, Missouri, 216, 280–81
Jardine, George, 16
Jaredites, 271n85
Jeremiah, 259
Jerusalem, 263–64
Jesus Christ. *See also* Godhead
Alexander Campbell's conception of,
92, 157–58
in Arianism, 75, 269n27, 269n28
Atonement of, 73, 171–73

Jesus Christ (*continued*)
in Campbell's restoration, 316
and creedalism, 80
doctrine of, 174
in first article of faith, 167–70
as fulfillment of law, 155
as fundamental principle of
Mormonism, 110–11, 137n102
knowledge of, throughout
dispensations, 124–25
nature of, 323
priesthood of, 326
in Trinitarianism, 75
in Unitarianism, 75–76
John 1:18, 202
Johnson, Richard M., 289
John the Baptist, 115–16
Jones, Abner, 54n34
Joseph Smith Translation, 105, 168–69,
181, 195n36, 206–11, 250n92

K

keys of salvation, 124
Kimball, Heber C., 277
King James Version, 203, 205
King, Joseph, 345
kingship, and Campbell's critique of
Book of Mormon, 260
Kirtland, Ohio
challenges facing church in, 274–80
missionary work in, 216
Kirtland Safety Society, 275–78

L

Lamanites, 256
Lane, George, 38n31
language, and Campbell's
restorationism, 83–84
Latonia, 21
law of Christ, 154–56
law of consecration, 231, 246–47n50,
280–81
law of Moses, 153–54, 261
laws, obedience to, 188–89
laws of conservation of mass and
energy, 336n37
laying on of hands, 17, 177–79
Lee, John D., 4
Lee, Robert E., 343
left wing Reformation, 269n15
Lehi, 255, 257–59, 270n35
"Letter to the Elders of the Church of
the Latter Days," 237–38
Liahona, 264

Liberty Jail, 286
"lick-skillets," 279
limited atonement, 73
Locke, John, 12, 25n21
logic, 58
Lord's Supper, 84, 107–8, 144
Lost Manuscript Found (Spaulding),
   234–35, 247–48n65, 248n68
love feasts, 86–87, 109
Lucas, General, 286
Luther, Martin, 72, 94

M

Maccalla, William L., 301–3
Macknight, James, 203
Madison, James, 343
Mahoning Baptist Association, 157–59,
   160, 223, 381–82
"Manifesto of the Mob, The," 182
marriage, 305, 330. See also plural
   marriage
Marsden, George, 43, 48
mass, law of conservation of, 336n37
Mather, Cotton, 184
McLellin, William, 291n63
Melchizedek Priesthood, 116, 258,
   270n35, 325–27
Mennonites, 98–99n11
Messenger and Advocate, 216
Methodism and Methodist movement,
   30, 34
Midgely, Louis, 195n41
Millennial Harbinger, 45–46, 160, 216,
   253, 308–9. See also Christian Baptist
millennialism, primitivism and, 45–49
Millennium, 129, 184–86, 306–15
Miller, William, 185
missionary work
   counsel for, 219n2
   in Kirtland, Ohio, 216
Missouri Mormon War, 219, 285
mob violence, 232–34, 281–82, 285–87,
   349–50. See also persecution
money digging, 133n38, 134–35n68, 234
Moore, George, 166
moral agency, 195n41
moral law, 154
Morley farm, 226, 245n17
Mormon, 256
Mormonism Unvailed (Howe), 235, 237
Moroni, 117–18, 134n54, 134n58
Mosaic law, 153–54, 261
Moses, 123, 207–9, 258–59

Mount of Transfiguration, 123, 130,
   136n91
Mulekites, 271n85
mummies, 335n8
Munzer, Thomas, 269n15
Murdock, Joseph, 233–34
Murdock, Julia Clapp, 233–34

N

Nauvoo Expositor, 349
Nauvoo Temple, 336–37n53
Nephi, 261, 271n85
Nephites, 252–53, 255
Newell, Grandison, 276
New Testament
   and apostasy, 40–42
   Campbell's edition of, 201–6, 210–11
   and Campbell's restorationism,
      80–81, 148, 157–59, 316, 343
   elements from, in Book of Mormon,
      252, 267
   and primitivism, 4
   and restorationism of Joseph Smith
      and Alexander Campbell, 51–53
   and restoration legacy of Alexander
      Campbell, 293–94
Nicene Creed, 194n13, 269n27
Noah, 150
Noll, Mark, 195–96n41

O

obedience, civil, 188–89
observation, 58
offerings, 85
offices, and Campbell's restorationism,
   87–90
"Of Governments and Laws in General,"
   188
O'Kelly, James, 54n34
olam, 334–35n4
Olbricht, Thomas, 346
Old Testament, 47–48, 52–53, 150, 252,
   330
Oliver, Peter, 2
On the Reasonableness of Christianity
   as Delivered in the Scriptures (Locke),
   12, 25n21
opinions, Alexander Campbell on, 313
ordinances, 172, 327–31
original sin, 72, 170–72, 195n41, 302,
   318n37
Owen, Robert, 227, 303–6

P

Page, Hiram, 291–92n63
Panic of 1837, 276, 290n19
papyri, 335n8
parable of vineyard, 87
Parker, Thomas, 126
Parrish, Warren, 277–78
"particular" redemption, 383n5
Partridge, Edward, 282
patronage, 11, 23n2
Paul, 189–90, 261–62
Pearl of Great Price, 193n5
pedobaptism, 69–70, 100n60, 175, 222,
   298–303, 318n37
Pendleton, William Kimbrough, 345
persecution, 187–90, 232–34, 281–82,
   285–89, 347, 349–50
perseverance of the Saints, 73
Pettigrew, David, 281–82
Phelps, W. W., 108, 283
Philippians 2:6, 202
plan of salvation
   of Alexander Campbell, 81–82, 96
   Atonement in, 173
   Joseph Smith on, 322
   knowledge of, throughout
      dispensations, 124–25
pluralism, religious, 56n64, 139–40
plural marriage, 330, 337n72
polygamy, 330, 337n72
poor, offerings for, 85
postmillennialism, 45
Pratt, Orson, 351
Pratt, Parley P., 64, 96, 126, 177, 179, 227,
   286, 351–52
predestination, 72–74, 106
premillennialism, 45, 185–86
premortal existence, 322–24, 326–27
Prentice, George D., 344
Presbytery of Chartiers, 144
priestcraft, 278
priesthood
   Aaronic Priesthood, 54n22, 115–16
   Alexander Campbell on, 82
   baptism and, 175
   and Campbell's critique of Book of
      Mormon, 257–58, 270n35
   and Campbell's restorationism, 87–90
   in fifth article of faith, 177–79
   loss of, 41
   Melchizedek Priesthood, 116, 258,
      270n35, 325–27
   restoration of, 54n22, 115–18, 197n86

priesthood keys, 123, 132n28, 136n91,
   328–29
primitivism
   and Declaration and Address, 146–47
   millennialism and, 45–49
   and restorationism, 42–45, 50–53,
      80–97
   and sixth article of faith, 178–79
promised land, 258–59
prophecies, and Campbell's critique of
   Book of Mormon, 262–63
prophets, false, 254
Protestantism, Mormon roots in, 43
Protestant Reformation, 1–2, 97, 310
psalms, 85–86, 108–9
Psalms, Hymns, and Spiritual Songs
   adapted to the Christian Religion,
   85–86
punishment, endless and eternal, 321–22
Purcell, John B., 344
pure speech, 83–84
Puritans, 1, 2, 6n2

Q

Queries of Highest Consideration, 7n3
Quincy, Illinois, 287–88
Quincy, Josiah, 348–49

R

race, 285
radical Reformation, 269n15
reason, 58, 60, 69
redemption. See also salvation
   need for, 171
   "particular," 383n5
Redstone Baptist Association, 152–53,
   156, 159
reductio ad absurdum, 306
reformation, 40, 71–80. See also
   Protestant Reformation; radical
   Reformation
Reformed Church, 11
Reid, Thomas, 10
religious freedom, 3, 7–8n8, 187–88
religious pluralism, 56n64, 139–40, 187
repentance, 173–76
restoration
   in Book of Mormon, 126–27
   defined, 39
   as part of Second Great Awakening,
      49–50
   perspectives on, 57

restorationism
  of Alexander Campbell, 69, 80–98,
    342–43
  of Alexander Campbell and Joseph
    Smith, 3–4, 339–40, 355–57
  apostasy and, 40–42
  and Campbell's views on baptism,
    69–71
  and Campbell's views on "-isms,"
    creeds, and confessions, 71–80
  defined, 39
  foundational events and revelations
    in Joseph Smith's, 109–23
  of Joseph Smith, 105–9, 129–31,
    346–47
  Joseph Smith and Alexander
    Campbell's contributions to,
    293–94
  other leaders of, 8n18
  and primitivism, 42–45, 50–53
  Puritan, 6n2
  restitution of all things in Joseph
    Smith's, 123–29
restoration legacy of Alexander
  Campbell, 293–94, 315–17
  baptism, 296–303
  defense of Christianity, 303–6
  Millennium, 306–15
  unity, 295–96
restoration legacy of Joseph Smith,
  293–94
restoration movement, 309
resurrection, 331–33, 338n81
Revelation 14:6–7, 307–8, 319n73
Revelation 22:18, 199n115
revelation(s)
  Campbell's views on, 60
  immediate, 253–54
  Joseph Smith on, 60, 132n27
  in Joseph Smith's restorationism,
    109–11, 340, 346–47, 355
  and Joseph Smith Translation, 207,
    210
  and ninth article of faith, 181–83,
    199n115
  received between 1830 and 1832, 215
  regarding degrees of glory, 219n1
  and restoration legacy of Joseph
    Smith, 294
  and Sidney Rigdon, 212n39, 236–37
  sources of, 105
  on spiritual gifts, 64–66
revivalism, 2, 34–36, 49–50, 61–63
Revolutionary War, 185, 307
Reynolds, John, 288, 350–51

Richards, Franklin D., 193n5
Richards, Willard, 350
Richardson, Robert, 23–24n3
Rigdon, Phebe, 227–28
Rigdon, Sidney
  and apostasy in Kirtland, 277
  arrest of, 286
  authority of, 177
  Campbell's attack on, 230–31
  and conflict between Joseph Smith
    and Alexander Campbell, 216–17,
    240–44
  defends Book of Mormon, 235
  defends church, 235–37, 238–39
  defends Joseph Smith, 276
  as JST scribe, 209, 250n92
  and Maccalla debate, 301
  reads Book of Mormon for first time,
    248n66
  religious history of, 221–30
  responsibilities of, 212n39
  strengths and weaknesses of, 230
  as victim of mob violence, 232–33
rituals, 327–31
Ryder, Symonds, 228, 231, 239, 273

S

Sabbath day, 84–85, 107–8
sacramental festival, 61–62
Saints, perseverance of, 73
salvation. See also plan of salvation;
  redemption
  Alexander Campbell on, 74, 100n60
  in Arminianism, 74
  Augustinian-Pelagian debates on,
    196n45
  interdependence of Mormon, 329–30
  Joseph Smith's concern over, 40–41
  keys of, 124
  in third article of faith, 172–73
Sandeman, Robert, 16, 26n45, 244n10
Scott, Walter, 96, 224, 230, 238–39, 241,
  244n10, 253
Scottish Common Sense Realism, 10,
  24n4, 140
Scottish Enlightenment, 16, 19–20
Scottish Presbyterianism, 61–62
scriptural language, 83–84
scripture. See also Bible; Book of
  Mormon
  in Campbell's restorationism, 316
  and continuing revelation, 182–83
  in eighth article of faith, 180–81
  interpretation of, 13

sealing, 329–30
Seceder Presbyterian Church, 24n11, 25n31, 146
Seceders and Secession movement, 11, 20, 23n2, 24n11
Second Coming, 184–86
Second Great Awakening, 1–3, 7n12, 34, 49–50, 57–58
secrets, 261–62
sectarianism, 76–77, 140
seekers, 7n3
seer stones, 133n38, 134–35n68, 262
seraphim, 308
"Sermon on the Law" (Campbell), 143, 153–56
Sharp, Thomas, 349
sin
    agency and, 195n41
    original sin, 72, 170–72, 195n41, 302, 318n37
    remission of, 154–55, 302–3
skepticism, 303–6
slavery, 281
Smith, Alvin, 32
Smith, Asael, 30, 193n9
Smith, Elias, 54n34
Smith, Emma Hale, 108, 119, 135n75, 243
Smith, Hyrum, 37n22, 121
Smith, Jesse, 30–31
Smith, John, 216
Smith, Joseph, Jr. See also Articles of Faith; conflict, between Joseph Smith and Alexander Campbell; eternalism of Joseph Smith; First Vision; Joseph Smith Translation
    arrest of, 286
    birth of, 29
    called false prophet, 254
    common experiences of Campbell and, 354
    common ideas of Campbell and, 355–56
    differences between Campbell and, 339–40
    on dispensation of the fulness of times, 137n100
    and enthusiasm, 58, 60
    followers of, 356
    formative years of, 33–36
    foundational events and revelations in restorationism of, 109–23
    history of comparisons with Alexander Campbell, 3–4
    illness of, 32

Smith, Joseph, Jr. (continued)
    knowledge of, of foreign languages, 213n43
    legacy of, 346–54
    and lost manuscript pages of Book of Mormon, 135n69
    and millennialism, 45–49
    petitions for redress, 288–89
    and plural marriage, 330, 337n72
    as premillennialist, 185–86
    as presidential candidate, 289
    priesthood keys conferred upon, 123, 197n86
    on primitivism, 43
    problems of, in Far West, 280–87
    problems of, in Kirtland, 274–80
    questions regarding leadership of, 273–74, 278–79, 283
    rejects religious pluralism, 56n64
    responds to "Delusions," 237–38, 267–68
    restorationism of, 3, 50–53, 105–9, 123–31, 356–57
    restoration legacy of, 293–94
    and revelations on spiritual gifts, 64–66
    and revivalism, 49–50, 63
    on sectarianism, 140
    understanding of apostasy, 40–42
    as victim of mob violence, 232–34
    weakness of, 130–31
Smith, Joseph, Sr., 29–34, 193n9, 216, 354
Smith, Lucy Mack, 29–32, 121
Smith, Samuel, 135n75
Smith, Sophronia, 32
Snow, Eliza R., 229, 246n36
Snow, Oliver, 228
Socinianism, 75
sola scriptura, 43, 48, 69, 98n4, 147, 180–81
"Son of God," 92
soul, 331–32
Spaulding, Solomon, 234–35, 247–48n65, 248n68
speculation, 274–76
speech, pure, 83–84
spirit matter, 323
spirit of Christianity, 87
Spirit of God, 93
spirit(s)
    foundational existence of, 335n14
    premortal existence of, 322–24, 326–27
    in soul, 332

spiritual creation, 323
spiritual gifts
    Alexander Campbell on, 14, 41, 61
    Joseph Smith on, 42, 48, 63
    revelations on, 64–66
    in seventh article of faith, 179–80
    Sidney Rigdon on, 236, 238
Stark, Rodney, 4
state, separation of church and, 3, 49,
    139
steamboats, 264
Stone, Barton, 54n34, 62–63, 160–61,
    164n87, 313–14, 343
Storch, Nicholas, 269n15
Stowell, Josiah, 133n38
Stubner, Mark, 269n15

T

Taylor, John, 348
telestial kingdom, 333
temples, 128, 260–61, 328–29, 331,
    336–37n53
Ten Commandments, 154
terrestrial kingdom, 333
theistic mental science, 10
theosis, 332–33
Toland, John, 25n21
tongues, gift of, 179–80
total depravity of man, 72, 171
treasure seeking, 133n38, 134–35n68,
    234
Trinity and Trinitarianism
    Alexander Campbell on, 75, 91–92,
        102–3n120
    Alexander Campbell's opposition to
        word, 91
    and first article of faith, 167–68, 170
truth(s), 56n64, 241, 249n84, 309
TULIP (Calvinism), 24–25n14, 72–73
typhus fever, 32–33, 37n18

U

unconditional election, 72–73, 106
Underhill, Samuel, 245n17
Unitarianism, 75–76, 193n9
unity
    called for in Declaration and
        Address, 147–48
    Campbells on, 310–15
    as motive of Restoration Movement,
        309
    and restoration legacy of Alexander
        Campbell, 293–96

Universalism, 193n9, 196n46
Urim and Thummim, 118–19, 183
utopian movement, 305

V

Van Buren, Martin, 288, 292n88
vineyard, parable of, 87
virtues of gospel, 189–91

W

Walker, John, 13, 298–301
Wentworth, John, 141, 142n9
Wentworth Letter, 141, 165, 178, 188,
    352
West, Robert, 8n16, 43
Whitefield, George, 57
Whitmer, David, 120, 283, 291n63
Whitmer, John, 283
Whitmer, Peter, Jr., 121
Whitney, Newel K., 109
wicked, punishment of, 321–22
Williams, Roger, 1, 6–7nn2–3, 7n39
"Word of God," 92
works, 94–95
Worrell, Frank, 349
worship, Christian, 84–85, 107–8

Y

Young, Alfonso, 4
Young, Brigham, 276, 351

Z

Zenos, 262
Zion, 128–29, 168–69, 183–87, 229–30,
    280–81, 310
Zwickau prophets, 269n15